JOHN MAYNARD KEYNES

VOLUME ONE

HOPES BETRAYED

1883–1920

JOHN MAYNARD KEYNES

VOLUME ONE

HOPES BETRAYED

1883–1920

Robert Skidelsky

MACMILLAN
LONDON

First published in 1983 by Macmillan London Limited

This edition published in paperback 1992 by
PAPERMAC
a division of Pan Macmillan Publishers Limited
Cavaye Place London SW10 9PG
and Basingstoke

Associated companies in Auckland, Budapest, Dublin, Gaborone,
Harare, Hong Kong, Kampala, Kuala Lumpur, Lagos, Madras, Manzini,
Melbourne, Mexico City, Nairobi, New York, Singapore, Sydney,
Tokyo and Windhoek

1   3   5   7   9   8   6   4   2

ISBN 0–333–57379–X Papermac
ISBN 0–333–11599–6 hardback

A CIP catalogue record for this book is available from the British Library

Printed in Hong Kong

TO

Augusta

Contents

List of Illustrations

Acknowledgements

A book is made possible by many people and things. My first debt is not to persons but to a place. This book would not be written, it was decided, unless I went away to write it. So in September 1981 we packed our bags and went to live for a year in La Garde Freinet, a mountain village in Provence. It proved an ideal setting for authorship, combining adequate isolation with a surprising atmosphere of intellectuality and culture. There were few occasions for frivolous distractions. For much of the year the wind blows ferociously; in the summer it becomes too hot to go out much; the sparse, prickly vegetation is regularly consumed by great forest fires. In our house, the telephone rarely rang, and when it did it was fortunately difficult to hear. The English-language newspapers were both expensive and late; even the stirring episodes of the Falklands War were lost in the crackling of the B.B.C.'s World Service. At the same time, La Garde Freinet has over the years attracted a lively and varied group of intellectuals, being cheap enough to be affordable, and sufficiently uncomfortable to banish guilt at actually being in the South of France. Few expatriates live there all the year round. But with the coming of spring an extraordinary number of academics and persons connected with the arts begin their annual descent, providing an array of captive expertise which would not disgrace the most eminent university or salon – but which had no impact on a local community equipped for survival and little else.

My debt to people starts with my family. My two small sons, Edward and William, were plunged into the village school, to be instructed in an unknown tongue. They adapted to this odd situation with admirable fortitude and good humour, acquiring over the year a mastery of amazingly idiomatic French. My wife Augusta was a tower of love and support. She made her own unique contribution to our stay by giving birth, in our house, to a daughter, Juliet, the first *vraie Gardoise* for seventeen years. This cheered up even the dour locals. My greatest sadness was that my father, Boris, and my mother-in-law, Elisabeth Hope, did not live to see the book finished. Beyond the world of Keynes, life continued to bring joys and sorrows.

My most valued intellectual companions were Professor Ian and Dobs Little, who live in La Garde Freinet for most of the year. On them I inflicted the first draft of successive chapters of the book. At a later stage the whole book was read by Professor Richard and Mrs Anne Keynes, the anthropologist Dr Polly Hill, vigorous with the blue pencil, Stephen Keynes, Dr Milo Keynes, Dr George (Dadie) Rylands, and Sir Harry and Lady Lintott. They will all know how much they have improved it.

Christopher Allsop, Professor Quentin Bell, Professor Phyllis Deane, Mrs Jean Floud, James Horwitz, Professor Terence Hutchison, Vijay Joshi, Professor Lord and Lady Kaldor, Dr Simon Keynes, Professor Adrian Lyttleton, Professor Marcus Miller, the Hon. Lady Mosley, Professor Austin Robinson, and Bernard Williams all made helpful comments on parts of the book. I would particularly like to thank Nicky and Clarissa Kaldor for their warm hospitality to me in Cambridge over many years. Talking to Nicky has been an intellectual and economic education of the rarest kind. At one moment in our year abroad our friend Carmen Callil came to stay. Her enthusiastic response to an early draft provided much-needed uplift when zest for writing was starting to flag.

In addition to those mentioned above I have greatly benefited from talking to Peter Avery, Professor Richard Braithwaite, Henrietta and John Couper, Peter Croft, the late Duncan Grant, Michael Holroyd, David Hubback, Professor Richard Kahn, the late Sir Geoffrey Keynes, Oliver Knox, the Rt Hon. Harold Macmillan, Professor James Meade, Roderick O'Donnell, Mrs Susan Rendell, Professor Joan Robinson, Lord Rothschild, Mrs Helena Shire, Richard Shone, Mrs Frances Spalding, Professor George and Mrs Zara Steiner, and Christopher and Baillie Tolkien.

Others who have helped me by correspondence are Lord Annan, Professor Charles P. Blitch, Neville Brown, Rohan Butler, Dr Christopher Cook, Dr H. J. Elcock, Professor H. J. Eysenck, Mrs Penelope Fitzgerald, Nicholas Furbank, Lady Harrod, Mrs S. C. Harding, Caroline Hobhouse, Niall Hobhouse, Professor John R. de S. Honey, Susan Hope-Jones, Lord Kennet, Paul Levy, John Luce, R. A. Luce, Sir Robin Mackworth-Young, R. D. Macnaghten, Professor Donald Moggridge, Sir Peter Proby, Priscilla M. Roberts, Paul Roche, Professor Richard Rose, Professor Stephen S. Schuker, Professor Quentin Skinner, Dr Iain Smith, Dr Charles Swithinbank, Professor Lynn Turgeon, Lady Barbara Wootton and Michal Vyvyan.

Much of my research was done in the libraries which housed collections of manuscript material. Such work is an essential part of the historian's craft; it can also be frustrating especially in those (few remaining) institutions where the researcher is reduced, through lack of photocopying facilities or librarian's dogma, to transcribing modern documents laboriously in pencil. This method, in addition to being a crashing waste of time, makes it much more difficult to quote accurately (or even to get the best quotation); and no doubt mistakes have crept into the final product through errors of transcription, though I hope only trivial ones. I was fortunate to have the help of three research assistants in the earliest stages of my work: David Morse and René Olivieri for the year 1975–6 when I taught at the Bologna Center of the School of Advanced International Studies, Johns Hopkins University, and Elizabeth McLeod in the following year when I was at the Polytechnic of North London. I would like to thank them, and the institutions which made them available to me.

My most persistent port of call was the Library of King's College, Cambridge, and I would like in particular to thank the Librarian, Peter Croft, and the Modern Archivist, Michael Halls, together with Miss Elizabeth Russell and other members of the Library staff, for their patient goodwill. I would also like to thank Professors Austin Robinson and Donald Moggridge, joint managing editors of Keynes's *Collected Writings*, for sending me proofs of the volumes as they became ready, and for allowing me to see originals in the Marshall Library; and their editorial assistant, Mrs Judith Allen, who was endlessly and graciously helpful.

My thanks also to Peter Gautry, Under-Librarian, Department of Manuscripts, Cambridge University Library; R. E. Macpherson, Registrary, Cambridge University; Marion M. Stewart, Archivist, Churchill College, Cambridge; F. J. Norton, Archivist, Pembroke College, Cambridge; Trevor Kaye, Sub-Librarian, Trinity College, Cambridge; D. S. Porter, Senior Assistant Librarian, Department of Western Manuscripts, Bodleian Library, Oxford; D. J. F. A. Mason, Librarian, Christ Church, Oxford; Dr B. S. Benedikz, Sub-Librarian (Special Collections), Birmingham University Library; Florence Bartoshevsky, Manuscripts and Archives, Baker Library, Harvard University; Mrs Elizabeth Inglis, Assistant Librarian, Manuscripts Section, Sussex University Library; Mrs G. M. Furlong and Mrs I. Percival, Archivists, University College Library, London University; Mrs Lola S. Szladits, Curator, Berg Collection, New York Public Library; The Keeper of the Manuscript Section, British Library; M. Moir, Deputy Archivist, India Office Library; H. S. Cobb, Clerk of the Records, Record Office, House of Lords; The Keeper, the Public Records Office, Kew; David Reed, Librarian, Percival Library, Clifton College; A. C. L. Hall, Librarian, Wodehouse Library, Dulwich College; and Michael Meredith, School Librarian, and Patrick Strong, Keeper of the College Library, Eton College.

For the use of manuscript material, most of it unpublished, I am indebted to: King's College, Cambridge, for Keynes's personal papers; the Royal Economic Society, for Keynes's economic papers, and for other items in the Marshall Library, Cambridge; the Strachey Trust and the Society of Authors for letters by Lytton and James Strachey; Mrs Angelica Garnett for letters by Vanessa Bell; Professor Quentin Bell for letters by Clive Bell; Mrs Henrietta Couper for letters by Duncan Grant; Trinity College, Cambridge, for the Edwin Montagu papers; Birmingham University Library for the Austen Chamberlain papers; Churchill College, Cambridge, for the Cecil Spring-Rice and Reginald McKenna papers; Eton College for records of the College Debating Society; Lord Kennet for Hilton Young's unpublished autobiography; Mark Bonham-Carter for Margot Asquith's diary; Richard Garnett for letters and diaries by David Garnett; the Trustees of the Thomas Lamont papers, Harvard University.

Money buys time to write a book. I am grateful to the Lehrman Institute of New York for giving me a Research Fellowship in 1975 on the recommendation of Professor David Calleo, my friend and former colleague at the Washington School of Advanced International Studies; to the Phoenix Trust for a grant for travel expenses in 1978, and to the Arts Council of Great Britain for a grant in 1981. In connection with the latter the encouragement and support of Miss Gillian Vincent of Macmillan was invaluable. My thanks go to Warwick University, which granted me four terms study leave in 1981–2; and to the Provost and Council of King's College, Cambridge, for making me a member of High Table during the Michaelmas Term of 1982. I would especially like to thank Mrs Joy Gardner, my Departmental Secretary at Warwick, for her efficiency and support at all times during the book's gestation.

An editor can be an author's best friend. Richard Garnett was an inspired choice by Julian Ashby. Richard's commitment to the book went far beyond the call of duty. I not only benefited from his great knowledge of the circle about which I was writing, but also from his fine sense of language. I dread to think when this volume would actually have appeared had it not been for his untiring efforts.

I am grateful to the following for writing to me with suggestions or corrections after the first publication of volume one: Robert Ackerman, Professor S. R. Dennison, Andrew Filson, Jennifer Hart, David Hubback, Mrs Marian Kenball-Cook, Norman Miller, Professor David Marquand, A. L. Rowse, Geoffrey Stone, Gerard Tallock, Julian Vinogradoff.

Preface

Writers of biography find themselves in a peculiar position. Lots of people enjoy reading their books; yet much more than writers of fiction, or drama, or history, they find themselves having to justify what they do. Like opera, biography is regarded with great suspicion by the high-minded. It is held to be an impure form; a coalition of unconnected, even repelled, parts, lacking a compelling logic, rarely achieving an aesthetic unity. It is fiction constrained by fact; voyeurism embellished with footnotes. Are biographers trying to tell a story or explain something?

When the first volume of my life of Keynes was published in 1983, the doubts about biography emerged in the form of the question: 'Does a great economist's life have anything to do with his economics?'[1] In his obituary notice of Keynes, published in 1946, Joseph Schumpeter, the great Austrian economist, had suggested that it does when he wrote: 'He was childless and his philosophy of life was essentially a short-run philosophy. So he turned resolutely to the only "parameter of action" that seemed left to him, both as an Englishman and *the kind of Englishman he was* – monetary management'[2] [my italics]. Keynes's childlessness was, at any rate partly, due to the fact that he was homosexual – even though in his early forties he married, very successfully, the ballerina Lydia Lopokova. Sir Roy Harrod, Keynes's first biographer, left out any mention of his homosexuality; I took the view that no 'life' of Keynes which left out such central emotional episodes as his love-affair with the painter Duncan Grant could seriously claim to be such. It was obvious that this would be to hand ammunition to critics of Keynesian economics. I took the view that Keynesian economics were robust enough to survive revelations about Keynes's private life.

Nevertheless, the question of the connection, if any, between Keynes's life and his thought, and with it the worth of biography itself, was posed. Critics of Keynes's economics took advantage of their opportunity. Thus Sir William Rees-Mogg argued that Keynes's rejection of 'general rules', which his homosexuality reinforced, led him to reject the 'gold standard which provided an automatic control of monetary inflation'.[3] Admirers of Keynesian economics moved, with a kind of reflex action, to insulate the 'life' from the 'thought'. Professor Maurice Peston wrote, 'It is obvious philosophical nonsense to suggest that there is a connection [between Keynes's sexuality and his economics]; the logical validity of a theory and its empirical relevance are independent of its progenitor. (What help is knowledge of the lives of Newton and Einstein in predicting the movements of planets?)'[4]

There was evidence of disciplinary divides as well. A sociologist, Christie Davies, asking whether there was a 'link between Keynes' homosexuality and his economics', wrote: 'It is an issue that is of no interest whatsoever to the economists who are merely concerned with whether or not Keynes' economics is valid. The . . . truth or . . . falsity of an economist's ideas can only be decided by testing them against reality and the fact that the economist may have been originally inspired by a weakness for necrophilia, a desire to commit bestiality with pink elephants, or a wish to be flogged by naked Australian police-women, is neither here nor there. However, it is an issue of interest to sociologists who are concerned with the question of the consequences (if any) of sexual deviation and its stigmatization by society for the behaviour and thinking of the individuals concerned'.[5] Professor David Marquand, the political scientist and biographer of Ramsay MacDonald, felt that the 'homosexual culture' in which Keynes lived his early life explained his ambivalent attitude to authority: 'Keynes . . . was not a true member of the Establishment after all. He merely took its shilling and wore its coat. Emotionally he was always an outsider, with outsider values and outsider loyalties'.[6]

These issues are worth exploring, for they touch on the validity of the biographical enterprise. To start with a basic question: does biography try to tell a story or to explain something? The answer is, of course, that it tries to do both. Biographies are written about people who have led interesting lives – whose lives make a good story. Undoubtedly we are initially interested in reading about such people because we already know that in some way they were famous or notorious or even 'relevant'. The name is the hook which catches the reader. But he will not stay hooked unless the life itself grips, or is made to grip by the biographer. Some people make marvellous subjects because their lives are crammed with events and emotions with which people can identify – even though their 'achievements' (except in the art of living) were mediocre. And some people of outstanding achievement make poor subjects because they led lives so dull that not even the biographer's art can rescue them. Keynes, unlike, I suspect, Marshall or Pigou, was both a great economist and a fascinating man; and the second would be justification enough for writing a biography about him even if he were not a great economist, though it might not be a life that Professor Peston would want to read. Most people read biography, I think, because they want to know more about a person, not because they want the person or his achievement to be 'explained' for them. And I see nothing wrong with supplying that demand.

The itch to 'explain' is peculiarly the biographer's. The biographer feels the need to 'make sense of' the jumble of facts and events he has to chronicle, to make of them satisfying patterns, to make the parts fit together. At root this has to do with the idea – which may be mistaken – that there is an objective, coherent, personality waiting for the touch of the biographer's magic wand to bring it to life. This leads to the view that outstanding achievement, whether in the world of thought, art, or action must be in some sense an expression of that personality, and therefore to be explained by reference to it. And even if we drop the strong assumption of coherence, we are still left with the feeling that there must be some connection, in the case of Keynes or any thinker, between mental events and the other events which are the proper subjects of a life. At its lowest: outstanding achievement in any sphere is usually the result of very hard, sustained work; the obsession with work is something a biographer can try to explain. Or can we not see original mental achievement as resulting from a particular conjuncture of personal qualities and personal and historical circumstances which biography is particularly well suited to explore?

Although a biographer is inevitably drawn to trying to explain why his subject was unusual, it has to be said that the scientific tools at his disposal are dreadfully inadequate. Most biographers come to the task with a smattering of psycho-analytic or sociological theory with the help of which they comb their subjects' lives for 'clues' that might 'explain' their achievements. Any good biographer should be aware of the main theories of personality, creativity, etc; as well as of the ways historians and sociologists go about the business of explaining the power of ideas (which Pareto, who was both an economist and a sociologist, once observed had very little relationship to their logical properties). But experience of reading many biographies has convinced me that the more systematic the theorising of the biographer, the less persuasive the results he achieves. The fact is that biographers are not in a position to discover causal relationships between different facets of the personality, between the 'life' and the 'thought', or between the 'thought' and the 'circumstances', even if such exist; and delude themselves if they think they can.[7] The most they can hope to do is to create aesthetically satisfying patterns of relationships – patterns that we intuitively accept as persuasive, because they conform to our feelings about the relationship between things.

What ideas, then, should a biographer bring to the task of connecting the life or personality of Keynes to his economics? The clue is given by Elizabeth Durbin when she writes that 'the focus on particular problems, the choice between different economic means, and even the use of one economic model rather than another, may . . . be affected by the values of the policy adviser.[8] In other words, behind the 'model' are the values of the theorist; and behind these the personal and historical circumstances that helped form them – the biographical terrain. Economists tend to be unhappy with this approach because they believe that theories issue from scientific research programmes and live or die according to whether they pass the test of successful prediction. The only midwives that interest them are the intellectual ones – the arguing out of the logical relationships involved in theory construction; the validity of a theory is measured by its success in doing the scientific work it claims to do – i.e., actually reducing unemployment or inflation. But this cannot be the only approach to understanding either the genesis or life-span of a theory; nor can it be a sufficient one, because we know, as a matter of fact, that all theorising or modelling takes place in contexts wider than those of the theory or model itself and that, strictly speaking, important theories in economics cannot be falsified, because it is never possible to set up the experiment which would do so. As Professor Hutchison has pointed out, the *ceteris paribus* condition is crucial to prediction in economics in a way it is not in the natural sciences.[9]

Take for example the quantity theory of money. In his youthful exuberance Keynes claimed that adherence to it was a test of scientific competence; that any denial of it was a sign of a 'natural deformation of the mind'. A few years later he cheerfully jettisoned it; in the 1970s back it popped. And there are many other examples: Keynes claimed that the theory of effective demand was one of them. If economics were really like physics, it would be impossible for ideas fundamental to the subject to disappear one moment and reappear the next – like the Cheshire cat in Alice in Wonderland. Clearly the rise and fall of ideas in economics is as much connected with attendant circumstances, including ideological and political circumstances, as with their logical properties or their power of passing any test of prediction. And by this I mean not only the use of such ideas by politicans or policy-makers but their hold on the minds of economists themselves. Part of the attendant circumstances are clearly the domain of the biographer; indeed biographies of great economists, written by economists with historical and cultural awareness, would greatly increase our understanding of the sociology of this particular branch of knowledge.

I have taken advantage of the lapse of time to correct some factual errors and to rewrite certain passages from the first edition. For those interested in making comparisons between the two, the changes of substance chiefly affect chapters 9, 12 and 15. I was at fault in not pointing the way forward more clearly from Keynes's pre-1914 interests in the quantity theory of money and the theory of probability to his interwar innovations in economic theory. A full appreciation of these connections will have to wait for the second volume; but I hope I have been able to indicate their general character.

References

1. Robert M. Fisher, *Economic Record*, June 1984, 196–7.
2. Joseph A. Schumpeter, 'John Maynard Keynes', repr. in *Ten Great Economists*, 1952, 275.
3. Sir William Rees-Mogg, *The Times*, 10 November 1983.
4. Maurice Peston, *New Statesman*, 9 December 1983.
5. Christie Davies, *Reviewing Sociology*, Summer 1984, 25.
6. David Marquand, *Encounter*, April 1984.
7. e.g., Bruce Mazlish, *James and John Stuart Mill*, 1975.
8. Elizabeth Durbin, *New Jerusalems*, 1985, 11.
9. T. W. Hutchison, *Knowledge and Ignorance in Economics*, 1977, 18.

Introduction

This is the first volume of the second full-length biography of John Maynard Keynes. A third, and even a fourth, biography are rumoured to be on their way. The study of Keynes's life is wide open again, after thirty years' domination by a single book, Sir Roy Harrod's *Life*, which came out in 1951.

I say 'study of Keynes's life' as distinct from the study of Keynesian economics or of Keynes as an economist. The literature on the last two subjects is vast, and still growing. There have been major interpretations, re-interpretations, and critiques of Keynesian theory. There is a huge literature of exegesis and pseudo-exegesis – what did Keynes say? What did he mean to say? What should he have said? What would he say now? Hundreds of thousands of students all over the world have been taught the Keynesian 'model' in their first-year courses in macroeconomics. What has been lacking is any up-to-date history of the man behind the model. It is the aim of this biography to supply one.

Although there is no need to argue the case for biography on utilitarian grounds, it is time Keynesian studies were given a proper biographical and historical context. As Joseph Schumpeter well put it in his obituary notice of Keynes in 1946:

> Every comprehensive 'theory' of an economic state of society consists of two complementary but essentially distinct elements. There is, first, the theorist's view about the basic features of the state of society, about what is and what is not important in order to understand its life at a given time. Let us call this his vision. And there is, second, the theorist's technique, an apparatus by which he conceptualises his vision and which turns the latter into concrete propositions or 'theories'.... The *General Theory* is the final result of [Keynes's] long struggle to make [his] vision of our age analytically operative.

If underlying Keynesian theory was Keynes's vision of his age, knowledge of his state of mind and the circumstances which formed it is essential, not only in order to understand how he came to see the world as he did, but also in order to pass a judgment on the theory itself.

Up to now our image of the 'man behind the model' has been formed almost entirely from Sir Roy Harrod's biography. Trying to improve on Sir Roy has been immensely challenging; not because a better life of Keynes could not be written but because writing about Keynes in the way one wants to write about him is a daunting, probably foolhardy, task. To gain proper understanding of his achievements one needs to capture his life in all its variety and richness; yet this calls for a combination of talents rarely found in a biographer. What makes most biography manageable is that the biographer does not have to know about too many different worlds. Most subjects, after all, are people of a single vocation and a limited milieu. Keynes inhabited many different worlds; his curiosities, his sympathies, his ambitions ranged over much of the thought, letters, arts, and practical affairs of his time: he even, fortunately briefly, hoped to make a contribution to genetics. He touched almost nothing without leaving a mark on it. It seemed to me, time and again, that I was having to write about things of which I knew nothing or very little, but which I sensed were important. What does one do? One learns as much as one can in the time available; and for the rest, one hopes, like Bernini, to create the illusion of solidity.

This was not the only problem. The atmospheres of Keynes's different worlds were very different, and so are the conventions for writing about them. Books about public men are usually very different from books about writers, artists, thinkers, etc. They are written by different kinds of people, in a different style. They tend to have different readerships. They even look different. Revelations or lines of enquiry which are considered shocking for one class of subject, are accepted without question for another. There are many explanations for this difference in treatment; but one of them has to do with an attitude to truth which, in turn, raises the question of biographical intention. Broadly speaking books by, or about, public men are much more Victorian than books by, or about, creative artists. Like Victorian portraits they try to conform closely to conventional expectations of what our public benefactors should be like – the ambitions they should have, the lives they should lead. No doubt in many cases, little enough in the way of truth is sacrificed. A surprisingly large number of public men do actually think and behave as we think they should. In other words they are not very interesting as people. Keynes was not like that, and it is no use writing about him as though he was. The fact that he did good does not mean that he was a conventionally good man, or even that he consistently strove to 'do good'. I hope this volume establishes these things, without in any way denigrating him. The worst, though most subtle, form of denigration is to make someone less interesting than he was.

This brings me back to Harrod's *Life*. I find that my Keynes is very different from Harrod's. This is not on the whole due to important differences in the information available to us. It is more nearly accounted for by the selection and arrangement of that information. Harrod left out many things which I thought essential to a proper understanding of Keynes's character and thought and, partly because of this, failed to make a number of important connections. Let me give some examples from the period covered by my book.

Since the publication of Michael Holroyd's *Lytton Strachey* in 1967, it has been known that Keynes was homosexual for much of his adult life, and that at least one love affair, that with the painter Duncan Grant, was supremely important to him. Roy Harrod omitted any mention of this side of Keynes, and the convention of not talking about his homosexuality has been followed even by those post-Holroyd writers on Keynes who have tried to provide a portrait of 'Keynes the Man' as a background to their economic discussions.* The result is a severely impoverished account of Keynes's feelings, his values, his friendships, and his cultural milieu. Harrod's omissions do not allow him to make sense of Keynes's remark about his pre-1914 existence that, of his prime objects in life, love came a long way first; and prudently he does not quote it. Yet the long time it took Keynes, whose genius was over-whelmingly practical, to escape from the coterie culture of the Cam-bridge Apostles and Bloomsbury, becomes much more understandable in the light of the specific protective functions which these groups had for him. No one who has read Keynes's correspondence with Lytton Strachey or Duncan Grant can doubt that homosexuality for him was not just a sexual preference, but part of the 'good life' as he then defined it; and while no one would want to argue that knowledge of Keynes's sexual and emotional leanings gives one a better understanding of his economic theory, there are interesting connections to be made between his economic outlook and what Schumpeter calls his 'childless vision', which Harrod precludes himself from exploring.

Harrod's discretion takes heavy toll of his understanding of Keynes's philosophic development. Much of this took place within the circle of the Cambridge Apostles, a select and secret discussion society. Harrod mentioned that Keynes was an Apostle, implied that the Apostles no longer existed (they still meet more than thirty years after his book appeared), and then wrote: 'But it is time to desist from prying into the affairs of that august body'. In his early to mid-twenties Keynes read the Society a dozen or so papers in which he developed his ethical position, and which include the earliest statement of his theory of Probability, dating from his last undergraduate year. Harrod must

* For example, D. E. Moggridge, *Keynes* (1976), and J. C. Gilbert, *Keynes's Impact on Monetary Economics* (1982). There is the gentlest of hints in Moggridge (p. 16) and Gilbert has a single footnote (p. 16): 'Whether Keynes's bisexuality is of much relevance is at present an open question.' On the other hand, literary biographers, and writers about Bloomsbury, have taken advantage of the new knowledge: for example, P. N. Furbank, *E. M. Forster* (1977) and Paul Levy in his essay 'The Bloomsbury Group' in Milo Keynes (ed.) *Essays on John Maynard Keynes* (1975). These are good examples of the differences in convention discussed above.

have seen all these papers, yet he refers to none of them, and postdates the start of Keynes's work on Probability by two years, thus removing it from the context of his ethical concerns. As a result he never puts himself into a position to discuss the links between Keynes's ethics, his Probability theory, and his economics. I suspect that Harrod found Keynes's ethical values, based on G. E. Moore, unsatisfactory, and decided that his purpose would best be served by hurrying on to more congenial matters.

Harrod is a master of selective quotation from Keynes's letters, the excluded matter almost invariably serving his purpose of 'cleaning up' Keynes's comments for public consumption. On 15 November 1905 Keynes wrote to Lytton Strachey: 'I find Economics increasingly satisfactory, and I think I am rather good at it. I want to manage a railway or organise a Trust, or at least swindle the investing public. It is so easy and fascinating to master the principles of these things'. The phrase 'swindle the investing public' is replaced by dots. Keynes wrote to his mother on 14 April 1918: 'Still and even more confidently I attribute our misfortunes to [Lloyd] George. We are governed by a crook and the results are natural'. The quotation continues with the second sentence omitted. Sometimes Harrod changes the words without saying so. He has Keynes writing to his mother on 22 February the same year: 'The course of politics at the beginning of the week was deeply shocking. Bonar [Law] could have become prime minister if he had liked, but funked it; and as no one else seemed inclined to take the job, the government struggled through ...' Keynes actually wrote 'the goat struggled through', the 'goat' being the Asquithians' name for Lloyd George. These points are trivial in themselves, but cumulatively the effect is to make Keynes smoother and blander than he was. He could be both *méchant* and wounding, and this often affected people's attitude to him. But it would not have suited Harrod to display this side at all prominently.

Harrod's most shocking biographical stratagems arise in connection with Keynes's attitude to the First World War. Keynes served with great distinction at the Treasury from January 1915 till his resignation in June 1919. But his attitude to the war was very ambiguous, and evolved in rough parallel to that of his Bloomsbury friends to whom the war became anathema. From the summer of 1915 to the end of that year he used his position at the Treasury to argue strongly in favour of Britain fighting a more limited war – one based more on subsidies to its Allies than on raising larger and larger armies to fight on the Western front. His financial memoranda dealing with this issue provided important ammunition for the anti-conscriptionists in Asquith's Cabinet, especially Reginald McKenna, his political chief at the Treasury. With the passing of the Military Service Act in January 1916,

Keynes came very close to resigning from the Treasury, together with
McKenna and other Ministers. What he did do was to apply for exemption from military service on the grounds of conscientious objection
(even though he was covered by a Treasury exemption). He came to
regard the continuation of the war as a criminal conspiracy on the part
of Lloyd George's government and particularly Lloyd George himself.
But he remained, outstandingly successful, at his Treasury job, locked
in a crisis of conscience. Two letters to Duncan Grant indicate his
feelings. On 14 January 1917 he wrote: 'God curse him [Lloyd George]
. . . I pray for the most absolute financial crash (and yet strive to prevent
it – so that all I do is a contradiction with all I feel)'; and on 15
December 1917: 'I work for a Government I despise for ends I think
criminal'.

Hardly a trace of this tension is to be found in Harrod's account,
though he had access to all the relevant facts. Of the 1915 period, when
Lloyd George himself recognised Keynes as the inspirer of the 'campaign which the Treasury were waging against my great gun programme' (*War Memoirs*, ii, 685), Harrod wrote: 'The work was extremely exacting. It does not seem to have given rise to major political
or interdepartmental crises. All went forward smoothly. It is a happy
nation that has no history'. Furthermore, Harrod omitted the fact
that Keynes had applied for a certificate of conscientious objection,
covering this up with language as slippery as that of any election manifesto. When this omission was pointed out many years later, first by
Clive Bell, later by Mrs Elizabeth Johnson (the first editor of Keynes's
Collected Writings), Harrod first simply repeated his denial that Keynes
was ever a conscientious objector, then admitted he might have 'over-
looked' the evidence, and finally promised to make changes in any
subsequent edition of his text (which he failed to do). His unrevised
account remains the standard one. It is not only very misleading in
itself, but it precluded him from adequately exploring the emotional
intensity which went into the writing of Keynes's *Economic Consequences
of the Peace*, with its savage condemnation of Lloyd George.

Harrod's omissions have to be understood partly as a result of cir-
cumstance, partly as a matter of biographical intention. He wrote his
book in the late 1940s. Biographical conventions were then quite different from what they are now. Any explicit statement of sexual irregularity, for example, was taboo. At best one might hint that matters
were not quite what they should be. It would be absurd to blame
Harrod for failing to write the kind of biography that would have been
possible only thirty years later. Nevertheless, he can be faulted on two,
connected, grounds. The first is for failing to make explicit the conventions and limitations under which he wrote. The second is for writing
about Keynes's private life and the Bloomsbury milieu at a length and

in a way which suggested that he was telling the whole story, whereas much of it is an exercise in covering up and planting false trails. Under the circumstances, to have candidly admitted suppression was the reputable course.

Harrod faced another difficulty which deserves sympathy. He started his book in 1947, a year after Keynes died; and so immediately ran into the problem of what Virginia Woolf called 'the widow and the friends'. She writes: 'Suppose, for example, that the man of genius was immoral, ill-tempered, and threw the boots at the maid's head. The widow would say, "Still I loved him – he was the father of my children; and the public, who love his books, must on no account be disillusioned. Cover up; omit!" The biographer obeys. And thus the majority of Victorian biographies are like the wax figures now preserved in Westminster Abbey ... effigies which have only a smooth likeness to the body in the coffin.'

Roy Harrod had to contend with not one, but a whole bevy of 'widows', vigorous, articulate and opinionated, of whom the least troublesome was his subject's actual widow, the delightful Lydia Lopokova. They were headed by Keynes's formidable brother, Sir Geoffrey Keynes. But there was also Keynes's sister, Margaret Hill, and his mother, Florence Keynes. Beyond the family there were his intimate friends of Bloomsbury, and his fellow-economists. All of them had, so to speak, stakes in the property. And between them they controlled practically all the primary source material which Harrod would need to use.

He faced formidable obstacles. Although Sir Geoffrey had commissioned the life, he soon decided to destroy some of the most important evidence – the run of letters between his brother and Lytton Strachey. Harrod took prompt action. He wrote to Clive Bell on 17 April 1947: 'I think probably the best thing would eventually be for me to approach Geoffrey K. quite frankly saying I know what to expect in the letters, that I am a discreet person and Maynard's friend, and that, since I am bound to discuss Maynard's friends in the *Life*, it is much better that I should do so from a background of real knowledge rather than from mere description by others...' In addition he got his and Geoffrey's mutual friend, John Sparrow, subsequently Warden of All Souls, to appeal to Sir Geoffrey's 'conscience as a bibliophile', and James Strachey, Lytton Strachey's brother, to claim that he wanted to 'collect all Lytton's papers'. That this correspondence, central to understanding the young Keynes, is still extant, is due to Harrod's efforts.

Another problem which Harrod faced is that although all the 'widows' had definite opinions about his subject, they were far from being the same opinion. To his family and economist disciples (of whom Harrod was one) Keynes was a hero, a statesman, almost a saviour. To Bloomsbury, who had to take his economic genius on trust, he was an intimate friend, who shared their somewhat unworldly values, though with regrettable backslidings. They shared a common allegiance to the Cambridge philosopher G. E. Moore, who had said that to 'be good' was more ethically valuable than to 'do good'. Harrod recalled a frosty interview with Leonard Woolf (who gave his book an equally frosty review): 'When I told him that I could not regard Moore's philosophy (as distinct from his personality) with respect, he seemed deeply offended and began to take up the attitude of a headmaster. I felt I was in serious danger of corporal punishment. A young man, such as I, must not presume to belittle a great philosopher. Unfortunately I knew a great deal more about philosophy than Woolf; his defence was quite trivial. I hastily changed the subject. Actually I am confident that my general estimation of Moore is one of the best things in the book and will stand.' (Harrod to Clive Bell, 22 November 1951).

Finally, every biographer has experienced that sinking feeling, when, his labours over, he waits for the 'widows' to comment on his manuscript. (I should add at this point that my 'widows' have been extraordinarily helpful and generous.) To one of Maynard Keynes's closest friends, David Garnett, Harrod wrote on 17 February 1950:

> Greatly as I should value your criticisms and suggestions on Maynard, and much as I believe they might improve the book, I am sorry to say that I do not wish to send it to you now.
>
> The fact of the matter is that I have come to have a crise de nerfs on the subject. I have had or am having to show the whole book to old Mrs Keynes, Geoffrey Keynes, Mrs Hill, Richard Kahn, and (for proof reading) R. H. Dundas. I have had to show large sections to the Treasury. I have had to show large sections also (about America) to Lionel Robbins, Frank Lee, and Lord Brand. Some time ago I showed the first part of the book to Duncan [Grant], Vanessa [Bell], Clive [Bell] and James Strachey. I have received much valuable help from these people and made numerous alterations; but it is not without nervous strain. I have now reached the end of my tether.

Harrod's book was written in an astonishingly short space of time, partly in order to get out a life of Keynes before Keynes's mother died (in fact she lived till 1958). Some of the carelessness in dating and quotation from letters, as well as the thinness of research in places (especially in the chapter on the First World War) can be attributed to this cause.

It would be unfair to minimise these problems. Yet I doubt if the presence of the 'widows' crucially determined the kind of book Harrod wrote. His own biographical intentions were sufficient censor. The most striking evidence for this is that when Mrs Johnson first uncovered the facts about Keynes's conscientious objection in 1958, the resistance to publishing them came not from Sir Geoffrey Keynes, but from Harrod himself.

Harrod's motives for writing the kind of book he did deserve respect if not approval. He loved and admired Keynes and wanted to protect him. Unfortunately his conception of what was to Keynes's discredit was excessively conservative. As Richard Kahn, who was also devoted to Keynes, shrewdly remarked in 1958: 'Roy seems to have the greatest difficulty in distinguishing [Keynes's attitude to conscientious objection] from the attitude of his parents, which we now know to have been highly conventional, like Roy's.'* As Lord Kahn surmised, Harrod was a much more conventional person than was Keynes, and perhaps could not honestly face facts about his hero contrary to his own view of what he should have been like. In particular, he was deeply embarrassed by Keynes's association with Bloomsbury. He found little to admire in the circle's sense of humour, its bawdiness, and its ethical values, all of which seemed to him an inadequate basis on which to build his subject's public achievements.

However, there was something else. Harrod was a biographer in the Victorian mould. He thought of biography as having an inspirational or exemplary purpose. Truth, in the sense of fidelity to the facts, was subordinate to uplift. Harrod was less concerned with hurting the 'widows'' feelings than with damaging Keynes's power to do good. He believed that if the world was to avoid a dark fate, governments must become 'Keynesian' – must be taught to run their economies at permanent boom by the methods of 'demand-management' which Keynes bequeathed. Specifically, he believed that a bright future depended on 'selling' Keynes to the United States. This required downplaying all those aspects of Keynes's character and thought likely to give offence across the Atlantic. Truth must sometimes be sacrificed to expediency. This was the opposite of what Keynes generally believed. Criticised for attacking President Wilson in his famous book, *The Economic Consequences of the Peace*, Keynes wrote: 'Attempts to humour or placate the Americans or anyone else seem quite futile, and I personally despair of results from anything but violent and ruthless truth-telling – that will work in the end, even if slowly.' Harrod's views were far less robust, and circumstances favoured his natural tendency to discretion.

The question of whether one should always try to tell the truth, or whether one should tailor truth to expediency admits of no clear answer, even for the purposes of biography. It is hard to believe that governments would have long resisted Keynesian policies on the grounds that they disliked his personality. Nevertheless, so deep-rooted

* In a letter to Sir Austin Robinson, dated 3 November 1958. I am grateful to Lord Kahn for permission to quote from this letter.

is the feeling that our great public benefactors must have admirable private characters that Harrod's emollient treatment may have eased acceptance of Keynes's ideas. In that case his biography would have served its political purpose. The biographer has a choice, after all: to tell the whole truth as he sees it, or to tell as much of the truth as is compatible with doing good. Fortunately the decision becomes easier the longer ago one's subject lived. The 'widows' pass away, and time rates all achievements at their proper worth. The biographer is free to become a historian, and to create something which may endure.

1 Dynastic Origins

ANCESTORS

John Maynard Keynes* was not just a man of establishments; but part
of the elite of each establishment of which he was a member. There was
scarcely a time in his life when he did not look down at the rest of
England, and much of the world, from a great height. He went to
England's best school, Eton, where he was both a Colleger, one of its
intellectual elite, and a member of Pop, its social elite. He was an
undergraduate and fellow of King's, one of Cambridge's top colleges,
and was a member of that select group of intellectuals, the Apostles. In
the Civil Service, he was at the Treasury, the top home department. He
was the intimate of one prime minister, and the counsellor of many. As
a favourite pupil of Marshall, he was right at the heart of England's
economics establishment. As chairman of the National Mutual Life
Assurance Society, he was at the centre of England's financial oli-
garchy. In the world of the arts, he was a member of the Bloomsbury
Group, England's most potent cultural coterie. His communications
with the educated public were always made from a position of unim-
peachable authority. This position was largely achieved by the force of
his dazzling intellect and by his practical genius. But he did not start
life without considerable advantages which helped him slip easily into
the parts for which his talents destined him. There was no nonsense
about his being in the wrong place or having the wrong accent. Of his
advantages the chief was being born at Cambridge, into a community
of dons, the son of John Neville and Florence Ada Keynes.

Maynard Keynes's path to the top had been smoothed by much toil.
When he was five his great-grandmother Jane Elizabeth Ford wrote to
him, 'You will be expected to be very clever, having lived always in
Cambridge.' The way the expectation was phrased is interesting.
Today a Keynes would be expected to have brains because he was born

---

* He was always known as Maynard Keynes; I will call him, depending on context,
Keynes, Maynard Keynes, or just Maynard, without further reference to the John
which his mother alone preferred, as being the name of her father.

a Keynes. But great-grandmother Ford wrote before the dynasty was established. Indeed all she would have known about the Keyneses was that they came from Wiltshire, that John Maynard Keynes's grandfather had been a successful businessman, and that her granddaughter Florence had married his son, a clever young Cambridge don called John Neville Keynes. Looking at the matter from the heights of provincial Nonconformity Jane Elizabeth Ford must have felt that there was something quite ordinary about the Keyneses.

Not till he was sixteen did her great-grandson have much cause to think otherwise. It was only at Eton that he discovered that the Keynes side of the family had some fairly impressive historical credentials. Working in the college library he constructed a family tree which started with the Keynes who came over with the Conqueror.

Something of the esoteric quality of Maynard Keynes's life is suggested by the name itself. When spelt right it is often mispronounced Keens; when pronounced right it is sometimes misspelt Canes. Such are the incidental penalties for having come from the otherwise desirable location of Cahagnes in the Calvados district of Normandy.[1] The name is probably derived from the late Latin word *casnus*, an oak, from which comes the modern French name *chêne*; alternatively it may come from *catanus*, or juniper bush.[2] Whatever the case, William de Cahagnes was a vassal of Robert, Count (later Earl) of Mortain, half-brother to Duke William of Normandy. He followed his lord to England, fought at the battle of Hastings, and received from Earl Robert a number of estates totalling over 5000 acres. The main ones were at Dodford in Northamptonshire – mentioned as being in the possession of 'William de Cahagnes' in the Domesday Book – and at Horsted Keynes in Sussex. Smaller properties were held in Buckinghamshire and Cambridgeshire. On William's death his estates went to his son and heir, Ralph; and on Ralph's death were divided between Ralph's three sons, Ralph, Hugh and William.[3]

The lines of the first two had died out by the fourteenth century. 'The Keyneses do not seem to have been a very warlike family' wrote the schoolboy Maynard. Prudently 'they went into battle only when their absence was likely to bring about a monetary fine'. The exception was Ralph's third son, William, from whom Maynard Keynes claimed descent. He captured King Stephen at the battle of Lincoln in 1141. As a reward, he received the manor of Winkleigh (later Winkley Keynes) in Devon. About 1330, William's descendant John de Keynes married Isabella Wake, who brought a considerable estate in Somerset into the family. In the sixteenth and seventeenth centuries, the Keynes family, now based at Compton Pauncefoote in Somerset, remained Roman Catholics and loyal to the Stuarts; a double mistake which resulted in their losing all their property. An extraordinary number of them became Jesuit priests. The most famous, John Keynes (1625–95), was Professor of Logic at the University of Liège. In 1683 he was appointed by the Pope to be Provincial of England and was one of Titus Oates's intended victims. He wrote *A Rational Compendious Way to Convince, without any dispute, all Persons whatever dissenting from the True Religion*. According to Maynard Keynes 'it seems likely that he was partly responsible, by his bad advice, for the fall of James II'. He had an elder brother, Captain Alexander Keynes, who was not a Jesuit. 'He fought for Charles I in the civil war; and the last remnant of the family estates was lost by him in the Royalist cause. The family now sinks into obscurity, and the next two links cannot be fitted in with any certainty. Alexander had several sons, most of whom became Jesuits. But as far as I can make out his son Henry was the father of Richard Keynes, of Wareham.'[4]

The line to our subject runs without problem from this Richard Keynes who died in 1720. There are three more Richards, then a John Keynes, who was the father of another John Keynes, Maynard Keynes's grandfather. These descendants of Captain Alexander Keynes, if such they were, start off as Anglicans but soon become Baptists; they also turn up in Salisbury as ornamental plasterers and brushmakers. By this time, Maynard Keynes noted, 'the tradition of their more interesting past seems to have entirely died out'.[5]

Family trees are apt to be tedious except to members of the family and genealogists. Nor are they always illuminating from a biographical point of view, since the laws of heredity are so little understood. Who knows what Maynard Keynes actually 'inherited' from all these Keyneses? The justification for the above account is that the subject of this biography discovered his Keynes family past at an impressionable age, was fascinated by it, and thought that he had a name to live up to. At Eton, he planned a family history. Its introduction, which he sketched out, contained the following passage:

> Some, however, I trust there are, to whom the great names of the past remain a living memory; who shape their course in this world under a deep sense of responsibility of bearing them; and fill their appointed positions and do their appointed work 'commanded by the dead gaze of all their ancestors'.

If his father's family recalled to Maynard Keynes vanished squirearchal glories, his mother's summoned him to moral and intellectual effort. His maternal grandmother traced her descent back to a Sussex smuggler, Thomas Ford, killed by the King's men in 1768. But repentance was swift and permanent. The smuggler's son, David Everard Ford, became a Congregational minister, 'subject to fits of depression possibly caused by the religious problems arising out of his interest in the study of fossils'.[6] In 1834 his son, also David Everard (1797–1875), who became Congregational minister at Lymington, Hampshire, married Jane Elizabeth Down, 'a young woman of outstanding energy and ability' who was descended on her mother's side from two old west-country families, the Haydons and the Langdons. She bore him ten children; she also ran a girls' boarding school at Lymington. When David Ford moved to the Richmond Congregational church in Manchester in 1843, she restarted her boarding school with her second daughter, Ada Haydon Ford. Jane Elizabeth Ford, the great-grandmother who expected Maynard Keynes to be brainy, was obviously a formidable – and not, one suspects, very agreeable – lady. Her husband was a well-known composer of religious music, and was not above treating in print such secular themes as 'Progressive Exercises for the Voice'. But his wife regarded music as frivolous, and made him give it up. Soon after his marriage he started writing religious tracts on the depravity of man. The most famous was *Decapolis; or the Individual Obligation of Christians to Save Souls from Death* which, published in 1840, 'produced a great and immediate effect upon the religious world of the time'.[7]

It was Ada Haydon Ford of the boarding school who married Maynard Keynes's maternal grandfather, John Brown. Born in 1830, the son of modest Lancashire business folk, Brown was apprenticed at fifteen to a printer. He decided to become a Minister, apparently as a result of reading the religious tracts he set up in print. He took his London Matriculation, studied classics at Owen's College, Manchester, and got his London B.A. in 1851. In 1855 he became Congregational Minister at Park Chapel, Cheetham Hill Road, Manchester, channelling his dramatic instincts into preaching. Running through Maynard's mother's family is a strain of didacticism and intellectual fancy lacking from the more recent Keyneses. The women especially had a strong capacity for moral indignation which Keynes may have inherited. But the ambiance of the Brown and Keynes families alike was very much Chapel and Trade. They were middle-class, even moneyed, but not yet gentlefolk as the Victorians understood the term.

II

JOHN NEVILLE KEYNES

It was Maynard Keynes's paternal grandfather, John Keynes of Salisbury, born in 1805, who restored the Keynes family fortune. Portraits of him as a youth and old man show a slight, spare figure, with shrewd eyes, an amused mouth, and a general air of satisfaction. John Keynes's satisfaction was that of the self-made man. An only son, apprenticed in his father's brushmaking business at eleven, he had built it up, by 1830, into a 'very lucrative manufactory'. But 'the soul of the flower', according to a gardening journal given to poetic exuberance, 'lodged in his breast'. At seventeen he won his first prize – a pair of sugar tongs – for his pinks. Determined to profit from his green fingers he gave up bristles and turned to dahlias. His one-man dahlia exhibition at Stonehenge in 1841 attracted thousands. This was the start of his reputation, and the foundation of his fortune. Dahlias made him. Cleverly developing new strains he helped promote the dahlia boom; when the dahlia bubble burst, he switched with equal success to roses. In 1845 he acquired some nurseries in Castle Street which were soon nationally known. They reflected 'in a very decided manner the tendency of Mr Keynes's mind for specialities'. He grew only for market – roses, dahlias, verbenas, and carnations – and only those that would sell well. 'No one has seen in the nurseries at Salisbury a general collection of plants. Their owner was too shrewd to embark money and strength in doubtful enterprises, but to make the round of his work complete, and squeeze rent out of glass at times when it might not be earning money, he developed a system of raising grape-vines in quantities of the trade. . . .'[8]

John Keynes had a legendary local reputation for business shrewdness. Stories were still told forty years later about how he had got the better of Mr Squibbs, evidently a somewhat dim-witted local florist. 'Business to him was a source of great pleasure; he had great confidence in himself, and his industry in business was astonishing; he kept all his books, it is said, up to a short time before his death.'[9] As he prospered, John Keynes diversified into banking and other commercial activities. Like most self-made Victorian businessmen he attributed his success in life to hard work and religious principles. He said his life had been happy because he had succeeded in all his enterprises, and sounded as if he meant it. He set great store by the education he had never had, supporting a number of local schools and becoming superintendent of the Baptist Brown Street Sunday School.

John Keynes's success was remarkable enough, but it was to be eclipsed by the performance of his son. He married twice. His first wife, Matilda Blake, bore him a daughter, Fanny, who later married a successful grocer, Edward Purchase. Matilda died of cholera and in 1851 John Keynes married Anna Maynard Neville, who came from an Essex farming family. Their only son, John Neville, Maynard's father, was born on 31 August 1852. If John Keynes took the first steps towards the production of Maynard Keynes by making money, John Neville took the decisive second step by getting himself established at Cambridge. It was a painful story.

Neville, as he was always called, grew up in a comfortable house in Castle Street, Salisbury, adjoining his father's nurseries. It seems to have been an affectionate home. Neville's relationship with his father is now difficult to reconstruct, though son always spoke of father with affection and respect. John Keynes was a religious man, who believed in religion as a moral discipline. His earliest surviving letter to his son dates from 21 January 1857: 'My dear little Neville is not going to be a naughty boy, the good Jesus was never a naughty boy and you must try and be like him.' Religious reinforcements were provided by John Keynes's mother who lived with them till her death in 1869 at the age of ninety-four. In her deaf old age she sat all day with a Bible on her knee, mouthing the words of the scriptures. There is no doubt that John Keynes put Neville under great pressure to succeed academically, once he showed signs of being clever. Academic success was the royal road out of trade; Neville, in any case, never shared his father's horticultural interests. However, John Keynes was not all stern Victorian paterfamilias. There was clearly a lighter, more companionable, side to him. He was a man of hobbies: he had built his fortune on a hobby. He and Neville played chess, Neville starting to beat him when he was twelve. John Keynes would take his son up to London for the pantomime, and later to plays and oratorios. From his father Neville thus got an ambiguous legacy. The pressure to succeed was there; but also the message that life was not wholly serious. Neville was to show the same divided character. He grew up with a pervasive anxiety, to which immersion in hobbies was his eventual answer.

Neville was very close to his mother. She died when he was well over fifty, and his grief was overwhelming. She was a warm, emotional, person, not stupid, but not intellectual and didactic as the women on Maynard's maternal side were apt to be. Nor had she any interest in social work. (She once tried to sell some Bibles, but never, we are told, repeated the experiment.) Also living at home was John Keynes's unmarried sister Aunt Mary, fussy, anxious, and devoted to Neville. Although John Keynes took part in civic affairs, Anna and Aunt Mary were purely domestic, devoting themselves to their two men. The close-knit character of his family made a great impression on Neville. He was to be first and foremost a family man, happiest in the circle of his family; unlike Florence, Maynard Keynes's mother, who after the first few years of her marriage, branched out into community work.

There was the usual complement of family friends – Tiffins and Chubbs, Williams and Todds. But the most important non-family influence on Neville was undoubtedly Henry Fawcett. His father, William Fawcett, was an old Salisbury friend of John Keynes. In an appalling shooting accident he had blinded his twenty-five year old son Henry, then a fellow of Trinity Hall, Cambridge. Undaunted, Henry

Fawcett went on to become Professor of Political Economy at Cambridge in 1863, and Postmaster General in Gladstone's government of 1880. It was an exemplary Victorian success story, in which individual courage and determination had triumphed over the most adverse circumstances. Fawcett's shining moral example was always before Neville as he struggled to fulfil his father's hopes in the face of much discouragement. Fawcett is also important in our story because it was he who set Neville's sights on Cambridge.

In 1864, when he was eleven, Neville started at Amersham Hall, a small, exclusive, Dissenting Academy of about a hundred boys at Caversham, near Reading, which under its headmaster Ebenezer West provided 'just the sort of education which was necessary to nullify the disabilities from which Nonconformity laboured in those days ...'.[10] There was no nonsense about games: John Keynes paid his £70 a year for examination results; though the boys were allowed to keep rabbits. Neville was prepared for the London University Matriculation, similar to modern O Level. Via this route Amersham Hall produced 'senior wranglers,* leading men in surgery, medicine, law, and literature'.[11]

How happy Neville was at Amersham Hall is difficult to say. When he went there he started the diary he was to keep till 1917, fifty-three years later. However, many of the pages covering his schooldays are missing – seemingly the first of a number of excisions of painful material which Neville was honest enough to record in his early years of diary keeping. Compared to Maynard, he seems to have been a late developer. Maynard would never have written at thirteen: 'I sit at a table near a jolly lot of boys. The one who sits on my right hand named Roselli is an awfully jolly fellow.'[12] However, by fourteen he was top of his matriculation class in mathematics, and second in classics. From that point his scholastic career took off, though not without alarms. A school report of April 1869 thought that in the Matriculation there would be 'marks lost through nervousness'. And so it turned out. He passed the Matriculation examination that summer respectably, but not brilliantly, being lucky to get a Gilchrist scholarship to University College, London.

On 5 October 1869, soon after his seventeenth birthday, he took up residence at University Hall, Gordon Square, Bloomsbury, a hostel set up in 1849 for Nonconformist students. Amersham Hall provided much of its intake, and Neville came up with a group of Amersham Hall friends, including Henry Bond, Arthur Spokes, and William Lord. Mostly the sons of self-made businessmen his fellow students knew they were expected through education to break out of trade into more highly valued professional careers. University College catered for this goal. Its educational system was based on examinations which were continually

---

* Those obtaining first-class honours in the Mathematical Tripos were known as Wranglers.

recurring and of 'portentous length'.[13] And for Neville this was not the end. Fawcett 'advised me to go for two years to London, & then on to Cambridge'.[14] As an only son Neville carried the whole burden of his parents' hopes. He used to say later he had never worked so hard in his life as in his years at University College. The strain told on his health and his personality. He began to complain of headaches, toothaches and chest pains, so much so that his mother feared the worst. 'You are very precious to us you know my own dear boy', she wrote him, 'and if we were to lose you I should lose my all.'[15] Until seventeen he was 'quite a chatterbox'. After that he started to dry up. By the time he got to Cambridge he was complaining in true pedant's fashion of idle chatter.[16] Coincidentally, he stopped growing, remaining stuck at 5 foot 4 inches, short even by Victorian standards.

As soon as he came to London he started recording the number of hours he worked each day, adding them up to make a grand yearly total – a habit which persisted until he gave up his diary. At University College he managed a ten-hour day. Yet he still had time for his hobbies. He played tournament chess. He collected stamps. He took up fives. Each weekend he escaped into the fantasy world of the Victorian melodrama, comedy, pantomime, opera; sometimes with his father up in London on horticultural business. Female company was confined to the holidays: skating with Flossie Williams, croquet and whist with Minnie Todd. Abandoning himself to passion he kissed Minnie's hand, receiving a lock of hair in return. But soon he was 'enjoying' himself with Flossie 'as if there was no Minnie Todd in existence'.

Neville's best friend at this time was Arthur Spokes, son of a Reading businessman. On 16 February 1871 he recorded in his diary that Spokes's father had given up his business, much to the annoyance of his son who did not think he could afford to; but 'Mr. Spokes was very ambitious to be no longer a tradesman'. Arthur Spokes – who later became Recorder of Reading – was evidently a gay dog in that high-minded company. Something of the flavour of their discussions on life is conveyed by a letter he wrote to Neville on 17 April 1871. He had decided not to marry a certain girl.

Do you know [he told Neville] I have finally given up all idea of going in for her, as I do not feel at present as if I could ever love her. In this decision I beg you to find a proof of the assertion which I made to you a few weeks ago namely that my ambition shd never interfere with my love or my pleasure. For to say nothing of the vast pecuniary advantage that wd follow the matrimonial step which I have contemplated, I cannot withhold from myself that it wd give me a very good chance of becoming M.P. for the town. Who could withstand the combined influence of two powerful municipal families?

In July 1870 Neville obtained a first-class in Part I of his B.A. For Part II in October 1871 he took Logic and Moral Philosophy Honours, being placed first equal. His first attempt to get into Cambridge as a mathematical scholar the following month was foiled by a skating accident in Regent's Park which gave him concussion. On 18 March 1872 he tried for Trinity Hall, Fawcett's college; but 'very much troubled' with toothache, he failed. On 3 June 1872, he sat the Pembroke College examination. This time he was successful, winning the first mathematical scholarship worth £60.

Neville had got to Cambridge, but the worst of his troubles were yet to come. The problem was he was in the wrong subject. He soon discovered that he hated mathematics. A better tripos for him would have been the Moral Sciences Tripos, established in 1848, and recently made available as a first degree.* However, not only were there hardly any scholarships in it (which is why Neville had entered Cambridge as a mathematics scholar), but he would have been very unlikely to get a fellowship by doing well in it, fellowships at the time being awarded almost exclusively for high places in the mathematical and classical triposes. The choice seemed to be between slaving away at mathematics which he disliked, or switching to moral sciences which held out no academic prospects. He could see only one escape: to leave Cambridge right away. He wrote two tormented letters to his parents on 19 and 20 October 1872. Would they take him away? They had 'perhaps naturally' overestimated his abilities. He was really fit only to be a solicitor, and had better start training for that straight away. 'I do not mind being laughed at & called a fool as I know I shall be. I think my best & bravest course will be to acknowledge an error which I now realise & manfully do that which I esteem most likely to turn out best for my future welfare'.[17] There was also the worry about being a financial burden to his father, already in his late sixties and in indifferent health.

His parents did not hesitate. On 22 October 1872 Neville noted laconically in his diary, 'They are very averse to my leaving Cambridge, so I have agreed to stay'. The plan was for him to persevere with mathematics till May 'and see how I liked it then'. But doing problems with Routh, Cambridge's renowned mathematical coach, filled him with despair. In the Christmas vacation he came to a decision. He wrote to his College tutor, C. E. Searle (later Master of Pembroke), that he meant to give up mathematics and read moral sciences instead. 'I did not ask for his advice, as I have quite made up my mind on the subject.' But the argument in Salisbury went on. Fawcett urged him to continue with mathematics. He returned to Cambridge on 21 January 1873 where a 'very bad attack of the blues commenced. I am seriously

* Tripos: Cambridge term for the examination leading to an Honours Degree.

doubtful if I took the right step when I came to Cambridge. My faceache still continues.' The next day he saw Searle.

> He was very kind & by dint of saying he thought I shd get a fellow-ship, his advice, added to that of Mr. Fawcett & to what I know to be Father's wish, has at last prevailed upon me to continue reading Mathematics till May. I do not myself consider the step to be a wise one, & I cannot begin to work with any 'go', but at any rate I suppose I please others.

He struggled on with mathematics till the summer and then, not liking it any better, was finally allowed to give it up. He did so in the belief that his fellowship chances were at an end.[18] That summer he started on his new intellectual regime. Up at college in the long vaca-tion he annotated the first volume of Mill's *Principles of Political Economy* and 'enjoyed it immensely'.[19] On 31 August, his twenty-first birthday, he started shaving.

Neville started reading moral sciences at a very interesting moment in the history both of the degree and the university. The ancient universities were in the course of being roused from their long slumber to a new sense of their responsibility to provide leadership in an age of industrialism, declining religious faith, rising democracy, and intellectual ferment.* Neville's presence at Cambridge was itself a sign of their new hospitality to intellectual Nonconformity, previously excluded by Test Acts dating from the seventeenth century. The Moral Sciences Tripos at Cambridge was one of the points of this awakening. It was attractive to scholars, because its component studies – moral and political philosophy, logic, psychology, and economics – were all in a state of flux, offering oppor-tunities for creative work. It was attractive to students like Neville whose logical grasp exceeded their mathematical facility. And parts of the moral sciences – especially moral and political philosophy and political economy – were coming to be seen as a source of social wisdom, replacing some of the functions hitherto performed by religion. Neville's switch to moral sciences determined the atmosphere in which Maynard Keynes was to grow up. He was a product of the Cambridge moral science tradition, in which Cambridge economics developed side by side with Cambridge moral philosophy.

By the end of the 1860s, though still a small school, the moral sciences were attracting able, dedicated young dons and a much better calibre of student. Henry Sidgwick had moved over from classics; Al-fred Marshall from mathematics: both 'new dons' with a high sense

---

* I shall have more to say about the circumstances which produced the awakening and the form it took in Chapter 2.

of intellectual and pastoral responsibility. William Cunningham, Herbert Foxwell, Frederic Maitland, and James Ward were distinguished graduates of the late 1860s and early 1870s; Arthur Balfour, the future Conservative prime minister, took second-class honours in the moral sciences in 1869.

Neville went to Henry Sidgwick for moral and political philosophy. Sidgwick, who had resigned his fellowship at Trinity College in 1869 because he could no longer subscribe to its 'dogmatic obligations', was a representative figure of the new age of intellectual doubt and high responsibility. He tried to construct a coherent system of secular ethics to replace religion, but his mind was far too critical for him to succeed. Neville, like almost everyone else, was very much attracted by Sidgwick's appealing personality, perplexed search for truth, and anxiety to do justice to every position; but, not himself troubled by religious doubts, he was not drawn to Sidgwick's brand of metaphysical speculation. Intellectually he was closer to Alfred Marshall, fellow of St John's, who taught him economics. Marshall had moved from mathematics to economics via ethics, which he abandoned as a waste of time. He was soon 'speaking very highly of some of the papers I have done for him, even in lecture'.[20] Neville went to Foxwell, another young fellow of St John's, for mental philosophy, and to John Venn, fellow of Caius, for logic. He showed great ability in the latter, though he thought some of Venn's lectures 'useless'.[21] At last in congenial intellectual territory, his self-esteem recovered. 'Spokes [who had also come up to Cambridge] informs me that he has heard my manner spoken of as very conceited' he confided to his diary.[22]

He continued to work at a furious pace in these years. He was never again to show such mental energy. In addition to his Cambridge work, he was also preparing for the London B.Sc., which he took in both parts, obtaining first-class honours in geology and chemistry in October 1874. Searle, his college tutor, advised him to try for the gold medal (awarded for top place) in the London M.A. examination in July 1875. He was only prevented from doing so by Fawcett, who advised him to postpone the attempt till after the tripos.[23] The object of all this extra-Cambridge work was to improve his fellowship chances; or if he failed to get a Cambridge fellowship, to have a fall-back position at London. As if this were not enough, he was gripped by 'chess mania'. He played first board for the university chess team, and took part in tournaments blindfolded, even though this gave him headaches.[24]

The reward for six years of nerve-racking exertion came in December 1875. He was declared Senior Moralist – placed first in the first class of the moral science tripos. Out of a possible 900 marks for each part, he got 684 in Logic, 617 in Political Economy, 620 in Moral and Political Philosophy, and 610 in Mental Philosophy – a wonderfully consistent performance.

> It was agreed unanimously [James Ward wrote to him of the examiners' meeting] that, as Marshall puts it, you have a very clear mind: for the rest, the Logic & Economy people rate you the highest. Jevons said that you floored the Logic papers & that your answers were a pleasure to read. I shd fancy that you pleased him better in Logic than in Economy: he evidently doesn't believe much in Marshall, & was amused by your curves. Foxwell praises your precision, but says you shirk difficulties and lack originality in philosophy.... All agreed that Pembroke ought to give you a Fellowship.[25]

The fellowship was not yet in the bag. There was a vacancy at Pembroke, but there were sure to be other candidates. Neville took out extra insurance by taking the London M.A. in June 1876, in political economy. Four days later he heard he could add the Gold Medal to the honorary fellowship which University College had already given him. Then on 10 August 1876 a 'Telegram came to say that I had been elected a Fellow of Pembroke ... unanimously & almost without discussion'.[26] His old headmaster, Ebenezer West, wrote to congratulate him: 'I am glad both as having helped your early steps along the road of learning and as a Dissenter at seeing this impartial recognition of merit as promising at no very remote day that social equality irrespective of creeds which priests ... do their utmost to hinder.' It was a double family triumph, for two months later his father was installed as Mayor of Salisbury, his nomination seconded by old William Fawcett, mayor as long ago as 1833, who described him as 'a man who had risen himself from the ranks'. Already in failing health, John Keynes had less than a year and a half to live.

The next four years of Neville's life are rather obscure because the diary, the main source of his early life, was either not kept or, more probably, is missing for the years 1877 to 1881. He had achieved his ambition; but he must already have known that it was a precarious security. The old system of fellowship tenures had been singled out for attack by the university reform movement. Lord Salisbury's denunciation of 'idle fellowships' in 1876 had led Parliament to appoint Commissioners to reform college statutes. One of the reforms they were sure to suggest was the abolition of the celibacy requirement for tenure of a fellowship. This would benefit Neville. He was the marrying type. The other proposed reform was not so good for him. This was to limit the tenure of prize fellowships – fellowships without teaching posts attached – to six years. Neville must have known that an unenviable choice was looming up; he would be able to retain his fellowship for life under the old statutes if he did not marry; he would be allowed to marry under the new statutes but would have to give up his fellowship in 1882. Pembroke, it seemed clear, would not provide a permanent resting place. In retrospect, what is important about the period 1876 to 1882 is Neville's failure to build on his achievement as Senior Moralist. When the time came for him to quit Pembroke he had written nothing. As a result, his career choices were constricted.

It is not easy to reconstruct what went wrong. Although his highest marks were achieved in Logic, he decided, under Marshall's influence, to specialise in economics. Twenty years later Marshall still regarded Neville as one of the two or three best students he had ever had. He had a firm grasp of theory and a balanced judgment; exactly the qualities Marshall was looking for to help him restore economics to what he regarded as its rightful authority. However, Marshall's advice was not always disinterested. Soon after he took the tripos, Neville signed a contract to write an elementary textbook on economics. This idea was abandoned. One can guess the reason. Some of the book would no doubt have been based on Neville's notes on Marshall's lectures; and Marshall, always touchy about the ownership of ideas, probably vetoed the project. (Mary Paley, another of Marshall's students, had a similar plan. Marshall married her and took over the main responsibility for her book, which appeared under their joint authorship as *The Economics of Industry* in 1879.) Instead, Marshall encouraged Neville to enter for the university's newly-established Cobden Prize. He started work in March 1877 on the set essay 'The Effects of Machinery on Wages', Marshall 'affording me considerable assistance'. In turn, Marshall was already starting to use Neville as a sounding board, sending him chunks of the manuscript of *The Economics of Industry*, and also draft chapters of the larger *Principles* on which he was working. By June 1877, Neville was sending parts of his own essay to be copied; 'my copyist causes me a good deal of annoyance. He seems to have given his wife some of the work to do. Her writing is not good, & some of her mistakes are atrocious.'[27] The essay, which came to 365 pages, failed to win the prize which went, on 4 March 1878, to Joseph Shield Nicholson who had taken the Moral Sciences Tripos a year after Neville. His prize essay was published in 1879 and helped him get the chair of political economy at Edinburgh a year later. Neville's essay has disappeared without trace.* Failure to win the prize must have been a

* In his *Scope and Method of Political Economy* (p. 275) Neville noted that 'the effects of machinery on wages' was an instance 'where the economist is more or less directly dependent on historical material'. It would seem likely that the topic set for the prize essay favoured Nicholson, with his strong historical and statistical bent, more than Neville whose strength lay in deductive reasoning. Neville seems also to have made the mistake of criticising the views of Cliff Leslie, one of his examiners. The other examiner was Henry Fawcett.

damaging blow to his self-confidence. In 1877, Marshall, having had to resign his fellowship at St John's on marrying Mary Paley, was appointed the first principal of the University College of Bristol. With his departure from Cambridge the incentive for Neville to continue economic work was temporarily gone. This did not stop him helping Sidgwick with his book on political economy.* He also sent Jevons criticisms of his book on Logic.† Neville was always generous with his time.

Marshall's departure had a further consequence. Foxwell took over the Economics teaching for the Moral Sciences Tripos from Marshall, leaving Neville, with Venn, to do the Logic teaching.[28] Neville was appointed lecturer in Logic at a number of colleges, including the two new women's colleges, Girton and Newnham. This took him away from economics and any thought of immediate writing on the subject.

Lecturing in Logic brought him into contact with the strange new species of women undergraduates just starting to establish itself at Cambridge. Not that women students at first pleased him. He found one of his Girton pupils 'far gone in transcendentalism; and her writing is shocking'. Another, a Miss Borckhardt, was a 'decidedly advanced thinker. . . . There is something repulsive to me in avowed infidelity in a girl.'[29] The arrival of women in Cambridge seemed to be connected in Neville's mind with 'the wide-reaching and increasing power of infidelity'.[30] But such shocking deviations from Victorianism were confined to words not deeds. One of the by-products of the higher education of women was the academic marriage. Marshall set the trend; and Neville followed in his footsteps.

In October 1878, the seventeen-year-old Florence Ada Brown, eldest daughter of the Rev. John Brown, came to Newnham Hall. Seventy-three years later, on her ninetieth birthday, she recalled the experience in a B.B.C. interview:

> Well, in those days Newnham was a Hall of Residence for only about thirty students. Our principal was Miss Clough – a great personality.

* Sidgwick's *Principles of Political Economy* appeared in 1883. A letter to Neville from Marshall at Bristol dating from 1880–1 may throw some light on the abortion of Neville's own project for a primer on economics: 'Foxwell', Marshall wrote, 'says you are helping Sidgwick on his economic book. Sidgwick & I differ on some questions of literary morality. For one thing we cd not agree in discussion as to the use which he (not you) wd be at liberty to make of your notes of my lectures & on hearing that he had asked you to help him with his book I asked Foxwell to give you my views on the subject.' (Marshall Library, Keynes Box 1, Item 75.)

† Jevons's *Studies in Deductive Logic* was published in 1880. Jevons wrote to Neville on 17 December 1880: 'The laws of thought form a very difficult subject & your criticism if not correct is in any case very acute & difficult to meet. I do not suppose I have got to the bottom of the matter. I confess I like to be criticised when the criticism is so acute.' (Marshall Library, Keynes Box 2, Item 92.)

She had been encouraged by Cambridge friends to become a pioneer of University education for women. And naturally she was most anxious that her flock should be well-behaved. There were a great many people in Cambridge all too ready to criticise us. So our Principal looked to us to be highly circumspect. For example, she wished us to be inconspicuous in our dress. But, unfortunately for poor dear Miss Clough, we were rather taken with the pre-Raphaelite style. And we liked to trail about in gowns of peacock blue and terracotta and orange.... Instead of being inconspicuous, we were observed of all observers![31]

Florence, at seventeen, was the youngest of Miss Clough's charges, 'I came up feeling very shy and inexperienced.' She assured her mother that she did not need a new dress: 'I do not care to go out much even if I am asked & Miss Clough does not at all approve of it.'[32] But she did emerge occasionally, under chaperoned conditions, and one such occasion was a party at the Bonds' in Brookside. William Bond, a successful local grocer, knew John Brown, and was keeping a friendly eye on his daughter. His son, Henry Bond, had been through Amersham Hall and University College, London with Neville, and was now, like him, a Cambridge graduate; his sister Annie had hopes of Neville. It was at Brookside that Neville and Florence met for the first time. On 17 May 1879, Florence wrote to her mother: 'Mr. Keynes invited Miss Crofts (our lecturer), Miss Martin & myself to lunch ... at Pembroke ... Mr. Keynes has invited me to go again on Tuesday ...' A year later, on 20 May 1880, he proposed, and she accepted.

III

FLORENCE ADA BROWN

The arrival of Florence at Newnham was a tribute to the power of Nonconformity to overcome the widespread Victorian prejudice against the education of women. Florence Ada, the eldest daughter of John Brown and Ada Haydon Ford, was born in Manchester on 10 March 1861. Three years later John Brown moved to Bedford with his wife and small daughter, to become Minister of Bunyan's Meeting. Alice, Jessie, Walter, Harold and Kenneth were added to the family later, Kenneth not until 1879.

At the Manse in Dame Alice Street, Bedford, a 'high standard of moral and intellectual effort' was demanded of both sexes; such effort being helped by the rigour of the environment. In her family memoir, Florence recalled a big, draughty, house, almost without heating, but filled with relics of John Bunyan, one of the first ministers of the Bedford Meeting. In the winter the River Ouse froze; so did the soap in the dish. The bedroom floors felt like ice, and there were no eiderdowns or hot-water bottles.[33]

To make up for the lack of heating there were books and sermons. Literary, political and theological interests flourished on both sides of the family. Florence remembered a childhood visit (she was six) to her Manchester grandfather, the Rev. David Everard Ford, grandson of the smuggler. 'Do you love Jesus?' he bellowed at her through a cloud of pipe-smoke in his book-lined study. Grandmother was 'very much the critical school-mistress'. In her extreme old age, she would instruct Maynard to send her 'a circle, triangle, etc., that I may be quite sure you know what they are'.[34] Florence's father, John Brown, despite an increasingly patriarchal appearance, was a companionable scholar, a man of reason, who quelled his own religious doubts by extensive lecturing and research on the history and doctrine of Nonconformity. His talks on Bunyan were expanded into a popular biography, published in 1885. A fine preacher, he became the Nonconformist 'bishop' of the area. Maynard Keynes's brother Geoffrey remembered him 'in his pulpit high above the congregation, with his white pointed beard, healthy pink face, and piercing blue eyes, preaching in his silvery voice to a rapt audience below'.[35] A convinced and active Liberal in politics, he would entertain his family with dramatic readings from Gladstone's speeches as Chancellor of the Exchequer.

Florence herself was a 'sadly delicate and nervous child' of whom sympathetic friends would say 'her mother can never hope to rear her'.[36] Her childhood was punctuated by intimations of mortality, as a succession of aunts passed away, with much solemnity and prolonged mourning, to higher things. There was a constant reminder, too, of duties to the poor in the long row of almshouses which faced the Manse. Ada Haydon Brown was busy in the London Missionary Society, the Charity Organisation Society, and Liberal politics. Like that of many late Victorians, Florence's sense of social obligation would prove more durable than her religious faith.

It was above all her mother who placed Florence in a position to meet the young don from Pembroke. A woman of forbiddingly 'active mind, unbounded energy and a full share of her mother's passion for education',[37] Ada Brown set up a school in the Manse to give her daughters the education they could not otherwise have had. As Florence later told it:

> Luckily for me, my grandmother and my mother were both great educationalists: and I was very well taught at home by my mother. My grandmother had eight children of her own. She managed to bring them up and run a successful school in my grandfather's large house – he was a parson. (She used to nurse a baby on her knees and stitch her husband's white shirts and teach the older children round the table all at the same time.) [My mother] began by teaching me

and my sisters in our Bedford home. Then friends asked if their children might join us. So Mother found herself with a school on her hands. She ran it for about twenty years, until other educational facilities for girls were developed in our neighbourhood.

In her determination to give her daughters the same educational opportunities as her sons Anna Haydon Brown was aligning herself with a movement of national importance. In 1869 Cambridge had started a Higher Local Examination open to women over eighteen, as a follow-up to the Local Examination for schoolchildren which dated from 1858. In 1870 Henry Sidgwick persuaded Anna Jemima Clough, sister of the poet, 'a fussy, and at times almost incoherent woman',[38] to take charge of a residential hostel for women from outside Cambridge who wanted to attend lectures being given by university dons for the Higher Local Examination. The hostel opened with five students at 74 Regent Street in October 1871. This was the start of Newnham College. Newnham Hall opened on its present site in October 1875. Simultaneously, Miss Emily Davies had started a women's hall of her own, first at Hitchin, then in 1873 at Girton, just outside Cambridge. These were all private enterprise efforts by university lecturers and outside educational reformers to avail women of the higher education facilities open to men, the ultimate aim being to make women full members of the university. The university was very suspicious. Women were allowed to attend lectures, on the invitation of individual lecturers (Foxwell refused to have them in his) but not to take the tripos examinations. As a way round this they were allowed, again on the initiative of the lecturers, to take the examinations informally. Under this arrangement two Newnham students, Mary Paley and Amy Bulley, took the Moral Sciences Tripos papers in 1874, the examination papers being carried from Senate House to Dr Kennedy's house in Bateman Street by 'runners' who included Sidgwick, Marshall, Sedley Taylor, and Venn. Maynard Keynes wrote later 'All the "runners" were familiar Cambridge figures of my youth. Apart from Marshall, they were all very short, and had long, flowing beards.... I see them as the wise, kind dwarfs hurrying with the magical prescriptions which were to awaken the princesses from their intellectual slumbers....'[39] Women were officially admitted to the tripos examinations in 1881, but not allowed to take their degrees till 1947.

With some outside help in languages and mathematics, Ada Brown was able to bring her daughter up to what would now be called 'O' level standard. At sixteen, Florence passed the Cambridge Local Examination well enough for her to gain a small exhibition at Newnham Hall to study for the Higher Local Examination. By this time she in turn was helping her mother run the Bunyan's Meeting Sunday School, promising to extend her family's pedagogical tradition into a third generation. She may have come to Newnham shy and inexperienced, but as the eldest daughter of the Manse, the oldest of six children, she had already tasted responsibility. Not for her the gloomy introspection of an only child.

It is difficult to know Florence in the way one feels one can know Neville. Her long life stretches out before us as dry and factual as the two books she wrote in her old age on Cambridge and on the Brown–Keynes connection, the two circles in which it passed. The facts and achievements are all there: but the personality behind them has been carefully hidden away by the impersonal style of writing. The things said about her do not help much either. *The Times* obituary of 14 February 1958 called her a 'Pioneer of Women's Rights'. A reporter wrote of her in 1916 that she was the 'busiest woman in Cambridge'. Notices of her are mainly catalogues of committees. Florence's energies and interests were too ample to be confined to the home. She came from a family devoted to improvement – their own and the world's. Her own era, coinciding with the growth of public and voluntary philanthropy, gave her much more scope than her own mother had had for participation in public affairs. Florence seized her chance. She confined her own activities mainly to Cambridge, but within Cambridge there was, by 1916, 'scarcely a social or public movement ... with which she is not or has been associated'.

But this picture of the energetic public woman forever in pursuit of good causes does not give the right impression of her personality. She was clearly a woman who charmed and persuaded rather than bullied her colleagues. All her work, one local correspondent wrote on her death, 'was done with such graciousness and kindliness that everyone found it a pleasure to work with her'. An interviewer found her 'most moving and kind', adding that 'she hides her great ability under a cloak of natural modesty'. To her children, noted *The Times* obituarist, she was 'both a mother and a companion'. Florence was not the kind of mother whose love of humanity is so intense that she has no time for her children. She was not demonstrative in her affection, but left no doubt that her first loyalty was to her husband and her family.

There was something else which was to be very important in Maynard's relationship with her. Florence had been bred in a hard school. Like many English women of middle-class, Nonconformist, background, her sympathies and tastes were high-minded, but narrow. Whole areas of aesthetic and emotional life were beyond her range. Yet she obstinately refused to become a period piece. She made her children's interests her own. More than Neville, whose flame flickered earlier than hers, she grew into the twentieth century with them. This enabled her to transcend her Victorianism – even to bridge, in an

extraordinary way, the gulf between the Bedford Manse and Bloomsbury. It was because she could grow up with her children that they
never outgrew home.

Photographs taken in the year of her engagement to Neville show a
serious, shy, young woman, looking older than her years, with a full
mouth set on a big chin, and big, steady, eyes; a handsome woman, who
nevertheless thought of herself as plain. Neville, taken the same year,
looks gauntly handsome, with deep-set eyes, side-whiskers and reced-
ing hair parted in the middle as was then the custom. Maynard got his
eyes from his mother; his full mouth is strikingly like that of his Bedford
Aunt Alice. Geoffrey, his younger brother, inherited the tight lips of his
father.

IV

A VICTORIAN COURTSHIP

Neville's diary resumes at the beginning of 1881. But the hand of the
censor is evident, since about one-third of the pages covering the next
eighteen months have been torn out. The missing and mutilated record
covers the period of Neville's transition from young bachelor don to
prosperous paterfamilias; a veritable valley of despair with Florence
alone beckoning him on and up to safety.*

Neville's father John Keynes died from stomach cancer on 17 February 1878. He left assets worth over £40,000 – a substantial sum in those
days. Of this, Neville's share came to £17,000, his sister Fanny's to
£12,000. His widow, Anna, got £12,000 in a trust, plus the Salisbury
house; the Keynes share in the Nurseries, and other businesses, being
sold off.†[40] With an unearned income of about £800 a year, Neville was
free to embark on marriage in substantial middle-class style – which
meant a spacious home and an adequate supply of servants.

* Geoffrey Keynes's comment in *The Gates of Memory* (1981) pp. 15–16, that his father's
diary for the period 1881–2 shows 'that they were very happy lovers, though he
sometimes tortured himself with the thought that he might not be worthy of his bride',
seems an inadequate summary. First, the record of the first year and a half of the
courtship and engagement is entirely missing. Secondly, it is possible to deduce from
context that the torn out pages for 1881–2 (about one-third of the total) deal with crises
in their relationship. Thirdly, a truer impression would be gained of the pages which
remain if 'frequently' was substituted for 'sometimes'.
† In his diary of 16 July 1877 Neville wrote: 'Father talks of leaving me £10,000 more
than he does Fanny. Mrs. Carter thinks he is fully justified in this; but I do not, & I
shall try to get him to alter it. He sometimes speaks very harshly of Fanny. I have no
doubt that he has often behaved badly to Mother, & done much to alienate his
affection.' In the end, whether through Neville's intervention or not, John Keynes left
Neville £5,000 in cash, the rest of the assets to be split equally between him and Fanny.

Soon after their engagement was announced, in May 1880, Florence passed her Higher Local Examination,* and went back to Bedford to help her mother run the School. There she continued to live until she married Neville two years later. He would go to Bedford, less than an hour away by train, once every three weeks. She would come to Cambridge occasionally to see him, staying at Brookside with the Bonds. They would take vacations together either at Bedford or Salisbury.

Their courtship took place in the full glare of family regrets. For much of it Neville was acutely depressed. Part of the cause was physical. On top of the toothaches which continued to plague him, he experienced headaches and colds which brought on attacks of acute hypochondria, against which he struggled in vain.[41] He was convinced that Florence was about to tie herself to an invalid whom she would have to nurse over an inevitably brief married life[42] – that is, if she herself survived. 'She is so often very poorly', his mother confided in him; 'she must be most delicate. I can't help sometimes feeling anxious about this – particularly as you are not strong. Still we must hope for the best.'[43] Anna Keynes and Neville were very close to each other. She wrote to him in 1882, 'You are *everything* to me. I thank God for such a son. You *do* make up in a great degree what I have lost in your beloved Father.'[44] To his disappointment at not being able to express his love for her adequately was now added the guilt of deserting her to get married. This was not helped by the fact that Anna Keynes found Florence unsympathetic. For her part Florence vetoed a proposal that his mother should come to live with them after they got married.[45] As a properly educated girl Florence probably found Anna Keynes frivolous and more than a little uncultivated, being entirely devoid of the intellectual interests and social concerns which flourished on both sides of her own family. Not till the summer of 1881 were there signs that Anna Keynes was becoming reconciled to Neville's engagement, and to Florence herself.[46] In the winter of 1881–2 mother and son went on a farewell holiday together in France and Italy, Neville finding Monte Carlo 'the most delightful spot on the Riviera'.[47] The trip, he concluded on their return, 'had been a great satisfaction to me in so far as I have been with her, & have been able a little, I think, to manifest my love towards her'.[48]

Meetings with, and letters from, Florence, while often delightful, sometimes bred the suspicion that her love for him was not as passionate or constant as it should be. Such thoughts induced the despairing reflection that he was unworthy of her. At other times they made him angry and critical. She was unfeeling, fickle, ungrateful. On

---

* Florence did not take the tripos, even unofficially, as Mary Paley had done. She was not, therefore, a 'graduate' of Newnham.

holiday in the summer of 1881 he treated her 'like a brute'.[49] Florence responded with spirit, 'Yes, you *are* a critical person. . . . I must make a study of your character in order to find out exactly what it is that makes continual criticism endurable';[50] while doing her best to reassure him: 'You talk as if any discovery I might make of shortcomings might possibly alter my love for you. Why, it wd only give me an extra reason for hoping that you wd not be too hard on mine. I love you & always shall.'[51] Such reassurances were reinforced by the good times they managed to spend together alone. At Bedford

> She lay on the sofa reading 'In Memoriam' to me, & I sat on the sofa too. . . . Afterwards, she sat on my knee with her arms round my neck, in her most loving way. She insists that she is spoiling me by being so good to me, and not shrinking as for a long time after we were engaged she wd have done from my embraces. But why shd she shrink? We love each other; and I feel just as much bound to her, as if we were already married.[52]

Florence herself was torn by a conflict of loyalties between Neville whom she loved and her family and work in Bedford. But she was never in danger of drowning in his flood of despair. Inexperienced as she was, she sensed that she was the stronger, and that her task in marriage would be to nurse not his body but his confidence:

> I too do sometimes have misgivings, but I am not fond of gloomy thoughts – I have a way of putting them off for consideration at another opportunity and meanwhile they generally vanish. My misgivings always arise from a contemplation of myself and my powers. At times I have such a scorn for this self, that I think it only natural & fitting that you shd have the same feelings towards it – and that I don't like. These are the thoughts that I think better on the whole to put to one side, for I believe a morbid investigation into oneself hinders growth rather than helps it. . . .[53]

Although to the outside world Neville would appear as the competent man of business, it was Florence who would keep the partnership afloat.

Not only did Neville's relations with Florence keep him agitated, there was also the uncertainty surrounding his future career. It was during the engagement that Neville revealed to Florence what she came to regard as his main fault: lack of ambition. When they became engaged she had reason to believe that he was destined to climb to the top of the academic ladder. But it was not to be. Early in their engagement he took a career decision which was to prove decisive, though it need not have. By the time they got engaged it had become clear that his Fellowship would expire in 1882 under the new statutes – six years after his appointment. There were no immediate academic jobs to be had at Cambridge. But there was a job in university administration. In 1858 the University had set up a Local Examinations Syndicate or Committee to set and mark examination papers for grammar school-boys. In 1873 another Syndicate had been set up to organise extra-mural lectures, as part of the University Extension Movement. The two syndicates had a single secretary, G. F. Browne, but each one had a separate assistant-secretary. At the beginning of 1881 the assistant-secretaryship of Examinations fell vacant. Most of his friends advised Keynes not to apply for it, but to concentrate on getting an academic job. A professorship in economics was going at University College, London, following Jevons' death. Marshall supplied him with a glowing reference, which even allowing for the exaggeration customary in such exercises shows the high hopes he had of him.

> Mr. Keynes [he wrote] has a great natural genius for economic science, and a wide knowledge of its subject matter. He is a clear and powerful thinker, distinguished preeminently for thoroughness of intellectual character. He has a quiet but strong originality which leads him to work steadily at great issues, & which is perhaps liable to be understated because it aims at producing that which is likely to live long than that which is most striking in its immediate effect. I regard him as an economist of the very highest promise.

When Neville was offered the administrative job, he decided to withdraw his application for the professorship, which went to Foxwell. His decision disappointed Florence.[54] Ambitious for her future husband, she found it difficult to come to terms with his low opinion of himself. The later successes of her children, especially Maynard, were to give her the pleasure which she never really got from Neville's career; while Neville who had a superb, but unambitious, mind was able to encourage his children without competing with them.

With a job in Cambridge came the need to find a Cambridge home. They decided to buy one about to be built in Harvey Road, as part of a new 'development' for married dons. Plans were approved in November 1881 with the architect Morley for a double-fronted structure of four floors, including basement. The house rose steadily through the winter and spring, signalling the start of a new life.

The marriage was set to coincide with the end of his Pembroke Fellowship in 1882. Neville was becoming more pleased with the Browns. 'At last Jessie & I kiss each other as sisters & brother ought to do', he noted on 12 February 1882. He confessed he was growing very fond of Walter,[55] found the baby Kenneth 'engaging'[56] and was enjoying Mr Brown's preaching more and more. He found it restful.[57]

John Brown wrote to Florence that Neville was a 'dear good fellow' and that he was quite reconciled to her going. 'It is better that life shd grow richer & more full of meaning for us under the guidance of our Heavenly Father, [and] it is a great comfort to me to know that you will always exercise in your new home the gracious influence of a truly Christian woman.'[58] Less able to take this objective view of the matter, Florence had 'fits of hysterical crying'.[59] Ada Brown could not stop crying either.[60]

There was much weeping in Salisbury too. On 17 July 1882 it was 'good-bye to Mother & Aunt Mary. I fear that to both it seems like the breaking up of the Salisbury home. But I trust that Mother at any rate will gain more than she loses by my marriage.' A week later Anna Keynes wrote, 'We are quite bright and cheerful now, dear Neville. It is the changes altogether that your marriage will bring that makes one feel sad at times – but I can heartily rejoice with you too.'[61] But Anna Keynes's deepest feelings came out in a letter she wrote to Neville just after the wedding, in which she discussed coming to live in Cambridge:

> Then again I shd get to know more of Florence. Like yourself she is very reticent, so that I cannot *quite* understand her. I am quite certain she does appreciate kindness – still one wd like a little more expression of it – and no doubt it will come in time. You know dear Neville what a loving and affectionate husband your dear Father was – all that love & affection I miss terribly – and the more so as time goes on – and this perhaps makes me more sensitive. Do you think that Florence wd be pleased for me to live in Cambridge? She has never *said* she shd like me to do so – neither has Mrs. Brown. . . Now all this is between ourselves dearest Neville. It will all come right, I know, still . . . I feel it a good opportunity just to say what I have all along felt. You know how much I rejoice in your happiness, and after all this is more to me than anything personal.[62]

As the wedding approached, Neville and Florence clung to each other for support. She affirmed her love in passionate prose;[63] he affirmed his in despondent verse.[64] She urged him not to harp on his unworthiness. He wrote 'My darling one! But she does not know yet all she may have to suffer for my sake!'[65] On 12 August he ceased to be a fellow of Pembroke. But for 'misgivings, hard to vanquish or control' his happiness would have been complete. 'My dearest maiden will very soon be my darling wife. If only I can keep tolerably well. . . .'[66]

Panic stricken to the end, Neville led Florence to the altar on 15 August 1882. The ceremony, at the Bunyan Meeting, Bedford, was very much a Brown occasion. The service, conducted by Florence's father, was 'deeply affecting by reason of its earnestness and simplicity'. The bride wore a dress of 'rich ivory satin broche with train, brocaded silk front, a tulle veil, and a wreath of orange blossom; she also carried a lovely bouquet of bridal flowers'.[67] At 5 foot 5½ inches she was an inch and a half taller than the bridegroom. Of the 120 presents, many of them vases, Neville was especially touched by some 'very handsome & valuable brass' given by his old Newnham students. They then went off to Switzerland for their honeymoon.

Their marriage lasted sixty-seven years, until Neville died in 1949. To all appearances it was a perfect love-match. On the fourteenth anniversary of his wedding, Neville wrote in his diary: 'We are happier together . . . than we have ever been before. But indeed all our married life has been a continuous period of happiness.' Three years later he wrote: 'Every year I congratulate myself more and more on the remarkable wisdom & foresight I shewed in the selection of my wife.' And indeed it is easy to believe that without Florence's rocklike support and moral strength, the iron discipline which kept Neville at his work would have disintegrated long before it did. Whether Neville was an ideal husband for someone of Florence's temperament is less certain. She was ambitious for her husband, more ambitious than he was for himself. As his life became gently becalmed, her ambitions inexorably transferred themselves from her husband to her sons.

Back in England from their honeymoon, they bought furnishings for their new home.[68] They slept their first night at No. 6 Harvey Road on 11 November 1882. By this time Florence, 'troubled with sickness more or less all day', had been told by her mother, 'what *was* the matter with her. We were both surprised.'[69] Now they were entranced by thought of parenthood. On 18 February 1883: 'We are so happy. Are we *too* happy? Do we need the discipline of suffering? We think & talk a good deal about "the little mortal".' On 26 March: 'It vexes me more than it should – the way Kenneth [Florence's youngest brother] is spoilt and allowed to overeat himself. I don't think it is because I dislike to see children enjoying themselves. Shall we manage the little mortal better?' On 18 May: 'Florence is keeping capitally well – and looking so pretty. I should fall in love with her over again merely through seeing her.'

On 5 June 1883, labour began at 3 a.m. Neville reported to his mother:

Florence was about yesterday as usual, and she felt well except for a kind of rheumatic pain in her legs. She went to bed between 10.30 & 11.0, & slept comfortably till a quarter to three. Then her pains began. We talked at intervals till five, and then I called Mrs. Brown. We dressed & got some tea for Florence. At a quarter to seven I went for Wherry [the doctor] & he was here at 7.30. I saw her at intervals till about nine, but after that they wd not let me go into the room. At 9.30 I went & listened outside the door . . . Florence was giving a slight groan every now & then (they say she was very brave) & at 9.45 I heard such a hullabaloo & Mrs. Brown just came to the door, & said that it was a boy. (This was rather a blow – I had wanted a girl – but I think *you* will be satisfied) . . . They say that the boy is the image of me. It's ugly enough ... Now what do you think of *John Maynard* for a name? That is what we propose....

John Brown wrote from Bedford, 'I like the name suggested – John Maynard Keynes sounds like the substantial name of the solid hero of a sensible novel.'[70]

2 Cambridge Civilisation: Sidgwick and Marshall

THE CRISIS IN AUTHORITY

Maynard Keynes was born into a certain civilisation at a particular moment of history, and was one of its foremost products. He inherited both its aspirations and its tensions. He grew up in the shadow of its great figures, notably Henry Sidgwick and Alfred Marshall, the teachers and colleagues of his father. His style of thought and way of life both bear Cambridge's unmistakable imprint. Roy Harrod, his previous biographer, often talks about the 'presuppositions of No. 6 Harvey Road'. But the presuppositions of Cambridge civilisation are more fundamental. Much of Keynes's life will not make sense unless this inheritance is set out.

Intellectual life in Victorian Cambridge was shaped by the crisis and eventual decline of religious belief. The 1860s were the decade when Cambridge men lost their religious faith: Edward Carpenter, Leslie Stephen, Henry Sidgwick, Alfred Marshall, Arthur Balfour were all from the 'doubting class' of the 1860s. The decade opened with the consequences of Darwin's *Origin of Species*, published in 1859, and closed with the results of the Second Reform Act of 1867. Occurring more or less simultaneously, the death of God and the birth of mass democracy wonderfully concentrated men's minds on the problems of social order and personal conduct.

The Victorian order rested on Evangelical religion and social deference. On the rock of these 'givens', the English and Scottish thinkers of the Enlightenment had erected political, moral and economic philosophies based on the sovereignty of the individual, his interests and choices. They never imagined that these interests and choices would be worked out other than in the framework of Christendom, would be other than constrained and harmonised by the existing social structure. The threatened breakdown of this protective system left them with nothing but their individualism to fall back on; and they were immediately faced with an adding-up problem. What guarantee was there that the sum of individual choices would result in a desirable social outcome? What assurance was there – heavenly rewards having been eliminated – that individual good would coincide with social duty?

Such problems were particularly felt by the Nonconformist intelligentsia, for whom morals were so bound up with personal belief that they could scarcely conceive of a godless society which remained good. This helps explain their trauma when they discovered that belief in the existence of God and the literal truth of the Bible could no longer be rationally entertained. It also helps to explain the preoccupation of so many mid- and late-Victorian intellectuals with the quest for some alternative ground for morals. But the attempt to build a 'scientific' system of morals and statecraft on nothing but individualist presuppositions ultimately proved impossible. One world was dead; the other was powerless to be born.

Of all the institutions, the ancient universities were the most directly affected by the crisis of Christian belief. Their intellectual activity had consisted largely of theological, or theologically-based, speculation. They provided the Established Church with its clergymen. They were thus an integral support of the inherited social order. But how could they continue to perform their social function in a situation in which theology was losing its power to do moral and political work, and in which their graduates no longer sought careers in the Church – or at least in such profusion?

Such questions dominated the movement for university reform. One response was the opening of the universities to Dissenters, as a result of which Neville Keynes himself had got established at Cambridge. The fundamental motive for this was conservative – to prevent the emergence of a rival, or dissident, intellectual class. In this it was successful: with the exception of the small group of Fabians, no one who had not been to Oxford or Cambridge made much impact on English thought over the next sixty years; in great contrast to the previous sixty years, when most of the seminal intellectuals were outside the university world. Undoubtedly, the relatively inclusive character of the English notion of a gentleman helped this consolidation of intellectual property. No one would have called Neville Keynes anything but a gentleman, although his father started work at eleven as an apprentice brushmaker.*

* Entry of Dissent into the ancient universities consolidated the 'intellectual aristocracy' of which Noel Annan has written in a well-known essay of that title (1955). Annan traced the growth of the nineteenth-century intellectual elite through a succession of family alliances. But he understates, it seems to me, the importance of university reform, particularly the admission to the ancient universities of both Nonconformists and women, in providing an institutional basis for this dynastic achievement, and in preventing the emergence of rival elites. He also leaves open the question of the relative importance of heredity, tradition and educational opportunity in perpetuating the intellectual aristocracy through time.

However, the unification of the intellectual class was only part of the answer to the decline of religion. What was required from it, or what many of its leading members set out to supply, was authoritative doctrine – authoritative in the sense of being able to command what Sidgwick called the 'unconstrained consent' of experts. Initially the task of producing such doctrine was left to philosophy, and particularly moral philosophy. It was moral philosophy which was expected to provide true beliefs for a secular age.

There were two main traditions in moral philosophy for the post-theological intellectuals to draw on: Intuitionism and Utilitarianism. Both had theological roots, but were capable of non-theological development, because both started with an appeal to human reason. The simplest way of distinguishing them is to say that Intuitionism claimed that certain ways of acting were right or wrong, whatever their results might be, whereas Utilitarianism said that conduct must be judged by results: good results being, in the Benthamite or hedonist version of Utilitarianism, results which increased human happiness. Two different aspects of human reason were thus being appealed to: in the first case, what might loosely be called conscience; in the second case, calculation. Both presupposed certain kinds of knowledge: Intuitionism, moral knowledge produced by a moral faculty; Utilitarianism, knowledge of consequences. A philosophy based on good motives confronted one which wanted good results.

This philosophic disagreement had considerable political implications. Utilitarianism had a radical edge. Institutions or practices must be swept away or reformed if they failed to pass the test of utility. It was the natural creed of those outside the Establishment. By contrast, Intuitionism was Establishment doctrine. As William Paley, an early Utilitarian, saw it, any system of morality built on innate ideas 'will find out reasons and excuses for opinions and practices already established'. This was certainly John Stuart Mill's view, too. He called Intuitionism 'the great intellectual support of false doctrines and bad institutions'. By its aid, he wrote, 'every inveterate belief and every intense feeling, of which the origin is not remembered, is enabled to dispense with the obligation of justifying itself by reason'.[1] On their side leading Cambridge Intuitionists such as Adam Sedgwick and William Whewell, both of Trinity College, regarded the London-based Benthamites as dangerous subversives. To Sedgwick, Utilitarianism prepared men for 'violent and ill-timed inroads on the social system, and the perpetration of daring crimes'. To William Whewell, it destroyed the 'reverence which, handed down by the tradition of . . . moral and religious teaching, had hitherto protected the accustomed forms of moral good'.[2] These polemics must not be taken too seriously: philosophical debate took place within the framework of a constitutional settlement which was generally acceptable, and within a theological tradition 'broad' (or exiguous) enough to satisfy most reasonable men. There was no real equivalent in nineteenth-century England to the Continental polarisation between reactionaries and liberals, clericals and anti-clericals. Intellectual energy which in much of the rest of Europe went into fighting for the forms of popular rule could in England readily be mobilised to limit its consequences.

In fact, the philosophical differences between the two schools could be resolved readily enough once their social perceptions had changed. After the middle of the nineteenth century intellectual Nonconformity, the main source of Utilitarian thinking, was being absorbed into the Establishment. Naturally the view from the inside was more attractive than the view from the outside. On the other hand, Intuitionists, seeing their theological supports crumbling, were more ready to accept the support of some overriding principle to which their Pandora's box of 'intuitions' could be related. Both sides were worried by the social question. In addition, historical, sociological and legal studies helped to bring the two views closer together, by emphasising the functional character of many institutions and customs which the earlier Enlightenment philosophers had been disposed to dismiss as mere superstitions. The result was the famous Victorian compromise, by which Intuitionists were persuaded to accept utility as the final test of doctrine and conduct; while Utilitarians agreed that existing social arrangements had some Utilitarian justification after all. By means of this philosophical merger the characteristic English tradition of improving conservatism received its adequate intellectual justification, and was able successfully to negotiate the industrial age. Even the working-class movement was compelled to pursue its political and industrial goals within a framework of ideas largely (though not exclusively) supplied by these intellectual representatives of property.*

Yet the intellectual synthesis between the rival philosophical traditions was by no means perfect. Philosophic agreement was possible so long as the subject-matter of discussion was society. The difficulty lay in the relationship between social and individual conduct. In the end it proved impossible to combine social and moral philosophy within a consistent non-theological framework of ideas. Social philosophy could not do without Utilitarianism; moral philosophy found it difficult to live with it.

To understand the way the difficulty presented itself one must recall

---

* The twin pillars of the post-1945 consensus – the Welfare State and the Keynesian full-employment policy – were based on ideas originating in Oxford and Cambridge. By comparison, the Fabian contribution to social, political and economic policy seems meagre.

certain features of the Victorian age. Put briefly, many aspects of Victorian life afforded the thinking person neither aesthetic satisfaction nor personal happiness. On the one hand, the division of labour between cultural and non-cultural activities had become much sharper. The old gentlemanly culture, which had included learning and the arts, now stood sharply opposed to the much expanded world of business, money-making, and politics. On the other hand, a generalised Puritan ethic had succeeded the morally more relaxed conditions of the eighteenth century; this made much greater moral demands on the individual in the name of social duty. On both counts Victorian civilisation paid a high price in cultural impoverishment and psychic strain for its material achievements and its social stability. Gertrude Himmelfarb may go too far when she says that Victorian intellectuals inhabited the 'plains of madness',[3] but certainly the sense that individual lives were being sacrificed to public duty was felt and was growing. Once theology ceased to provide for the thinking Victorian an axiomatic connection between morals and social requirements the tension between the ideals of civilised living and the 'needs' of society, between personal happiness and social obligation, came out into the open.

These tensions were at the heart of the university reform movement. The problem as it presented itself to the reformers was how to maintain cultural standards *and* serve the needs of a society organised round money-making. The solution adopted, as Sheldon Rothblatt has brilliantly shown,[4] was to admit a more representative elite, but to educate it in the old gentlemanly culture. Greek was kept as a compulsory entrance requirement; the curriculum, based on classics and (at Cambridge) mathematics, remained sternly non-vocational. By these means the universities ensured both that they would not be swamped by the sons of businessmen and (more importantly) that their graduates would not go into business life. Previously most of them had become clergymen. Now they went into education, public service and the learned professions. The upshot was to place at the head of British public life in the first half of the twentieth century men whose education had left them quite uncontaminated by knowledge of industrial society, and with an ingrained dislike of the profit motive. Whether this proved good or bad for Britain is still endlessly debated.[5] It had also, to a lesser extent, given Britain a ruling-class which regarded public life as a diversion from more valuable private pursuits.

The growing feeling that private life should be distanced from public life, and was in some sense opposed to it, wrecked the philosophic attempt to reconcile the two. Specifically it destroyed John Stuart Mill's attempt to combine social and moral philosophy under the unifying principle of utility. In one sense, Mill was successful. Setting out to provide a 'unifying social doctrine' by incorporating the 'major positive views' of his Intuitionist critics,[6] he succeeded in giving Utilitarian justifications for many current social practices. Where Mill was much less successful was in linking his social doctrine with his morals.

The clue to that failure is given in his *Autobiography*. At the age of twenty he discovered that working for humanity made him ill. He could not accept the alternative of 'wine, women and song' because he had little taste for any of them, and had, moreover, been brought up by his father James Mill to feel an overriding sense of social duty. Mill eventually concluded that men could be got to take pleasure in working for humanity if their sympathies had been cultivated by music and poetry. Such benevolent sympathies would furnish motives for altruistic behaviour. This implied that men should cultivate what he called the 'higher pleasures' rather than the lower ones. But to say that we should prefer some pleasures which may be less pleasant than others is to raise an impossible problem for Hedonism. Mill raised two problems about the Benthamite tradition as it applied to moral philosophy between which he did not carefully distinguish. The first concerns the egoism–altruism split. How was one to behave if the claims of private and public happiness did not coincide? The second, evaded by the formula of 'higher pleasures', concerns the adequacy of happiness or pleasure itself as an end to which individual conduct should be directed. Were there not some things worth doing, some dispositions worth cultivating, which were valuable in themselves, irrespective of any Utilitarian justifications they might have? Was it not better to be Socrates dissatisfied than a fool satisfied?

Mill's efforts – both his successes and failures – are vital for understanding the Cambridge civilisation of Keynes's day. What Mill succeeded in doing was to make Cambridge Benthamite in that aspect of its thought which related to social policy. Mill's Utilitarianism, Cambridge mathematics, and Cambridge's Nonconformist conscience were the chief constituents in what became the Cambridge School of Economics, whose founder was Alfred Marshall. What Mill failed to do was to make Cambridge moral philosophy Benthamite. Henry Sidgwick, Marshall's great contemporary, tried but failed to repair Mill's breaches in the Benthamite fortress. His failure left the way open for G. E. Moore, drawing on certain other features of the Cambridge tradition, to construct a Cambridge School of Moral Philosophy which was anti-Benthamite. Social and moral philosophy as Cambridge conceived them had come apart and were never put back together again. Maynard Keynes spent his life zigzagging between the two.

II

THE CAMBRIDGE SETTING

In the context which interests us the two dominant figures in late Victorian Cambridge were Henry Sidgwick and Alfred Marshall. Curiously there has been no biography of either, a great omission since full understanding of what they tried to achieve requires a biographical dimension.

They were near contemporaries, Sidgwick being born in 1838, Marshall in 1842. They both taught for the Moral Sciences Tripos. Sidgwick became Professor of Moral Philosophy in 1882. Marshall became Professor of Political Economy in 1885. Both inherited the problems of a collapsing theology and both engaged in essentially the same enterprise: the attempt to find authoritative theology-substitutes. Both realised that this attempt had to come to terms with the Victorian mood. Like Mill, they were both compromisers and synthesisers. But whereas Sidgwick's efforts were conceived in the sphere of ethics, Marshall concentrated his on a branch of applied ethics, which he took economics to be. This difference is accounted for by differences in intellectual equipment and temperament. Sidgwick was mainly a classicist; Marshall was mainly a mathematician. The loss of religious belief was also a much greater personal shock to Sidgwick than it was to Marshall. Sidgwick's ambition was thus the greater. It was nothing less than to attempt to substitute a secular philosophy for theology as the scientific foundation of all social and individual conduct. Marshall quickly realised that this attempt was doomed to failure. Economics, he saw, had a far greater potential for scientific development if it was detached from moral philosophy. In terms of the organisation of Cambridge studies this disagreement led to the long-drawn-out battle Marshall waged against Sidgwick to liberate economics from the Moral Sciences Tripos, a battle which he won only after Sidgwick's death. Sidgwick lost both the intellectual and the institutional battles. His *Methods of Ethics* (1874) was widely recognised, not least by himself, to have fallen short of the goals he had set, whereas Marshall's *Principles of Economics* (1890) was immediately accepted as authoritative. Yet Sidgwick's failure was by no means so complete as to deter others from attempting to place ethics on a scientific basis. For many intellectuals brought up on Christianity still felt the need for authoritative guidance on how to conduct their lives – which they did not get from economics.

Sidgwick's enterprise was, in fact, undermined from two sides. Marshall simply took the view that ethics could not be made scientific, but economics could. But there were those who mistrusted the whole attempt to provide a social context for ethical theorising. The primary ethical question, they would have said, was: What is good for its own sake? not: What is good for society? This was the tradition of the Saints: personal sanctity took precedence over social virtue. This tradition found its most characteristic expression in Cambridge's most select group – the Apostles, or the Cambridge Conversazione Society, or more simply the Society. We shall have much more to say about this circle when we come to Maynard Keynes's time at Cambridge. It was founded in 1820 by a group of friends who came together to pursue a common interest in working out a philosophy of life. They recruited to their number the most 'apostolic' or philosophically-minded undergraduates of each generation (largely from a handful of public schools and two or three colleges), bound them together in secrecy and friendship, and maintained a collective life which stretched far beyond their junior years and to which younger Apostles were successively admitted on the same terms of intimacy. Over a long and continuous existence – the Society still perseveres – the content and focus of philosophic discussion naturally shifted with changing intellectual and political fashions. Nevertheless, the concern with establishing a philosophy of life, the commitment to lead one's own life in harmony with its principles, the feeling that one sullied one's hands by meddling in the affairs of the world, remained fairly constant. The Society's ideal was, in fact, monastic, with love of truth and communion with friends replacing the service of God as the inspirer of conduct. Sidgwick wanted to make the Moral Sciences Tripos into a nursery for intellectual statesmen. Yet he had served his own philosophic and emotional apprenticeship in the Society. He was its dominating figure in mid-century, reading it thirty-two papers in his nine years of active membership from 1856 to 1865. In his own person he symbolised the conflict between the private and the public, between the good life and the useful life.

III

HENRY SIDGWICK AND THE DILEMMAS OF MORAL PHILOSOPHY

Henry Sidgwick was a dominant figure in the Cambridge in which Maynard Keynes grew up. He was a man of considerable parts: the trouble was they did not fit. He spent his life trying to work out a philosophy which would make them do so; and failed. His contradictions could be reconciled only in eternity; and eternity was the one thing Sidgwick could not believe in. He was Carlyle's typical Victorian intellectual, 'devoid of faith, and terrified of scepticism'.

Born the son of an Anglican clergyman, Sidgwick was elected an Apostle in 1856. Two years later he took a 'double first' in classics and mathematics. He became a Fellow of Trinity College at a time when Mill's influence was at its height and when theology was in retreat. Not surprisingly he swallowed Mill's Utilitarianism and lost his faith, though not his need for it. Eventually he resigned his Fellowship in 1869 after he found he could no longer subscribe to the 39 Articles of the Church of England. Sidgwick became one of the best connected figures of his day, moving effortlessly – if not painlessly – between the several worlds of Victorian *Angst*. Through his sister's marriage to E. W. Benson, the future Archbishop of Canterbury, and his own to the sister of Arthur Balfour, the rising Conservative politician, he gained access to the worlds of high Anglicanism and high politics. But not even the Church and the Cecils in combination could tell him what he ought to do. The search for an answer to this question drove him into prodigies of inconclusive enquiry ranging from the Arabic language to investigation of psychic phenomena. In addition, he was deeply involved in the problems of homosexual friends like John Addington Symonds, quoting poetry at them and burning theirs. His mind is a window into the whole range of Victorian infirmity.

This is certainly how he struck Maynard Keynes. In 1906 Keynes, who had played golf occasionally with Sidgwick, wrote of him with wicked accuracy: 'He never did anything but wonder whether Christianity was true and prove that it wasn't and hope that it was.' Yet Sidgwick was not unlike Keynes – part Apostle, part Benthamite, part poet, part scientist, part coterie figure, part statesman. The difference was that Sidgwick had a need, which Keynes never had, to find a way to bring all these things into a rational, coherent, relationship with each other. And that, as he came sadly to realise, needed the Christianity he could no longer believe in. When it came to the crunch he would not sell his reason for a 'mess of mystical pottage'. But as a result he remained, in his own words, a 'maimed intellect'.

Sidgwick had an unerring instinct for spotting weaknesses in arguments, especially his own. In his notes for his obituary notice of Sidgwick, Neville Keynes wrote: 'He sometimes humorously complained that he had never been able to found a school at Cambridge ... How could he found a school of followers who so temptingly placed before us the claims of so many different philosophies?' *The Times* obituary agreed: 'he loved solutions which were compromises or coalitions of repelled elements; and such was the repugnance of his mental constitution to the blunt answers of plain men that he was never, it has been said, entrapped into saying "Yes" or "No" to any question'. Sidgwick's inability to give plain answers was enhanced, almost symbolised, by his stutter. He had his share of unexplained medical and nervous disorders; and in middle age took to running through the streets of Cambridge to strengthen his health; a delicate gowned figure with a flowing white beard. He was much more decisive in practical than in intellectual matters. He was the leading Cambridge reformer and politician of the 1870s and 1880s, and was largely responsible for bringing women to Cambridge. He met his death from cancer of the stomach in 1900 bravely and without fuss.

Sidgwick's problem was the same as Mill's: he could not bring the private and public life into a rational relationship. People, he thought, ought to conduct their lives in such a way as to promote the general happiness. But how could they be justified in doing so at the expense of their own happiness? Then again there were certain qualities, states of mind, ways of life he instinctively felt were good or bad independently of whether they increased or diminished our, or the world's, happiness. These dilemmas are set forth formally, but not satisfactorily resolved, in Sidgwick's *Methods of Ethics* published in 1874. The three 'methods' for reaching ethical judgments he calls rational egoism, intuitionism, and rational benevolence.

Sidgwick called the relation between rational egoism (aiming at my own happiness) and rational benevolence (aiming at the universal happiness) the 'profoundest problem of Ethics'. He thought that people ought to act in accordance with the latter. But he could not persuade himself that it would make them happy to do so. He wrote that 'the inseparable connection between Utilitarian Duty and the greatest happiness of the individual who conforms to it cannot satisfactorily be demonstrated on empirical grounds'. The reason was that there was no 'empirical' evidence for the existence of God. The demonstration of the inseparable connection between egoism and altruism, he thought, required God's existence, since divine sanctions 'would, of course, suffice to make it always in everyone's interest to promote universal happiness to the best of his knowledge'.[7]

Sidgwick felt he had made more progress in resolving the second dilemma, that between the claims of intuition and rational calculation. Intuitionism, he said, was not opposed to Utilitarianism since our intuition tells us that universal happiness is the sole good: that the things we think of as good tend to make the world a happier place. Thus most of our intuitive moral judgments and the moral rules deriving from them could also be given Utilitarian justifications. Undoubtedly Sidgwick hoped to make his Utilitarian mansion spacious enough to include qualities and dispositions not mainly commended on Utilitarian grounds – such as affection, aesthetic emotion, loyalty, honesty, etc. But the result, as Bernard Williams has pointed out, was a 'deeply uneasy gap or dislocation in this type of theory between the spirit that it supposedly justified and the spirit of the theory that supposedly justifies it':

Unsurprisingly [he writes] Sidgwick has to treat these dispositions, when he is talking about them theoretically, in a very instrumental way, and the arguments that he produces about them are very linear. The dispositions are regarded just as devices for generating certain actions ... those that most minister to the universal good.... [But] the dispositions will do the job which the Utilitarian theory has assigned to them only if the agents who possess those dispositions do not see their own character purely instrumentally, but rather see the world from the point of view of that character. Moreover, these dispositions require them to see other things in a non-instrumental light. Though Utilitarianism usually neglects the fact, they are dispositions not simply of action, but of belief and judgment; and they are expressed precisely in ascribing intrinsic and not instrumental value to various activities and relations such as truth-telling, loyalty and so on ... it was these possessors who, just because they had these dispositions, were so strongly disposed to reject Utilitarianism and insist on the intrinsic value of these actions and ends other than universal good.

What Sidgwick, and for that matter Mill, might have said had they not been so concerned to keep moral philosophy Benthamite was that many of the qualities and dispositions we regard as most ethically valuable need have little or no hedonistic value – that is, little or no tendency to make us or the world happier. G. E. Moore did say this in his *Principia Ethica* (1903) and thus fractured Sidgwick's system at one of its most vulnerable points. Sidgwick's own solution was different. It was, in effect, to justify double standards – one for exceptional, another for ordinary people:

Thus, on Utilitarian principles, it may be right to do and privately recommend, under certain circumstances, what it would not be right to advocate openly; it may be right to teach openly to one set of persons what it would be wrong to teach to others; it may be conceivably right to do, if it can be done with comparative secrecy, what it would be wrong to do in face of the world .... These conclusions are all of a paradoxical character; there is no doubt that the moral consciousness of a plain man broadly repudiates the general notion of an esoteric morality, differing from what is popularly taught; and it would be commonly agreed that an action which would be bad if done openly is not rendered good by secrecy. We may observe, however, that there are strong utilitarian reasons for maintaining this latter common opinion .... Thus the Utilitarian conclusion, carefully stated, would seem to be this: that the opinion that secrecy may render an action right which would not otherwise be so should itself be kept comparatively secret; and similarly it seems expedient that the doctrine that esoteric morality is expedient should itself be kept esoteric.

Such an outlook, Williams argues, 'accords well enough with the important colonial origins of Utilitarianism. This version may be called "Government House Utilitarianism".'[8] However, it may well be that in this passage Sidgwick is seeing himself less as a Machiavelli instructing rulers than as an Apostle justifying special standards for his friends; provided they are kept secret, since their complicated utilitarian justifications would not be understood by the 'plain man'.

It should be noted, in conclusion, that both problems in Sidgwick's philosophy – the difficulty of reconciling the two 'methods' of rational judgment, and of giving utilitarian justifications of valuable dispositions – arise from the breakdown of belief in God; hence from the need to substitute results pleasing to man for results pleasing to God.

Having established immortality as a necessary condition of a fully coherent ethical system, Sidgwick spent much of the remainder of his life trying to discover empirical evidence for its existence. He attempted to get in touch with the dead, accepting the presidency of the Society for Psychical Research. Unfortunately, the main result of these researches was 'a considerable enlargement of my conceptions of the possibilities of human credulity'.[9] His election to the Knightbridge chair of moral philosophy at Cambridge in 1883 led to a mental crisis which is captured in the following excerpt from his journal:

28 January 1887:

I have been facing the fact . . . . that we have not, and are never likely to have, empirical evidence of the existence of the individual after death. Soon, therefore, it will probably be my duty as a reasonable being – and especially as a professional philosopher – to consider on what basis the human individual ought to construct his life under these circumstances. Some fifteen years ago, when I was writing my book on Ethics, I was inclined to hold with Kant that we must *postulate* the continued existence of the soul, in order to effect that harmony of Duty with Happiness which seemed to me indispensable to rational moral life. At any rate I thought I might *provisionally* postulate it, while setting out in the serious search for empirical evidence. If I decide that this search is a failure, shall I finally and decisively make this postulate? Can I consistently with my whole view of truth and the method of its attainment? And if I answer 'no' to each of these questions, have I any ethical system at all? And if not, can I continue to be Professor. . .?[10]

As Sidgwick himself admitted, he was always mixing up 'personal and general questions'. The conflict between private and public duty presented itself to him and his friends primarily as a personal conflict which made them feel ill. This was not only because the Victorian code offered so little legitimate outlet for the sexual pleasures but because they had been brought up to believe that aesthetic pursuits had little or no utilitarian justification. The result was that when religious feeling began to wither away, a great void appeared in their lives which intellectual work alone could not fill. For Sidgwick's intimates – his brother Arthur, and his friends Roden Noel, Oscar Browning, Graham Dakyns, and John Addington Symonds (the first three being Apostles), the conflict was quite specific for they were all homosexuals with strong leanings towards the arts.[11] Sidgwick could not help but be aware that his philosophic endeavours offered them little in the way of guidance or comfort. In the absence of the afterlife he could discover no convincing reason why they should renounce personal happiness for the sake of duty, although as a Victorian moralist he felt they should. And he could offer only the lamest Utilitarian justification for their poetic leanings, although he felt these to be valuable.

Sidgwick's professional and personal dilemmas fused with his wider social concerns. Christianity, he felt, was indispensable from the 'sociological' point of view. To his friend, the mathematician J. R. Mozley, he wrote in 1881:

> while I cannot myself discover adequate rational basis for the Christian hope of happy immortality, it seems to me that the general loss of such a hope, from the minds of average human beings as now constituted, would be an evil of which I cannot pretend to measure the extent. I am not prepared to say that the dissolution of the existing social order would follow, but I think that the danger of such a dissolution would seriously increase, and that the evil would certainly be very great.[12]

Sidgwick's failure to prove his 'postulate' of immortality came at a particularly worrying moment. The economic reversals of the 1880s caused the ominous word 'unemployment' to appear for the first time in *The Oxford English Dictionary* in 1888. The coincidence of economic troubles with the further extension of the franchise to the working-class in 1884–5, the terrorism and mass disaffection in Ireland, the revival of socialism, and the appearance of demagogues, like Parnell, Joseph Chamberlain and Lord Randolph Churchill, all pointed to a new and highly disturbing era in which ignorance and madness would take the place of reason in politics. The following quotations from Sidgwick's Journal of 1885–6 need to be set against Roy Harrod's picture of confidence in a 'strongly upward' trend in England's material development:[13]

26 January 1885:

Reading the growth of England's commercial greatness rouses a mixture of curiosity and patriotic anxiety; it seems clear that we are past all culmination, relatively speaking, and it would be contrary to all historical precedents that we should not go down hill; but will it be by destructive, disastrous shocks, or gradual painless decline? That, I fear, is the only question of practical importance; but who can answer it?

Sidgwick felt that, like decline, some form of socialism was inevitable, indeed was its inevitable accompaniment. The sole question was whether it would take violent or moderate forms. This depended on the quality of leadership on which, unfortunately, it was impossible to be optimistic:

17 March 1886:

My recent fear and depression has ... related rather to the structure of Government than the degree of its interference with property and contract. I have hitherto held unquestioningly the Liberal doctrine that in the modern industrial community government by elected and responsible representatives would remain the normal type. But no one has yet found out how to make this kind of government work, except on the system of alternating parties; and it is the force of resistance which this machine of party government presents to the influence of enlightened and rational opinion, at crises like this,* which alarms.[14]

By the time Sidgwick wrote these words his intellectual system had broken down, his philosophic ambitions turned to dust. Not just the fact of his failure, but its form was important. Despite his inability to build a system, Sidgwick had made Cambridge Benthamite in its social reasoning. Perhaps this development was always inevitable in a university which had aimed to turn out mathematical rather than classical curates. But it had important consequences. Only a philosophy based on a hedonistic calculus could provide exact reasoning about social policy: Alfred Marshall was a product of Sidgwick's Cambridge. On the other hand, Sidgwick left moral philosophy in a mess. Intuitionist ideas revived, with an admixture of Hegelianism, in the more dynamic form of Idealism. But its headquarters were at Oxford rather than Cambridge; its high priests the Oxford philosophers Bradley and T. H. Green. Cambridge had become too critical, too empirical, to accept its ethics in metaphysical form. The way was open for G. E. Moore to construct a Cambridge system detached from both Benthamism and metaphysics. Moore was as much a product of Sidgwick's failure as was Marshall.

---

* A reference to the Irish Home Rule crisis.

IV

ALFRED MARSHALL AND THE CAMBRIDGE SCHOOL OF ECONOMICS

Although he was a good and, in some ways, influential economist, Sidgwick remained stuck in ethical speculation. To his students he transmitted nothing but doubts. Alfred Marshall gave his students a sense of mission; more broadly, he put Cambridge's sense of social mission on solid intellectual foundations. This could be done only by leaving the inconclusive fields. 'We are not at liberty', Marshall said, 'to ... exercise ourselves on subtleties which lead nowhere'. Marshall was the real founder of English academic economics. What he did was to give it a new scientific and moral authority, which equipped it to take over at least part of the political work which theology had done, and which philosophy could not do.

Marshall was yet another product of the well-connected clerical families which colonised English intellectual life. The clerical calling had been briefly submerged with his father, a cashier at the Bank of England, who, however, himself 'cast in the mould of the strictest Evangelicals [and] the author of an Evangelical epic', intended Marshall for holy orders.[15] At Merchant Taylors School, Marshall developed a flair for mathematics. This meant Cambridge, not Oxford. In 1861 he went to St John's College, then the centre of Cambridge mathematics, with the help of an exhibition and a loan from a rich Australian uncle; and in 1865 he graduated as Second Wrangler. The study of mathematics, however, had not yet interfered with his own or his family's plans for his ordination; and, as Maynard Keynes remarked in his beautifully written memorial of Marshall, 'the double character of scientist and preacher clung to him for the rest of his life'. Both played a part in moulding the Cambridge tradition of economics. The familiar crisis of religious doubt occurred only in the mid-1860s, and coincided with his first contacts with the Sidgwick circle. Until then, Keynes remarks, 'there is no evidence of Marshall's having been in touch with the more eminent of his contemporaries'[16] – possibly a tactful reference to the fact that he had not been an Apostle.

Marshall was part of the great exodus from theology. He was soon convinced that Christian dogma was untenable and, Keynes writes, 'after a quick struggle his religious beliefs dropped away and he became ... an agnostic'.[17] Marshall's ethical beliefs, though, remained unchanged; and unlike Sidgwick he never seems to have regarded them as problematic. He never seems to have felt personally the loss of theological support for morals, or a stirring of new possibilities which it created. The truth is he never needed Christian belief to keep him 'good' in the conventional sense, for he seems to have had little capacity for pleasure, and few aesthetic yearnings. His work was his life. He simply redirected his intellectual and moral energies from the service of God to the service of economics. Why economics? Because he thought that alone of the social sciences it could become as 'hard' (undisputed in its first principles) as theology had been; and because he thought it could take theology's place as the saviour of souls. This latter conclusion came to him after he had spent several vacations walking through the slums of great cities looking at the faces of the poorest people. He convinced himself that morality is largely a function of social conditions. Like so many people, Marshall generalised from his own character-type. To him efforts were always more vivid than wants; and he was able to persuade himself that with every increase of income up to a certain point people's efforts would increase relative to their wants; or, as it seems more reasonable to say, their wants would become more moral and social in character. Marshall was very much of his class in believing that the very rich and the very poor constituted the ignoble elements in society. Their joint elimination – partly through the mechanism of redistribution of wealth – would increase the aggregate of goodness or benevolence in society, which in turn would stabilise the capitalist social order.

But in order to get economics into a position where it could serve as an engine of moral progress and instrument of social stability much reconstruction needed to be done. Marshall began his life's work as an economist at a time when the scientific foundations of the subject were being knocked away, and its very survival was in doubt; a situation not unlike that facing economics today. The centrepiece of classical value theory, the theory that the price of a good depends on its cost of production, had been challenged by Jevons, and others, in the name of subjective utility. Much more threatening to economics than the confusion (or profusion) of theory was the crisis of method. The claim of economics to be a science with its own laws invariant through time and place was challenged on the one side by sociologists who claimed that it gave only a very partial account of human behaviour, and on the other hand by the German historical school which argued that each epoch was subject to its own laws of development which could be uncovered only by history. These issues were fought out in an environment in which it was not exactly clear who was or who was not an economist. Many of the arguments about scope and method, for example, were possible only because there was no frontier to the profession, no agreed professional training required for a person to set up in business as an economist. By the early 1870s it appeared to Foxwell 'as if science had been replaced for war of opinion'.[18]

The moral authority of economics was also at a low ebb. The classical political economy founded by Adam Smith and his followers was out of tune with Victorian evangelicalism because it offered no scope for the benevolent motives. Of the three methods of ethics discussed by Sidgwick, the classical economists accepted the need only for the first: rational egoism. If everyone pursued his own self-interest the invisible hand of the market would so arrange things that everyone would gain. Indeed, classical economists (or at least their political spokesmen) never stopped pointing out that policies undertaken for humanitarian or protective reasons would slow down, or even reverse, the increase of wealth. The idea that private vices, like love of money, would produce public benefits was repugnant to many, perhaps most, thinking Victorians. They regarded it as the self-interested creed of Manchester calico-manufacturers who simply wanted to destroy all social obstacles to their own enrichment. Few offered any alternative theory: what they demanded was the right to judge wealth-creating activities by ethical standards. Ethical concerns merged with political ones. The great Victorian moralists like Carlyle and Ruskin argued that social policy based on the teachings of classical economists would, by destroying existing social relations, prepare the way for anarchy and revolution. This touched a responsive Victorian chord.

By the early 1870s, when Neville Keynes was reading Moral Sciences at Pembroke, Marshall was already lecturing in economics at St John's. He spent the summer of 1875 in the United States studying business conditions there. But soon after his return came a profound crisis, whose origins and ramifications are now obscure. In 1877 he married Mary Paley and, forced to resign his Cambridge Fellowship, became the first Principal of the University College of Bristol. 'Soon after his marriage', Maynard Keynes wrote, 'his health and nerves began to break down, chiefly as a result of a stone in the kidney'.[19] From 1879 to 1885 when, as Keynes says, he should have been 'giving his all to the world', he was a semi-invalid, and for the rest of his life a prisoner of his 'nerves'. Beatrice Webb wrote of him, in 1889, when he was forty-seven: 'A small, slight man with bushy moustache and long hair; nervous movements, sensitive and unhealthy pallid complexion, and preternaturally keen and apprehensive eyes, the professor has the youthfulness of physical delicacy. In spite of the intellectuality of his face, there is a lack of the human experience of everyday life....'[20]

In 1883 Benjamin Jowett brought him to teach economics at Balliol College, Oxford, but he remained there only four terms, before being appointed Fawcett's successor as Professor of Political Economy at Cambridge. In his inaugural lecture entitled 'The Present Position of Economics', delivered in February 1885, he set himself three inter-related tasks: to strengthen the scientific authority of economics; to align it with the Victorian moral and political mood; and to draw the best Cambridge men into the subject. For the twenty-three years of his occupancy of the Cambridge chair Marshall pursued them all as energetically as his hypochondria would allow.

Maynard Keynes has himself provided a summary of Marshall's main analytic contributions.[21] Marshall produced no great theoretical breakthrough: like Sidgwick he was a synthesiser of previously repelled, or disparate, ideas. But his subject matter, not being concerned with the whole range of human conduct but only with the calculable or measurable aspects of it, could much more readily be made scientific.

Marshall reconciled the cost of production and subjective utility theories of value by his famous simile of the two blades of a pair of scissors, thus establishing continuity with the older doctrine whereas Jevons had sought revolution. He generalised the underlying proposition of his value theory – that value is determined at the equilibrium point of demand and supply – to cover the theory of distribution and the theory of money, hitherto regarded as subject to separate laws. Almost as important, he did not write too much – at least in his prime. Some thinkers kill subjects, and thus their own achievements. Their books become unread classics. Marshall left an 'oral tradition' and lots of minor puzzles and fertile suggestions which provided an apostolic succession of students with an extensive research programme. Anglo-Saxon economics in the thirty years after 1890 was largely what Donald Moggridge has called 'glosses on Marshalliana'.

Marshall also played a key part in ending the methodological dispute. His redefinition of economics as a science of 'measurable motives' strengthened it enormously on its deductive side. By means of this redefinition he got rid of that unlovely abstraction 'economic man' assumed to be solely concerned with lining his pocket which so offended the Victorians and which rendered the discipline vulnerable to attack on the grounds of the unrealism of its psychological assumptions. In Marshall's formulation there was a calculable or economic aspect to all activities which involved scarcity and choice; he did not claim that everyone acted only to increase his material wealth. Marshall was also much more receptive than his predecessors had been to the use of history to discover economic laws – the so-called inductive as opposed to deductive method – though he rejected the main contentions of the German historical school (which would have destroyed economics' claim to be a science), and his own history was, according to J. S. Nicholson, 'vague, old-fashioned and excessively weak'.[22]

Finally, Marshall played a crucial role in making English economics a profession with a specialised training and agreed standards of performance. His main contribution to this end was to establish the Cambridge Economics Tripos in 1903. It had taken him eighteen years and was accomplished only after Sidgwick's death. Neville Keynes was

very much involved in this battle, and its echoes must have rever-
berated round 6 Harvey Road. Maynard's own ambiguous attitude to
Marshall can probably be traced to these youthful memories, since his
father was frequently exasperated by Marshall's aims and tactics.

Marshall's attitude to the Moral Sciences Tripos, Sidgwick's creation, was always lukewarm, and became progressively more so. Already in his Inaugural Lecture he complained that its 'metaphysics'
put off able men who would otherwise have studied economics. This
brought an immediate complaint from Sidgwick. By 19 April 1885
Neville Keynes wrote in his diary that: 'The state of things between [Marshall] and Sidgwick is really becoming very painful.' Rows
between Sidgwick and Marshall on the Moral Sciences Board became
frequent, with Marshall 'so narrow and egotistical'.[23] By 1888 the
disagreement between the two men over the place of 'metaphysics' in
the Tripos had become so acute that Sidgwick thought of resigning his
chairmanship. There were many more 'painful scenes' in 1894. The
basic issue was simple. Sidgwick supported by the majority of the
Board was trying to hold the Moral Sciences Tripos together, and was
insisting on the necessity of a philosophical training for would-be
economists. Marshall was convinced that what he called 'metaphysics'
was putting off people from reading economics. 'Practically the only
man for Part II was a negro, Talma', he wrote to Neville Keynes on 2
November 1895, 'a delightful man, but no good at examinations....
Were it not for such men as Berry, Flux & Bowley who do not take the
Tripos at all, & who learn what they do from me chiefly in private
conversation, it would be little better than hack work to teach Pol. Ec.
here. Sanger is the only student (man or woman) who has taken up
economics for Part II & was really worth teaching.'[24]

Marshall's last attempt to work within the confines of the existing
Tripos came when, after Sidgwick's death in the summer of 1900, he
tried to engineer the appointment of Neville Keynes as chairman of the
Moral Sciences Board. He explained 'with great frankness' to James
Ward, since 1897 Professor of Mental Philosophy, why Neville Keynes
rather than Ward should succeed Sidgwick:

> In brief it came to this [Ward wrote to Keynes]: that I was so
> impatient & so indifferent whenever questions relating to Economics
> were before the Board that he felt the subject wd. not receive fair &
> dispassionate treatment if I were in the Chair. Though he said
> economic questions had not in fact occupied five per cent of the
> Board's time, I had rarely failed to make it plain that I grudged them
> even this. Rarely as he had had occasion to speak at our meetings
> he believed that the occasion was still rarer on which I had not

attempted to cut him short by 'disparaging' or 'fractious' remarks.

Whatever the Board will do, I cannot say, but I feel strongly that I do not deserve the snub which Marshall had thought fit to administer. Impatient with *him* I have been, I know, & disgusted too with *his* contemptuous attitude not only towards what he lumps together as metaphysics but towards the Tripos as a whole & the working of the Board.[25]

When this plan was defeated Marshall decided to force the issue. Neville Keynes noted in his diary on 21 January 1902: 'Marshall is starting his agitation for the establishment of an Economics & Politics Tripos, & he has written a paper on the subject with which I am in considerable disagreement.... I want to nip it in the bud if possible.' To Neville Keynes, Marshall wrote on 30 January 1902:

Put yourself in my position. I am an old man .... I have no time to wait. Economics is drifting under the control of people like Sidney Webb and Arthur Chamberlain. [A reference to the London School of Economics and Birmingham's new School of Commerce.] And all the while, through causes for which no one is in the main responsible, the curriculum to which I am officially attached has not provided me with one single high class man devoting himself to economics during the sixteen years of my Professorship.... In fact McTaggart is the only first class man whom I have caught; and him I have only half caught.[26]

To Foxwell he also complained that the only high-class students had come from other triposes or other universities: 'the fresh strong beautiful youthful minds that used to come largely to the Mo. Sc. Tripos are now scarcely even seen there'. For example, Pigou 'who has *no* memory' and was 'rather bothered by want of it in the History Tripos' should have been studying economics. 'The oppression & suppression of economics by the incubus of Moral Sciences seems to me at once so cruel & so great a national evil', Marshall concluded, 'that I should be a traitor to my trust if I allowed my personal regard for Keynes & others to prevent me from appealing to the judgment of the impartial University for redress.'[27]

Marshall's appeal proved successful. An Economics and Political Tripos was set up in 1903 with Economics as the major, Politics as the minor, subject. The 'fresh strong beautiful youthful minds' were slow to take advantage of the new opportunity but Marshall's hopes were eventually realised. By the 1920s over two hundred students were reading economics; by 1980 there were 450. Most of them did not, of course, become professional economists but this had never been Marshall's aim. His Economics Tripos was designed to educate not just potential economists but potential legislators, civil servants, higher managers, country gentlemen and philanthropists:[28] to permeate the intellectual aristocracy with the new wisdom. In this ambition he has not been entirely unsuccessful.

Marshall's second ambition was to align the reconstructed science with the ethical aspirations of the enlightened middle-class. This he managed to do most skilfully by inserting into his economics a theory of moral evolution. As Talcott Parsons has pointed out, if on its 'scientific' side Marshallian economics is a study of the rational process of individual want-satisfaction, on its evolutionary side it contains 'a theory of the progressive development of human character and activities in relation to economic wants and want-satisfaction'. The agent of moral growth is no less than business life itself. Specifically, 'free industry and enterprise' are associated with the development of two sets of virtues: energy, initiative, and enterprise; and rationality, frugality, industry, and honourable-dealing. Marshall also believed that improved material conditions automatically produced an improved – that is, more energetic and self-sacrificing – character-type, by having a direct effect on the genetic equipment (see below p. 226n). In all this there was a considerable confusion between different types of progress – progress in rationality, in health, in morals. Specifically he confused economic progress with the growth of what he called 'earnestness', which was simply the Victorian code of his day. Like other Victorians, Marshall was fascinated by biological analogies, drawing support from Darwinism for his theory of moral evolution.* But these confusions, one feels, were necessary for Marshall's purpose, which was to show that economics was a science of life in its higher rather than lower manifestations. And this in turn had the important effect of legitimising the economic organisation which produced these higher qualities. The long-run effect of capitalism, in Marshall's scheme, was to 'moralise' wants. As Talcott Parsons put it, 'While to some extent, this moral advance facilitates an extension of government functions to a large extent it tends to make them unnecessary and to make a system of economic freedom workable with a minimum of regulation.'[29] This is because, with the growth of earnestness, society could increasingly rely on voluntary sacrifices from capitalists and workers to sustain

---

* Marshall had an interesting correspondence with the Social Darwinist Benjamin Kidd. Kidd's book, *Social Evolution*, appeared in 1894. Marshall wrote to him that 'it is a long time since I was so much excited by a book'. But he objected strongly to Kidd's view that Christianity was opposed to the evolutionary struggle and that Christian ethics, if universally adopted, would bring economic ruin. 'For as to Darwin', he wrote to Kidd on 6 June 1894, 'he seems to have done, what you seem to hold he has not done, emphasize the dominance of sacrifice for future generations as an or even *the* essential element of progress.' (CUL Add. 8069: M.251.)

economic progress. An additional benefit of Marshall's evolutionary perspective was that it enabled him to incorporate history into economics, but as a servant, not master: a useful way of accepting the letter, but not the spirit, of the criticisms of the German historical school.

Marshall's view of business life as the forcing house for morals was unusual, to say the least, in Oxford and Cambridge circles. He was unique among contemporary economists in building bridges to both the business community and the working-class. On the one side he was fulsome in his praise of the moral qualities of the entrepreneur and the business vocation. He took special pains to study business conditions, and to make his writings accessible to businessmen. He encouraged graduates to go into business. He realised that unless the effort was made to assimilate business life to the prevailing moral consensus, capitalism would always be vulnerable to the moral distaste of the ruling-class for mere money-making. On the other side he took equal pains to support and educate working-class aspirations. He condemned poverty and drudgery as productive of moral waste. 'No one', he wrote, 'should have an occupation which tends to make him anything less than a gentleman.'[30] Higher incomes, he argued, would increase not the quantity of labourers, as the Malthusians had claimed, but their quality or efficiency, thus making possible continued economic advance. He supported a moderate redistribution of wealth, on the ground that it would 'pay' society in increased productivity and social contentment to spend money on improving working-class housing and health care. He warmly supported the Cooperative Movement, which he saw in a double sense as developing workers' sense of responsibility and pooling together their small capitals. But noticeable in his Presidential address to the Cooperative Society in 1889 is the way he downgrades the desire for wealth as a worthy motive for human action. His message was that the workers should not ask for too much. Morality did not require great wealth. The *nouveaux riches* and their children, Marshall told the delegates with a fine Cambridge disdain, were not 'truly refined'. Nor, Marshall warned in the spirit of the modern environmentalist, should the production of wealth be carried to the point of destroying natural beauty.[31]

Like Gladstone, Marshall tried to deflect material demands onto a higher moral plane. Indeed, his conviction that the object of working-class endeavour should be to increase not wealth but nobility seems to have grown parallel with the growth of organised labour, and its demands on the rich. Thus he argued in a lecture of 1897 that the growing scientific authority of economics should, when the occasion arose, be used to oppose 'the multitude for their own good'.[32] To Benjamin Kidd he wrote in 1902:

As things are I confess that I am inclined to think that a race which has prospered under the influence of natural selection through struggle, & in spite of bad provisions for the health of mind & body of young and old, might *conceivably* continue to progress under the influence of better physical and moral conditions of life, & in spite of the cessation of the struggle for survival.

On the other hand I cordially agree with you that the true danger of socialism lies in its tendency to destroy the constructive force of variation & selection: & that in the permanent interests of the race we cannot afford to diminish suffering by means that appreciably choke up the springs of vigour.[33]

The same year we find him writing to Mrs Bosanquet, the founder of the Charity Organisation Society:

I have always held that poverty and pain, disease and death are evils of much less importance than they appear, except insofar as they lead to weakness of life and character; and that true philanthropy aims at increasing strength more than at diminishing poverty. And now that democratic economics are so much more popular than they were a generation ago; now that the benefits of socialistic and semi-socialistic action are so much more widely advertised, and its dangers so much underrated by the masses of the people, I think it is more important to dwell on the truths of Mill's *Liberty* than on his *Essays on Socialism*.[34]

To trade unionism of any but a Friendly Society kind Marshall was vigorously opposed. To the trade union desire to 'make work', and the increase in their power to do so, Marshall attributed in large part England's industrial decline. When the Engineers struck in 1897 against proposals for the dilution of labour, Marshall wrote to the new Master of Balliol, Jowett's successor: 'I want these people beaten at all costs: the complete destruction of Unionism would be ... not too high a price'. Noting that three Glasgow men were required to do the work of one American, Marshall put one-quarter of the blame on employers, and one half on the new unionism: the remaining quarter he saw, characteristically, as a net gain to welfare.[35]

Marshall could not complain of being misunderstood. When his *Principles of Economics* appeared in 1890, its success, as Maynard Keynes wrote, was 'immediate and complete'. According to the *Pall Mall Gazette*, 'It is a great thing to have a Professor at one of the four old Universities devoting the work of his life to recasting the science of Political Economy as the Science of Social Perfectibility.' Benjamin Jowett wrote from Balliol:

It will be of great value both to the capitalists & to the working classes. It seems to me just what was wanted to mediate between the old political economy and the new or rather between the old state of individual society & the new. Neither employers nor employed have any reason to regard you as otherwise than a friend. Ricardo himself would not have objected to your a priori reasonings supplemented & modified by your facts.

Also I think it most excellent in an education point of view. It is very clear & interesting & goes back to great principles. It answers implicitly the question so often asked: 'What is the relation of Political Economy & Ethics'? I think the style admirable – I am also pleased that you have not overloaded the subject with Mathematics – and have rather diminished than increased its technicality.*[36]

By 1907 Marshall was ready to step down. He arranged, successfully, that he should be succeeded in his Cambridge chair by his disciple Pigou, rather than by his old colleague, Foxwell, who had always taken an independent stand on method and policy. More importantly, as Marshall explained to Neville Keynes, 'Pigou & I care for the men: & I think I may truly say for the men only. Foxwell does not seem to be able to understand this sort of aim....'[37] He looked back on what had been accomplished. In the previous thirty years, the different schools of economic thought had converged. Methodological dispute had ceased; analysis and the search for facts being reconciled as the right and left foot in walking. There had been a similarly gratifying, though less complete, convergence of social ideals. Most economists agreed that there was a very large expenditure by the rich which contributed little towards social progress and conferred only unworthy satisfactions on the spenders. This sum could be used to open up a more worthy life for the poor. But there remained one mortal threat to further progress, namely, the 'ill-considered measures of reform by Utopian schemes', particularly plans for wholesale nationalisation and municipalisation which would merely lead to the shrivelling up of effort under a deadening bureaucracy. This kind of socialism could still be avoided by what Marshall called 'Economic Chivalry' – a moral government, employing class, and working-class, each doing its duty. The state, Marshall thought, had attained to sufficient morality to make beneficial interventions in spheres closed to private enterprise, though he doubted whether it yet had sufficient intelligence. Wealth could similarly be 'moralised' through being employed in both voluntary and enforced philanthropy. This would in turn waken the chivalrous instincts in the working class for:

under such conditions the people generally would be so well nurtured and so truly educated that the land would be pleasant to live in. Wages in it would be high by the hour, but labour would not be dear. Capital would therefore not be very anxious to emigrate from it, even if rather heavy taxes were put on it for public ends; the

* Beatrice Webb was one of the rare sceptics: 'It is a great book' she wrote in her diary, 'nothing new.... Economics still has to be re-made. Who is to do it?'

wealthy would like to live in it; and thus true Socialism, based on chivalry, would rise above the fear that no country could move faster than others lest it should be bereft of capital. . . . If we can educate this chivalry, the country will flourish under private enterprise.

Economics, Marshall concluded, could not do the educational job alone. But its share in it would be 'very large'. For only economics could provide the correct reasoning for the achievement of the chivalrous society.[38]

V

BEING GOOD AND DOING GOOD

Through Marshall's life and work the Victorian demand for authoritative social doctrine found one of its most important expressions in the Cambridge School of Economics. Maynard Keynes's relationship to that tradition is one of the central themes of this biography. That relationship was never unproblematic, because Marshall's achievement was incomplete. He had shown how the existing moral code could be made to serve society rather than God. But there was nothing in his work to show how it could be altered so as to make it possible for individuals to lead happier or more civilised lives. Marshall himself seems not to have felt any pressure to do so. But Sidgwick had; as had many other thinking Victorians. It was the reorganisation of personal life rather than the reorganisation of society which seemed the urgent problem for the next generation, especially once the social and economic clouds of the 1880s and 1890s had given way to the bright sunlight of the Edwardian age.

3 Growing up in Cambridge

6 HARVEY ROAD

Maynard Keynes was the first of three children: a sister Margaret was born on 4 February 1885, and a brother Geoffrey on 25 March 1887. He grew up at No. 6 Harvey Road, a house 'without charm or character'.[1] It was part of a new housing development for young married dons, on land owned by Caius College then on the outskirts of the town. It was double-fronted, bay-windowed, and depressing, of dark yellow brick – 'corpse bricks' as the children called them – and stood on four floors including the basement. Leading off from a tiled entrance hall were Neville's study, and the dining-room with blue and crimson William Morris wallpaper and a dining-table with legs shaped out of old oak beams from a church tower; at the back the drawing-room, with its potted plants and its walls covered with etchings and family photographs, opened out into a small garden. A veranda was added later. On the first floor were the family's bedrooms. The servants' bedrooms were in the attic. In the basement was the kitchen and servants' room. The house was comfortable, but not excessively large, considering that with all the staff nine or ten people had to live in it. Some of the solid furniture came from Neville's rooms in Pembroke; the rest was ordered from Webbs in Salisbury and Maples in London: Neville treated himself to a desk from Maples in 1884 costing £15 15s. The furniture was made to last a lifetime and it did. The dining-room was hung in 1884 with William Morris wallpaper. Prudently Neville and Florence bought extra rolls, so the walls still looked the same when Florence died in 1958.

The year Maynard was born, Neville bought the house next door, the idea being that his mother might come to live there. This plan did not materialise, Florence dreading the 'implicit criticisms on small matters which Mother does rather keep on about'.[2] Instead, Anna Keynes moved to Sidney Villa in nearby Bateman Street in 1885. Most Sundays Neville would take the children to have tea with her, falling happily asleep himself. When she died in 1907 Maynard remembered her as 'Simply affection. Everything including herself was merged in it.

There never was anyone quite so free from all unkindness.' Much later Neville colonised one room of the ground floor of No. 5 Harvey Road as his study; the rest of the house being let to academic families. His property acquisitions continued with the purchase of 55 Bateman Street, next door to his mother's, for £1,070 in 1895.

There was nothing in either Keynes family home to stimulate the aesthetic sensibilities. Neville's father had bought pictures in Salisbury, but with the exception of a small George Morland, they were unremarkable, even by Victorian standards. Florence and Neville rarely bought new ones, though in 1889 she hung an engraving of Fred Walker's called *A Rainy Day* in the drawing room.[3] Nor was music then part of their lives, except for an occasional visit to a Gilbert and Sullivan, though Neville later collected records of operatic arias.

In place of Art there was Nature. Harvey Road itself adjoined open country. Florence later wrote 'My children looked from their nursery window across "Bulman's field", where the drovers kept their cattle over the week-end, ready for the Monday market, and the lowing of cows was a familiar sound. With the exception of the houses in Station Road there was, indeed, little or nothing between us and the Gogs [Magog Hills].'[4] To get from Harvey Road to the town one walked, or took the horse-drawn tram or a hansom cab. Unlike grander Cambridge families, such as the Jebbs, the Keyneses did not have a carriage. Bicycles started in the 1880s, but the Keyneses did not acquire any till 1895 when Maynard was given a free-wheel one for his twelfth birthday. He promptly collided with a hansom cab damaging his little finger.[5] His parents' efforts to master cycling a year later were not successful either, Neville finding it almost impossible to get on and off, and Florence forgetting to put the brakes on. She fell off her bicycle so often that Neville tried to stop her using it.[6]

Nature farther afield was increasingly accessible to cheap travel by railway and not yet ruined by tourism. Neville and Florence liked to escape from the family in July for a fortnight in Scotland or Switzerland. Then for August and part of September the whole family would set off, children, servants, relations, to Norfolk, Devon, Yorkshire, or Cornwall, renting a house for six weeks. In the 1890s they went for four years to Lealholm Hall in Yorkshire, remembered by Geoffrey as a self-sufficient farm near Whitby, surrounded by unspoiled moors, where the children 'learnt the Facts of Life without surprise or shock'.[7] Neville almost bought it. In the later 1890s the family spent a number of summers at Tintagel in Cornwall. Christmases would be spent at the Manse, Bedford, where there would be skating on the frozen Ouse and full observance of the Sabbath. Neville enjoyed these visits to his in-laws provided they kept off politics and religion. Both Dr and Mrs Brown were uncritical admirers of Gladstone and strong supporters of

Disestablishment at a time when his own views had moved somewhat to the right of Lord Hartington. Finally there would be visits – often at Easter – to Weybridge, Surrey, where Aunt Mary lived with Fanny, married to Edward Purchase, and where there was also a 'Cousin Keynes' with a billiard table.

Like most middle-class Victorians the Keyneses read a lot. Reading novels was the main family entertainment, much of it done aloud and for the whole family, especially on holidays. They read the Victorian classics, but also lighter writers like Anthony Hope and Rider Haggard. Both Neville and Florence found French literature unedifying, Florence commenting after one novel that 'no one could believe in the existence of such wretches here'.[8] But they thought *Anna Karenina* 'a wonderful book'.[9] They shied away from any unpleasantness or vulgarity on the page, Neville taking as his measure anything likely to offend Florence. The same test was applied to friends, poor Alfred Spokes (later Recorder of Reading) often failing it because of his tendency to make risqué jokes. Plays were judged by the same standard. Neville was an enthusiastic playgoer in Cambridge and London. But his taste was conventional. Although he found Ibsen's plays 'very interesting', he couldn't be an Ibsenite, finding it impossible to justify Nora's desertion of her husband and children in *A Doll's House*.[10] Life was enough of a vale of tears as it was, and one looked to Art for uplift or escape, not to add to one's depression.

Apart from the odd visit to the theatre or pantomime families had to entertain themselves. They were saved from boredom not only by reading but by a multitude of games and hobbies. With Neville hobbies amounted to an obsession: absorption in them stopped him from feeling ill. (Something else which helped was the removal of his upper teeth in 1884, finally bringing his face-aches to an end.) Not least of his virtues as a father was the ability to enter into his children's interests and make them his own, without taking them over. As a young unmarried don he played chess and tennis. These continued, though less intensely. He started Harvey Road Book and Whist Clubs.[11] At the age of three, Maynard was showing an interest in stamps, and on 20 March 1887 we find the significant entry in Neville's diary: 'In my old age [he was thirty-four] I have actually begun stamp collecting again.' He started to buy regularly at Cheveley's and to swap through a local Stamp Exchange. His passion grew with his collection, and was to prove lifelong. By 1895, he had 8,000 stamps, which Maynard valued for him at £2,000.[12] In the evenings at Harvey Road he would arrange them lovingly while Florence read to him. Every Sunday morning he would lay a pile of his rejects on his study table, allowing the children to choose one in turn till the pile was exhausted. 'Armed with a catalogue they studied the values carefully and chose accordingly. In this way

they learnt how to use a catalogue and acquired a considerable knowledge of other countries,' commented Florence didactically.[13] On 3
August 1895 there is the first reference to butterflying with Geoffrey
and Margaret. Geoffrey was to add to this entomological enthusiasm
a passion for collecting and classifying bones; his father helping him
with the knowledge he had acquired in preparing for the London B.Sc.
This collecting trait, stamps, butterflies, books, pen nibs, was later to
be extended by both brothers, though not by the father, to books.
Margaret was more interested in handicrafts, painting and gardening.
In the latter, at least, Florence, not Neville, was her mentor. The son
of a famous horticulturist, Neville never showed much practical
interest in gardening.[14]

From 1892 dates the start of Neville's greatest passion of all, one
which was to dominate his middle age. On 20 September his friend
Henry Bond initiated him and Florence into the mysteries of golf, at
Sheringham, Norfolk, in the pouring rain. Neville's diary entry, listing
an 'uncommon lot of foozlers', was the first of dozens of such, often of
enormous length, in which he struggled with the problem of his
recalcitrant swing in much the same spirit as other Victorians wrestled
with sin, and equally unavailingly. Neville managed to get Maynard
keen on golf; an interest which proved more enduring than stamps,
Maynard continuing to play golf with his father till the First World
War. In the 1890s they often went out together to the links at Royston,
a few miles from Cambridge; Maynard played a round there with
Henry Sidgwick a few weeks before Sidgwick's death in 1900. In the
1900s Maynard would accompany his father on golfing holidays. In the
holidays, too, the whole family would collaborate to produce a newspaper. A succession of these ran through the 1890s.* Maynard and his
father were both fascinated by word games, especially puns. They
enjoyed exchanging Spoonerisms. Like many children who have no
aptitude for games, Maynard was entranced by them in their statistical
aspect. He compiled lists of batting and bowling averages. In 1896 he
spent every spare summer afternoon at Fenner's Cricket Ground,
which adjoined Harvey Road, watching the University play. He and
his father relentlessly kept their golf scores. Activities which lent themselves to measurement, or the measurable aspect of activities,
fascinated them both.

* The Lealholm and Langston *Gazettes*, edited by Kenneth Brown, Florence's youngest
brother, four years older than Maynard, date from the family's summer holidays at
Lealholm and Langston between 1893 and 1895. The illustrated *Gem* was started on
7 January 1896 under Margaret's editorship. It was a joint production by the Keynes
and Glazebrook children, the Glazebrooks being one of the academic families in Harvey Road. The first number of the *Acorn* (derived from Keynes = oak) appeared in April
1899 under Maynard's editorship. He solicited contributions from his Eton friends.

Servants were a permanent, indispensable, part of the background of this world. For most of Maynard's childhood, the Keyneses had three: a cook, a parlour maid, and a nursery maid. Temporary reinforcements would arrive during Florence's confinements and after delivery. In 1892, a governess, Miss Laxton, made her appearance. She stayed for two years, and was followed by two German ones in succession. Mostly we know the servants only as names as they passed through Harvey Road on their way to unknown fates. They emerge as human beings only when scandal struck. In April 1887 Neville had to sit in moral and disciplinary judgment on Lillian Austin, the parlour-maid, who had entertained a young man in the kitchen, apparently with the cook's connivance, when the family were away in Bedford. Cook's male cousin had also been seen. Neville held long interviews with the cook, with Lillian, with Lillian's mother and sister, and the other servants. Stories were checked and cross-checked. More alarming details began to emerge. The young man had been seen going into a bedroom. Lillian had a lady friend who was 'on the town'. Young men had been heard to say that if one wanted a girl, Harvey Road was the place. The basements were buzzing with gossip. With much heart-searching, Neville came to his decision: Austin and cook had to go. On 29 April he wrote in his diary: 'We have engaged a new cook who admits to 48 & who looks older.'[15]

The German governesses, Fräulein Rotman and Fräulein Hubbe, gave Maynard a good grounding in German, which was to prove indispensable to him when he came to write his *Treatise on Probability*. Maynard grew up in a pro-German household. This was not unusual, particularly in educated circles. Germany was still the home of philosophy and science, not the jackboot. Florence had spent several months with a pastor in Bonn, a friend of Dr Brown's, just before going up to Newnham. Margaret and Geoffrey would also spend a year in Germany in their late teens. The Keyneses were not unusual, either, in holding the French in fairly low esteem. Traces of this early conditioning come through in Maynard's adult opinions.

The Keynes life-style was sustained by an income which was never less than comfortable, and grew more so. Marshall thought that a family man 'whose brain has to undergo continuous great strain' needed £500 a year at least.[16] Neville and Florence started married life with £1,000. Of this £600 was income from Neville's inherited capital (part of which now included the two houses at Harvey Road which had cost just over £2,000). £400 came from his stipend as assistant secretary for examinations, and various fees he received for lecturing and examining. Tax was paid at the less than punitive rate of sixpence in the pound. There were no dependants to support, Anna Keynes being amply provided for with an income which came to £700 in 1891.[17]

Neville usually managed to save £400 a year to add to capital. Out of the £600 they spent annually they could afford two substantial holidays. The expenses of these were not great. It cost about £5 a week to rent a big farmhouse in the summer. In 1889, Neville and Florence spent ten days in Belgium for £23.10s. inclusive. A month in Switzerland in 1891 cost them £68.

As Maynard grew up his parents grew steadily more affluent. Capital and earnings went up, while prices went down. By the late 1880s the Keyneses' annual income averaged £1400, and their expenditure £1000. In 1892, when Neville became secretary for local examinations, his salary went up to £500; in 1896, to £775. Neville was a nervous manager of his money. In the late 1870s, as a bachelor of independent means, he had invested part of it with Frank Tiffin, his boyhood friend from Salisbury, and an underwriter at Lloyds. But Tiffin proved unreliable, and Neville, finding that the profits from underwriting failed to balance the 'worry and anxiety' of it, withdrew.[18] On 30 June 1888 he felt very worried by the fall in the price of tin, in which he had speculated to the tune of £600. By January 1894, when he conducted his annual stocktaking, he felt so discouraged by the performance of his equities that he thought of putting all his future savings into Consols. However, there then followed some very satisfactory years. By 1900 his capital was over £24,000. It had, he noted, been going up 'by leaps and bounds for some years past, and it will I am afraid soon be the turn of another period of stagnation as we had from 1892 to 1895, and previously from 1882 to 1886'.[19] With his mother's death in 1907, Neville inherited more money, and by 1908 he had £38,000. His temperament was such that with every downturn he saw ruin staring him in the face. But what strikes one today is how secure his position was. He just went on getting richer and richer without any great effort on his part. That is what the Victorians meant by progress.

Neville found his affluence all the more agreeable because his enjoyment of it was unclouded by any sense of guilt. With his Baptist background he started as a conventional Liberal in politics, though without the slightest passion for Reform. He had breakfasted with Gladstone in 1878 and knew his mother would be 'glad that such a good thing has fallen my way'. But he was too pessimistic and anxious by nature to make a convinced Liberal. Disenchantment starts with the 'tragic fall of Khartoum' in 1885.[20] He thought Gladstone's first Home Rule Bill 'a thoroughly bad Bill' and Chamberlain and Hartington 'excellent' in their arguments against it.[21] On 8 June 1886 he noted in his diary, 'My faith in Gladstone is shattered; and I fear my faith in democracy, which was never very strong, will be shattered also.' Increasingly, he looked to Lord Hartington to save the nation; a man 'whose perfect honesty and straightforwardness is entirely above suspicion'. Like many other

Cambridge academic Liberals he voted Tory in 1886. In the 1890s Neville would have described himself as a Liberal Unionist; in the 1900s as a Liberal Imperialist. But for a long time his deepest instincts had been conservative. In 1898 as well as in 1900 he allowed his name to go forward on the Conservative as well as the Liberal ticket for elections to the University Council. His references to socialists, socialism, and working men became increasingly unsympathetic, though never cholerically so.

One important root of his conservatism was his love of ceremonial. He was moved by the pageantry of politics, not the issues. He was also something of a social snob. Encounters with, or even close proximity to, aristocrats produced a warm glow of satisfaction. Royalty left him starry-eyed; the deaths of royal persons moved him to bathetic expression. He wrote to the eight-year-old Maynard: 'We have had the honour of travelling in the same train as the Archduchess Valerie, daughter of the Emperor of Austria.'[22] This is typical of the sentiment such figures evoked in him. It is in sharp contrast to Maynard's own generally irreverent and mocking attitude to figures in authority. But Maynard had something of the same overvaluation of outward forms, of inherited position. It was part of the psychological adaptation of the Nonconformist intelligentsia to life inside the Establishment.

Florence's Liberalism was of a more robust variety. Her instincts and family tradition alike moved her towards self-improvement and do-gooding. Once the joy of reading each other romantic poetry had worn off somewhat,[23] Florence took to night school, mothers' meetings, and Marshall's lectures.[24] In the summer of 1888 we find her presiding over a Mothers' Tea Meeting of two hundred. That autumn she attended cookery classes. The following spring she learnt about the dangers of cold baths at ambulance lectures. That summer she joined the Care of Girls Committee. In the autumn of 1890 her own lectures on Health to mothers drew far larger audiences than Neville's on Logic to Girton girls. Florence was genuinely interested in medical matters. Her brother Walter and her sister Alice became doctors. She was deeply concerned about the health of her children, stuffing them with tonics and taking great precautions against draughts, possibly in reaction to the neglect of such things by her parents. She followed her father's example, though, in other ways, lecturing on *The Pilgrim's Progress* at her Bunyan readings. On 22 February 1895, Florence's public life took a definite direction when she became Cambridge secretary of the Charity Organisation Society. From then onwards her social work expanded in true Brown fashion. 'What a devoted woman she is!' Neville wrote to Maynard at Eton five years later. 'If there is anything in heredity, her children certainly ought to have a sense of duty.'[25] But privately he chafed at Florence's sense of duty and was always trying to get her to reduce her public work. He hated it when she was not at home.[26] Neville was wholly a family man. Florence was a conscientious wife and mother, but she needed larger causes to engage her full sympathies. Here again, quite apart from what she herself accomplished, Maynard was able to give her the vicarious satisfaction she could not get from Neville. So from his family Maynard got a divided legacy, his father standing for the private, his mother for the public, pleasures.

II

NEVILLE'S ANXIETY

By the time Maynard was ten, his father had become a full-time university administrator, and had switched his intellectual energies from his own academic work to worrying about his children's. Neville's failure to build on his achievement as Senior Moralist came as a great disappointment to his colleagues but was inherent in his temperament.* Although his mind was judicial rather than creative (he would have been a fine judge or civil servant) the real barrier to a successful academic career was not lack of originality, but anxiety. Neville's life's strategy was an attempt to reduce the pressure on himself. The tasks he set himself once he did not have to 'please others' were such as to minimise strain. Immersion in hobbies was one solution; immersion in work which was intellectually undemanding was another. Unlike Marshall, who early in life abandoned activities which 'led nowhere', Neville increasingly abandoned himself to them. To put himself beyond the judgment of his intellectual peers, to be judged by less exacting standards, became his goal.

This was not achieved quickly. There were considerable expectations of vigorous intellectual performance, which Neville himself shared. With Maynard safely born, he started, on 5 July 1883, 'a small book of Problems and Exercises in Formal Logic' which had arisen out of his teaching. Writing with great speed, he had already completed sixty-two Problems by 14 July, poor Florence having to spend her holiday evenings doing them. By 27 July he was expanding the book to include Terms, Propositions, and Syllogisms. On 17 September, with 373 Problems, it was almost finished. The experience had not been entirely encouraging. He regretted his inability to do 'really sterling literary work'.[27] On 27 October 1883 he noted that James Ward had been 'rather crushing on the subject of my book. The best he wd say was

---

* Harrod's comment (p. 10) 'Meanwhile [i.e., while Maynard was growing up] John Neville was going from strength to strength' is far from the truth if one compares his actual academic achievements with the expectations held for him as Senior Moralist.

that it was *accurate* – but that of course he would naturally anticipate from me'. *Studies and Exercises in Formal Logic* was published by Macmillan in February 1884 to a chorus of praise from his Cambridge friends. Marshall thought it 'a beautiful specimen of thorough Cambridge work';[28] Alfred West, the son of his old headmaster, thought that 'a chair of logic in the United Kingdom ... can now be yours for the asking'.[29] The fundamental criticism came from Francis Edgeworth, then lecturing at King's College, London, who wrote that Keynes 'follows up the achievements of Aristotle; he relinquishes the aspirations of Boole'.[30] This is now the generally accepted verdict. Although it was widely used as an advanced textbook, and although claims were made for its originality,[31] *Formal Logic* is essentially a summing up of the deductive system bequeathed by Aristotle, already being undermined by the onset of symbolic, or mathematical, logic. This was the trouble, James Ward wrote to Neville on 1 October 1894:

> I used to try twenty years ago to persuade you that there is no such thing as Formal Logic. I daresay you have forgotten it; but I must confess to some private satisfaction in the fact that what then seemed reckless heresy is fast becoming the prevalent view.
>
> But while regretting that you are – as I think – so 'conservative', I am quite awake to the great excellence of your work. ... Within the limits that you allow yourself you are, indeed, the most exact & thorough writer I know. That you will some day see fit to extend your range is the hope of your old friend.[32]

Neville revised his book several times before the definitive edition of 1906; as late as 1912 he contemplated reducing it to an elementary textbook. But despite James Ward's plea, he played no further part in the development of the subject. Within his range he had reached a dead-end.

What the book got him, as it was intended to do, was a university lectureship in Moral Sciences. His next book was also a by-product of a teaching commitment. In his diary of 16 February 1885 he wrote: 'I have decided to lecture at Oxford on the Methods of Political Economy; and I have an idea of writing a small book on the same subject. This wd be my work during the Long Vacation.' It was Marshall who had brought him back to economics. A letter from Oxford, where Marshall had gone after leaving Bristol, hinted at talents running to waste in the Syndicate. In November 1884 Henry Fawcett died, and Marshall was elected to succeed him as Professor of Political Economy at Cambridge. This meant he had to leave Balliol College, Oxford, after a very successful four terms there. He summoned Keynes to succeed him, enlisting Florence's help. She wrote to her husband on 17 December 1884:

[Marshall] is not altogether satisfied with your position here. He does not at all like you spending your energies on the Local Exam. work while there is such a fine career there for the right man ... The pay is merely nominal, £120 for the Indian students ... plus £80 for the rest.... Still, there is a good chance of a Professorship to come.... Of course, we shd both very much dislike the thought of leaving Cambridge – but your work must be considered first of all – & you might have more congenial work at Oxford. At any rate you wd be able to devote yourself to Political Economy wh is the subject I believe you are really most interested in. And so long as we had each other & the boy we could get on happily anywhere.[33]

This persuasive appeal failed to budge Neville. Marshall, unrivalled in his use of flattery to advance the sacred cause of economics, inundated him with telegrams and letters. He was extremely anxious to establish an outpost of 'scientific' economics at Oxford, and considered that Neville, his best student, was the person to man it. Oxford undergraduates, he wrote to him on 28 December 1884, were being taught economics, if at all, by 'those who have taken it up so to speak as a plaything. What with your singular power of lucid exposition, you wd be certain to get hold of the best of them. If you have any want of rhetorical power – & on that point I have no information beyond what Mrs Keynes said – it would only influence the numbers at the fag end of your class – and they do not matter.' He begged Neville to give Oxford a six months' trial. 'If you do go to Oxford you will have the formation of a very considerable part of the thought & feeling of the English people in your own hands.' Marshall went on:

I want you to consider this: you have, what I have not, the strength to carry through the work single-handed at Oxford. You *wd* be alone there. There is no one else who has given the best part of his life to mastering economic theory. On the other hand teachers of history abound there; there is a plethora of them. Putting aside all personal considerations, that seems to me (& I think it will to others) to be a sufficient ground for believing that you are *the* man wanted. And if others think that you are ... then surely you must be bold enough to think it probable you will succeed. If you do succeed you will probably be Professor in three years time.[34]

Marshall's energetic lobbying secured Neville the offer, from Balliol, of a temporary lectureship. Under this pressure Neville developed shooting pains in his chest, which made him wonder how much longer he had to live.[35] Finally he yielded to Marshall's urging sufficiently to agree to go to Oxford one day a week in the Hilary, or Summer, term of 1885. Oxford was definitely a finer town than Cambridge, Neville decided. His lecture audiences, composed largely of candidates for the

Indian Civil Service Examination, were large and appreciative. But Neville never developed Marshall's zeal to fertilise Oxford's barren economic culture. Although Balliol under Jowett was, as Maynard Keynes later wrote, 'at its highest point of brilliance and fame', Neville never took to it. He disliked Oxford men; he felt that Balliol 'might have paid me rather more attention'.[36] The experiment was not repeated. After the Oxford visit Neville practically gave up teaching economics in Cambridge also, Marshall's return having reduced the demand for his services.

The book on which Neville embarked was essentially an exercise in the Marshallian art of harmonising the views of various schools in order to regain for economics what Foxwell called its 'rightful authority in legislation and affairs'. J. S. Nicholson complained in 1885 that what economics needed was not more discussions on method but 'useful applications of the right method'.[37] Keynes's reply was that until the methodological issue between the deductive, inductive and ethical schools had been resolved, economics could have no practical influence. The point had some validity in 1885. By 1891 when Neville's book appeared, the methodological issue was just a little *passé*. Neville's 350 pages were a definitive summing-up of the terms of a contract or *modus vivendi* between the rival methodological persuasions which had already been established. His second book, no less than his first, 'killed' the subject – not least for him.

The book's long gestation – it took over five years – can be explained partly by the time taken up by Neville's other work, partly by the discouraging effect of criticisms. The Cambridge habit of circulating work in progress was designed for people with a more robust self-confidence than Neville had. By 1888 he had a first draft ready, which he showed to Marshall. Marshall killed his hopes of early publication. He 'depressed me very much' Neville wrote in his diary on 21 April 1888. 'He practically wants me to give a year to studying the Germans and then to rewrite entirely.' In a letter of 26 April 1888 Marshall wrote, 'A new book on the subject ought to be very German & based more on "new school" difficulties as felt in Germany & in America and England. Too much prominence is given to the doctrines of writers who are sinking out of memory; too little in comparison is said in anticipation of the difficulties of the coming generation.' Marshall was clearly having doubts about the value of Keynes's enterprise. 'I should have thought something might be said as to *why* there is so much more dispute as to the method of studying P.E. than there is about studying anything else. It always seems to me that some apology is needed for talking about Economic Method, when we never bother ourselves about method in the other sciences.'[38] The disaster was compounded by the fact that Neville did not read German. So Florence was set to work on the German economists. At the same time throughout 1888 and 1889 Marshall was sending Neville massive chunks of his draft *Principles*. Keynes generously responded with long, conscientious comments, though in the opinion of one observer he was 'too diffident and self-deprecatory' to make a completely effective critic.[39] Partly as a result, Marshall's book surged on to publication in the summer of 1890, while Keynes's more slender effort lagged behind. Keynes's other commitments also interfered with his book's progress. In 1887 he worked 2051 hours altogether, but of this 688 hours was Locals work. And yet he felt that if he gave up his administrative job he would only relapse into idleness.

A fresh stream of criticisms from Marshall in the autumn of 1889 depressed Neville once more. This time Marshall accused him of being too pro-German, and consequently 'most harsh & unfair to your own countrymen.... I think the picture you give is a general libel on England.' Mary Marshall added insult to injury by saying that the discussion of method was really a German not an English habit: 'the best work in England has been done by the best available methods without troubling to say what the method is'. By now Marshall had come to realise that Neville's training as a philosopher was not necessarily an advantage when it came to trying to bridge differences. He was too keen on precise definitions. 'Every one of your contrasts & oppositions is too sharp for me.... You talk of the inductive & the deductive methods: whereas I contend that each involves the other....'[40]

Some years later Marshall complained to Foxwell: 'Even Keynes himself when he mounts his logical horse seems to me to incline to make his classifications with a view to logical symmetry rather than to nature & the facts of life.'[41] Yet if Marshall found some of Neville's contrasts too sharp, he joined with J. S. Nicholson in criticising his failure to distinguish properly between the 'ethical' and the 'realistic' schools. Both Marshall and the philosopher W. E. Johnson found Neville's definition of economics in terms of wealth and 'economic man' old-fashioned and counter-productive. Johnson found some difficulty in following the section on Historical Method. 'I evidently don't succeed in making my points clear,' a disconsolate Neville wrote in his diary on 6 October 1890. And so the re-writing went on.

On 13 January 1888 the Professor of Political Economy at Oxford, Bonamy Price, died. Marshall wrote quickly to Neville: 'I was very glad to hear you intend to be a candidate....' Neville commented: 'This is the first I had heard of it.' He reflected that 'it is rather unfortunate that my book is not yet published. On the other hand, I should feel leaving Cambridge & my work here horridly.'[42] Sidgwick, Ward and Marshall all advised him to stand. So did his father-in-law, Dr

Brown, who felt 'that your present work in connection with the Local Exams is not commensurate with your intellectual power ...'.[43] Foxwell urged him to stay put:

> Pray don't go. It is much better that a study should be concentrated in a particular place. There arise many of the same advantages as in the localisation of an industry. Your departure would leave a nasty ragged wound in our Moral Sciences organisation.

He continued in lighter vein:

> What is the use of being a settled family man if you are to drift from your moorings in this fashion! Think of the effect your move may have on your son. He may grow up flippantly epigrammatical, & end up becoming the proprietor of a Gutter Gazette, or the hero of a popular party, instead of emulating his father's noble example, becoming an accurate clear headed Cambridge man, spending a life in valuable & unpretentious service to his kind, dying beloved of his friends, venerated by the wise, & unknown to the masses as true merit & worth mostly are.'[44]

Neville applied for the chair without hope, and seemed pleased enough when the economic historian Thorold Rogers got it.

But Marshall was not finished with his nagging. Plans were afoot to start an Economic Association (later the Royal Economic Society) with its professional journal (the first issue of the *Economic Journal* appeared in 1890). Marshall wanted Keynes to edit it. 'The salary is to be £100. It may not last for ever: but very likely it will: & anyhow it will get you in the way of writing on economic subjects. ... You are the right man for the work, & it is very important work.'[45] Keynes declined. It would 'worry me beyond measure', he told Marshall.[46] Instead Edgeworth took it on. He was succeeded in 1911 by Maynard Keynes who never shrank from such challenges. Edgeworth tried hard to get Neville to write, without success: 'Unfortunately I have not the pen of a ready writer, & I cannot do literary work of any kind quickly.'[47]

The Scope and Method of Political Economy was finally published by Macmillan in January 1891. Neville dissolved the methodological dispute between the different schools into a matter of taxonomy or correct classification. He accepted the primacy of the deductive approach – 'the preliminary determination of the principal forces in operation and the deduction of their consequences'. But deductive conclusions needed to be tested and modified by history and statistics. The role of ethics was to provide standards for judging economic arrangements. Economics properly conceived was a broad church in which the theorist, historian, and moralist could all work together provided each knew his place and stuck to it; or in which the economist might, and perhaps should, be all three, provided he did not confuse his roles. The book was praised for being 'so widely read, so impartial, and exact'.[48] On the strength of it, Neville received a doctorate in science, Geoffrey enquiring anxiously whether he 'would still live with us when he was a doctor'.[49] Florence, who was largely responsible for the book's much noticed mastery of German sources, failed to get an ackowledgement[50] – an omission her husband failed to repair in subsequent editions. Running through the encomiums was a sense of relief that the final word seemed to have been said. 'For we cannot conceal', wrote Edgeworth in the *Economic Journal*, 'a certain impatience at the continual reopening of a question on which authorities appear to be substantially ... agreed.'*

In producing one book on pure, and a second on applied, logic, Neville had circumnavigated the range of his intellectual interests. He was thirty-eight. He lived another sixty years. Apart from a few contributions to Inglis Palgrave's *Dictionary of Political Economy* and the odd essay, his pen was henceforth confined to revising previous work, writing his diary and letters, and drafting minutes. Had he finished his second book earlier, and got a chair when he was still relatively open to the idea of moving, a sense of duty, if not intellectual energy, might have led him to write more books in his lucid, painstaking, manner.

Perhaps he is to be admired, rather than pitied, for keeping silent when he had nothing to say. As it was, soon after the publication of *Scope and Method*, his chief at the Syndicate, G. F. Browne, was made a canon of St Paul's. In 1892, Neville succeeded him as Secretary for Local Examinations at a salary of £500 a year. Marshall finally acknowledged defeat: 'I never felt quite sure', he wrote to him, 'that the work was the right thing for you; but I was always sure that you were the right man for the work.'[51] The feeling of being master at Syndicate

---

* In her introduction to a new (Italian) edition of *The Scope and Method of Political Economy*, Phyllis Deane makes the point that J. N. Keynes's classificatory scheme enabled the theoretical economist 'to insulate his fundamental theorems from accusations of ideological bias, or immorality or relativity or from the failure of practical economic policies'. She summarises JNK's thesis thus: 'Abstract economic theory, its exposition sharpened by mathematical techniques of analysis, was to be based on assumptions chosen for their simplicity and relevance to the real world and to be verified by a logically-designed compilation of empirical observations'. My account of JNK's book was written before I read her introductory essay, but she confirms that its main achievement was to sum up the existing consensus, and she quotes C. D. Broad's obituary notice on JNK in *E.J.* (1950), 406: 'The consensus amongst orthodox economists which Keynes's *Scope and Method* was designed to document was sufficient to render the text superfluous. ...' She herself notes that it is 'doubtful if it was widely read, even in Cambridge'. JNK had no important English successors, except possibly Lionel Robbins. In general her biographical sketch of JNK ignores the psychological factors, emphasised here, which made intellectual work a burden to him. In particular she ignores the evidence that JNK disappointed the expectations of Marshall and others.

Building pleased him.[52] His administrative work now took up more and more of his time. Later that year he was elected to the Council of the Senate. Six months later, he became its honorary secretary, and thereafter indispensable. Rejecting an offer of a professorship of political economy at the University of Chicago in 1894, Neville wrote back that he was 'far too firmly rooted at Cambridge to be able to think of moving'. He crossed out a final sentence, 'I feel I am settled here for life.'[53]

For the next thirty years indeed Neville was to be at the centre of university administration at Cambridge, eventually succeeding J. W. Clark as Registrary in 1910. No university committee, it seemed, was to be deprived of his calm and balanced judgment. His period of service coincided with the exhaustion of the movement for university reform. This suited Neville perfectly. Unlike Sidgwick he had no programme. Indeed his instincts were profoundly conservative. Although he became Vice-President of Newnham in 1902, he opposed women's admission to degrees on the well-known principle of the unripe time.[54] It was enough to be addressed by Vice-Chancellors as 'Dear Hewer and Drawer of Agenda and Graces'.[55] Or almost enough: he had hopes of the Mastership of Pembroke on the death of the Master, Sir George Gabriel Stokes, in 1903; instead the college elected the professor of Divinity, Arthur James Mason. Neville would have made a good Master, and he would have loved the ceremonial aspects of the job. In these ways, his academic career finally petered out, as it had always threatened to do, under the accumulation of routine, undemanding, business, which nevertheless left him enough time to pursue the obsession of his middle years, golf, and devote himself to the education of his children.

III

MAYNARD'S EARLY YEARS: 1883–1897

Both parents were besotted with baby Maynard: Neville felt he could watch him for hours on end, though typically worried that he might not grow up 'sturdy in mind and body'.[56] He was born tongue-tied.[57] A small operation enabled Florence to nurse him normally till he was weaned at nine months; but, whether or not as a result of this, he lisped slightly as an adult. On 24 March 1884 Neville wrote in his diary, 'Florence says she loves Baby so much that it is quite painful. For myself I can say that his smiles and his little arms put out to come to me constitute one of the greatest joys that I have ever had in my life.'

Doting on Maynard did not exclude chastising him for his misdemeanours. From Maynard's second to seventh year there are frequent slappings and even 'whippings'. Then they stop, presumably with the dawn of 'reason'. Maynard was whipped when 'he got a spirit of wickedness into him that would not let him be good'.[58] Amateur psychologists might have a field day speculating on the effects of Maynard's late circumcision. He and Geoffrey were both circumcised as young boys, the most desperate of the measures taken to stop them masturbating.[59] The date of these operations cannot be placed with certainty, but they were probably done in London in 1891 when Geoffrey was four and Maynard eight.[60]

Within the limits of the moralistic conventions of the day, Neville and Florence were loving and careful, even over-careful, parents. Neville's diary makes it clear that from the start he was fascinated by Maynard – more so than he was to be by his other two children. Florence, it seems, did not keep a diary, so it is difficult to discover her own feelings about her children, or what she was like as a mother: a deficiency not repaired by Geoffrey Keynes's memoirs in which Florence and Neville get one unilluminating sentence as parents.[61] It is by no means clear that Maynard was Florence's favourite. Interests and companionship bound her more closely to Margaret than to either of the boys. She was more shy than was Neville about showing her feelings. There was also this difference between father and mother: that as the children grew up his interests came to narrow increasingly on the family whereas hers broadened outwards to the community.

Maynard's feelings towards his mother naturally waxed and waned at different times. He felt particularly close to her between the ages of six and eight, tending at this time to distance himself from his father. It is in this period that he calls Florence his 'greatest friend in the world' and his 'city of refuge'; when looking at her alone makes him incredibly happy, when he wants to be exactly like her, never to leave her or, alternatively, wants Neville to choose a wife for him just like her. Appeals to his love for his mother can get him to be good when all others fail.[62] From 1891 Father starts to come much more into the picture. He and Maynard are drawn to each other by their love of stamps. From eight onwards, right through school, university, and into adult life, Maynard's relationship with his father is the essential one. Later things changed again as his father withdrew into apathy. One is talking about relationships which, most unusually, lasted for sixty-two years. All three had plenty of time to adapt to the evolving personalities and interests of each other.

As one might suppose, Maynard was closer to his sister Margaret than to his brother Geoffrey, a twenty-month gap being easier to bridge than a forty-five-month one. Margaret was the first outlet for his didactic urges. But apart from the age difference, his mental development was much quicker than that of the other two, and this alone would have drawn him to older people. An early memory of Geoffrey's which obviously crystallised for him his childhood relationship with Maynard is of rushing up to embrace his brother when he got his Eton scholarship in 1897, only to be pushed impatiently aside.[63] Of relations near his own age Maynard was probably closest to 'Uncle' Kenneth, Florence's youngest brother, only four years his senior. Harvey Road was full of dons' children. The Keynes children seem to have seen most of the Glazebrooks. But Maynard was not particularly close to them. Friends started to be important to him only at Eton.

He was a thin, delicate, lanky child. Florence and Neville quickly concluded that he was not robust, an opinion shared by their family physician, Dr Wherry, 'a tall man with a melancholy face and manner'.[64] Suffering frequent sickness and diarrhoea in his first three years, and 'feverish attacks' from then onwards, Maynard grew up, his parents felt, with a mind too active for his enfeebled body. He was frequently taken away from school or let off school work. Part of the problem may have been caused by his uneven physical development. His childhood is punctuated by fierce spurts of growth which left him exhausted, and by the age of fourteen already taller than his father.

From the age of six Maynard was convinced that he was 'remarkably ugly. He thinks no one ever was quite so ugly.'[65] This was not just a childhood fancy, but as he told Lytton Strachey many years later a 'fixed, constant, unalterable obsession' from which he had 'always' suffered. (see below p. 169). This is surely important. An uncoordinated body which left him bad at games and a conviction that he was physically unattractive played their part in making his childhood so cerebral. Perhaps they also contributed to the periods of depression – 'natural sadness' Maynard called them – which Geoffrey remembers in a brother who was 'normally cheerful, witty, and full of self-confidence'.[66] Maynard's conviction of his own ugliness can be set against the photograph of him taken with the other two children about this very time. His appearance here is certainly far removed from that physiognomy, described by George Eliot, 'in which it seems impossible to discern anything but the generic character of boyhood'; but it is far from unattractive. The photograph shows that, at six, he had a most unusual face, intelligent, alert, full of personality, besides which his younger sister and brother seem merely pretty. The 'little shrimp' as his father called him, with the distinctive high cheek bones and the most delicate hint of laughter in eyes and mouth, is already recognisably the father of the man.

Surrounded as he was by the conviction that he was bound to be clever, Maynard would have disappointed more people than great-

grandmother Ford had he turned out not to be. However, there was no
fear of that. Even before he was two, Florence worried about his 'working his brain too hard'.[67] Such was Maynard's reputation for precocity
that years later his Cambridge colleague, C. R. Fay, wrote jokingly, 'I
have heard that when a few months old he confuted his nurse who was
urging him to drink a noxious medicine by a carefully reasoned argument which proved conclusively that the Elasticity of his Demand for
the commodity in question was zero.' However, most of the evidence
of budding genius recorded by his father are no more than the bright
remarks of a bright boy. There is certainly nothing approaching the
John Stuart Mill standard of achievement. However, a connoisseur of
precocity might savour the definition of interest given by the future
economist at the age of four and a half: 'If I let you have a halfpenny
& you kept it for a very long time you would have to give me back that
halfpenny & another one too. That's interest.'[68] That his economic
understanding was not complete, however, is shown by his wonder that
all the chairs (rather than shares) should come tumbling down after a
warlike speech by Kaiser William II of Germany.[69] He developed the
bright boy's habit of blurting out embarrassing things. As the family
were leaving chapel one Sunday he said in a loud clear voice 'It's the
prayers I dislike most.'[70] When one Easter at Kington Aunt Mary
Keynes in a 'rare mistake for her' said ''im instead of him', Maynard at
once remarked drily and seriously, 'I *think* "him" is spelt with an "h".'
He was not quite six. Nor was he at all put out when his parents told
him that it was wrong to hurt other people's feelings. 'Father & Mother
often hurt *my* feelings', he replied.[71] On his sixth birthday he reduced
his sister Margaret to tears by proving to her that she was a *thing*. 'She
wouldn't like to be nothing, and if she wasn't nothing she must be
something, & if she was something she was a thing.' The logician
W. E. Johnston, visiting the Keynes house, decided to pursue the
conversation further. 'You call Margaret a thing,' he said, 'but can
things talk? Is this table a thing?' 'Yes.' 'Well, it can't talk, and Margaret can talk.' Unabashed, Maynard replied, '*Some* things can't talk,
but *some* things can.'

As an adult, Maynard looked back with affection on his father's circle:

> In the first age of married society in Cambridge, when the narrow
> circle of the spouses-regnant of the Heads of Colleges and of a few
> wives of Professors was first extended, several of the most notable
> dons, particularly in the School of Moral Science, married students
> of Newnham. The double link between husbands and between wives
> bound together a small cultured society of great simplicity and dis-
> tinction. This circle was at its full strength in my boyhood, and, when
> I was first old enough to be asked out to luncheon or dinner, it was
> to these houses that I went. I remember a homely, intellectual,

John Keynes of Salisbury

Anna Maynard Keynes

Dr John Brown

Florence Ada Keynes   John Neville Keynes

Maynard at the age of three

Margaret (4), Geoffrey (2½), Maynard (6)

Maynard aged ten

Maynard shortly before he went to Eton

Sheridan's *The Rivals* at Eton
Harold Butler as Sir Lucius O'Trigger, Maynard as Bob Acres

Maynard Keynes, Bernard Swithinbank, Gerard Mackworth Young

Oscar Browning

Alfred Marshall

Arthur Cecil Pigou

The Committee of the Cambridge Union, 1905

A.C.O. Morgan
(Trinity)
W.E. Bousfield
(Caius)

A.P. Hughes-Gibb
(Trinity)
E.S. Montagu
(Trinity: Ex-President)

H.M. Paul
(Junior Treasurer: Oxford Union)
J.K. Mozley
(Pembroke: Vice-President)

G.S.C. Rentoul
(Oxford Union)
J.M. Keynes
(King's President)

H.A. Hollond
(Trinity)
J.R. Tanner Litt.D.
(St John's Treasurer)

A.R. Churchill
(Caius)
H.W. Harris
(St John's Secretary)

Stanley S. Brown
(Chief Clerk)
J.T. Sheppard
(King's Ex-President)

Lytton and Pippa Strachey

Duncan Grant

Arthur Lee Hobhouse

Duncan Grant, Self-Portrait, 1909-10

Maynard Keynes, portrait by Duncan Grant, painted on Hoy, 1908

atmosphere which it is harder to find in the swollen, heterogeneous Cambridge of to-day.*[72]

Geoffrey adds that Maynard was 'ready from an early age to join in learned discussions'.[73] W. E. Johnston, who joined subtlety of mind to sweetness of disposition, was Neville's closest friend. His sister Hattie ran a Dame's school attended by Margaret and Geoffrey. Maynard remembers him and Neville discussing logical points over interminable lunches. The austere but charming Sidgwick with his white flowing beard was a golf as well as a dinner companion. Another friend was the philosopher and psychologist James Ward, 'a testy, irritable thing' as he called himself: the Keynes and Ward families would picnic together on the river in the summer. The bibliophile economist Herbert Foxwell, another friend, moved to Harvey Road on his marriage in 1898. The absurd but fascinating Alfred Marshall was a frequent visitor at No. 6 Harvey Road, not so much for dinner as for discussion. Neville's friends included economists from outside Cambridge too – James Bonar, Paul Wicksteed, Robert Giffen, and Inglis Palgrave. It was no doubt the educational effects of such a society which great-grandmother Ford had in mind when she wrote to Maynard that 'you will be expected to be very clever, having lived always in Cambridge.'

When he was five and a half he started going to the kindergarten of the Perse School for Girls. By the end of 1889 he was showing 'talent' at arithmetic. But 'Maynard's nerves seem very much unstrung', reported his worried father on 10 October 1889. 'He is constantly blinking his eyes & sometimes he turns them up in a dreadful way so that only the whites shew.' The twitchings had become so 'dreadful' by 30 October that he was removed from school after Wherry had diagnosed Sydenham's chorea, or St Vitus's dance, probably an after-effect of the attack of rheumatic fever he had had in the summer. A year later, in December 1890, Maynard was showing 'power' at arithmetic; but then for some reason he was removed from the kindergarten for good and taught at home for a year.

In January 1892, he started as a day boy at St Faith's Preparatory School in the Trumpington Road. It was founded and run by Ralph Goodchild, a tough Victorian pedagogue who recognised 'scholarship material' when he saw it. Neville moved quickly and sensibly to stop Maynard being exploited:

It is clear [he wrote to Goodchild on 12 February 1892] that Maynard finds the afternoon work rather long. He sometimes comes

* C. D. Broad, too, remarked on 'how much the Cambridge school of moral science in the nineteenth and early twentieth centuries owed to cultivated Liberal Nonconformists ... with their tradition of plain living and high thinking, and their passion for freedom of thought.' (*Proceedings of the British Academy*, xvii, 1931.)

home – as to-day – quite overdone. I shall be very much obliged if instead of being kept in to write out his mistakes he can come home directly school is over, & write out his mistakes in the evening.... He also complains of being knocked on the head with a ruler & having his wrists twisted by a boarder named Watson – two years older than himself – when they are left in the schoolroom together. The boy himself does not like the idea of my writing to you, & I shall therefore be glad if you will say nothing about it at present to Watson or the other boys. I will write to you further if I hear of anything of the kind happening again.

By March, his father noted that Maynard was 'very quick at Arithmetic and Algebra'. He concluded, though, that he was 'not likely to excel in sports any more than his Father did'.[74] The main problem was to resist Goodchild's efforts to hurry him along. Before he was ten, Maynard had finished Book I of Euclid, was doing Quadratic Equations in Algebra and Stocks in Arithmetic, Ovid and continuous Prose in Latin, and *Samson Agonistes* in English.[75]

Worried by the effects of all this on his health, his parents removed him to Bedford for the autumn of 1893, where his Brown grandmother re-opened her schoolroom for his benefit. Maynard was a cheerful correspondent.

Sunday, 1 October 1893:
... I have been reading lately two books by Henty called 'Condemned as a Nihilist' and 'Through the Fray'. To-day I read through a 'Crown of Success'. As I was at chapel this morning you will see that I read it rather quickly.

8 October 1893:
... Have you got the sequel to 'Kidnapped' or the 'Refugees' yet. I am reading the second scene of the New Arabian nights so I should either like the first series or either of the two above named books. I see that the Cook Island stamp has now got the cook on.

5 November 1893:
... This evening Grandpa will lecture on the Reformation.... On Monday they are going to have in the Grammar School field a grand display of fireworks ... a dancing skeleton, a balloon, etc., etc.... Have Margaret and Goeffrey [sic] taken up bubbles, if they have White Castile Soap is best.

Mrs Brown was much struck by Maynard's 'general ability and the interest – quite beyond his years – wh. he shews in literature. She says he is very intense while at work, but finds steady application more difficult' – a standard comment about this time.[76] But Neville was not completely satisfied with the results of the Bedford experiment. 'Maynard has come back not quite up to the mark,' he noted on 2 January 1894. 'Perhaps Florence pays rather too much attention to his ailments, but at Bedford they go to the opposite extreme, paying no attention to his diet, & laughing at him when he professes himself not well.'

Nevertheless, it was after his return from Bedford that Maynard's scholastic work really 'took off'. In July 1894 he came top for the first time in examination and classwork, after being coached by Neville in examination technique. His ascendancy, which was not shaken while he remained at St Faith's, was firmly based on mathematics, for which it was now accepted that he had a definite bent. From October 1894 he started two hours' extra coaching in it, four days a week. On 30 November 1894 his father noted that 'Maynard has himself discovered the method of squaring a number of two figures by applying the formula $(x+y)^2 = x^2 + 2xy + y^2$' – a first sign of the facility in Algebra which would be his main strength as a mathematician. By December 1894, his teacher Holt, himself a Wrangler, reported that Maynard 'now and then does really brilliant work, but soon tires & has not the perseverance in the face of a difficulty'. The following July a relieved Neville noted that 'his work does not seem to be any great labour to him, & he seems much more robust than he used to be'. Extremely quick to grasp the point, Maynard was careless about details. Goodchild told Neville that 'work that may take two hours is finished in less than half the time given'. The annoying thing, Goodchild continued, was 'that he corrects his mistakes when I am looking them over before I have seen them myself'.[77] Maynard was so obsessed by his Algebra at this time that in family prayers he found himself praying, 'Let Mother equal x and let Geoffrey equal y.'[78]

The days when he was bullied in the schoolroom had been left far behind. Already tall for his age, soon after his return from Bedford he started shooting up in height. When Goodchild wrote to Neville at the end of 1896 that Maynard stood 'head and shoulders above all the other boys in the school' he meant physically as well as mentally.

There can be no doubt [his brother recalls] that ... he was regarded almost with awe by his schoolfellows. The stories of his slave, who walked behind him carrying his books in return for help and protection, and of the other boy with whom he had 'a commercial treaty', sealed with blood and enacting that he should not approach at any time nearer than fifteen yards, are not apocrypha. I can still name the second one.[79]

He established something of an ascendancy at Harvey Road, too. The whippings long forgotten, Maynard now stayed up late at night and disdained, in the holidays, to come down to breakfast before mid-morning. He worked with Neville in his study. When his parents went away on holiday, Maynard expertly sorted out their mail, Neville thanking 'My dear Private Secretary'. The basis of Maynard's domestic position was parental admiration which became more unstinted with each prize he notched up. 'I am already too proud of the dear boy,' Neville noted on 12 January 1897. 'My pride in him and my love for him feed each other.'

Despite worries about his increased stammering, his parents decided, at the end of 1896, to enter him for the Eton College Scholarship Examination in July the following year. Maynard would have gone to public school in any case – Goodchild advised Tonbridge – since his parents were no longer members of a Dissenting sect but part of the Establishment, and well pleased to be. But it was Maynard's brains which opened up Eton for him, for his parents would never have dreamt of placing him among the aristocratic or wealthy Oppidans. Eton meant Eton College to which each year about fifteen boys were 'elected' on the results of a competitive examination. It was Maynard's first chance to measure himself against a cross-section of England's budding intellectual elite.

Neville, as can be imagined, was determined to leave nothing to chance. Special tutors were engaged. Father and son started getting up at 7 a.m. every morning and working together before breakfast to accustom Maynard to the times of the scholarship papers. Not surprisingly Neville started to feel 'very tired'. To his depression whenever he dwelt on Maynard's prospects was added his 'grief to ... think that the dear boy will not in any case do his work very much longer with me in the study'.[80] By the time he, Florence, and Maynard left for Eton on Monday 5 July, he was in a 'fearful state of worry'. To make matters worse their hotel in the High Street was 'frightfully noisy', so that he lay awake all night with his gloomy thoughts.

They all got up at 6.15 a.m. on Tuesday, 6 July to send Maynard off to Upper School in good time for Latin Composition. Before Neville could start to meet Maynard at the end of the paper, his son walked cheerfully into the hotel having finished it early. Latin Translation and Mathematics followed. Next morning, Maynard, despatched to Greek Grammar fortified with Valentine's Beef Extract, was out early again.

Harder Mathematics followed: he left the afternoon's Greek Translation early once more, complaining that 'the days seem dreadfully long'.
His parents meanwhile had formed a most favourable impression of the
manners of the Eton boys. On Thursday morning Maynard did Latin
Verse, and the examination ended with the General Paper 'which
didn't suit [him] very well'.*[81]

Worrying about the examinations was followed by worrying about
the results. Depressed by Goodchild's pessimistic appraisal of Maynard's examination notes, and alarmed by the lack of geniality of the
Vice-Chancellor, one of the Eton examiners, Neville despaired. 'Well,
the dear boy has I am sure done his best.' As no news came on Monday
he and Florence gave up hope. It would have to be Tonbridge after all,
or perhaps Rugby. And yet 'after visiting Eton we are the more keen
about the school: & after all the expectations raised about the boy, we
cannot think of his failing at his first public trial'. At last a telegram
came at 5.30 p.m. 'Maynard 10th College Scholar'. His mathematics
had pulled him through after all, and he was placed first equal in that
subject. 'This was I think the most delightful telegram I ever received,'
a thankful Neville wrote in his diary. 'My own successes never gave
anything like the pleasure this has done.' It was to be the first of many
such pleasures for however often his father revised his expectations
upwards Maynard was to be equal to them.

That summer, at Leigh Farm, Tintagel, Neville observed his 5 foot
5 inch son with fond indulgence. 'Maynard', he wrote, 'is just now a
curious combination – quite childish in some things, thoroughly entering into the simplest enjoyments such as Geoffrey or even younger
children can share with him, while in other things he is thoroughly
grown up, entering most sensibly and seriously into what are quite
men's ideas.'[82] Goodchild wrote, 'He leaves me with a great reputation
for every good quality.'

---

* The first question in the General Paper was: Write not more than 30 lines on one
of the following:
  a. The uses of an aristocracy.
  b. Your favourite poet with reasons for the choice.
  c. Westward the tide of empire holds its course.
  d. God made the country, but man made the town.
  e. Free Trade and Protection. Their respective advantages and disadvantages.

The following is a typical question from the first mathematics paper:
  5. Find, to the nearest penny, the amount at compound interest of £1250 in 4 years
     at 4 per cent per annum.

4 Eton

AN ETON EDUCATION

As Tenth King's Scholar Maynard was given a place in College for September 1897. Boarding was a new and no doubt frightening experience for him, and as the time for him to go to Eton approached he became depressed and irritable. As if in protest he developed a heavy cold and so had to miss the start of his first half (at Eton a term was known as a 'half': three 'halves' made a whole). 'It is most unfortunate that the dear boy should not be able to put in an appearance at Eton on the proper day,' noted his father, worried equally about Maynard's health and the proprieties. Eventually Maynard was able to leave Cambridge with his mother on 26 September, four days late, still looking 'like an invalid'.* The College matron, Miss Hackett, was not very welcoming. 'This is not a hospital,' she told Florence crossly. But one of the boys' maids, 'such a nice motherly woman', unpacked Maynard's clothes in his cubicle in Chamber. Florence was relieved to find them all correct. On 4 October Maynard wrote to his brother:

> Dear Boff,
> ... We feel [sic] baths with pipes which we call siphons. Any insubordination is punished by a whacking with one of these and it is called siphoning. I played to-day at the Wall Game for the first time. It is a most indescribable and extraordinary game and you dress in most indescribable and extraordinary costumes called Wallsacks.
> Please tell mother that I received the box containing stockings and books to-day
> I remain
> Your affectionate brother
>
> JMK
> Hallelujah

One benefit of arriving late was that Maynard missed the new boys' traditional first encounter with the headmaster in Upper School. The

---

* Curiously he had to miss the start of his second year, too, Dr Wherry telling Neville that he had 'just escaped being jaundiced'.

Rev. Edmond Warre, immensely muscular and immensely Christian, always used the occasion to deliver a warning about the dangers of 'filth'; a warning made more impressive and mysterious by the fact that few other words in his discourse were audible.[1] Maynard's Brown grandmother moved quickly to fill the gap in his education. 'Never do or say anything you would feel ashamed of if your mother were by,' she wrote to him. With these traditional injunctions ringing in their ears, Maynard and the other boys of his 'election' submitted themselves to be reshaped into Etonians.* He emerged five years later very recognisably the adult he was to be for the rest of his life. What sort of experience had it been?

He was outstandingly successful at Eton, and predominantly happy there. These facts help one understand the part he came to play in English life. Many gifted English middle-class boys have been made miserable by their parents or by their boarding-schools; some of them, as a result, become rebels. In an eloquent passage with a Bloomsbury ring Clive Bell explained why any English boy born with 'fine sensibility, a peculiar feeling for art, or an absolutely first-rate intelligence' was bound to find himself 'at loggerheads with the world in which he is to live'. The basic reason was that middle-class education was 'so smug and hypocritical, so grossly philistine, and at bottom so brutal, that every first-rate Englishman necessarily becomes an outlaw. He grows by kicking....'[2] However true this may be of some middle-class experience it does not fit Keynes. He is an example of a 'first-rate intelligence' who never became an 'outlaw'.

One reason for this is clear. He never felt the need to rebel against his home. The values of his parents were scholarly and intellectual, not hearty; and he never repudiated this part of his legacy. But Eton, too, must take some of the credit. His experience there did not turn him into a rebel. Perhaps the most important reason was that all the seventy scholarship boys lived together in the same house – College – rather than being scattered round the school. In College his intelligence could grow in congenial company and an environment favourable to learning. And the existence of College itself helped leaven the rest of the school. Maynard never had to 'kick' against the rampant philistine and athletic values which reduce so many clever boys to a state of misery and boredom. At home, at Eton, and later at King's College, Cambridge, the development of his mind was supported by the surrounding conditions, not twisted by them.

* Maynard's election consisted (in order) of Knox, Balston, Hamilton, Duncan, Young, Herringham, Hope-Jones, Dundas, Keynes, Ainger, Olphert, Micklem, Lightfoot, and Swithinbank. The first ten came with Keynes, the rest arrived one or two halves later as places became available. Several boys had meanwhile dropped out; that is why Keynes entered in 9th place, although he had been 10th in the scholarship examination.

College was a unique historical survival in the public school world. It dated from the fifteenth century, when its founder, King Henry VI, set out to provide a free education for seventy poor scholars, as well as a separate fee-paying one for twenty commoners lodged in the town of Eton. The plan misfired, as even monarchs cannot control events from beyond the grave. While College languished, its endowment income appropriated by its rapacious Fellows, fee-paying or Oppidan Eton swelled in size and prestige to become the foremost aristocratic school in England. Its proximity to Windsor Castle gave it a social cachet no other school had. George III was its greatest patron, and to this day Etonians celebrate his birthday, the Fourth of June, and wear their black suits in mourning for his death.

But College survived even the horrors of Long Chamber, the big dormitory where the scholars were locked up every night with the rats, their revels and cruelties to each other disturbed only by the occasional entrance of the headmaster to deliver a mass flogging. By the time Maynard arrived, evangelicalism had done its work. New Buildings had been added to Long Chamber in 1846, which provided bed-sitting rooms for fifty-five Collegers, leaving only fifteen cubicles or 'stalls' for the most junior arrivals. A master now lived in College to keep an eye on things. Collegers were decently fed and adequately washed. When Maynard came there were still seventy of them – as against ten times that many Oppidans – whose board and tuition were provided free, living on the east side of the chastely beautiful front quadrangle known as School Yard. College's prestige also stood high. There were few, if any, 'poor' scholars. Most were from professional or academic families, many connected with the school and with the ancient universities.

The reform of College was part of the general modernisation and moralisation of Eton under the Arnoldian influence. Its curriculum was broadened from the classics to include mathematics, history and modern languages. New classrooms were built and the quality and status of the assistant masters improved. Relations between masters and boys and the boys themselves were humanised. Although these reforms went hand in hand with the characteristic Victorian emphasis on games and character-building Eton as a whole never surrendered to the excesses of muscular Christianity. The school's very position, at the apex of the public school world, permitted a more humane, less repressive, internal culture than was found elsewhere. Its parents took gentlemanly status more for granted, and exerted less pressure on the school to produce a standardised product. Enlightened schoolmasters like William Johnson and Oscar Browning, who believed in cultivating the mind and feelings rather than the body, could flourish, at least for a time, in remarkable independence of the headmaster, aided in this by another unique Eton institution, the tutorial system. Above all, each boy (in College after his first year) had the wonderful boon of his own bedroom-study, which meant privacy. Right through the school there was less pressure to conform than in other public schools. Eton, as one old Etonian described it, was a place where 'you could think and love what you liked: only in external matters, in clothes, or in deportment, need you do as the others do'.[3]

There remained a considerable difference between College and Oppidan Eton. College, in Bernard Crick's apt phrase, was 'an intellectual elite thrust into the heart of a social elite'.[4] One of the practical consequences of this was captured in a letter Maynard wrote home in his third year (28 January 1900):

> Goodhart [the Master in College] gave us a lecture after prayers yesterday on the growth of slackness and extravagance in imitation of the Oppidans in College.
>
> His points were quite sound: that Collegers would have to earn their own livings and therefore must work now; that those who can afford to be extravagant ought not to be in College, and that those who can't shouldn't.

The atmosphere of College was cerebral and unworldly. It tended to produce clergymen, scholars and schoolmasters; Oppidan Eton soldiers, statesmen, bankers. Tugs, as Collegers were known, were expected to work or 'sap' harder than Oppidans. They wore gowns for school, and surplices for chapel. They had their own sports ground, College Field, where they played an incomprehensible game of their own, the Wall Game. They had their distinctive social organisation and vocabulary. Geographically College, in School Yard, was at the heart of the school, whereas the Oppidans had their houses in the town. Until his last couple of halves all Maynard's habitual interests, activities and friendships were College-centred. Even though he would do his schoolwork with Oppidans, he and the fellow-Collegers of his election formed an intellectual minority at the top of each division, competing with each other for the prizes.

Despite the Victorian reforms, Eton's curriculum remained remarkably narrow. Two subjects dominated – classics and mathematics, with a heavy emphasis on the former. History came a poor third. A little French was taught by two stage Frenchmen. Natural sciences were not something a gentleman need bother himself with. Even in classics the teaching was intensive rather than extensive. Schoolwork was spent in learning a few Latin and Greek books by heart, construing, and practising writing Greek and Latin verses and prose. Mathematics was dominated by weekly Problem Papers, at which boys acquired skill, through endless repetition, in solving simple Algebra problems. (These typically had to do with buying stocks and shares, and calculating times or distances of trains which invariably ran between London, Oxford, and Cambridge.) The work done in class, or divisions as they were known, was examined in 'Trials' each half, as a result of which a boy could earn his 'remove' to the next level, and so on all the way up the school till he reached the First Hundred. A somewhat depressing feature of the system was that boys moved up the school in a definite order, determined by these examination results; many of them, no doubt, never moved very far. Performance was stimulated by an extraordinary quantity of prizes; but inevitably most of them were appropriated by the few.

None of this diverged significantly from the standard pattern at dozens of other public-schools. But side by side with school work ran a parallel system of instruction given by a boy's tutor in his pupil-room. Each boy was assigned a tutor for his years at school. The tutor saw that his pupil knew the lessons for his division master, read 'extra books' with him, and gave him religious instruction and general counselling. As Oscar Browning saw it: 'Eton possesses two elements, which are an essential part of a good education, the firm and uniform course of the school curriculum . . . and the work of the tutor's pupil room, subtle and adaptable, fitted for every kind of mind and capacity.'[5]

Two people above all shaped Maynard's life at Eton. The first was his tutor, Samuel Gurney Lubbock, newly returned to Eton himself as an assistant-master, having taken a first-class in classics at King's College, Cambridge. Neville had selected him personally for the job, after making enquiries at King's. It was an excellent choice. Lubbock was a true gentleman scholar, with an ideal of all-round development. He immediately recognised in Maynard a boy with an exceptional range of ability and interests and encouraged him to spread himself. Maynard, who as we shall see was no instinctive admirer of authority, liked and respected his tutor. Lubbock's influence can be seen in Maynard's decision to try for King's College, Cambridge and in his refusal to specialise in his strongest subject, mathematics. It was Lubbock, too, who planted his interest in mediaeval Latin poetry. However, it is not true that Lubbock had 'complete control of the boy, body, mind, and spirit' as Oscar Browning says a good tutor was bound to have. This honour Lubbock was obliged to share with Neville Keynes himself. Neville appointed himself Maynard's director of studies. 'Let us know each week how you are getting on with your work,' he wrote to him soon after he arrived. Maynard obliged. In return he got back a stream of instruction on methods of study, examination technique, prose style, and general conduct.

Neville soon got to know his son's academic, social, and competitive situation in College almost as well as did Maynard himself. His weekly letters were directed, above all, to keeping Maynard 'up to the mark', to making sure that he mastered his bookwork, acquitted himself well in the examinations, and entered and thoroughly prepared for the main prizes. If Lubbock's influence was exerted on behalf of breadth of culture, Neville's emphasis was on strenuousness of effort. Yet in the end it is probably wrong to say that he controlled his son's 'body, mind, and spirit' any more than Lubbock did. Maynard certainly took Neville's academic advice, but he pursued his own intellectual interests independently. Above all, his rhythm of work was different. To Neville academic achievement was always associated with pain; to Maynard it came much more easily. As the prizes came flooding in Neville's tone gradually changed from one of exhortation to one of awe: 'These things seem to come to you whether you will or not,' he wrote on 4 February 1901. It was an admission of defeat.

II

THE SCHOOLBOY

There is much about Maynard's schooldays at Eton which is probably beyond recall. We have a complete run of his school reports, of his letters home. A number of his essays and notebooks survive. He kept a diary for most of his last three years, much of it compiled later from his memory and letters to his parents. From these we can get a fairly good idea of his mental growth, his interests, his sporting activities, his opinions on a variety of topics, his literary style, and those aspects of his personality which he chose to expose to his teachers and parents. On the other hand the quality of his inner life, of his relations with his schoolfellows has to be, at best, inferred from very slender evidence. This was before Keynes and his friends exchanged copious quantities of letters analysing their 'states of mind'. The few letters which survive between Keynes and his schoolfriends are rather impersonal. They give one the feeling that they could be read, if necessary, by parents.

From his school reports Maynard emerges as a model pupil. Gurney Lubbock's first one sets the tone of much of what was to follow. Mathematics was from the start his 'forte', but he was also very good at classics. 'At construing, especially construing at first sight privately with me he is really remarkably good; he has a fair vocabulary and is wonderfully quick at grasping a passage. . . .' But his verse composition was moderate only – 'he does not really know the difference between a good verse and a bad verse'. He had displayed a 'real healthy interest in all the doings of the College, athletic and otherwise'. Lubbock concluded, 'Certainly if all boys were like him the schoolmaster's life would be an easy one.'

In the terms which followed, a number of mental and personality traits are repeatedly singled out for mention. There was the speed at which he did his work, based on quickness in grasping and retaining facts, and understanding essential points. His command of the English language is often noticed. This was particularly important in all the translation and essay side of his work in classics. However, his verse composition remained 'wooden', his Latin prose subject to 'strange blunders'. He was thought to lack the imagination, and take insufficient pains, to become a really good versifier. Yet though his domination of mathematics, based on exceptional facility in Algebra, became so complete that he had to be barred, in his third year, from the Problems Prize, no one except Gilbert Harrison Hurst, his mathematics master, wanted him to specialise in his strongest subject. Luxmoore, Eton's best-known classicist, hoped that 'the more accurate sciences will not dry the readiness of his sympathy and insight for more inspiring and human subjects. His little essay on "Antigone" was not like the work of one made for mathematics' (April 1901). Marten, his history master, reported him the 'ablest boy in the division' with a 'decided talent for history' (December, July 1900). Only his French seemed to make little progress: 'grammar weak – composition poor – general knowledge unsound' (December 1898).

Keynes was a prodigious prize-winner at Eton. He won 10 in his first year, 18 in his second, 11 in his third: a total of 63 volumes in all. He won all the school's main mathematical prizes, and even managed to pick up a chemistry prize on the way. Yet what particularly pleased Lubbock was the absence of any 'mercenary spirit' in Maynard's work. He worked for the pleasure of the work not for the pleasure of winning prizes. 'He is one of the very few who seems to appreciate the value and merits of the books he is working at' (December 1898). Here Geoffrey Keynes may give a somewhat one-sided view of his brother. Their father, he wrote, 'set great store by our marks and position in class, and this stimulated a sense of competition in Maynard, who enjoyed his own capacity of leaping ahead of other boys'.[6] The first part of this statement is undoubtedly true. Neville's letters to Maynard are full of remarks such as 'You didn't tell me how much you were behind Herringham and Bailey in the first fortnightly order in Classics' (28 February 1898); 'Ainger seems to be coming on well. You must not let him beat you in Trials' (12 May 1898); 'You must not let Knox and Bailey go on beating you in Problems' (9 February 1899); 'You must not allow yourself to be beaten every fortnight by Ainger and Lightfoot' (5 March 1900). How far Maynard needed this competitive stimulus is open to question. The truth seems to be that Neville, influenced by his own experience, could never appreciate the intensity of the pleasure which Maynard got out of work for its own sake.

Two examples of this from his Eton time, which had nothing to do with prizes, are his researches into his family history, which occupied much of his fourth year, and his love of medieval poetry. Such diversions from the main line of his school work worried his father. All his life Maynard had this capacity for getting hooked on something which seemed a diversion from his main efforts, yet in the end enriched them. Extra-curricular interests give an added dimension to his economic writings.

Keynes's interests, in or out of class, were far from being confined to things of the mind. At first Lubbock found his manner a trifle spinsterish, but by his second term was able to note, with relief, that he had 'become a little more boyish' (April 1898). Keynes, he wrote in August of that year, was 'thoroughly interested in Athletic and School matters'. His cricket performances were modest. 'My scores have been 5, 3, and 2,' he reported to Neville on 22 May 1898 with his usual precision. But cricket, and cricketing occasions, produced the usual schoolboy emotions. He was 'frightfully pleased' by Eton's performance against Winchester, but 'horribly disappointed' when Cambridge lost to Oxford. 'Strawberries and iced devonshire cream is spiffing,' he told his sister Margaret with full boyish appreciation on the occasion of his first visit to the Eton and Harrow match at Lords. In his second summer he became a 'wet bob', and enjoyed to the full the life on the river, languidly sculling up the Thames with his friends to favourite spots for a bathe and tea.

His ability to share the normal schoolboy enthusiasms made him less formidable, and thus less remote, to his schoolfellows. 'It says much for him', Lubbock wrote on 5 August 1899, 'that some very illiterate members of my pupil room, with whom he comes into contact, like and respect him a good deal.' Members of his election looked on him as a natural spokesman.[7] He was a little older than most of them, having come at fourteen, rather than thirteen. He was very tall – in his first year he towered over his fagmaster, Macnaghten – which meant that he had to go straightaway into 'tails' – a black morning suit, black silk top hat, and white bow tie. (Florence used to buy his ties by the gross, to wear once and throw away.) His voice had already broken: a Colleger remembers 'a rather tall, incredibly angular' boy singing *Three Blue Bottles* at Chamber Singing 'with great gusto and entire indifference to tune'. At the end of his first half he was elected to Chamber Pop (College's junior debating society) and took an active part in its speechmaking, his father furnishing him with topics and technical advice. (They refused to debate the Dreyfus case, but sympathised 'unanimously' with Spain in its war against the United States). In his third half Maynard became Captain of Chamber, a position which 'I don't at all dislike', he told Neville. There is no evidence of teasing: Maynard's personality commanded respect from his peers.

He made an equally good impression on his teachers. 'Always most pleasant to deal with' (Donaldson), 'a very pleasant companion' (Vaughan), 'a capital fellow' (Broadbent), 'I like Keynes much' (Luxmoore) are typical comments. His modesty of disposition, his lack of priggishness, his thoroughness, his willingness to do what was asked of him, were all noted and appreciated. He rarely got into trouble with his boy seniors, managing to avoid being 'worked off' (caned) till his fifth term, and then 'absolutely unjustly', he wrote in his diary 3 July 1899. His one consistent failing in the eyes of the authorities was his inability to get up in the mornings. This was his only sign of rebellion. There is something here which is curious. So much intelligence and so much acquiescence in things which must have seemed to him unjust, irritating and unintelligent poses a problem. David Garnett gives a clue to the answer in a letter he wrote to Maynard during the First World War. Maynard was winning golden opinions from his official superiors at the Treasury for the excellence of his work on behalf of a cause in which he did not believe. His friends were puzzled by his attitude and often discussed it with him. Garnett wrote:

> It all comes back to what you and Ottoline [Morrell] were talking about after dinner. Whether one minds being caned at school. You guided by your intellect have set yourself in a position where you won't be caned. I, guided by my body, have aroused in me a degree of hate that comes to nothing more practical than intestinal derangement.

Keynes neither wanted to beat or be beaten. Intellect offered a way out. He had already used it to get his own way at home. Later he would use it to offer the world an alternative to rebellion or submission.

That Keynes was already less pleased with authority than authority was with him comes out clearly in his letters home. They are full of sharp comments directed at the stupidity or dullness of examiners, masters, preachers, bursars, matrons, etc. Even at Eton he did not suffer fools gladly. He always seems to have had a lower opinion of examiners than examiners did of him. The one whose papers won him the Junior Mathematical Prize in his first year should have been 'locked up as a dangerous lunatic', he wrote home on 3 July 1898. This is already vintage Keynes. His constant irritation with the College matron – 'the Hackett' as she was known – earned him a rare parental reproof: 'You must not let her little foibles blind you to her good points.' On 14 October 1900 he complained of the lack of hot water: 'But what can you expect of a Bursar, who thinks such things superfluous because he cannot remember any hot and cold water arrangements in the Ark, where he spent one of his summer holidays with his old friend Noah?' The Bursar of King's was later to squirm beneath that withering scorn, until Keynes took over from him.

He liked masters like Luxmoore who could instruct or amuse him, but hated being bored. His *bête-noire* on the teaching staff was 'Mike' Mitchell, a cricketing fanatic, to whom he was 'up' in classics in his third summer. Maynard could 'hardly have imagined that a man could be so dull; anyhow I shall not suffer from want of sleep this half' (6 May 1900). Two weeks later: 'we have not yet succeeded in probing the depths of his ignorance. It must, I think, be bottomless.' Mitchell set him the first 300 lines of the First Georgic for persistent talking in class. In his diary Keynes wrote on 30 June 1900, 'One must talk for want of something else to do. I suppose he was justified in giving me a poena but he might have given us something that was less blatantly useless. I grudge an hour and a half.' Mitchell's report struck the only sour note in the ecomiums showered on Maynard at school. 'Rather a provoking boy in School – reads notes often when he ought to be attending to the lesson, apt to talk to his neighbour unless severely repressed. He gives one the idea of regarding himself as a privileged boy, with perhaps a little intellectual conceit.' This strikes an authentic note: so many gifts and so much modesty as Lubbock portrayed suggest an implausible perfection. The truth is that Maynard could be charming to those he liked and respected, but awful to those he thought foolish or boring. The charm remained, but the rudeness grew with the years.

Preachers in chapel provoked in him most un-Christian feelings. On 12 November 1899 he 'sat and squirmed for twenty-five minutes'. The preacher 'was an archdeacon, but you must have guessed it. I think that he can almost preach badly enough to become a bishop.' Four months later (4 March 1900) he registered a 'revolting performance. They ought to make him an archdeacon at once. He has got all the qualifications.' A year later 'an atrocity was perpetrated in the pulpit, a revolting and merciless atrocity in a loud voice' (17 February 1901). On 17 October 1901, Welldon, the headmaster of Harrow, whom Keynes had found 'hideously ugly' on a previous visit, was back again to preach on the subject of 'Christian Imperialism'. 'He can get a fine roll on the words "British Empire",' Keynes remarked. Preaching offered unrivalled opportunities for sonorous nonsense. It combined the two things Maynard disliked most: imprecise thought and the waste of his time.

Keynes was already a precisian. He wanted exact meanings. 'What is the "imperishable plinth of things"?' he asked after reading one of Kipling's poems. He had a passion for exact information, particularly when expressed in numerical form. On 1 July 1900 he reported 'some investigations ... about the comparative length of some long poems'. The tabulations in a neat hand – William Morris's 'Earthly Paradise' came out top with 40,000 lines – are preserved in his papers at King's. His letters are full of times of trains, people's heights and weights, his own temperatures, their rise and fall, his financial accounts, and so on. In his diary he followed his father's habit of recording hours worked per day (mornings, afternoons, and evenings), books read during the year, visits to theatres, annual accounts (he spent £24 6s. 6d. in 1900, £28 19s. 9d. in 1901), even golf scores. He was constantly monitoring his own time, noting down how long it took him to do this or that. On 29 July 1900 he reported 'covering sixteen pages' of History in the hour and a half allotted for the examination. 'I have never accomplished more than fifteen before.' To Florence he wrote on 2 May 1902, 'This letter is a very creditable performance having not taken me more than 10 minutes by the clock.' At the end of 1901 he astonished his father with an article he had written for the *Eton Chronicle* at one minute's notice and which was in the printer's hands an hour later. 'The article,' commented Neville, 'is very ingenious; and the composition, considering the circumstances, is quite admirable in style and finish.' Maynard rushed through life with the clock ticking in his ear, yet rarely gave the impression of being hurried.

Many of his comments on life outside the school betray, as one would expect, a bias in favour of his own class, the 'educated bourgeoisie' as he later called it. His attitude to the royal persons who thronged Windsor was robustly irreverent, in contrast to his father's star-struck remarks. Neville's own account of the visiting Swedish King at Cambridge – 'a magnificent-looking person – every inch a King' (15 May 1900) – contrasts with Maynard's much lighter descriptions of Kaiser Wilhelm II (26 November 1899): 'I was much impressed by his kingly bearing and his moustache was quite up to my expectations.' Neville was loyally anxious that Maynard should catch a glimpse of 'Her Majesty'. He finally saw the 'good lady' close-up, but 'doubtless owing to the coldness of the day, her nose was unfortunately red' (20 May 1900). Not that he took greater pleasure in lower forms of life. 'Windsor has got an extraordinarily ruffianly population,' he wrote home on 26 November 1899. Visiting his sister Margaret at school in High Wycombe he deplored, 'the entire absence of moderately wealthy middle class residences' in the town (2 November 1899). When the Australians managed to draw a Test match by scoring 89 in five and a half hours, Maynard commented: 'But what can you expect of a team of bricklayers and such like' (19 July 1899). The interesting thing about such attitudes is not that he held them at this time of his life but that they never changed much later. Aristocrats were always absurd; the proletariat was always 'boorish'. The good things in life always sprang from the middle-class.

No economist has wielded the pen as well or to such effect as Maynard Keynes; and the distinctive Keynes touch is already beginning to show in his letters home, though not in his rather uninspired diary. His ability to go straight to the point was coupled with the realisation that the point was often absurd. Thus on 11 October 1898 he wrote 'On Sunday Tuck preached in chapel about bicycling, comparing it to life. He compared the telegraph poles to Guardian Angels. He has promised them one on football next Sunday.' He was already telling sly jokes. Anticipating the visit of the Kaiser in 1899 he wrote, 'Last time he was here he asked to see a body swiped but the head excused himself on the ground that no one happened to be in need of punishment. William immediately offered to place a member of his suite at his service.' He had an excellent turn of phrase: tea with 'Toddy' Vaughan, a classics master 'was more agreeable to the spirit than to the flesh ... I was regaled with three biscuits and two microscopic pieces of bread and butter.' He delighted in verbal games, and bombarded his father with Spoonerisms: 'Mr. Spooner seeing a gang of navvies at work remarked on "these sturdy tons of soil"' (1 October 1899).

Maynard's style was economical, direct, limpid. He wrote in short sentences and paragraphs, going from point to point. He almost never crossed out. He described events, but rarely people, and never states of mind. He found it much easier to record facts than to paint pictures, admitting, in another context, that 'I have no imagination' (17 February 1901). But he worried about what he called his 'telegraphic style'. On 20 November 1898 he wrote, 'I wish I could write a less disjointed letter.' Two days before his sixteenth birthday he wrote: 'I have just read my letter through and it is a beastly series of very short jerky sentences. How can I improve on it?' Neville replied (9 June 1899): 'I do not think that the composition of your letter was at all bad. There is indeed a distinctive merit in short sentences, if the transition from one to another is not too abrupt. That is a point you might attend to but I have no doubt that with practice you will attain to a good English style.' Fortunately, despite some tendency to High Table phrases – 'I have replied in the negative' – Maynard did not model his style on Neville's which, while lucid, is a good example of the academic pompous. Curiously, he never did entirely master the problem of the transition from one argument, or level of argument, or one subject, to another. The reason is that his ideas and interests, like the different facets of his personality, tended to be kept in separate compartments. The virtue of the defect was his uncanny power of 'turning off' one subject and turning to another with complete concentration. Without it, he would never have been able to do so many things, and so well. The penalty was a certain brittleness. The lack of satisfying shape to his letters was reproduced in his life.

The picture we get of Maynard is that of an exemplary pupil, brilliant at his work, modest in manner, conscientious in all his undertakings; who is also an amusing and amused, witty and irreverent, schoolboy, very quick, logical, precise, statistical, but saved from narrowness by his very speed in understanding, a compulsion to do many things well, and a great curiosity about the world. That his final bent would not be towards mathematics but to something more eclectic and practical was already foreshadowed. But this is not the whole story. What the reports and letters home leave out is one side of his personality which was already very important and was to become centrally so: his need to give and receive affection.

Maynard's first important friendships date from his time at Eton. In adolescence his feelings started to catch up with his intellect – not unusual in a clever boy. Some boys find their main emotional outlets in poetry or religion. Their feelings can be aroused by natural beauty or heroic exploits. Maynard was too rational and ironic to be much affected by such things. Poetry gave him genuine pleasure but, as we have seen, it was as likely to produce statistical as spiritual ecstasies. In his third year he read romantic novels but, as he told his father, found it hard to get absorbed in them (20 May 1900). Nor did chapel awaken religious feelings. True enough, he was moved by some of the hymns. He even seems to have been confirmed in his third year, at what he called an 'awful service' (31 March 1900). But he was never able to take religion seriously, regarding it as a strange aberration of the human mind. Even at school he delighted to puncture his friends' religious beliefs by refuting arguments for the existence of God. With little capacity for poetic or aesthetic experience Maynard came to concentrate his feelings on two points: his work and his friendships. Both became highly charged for him. And there must have been pain as well as happiness for him in them, especially in the latter. He was not a pretty or handsome boy. Indeed, according to Geoffrey Winthrop Young, who came to Eton as an assistant master in 1900, Maynard was 'distinctly ugly at first sight, with lips projecting and seeming to push up the well-formed nose and strong brows in slightly simian fashion'.[8] Probably as a result of his appearance he was nicknamed 'Snout' by his friends. In fact this impression of ugliness was soon dispelled. Maynard had very expressive eyes, his face, in animation, was distinctly attractive, and he had a sympathetic voice. Nevertheless, he was convinced of his own ugliness. Lack of physical confidence and athletic prowess can be agony for a schoolboy, however clever; and this, too, helped make those friendships which Maynard did form particularly important for him.

Naturally enough his early schoolfriends were boys from his own election. A number of names flit through his correspondence: Robert Hamilton Dundas, from a Scottish legal family, already showing the signs of primness, verging on prurience, which he later exhibited as a long-serving classics don at Christ Church, Oxford; Granville Hamilton, the grandson of the Earl of Donoghue, 'a dear chubby boy' as Maynard called him; Gerard Mackworth Young, from an Anglo-Indian family, with whom Maynard collaborated on a book of limericks and doggerel called *Tommy Rot*, and whom he startled one day in Hall by proving that infinity was a curve.* (Geoffrey Winthrop Young was his cousin, as was Maynard's later friend Edward Hilton Young, lawyer and Liberal politician.) But undoubtedly Maynard's first important Eton friend was Dilwyn Knox, with whom he 'messed' or took his meals during several halves in his first four years.

'Dilly' was the second of four remarkable sons of a bishop. Although he was two years younger than Maynard, he and Maynard were the cleverest boys in their election. Dilly, who looked a bit like a scarecrow, was Maynard's main rival for Eton's mathematical honours; he was a brilliant, if narrow, classical scholar. He was also much the most interesting of Maynard's friends. After the early death of his mother he and his brothers had determined, says his biographer, 'not to care too much about anyone or anything again'.[9] Their method was to convert life into a game. Ethics, logic, poetry, all would be reduced to the level of billiards or ludo. 'Cheating was instantly detected. It was cheating to show fear, cheating to give up. A monstrous rule, superimposed on all the others by Dilly, was that 'nothing is impossible'. But, inconveniently enough, 'the emotions are exempt from rules, and ignore their existence'[10]. Dilly drew Keynes into his games. How much the emotions were involved is difficult to say: probably more on Keynes's side than Knox's. The quality of their relationship is suggested by two letters Keynes wrote a few years later. The first, dated Christmas day 1905, was to Dilly himself. He never sent it. It concluded, 'But ever since we first messed together, even through the curious incidents which marked our last two years at Eton, there has been a kind of affection between us. . . .'[11] The incidents were almost certainly sexual. As Keynes wrote to Duncan Grant on 22 December 1908: 'I told him [Swithinbank] about Dil and me long ago at Eton. I've never seen any one so surprised and so jealous. Apparently, he longed to do likewise himself and had never dared. . . .' Penelope Fitzgerald puts it as follows:

* Hamilton appeared thus in *Tommy Rot*: 'I thought I saw fat Hamilton/ Wallowing in dirt and ink./ I looked again, and lo! it was/ The famous missing link./ "Dear Sir" said I "How old are you?"/ It said "I cannot think".'

'God once dismissed, Dilly and Maynard had calmly undertaken experiments, intellectual and sexual, to resolve the question of what things are necessary to life. Pleasure, like morality and duty, was a psychological necessity which must therefore be accepted, but without much fuss.'[12] To Keynes life was never just a game. Dilly's tragedy was that he could never succeed making it more, though his puzzle-solving mind made him a brilliant breaker of enemy ciphers in both world wars.

III

HISTORY AND ITS USES

On 24 May 1899 Queen Victoria celebrated her eightieth birthday, having reigned for sixty-two years. In honour of the event Maynard was set an essay on 'Victorian Achievements' which survives in his papers at King's. As an adult he was never a great admirer of the Victorian era which he came to think of as 'pathological' in its denial of the 'arts of enjoyment'. Apart from his school prizes there are hardly any Victorian books in his book collection: the seventeenth and eighteenth centuries pleased him much better. It is interesting to compare his mature view, as set out in the first chapter of his *Economic Consequences of the Peace* or in *Economic Possibilities for our Grandchildren*, with this schoolboy essay which gives a glimpse of his style and views just before his sixteenth birthday.

Maynard briskly ticks off the Victorian achievements, under eleven heads, in his 'telegraphic' style. First came the progress in education.

> The crass ignorance and superstition of the lower classes has given way to at any rate a smattering of education, while they now have facilities for leaving their native towns which must of necessity broaden their mental horizons. A smattering of education has no doubt in some cases had a bad influence. It is very well to encourage a labourer to think for himself . . . but when his little knowledge leads to strikes, it must be admitted that it is a dangerous thing.

Secondly, Keynes praised the advance of morality. 'A drunken clergyman is now almost unknown . . . and the upper-classes must at any rate keep up a semblance of decency.' As a result of Parliamentary Reform 'it is no longer necessary for a member of Parliament to distribute wholesale bribes amongst his constituents. It is thought sufficient if he subscribes to all local charities, deserving or otherwise.' Naturally enough Maynard welcomed the advance of religious toleration. 'The nonconformists have a far better position than ever before and it was a great step when the universities were opened to them.' The public finances had been reformed ('free trade is firmly established') and Maynard noticed in an amused way the change in the position of women: 'Women have now entered almost every walk of life except perhaps the law and the church. But the movement is still young; Portia practised the former and the genus clergywoman is not entirely un-known in the United States.' He remarks that 'the football field has taken the place of the prize ring' and that 'the philanthropist is more rampant than ever before in the history of the world'. After despatching the Penny Post and the standard of comfort, Maynard ends:

> It is only in the present reign that we have begun to realise the responsibilities of Empire and to see our duties to subject races.
>   We have begun to see that Great Britain may have a high destiny and a great future before her. We have perforce taken up the 'white man's burden' and we must endeavour to wield the powers of Empire with more lasting effect and to greater good than the mighty empires which have risen and fallen through the course of history.

The responsibilities of empire were to dominate much of Maynard's third year at Eton. 'I don't know what to think about the Transvaal business,' he wrote to his father on 8 October 1899, 'but I think I am getting more and more anti-war.' In his diary he wrote three days later: 'The Boer ultimatum expired to-day at 3.10. Herringham who was up to Allcock took out his watch at that hour and said "Please, sir, it's war". He got 200 lines and a ticket.'

Keynes was at or near the centre of British government in two world wars. Much of his life after 1914 was spent thinking about the national interest and his own relation to it. In 1899 these kinds of questions forced themselves on his mind for the first time. On the whole his schoolboy attitudes foreshadow his later ones; they were, of course, largely the attitudes of his home.

His parents took a moderate position. 'Of course I want to win,' wrote Florence on 20 October, 'but I confess I find it blood-curdling to read of these white men killing each other – The Dervishes did not seem so bad – I mean the slaughter of them.' Maynard wrote home on 22 October: 'I am no more jingo than I was previously, but now that the war has begun, one must perforce be reconciled to it.' His father agreed, and approved.[13]

Soon the heavy losses the Boers inflicted on Buller swung the Keyneses more firmly behind the war. 'Your mother & I dined on Monday evening with the Marshalls,' Neville wrote to Maynard on 13 December. 'Prof. Marshall is a pro-Boer & we find him very irritating.' The war started to present itself to Maynard in historical perspective, perhaps the first product of the history teaching he was getting from C. H. K. Marten. He wrote to his father on 17 December 1899:

In the battle of Albuera nearly a hundred years ago in the Peninsular war our losses were seven times as heavy per cent, as at the Modder river. Yet we won.... It is rather deceptive to include in the term 'losses' wounded and missing as well as killed .... It is hard luck on generals that news should be transmitted so quickly. The people don't see the result of the campaign, but seem to gloat over every little loss. Seventy men killed in battle is terrible for their families but it is a tiny thing in a nation of thirty million.

In the new half – and century* – the war came directly into the lives of Collegers. Herringham of Maynard's election left at sixteen to join the Army. On 29 January 1900 Maynard wrote 'After 12 the Head gave the upper part of the school [a talk] on the subject of the Volunteers. He said that at a national crisis like the present it is the duty of everyone to do what he can to make himself efficient by joining the Volunteers.' He wrote to his parents: 'Am I to join? I am not keen & the drills will be a nuisance, but I am perfectly willing to do so if I ought. It would be unpleasant to be the only non-shooter.' His mother pondered the familiar dilemma between moral and social duty, or how to reconcile the values of Bedford and Eton: 'As you know,' she wrote on 4 February, 'we were never very anxious for you to join the Volunteers, and we are no more anxious now – in fact, we prefer that you should not. At the same time, if you feel that it would be the right thing to do, and that you would be in an uncomfortable position if you did not join, we shall raise no objection....' Maynard took the robust line. 'I wavered a little and hey presto! it was done – or rather it was not done. I think that without your letter which amounted to a refusal I should have been engulfed in this marvellous martial ardour that has seized the school. Some say that patriotism requires one to join the useless Eton shooters, but it seems to me the sort of patriotism that requires one to wave the Union Jack.' The decision was the more difficult for Maynard because his particular friends Hamilton and Dundas had joined.[14]

The relief of Kimberley stirred Maynard's father to patriotic enthusiasm. 'There is one thing upon which the whole country is agreed,' he noted in his diary of 18 March 1900, 'and that is admiration for Lord Roberts.' Under the influence of this emotion he applied for £4000 of War Loan, though securing only £500. Maynard took a more detached view: 'The Head is quite dotty with war enthusiasm, and can't talk about anything else,' he wrote home on 18 February. 'He came in the other day to talk about grammar ... and told us that it was

* There was much argument as to whether the nineteenth century had in fact come to an end. Maynard's diary of 1 January 1900 reports 'a great correspondence in the "Times" as to when the twentieth century begins. "The Times" takes the obvious view that Jan 1 1901 is the day very strongly. Sentimentally however there is much to be said in favour of to-day and the dear old Kaiser has authoritatively decided that this is so.'

by persevering with such things that England's battles were won.' And to counterbalance his father's enthusiasm he wrote, 'Roberts' triumphal procession through the Orange Free is grand, but I think that too much has been made of the joy with which the inhabitants of Bloemfontein received him; for, after all, the majority of those that are left are of British descent.'[15]

On 19 May 1900 Maynard took part in the riotous celebrations over the relief of Mafeking, but kept his usual detached note in his letter home.

> The papers call it a 'fervent thanksgiving from the heart' [he reported]. But I do not think we are such hypocrites here. Most of us know that Mafeking is a glorious pretext for a whole holiday and for throwing off all discipline. We do not break windows because we are mad with joy, but because we think that under the circumstances we can do so with impunity.

The celebrations of the Windsor 'mob' on the other hand struck a discordant note:

> The men were reeling drunk, and the women offensive & gross beyond words. It is a good thing it was Mafeking and not the Royal Borough of Windsor that was besieged.

He concluded, 'The town of Windsor is the fungus on the Royal oak.'[16]

In his essay 'The English National Character', written in March 1901 against the background of the war, Maynard developed his conception of a proper patriotism. The typical Englishman he said was 'neither reactionary nor radical'. In this vein he endorses Kipling's view of the obtrusive patriot as a 'jelly bellied flag flapper', but 'no less to be abhorred', in his opinion, is the obtrusive 'patrophobist' who has, unfortunately, become a 'characteristic figure' of the time. 'It is in part a reaction against modern imperialism, in part the effect of an increased tolerance in thought and speech, but it is largely due to a certain love for the minority which seems to possess a certain class of Englishman.' Keynes was already the thinking patriot he was to remain. His imperial confidence survived the Boer War. He was too young to identify with the anti-imperialism of the older generation of anti-war Radicals like J. A. Hobson, especially as there was no pressure in that direction from home. Throughout his life he assumed the Empire as a fact of life and never showed the slightest interest in discarding it. At the same time he was too much of an economic liberal to develop any sympathy for the attempts of Joseph Chamberlain and others to weld it into an economic bloc. He never much deviated from the view that, all things being considered, it was better to have Englishmen running the world than foreigners.

How much did he learn from history? He took it up as a separate study in his third year under C. H. K. Marten, author of Eton's famous rhyming history verses ('End of Roses War we see /1485 A.D./ Henry, Seventh of the name, /To the shore of England came', etc.) and was soon producing notably taut pieces of historical summary. In the first half of his fourth year he entered for the Richards Essay Prize, for which the essay set, to be done under examination conditions, was on 'The Character of the Stuarts: How far is it responsible for their Misfortunes?' 'I can't say it is a very congenial subject,' Maynard complained as he spent his mid-term leave reading it up, while Florence busied herself making helpful notes. Back at Eton he managed twenty-two pages in three hours and won the prize, valued at £10 10s. The essay is not particularly good, despite its epigrammatic flavour, but the main conclusion, that the dynasty collapsed because it failed to choose brainy advisers, is of some biographical interest. In an essay on Cromwell dated 14 June 1901, he remarks interestingly that Cromwell should not be judged by later standards. It was 'the conditions of the times' which forced him to rule through the army. An essay on 'The Differences between East and West' written in the autumn of 1900 argues that the differences are in fact immutable: 'In the West it is the individual that is all important, in the East the mass.' From this flows the difference between democracy and despotism, progress and stagnation. Indicative of contemporary attitudes is the example he gives of the Jews as an Eastern people who, on account of 'deep-rooted instincts that are antagonistic and therefore repulsive to the European', can no more be assimilated to European civilisation than cats can be made to love dogs. Racial characteristics, he concluded, 'are unchanged by lapse of time and by revolution'. In 'The English National Character' Keynes took the view that England's liberal institutions were the product of a specially favourable situation. Maynard never became a professional historian. In later life he is said to have used, even abused, history to support his economic theses. Perhaps it is not too much to claim that he got from it a sense of *'autres temps, autres mœurs'*. One never feels that he had a sense of a single current of history carrying the world forward to the natural order described by the classical economists, or some other kind of utopia. Rather he was always impressed, some would say over-impressed, by the fragility of the civilisation inherited from the Victorians, by the feeling that it was an exceptional episode in human history.

In January 1901 the long Victorian age came to an end. Etonians had a ringside view of the funeral. On 3 February 1901 Maynard wrote home that of all the monarchs 'the Kaiser was the only one who was not an ordinary man. He was the only one who could have been nothing but a king.... The King of Portugal is considerably more grotesque than his photographs. He has an absolutely enormous pot belly and it was as much as he could do to waddle.' Maynard also liked the look of the German Crown Prince. King Edward VII 'did not look either young or healthy'. Of the rest he was 'most pleased with the small band of picked Germans'. The only blot 'was the French mission; they chatted and strolled along as if they were smoking cigarettes on their native boulevards'. With these pro-German, anti-French, emotions, Maynard saw out the Victorian era.

IV

GLITTERING PRIZES

By his fourth year, Maynard had reached the First Hundred, or what was, in effect, the Lower Sixth form. He was now free to specialise. Hurst, his mathematics master, wanted him to drop all his other subjects. This annoyed Maynard very much. His curiosity was expanding, not contracting. In classics he was up to Luxmoore, whose sarcastic manner he found wholly congenial, regretting only his tendency to set verses on such unpromising subjects as Nuts. He thoroughly enjoyed his History 'extras' with Marten on the Gunpowder Plot, wondering whether it was really a plot hatched by the authorities to discredit the Catholics. (He was full just then of his Jesuit ancestors whom he had discovered in the course of his researches into his family history, conducted on Sunday afternoons in the Fellows' Library). In the summer half of 1901 Lubbock opened up yet another interest, when he and Maynard read together an 'extremely fine poem' by Bernard of Cluny, *De Contemptu Mundi.* 'Mediaeval Latin poetry is now one of his hobbies,' noted Neville in his diary of 22 June 1901. How could one think of giving all this up for mathematics? Hurst now had an additional argument. In June 1901, R. G. Hawtrey, ex-King's Scholar, and future Treasury official, only managed 18th Wrangler in the Mathematics Tripos. Hurst cited him as an awful warning of someone who had spread himself too thin. Maynard was unconvinced. Hawtrey, he wrote to Neville on 16 June 1901, was not a person of 'surpassing mathematical ability'; and anyhow it was ridiculous of Hurst to think that 'he has lost his soul in knowing something besides Mathematics'. Both observations offer a clue to Maynard's refusal to specialise; a refusal endorsed by his father who remembered, perhaps, his own sufferings as an undergraduate mathematician.

Maynard's interests extended to sport. He was not good at games, but neither was he a complete 'scug'. In the Michaelmas Half he played a primitive form of soccer known as Eton football. In the Second Half he would play an almost equally esoteric game called Eton Fives, originating centuries earlier from the pastime of banging a ball around in the spaces between the chapel wall and its buttresses. He took up racquets in 1900, finding it a 'very excellent game'. He also rowed, getting his College boating colours in February 1901. Competitive rowing in the icy wind and driving rain gave him little pleasure. He sensibly concluded that 'the labour and time involved in becoming a good oar is not commensurate with the advantage gained' and welcomed his 'promotion' to the Monarch, a boat for bad oars where one bought 'cultured ease by giving up ambition' (12 May 1901). Maynard loved going on the river with friends. Hilton Young remembered him as a 'dark slip of a young colleger, soft of voice, swift and intense of speech, and obviously of penetrating intelligence. He could not however keep good time with his oar, because he must stop, lean forward, and dart into the conversation some barbed shaft of question or criticism.' In the summer Maynard would also join other wet-bobs in a light-hearted game of cricket known as Aquatics, played in College Field.

But the sport which gave him the greatest thrill was the Wall Game. This was yet another of Eton's sports based on special geographical features, in this case the existence of a wall, a gate and a tree in a corner of College Field. From these landmarks generations of Collegers had fashioned a game of exquisite boredom for the spectator, but one which roused its participants to ecstacies of joy. Two sides formed a scrimmage against the wall, each one hoping to gain ground with the ball by pushing the other one back. Proceedings could be brought to a virtual halt by one player sitting on the ball for an inordinate length of time. Maynard thought it a 'glorious game'. Several afternoons a week he would return to his room, muddy, exhausted, exhilarated. Not even the 'awful' inability to breathe beneath a tangle of limbs and bodies dampened his enthusiasm for it; and he was wont to discuss with great seriousness, deploying finely balanced arguments, proposals for some minute change in the rules. Maynard was too light to make a really good 'wall', but his height and pluck made him a valuable player. Every 30 November, on St Andrew's Day, came the great annual game between College and Oppidan Eton, which resembled the battles on the Western Front in the First World War in the mighty exertions they inspired without visible gain of ground. Maynard was College's 12th man in 1900. The following year he played regularly as College '2nd wall', once remaining on the ball for eight minutes in a prodigious display of valour against gigantic opponents. His parents came up to see him play on St Andrew's Day, 1901, without much pleasure: 'Maynard and the others looked frightfully exhausted,' Neville wrote in his diary. 'He said at one time he thought he was done, all the bully being on top of him and he could not either breathe or call out.' Lubbock was delighted that 'he was so keen about such things'.

Maynard was now a person of some consequence in College. In the Michaelmas Half of 1900 he 'messed' in great style with Hamilton, Dundas and Young in upper tea room, of which he was captain. 'Yesterday evening,' he wrote to Neville on 30 September, 'we ordered 3/– worth of cutlets for tea, then I had a sort of sausage roll business, concluding with some most superlative jam Young brought from home, and cake. This morning after porridge we had buttered eggs made from 15 eggs, then sardines and jam.' His mother worried about such indulgence. 'But, really, my dear son, you will be laying up a bilious attack in store for yourself if you go on like this.' The collapse a few weeks later took the form of boils on the knees, brought about by scratches which had become infected from the mud of the Wall Game. Maynard's blood, the doctor concluded, was not sound.[17] As throughout his life, Maynard's work-load was kept going in face of uncertain health. He had measles in his second term, facial twitchings in his fourth. He was prone to mysterious fevers which he called his 'periodicals'. Florence and Neville had no doubt that he was delicate. They urged him to wrap up against the cold, unwrap against the heat, avoid draughts. They bombarded him with tonics and dietary instructions. He must be sure to wear a large white cotton hat for rowing, Florence wrote, 'for I am sure it cannot be safe to have your head and neck exposed'.[18] She signed herself 'your over-anxious mother'. Maynard never showed the slightest resentment at this nagging, which his good humour soon converted into a family joke.

In January 1901 his standing with his fellow Collegers was confirmed when he was elected to College Pop, or Debating Society, the third of his election to make it, behind Dundas and Hamilton. It met on Saturday evenings under its president in College Reading Room. As the name suggests, election was a mark of a boy's popularity with his seniors, since someone could be blackballed almost indefinitely. Maynard took an active part in its proceedings, making witty speeches on such subjects as 'This House would rather England be free than sober'. He also took a close interest in Private Business, at which members of College Pop decided on the regulations and policy of the Reading Room. The future economist appears in this comment on the practice of fining people for leaving their possessions in the room (3 March 1901): 'I do not think it is a good policy to make fines a source of revenue; it is an extremely vexatious form of indirect taxation and one which involves a considerable trouble in collection.... I should prefer a fixed subscription in lieu of fines.' By such a lofty appeal to general principle did Maynard hope to lessen his own contribution to the Reading Room's revenue, as a result of constantly leaving his fives gloves there. His administrative activities burgeoned in his last year. He found himself on the Library Committee, which expelled 112 books from the College Library; on the Committee of Management of the School Stores, in which capacity he spent hours carrying out an inventory of the School shop; and on the Committee of the Athletic Society. 'I am finding like you,' he wrote to his father on 9 February 1902, 'that when I am appointed to a committee I am invariably made to do all the work.'

In these ways his Eton life remained full of interest and activity. There was no question of Maynard being bored at school, a common experience of many bright boys. He wished a day had thirty-six hours, a week fourteen days, he told his father, so that he could do justice to all his interests.[19] Apologising for the abrupt termination of one letter home he wrote, 'In a minute and a quarter my light has to be put out and I have many things do before then.' It was to be thus all his life.

Eton's two main school prizes were the Newcastle for Classics and Divinity, taken in March, and the Tomline for Mathematics, taken in June. In his fourth year, Maynard decided to concentrate his efforts on the second. Neville took charge of the preparations with his usual thoroughness, recording in his diary:

11 April 1901
Maynard is working steadily about 3 hours a day under my direction. I feel quite like a trainer, as if I were training him for a race or a prize fight.

13 April 1901
The boy works in the mornings but is disinclined to put in another hour in the evenings. He is more interested in the Keynes genealogy, though I think he likes his mathematics when once he settles down to it. Florence induced him to do an extra hour after dinner this evening. I am quite convinced that his only chance for the Tomline and afterwards is to grind hard at his bookwork this vacation.

14 April 1901
So far as I can gather from conversation with Maynard, Hurst has given him very little systematic instruction; and he has done remarkably little in the way of getting up bookwork. I am rather depressed in regard to his chance in Mathematics.

19 April 1901
Maynard has today been doing some Mechanics and some Geometrical Conics. He settled down to his work fairly well. But he doesn't quite rise to the occasion and devote himself to it as I should

like to see him do, considering how much is needed in order that he may be properly prepared for his approaching examinations (Tomline in June, Certificate in July, King's in December). But perhaps I expect too much.

25 April 1901
[The Master of Sidney Sussex College] agrees with me that Maynard's mathematics has been wrongly taught, an inordinate time being spent on examples and insufficient time being given to mastering the bookwork.

26 April 1901
I am feeling very much dissatisfied with the teaching in mathematics that Maynard has got from Hurst. The boy has worked well today. I think he now feels how much still remains to be done.

30 April 1901
It seems quite clear that ... his Classics will help him towards a scholarship [at King's] and that he must not drop his Classics.

2 May 1901
[Maynard back to Eton] He has certainly during the vacations done work that will be very valuable to him.

The Tomline examination started on 5 June 1901, Maynard's eighteenth birthday. 'The Algebra and the Analytical Conics were ridiculously easy,' he told his father, 'but the Differential Calculus and Theory of Equations were I think distinctly harder than usual.... I went on the plan of looking up very little during the examination.' He and his father had decided that the contest lay between him and Dilwyn Knox; in fact, he won it quite comfortably from Bailey; Knox only just managed the Select.* Knox, Maynard thought, had been undone by his Mechanics and lack of lucidity. 'He has got one of the most confused brains I have ever come across,' he wrote to Neville on 15 June. 'Even in conversation he is wholly incapable of expressing the meaning he intends to convey; in addition to this he is quite abnormally untidy in his work & always forgets to write down the most necessary steps.'

When Geoffrey heard the news of Maynard's success he said 'Poor fellow, he can't help it.' This was Maynard's biggest prize to date – £32 worth of books. He had already started buying books from David's

* Those who gained a certain minimum number of marks were deemed to be in the 'Select'.

second-hand book stall in the Cambridge market, and was determined to take some of his prizes in non-regulation bindings (the rule was that they had to be bound in leather) in order to increase the quantity of his purchases. He finally got the headmaster to agree, and as a result was able to buy forty-five volumes.* By the time he left Eton his book collection already numbered over three hundred, of which about half were school prizes. His leaving present to the College was a fine psalter owned by Nicholas Udall, an Eton headmaster of the 1530s.

The Tomline over, Maynard could relax for a few days with his friends on the river before the next bout of examinations. In the last week in July he 'perpetrated' thirty papers for the Cambridge Higher Certificate – the same examination Florence had taken at Newnham. The main bait was the Chamberlayne Prize, a £60 scholarship for four years, which Eton awarded to its candidate with the highest marks, and which would contribute to Maynard's university fees. Maynard had 'never worked so hard before', he told his father, adding characteristic details: 'Before last week I have never done more than 10 hours in a day or more than an average of 7½ for a week, but for the last week I had an average of 10½ hours a day and on Thursday I worked for 12½ hours.' He thought that the mathematics was much harder than in the Tomline. Nevertheless they and history combined won him the overall first place, since he was way down in the classics. 'Even I,' Lubbock wrote to Neville on 2 August 1901, 'was fairly dazzled by the actual result. It is an extraordinary performance. He certainly does command success to an amazing extent but then no one ever deserved it better. His way of accepting it is characteristic; just as quiet, frank, and modest as ever.... I hope he has not overdone himself.'

It was accepted that Maynard should try for a university scholarship in his last year. There was no problem about which university: 'I don't want to go to Oxford at any price' (24 November 1901). It had long been established that he should try for King's College, Cambridge, Eton's sister foundation, but in the Michaelmas Half of 1901 Hurst and Marten both started urging the claims of Trinity College, on the grounds that mathematics was at such a low ebb at King's. 'For myself,' Maynard wrote to Neville on 4 October 1901. 'I still think that I would rather go to King's.... I have been imagining myself going there for some time and it is difficult to dispel the "fixed idea".' Neville replied on 6 October: 'Perhaps the strongest point in favour of Trinity

---

* His books were: Gardiner's *Cromwell* 'magnificently bound'; Jebb's *Sophocles* in 8 vols, in morocco; Browning's *Poems* in 9 vols, half-morocco; Burke's *Complete Works* in 12 vols, published binding; *The Roll of Battle Abbey*, 3 vols, in vellum; Matthew Arnold's *Essays in Criticism*, 2 vols, speckled calf; Spenser's *Faerie Queene*, 6 vols, half-morocco, Macaulay's *History of England*, 4 vols, calf.

is that you would have much more competition there, & so might have a stronger inducement to work hard. Is the spur of competition needed to keep you up to the mark? That is really an important question.' On the other side, at Trinity there would be 'much more severe competition in the scholarship examination; so that, as you say, there would be considerable risk of you not getting anything decent. Some of your competitors would have specialised in mathematics for years.' An extra advantage at King's was the existence of scholarships for which only Etonians were eligible. So King's it proved. 'There is nowhere else worth going to at Cambridge,' Maynard finally decided. The subject in which he should try for a scholarship was also carefully discussed. Lubbock considered Maynard safe for a first-class honours in classics if he read it; Hurst thought he was certain to be in the first twelve wranglers in mathematics.[20] Mathematics, Maynard's stronger subject, was decided on; but even then there was a question whether he should take just the mathematics papers or offer some classics in addition, as he was allowed to do. Hurst wanted him to take the mathematics papers only. But Maynard had the truer instinct that he would appear more impressive if he offered a combination. In one sense, he was paying the price for his refusal to specialise. Yet that refusal was based on a shrewd suspicion that mathematics was not his life's vocation. Neville supported him; he was also able to use his contacts at King's to direct Maynard's revision particularly to Latin verses. Lubbock, too, made discreet enquiries of the King's classics tutor, Nathaniel Wedd, as to 'what he will have to do in the way of composition'.[21] What strikes one about these preparations is how little was left to chance. Maynard came up to take his scholarship in December like a perfectly trained racehorse, whose capacities, as those of his rivals, were exactly known, for a race whose every obstacle had been foreseen and prepared for. The result could be predicted within a small margin of error. All this was, of course, made possible by the closeness of the connection between a few schools and a few colleges.

Ninety-five candidates in classics, and sixty in mathematics competed for ten open scholarships; of these four from each camp offered the other subject as well. In addition, there was a general essay question: Maynard wrote on 'Money'. Neville got into his usual flap. He thought Maynard had done badly in Mechanics and Differential Calculus. He tried to pick up hints about his son's performance, and couldn't sleep at night. By 9 December he was out of his misery: Maynard would have won one of the closed scholarships in any case. The addition of his classics converted it into an open scholarship, worth £80. Of all the mathematicians, Neville was told, his essay was the only one worth reading. The Provost, Austen Leigh, wrote to Maynard: 'It is a special compliment, and you will get tuition free besides the £80, and also rooms rent free till your first degree.'[22] This was not the end of December's good news. 'You will scarcely believe me,' Maynard wrote to Neville on 15 December, 'I have been elected to Pop.' He had arrived socially as well as academically. Pop, or the Eton Society to give it its proper name, was Eton's most exclusive social club, of whom Roy Harrod remarked, 'these young men govern the school for a time – as they expect ... or used to expect, to govern the country later.'[23] Maynard was an unusual choice since Pop was notoriously a society in which athletes dominated. Certainly, neither he nor Neville had expected the honour. With membership of this grand order went a whole set of sartorial and disciplinary privileges; but though it widened somewhat Maynard's Etonian circle, his best friends remained Collegers.

Even now there was no thought of relaxation. Neville was already planning the future. On 14 January 1902 he wrote in his diary: 'I have been looking up the King's Statutes and find that Maynard will probably be superannuated for a Fellowship after the Michaelmas T. 1908. I suppose he will take his Tripos in 1905, and his C[ivil] S[ervice] Exam^n in 1906; so this leaves a good margin for writing a Fellowship dissertation.' Thus the next six years were mapped out. Meanwhile there was one prize at Eton which Maynard had not yet won: the Newcastle. He had promised his parents to have a go at it. On 19 January 1902 he wrote to Dundas:

> The sap I have done these holidays is directed towards Kirk, History and the works of one Luke a physician. I have found myself rather apt to go off at great length on questions interesting to me but not very utilitarian from the point of view of the Newker.... You know Theology is damned interesting; Arius and all his works I would gladly consign to the devil, the father of bores; but some heresies are perfect doves.

He sat for the Newcastle on 21 March 1902 without much hope, since there were better classical scholars than he in for it. He wrote thirty pages on St Luke in two hours, finding the paper 'ridiculous'. General Divinity was 'stupid'; and Church History 'not nearly hard enough to suit me'.[24] He did well enough to make the Select, in seventh place, his father noting that this was the first time a Tomline Prizeman had done so since 1888. Neville worked out that Keynes had done best of his election at Eton. He started in tenth place, but had come seventh in the Newcastle, first in the Tomline, and first in the Certificate Examination. Knox, who had passed into College first, came nowhere in the Newcastle, fourth in the other two. Nearest to Keynes's achievement was Ainger who had, however, done nothing in the Tomline. Moreover, Maynard had been the only one to achieve a position in all three.[25] Long ago, Neville recalled, Mrs Goodchild had said Keynes 'was a genius', with a particularly marked 'general ability', and these results proved it.[26]

In his last year at Eton Maynard emerged into the sunlit eminence which English public schools briefly confer on their cleverest and most popular boys, and compared to which the rest of life seems for many who have attained it a long anti-climax. He was now one of the school-boy rulers of College, exercising, according to his father, 'a wholesome influence on the Elections below his own'.[27] As a sixth former he was entrusted with maintaining general school discipline. And no doubt he excited the usual feelings of awe and envy from lesser mortals as he grandly sauntered round the school grounds, white-waistcoated, and linked arm in arm with a fellow member of Pop. He blossomed on Eton's public occasions with the sartorial splendour they required – declaiming Burke's panegyric on Fox in February Speeches in dress clothes, knee-breeches, and black silk stockings, appearing on the Fourth of June in a 'perfect dove of a waistcoat – lavender with pale pink spots'. His social success was, in a way, more remarkable than his intellectual success, and as significant for the future. No one in England gets far on brains alone. Maynard lacked the famous Eton charm. But he already showed a remarkable ability to win the respect and appreciation of the authorities and his schoolfellows. His intelligence was neither narrow nor abrasive; it was at the disposal of the community. And with it went a sympathetic, quietly authoritative manner, which was very appealing. Later Maynard's arrogance grew more pronounced to those outside his circle. And his values became more self-consciously private. Yet the nature of his gifts continued to tether him to society. He never lost the ability to get the best of both worlds – the respect of both his intellectual and his social peers.

To this one should add: the ability to retain the love of his friends. Despite his public successes he remained at his best and happiest in small groups. Two partly overlapping circles dominated his last two terms at school. This first was College Pop. Curiously, he never became an officer of this club, being defeated for President by a boy called Pallis in December 1901. But all his old friends, bar Mackworth Young, were now in it, and three new ones: Bernard Swithinbank from his own election, Harold Butler from the election of 1896, and Daniel Mac-millan from the election of 1898. Maynard spoke practically every week, and to some effect, telling his father that 'I have no modesty when on my legs even before a strange audience'. A few of his contributions are worth noticing. On 8 March 1902 he proposed that 'this House would rather see Lord Rosebery in power than the present government' in a speech lasting twenty-five minutes delivered without notes. It is chiefly interesting for the summary he gives of 'true' Liberalism:

It is not root and branch reform, it is not the exaltation of the ignorant at the expense of the privileged. It is the spirit that frankly
faces the current evils ... and makes a statesmanlike commonsense
effort to correct them. It is, as far as possible, free from prejudice; it
is always desirous to probe and investigate; it will respect institutions
for their antiquity, but will not take this antiquity as a passport of
their merit. Abroad it will answer the interests of humanity as well
as those of England; it will accept things as they are and practise
what is noble so long as it is consistent with what is practicable.

On 3 May 1902 he spoke in support of Cecil Rhodes's dream of 'the
supremacy of the Anglo-Saxon race', a vision, Maynard averred, 'worthy of this house's greatest admiration'. On 6 July, in a speech on the
French Revolution, he tried 'to show how distinct the intellectual
revolution for which we value the eighteenth century was from the
violent upheaval known as the French Revolution'. The abuses of the
ancien régime could have been removed by 'less violent and somewhat
more constitutional means'. Maynard never deviated significantly
from these views.[28]

His second circle was the Eton Literary Society which he and Harold
Butler rescued from a moribund condition in February 1902, Maynard
becoming its President. Other members included Charles Buxton and
Humphrey Paul, both Oppidans, and Bernard Swithinbank from
College. They met a couple of times a term to read each other papers
on literary topics. The apprentice don comes out in this comment of
Maynard's on Paul's paper on Charles Lamb: 'It was very good indeed
and distinctly the best we have had. I should, however, have dearly
loved to use the Blue Pencil in one or two places; his taste is, to my
mind, not always quite perfect, especially with regard to topical
allusions.'[29] Maynard went on seeing Paul, who became a civil servant,
for a number of years after he left Eton.

His own contribution to the Society was a paper on Bernard of Cluny
which he read on 3 May 1902. He had spent almost the whole of the
Easter holiday researching and writing it, much to the consternation
of Neville, who wanted him to re-start his mathematics in preparation
for Cambridge. The paper consists partly of literary and philological
exegesis. But Maynard was as much attracted by the character as by
the poetry of this Benedictine saint who forsook the world for the
cloister, reading an expanded and revised version of the same paper a
number of times later. His theme is the gentleman's choice: between
the life of action and the life of contemplation; the vanity and corruption of this world and the 'calm and joy and light' of the celestial city.
The style is excellent, if a little clipped, throughout. And one wonders
whether it was a sense of self-recognition that prompted him to end his
paper with the following lines from Bernard's *De Contemptu Mundi*:

Not only those
Who hold clear echoes of the voice divine
Are honourable – they are blest, indeed,
Whate'er the world has held – but those who hear
Some fair faint echoes, though the crowd be deaf,
And see the white gods' garments on the hills,
Which the crowd sees not, though they may not find
Fit music for their visions; they are blest,
Not pitiable

A day after he read this paper he wrote to his father: 'It has at any rate inspired Bernard the Luny [Bernard Swithinbank] with a desire to read the complete works of Bernard the Cluny.' A year younger than Maynard, though of the same election, Swithinbank, the son of an Anglican clergyman, had come to College two terms after him. As a result their paths had not crossed much academically or in College till Swithinbank was elected to College Pop in July 1901. After that their friendship grew quickly and in his last year Swithinbank was Maynard's best friend. Maynard rarely described how his young friends looked; but Swithinbank must have struck him as only a slightly more youthful version of the Oxford undergraduate Lytton Strachey met three years later:

In appearance he's tall ... and rather large footed and essentially solid; but by no means looks a strong and bulky person, his face is pale, ill and intellectual. The expression is often cat-like – the eyelids droop, and the mouth broadens; the features are well-shaped and boyish. The general impression he gives is undoubtedly one of vagueness. One sees at once that he's kind, nervous and impractical; and one's a little inclined to think that that's all. But it by no means *is* all. To begin with, there's his humour, which is always faultless and always wonderfully his own. Then his character is a real character. It's poetical – untrammelled. I mean by actualities; and quite unafflicted by contortions and affectations; it shines with a pale sincerity.[30]

In his speeches at College Pop Maynard half-jokingly referred to the 'epigrammatic lips of Mr. Swithinbank' and praised him as 'that child of all that is best in the eighteenth century'. He certainly confirmed Strachey's impression of his vagueness, in this account of a meeting of the Literary Society (16 March 1902):

Swithinbank read a paper last night on Ben Jonson. His behaviour was typical; though he has had several weeks in which to prepare it, he did not begin writing anything down until 5.15. He then wrote as hard as he could till 7.0., the hour at which he had to read. He had not however had time to write a peroration; he was saved by a great

stroke of genius. He read us out the peroration of an article on the
same subject he had got hold of.

Swithinbank, a fine classicist, was good-looking, poetic, tender, vulnerable, unworldly: a combination which Maynard always found appealing. He regarded him as a delicate work of art, to be worshipped
and protected against breakage. The same feelings inspired the two
great later loves of his life – Duncan Grant and Lydia Lopokova. Once
again, the exact timbre of their friendship is difficult to recreate, since
the letters which passed between them at this time have probably been
destroyed. But we get a glimpse of their world from Maynard's pen in
1905:

> On Sunday [he wrote to Lytton Strachey on 27 March 1905] I went
> through all my papers and documents . . . the thing that interested
> me was the astounding apostolicity of the goings on of my circle
> during my last year at school – especially with Swithinbank. I had
> no idea of it – the thing was complete.
> The amours – Swithinbank and I in agreement and corresponding
> about the object. The solid indecency – laughingly quelled by
> Dundas. . . . And the complete lack of Christianity.
> Swithin and Young continually poetising. (Swithin imitating
> Swinburne for the most part). Much laughter.
> The whole thing very lighthearted but tempered for Swithin at any
> rate by fits of depression. Long speeches at College Pop. Walks in
> which the doctrine of the Resurrection of the body alternated with
> the problem as to whether a kiss should be followed with a cop[ula-
> tion].
> A little box of letters brought the whole thing back – I had quite
> forgotten it.

The chief 'object' of their joint attentions was Daniel Macmillan,
then sixteen, a clever, beautiful, boy, who remained Maynard's lifelong
friend and published all his books. Bernard Swithinbank later
described the emotional atmosphere as he remembered it:

> In College emotion and desire were directed almost exclusively
> towards the male sex – I knew hardly anyone who ever thought of
> women. This does not mean that there was a great deal of 'vice';
> indeed, it was looked on with disapproval, not untinged with envy,
> by the many who repressed their desires through shyness or virtue.
> M[aynard] shared the general feeling. I do not know that he was
> reputed to indulge in it. At Cambridge, he was deeply moved by
> Plato's pictures of passion spiritualized.[31]

Maynard's Eton life ended as strenuously as it had begun. He and
other members of the Shakespeare Society performed part of *Much Ado
about Nothing* for Fourth of June Speeches (Maynard acting Dogberry);

Maynard also acted Acres opposite Harold Butler's Sir Lucius in an act of Sheridan's *The Rivals*. Early in July he was briefly ill with one of his 'irrational fevers', Swithinbank nursing him 'in a most devoted way'.[32] At the end of July, much against his inclination, but no doubt as an antidote to idleness, he retook the Cambridge Higher Certificate, once more coming out top, despite lack of preparation. He was now nineteen; Eton had no more to give him. On 30 July he wrote to Neville: 'I have just reached the very melancholy stage. Last night I received a vote of thanks in College Pop, a thing I desired perhaps more than anything else that remained to be got here – Eton has been much kinder to me than I have deserved.' Lubbock wrote:

He leaves regretted by everyone who knows him. He has I think been lucky in his time here: the leading boys here during the last year or two seem to me to have been extremely nice: & well has he taken his part among them. He has no doubt a very fine mature mind, & he is not in the least overweighted by it as many boys of his age might be; I have rarely known any boy so clever, & yet so far removed from any trace of priggishness ... I fear it may be long before I have again a pupil who will combine ability & industry so well; of his character I will only say that I think he is a boy on whom one can depend entirely. With all his cleverness he accepts the duties put before him with the readiest obedience & without any questioning as to whether he himself after all does not know best.

5 The Cambridge Undergraduate

I

KING'S COLLEGE

At Cambridge Maynard experienced a philosophic, aesthetic, and emotional awakening which shifted his values. He never lost his inherited sense of public duty, which his Eton education had reinforced. But from his undergraduate years onwards he was to balance this against the claims of leading a civilised life and of personal happiness, which sprang from the emotional and philosophic atmosphere of his Cambridge world, and to which one part of him strongly responded. In this shift of values King's College played an important part.

It had been founded by King Henry VI in 1441 as the sister foundation of Eton College. The king's intention was that 'our poor scholars of our Royal Foundation of St Mary's of Eton, after they had been sufficiently taught the first rudiments of grammar, shall be transferred thence to our aforesaid College of Cambridge ... there to be thoroughly instructed in the liberal arts ...'. Four hundred years later this scheme was still in operation. King's College 'numbered seventy members, partly Fellows and partly scholars, varying inversely with each other .... An Eton Colleger went in due time to King's, if there was a vacancy for him, became a Fellow, took his degree without examination, and remained till the end of his days with increasing income and dignity unless he married or took a living.'[1] But what was potentially, at any rate, 'a magnificent system for the endowment of research' had by then become 'a sort of life-long rest-home' for those who had survived the horrors of Eton's Long Chamber.[2]

In the first half of the nineteenth century King's must have given the impression of a beautiful, but largely deserted, stately home. Two buildings of great splendour, the Chapel, completed in 1515, and the Fellows' (or Gibbs) Building dating from 1725, were set in beautiful parks and lawns. But there was no intellectual life, and few signs of physical life. Most of the fellows, having no teaching duties, were non-resident, though they continued to draw handsome dividends from the College's estates. The scholars never numbered more than a dozen or so. Lack of inhabitants did not prevent the multiplication of buildings.

In 1828 the architect William Wilkins was commissioned to complete the great front court. He designed a screen and gatehouse facing King's Parade on the east side, joined on the south side to a Hall, Library, and Provost's Lodge of frigid gothic. The gatehouse was derisively called the Decanter and Wine Glasses.

Both Royal Foundations were wakened from their torpor by the magic wand of Victorian reform. The revival of King's dates from the 1850s, and was accomplished by a mixture of external pressure from Parliament, and the internal pressure of new arrivals from a reformed Eton. In 1852 the College established quality control by renouncing its right to confer its own degrees. By a reform of 1861 the number of Fellows was reduced to forty-six and the number of scholars increased to twenty-four. In 1865 the limitation on overall numbers was finally dropped and twenty-four Open Scholarships created – open, that is, to non-Etonians. These reforms met with strenuous opposition from Provost Okes and the old life-fellows. Forced to accept non-Etonian fellows, the Provost welcomed the first of them, William Parker Brooke, Rupert Brooke's father, in 1873, with the ungracious words, 'Let us hope that this *noo* leaven will not leaven the *whoole* lump'.

When Maynard arrived, King's was on the crest of a wave. 'The decade 1875–1884,' he recalled much later, 'was a period of exceptional distinction, the full prestige of which the college was enjoying when I was young.'[3] By basing its intake on Scholars, and by insisting that all its undergraduates took the tripos, King's deliberately set out to educate an academic elite. Of 34 undergraduates in residence in 1873, no less than 19 obtained first-class honours. By the time Keynes came up King's had 30 fellows, 30 postgraduates, and over 130 undergraduates (there were 3000 undergraduates altogether at Cambridge) and only Trinity and St John's, much larger colleges, rivalled it in academic and social prestige. But although there were the usual divisions into Scholars and Hearties, as well as Etonians (now reduced to 13 per cent) and the rest, he entered a society very similar to the one he had left – where intellectual values were prized and which had inherited from Eton a tradition of intimacy, and close contact between dons and students. King's Fellows of the late nineteenth century were characteristically outstanding teachers rather than scholars, though there were some eminent scholars too, like Charles Waldstein (later Walston), the archeologist who started the triennial Greek play, Walter Headlam the classicist, and George Prothero the historian. But men like Augustus Austen Leigh, Oscar Browning, Nathaniel Wedd, and Lowes Dickinson were above all devoted to the young men – to the formation of their characters and minds. Kingsmen carried the special atmosphere of the place and the influence of these teachers with them all their lives.

The King's of Keynes's day was shaped above all by Oscar Browning. 'The O.B.' as he was known in recognition of his uniqueness was
Cambridge's most famous 'character'. 'A genius flawed by abysmal
fatuity' is E. F. Benson's well-known, but inaccurate, pre-Freudian,
verdict. In fact O.B.'s genius – as an educator, for he had none as a
scholar – was built on his 'flaw', the flaw being a love of boys and young
men. O.B.'s homosexuality, and the way he coped with it, is *the* central
thing about him. The only woman he loved was his mother, who
provided him with a home until he was fifty. He was a member of that
group round Henry Sidgwick, in whom forbidden emotional desires
were sublimated into high educational ideals; ideals which were at
constant risk from unsatisfied longings. It was a precarious psychological balance, whose collapse could bring scandal and ruin. O.B. was one
of the great Victorian survivors. His secret was his style. He was
outrageous, bawdy, witty, catty, artless, snobbish, egotistical, affectionate, amorous; but not overtly lecherous. In that repressed era,
when intimacy was sought but denied, O.B. broke down barriers: his
absurdity made them seem absurd. His gift was to put all kinds of
people at their ease. As a result he got and gave a good deal of affection
without overstepping the limits of what was permissible, though his
behaviour was certainly highly eccentric.

O.B.'s aim was to provide an education fit for statesmen. To this end
he opposed the two main educational tendencies of his day – the worship of athletics and the trend to specialisation. Like his university
colleague, J. B. Seeley, Regius Professor of Modern History, he
believed that the kind of education he had in mind could best be done
through history and politics. Browning was appointed College Tutor
in history in 1880, and a university lecturer in 1883. In his day, King's
became the college to go to for history, though O.B. was an indifferent
tutor, sleeping soundly through his students' essays. His didactic purpose depended not on exact scholarship or criticism but on a new
relationship between dons and undergraduates. He founded his famous
Political Society, instituted his Sunday evening 'At Homes', and
associated himself with numerous undergraduate activities (as
president of the University Bicycle Club he once crossed the Alps on
a tricycle). As he had done while an assistant-master at Eton, he took
favoured pupils on the continental grand tour to widen their cultural
horizons. Nor was working-class education neglected. O.B. was founder and for eighteen years principal of the Cambridge Teachers Day
Training College. He took an active interest in the Cambridge branch
of the Navy League; his biographer H. E. Wortham recording that 'one
of the many soft spots in his heart he kept for sailors'. He would take
groups of them to see plays in London. He kept working-class youths

as his servants. They slept in his room and scrubbed him in his bath; he taught them to play musical instruments.

In O.B.'s educational designs there was a considerable element of misapplication which was part of his absurdity. His tally of statesmen was meagre — Lord Curzon at Eton, possibly Austen Chamberlain. He had no gift for it, having neither Seeley's vision nor Jowett's high seriousness. O.B.'s arts were conspiratorial. His genius was to make young men feel he was on their more interesting side against authority and convention. It was O.B. who, according to Desmond MacCarthy, dissolved for many King's undergraduates the connection between 'good' and 'good form'. His continental tours were riots of irreverence and snobbery. J. T. Sheppard (later Provost), who came up two years before Keynes, was taken by O.B. to Bayreuth. As the curtain rose to reveal the swimming Rhine maidens, O.B.'s voice boomed out, 'I say, Jack, isn't it just like an aquarium.' Any serious intent of his history lectures would be undermined when O.B. would suddenly pause. 'Such a *nice* Emperor,' he would purr, before embarking on one of his more spectacular feats of name-dropping.

His importance in our story is not that he and Maynard were particularly close, but that the social atmosphere of King's in Maynard's time and for many years afterwards was largely O.B.'s doing. His Sunday evening 'At Homes' were a strange contrast to the contemporary student disco. At these, O.B. aimed to provide, in his own words, 'very good music, classical trios, quartettes, and other pieces executed by most competent performers'. And no doubt he often did: the violinist Gompertz was frequently there. But Desmond MacCarthy who came up to Trinity in 1894 has left a different impression of the first impact of an O.B. evening on a seventeen-year-old fresh from public school. One entered O.B.'s suite of rooms, lined from floor to ceiling with dusty, unread books, to the sight of tables loaded with whisky bottles, cakes, and lemonade jugs. The air would be blue with tobacco smoke. A weird cacophony of sound emanated from the oddest collection of people. In one corner a famous metaphysician – presumably McTaggart – was being badgered by a couple of undergraduates. In an armchair, an elderly peer, somewhat the worse for drink, was expounding his political views to a circle of squatting young men. Discordant chords crashed out from the piano. By the fire a soldier in scarlet uniform was shaking the spittle of his clarinet into the flames. Seated here and there were pairs of friends 'conversing earnestly in low tones, as oblivious as lovers of their surroundings'. MacCarthy goes on:

> my host astounded me: a very short, globular old man with an enormous yellow bald head and a broken coronal of black, un-

pleasant curls, came rolling towards me as though the cup of his happiness was at last full. I was led with many pats and smiles up to a youth shrinking with shyness, who turned out to be ... a non-Collegiate student, one of 'O.B.'s' numerous beneficiaries. With an affectionate hand on the shoulder of each of us, and bringing us almost nose to nose, he seemed to be performing a sort of marriage ceremony; then with the confident assertion that two such charming people must like each other, he rolled off into the next room, throwing as he went a rapid Spanish sentence at a professor from Madrid, who remained for the rest of the evening sadly stinted of conversation. Presently the piano began in the room beyond, and we went in to watch our host trolling out *Voi che sapete* with immense gusto. At the close of his performance the clarinet-player gave him a spanking which I thought a most undignified incident.[4]

In 1908, O.B., by then seventy-one, lost both his college post and his principalship of the Day Training College, on general grounds of age, and specific grounds of non-performance of duties. He felt he had been badly treated, and though still a Fellow of King's, decamped to Rome where he lived, 'a by no means extinct volcano',[5] till 1923. Maynard, by then also a Fellow of King's, made it a point to keep up with him and help him with his tax problems. One of O.B.'s last letters to Maynard from Rome is dated 19 January 1918: 'I am engaged in the fascinating occupation of writing a History of the World – the only History worth writing,' O.B. wrote. He added, 'I like being 81.'

A less overpowering personality than O.B.'s who helped shape the King's of Maynard's day was a bachelor history don called Goldsworthy Lowes Dickinson, a Fellow since 1887. If O.B. represented, notionally at least, the outgoing spirit of the college – he stood unsuccessfully for parliament three times – Goldie represented it in its aspect as shelter from the world. This was so by temperament, not conviction. He wanted to serve humanity; but he could never hit the right keys on his typewriter. So he retreated into King's, and erected, as he himself admitted, a philosophy on a defect. Needing to love, and be dominated by, heterosexual men, he depicted in his writing an ideal world united by the love of comrades. His most influential books were in the form of Socratic dialogues; he made his educational impact at King's not through formal instruction but through his Discussion Society modelled on a Platonic symposium. At meetings of this body, writes Esmé Wingfield-Stratford, a Kingsman of Keynes's time, 'a convention of cultivated irreverence' coexisted with 'an atmosphere of a certain Grecian suggestiveness'. Wingfield-Stratford saw him as 'the best type of old maid, rather prim and fastidious' who would 'come out with some gentle little half-aside; this would have the effect of a needle pricking a bladder'.[6] There was, in fact, something soft at the centre of

Goldie's philosophy, captured in a parody by *Basileon*, the College undergraduate magazine, of a Goldie discourse to his Discussion Society on the theme 'Is Life Worth Living?':

> Mr Dickinson said life, like a dome of many-coloured glass, stained the white radiance of eternity. Many people had tried to solve this problem, which had interested the philosophers of all ages. The difficulty was that we couldn't be certain that we would stop living, if we took measures to end our present existence – he had written three books about 'Immortality' and so knew more about it than anyone else, and all he knew was that he didn't know anything about it. He admitted that biology, psychology, and metaphysics had proved up to the hilt that life was not worth living. The fact that the sciences mentioned above proved that life was not worth living, condemned not life, but the said sciences.[7]

While setting a standard in cultivated discussion, Goldie lacked the power to move either to intellectual or emotional passion. When in 1914 the great fire of war swept away his hopes for sweetness and light, he blamed himself 'since I could never so speak and act that men had to attend to me'. At King's, though, many did, like E. M. Forster, his friend and biographer, and his influence was overwhelmingly on the side of the private affections and allegiances. Like Sidgwick and Browning, Goldie was a characteristic late-Victorian intellectual in whom a vestigial sense of public duty was constantly at war with unfulfilled private passions; unable to separate them in his mind, he was unable also to bring them into harmony with each other.

There were many other dons who contributed their quota of distinction and eccentricity – Nathaniel Wedd, a classics tutor who affected red ties and blasphemy, J. E. Nixon, a famous hoarder of umbrellas, 'Monty' James, a bibliophile of immense erudition and pedantry, who entertained his favourite Etonians by reading them his own ghost stories. The main point is that King's, contrary to Browning's hopes, was never cut out to be a nursery for statesmen. It was 'a perfect forcing house of unique characters, varying between the extremes of greatness and absurdity'.[8] It could remain a perfect shelter for those too shy or eccentric to face the world: a society of clever, dotty inmates, provided with a continuing supply of charming and clever youths to stir atrophied emotions. Maynard Keynes while appreciating to the full what King's had to offer was built for a less cloistered existence. Nevertheless, King's became, with Eton, an object of his passionate loyalty, to be cherished and preserved by all the exertions of his practical intelligence.

II

THE FRESHMAN

In his first year he was lodged in a poky house in King's Lane.* A fellow
freshman, Charles Rye Fay, later an economic historian, remembered
a young man with 'a moustache and fancy waistcoat' inviting him to
tea his first day. 'My name's Keynes. What's yours?' Fay became a
good, but not close, friend. Maynard's best friend at King's was
another Lane freshman, Robin Furness, a clever, elegant, Rugbeian
classical scholar, with an exceptional mastery of the obscene in the
literature of all languages and ages. His experience was not confined to
books, or so he led Keynes to believe. 'Fallen in love? Five times only
to be exact,' he informed him his second term. '3 women – one married
– and 2 boys.' With Furness, Maynard could indulge in the sexual
gossip which had delighted him at Eton. Not that Eton friends were
ignored. He was in close touch with Granville Hamilton and Harold
Butler who had gone to Oxford; Dundas and Swithinbank, still at Eton,
regaled him with school news; he kept up a somewhat one-sided correspondence with Daniel Macmillan. Another freshman inhabitant of the
Lane was William Norton Page, a mathematical scholar, with whom
Maynard went for coaching to Ernest Hobson, later Sadlerian
Professor of Mathematics, and elder brother of J. A. Hobson, the un-
orthodox economist. For many years Maynard had a higher regard for
the mathematician Hobson than for the economist Hobson. He found
he had little in common with Page, complaining that he cared for
nothing except doing well in the Tripos.

No more than at Eton was Maynard prepared to be boxed into
mathematics. He would not, he told his father, devote himself exclusively to it, even 'if he could thereby be Senior Wrangler'.[9] Soon
after he arrived he went on a book-buying spree; he also took up rowing
for the college. But above all he found himself in a society honeycombed
with clubs and discussion groups, many of them based on King's and
Trinity. Although some of them were quite up to the Etonian standard
of exclusiveness, Maynard, who arrived with a big reputation in a small
world, soon found himself besieged with invitations. There was Oscar
Browning's Political Society and Dickinson's Discussion Society.
There was the Trinity Essay Society at which, on 10 November 1902,
he heard Lytton Strachey deliver what he called a 'most brilliant satire
on Christianity' – probably his first sight of Strachey, then a third-year
undergraduate. Soon Maynard was a member of four debating

* The Lane was demolished in 1967 to make way for the Keynes Building.

societies, one of them the *Decemviri* made up of ten invited undergraduates from King's and Trinity.

Some mathematics was done in Maynard's first Christmas vacation; but this was coupled with a study of 'the works of Peter Abelard, my intention being, at present, to write a paper upon the aforesaid gent'.[10] Keynes complained to Swithinbank about his Harvey Road routine. 'One disadvantage I do find in living at home; I am compelled to go to bed just when my brain is ceasing to be that of a dolt; in the mornings I am fatuous and comatose and then I am supposed to work; in the early evening my dinner is too near the surface, and as soon as I am beginning to become rational, off I go to bed.'

He continued to find Peter Abelard 'a most entrancing subject'. The essay he was writing on him was getting more and more unwieldy but 'never mind, I do it for my own amusement rather than for my hearers' and they may go to the devil'.[11] Once again he was showing his ability to get totally absorbed in a subject remote from his official interests. The following term at a meeting of the King's Appenine Literary Society, Maynard read his paper on Abelard, the twelfth-century theologian, who had been the lover of Heloise and was condemned for heresy at the instigation of Maynard's old hero Bernard of Cluny. What Maynard admired in Bernard were his ascetic ideals; what he praised in Peter Abelard was his belief in reason. He quoted his words: 'Not because God has taught it, is a thing to be believed, ... but because it is proved to be so.' In his paper on Bernard Maynard had set up the conflict between monastic ideals and the life of action. In his paper on Peter Abelard he contrasted the claims of reason and love with those of faith and conventional morality. He was growing up into adulthood, and into the Edwardian age.

Maynard was as eager as ever to taste anything which seemed intellectually worthwhile. Thus in his second term he dragged Fay, reading History, to G. E. Moore's lectures on Ethics, and J. E. McTaggart's on Metaphysics. McTaggart covered the metaphysical aspects of time, and soon Keynes was writing a paper on 'Time and Change' to be read to another King's College society, the Parrhesiasts. He helped form a Baskerville Club with fellow book-collectors like Arthur Cole. He took up bridge with the old Etonian Stephen Gaselee. 'It is too much' Neville noted disconsolately.

Neville himself was responsible for opening up one avenue of escape from mathematics. He had made Maynard a life member of the Cambridge Union, or Debating Society, and on 4 November 1902 Maynard made his maiden speech – 'the bravest thing I ever did' he told his father. *Granta*, the undergraduate newspaper, thought it excellent. So did the President of the Union, Edwin Montagu, who invited Maynard to deliver a speech 'from the paper' a fortnight later. Montagu, a rising

Liberal politician, was Keynes's first and most important political patron. He was a hideously ugly man, whose ugliness, however, was redeemed by charm, a cynical intelligence, and a passion for gossip. Maynard had much reason to be grateful to him in the early part of his career. At the Union, Montagu was more taken by Keynes's logic than by his delivery, which was not impressive. Keynes spoke regularly throughout his first year on the political subjects which were the staple of debates, and in June 1903 was elected to its Committee at his second attempt.

The lack of passion in Maynard's oratory reflected the lack of passion in his political beliefs. He joined the University Liberal Club, because the Liberals were the party of intelligence, not because he had any enthusiasm for reform. Thus in May 1903 we find him at the Union opposing Home Rule for Ireland on practical grounds. He could speak much more eloquently when aroused, as he invariably was when the subject was Christianity and its iniquities. In his second term he and fellow Kingsman Jack Sheppard mobilised the forces of College anti-clericalism to stop the establishment of a mission to the East End of London, one of the main outlets for the do-gooding impulses of the time:

> During the last week [he wrote to Swithinbank on 5 February 1903] the whole of King's has been turned upside down by a religious controversy – as to what lines a mission, which it is proposed that the College should start, is to be run on. It was, at one time, to be high Church, but Sheppard and I and several others helped to organise a regular opposition and we finally carried the College meeting by a majority of 75 to 25 that the scheme should be on a purely *secular* basis .... It was a tremendous triumph ... I had to make a speech before the Provost, almost the whole College, and a no. of dons....

Maynard's speech was remembered years later as a triumph of the forensic art.

His fellow anti-clerical John Tressider Sheppard, the son of a Baptist pastor in Balham, was one of the products of O.B.'s liberating touch. He became one of Cambridge's 'characters', declaiming and dancing his way though the Union, of which he became President. The Greek tragedies were his real love. His approach to them, as to life, was histrionic rather than scholarly; and he lectured on the pagan ethic with all the eloquence of the Baptist preacher. Later his referees complained of an 'unfortunate lightness of touch' in his (successful) Fellowship dissertation, which they thought might be cured by a 'year in a German seminar'. He was slight and cherubic when Maynard first knew him. Sheppard's first impression of Maynard was of 'sensitive, expressive hands and of the beauty of his eyes'. They soon became friends, and were to be lifelong colleagues.

Maynard's insatiable passion for everything except mathematics alarmed Neville. Hobson was adamant: Maynard must 'wear blinkers' if he was to do well in the Tripos. 'Probably his heart is not in the subject,' wrote Neville in his diary, remembering his own disastrous first year. Although Maynard confessed to be 'sick of mathematics', telling his father that it was his 'worst subject',[12] it was Neville who suffered more than he did. Maynard always had a great capacity for applying his mind to something which had no connection with his heart. Nevertheless, he could manage no better than fifth out of six in College Mays, the freshman's examination in his third term. His tutor, Arthur Berry, 'an extremely solemn and worthy agnostic',[13] began to sound more and more like Hurst at Eton. Neville wrote, 'He thinks the boy decidedly clever in Mathematics ... but he considers him unwise in practically refusing to go to lectures, and he does not seem very sanguine as to the future ... I just now feel very much depressed .... I keep wondering whether we did the right thing in letting him read Mathematics. No doubt if he would work regularly six hours a day it would be alright.' The diary tells a familiar story. Neville, when he was not worrying about his golf, was worrying about Maynard's future. Maynard appeared to live only for the present, but he always managed to do enough to ensure his future, too.

III

APOSTLES AND PHENOMENA

In the December of his first term Maynard received a visit from two tall young men, one thin and etiolated, with moustache and pince-nez, the other dark, with a long mournful face. They introduced themselves as Mr Strachey and Mr Woolf. Sir Roy Harrod assures us that a lively conversation ensued. More probably the occasion lent itself to one of those famous Bloomsbury silences. Maynard was supposed to have no inkling of their purpose, which was to consider his suitability for election to the University's most selective society, the Cambridge Conversazione Society, or Apostles. Its existence was meant to be secret, partly to avoid offence to friends of Apostles who were not themselves Apostolic, and partly as a means to privacy. But the secrecy was not total; more aspired than were chosen. Maynard would not have been hard to spot as an 'embryo' or likely recruit to a Society whose field of scrutiny was virtually confined to two colleges – Trinity and King's. Both abounded in Apostles, active and emeritus. Maynard would already have been known to most of them by his brilliant reputation at

Eton, his exceptional scholarship performance, and as Neville's son. In his first term, Oscar Browning and Lowes Dickinson, both 'angels' or retired Apostles, had observed him approvingly. Sheppard, an undergraduate Apostle, had met him through the Cambridge Union. Following the visit by Strachey and Woolf he was subjected to a secret selection procedure organised by Strachey, who was secretary, and consisting of breakfast and tea parties at which other Apostles would look him over. In these ways he was judged and found worthy. On Saturday 28 February 1903 he was initiated or 'born' into the Society with the usual paraphernalia of the secret curse and other time-hallowed rituals. Sheppard was his 'father' or sponsor. It was a rare honour for a freshman, but Maynard was a rare freshman. The philosopher McTaggart wrote him a letter of welcome:

Dear Keynes,
    Best congratulations on your election. I hope you will always enjoy the Society as much as I have.
    I am always in my rooms on Wednesday's 9.30–12. If you ever cared to look in, you would generally meet some of the brethren, and not infrequently an embryo.
    Yours fraternally,

J. Ellis McTaggart[14]

Maynard was Apostle no. 243 in an unbroken sequence stretching back to George Tomlinson, the Society's founder, in 1820. The proceedings were very much what they had been in Sidgwick's day. Every Saturday evening in term time the active brethren would meet, behind locked doors, in the secretary's room. Angels would often join them, though not obliged to do so. A 'moderator' would read a paper on a topic previously agreed; it would be discussed by members, speaking from the 'hearthrug', in an order determined by lot, and a question arising from it put to the vote. These intellectual activities were accompanied by the consumption of anchovies on toast – known as 'whales' – and tea or coffee. The object and atmosphere of the meetings seem not to have varied much over time. They were summed up by Sidgwick as 'the pursuit of truth with absolute devotion and unreserve by a group of intimate friends'. The papers often had humorous titles, and serious themes were thought to be improved by witty and amusing treatment. Meeting every Saturday, and practically living in each others' rooms in the intervals, the Apostles were more like a family than a club. Their discussions were full of in-jokes, personal allusions, private meanings. Their talk would be spiced with blasphemy and sexual innuendo, much as it had been at school.

Maynard's new companions were clever, philosophical, irreverent, and unworldly. The active brethren at the time of his election consisted of three undergraduates from Trinity – Lytton Strachey, Saxon Sydney-Turner and Leonard Woolf – and two from King's – Jack Sheppard and Leonard Greenwood. Other Apostles like E. M. Forster, Ralph Hawtrey, A. R. Ainsworth, and H. O. Meredith, all recent graduates of King's, would often come up for meetings. Further back were the 'angels' of the 1890s, notably Charles Percy Sanger, Bertrand Russell, R. C. and G. M. Trevelyan, G. E. Moore, G. H. Hardy, and Desmond MacCarthy, all from Trinity. Stretching further back were the Davies brothers (Theodore and Crompton), Roger Fry, McTaggart, Lowes Dickinson, and A. N. Whitehead. The O.B. was the most ancient fount of Apostolic lore, and had donated a cedar trunk (known as the ark) in which the Society kept its records.

Membership of the Society affected Maynard's life in a profound way. It gave him most obviously a new circle of friends; and one which was constantly replenished from the same source, as the Society gave 'birth' to new Apostles, to whose selection and cultivation Maynard gave considerable attention. Much of the rest of his life would be spent in the circle of Apostles, old and new, and their friends and relations. Two close Trinity friends of Lytton Strachey, Sydney-Turner, and Leonard Woolf must count as part of this circle – Thoby Stephen and Clive Bell. A little later they played a key part in creating that London extension of Apostolic Cambridge known as the Bloomsbury Group. Not that Maynard's old friends fell away immediately: Dilly Knox (who came to King's in 1904), Bernard Swithinbank and Daniel Macmillan (who both went to Balliol College, Oxford) remained his main links with his Eton past. He remained friendly with Furness and Fay, especially the former. But he had entered a new world, which became more central to him than his old one.

With a change in friends came a change in values. Part of it was no doubt due to growing self-awareness; but membership of the Society reinforced it. At Eton he had been a schoolboy with an exceptional range: a scientist with an 'artistic' side, an intellectual with a marked practical flair. After 1903 the partition of his life into a private and public sphere becomes more obvious. On one side were ranged philosophy, aesthetics, friendship; on the other political and practical affairs. Not only did Maynard keep the two sets of activities more or less separate; but there was little flow of feeling from one to the other. It is also noticeable that from this time onwards he started to give much more priority to the first than to the second. This represented a choice of values. Maynard's genius shone through in whatever he did; but from 1903 onwards his passions were most deeply engaged by private aims, however 'pleasant', 'agreeable', or 'amusing' he found politics or administration. This priority he gave to the private sphere reflected a particular kind of conditioning which started with his membership of the Apostles. The Society gave him the opportunity, incentive, and justification for becoming the kind of person he wanted to be.

The shift can be summed up in terms of the Society's own Kantian joke: it alone was 'real'; the rest of the world was 'phenomenal'. When McTaggart unexpectedly married late in life he assured the brethren that he was merely taking a 'phenomenal' wife: Maynard himself would refer to non-Apostles as 'phenomena'. What all this meant was that the world outside was regarded as less substantial, less worthy of attention than the Society's own collective life. It meant it was being judged by esoteric standards and found wanting. It was a joke with a serious twist.

Whence came the Society's potency, its ability to transform the lives of its members? How could a club which in many ways was 'a typical undergraduate debating society and typically silly'[15] have this effect? One should never underestimate the effect of secrecy. Much of what made the rest of the world seem alien sprang from this simple fact. Secrecy was a bond which greatly amplified the Society's life relative to its members' other interests. It is much easier, after all, to spend one's time with people from whom one does not have to keep large secrets; and spending much time with them reinforces whatever it was that first drew them together. Also important was the fact that membership was for life. Older Apostles did not simply disappear into their careers. They took wing – but often no further than to the nearest combination room whence they could maintain their involvement in the Society's affairs. From 1903 until 1908 or 1909, that is, from the age of twenty till twenty-five or twenty-six, most of Maynard's private life, talk, and gossip had reference to the Society. Such a prolonged exposure to a small group of people of like mind can implant a lifelong stamp to one's values and attitudes.

Membership of the Society undoubtedly bred an attitude of superiority to the phenomenal world and its concerns. No member doubted that he was one of the pick of young Cambridge. 'It was owing to the existence of the Society that I soon got to know the people best worth knowing,' wrote Bertrand Russell.[16] Such self-perception was only partly accurate: as Stephen Toulmin has remarked, most of the great nineteenth-century Cambridge scientists – Darwin, Rayleigh, Jeans, and Eddington – managed to slip through the net.[17] So did Galton and Karl Pearson, Alfred Marshall and Pigou. Nevertheless, it was all too easy to feel that one was living on a lofty, and lonely, eminence. 'Is it monomania – this colossal moral superiority that we feel?' wrote Maynard to Lytton Strachey a couple of years later. 'I get the feeling that most of the rest never see anything at all – too stupid or too wicked.'[18]

'The undergraduates who made it into the Cambridge Conversazione Society,' Toulmin continues, 'were (it seems) the ones who had a way with words ...'. This is important. The Society's tradition was philosophical. From the days of Maurice and Sterling in the early nineteenth-century through Henry Sidgwick to McTaggart and Moore, philosophy, especially moral philosophy, had been a leading preoccupation. The Society of Maynard's day contained Whitehead, McTaggart, Russell and Moore, all destined to be world-famous philosophers. It is hardly surprising that Maynard's first sustained intellectual interest should have been in philosophy rather than economics, though here we must add the influence of his own home and the endless discussions between his father and W. E. Johnston on logical problems. But the important point about this philosophic apprenticeship is that successive generations of Apostles, and Maynard's was no exception, emerged with tough-minded, and therefore robust, theories about how they should lead their own lives. Maynard's election to the Society was followed, six months later, by the publication of G. E. Moore's *Principia Ethica*, the most important book in his life. We will discuss the ethical beliefs he got from G. E. Moore in the next chapter. The key point to note is that they were far from being the wishy-washy things which emerge from most student discussions over midnight coffee. They were capable of giving direction to lives. A second important interest of the Society's in Maynard's time was aesthetic. Apostles like Desmond MacCarthy, H. O. Meredith, E. M. Forster, Saxon Sydney-Turner, Lytton Strachey and Sheppard, as well as Clive Bell and Thoby Stephen, were more interested in literature and painting than in philosophy as such. Nevertheless, their orientation to these things, the value they placed on them, the way in which they talked about them, was largely determined by philosophy and particularly by Moore's philosophy. Both streams, philosophic and aesthetic, flowed into the Society's 'search for truth' in Maynard's time, and his own papers to the Apostles can be broadly divided into these two groups. Economics was hardly represented at all. Nor was politics.

The focus of the Society's interests suggests another feature: its unworldliness. Most of the Apostles were dons: embryonic, actual, or manqué. They were selected for membership precisely because they combined great cleverness with great unworldliness. The source of this unworldliness differed from case to case. G. E. Moore was a genuine saint, whose innocence was palpable. Lowes Dickinson was simply defeated by the world. Lytton Strachey, as his biographer Michael Holroyd remarked, was 'not unambitious only unconfident'. Another characteristic is more common. The Apostles of Maynard's day, with one or two exceptions, were distinctly deficient in charm and beauty, the qualities which tether people to society. Not only were they lacking, as Virginia Woolf later remarked, in 'physical splendour'; they had no small talk; they were arrogant, prickly, withdrawn. They compensated by the brilliance and fearlessness of their cerebration to each other, by the exaggerated unworldliness of their ideals, and by the inelastic standards by which they judged the human drama unfolding outside. They were men whose lives tended to be devoid of feminine company, except that of their female relations. This was a common Cambridge, even Victorian, pattern in young adulthood; but it was exaggerated by precisely those other features which cut off the Society from the world. In these ways the Society functioned as a 'protective coterie' for members who were too shy or awkward or clever to be fully comfortable in the world and who needed each other to sparkle or for social therapy. At the same time, one must not ignore the positive power of the unworldly ideal for clever young men bred both in the classics and gentlemanly ideals, to whom much of Victorian life seemed ugly and oppressive

The Apostles had a bad press at the time of the spy scandals, when it came out that two of the 'Cambridge' spies, Burgess and Blunt, were members of the Society. It was widely, if implausibly, suggested that the Society had fostered, or its secrecy in some way facilitated, their treacherous activity. There were strident editorials in the newspapers concerning the consequences of people cutting themselves off from 'ordinary morality' to indulge their esoteric tastes. Yet the most striking thing about the Apostles is their quintessential *Britishness*. Their own exclusiveness was rooted in the larger exclusions of English life: exclusions which ensured their own membership was drawn from the small group which had survived an elaborate selection procedure which started with birth. Their own sense of special worthiness was echoed by every group in England which felt able to look down on some other group as deficient in the special virtue it felt itself to possess. They were a product of a very English reaction to industrial life, based on the cult of dead languages, chivalry, moral utopias, and the rejection of commercial careers. They were a civilised response to the barbarities of English public-school education and the stifling moralism of English family life; and at the same time an expression of the peculiar English capacity for keeping its upper-class males in a state of petrified adolescence. Finally, they reflected one side of an ancient university civilisation – Cambridge's image of itself as a world of learning and beauty set in a land of barbarians and philistines. Theirs was the donnish ideal of Elysium on the Cam.

From all that we have discovered so far, and from what we know of Maynard's career, it is clear that the Society appealed only to certain sides of his character. He could get enjoyment out of life in its more vigorous aspects. In May 1903 he attended a dinner given for Sir Edward Grey whom he considered a 'very commanding and reliable statesman' – a fallible judgement if ever there was one. 'I have been waxing quite political lately – a most amusing game and a very fairly adequate substitute for bridge,' he told Bernard Swithinbank. His letter continued with a mixture of Apostolic and Etonian gossip. 'Strachey is very well and as godless as ever. Sheppard also. Gaselee wears starched pyjamas in bed .... Quirk [an Etonian] prefers the company of pansies to that of men; Capron [another Etonian who lived in the rooms below him in the Lane] thinks there is more in palmistry than is dreamt of in my philosophy at any rate.'[19]

With Maynard at Cambridge, his parents gave up the family's traditional August holiday: it was important that their eldest son go on working at King's which provided residential facilities for a six-week term in the long vacation. On 12 July 1903 he moved into his new rooms on Staircase A of Wilkins building, facing the chapel. Neville and Florence bought him a new desk, no doubt to encourage mathematical endeavour. There were the usual interruptions. Eton friends came to stay; at the end of August he spent a week with Humphrey Paul in Sussex. He returned to Harvey Road where, he told Swithinbank, 'I am enjoying a useless existence in the study of electricity, dynamics, and golf.' He was also engaged on a compulsory essay on Dickens, which King's inflicted on its undergraduates. 'He is an author whom I am physically incapable of reading, so that I have to invent purely imaginary theories about him – and then find not unnaturally that I have no illustrations ....' On 25 September he left with his father for a week of golf, mathematics, and double dummy bridge at Sheringham. Maynard only worked efficiently at his mathematics under his father's eagle eye. Neville, who was having one of his attacks of 'golf pleurisy', noted that Maynard had quite 'recovered his driving power' by the end of the vacation.

He could have done with some of it at the Union where, on 24 November 1903, he defended Free Trade in a speech which, according to *Granta*, displayed 'such an utter lack of animation and rhetorical verve' that Neville contemplated lessons in voice production.[20] But Maynard had sufficiently increased the vigour of his delivery by the end of his second year to be elected secretary of the Union, thus ensuring his automatic ascent to the Presidency. The Free Trade–Protection controversy, which broke out in 1903 with Joseph Chamberlain's call for Protection and Imperial Preference, stirred Maynard to economic as well as political activity: his father records him studying Political Economy in September 1903.[21] Like most Cambridge economists (Marshall headed a Free Trade Manifesto published in *The Times* on 15 August 1903 which confidently declared that no unemployment could result from an increase of imports) Maynard was a staunch free trader; in fact free trade was his only political cause before the First World War. 'Conservatism had died and been born again, a lower animal,' he told the Cambridge Union a little later.[22] To Swithinbank he wrote on 15 December: 'Sir, I hate all priests and protectionists . . . . Free Trade and free thought! Down with pontiffs and tariffs. Down with those who declare we are dumped and damned. Away with all schemes of redemption or retaliation.' A further distraction that term had been Cambridge's triennial Greek play, in which Sheppard had clowned his way through the part of Peisthetaerus in Aristophanes' *Birds*. Hamilton, Swithinbank and Dundas came over from Oxford; Daniel Macmillan from Eton. 'The naughty boy had already been twice to the Greek play,' Neville noted on 27 November 1903. The next night he went again with Florence and the Eton party. 'Maynard cannot be doing much Mathematics,' his father observed on 2 December. 'For 14 consecutive days he has only one free evening.' But discipline was re-established in the holidays. To Swithinbank he wrote on 22 December: 'All the term long I talk and behave and talk and am desperately normal. And in the vacation I sit and read and write and the most mad things come into my head and I pass through every variety of mood in a week.'

Family business of a more agreeable kind occupied Maynard in his next vacation. His sister Margaret, 'exceedingly pretty and winsome' in Neville's eyes, had been packed off to Germany in October 1903 after having failed her examinations at Wycombe Abbey, where she spent a miserable six months with an impoverished aristocrat, Baroness von Gissing. In mid-March 1904 Florence and Maynard set out to rescue her. It was his first trip to Germany and they did some sight-seeing, as well as visiting his old German governess, Fräulein Rotman, now married. From Dresden Maynard wrote to Swithinbank on 24 March:

> Every painter is here, but I find the Germans of the early sixteenth century most to my taste, – the Dürers, Holbeins, and Cranachs. I should like to analyse my reasons – if I have any. In Berlin we saw more pictures – especially one Holbein, and both here and there much statuary, Greek and Roman and later; at Berlin two most beautiful boys' busts of the Augustan period, and a most magnificent bust of Scipio Africanus – but the list is endless . . . . At Berlin we saw Ibsen's 'Wild Duck' supremely acted. The more I contemplate it the greater does the play appear . . . . The book-sellers' shops in this country are rather an interesting contrast to ours – innumerable translations from French and English (particularly Bernard Shaw and Maeterlinck), very little native modern literature, but the Classical writers of all languages translated and fabulously cheap.

On his return Maynard read a paper on 'Beauty' to the Apostles (30 April 1904) in which he tried to show that it was better to love nature than pictures and statues, but statues were more beautiful, because more like nature, than pictures. A faithful enough account of

middlebrow Victorian aesthetic theory, it does at least show that Maynard's interest in the visual arts antedated his connection with Bloomsbury. Maynard's new life was too full for him to have much time to give
to his sister and brother. Margaret took up weaving, gardening and
social work. Geoffrey had left St Faith's for Rugby in 1901, without a
stain on his character, but also with only one prize to show for his time
there. Soon after his arrival at Rugby – his housemaster was the Kingsman William Parker Brooke, Rupert's father – he attended a 'ripping'
lecture on spiders. He had become a passionate collector of butterflies
and bones. Geoffrey's interests, as well as his rhythm of development,
were quite different from his brother's, and this, as well as the age
difference, kept them apart.

On 5 June 1904 Maynard became twenty-one. He received a watch
from Neville and Florence, and many other presents from members of
the family. Although one part of his life had moved beyond the control,
even knowledge, of his parents, their involvement in his future had not
diminished. Berry's report to Neville on Maynard's mathematics was
moderately encouraging: 'He thinks the boy has not got stale ... as at
one time he feared would be the case.' Far from reassured Neville
'made some suggestions' for future work to Maynard's new coach,
Leathem of St John's.[23] Whatever happened in term-time, the old work
regime was renewed in the holidays. Indeed, it would not be too much
to say that most of the mathematics Maynard did in his three undergraduate years at Cambridge was done in the vacations under his
father's supervision. But the role of No. 6 Harvey Road was not confined to this. In term-time it was a second home. Each weekend
Maynard would take his friends there for meals. What Neville and
Florence made of the squeaky, disjointed Lytton and trembling
Leonard Woolf, is not recorded. But their hospitality was not of the
prying sort. Manners held together the Victorian and Edwardian
worlds even after their values had started to drift apart. No doubt
Neville and Florence tried a little match-making. There were plenty of
young women on Harvey Road occasions, daughters of Neville's
colleagues, or students at Girton and Newnham, where he still lectured
on Logic. Neville, with his old-fashioned gallantry, was probably more
interested in them than was Maynard. There were also the usual invitations to dances and balls, which Maynard either refused, or accepted
with bad grace. He hated dancing. 'Thank heaven I have refused *all*
parties this year,' he wrote to his sister Margaret on 23 December 1903;
'not a single dame has ensnared me ...'.

Maynard's Cambridge friends were now a mixture of Apostles and
phenomena. In June 1904 he stayed with Fay in Liverpool, where Fay
remembers his brilliant disproofs of Christianity and his execrable
golf.[24] In the middle of July he spent what was meant to be a restful

weekend with Bertrand Russell and his wife Alys in their cottage near Farnham. Twenty-six guests arrived unexpectedly.[25] Russell's *Principles of Mathematics* (1903) had just established him as one of the world's leading philosophers. To Lytton Strachey Keynes wrote, 'For hours on Saturday night Russell wiped the floor with a man called Leonard Hobhouse – a most superb display.'[26] Russell formed the highest opinion of Keynes's intellect. It was 'the sharpest and clearest that I have ever known. When I argued with him, I felt that I took my life in my hands, and I seldom emerged without feeling something of a fool.'[27] On 29 August 1904 Maynard set off for a week's walking tour in Wales, knapsack on back, with another Apostle, Leonard Woolf. They climbed Snowdon, staying on the way with Sanger and his wife Dora in Aberdaron. Maynard was never a great walker or climber, and he and Woolf were never particularly close. On this holiday, however, Leonard remembered him as an 'extraordinarily good companion' with whom he talked philosophy all day and played bezique in the evenings.[28] At Cambridge in the Michaelmas Term of 1904 Maynard took to walking on Sunday afternoons with the Angel George Trevelyan, also of Trinity, a historian and doughty walker of the old school. Maynard had just become both president of the Liberal Club and of the Cambridge Union, speaking in debates at both Oxford and Edinburgh. He also took a King's team to Eton to play College at wall. 'I do think Eton is the most astounding place in the world,' he wrote to Swithinbank on 5 November 1904, 'of all complex entities the most a priori improbable'. Trevelyan urged him to a political career. 'You are born to be a politician I should guess,' he told him – a judgment singularly lacking in perception.[29]

An interesting contemporary assessment of Maynard by Pigou was published in *Granta* on 4 June 1904:

> The walls of his rooms [Pigou wrote] bespeak wide interests – hundreds of ancient and curious books; Ibsen's picture for love of drama; Erasmus' for Protestantism; the card of the Liberal Club for politics; the menu of its dinner for gastronomy; readable volumes on philosophy; unreadable ones on mathematics; photographs of Etonians robed for the wall-game; a terrifying portent to signify 'projective geometry'.
>
> ... there is something more; a document in diaconal calligraphy, beginning – is it possible? – with a jest. This, then, is one of Mr Keynes's characteristics; he is not of the strenuous youth whom stern patriotism impels to the glorious ineptitude of pre-breakfast trench-digging in the rain; reason is his strong point, and he rises at a 'reasonable' hour. There is one further fact. Mr Keynes is secretary of the Union; something may be gathered from the speeches which

he makes. Clear-headedness more than human; a petrifying logical-ity; judicial impartiality worthy of a Rhadamanthus: these and a stern resolution that never in his presence shall confusions between 'good as means' and 'good as end' pass without challenge,* are the chief characteristics of his oratory.

These things are solemn truth .... But ... they do not resolve for us the enigma of Mr Keynes. As a rule there is nothing so irritating as conspicuous logicality, except its conspicuous opposite. Mr Keynes however, contrives to be clear-headed without making muddle-headed people hate him. That is a remarkable thing, which demonstrates that, besides the minor gift of cleverness, he has the major one of sympathy.

IV

STATES OF MIND

Maynard's best friend at Cambridge in his last undergraduate year was Giles Lytton Strachey. The future author of *Eminent Victorians* was then a postgraduate at Trinity, writing a dissertation on Warren Hastings. In one respect, Strachey was the most important friend Maynard ever had. He was the only one who ever exerted on him an appreciable moral authority. In the usual pattern of Maynard's close friendships, Maynard was the one who dominated. He was cleverer, more articulate, more worldly, more practical than his friends. As his achievements piled up, he came to be regarded (and to regard himself) as an arbiter on every subject. In his friendship with Strachey, the roles were reversed. Strachey was three years older than Keynes and a much more formed and definite character. He did not become a professional philosopher, but he had a very sharp, analytical, mind, even being able to hold his own with Russell.† Strachey was a philosopher of the tastes and the emotions. Long after the intimate phase of their friendship expired in 1908, he retained his power to make Maynard feel morally uncomfortable.

Born into London's intellectual aristocracy, the eighth of ten child-ren of parents with strong connections with Indian administration, Strachey grew up into a 'very queer gentleman'. His appearance when Keynes first knew him was disconcerting, even to himself. He was

* This was the central distinction of Moore's *Principia Ethica*; see Chapter 6.
† Maynard gave the following example in a letter to Swithinbank dated 6 November 1904, of an exchange between Russell and Strachey, on the question: Ought we to make all things new? Russell: God certainly ought to, and there is no reason why we should be so modest as to say that we ought not to do what God ought to do. Strachey: But he never made things new; doesn't it say somewhere that he made man in his own image? Russell: Ah yes, of course that was the mistake.

long, thin, pale and disjointed, with spidery legs and arms; short-sighted, big-nosed, and with what his biographer calls 'calamitous equine teeth'. His voice never managed a decisive transition to a lower register, periods of deep masculine sound alternating with squeals in piping falsetto. His family home, 69 Lancaster Gate, Lytton himself described as 'a house afflicted with elephantiasis'. Here he grew up with six sisters and numerous relations, all talking, usually simultaneously, with those piercing voices and exaggerated emphases which came to be recognised as Stracheyesque. His education had been alarmingly spasmodic, mainly due to the inattention of his mother, intervals of the bizarre alternating with long stretches of the substandard. The Trinity College porter was very suspicious when the spindly Lytton first presented himself at Cambridge in 1899. 'You'd never think he was the son of a general,' he remarked. Nor did most of his fellow-undergraduates. Lytton Strachey soon retired with a few choice spirits into a network of tiny literary societies, from which he graduated, in 1902, into the Apostles.

Out of these unpromising ingredients, Strachey fashioned a personality of unusual authority, if limited appeal; he was able to impose himself on his intimates by the definiteness of his views and sheer weight of his mannerisms. The two were intimately connected: Strachey was one of those people able to put behind a particular outlook on life the whole weight of a 'character'. The key to his power was the style and tone of his utterance which, in its unusual stresses, its joky private vocabulary, and its chilling silences, conveyed a whole world of approval and disapproval. Much later Keynes wrote that he 'used to hear the Stracheys talk about someone being "dim" forty years ago, and it was only after that that it came into general circulation. They also had another, more extreme expression for someone who was still worse than dim, who was so to speak perniciously dim. He would be known as a "death packet".' Strachey delighted to shock people out of Victorian taboos. Discussing sex differences with a dowager at a dinner-party, he remarked, 'The whole matter turns, as in golf, on the question of holes and balls?' His subversive wit which was such a joy of his conversation, his letters, and later his biographies was similarly always in the service of his own set of values. These values were largely derived from G. E. Moore, but Strachey invested them with his own apparatus of certainty. People, activities were either inside or outside the pale. His descriptions of his friends and enemies were masterly; his dissection of their characters merciless. He loved clever people and that is one reason he loved Keynes. 'He analyses with amazing persistence and brilliance. I have never met so active a brain,' he told Leonard Woolf. 'His conversation is extraordinarily alert and very amusing. He's interested in people to a remarkable degree.'[30] On the other hand, he never wholly approved of Maynard. He did not think that, on the whole, he had a 'good character'; an assessment in which there was a good deal of jealousy, as we shall see. Maynard on the other hand worshipped Lytton, even if he must often have been made uncomfortable by him. He had reached the point in life where he was ready to be shocked out of the conventions of Harvey Road. He and Lytton could now indulge in a common taste for blasphemy and attractive young men.

Their friendship almost broke up soon after it had started, over competition for the affections of a young Trinity freshman called Arthur Lee Hobhouse. Hobhouse was a stunningly handsome product of Oppidan Eton. He was spotted by Strachey, who introduced him to Keynes as an 'embryo' or possible Apostle. To Woolf, now banished for seven years to an administrative post in Ceylon, Strachey enthused on 30 November 1904, 'Hobhouse is fair, with frizzy hair, a good complexion, an arched nose, and a very charming expression of countenance. His conversation is singularly coming on .... He's interested in metaphysics and people, he's not a Christian and he sees quite a lot of jokes. I'm rather in love with him, and Keynes who lunched with him today ... is convinced that he's all right ... he looks pink and delightful as embryos should.'[31] Largely as a result of Strachey's energetic canvassing, the agreement of the brethren (including the important assent of G. E. Moore) was secured for Hobhouse's election. However, Lytton soon discovered that Hobhouse was much fonder of Maynard than of him; and it was Maynard, in fact, who sponsored the new 'birth' on 18 February 1905. Hobhouse's defection (as Lytton saw it) was a damaging blow to his own feeble sexual confidence. He broke off relations with Maynard. 'He repels me so much,' he wrote to Woolf in Ceylon, 'that I can hardly prevent myself ejaculating insults to his face.'

The election of Hobhouse to the Apostles has been interpreted as marking a new phase in the Society's history, one in which the criterion for election became good looks rather than mental or spiritual qualities. In his autobiography, Bertrand Russell wrote that following a 'long drawn out battle between George Trevelyan and Lytton Strachey ... homosexual relations among the members were for a time common, but in my day they were unknown'.[32] This is not only untrue in general, but is misleading insofar as it refers to the reasons for Hobhouse's election. Perhaps Strachey and Keynes were influenced mainly by his looks, but George Trevelyan favoured his election on different grounds: 'I am immensely glad about Hobhouse,' he wrote to Maynard in February 1905. 'I remember him very well and thought he had a *distinction* of mind which raised him above the other candidates.'[33]

This comment suggests that Hobhouse was more than just a back-woodsman from Somerset, whose brightest feature was his hair. He came from a well-connected Liberal family; his mother, Margaret Potter, had been Beatrice Webb's favourite sister. His father, Henry Hobhouse, was a Liberal M.P. and privy councillor. Before coming to Cambridge Arthur had studied medicine for two years at St Andrews University; at Cambridge he read natural sciences. He later became a lawyer, but would probably have done better to have read Moral Science. But he was never one to do what he wanted to do, or what he might have been good at. He did what was expected of him. The Hobhouses lived by the duties of their class and station; and this was to cripple Arthur, in the opinion of Maynard who had initially sensed something more to him than his yellow hair and aquiline features.

Schoolboy experiments apart, Hobhouse was the first great love of Keynes's life. Over the next seventeen years he had several love affairs with men, one of them of central importance, as well as a certain amount of casual sex. This side of his life was entirely omitted from Roy Harrod's biography. There were good reasons for this at the time. But insofar as he tried to justify the omission he fell back, in private conversation, on the notion that homosexuality was a 'phase' in Keynes's life – a 'delayed adolescence' he called it – out of which he grew, and which did not therefore require attention in its own right. Much of Keynes's early life and beliefs are disposed of by Harrod in this way. And there is this much to be said for his view: that Keynes at forty-five was not the same person as he was at twenty. He was famous and happily married. But this does not mean that a 'phase' which lasted some twenty years was not a central part of his life, crucial to him, and for understanding the kind of person he was.

There is no satisfactory explanation of homosexual tendencies. Both Maynard's brother and sister had bisexual inclinations. But what, if anything, there was in the family situation to produce them in all three is difficult to say. More suggestive is the fact that Maynard, and many young men similarly situated, passed their adolescence and much of their adult life in an environment which excluded women, apart from family, either as companions or as providers of conveniences and comforts. There was little need to break patterns of relationships established at home and at boarding school. Yet surely the break would have been made had the urge to do so been strong enough.

Alienated intellectual ex-public schoolboys sought through homosexuality contact with the normal and uncomplicated. Writing to Sheppard in 1903 about a young subaltern who had taken his fancy, Lytton Strachey observed: 'It is what all of Us – the terribly intelligent, the unhappy, the artistic, the divided, the overwhelmed – most intimately worship, and most passionately, most vainly, love'. It was easy to build on an inaptitude for ordinary human contact an ideology of a higher form of love. Keynes and Strachey had been brought up to believe that women were inferior – in mind and body. Love of young men was, they believed, ethically better than love of women. They built an ethical position – the 'Higher Sodomy' they called it – on a sexual preference. Keynes was fully alive to the dangers of his choice. Oscar Wilde's conviction and disgrace were recent memories. 'So long as no one has anything to do with the lower classes or people off the streets,' he wrote to Strachey on 20 June 1906, 'and there is some discretion in letters to neutrals, there's not a scrap of risk – or hardly a scrap.' In their letters to each other there was less need for discretion. Keynes and Strachey felt that later generations would regard them as pioneers, not criminals. They carefully preserved their correspondence and expected that one day its contents would become public knowledge.

By March 1905 Maynard's friendship with Hobhouse had progressed sufficiently for them to plan a 'working holiday' together in Truro. He wrote him a letter on 27 March:

I don't think one realises how very discrete (in the mathematical sense) one's existence is. My doings at school don't seem to have the remotest connection with my doings up here: nor my life in one term with my life in any other.

One's always first cousin to oneself, but the relationship is not much nearer.

I am reading six different books and am making a particular study of the Integral Calculus; I play record rounds of golf and pet my dog. Your company – and the thing would be complete.

I wonder if you are right that I ought to be canvassing for Montagu, and addressing a boy's club on the subject of self-abuse every evening; attending mothers' meetings in the afternoon, and entertaining a kaleidoscopic tea party judiciously composed of improvers and improvés at 4.30pm.

But I admit your point – at least a little of it.

But don't you agree that it is only by becoming respectable yourself that you are likely to make the quality infectious, and that there is more hope of climbing peaks if you organise a walking tour with your friends, than if you pay Messrs Cook and Sons for the first fifty the highways and hedges provide ...?

However – I have been conversing with you for thirty-five minutes precisely and seem to have had most of the conversation.

You know my feelings – I shall know yours in time.

Ever yours

J. M. Keynes[34]

Maynard, who was now coming up to his finals, had just completed his term as President of the Cambridge Union. His farewell speech attacking the Conservative Government was, according to the *Cambridge Review*, 'in the retiring President's best style – cool, logical, yet full of regard primarily, and above all, for the highest and best moral principles of statesmanship. ... We look forward to a great career for him in other circles.'[35] On 30 March he and Hobhouse left for their three-week holiday. In his letters home Maynard emphasised his preparations for the Tripos. On 6 April he wrote: 'I have revised Dynamics & Elliptic, Legendre, and Bessell Functions, and am now engaged upon astronomy – about 6 hours a day.' And on 16 April: 'This is the most industrious week I have had this year. Astronomy finished, Solid Conics, Optics begun. ... I am coming back next Thursday – in the meantime there is nothing to tell you – except that my morning hours would surprise you.' Maynard, a relieved Neville noted, 'seems to be having a quiet but pleasant time.' To Swithinbank Maynard could speak his mind more freely. If Jesus Christ had had to face a competitive examination to elect a Messiah, he wrote him on 18 April 1905, 'we should have heard even more about the generation of vipers and outer darkness and wailings and gnashing of teeth.' He went on:

> I find my chief comfort more and more in Messrs Plato and Shakespeare. Why is it so difficult to find a true combination of passion and intellect? My heroes must feel and feel passionately – but they must see too, everything and more than everything.
> What is there worth anything except passionate contemplation?

Maynard revealed more of the true story of his three weeks at Truro in a letter written on 23 April 1905 from Harvey Road to Lytton Strachey, with whom somewhat wary relations had been restored:

> That episode is over; I wonder if you will ever know exactly what happened. ... I swear I had no idea I was in for anything that would so utterly uproot me. It is absurd to suppose that you would believe the violence of the various feelings I have been through.
> However – perhaps you will gather a little when we meet. All I will say is that for the moment I am more madly in love with him than ever and that we have sailed into smooth waters – for how long I know not. ...
> We had some phenomenal troubles in Truro, which brought their depression with them.
> I was working six hours a day at work I was actively loathing almost the whole time I was at it.
> He – without intermission – was ill in health and attempting to force himself to do more work than he was fit for.
> However, it was – *ethically* – the most valuable three weeks I have ever spent.

From the Royston Golf Club Maynard wrote to Hobhouse on 27 April:

> Despite your treasonable thoughts, I very much want to see you again. Yes, I have a clever head, a weak character, an affectionate disposition, and a repulsive appearance. My latest disease is novel reading; I have not had an attack for years, and now it has come to find me absolutely defenceless. . . .
>
> Anyhow get well, keep honest, and – if possible – like me. If you never come to love, yet I shall have your sympathy – and that I want as much, at least, as the other.
>
> Your importunate, affectionate,
>
> JMK

Hobhouse had not allowed any physical intimacies at Truro; as he later told Lytton Strachey's brother James, 'Whenever his [Keynes's] demonstrations of feeling became very intense I couldn't help suffering a revulsion in mine'. Maynard remembered that 'he [Hobhouse] used to lead me on with one hand, and then every three days tell me, for the sake of honesty and sincerity and to show he was apostolic, that he hated me.' On the anniversary of the Truro holiday, Keynes wrote Hobhouse a letter which he signed 'Your constant true love, JMK.' Memories of Truro still brought tears to his eyes; he doubted whether a second affair could ever have all the supremacies of a first. But gradually the intensity of his feeling faded in face of Hobhouse's limitations. 'He simply does not know what the thing means,' he told Lytton Strachey; he was 'devoid of passion'. This may have attributed to Hobhouse an innocence he did not possess; he was adept at masking his understanding.

One of Maynard's most useful traits was his ability to switch off the last subject completely when his mind needed to be given to the next. With the approach of the Tripos, Hobhouse was banished from his mind as the Harvey Road examination machinery went into action. His father resumed his familiar role. 'Maynard has planned out his work very methodically. There is a great amount of ground to be covered.' By 11 May Neville was starting to feel depressed; on 15 May, the Tripos started. 'I went round to Maynard's room early to make sure he was getting up.' Neville followed his son's progress with growing anxiety. He did badly in Geometry, but better in Algebra and Trigonometry. Optics and Astronomy were poor, as were Hydrostatics, Heat and Electricity. Problems were a disaster. At the end of the first week Neville was 'feeling very tired & depressed. . . . I think he is going to do badly, & I am oppressed by the idea that I ought not to have encouraged him to read mathematics at all. He has throughout found the subject irksome.' A week's pause now followed, filled with strenuous revision. 'What he finds difficult is not the intellectual effort but the moral effort necessary to due concentration of attention.' Neville was still going to King's every morning to get him up. 'He has drawn out a plan of final revision that gives him no time to spare, & he is already a little behind with it. He is certainly working hard now.... Page is working still harder.' On Saturday Maynard was revising Electricity and Elliptic Functions; on Sunday, Integral Calculus. By Monday, his father was exhausted.

The second part of the examination started on Tuesday 30 May, Neville again coming in to get Maynard up each morning. On Friday he found him in his bath twenty-five minutes before the paper was due to start. The examination finished with Problems on Saturday at which Maynard did not do well. At last it was all over. 'Maynard thinks he may be as high as twelfth wrangler; but I am afraid he is too sanguine.' Maynard had judged his final sprint to perfection. In his three years as an undergraduate he had done all he wanted, and still managed to come out twelfth wrangler, four below the blinkered Page. 'On the whole we are satisfied,' a relieved Neville wrote 'though the boy might of course have done better had he devoted himself more exclusively to his mathematics. Most people congratulate me, a few condole (having expected him to get a Fellowship place). At King's they appear to be very well pleased....' Neville could not quite reconcile himself to the result: 'I fancy Maynard was not very well or wisely taught for Tripos purposes....'[37] In fact, Maynard had followed his father's programme almost to the letter. That he would not be a top wrangler had always been foreseen. Mathematics could finally be put aside for more interesting intellectual pursuits. On 28 June 1905 he started work on Marshall's *Principles of Economics*.

6 My Early Beliefs

G. E. MOORE AND *PRINCIPIA ETHICA*

On 9 September 1938 Maynard Keynes read a paper to Bloomsbury's Memoir Club called 'My Early Beliefs'. It was published posthumously by his friend David Garnett in 1949 and is also reproduced in volume x of his *Collected Writings*. It is a key document for understanding his life's work; and that for one main reason. He was close enough to the 'believing' generation to have a need for 'true beliefs'. This is perhaps the characteristic of his age which separates it most strikingly from our own. It is not so much that we have lost our beliefs as that we have lost the belief in the possibility of having true beliefs. And this must mean that our beliefs make less claim on us. The importance Keynes attached to the discovery of true beliefs, the amount of intellectual attention he devoted to the relation between belief and action, the constant need he felt for justifying his actions by reference to his beliefs, all presuppose a mental outlook which has virtually disappeared, except among Marxists. It was an outlook which also enabled Keynes to exert moral authority. His calculations and actions were in the service of ends he believed to be true.

Philosophy provided the foundation of Keynes's life. It came before economics; and the philosophy of ends came before the philosophy of means. Keynes's philosophy was worked out between 1903 and 1906, in his last two years as an undergraduate, and in his first and only postgraduate year. It was elaborated mainly in the circle of the Apostles, being conceived as a set of answers to the questions which chiefly interested them. Fortunately we do not have to rely entirely on his 1938 paper for an account of what that philosophy was. A number of essays and fragments have survived from these early years, in which we see him wrestling with the problems of value and conduct, his solutions to which are given retrospectively, not always accurately, and certainly not completely, in his Memoir Club paper.

The heart of this paper is an account of G. E. Moore's *Principia Ethica*, and the effect it had on him. His testimony on the latter point is unequivocal. 'Its effect on *us*,' Keynes said, 'and the talk which preceded and followed it, dominated, and perhaps still dominates, everything else.' He went on, 'It was exciting, exhilarating, the beginning of a new renaissance, the opening of a new heaven on earth.' These were not retrospective judgments. A few days after the publication of *Principia Ethica* he wrote to Swithinbank (7 October 1903): 'it is a stupendous and entrancing work, *the greatest* on the subject'. And on 21 February 1906 he wrote to Lytton Strachey: 'It is *impossible* to exaggerate the wonder and *originality* of Moore; people are beginning to talk as if he were only a kind of logic chopping eclectic. Oh why can't they see. How amazing to think that only we know the rudiments of a true theory of ethic; for nothing can be more certain that the broad outline is true.'

Moore's *Principia Ethica* was a product of a time, place and personality. In philosophic terms, it can be seen as a continuation of the enterprise of moral philosophy from the point where Sidgwick had left it, which was in a mess. It inherited the problems which had given rise to Sidgwick's project, and tried, where Sidgwick felt he had failed, to overcome them – the problems of a Godless universe ushering in a 'cosmos of chaos', of the inadequacy of Hedonistic Utilitarianism, of the demand for a philosophy which would lighten the burden of conventional morality. Whether Moore made any real progress, or whether it was the case that 'what Sidgwick portrays as a failure Moore takes to be an enlightening and liberating discovery',[1] is a question which lies behind practically all the questions which need to be asked about Keynes's life and work. For the moment, it is enough to note that Moore's disciples did feel that he had made progress, and in so doing had provided them with the 'rudiments of a true theory of ethic'.

The demand, which Moore's theory supplied, was for a rational justification of a rearrangement of values, such that duties could be attached to goods which the Apostles felt were valuable rather than to those which society felt were useful. A shift in outlook which had already occurred among the Cambridge Apostles was waiting to be legitimised. Moore's book was more a result of this shift than its cause, though he provided the rational weapons for its defence and reinforcement. The change in outlook has been amply documented, most notably in a paper which Desmond MacCarthy read to the Society in December 1900. In it he contrasted his generation's attitude to life with that of its Apostolic predecessors. The key difference was that his generation took 'everything more *personally*' than they did. 'We see the relations of men to each other and to other aims on the whole less broadly.' The change was due, MacCarthy explained, to 'all institutions, the family, the state, laws of honour, etc., which have a claim on the individual . . . having failed to produce convincing proofs of their authority'. He went on:

But there is another characteristic, which is the result of a shaken belief in rules of thumb and the usual aims in life, which also contributes directly to the greater interest taken in personal relations.

They [the previous generation] did *not* trust their immediate judgments as completely as we do, which simplified for them the social as well as the other relations in life. They had more rules which they trusted to instead.... Hence an apparent paradox, that though they did not analyse so much, they trusted their eyes less and we who do analyse more also trust our eyes more.

MacCarthy is making the very important point that the more one analyses, and the more one's analysis disintegrates the 'rules of thumb' and 'usual aims in life', the more one is forced to rely on 'immediate' judgments of value to orient oneself to one's fellows. But such 'immediate' or what we would now call 'intuitive' judgments have precisely the effect of cutting one off from 'broad' aims and turning one towards a shared companionship with those who share one's own particular 'intuitions'. It was the increased importance of the 'state of personal relations at any particular time' in relation to 'their other aims' that MacCarthy found to be the distinguishing feature of the brethren of his day. 'The previous generation did not think less *of* their friends; but they thought less about them, not less of friendship, but less of intimacy.'[2] Moore's achievement was to provide a particular kind of language for justifying this shift, for making people comfortable with it.

Moore's own personality played a vital part in this achievement. Leonard Woolf called him a 'great man, the only great man I have ever met'.[3] He was honoured not just for his qualities of mind, but for his charisma. Indeed, his single-minded dedication to the pursuit of truth was part of that charisma. He was the son of Daniel Moore, a doctor, and Henrietta Sturge a descendant of one of the Quaker families of the Clapham Sect. Educated at Dulwich College in South London, he 'caught' religion so intensely at the age of thirteen that for two years he would ask of all doubtful cases, 'What would Jesus do?' The loss of his Christian faith was so traumatic that he determined thereafter to question all propositions. In 1892 he came up to Trinity College, Cambridge, on a classics scholarship. After two years he switched to the moral sciences, and in 1898 won a prize fellowship at Trinity with a dissertation on Kant.

Moore was elected an Apostle in 1894. From the beginning his combination of looks, philosophising passion, and obliviousness to ridicule, had an explosive effect on the Society. 'He was in those days beautiful and slim,' writes Russell, 'with a look almost of inspiration, and with an intellect as passionate as Spinoza's. He had a kind of almost exquisite purity.'[4] The theme of Moore's opening remarks to the Apostles was that 'we should spread scepticism until at last everybody knows that we can know absolutely nothing'. At this point he was overcome with hysterical laughter. 'We all felt electrified by him,' Russell continued to his fiancée Alys Pearsall Smith, 'as if we had slumbered hitherto and never realised what fearless intellect pure and unadulterated really means.' Three days later Russell wrote to Alys: 'I find it impossible either to like or dislike him, because I have seen no trace of humanity in him yet: but there is an odd exhilaration in talking to him: his criticism is like the air of the High Alps.'[5]

Moore's scepticism was directed against both Idealism, represented in the Society by McTaggart and Lowes Dickinson, and the Utilitarian tradition bequeathed by Sidgwick. In the McTaggart–Dickinson version of Idealism, the Absolute was 'a state of communion of immortal souls in the perfect love of friendship'.[6] Moore had no objection to this as an ideal – in fact his own Heaven was very similar – but he could not accept a style of philosophising which attempted to deduce it from the existence of an unknowable world: a theistic philosophy with God left out. Moore was equally disenchanted with the language and mood of Utilitarianism. This comes out in a comment on the Fabian Graham Wallas whom he met in 1896: 'A beastly fool ... everything is to subserve his wretched utility – educating the masses! Educating them for what? He cannot tell you. He is the blind leader of the blind. ...'[7]

Moore's mistrust of social and political passions was in line with the change towards introspection described by MacCarthy, but was carried to extreme lengths. 'It is remarkable,' Keynes wrote in his 1938 paper, 'how oblivious he managed to be of the qualities of the life of action and also of the pattern of life as a whole.' On 24 February 1894 Charles Percy Sanger read a paper to the Society called 'Which Wagner?' – the composer Richard or the economist Adolf, art or world-improvement. Sanger, McTaggart, and Moore supported the cause of art, Moore, according to Russell, 'because he is a Stoic and thinks happiness doesn't depend on externals such as food or clothing'. Russell was on the other side. He thought that 'fine emotions were to be got out identifying yourself with a great movement, *even if it did have some practical utility*' (my italics).[8] Interestingly, Sanger became an economist, and was to encourage Maynard's interest in statistics. But he did not see economics as a means to welfare, advising Russell to stick to philosophy. 'The few poeple who, like myself, think that it [economics] ought to be a science naturally do not much mind whether it means anything or not.'[9] Such attitudes were far removed from Marshall's 'earnestness'.

The secret of Moore's power as a philosopher was his literalness of mind. He took words seriously, especially the words used in everyday language. When people called something good or bad, beautiful or ugly, intelligent or stupid, he thought they meant just that, not something else; they were referring to *things* which were as real as any natural objects. Keynes wrote, 'Moore had a nightmare once in which he could not distinguish propositions from tables. But even when he was awake, he could not distinguish love and beauty and truth from the furniture. They took on the same definition of outline, the same stable, solid, objective qualities and commonsense reality.'[10] It was only by holding onto the truth that words meant exactly what they said that Moore felt one could make progress in philosophy; that by exposing the tricks which philosophers play with words one could expose the falsity of the systems constructed on the tricks. The motto from his *Principia Ethica* was taken from Bishop Butler: 'Everything is what it is, and not another thing.' The effect of Moore's methods of argument were devastating. 'What exactly do you mean?' was his favourite question; and if he got an unclear answer he would assume an air of amazement that anyone could be so idiotic. As Keynes remarked, he was adept in his use of the 'accents of infallibility'.[11] His stream of expostulations, his violent shaking of the head, his desperate attempts to light his pipe were all integral parts of his philosophical performance. With the aid of his pipes, his gestures, his tone, and his arguments, Moore exorcised the spirit of Idealism from Cambridge. McTaggart was defeated, but unrepentant. He stuck to his Idealism for the comfort it gave him. All he would say was 'Well, anyway, I'm sure Moore is wrong.'[12] Lowes Dickinson gave up philosophy altogether. 'I'm fagged to death,' he wrote to R. C. Trevelyan in 1898, 'the result of a metaphysical talk with Moore. What a brain that fellow has! It desiccates mine! Dries up my lakes and seas ... in arid tracts of sand.'[13]

Paul Levy was right to notice that much of Moore's authority derived from his character, which had in it something of the Divine Simpleton. He had a childlike capacity for total absorption in the activity of the moment, whether is was philosophising, singing German lieder in a light tenor, or playing the piano or fives. He had no small talk: all statements were taken with immense seriousness. He had no sense of fancy: his mind, as Keynes put it, was unadorned. Equally impressive was the agony which his thought processes gave him, the anguish he suffered if he failed to communicate something which seemed to him supremely important. 'Only a passionate sense of duty,' Keynes wrote to Lytton Strachey on 16 March 1906, 'could persuade him [Moore] to produce [his paper on 'Objects of Perception']. When one reads some philosophy, the pleasure of the writer is obvious. But this is not like that. It is wrung out, squeezed with pain and contortion through a constipated rectum.' There is an account of Moore at a philosophical conference tearing his hair in despair. 'Look here!' he cried. All looked while Moore tapped the table with ferocious fingers. 'This table does not exist. IT DOES NOT EXIST.' Levy has emphasised Moore's innocence. He confessed to the Society that when he came up to Cambridge he did not know that there would be a single man there who fornicated, or that sodomy was ever practised in modern times.[14] Knowledge that these things went on in Cambridge did not change his attitude to them. He remained a Puritan. Good states of mind always seemed to him to involve much pain. Such a man was easy to revere, difficult to feel cosy with. 'He is too remote for ease or intimacy,' Keynes wrote to Strachey on 20 December 1905, 'but one could hardly treat him as a stranger.' And a little later (25 January 1906), 'Moore has, for me become too mythical for inclusion in the list [of lovable Apostles]. I seem to know him by description only, and he lives with Socrates, Shakespeare, and Tomlinson – the trinity of our holy faith.'

Principia Ethica was written with all the sense of struggle, vehemence of utterance, and passionate desire to convince which marked Moore's conversation:

Philosophical questions are so difficult, the problems they raise are so complex, that no one can fairly expect, now, any more than in the past, to win more than a very limited assent. And yet I confess that the considerations I am about to present appear to me to be absolutely convincing. I do think that they *ought* to convince if only I can put them well. In any case I can but try. *I shall* try to put an end to the unsatisfactory state of affairs, of which I have been speaking.[15]

Moore's method of arguing his points was, like Strachey's vocal cadences, so distinctive that it was hard for people under his spell not to start thinking and talking like him. The flavour of that style, and also something of the argument, is conveyed in a passage from a paper Strachey read to the Apostles, in which Moore's unmistakable accents are heightened by parody:

there remain to be considered the evils likely to be produced by the extreme proximity of two bodies. The question as to whether the sexual emotions are not bad in themselves is immensely complicated by the great variety of such emotions. It is certain that they are sometimes bad; but they seem to be less bad in proportion as they lose the characteristics of what I am obliged to call, for want of a better term, pure lust. Pure lust is I think best seen in the case of self-abuse; nor can I imagine what the state of mind of a person abusing himself is other than very bad. But the characteristic which distinguishes this state of mind from other states of sexual feeling is that it is peculiarly devoid of fervent emotion, that it is on the contrary coldly deliberate, and that it is only exciting with the sort of excitement which is present in the scratching of an itching sore. The form of sexual emotion furthest from this – the most fervent, the least deliberate, the most exciting – is undoubtedly to be found in the sort of love which is depicted in Romeo and Juliet; and surely it is true that the feelings of Romeo and Juliet are good in themselves, in spite of the fact that they are certainly sexual.[16]

There were four main building blocks in Moore's ethical system. The first was the notion of the indefinability of good. Good is the name of a simple, indefinable, non-natural property, analogous to 'yellow', which can be identified only by direct inspection or intuition. It is indefinable because, Moore argues, it can be shown that any attempt to define it – that is, to make it mean something else like 'pleasant' or 'beautiful' or 'more evolved' – breaks down. Of any state of affairs which is one of these things it can always still be asked whether it is good. Attempts to identify good with such other properties Moore called 'the naturalistic fallacy'. Much of the ground for these assertions had already been laid by Sidgwick. According to Sidgwick, the proposition 'pleasure is the sole good', which Sidgwick held to be true, was unprovable: it was mankind's 'intuition'. Moore's counter-argument was that it was not mankind's intuition.[17] Common to both Sidgwick and Moore is the abandonment of the attempt to ground Hedonism in the facts of human nature – to infer what is desirable from what is desired. Moore just carries the process further by breaking the link Sidgwick had tried to keep between goodness and happiness. He threw out the baby with the bathwater.

Moore's second building block is the assertion, in his famous last chapter 'The Ideal', that the only things valuable in themselves are states of mind, of which the most valuable are 'the pleasures of human intercourse and the enjoyment of beautiful objects'.[18] Of the many implications of this view, one which may be immediately noticed is that mental states are given clear priority over states of action. Action itself can never be intrinsically good, but at best a means to good states of mind.

The third element in Moore's system is the doctrine that right action is aimed at bringing about desirable states of affairs – at the limit those ultimately valuable states of consciousness.[19] In defining right actions as actions which do good rather than actions which are good, Moore gives a Utilitarian justification of duty. He has been called an 'ideal Utilitarian'. He rejected Egoism, the doctrine which held that action should be aimed at 'my own good', by pointing out that it is self-contradictory: each man's good cannot be the sole good.[20] Thus Sidgwick's insoluble conflict between Rational Egoism and Rational Benevolence is illusory: the sole good cannot be egoistic in character.

At the same time Moore undermines much of the force of this conclusion by asserting that egoistic action is generally the right means for the attainment of the universal good: 'Egoism is undoubtedly superior to Altruism as a doctrine of means: in the immense majority of cases the best thing we can do is to aim at securing some good in which we are concerned....'[21] The main reason Moore gave for this choice – the impossibility of calculating the remote and indirect consequences of action – also led him to argue that present or immediately realisable goods are to be preferred to future ones and that in many cases the best Utilitarian results are to be achieved by following the rules of common sense morality. Moore's position on practical Ethics can be described as Utilitarian in aim, Egoistic and Common Sense in method: a position which is identical to that of classical economics in its evangelicalised form.

Finally, Moore's view that action should be aimed at bringing about desirable states of consciousness was qualified by the doctrine of organic unities, which stated that the best achievable states of affairs are bound to be 'complex wholes', the value of which do not add up to the sum of the value of their parts.[22] By this he meant that goods which on their own had a zero or even negative value might, in conjunction with intrinsically valuable goods (states of mind), form a whole of greater value than good states of mind on their own. The chief use of the principle of organic unities was to limit the power to sum goodness by reference to isolated states of consciousness on their own. By including in the notion of good states of affairs attributes, including those of action, which were not themselves good, Moore left the door open for the 'usual aims' in life which MacCarthy had talked about. Whether by means of this device he had succeeded in building a secure bridge to other ethical systems was something Keynes and his friends endlessly discussed.

As we have seen the Apostles were looking for an ethic which could direct attention to ends other than the duties set before the Victorian gentleman. This Moore provided for them. He unshackled contemporary ethics from its connection with social utility and conventional morality by locating its ultimate ends in goods which stood apart from the Victorian scheme of life, and by making 'ought' correlative to these goods. By dropping Hedonism and by proclaiming as intrinsically valuable dispositions and states of mind which Mill and Sidgwick had been forced to treat instrumentally he had evaded the problems which had wrecked their attempt at coherence. No one serious about achieving Moore's goods could take Victorian morality entirely seriously again. What Moore had not solved was the problem of how to relate his goods to the practical business of life, most of which had no connection with them. It turned out that Sidgwick's difficulty of effecting a harmony between the private and public sphere, between the good life and the useful life, had not been overcome by Moore: it had merely been restated in a new way.

II

KEYNES AND MOORE

In his 1938 paper to the Memoir Club Keynes gave the following account – and critique – of his 'early beliefs'. The key statement, on which the whole account hinges, is:

> Now what we got from Moore was by no means entirely what he offered us. He had one foot on the threshold of the new heaven, but the other foot in Sidgwick and the Benthamite calculus and the general rules of correct behaviour. There was one chapter in the *Principia* of which we took not the slightest notice [the penultimate chapter 'Ethics in Relation to Conduct']. We accepted Moore's religion, so to speak, and discarded his morals. Indeed, in our opinion, one of the greatest advantages of his religion was that it made morals unnecessary – meaning by 'religion' one's attitude to oneself and the ultimate and by 'morals' one's attitude towards the outside world and the intermediate.[23]

The rest of the paper is an elaboration of this theme. First, Keynes gave an account of Moore's 'religion':

> Nothing mattered except states of mind ... chiefly our own. These states of mind were not associated with action or achievement or with consequences. They consisted in timeless, passionate states of contemplation and communion, largely unattached to 'before' and 'after'.... The appropriate subjects of passionate contemplation and communion were a beloved person, beauty and truth, and one's prime objects in life were love, the creation and enjoyment of aesthetic experience and the pursuit of knowledge. Of these love came a long way first....
> Our religion closely followed the English puritan tradition of being chiefly concerned with the salvation of our own souls. The divine resided within a closed circle. There was not a very intimate connection between 'being good' and 'doing good'; and we had a feeling that there was some risk that in practice the latter might interfere with the former. But religions proper, as distinct from the modern 'social service' pseudo-religions, have always been of this character; and perhaps it was a sufficient offset that our religion was altogether unworldly – with wealth, power, popularity or success it had no concern whatever, they were thoroughly depised.[24]

Although Keynes called the New Testament a 'handbook for politicians' compared with the unworldliness of Moore's Ideal, he makes it clear that he and his friends practised what Moore preached: they

> lived entirely in present experience, since social action as an end in itself and not merely as a lugubrious duty had dropped out of our Ideal, and not only social action, but the life of action generally, power, politics, success, wealth, ambition, with the economic motive and economic criterion less prominent in our philosophy than with St. Francis of Assisi, who at least made a collection for the birds.[25]

As these quotations suggest, Moore's religion was attractive to Keynes in part because he could see it as a latter-day version of the monastic ideal which had excited his admiration as a schoolboy. It was, Keynes points out, suitably austere:

> in our prime, pleasure was nowhere. I would faintly urge that if two states of mind were similar in all respects except that one was pleasurable and the other was painful, there *might* be a little to be said for the former. But the principle of organic unities was against me. It was the general view (though not quite borne out by the *Principia*) that pleasure had nothing to do with the case and, on the whole, a pleasant state of mind lay under grave suspicion of lacking intensity and passion.[26]

'Thus we were brought up,' Keynes concludes, 'with Plato's absorption in the good in itself, with a scholasticism which outdid St. Thomas, in calvinistic withdrawal from the pleasures and successes of Vanity Fair, and oppressed with all the sorrows of Werther.'[27]

Moore's purpose, Keynes pointed out, had been to 'distinguish between goodness as an attribute of states of mind and rightness as an attribute of actions'.[28] Moore's morals, as we have seen, were based on the Victorian compromise between what Keynes called the 'Benthamite calculus' and 'the general rules of correct behaviour'. These morals, Keynes claimed, were rooted in a double error of reasoning. Moore's handling of the probabilistic calculus was 'riddled with fallacies'. And Moore's 'general rules' had little enough sanction behind them except Christian 'hocus-pocus'. These errors were sufficient grounds for repudiating them. Keynes describes his rejection of the morals (as distinct from the religion) of *Principia Ethica* as follows:

> We entirely repudiated a personal liability on us to obey general rules. We claimed the right to judge every individual case on its merits, and the wisdom to do so successfully. This was a very important part of our faith, violently and aggressively held, and for the outer world it was our most obvious and dangerous characteristic. We repudiated entirely customary morals, conventions and

traditional wisdom. We were, that is to say, in the strict sense of the term, immoralists. The consequences of being found out had, of course, to be considered for what they were worth. But we recognised no moral obligation on us, no inner sanction, to conform or obey.[29]

In retrospect Keynes felt that his 'early beliefs' had brought him both gain and loss. The gain was that 'we were amongst the first of our generation, perhaps alone amongst our generation to escape from the Benthamite tradition', with its 'over-valuation of the economic criterion'. This had protected 'the whole lot of us from the final *reductio ad absurdum* of Benthamism known as Marxism'.[30] The loss lay in a 'disastrously mistaken' view of human nature. He and his friends, repudiating original sin, had believed that human beings were sufficiently rational to be 'released from . . . inflexible rules of conduct, and left, from now onwards, to their own . . . reliable intuitions of the good'. This view ignored the fact that 'civilisation was a thin and precarious crust erected by the personality and will of the few, and only maintained by rules and conventions skilfully put across and guilefully preserved'. Secondly, he and his friends had ignored 'certain powerful and valuable springs of feeling', both the blinder passions of the human heart, and 'the many objects of valuable contemplation and communion beyond those we knew of – those concerned with the order and pattern of life among communities and the emotions which they can inspire'.[31]

Keynes's story of his early beliefs did not find unanimous favour either with his own circle or with later writers. Some argued that Moore's doctrine could not have been so naive as Keynes made it out to be; others that Keynes's beliefs could not have been so naive as his account makes them appear. Still others have claimed that Keynes's memoir shows how trivial and immature Cambridge civilisation at the turn of the century had become. One must not forget that his paper was read to a special audience of young and old friends, and certain liberties with strict truth for the sake of effect and amusement would have been natural. Also he was no doubt exaggerating the unworldliness of his generation by way of drawing a contrast with the same kind of young people of the 1930s who were steeped in Marx and Freud. But when all allowances have been made under these heads, people's disquiet with the paper remains. Somehow his account is felt to reduce either Moore's or his own moral stature; or that of both. Three groups of critics can be identified.

The first have been concerned to defend Moore against the view of his philosophy presented by Keynes. Thus Bertrand Russell writes in his autobiography:

The generation of Keynes and Lytton [Strachey] did not seek to preserve any kinship with the Philistine. They aimed rather at a life of retirement among fine shades and nice feelings, and conceived of the good as consisting in the passionate mutual admirations of a clique of the elite. This doctrine, quite unfairly, they fathered on G. E. Moore, whose disciples they professed to be. Keynes, in his memoir 'My Early Beliefs', has told of their admiration for Moore's doctrine. Moore gave due weight to morals and by his doctrine of organic unities avoided the view that the good consists of a series of isolated passionate moments, but those who considered themselves his disciples ignored this aspect of his teaching and degraded his ethics into advocacy of a stuffy girls-school sentimentalising.[32]

Leonard Woolf too writes that Keynes gave a 'distorted picture of Moore's beliefs and doctrine ... and of the influence of his philosophy and character upon us ...'. He goes on:

we were not 'immoralists'; it is not true that we recognized 'no moral obligation on us, no inner sanction, to conform or obey', or that we neglected what Moore said about 'morals' and rules of conduct.... Moore himself was continually exercised by the problems of goods and bads as means of morality and rules of conduct and therefore of the life of action as opposed to the life of contemplation. He and we were fascinated by questions of ... what one *ought* to do. We followed him closely in this as in other parts of his doctrine and argued interminably about the consequences of one's actions, both in actual and imaginary situations.[33]

Paul Levy has adopted a more radical strategy in his biography of Moore. The fact that the Apostles took from *Principia Ethica* 'only that which interested them, which was by no means all it had to offer' shows, in his view, that 'Moore's influence upon them was not importantly doctrinal at all, but personal'. They showed their allegiance to him as a person by proclaiming their allegiance to his ideas, but these ideas were never properly studied. Moorism was an example of the 'cult of personality' in philosophy. Keynes's account had little to do with the main philosophic content of *Principia Ethica*.[34]

A second group is concerned to defend Keynes's reputation from his own account of his beliefs. No one, they say, who really believed what he said he believed could have achieved what he did. Thus Keynes's first biographer, Roy Harrod, while not disputing that Keynes as a young man might have fallen under the spell of Moore's 'cloistered and anaemic' values, with their neglect of duty, regards Keynes's life work as proof that he escaped from them. In his summary of Keynes's 1938 paper he lays great stress on Keynes's own criticisms of *Principia Ethica*. Moorism, in Harrod's eyes, was yet another of those adolescent stages through which his hero passed on the road to maturity.[35]

In this group also comes R. B. Braithwaite, former Knightbridge Professor of Moral Philosophy at Cambridge. He objects to Keynes's statement that he and his friends took 'not the slightest notice' of Moore's chapter 'Ethics in Relation to Conduct'. Like Harrod, Braithwaite feels this remark is inconsistent with Keynes's achievement as a 'humane Utilitarian'. Unlike Harrod, Braithwaite does appear to believe that Moore left a coherent system in which his 'religion' entailed his 'morals'; and that Keynes had simply made a mistake in describing himself as an immoralist. The explanation for this mistake Braithwaite finds in the fact that 'the consequentialist teaching in *Principia Ethica* was no exhilarating novelty, since it was part of the classical Utilitarianism which Keynes had absorbed through his childhood'. Keynes was always a moralist; it was just that later in life his moral practice changed as he came to realise that human beings were less rational than he had believed.[36]

The third line of criticism is represented by the literary critic F. R. Leavis. The starting point of Leavis's remarks – as indeed of Keynes's own paper – was a much earlier attack on Bloomsbury by the novelist D. H. Lawrence who, in the First World War, had been driven 'mad with misery and hostility and rage' by the brittle chatter and irreverence of Keynes and his friends. Leavis finds in Keynes's 1938 paper ample justification for Lawrence's distaste. Moorism as Keynes interpreted it was the expression of the immature culture of an undergraduate coterie masquerading as a new civilisation. The telling point, in Leavis's eyes, was how little the mature Keynes repudiated it:

Keynes, looking back, describes the intellectualities of the coterie and its religion with a certain amused irony; but it is not the detached irony of a mature valuation. Still in 1938 he takes them seriously; he sees them, not as illustrating a familiar undergraduate phase which should in any case be left behind as soon as possible, and which the most intelligent men should escape, but as serious and admirable – even, it would seem, when cultivated well beyond undergraduate years.... Of course, Keynes criticizes the 'religion' for its deficiencies and errors. But he can't see that, 'seriously' as it took itself, to be inimical to the development of any real seriousness was its essence.

Leavis concludes with a question:

Keynes was a great representative Cambridge man of his time. Cambridge produced him, as it produced the 'civilization' with which he associated himself and which exercised so strong a sway over metropolitan centres of taste and fashion. Can we imagine Sidgwick or Leslie Stephen or Maitland being influenced by, or interested in,

the equivalent of Lytton Strachey? By what steps, and by the operation of what causes, did so great a change come over Cambridge in
so comparatively short a time? ... The inquiry into which the second
[question] would lead, if seriously pursued, would tell us about a
great deal more than Cambridge.[37]

Though the critics are right to feel disquiet at the story Keynes told,
only Harrod and Leavis get close to the biographical problem the paper
poses. Levy is simply wrong to say that Keynes was not interested in
the logical status of Moore's arguments. The inside covers of Keynes's
own copy of *Principia Ethica*[38] are covered with pencilled notes, chiefly
about the difficult question of 'indefinability of good'; also Levy has not
seen Keynes's papers and notes in the Marshall Library dealing with
this subject, Egoism, and many other *philosophical* matters arising from
Principia Ethica, to be discussed in the next section. Russell, Woolf, and
Braithwaite are all concerned to assert that Moore's ethics or religion
did entail socially-concerned conduct; and, by extension, gave a war-
rant for Keynes's later preoccupation with economic reform. But this
ignores the crucial point that Moore provided no logical connection
between ethical goodness and political, social or economic welfare:
economic welfare, for example, is clearly not the *same* as ethical goodness; and there is nothing in Moore's argument to show that it is a
necessary condition of it. Any link between the two has to be supported
by further argument from outside Moore's system. To the extent that
Russell and Woolf were able to busy themselves with problems such as
preventing war or ending colonialism they were drawing, no doubt
sensibly, on older moralities. But this makes them Moorites and something else. Harrod does recognise that Moore failed to provide a complete ethical system, but falls into error when he implies that Keynes
outgrew Moore. Of course it was easier to live a 'Moorite' life as a
young man. But Keynes always remained a Moorite, though even as
an undergraduate he was never exclusively so.

Leavis's remarks draw attention to a point already made – that
Moore's philosophy was very much a product of time and place. By
the 1890s the Victorian reform movement had run out of steam,
without making political reaction any more reputable. Social stress
had been relieved, but not emotional stress. The times, as Harrod
observed, seemed ripe for new experiments in living. 'Cambridge',
wrote a commentator in the *Times Literary Supplement* of 20 May 1949,
'had, in fact, taken Oxford aestheticism by the neck, given it a good
shake, and turned it into analysable propositions'. Moore's teaching
was also a response to the specific dilemmas of Cambridge moral
philosophy; especially Sidgwick's failure to reconcile public and
private ends, my own good with the world's. Moore abolished the

problem by abolishing the set of ethical goods connected with public life. But anyone whose temperament and upbringing was such as to make him take both Moore's ends (good states of mind) and Sidgwick's end (general happiness) seriously was bound, sooner or later, to discover that Moore had not solved Sidgwick's problem; that the problem of bringing them into a logical relation was, in fact, insoluble with the intellectual tools available. Moore's philosophy was simply a temporary halting-post on the road to the complete disintegration of a unified world-view.

III

KEYNES'S PHILOSOPHIC APPRENTICESHIP

The above account presupposes that Keynes took his moral philosophy seriously; that he felt a need for 'true beliefs'; that he needed to justify his actions by reference to his beliefs; that his actions were in fact influenced by his beliefs. Much of the preliminary evidence for these assertions comes from hitherto unpublished papers and notes dating from his undergraduate and post-graduate years. The best intro- duction to these early writings is from some notes he made between July and September 1905, just after his Tripos examination, which he called 'Miscellanea Ethica':

My scheme of a complete ethical treatise would be somewhat thus: the first division would be twofold – into Speculative and Practical Ethics.

Speculative Ethics would concern itself, in the first instance, with certain quasi-metaphysical or logical questions; it would establish the usage and significance of the more fundamental terms. Out of this would follow an analysis ... of the notion of 'good' in itself. It would, in fact, include (in Moore's words) 'Prolegomena to any future Ethics that can possibly pretend to be scientific'. Moore him- self might be employed (at a small but sufficient salary) to write it under direction.

Upon this basis could be raised a Catalogue Raisonné of fit objects and good feelings. Bad feelings would come in for their share of attention; and there would be very little in the field of experience or of passion, which the writers could not introduce if they had the mind for it.

The nature of beauty and tragedy and love and attitude a man should have towards truth would prove of interest in the discussion, though the conclusions appear in the result no wiser than Aristotle's.

The second division – of Practical Ethics – would concern itself with conduct; it would investigate the difficult question of the probable grounds of action, and the curious connexion between 'probable' and 'ought'; and it would endeavour to formulate or rather to investigate existing general maxims, bearing in mind their strict relativity to particular circumstances. It would also concern itself with the means of producing (*a*) good feelings, (*b*) fit objects. Perhaps this division would be less interesting than that of Speculative Ethics, but it might attempt to answer such questions as the following:–

   (i) the nature and value of virtue
  (ii) the theory and methods of Education
 (iii) the theory and methods of Politics
 (iv) the practical expediency and proper limits of Egoism – i.e., the extent to which we ought to regard ourselves as ends and means respectively
  (v) the exceptions to the rule that truth stands first.

The whole would be printed in Baskerville type and published in 150 volumes.[39]

This passage sufficiently indicates that Keynes's interests were from the first concentrated on the connection between 'speculative' and 'practical' ethics and the problems to which Moore's treatment of these connections gave rise.

His first target was Moore's confusing doctrine of 'organic unities'. Moore had said that 'good states of affairs' were good states of mind *plus* things which were not good in themselves. Thus the states of 'aesthetic enjoyment' and 'personal affections' were said to contain respectively material objects (things of beauty) and mental objects (qualities of intelligence) which it was good to contemplate. Keynes regarded these assertions as perverse: it might be desirable that such objects should exist, but they could not be part of ethical good, which consisted solely of good states of mind. We have it on his testimony that 'one Saturday evening the principle of organic unity was abolished'.[40] When this momentous event took place is not recorded, but it must have been in 1905. Thereafter the Apostles confined the notion of ethical goodness to states of mind alone, and considered their duty to the Universe adequately fulfilled if they attained to a succession of such states – largely conceived as states of being in love – for themselves. In place of the rejected doctrine, Keynes proposed an alternative, based on a distinction between goodness as an attribute of states of mind and fitness as an attribute of objects. His discussion can be followed in a portmanteau quotation from his paper 'A Theory of Beauty' written in September–October 1905 and in his 'Miscellanea Ethica':

Mental states alone are good; those objects which directly inspire good feelings are fit. . . . Corresponding to every good feeling there is a fit object and we may say that . . . a fit object is one the contemplation of which *ought* to give rise to a state of mind which is good.

But the process of specification cannot be reversed; not *all* feelings towards fit objects are good, [even though they may be appropriate]. . . . The *appropriate* feeling must always be the best possible under the circumstances, but it need not, for that reason, be absolutely good.

A Universe, for instance, entirely peopled by persons whose only opportunities lay in appropriate emotions towards dunghills would lack intrinsic value. It would be better, no doubt, than if all the inhabitants were to be persons of inaccurate taste in the matter of dunghills, but I dispute its absolute worth. An ugly or unfit object, is therefore, one towards which the appropriate and best possible state of mind is nevertheless bad.

There are, I think, different types of classes of fit objects roughly corresponding to the vulgar use of the words 'beautiful', 'interesting', 'important', 'exciting', 'amusing', 'loveable', 'pitiful' . . . Amongst fit objects, the beautiful forms a large and important class.

I have, in fact, split up the whole Universe of entities that are relevant for ultimate Ethics into two divisions – the feelings of conscious minds, and the objects mental or otherwise towards which these emotions are felt.

In splitting up Moore's organic wholes into the two classes of feelings and objects, Keynes was making a logical point: if only feelings are good, objects cannot be good also. But his argument had a potential bearing on practical ethics: for if good feelings required the presence of fit objects, then it was surely the task of practical ethics to create a universe of them. This consideration was reinforced by the importance which Keynes, following Moore, attached to *true* belief as an attribute of goodness. Truth was a necessary, but not sufficient, condition of a good state of mind.

Keynes next turned to another problem. Given that ethical good consists solely of states of mind, should our aim be to improve our own states of mind or the state of mind of the Universe? Moore had claimed that the latter was the only rational ethical aim; he rejected rational egoism as an end. But this rejection, Keynes claimed, rested on assertion only. Against it were two powerful arguments. First 'as we never have the opportunity of direct inspection [of other people's states of mind], it is impossible to tell what kinds of action increase the goodness of the Universe as a whole' ('Miscellanea Ethica', 6 August 1905). Secondly, Moore has failed to provide any rational grounds of obligation to pursue the universal good if it is at the expense of one's own good. The second was the position Keynes argued in his paper on 'Egoism' read to the Apostles in 1906. The egoist, Keynes said, 'denies that he ought, on occasion, to make himself *bad* in order that others may be good'. The flavour of his argument is captured by the following quotation:

For those who have no faith in the maxims of utilitarianism or in the sanctions of religion and who agree with the general principles of Moore, this is, in my opinion, the crux:– and Moore slurred it over. . . .

Are we not, each of us, an end to ourselves?

Suppose the decree has gone forth: It is good as a means that you should be bad in yourself: Am I to submit? Am I to *choose* to be bad in myself in order that some devils whom I neither know nor care for should wallow in heaven? Am I to go to hell that some stranger may sit at the right hand of God?

It may be that by such action I shall increase the general good, that I shall be *doing* good. But is the obligation to *do* good? Is it not rather to *be* good? . . . Suppose they conflict: which is then to be paramount? . . . I ought to sacrifice my happiness, everything indeed that is mine; but ought I to sacrifice *myself*, my own goodness on the altar of humanity?

The atonement of Jesus Christ was a very bogus business, if we weigh it with the highest claims of the principle of benevolence. Suppose he had freely consented to *become* the devil, in order to save mankind; that would be something to respect him for . . . . But perhaps he was right to hang back from the real crucifixion, the crucifixion of his goodness.

I wonder if in our heart of hearts we would blame a man who chose the most splendid flights of passionate and mutual affection or who elected to sup with Plato and Shakespeare in Paradise, *rather* than linger through eternity in a state of sordid and disgusting pain combined with the lowest and most degraded feelings and with the foulest and most malignant desires . . . although the sacrifice were to lead to the enlightenment of two negroid negroes from Central Africa and to their participation in the paradisiac supper party.

It was Christianity, Keynes said, in unconscious echo of Nietzsche, which had introduced the 'negroid negro question' into morality.

But it is noteworthy [he goes on] that with the exception of Moore the long train of English ethical philosophers have either accepted the paramount authority of Egoism or have expressly reconciled the conflict and harmonised the moral consciousness by invoking the Justice of God or the essentially just order of the Universe. They have even argued to the existence of a God from the alleged necessity of introducing order into the moral chaos. Unless we suppose a God, they say, our common morality is contradictory.

Then comes Moore; and, as I say, the problem arises in its acutest form.

For goodness no longer consists in the formation of character, or in obedience to the laws of God or the so-called Laws of Nature or Categorical Imperatives or Laws of any kind. It is to be found only in certain specific states of consciousness, any one of these states being logically independent of any other.

Despite Moore's claim to have refuted Egoism, my good starts off more clearly differentiated from your good than ever before, and both of our goods from the good of the Universe. In fact if he presses his principle of Organic Unities in its extremest form the good of the Universe has not even a necessary connection with individual goodness.

My goodness and your goodness no longer consist in obedience to a Common Law; my goodness demands that *my* states of mind should be as good as possible, and yours depend upon your states of mind; and there is nothing whatever to prevent these two competing.

Yet Keynes was clearly not happy with a purely Egoistic Ideal:

> There can plainly be no method of solution save that of direct inspection; and, as I tried to show, ... a solution by this method seems peculiarly difficult.
>
> For my goodness and the goodness of the Universe both seem to have a claim upon me and claims which I cannot easily reduce to common terms and weigh against one another upon a common balance.
>
> I am a good friend of the Universe and I will do my best for it: but am I willing to go to the devil for it?

Keynes thus accepted two sets of claims which the Universe might make on the individual which might be in conflict with Moore's injunction that he 'make himself good'. The first had to do with the creation of 'fit objects' which were not good but desirable – e.g. Beauty and Intelligence. (In a 1921 paper he added Justice and Virtue.) The second had to do with making the whole world good, even at the expense of making oneself bad.

As a major practical difficulty in the way of the latter, Keynes had drawn attention to the inadequacy of causal knowledge. This was to be such an important intellectual thread in his life, extending into his economics, that something must be said about it here. In a consequentialist or Utilitarian philosophy, action is aimed at producing certain desirable results. I must therefore have knowledge of the likely consequences of my actions. The question is: what kind of knowledge is necessary for a consequentialist system to be possible? And how is it to be acquired? The answer must be: knowledge of probabilities, since we can never know that our actions will certainly produce the results we aim for: hence the importance of Keynes's phrase in his introduction to 'Miscellanea Ethica' about the 'curious connexion between "probable" and "ought"'. But this raised the question of what was meant by probability.

Keynes's investigation into the meaning of probability was to occupy most of his leisure from 1906 to 1914. But his first discussion on the subject dates from 23 January 1904 when he read a paper to the Apostles entitled 'Ethics in Relation to Conduct'. This makes it clear that his interest arose directly out of the intellectual ferment caused by the appearance of *Principia Ethica*. The paper, which Harrod failed to notice, already contains the main idea of what was to become Keynes's *Treatise on Probability* which was not published till 1921. It is, therefore, of key biographical importance. In order to understand its context one must go back to Moore's argument in his chapter of the same title.

This chapter was, in the main, a justification of accepted rules of conduct, a position which was anathema to Keynes. What Moore says is this. Given the inherent difficulty of calculating the remoter and indirect effects of action, it is rational to aim at our own immediate good; but *only if* there is a reasonable probability that so acting will increase, or at least not diminish, the good of the Universe. To the extent that we are unlikely to have such an assurance, we can do no better in most cases than to follow the existing rules of morality. Thus Moore accepted Egoism as a doctrine of means (though not of ends); but so qualified it by his rationality stipulation as to leave it very little scope. Following accepted rules would, in the majority of cases, bring about the best results possible. Keynes wanted to show that we can do better than that. He wanted to show that we can make a rational probability judgment without possessing the kind of knowledge which Moore seemed to suppose we must possess before we can rationally decide for ourselves what we ought to do. But this attempt involved a redefinition of the meaning of probability.

The text for Keynes's 1904 paper[41] is taken from Moore's argument on pp. 152–3 of his *Principia Ethica*:

we can certainly only pretend to calculate the effects of actions within what may be called an 'immediate' future . . . in general, we consider that we have acted rationally, if we think we have secured a balance of good within a few years or months or days. Yet, if a choice guided by such considerations is to be rational, we must certainly have some reason to believe that no consequences of our action in a further future will generally be such as to reverse the balance of good that is probable in the future which we can foresee. This large postulate must be made, if we are ever to assert that the results of one action will be even probably better than those of another. Our utter ignorance of the far future gives us no justification for saying that it is even probably right to choose the greater good within the region over which a probable forecast may extend.

'Failing such a proof,' Moore concludes, 'we can certainly have no rational ground for asserting that one of two alternatives is even probably right and another wrong.' It is on the difficulty of being able to prove his postulate that Moore bases his justification for 'general rules of conduct'. And this is the point on which Keynes directly engages him. 'It is not obvious,' he writes, 'that any such proof is required before we are able to make judgments of probable rightness.' In other words, for action to be rational we are not required to have any grounds for believing that 'no consequences of our action in a further future will be such as to reverse the balance of good that is probable in the future which we can foresee'. We can act with good conscience in the pursuit of *immediate* good.

Moore's argument, Keynes says, shows that he must have been working with an empirical or frequency theory of probability, according to which a probability statement depends on *certain knowledge* that 'A will happen more often than B'. Such certain knowledge of the far future might well be unattainable. But we need not thereby be reduced to conventional morality. Keynes insisted that something else was meant by the statement 'A is more probable than B'. He continued: 'I mean something of the nature "I have more evidence in favour of A than in favour of B"; I am making some statement concerning the bearing of the evidence at my disposal; I am not stating that in the long-run A will happen more often than B for certain.' And later in the paper Keynes asserts: 'A statement of probability always has reference to the available evidence and cannot be refuted or confirmed by subsequent events.' In other words to say that an action was probably right was not to say that in the long run it would lead to result A more often than to result B. It was to say 'This is the best estimate of results I can form under existing circumstances.' Probability statements were judgments about the bearing of evidence on conclusions, not forecasts of results. Later Keynes was to put this more precisely: probability was concerned with the logical relation between the premise and conclusion of an argument; it was a branch of logic, not of statistics; it was a relation not anything in itself. All this has been of great interest to philosophers; it may even have some bearing on Keynes's economic thought. But its immediate purpose was to cut the moorings which still kept Moore's airship earthbound – grounded in 'Sidgwick and the Benthamite calculus and the general rules of correct behaviour'.

Keynes's argument, then, can be interpreted as an attempt to free the individual to pursue the good (whether he defines that as his own good or the good of the universe) by means of egoistic actions, since he is not required to have certain knowledge of the probable consequences of his actions in order to act rationally. It is part, in other words, of his continuing campaign against Christian morality. This would have been appreciated by his audience, although the connection is not obvious to the modern reader. More generally, Keynes links rationality to expediency. The circumstances of an action become the most important consideration in judgments of probable rightness; rules are not nearly as important as Moore supposed. By limiting the possibility of certain knowledge Keynes increased the scope for intuitive judgment. Such judgment was, of course, applicable not only to ethical action but to all kinds of action.

Keynes's theory of probability provides a logic of action which also enables one to choose which of the possible objects of action is most appropriate in the given circumstances. This is relevant to his view of the connection between ethical and non-ethical ends. Keynes did not believe that political, social and administrative ends were good in themselves; or that they were necessarily good as means; or even if they were good as means that one was obliged to pursue them at the expense of one's own good. But he did think that they had some value in themselves (for example, they might afford pleasure) and that they also had a valid, and perhaps overriding, claim on the individual in certain circumstances. The claims of public life, Keynes might have said, were the claims the Universe makes on the individual as a citizen. It was extremely hard for the son of Neville and Florence Keynes, brought up in a tradition of duty, and endowed with great practical competence, not to feel the force of such claims. They existed outside the Moorean system of ethics, but could be given a Moorite justification under certain circumstances – when, for example, the ordered existence of society, which was the ultimate condition of the possibility of good states of mind, was threatened. If one is looking for the logical link between Moore's ethics and Keynes's economics it is in this area that the search must be made. It is important to remember, though, that the connection for Keynes was never mechanical, always problematic.

Keynesian economics was conceived, above everything, as a contribution to the art or science of statecraft. Keynes never wrote a treatise on politics, but in his papers there is a 99-page undergraduate essay on 'The Political Doctrines of Edmund Burke'.[42] This is his most extended treatment of the 'theory and methods of politics'. It was submitted for the University Members Prize for English Essay in November 1904 and duly won it. Keynes's interest in Burke dated from his time at Eton. If by no means an uncritical admirer – he attacked the extremism of Burke's reaction to the French Revolution – nevertheless he did think Burke one of the great political thinkers of all time. If Moore was Keynes's ethical hero, Burke may lay strong claim to be his political hero. Certainly he was the only one he ever acknowledged as such.

The science of politics, for Burke, was a 'doctrine of means' designed to attain the 'sole and ultimate end' of government, which Keynes variously summarises as 'general happiness', 'the wide dissemination of comfort', the 'general advantage' and 'equity' (Keynes virtually ignored Burke's treatment of the last aim). Politically Burke 'may, without serious inaccuracy be described as a utilitarian; but ethically he can in no way be said to have anticipated his distinguished contemporary [Bentham]'. Keynes makes the following comment on Burke's political theory:

> He did not much believe in political ends good intrinsically and in isolation. The happiness of the people was his goal, and the science of government worthless except in so far as it guided him to that end. Whatever the doctrines of utilitarianism may be worth abstractedly [sic] . . . they do not offer an unsatisfactory basis to a political theory. The tastes and the emotions, good feeling and right judgment, these government cannot directly do much to foster and develop on any scheme or theory. Physical calm, material comfort, intellectual freedom are amongst the great and essential means to these good things; but they are the means to happiness also, and the government that sets the happiness of the governed before it will serve a good purpose, whatever the ethical theory from which it draws its inspiration.

Keynes thought that the most important consequence of Burke's political utilitarianism was his championship of 'expediency against abstract right' – whether these were the rights claimed by revolutionaries or counter-revolutionaries. Burke's most famous political stand on this maxim, his opposition to the coercion of the American colonies, put him, in Keynes's view, into the ranks of the 'very great', and he quotes him approvingly: 'The question with me is, not whether you have a right to render your people miserable, but whether it is not your interest to make them happy. It is not what a lawyer tells me I *may* do, but what humanity, reason and justice tell me I ought to do.' Keynes notices that a corollary of this attitude was Burke's 'extreme timidity in introducing present evils for the sake of future benefits', a principle, he thought, 'often in need of emphasis':

> Our power of prediction [Keynes writes] is so slight, it is seldom wise to sacrifice a present evil for a doubtful advantage in the future. Burke ever held, and held rightly, that it can seldom be right to sacrifice the well-being of a nation for a generation, to plunge whole communities in distress, or to destroy a beneficent institution for the sake of a supposed millenium in the comparatively remote future. We can never know enough to make the chance worth taking, and the fact that cataclysms in the past have sometimes inaugurated lasting benefits is no argument for cataclysms in general. . . . It is the

paramount duty of governments and of politicians to secure the well-being of the community under the case in the present, and not to run risks overmuch for the future. . . .

In addition to the risk involved by any violent method of progress, there is this further consideration that is often in need of emphasis: – it is not sufficient that the state of affairs which we seek to promote should be better than the state of affairs which preceded it; it must be sufficiently better to make up for the evils of the transition.

Thus while criticising Burke for not seeing the potential good in the French Revolution, Keynes insisted that 'Even at the present time it is difficult to deny that another method milder both in its methods and in its immediate achievements might have been productive of incalculably greater good for Europe.'

Keynes strongly supported Burke's 'timidity' in embarking on war – 'with much prudence, reverence, and calculation must it be approached', he quotes, and endorses his flexible attitudes to *laissez-faire* and the functions of government. He admires Burke's readiness to bring into power people of weight and character – 'The machine itself he believed to be sound enough if only the ability and integrity of those in charge of it could be assured' – and has sympathy with his defence of establishments and reverence for organic growths. But Keynes often felt that Burke's timidity prevented him from doing full justice to his principle of expediency: it was true that society was a seamless web 'but Burke was often as anxious for the outworks as for the central structure itself'. An example of this was the lengths to which he carried his defence of existing property arrangements. Keynes cited his arguments against redistribution of wealth, but thought he carried them much too far. While agreeing with Burke that men have no right to direct self-government, since they have rights only to what is reasonable and for their own benefit, he derided Burke's dream of a 'representative class' and thought that democracy had important 'educational powers'. Keynes's assumptions about the character of the democracy of his day are important for understanding what he thought government could achieve in the way of successful economic management, so it is interesting to read the 1904 reflections:

Democracy is still on its trial, but so far it has not disgraced itself; it is true that its full force has not yet come into operation, and this for two causes, one more or less permanent in its effect, the other of a more transient nature. In the first place, whatever be the numerical representation of wealth, its power will always be out of all proportion; and secondly the defective organisation of the newly enfranchised classes has prevented any overwhelming alteration in the preexisting balance of power.

Burke's philosophy, Keynes concluded, must be explained by his particular genius and temperament:

> His goods are all in the present – peace and quiet, friendship and affections, family life, and those small acts of charity whereby one individual may sometimes help his fellows. He does not think of the race as marching through blood and fire to some great and glorious good in the distant future; there is, for him, no great political millenium to be helped and forwarded by present effort and present sacrifice.... This may or may not be the right attitude of mind. But whether or not the great political ideals that have inspired men in the past are madness and delusion, they have provided a more powerful motive force than anything which Burke has to offer.... For all his passions and speechmaking, it is the academic reasoner and philosopher who offers us these carefully guarded and qualified precepts, not the leader of men. Statesmen must learn wisdom in the school of Burke; if they wish to put it to any great and difficult purpose, the essentials of leadership they must seek elsewhere.

Moore and Burke: Keynes's life was balanced between two sets of moral claims. His duty as an individual was to achieve good states of mind for himself and for those he was directly concerned with; his duty as a citizen was to help achieve a happy state of affairs for society. The two claims he thought of as logically independent of each other. He attached greater priority to the first than to the second, except when he thought the state was in danger. He was as timid about his expectations of realising good states of mind on a large scale as he was bold in his expectations about the amount of happiness or utility a government could deliver. In both sides of his moral thinking he gave priority to immediate goals over future ones, reinforced in this by his theory of probability: rational actions were the best possible in the circumstances. The duty of the state was to realise happiness and not ultimate goods, though the latter might follow as an indirect consequence of the former. He was thus both an aesthete and a manager. But he rejected the role of therapist, believing that truth took priority over expediency.

A final aspect of Keynes's considerations of ethical problems deserves notice. What kind of personality, and of vocation, had the highest ethical value? He tended to see human beings as embodiments of types or states of mind – the Artist, the Scientist, the Businessman, the Politician, the Philanthropist. He was interested in the relation between appearance and character, beauty and intelligence. These discussions are coloured by a lively sense of his own contradictions. Keynes was (or felt himself to be) an ugly man who worshipped beauty, a scientist who would have preferred to be an artist; a Moorite who got pleasure out of politics and money-making; an intellectual whose habit of analysis kept getting in the way of his feelings. The implied personal references give his reflections on character an added biographical interest.

One of the favourite Apostolic discussions of Keynes's time concerned the relationship of beauty and intelligence; a topic highly relevant to the value of 'states of mind'. Moore had pointed out that 'wherever the affection is most valuable, the appreciation of mental qualities must form a large part of it.... But it seems very doubtful whether this appreciation by itself can possess as much value as the whole in which it is combined with an appreciation of the appropriate *corporeal* expression of the mental qualities in question.'[43] Unfortunately in the experience of the brethren, beauty and intelligence were seldom adequately present in the same person. 'It's that damned law of nature,' Keynes wrote to Lytton Strachey, a fellow-ugly, on 5 November 1905, about Swithinbank. 'I suspect he wouldn't be half so beautiful if he did analyse a little more.' The best Keynes could do was to conclude, comfortingly, that 'the character and the appearance have very little connection with each other'.[44] Analysis was also relevant to the question of beauty of soul: the power to have appropriate feelings. On this matter he wobbled. Simplicity was a 'good complexion of the soul'. He wrote: 'We should all like good complexions – superimposed. But that is the difficulty – they do not come that way, they imply all sorts of other things which if we changed, we must be willing to accept as well.' As for himself, 'I do not want to be good if it precludes me from knowing what's what and, incidentally, what's good.' But perhaps this was a false dilemma after all: analysis, it may be, does not 'kill feeling: it stimulates it'.[45]

Keynes's most extended discussion of personality came in a paper he read to the Apostles on the opposition between Science and Art.[46] He considered this in two aspects. Does excellence in Art require a different cast of mind from that which is necessary for excellence in Science? And, if so, which excellence is more ethically valuable? In developing his answer to these questions Keynes gave his own ranking of human qualities:

> I, the moderator, believe that the scientist should take an intermediate position in the world. It is certain that he spends his time much better than the business man does his. The beauties of argument and the excitement of discovery are not imaginary goods. The life of the business man is partly one of irksome toil and partly one of bridge. The element of bridge comes a good deal into science, but differently. But is it not almost as certain that the good artist stands to the scientist very much as the scientist stands to the stockbroker? Putting moneymaking and capacity aside, is there any brother who would not rather be a scientist than a business man, and an artist

than a scientist? (There are two other classes, of course, the philanth-ropists and the politicians and there is every possible cross and mixture – but we need not discuss these now). This, then, is the first step towards peace, the scientist must admit the artist to be his master.

But, on the other hand, the scientist is nearer in kind to the artist than he is to the stockbroker, and it is not easy to say of some activities to which class they properly belong. The metaphysician, for example, may partake more of the artist's nature than of the scientist's, and certainly he belongs to both. There are few arts also in which there is no science. The scientist is lower than the artist, not because his activity is one of use and not one of value, but first because, probably though not inevitably, his quality is lower, and secondly because he will spend a large part of his time in what has no intrinsic value whatever. Nobody pretends that the ecstasies of the scientist, whatever they may be worth, are very frequent. For the greater part of his life he is busied with the preparations. This is true also, I should suppose, of most artists. But of the two the scientist is occupied for by far the greater proportion of his time with mixing the paints. . . .

There remains the question, assuming that someone else mixes the paints both for the scientist and for the artist, of the *quality* of the two activities. Here too I am inclined to believe that the artist has the advantage. But such a judgment of value is the most doubtful thing possible. I had better try to describe what the activity of the scientist seems to be like.

He is presented with a mass of facts, possessing similarities and differences, arranged in no kind of scheme or order. His first need is to perceive very clearly the precise nature of the different details. . . . He [then] holds the details together clearly before his mind and it will probably be necessary that he should keep them more or less before his mind for a considerable time. Finally he will with a kind of sudden insight see through the obscurity of the argument or of the apparently unrelated data, and the details will quickly fall into a scheme or arrangement, between each part of which there is a real connection. He is dealing with facts regarded as facts, very much as the artist is dealing with perceptions regarded as perceptions. His activity runs the risk of being thought the less valuable on the unfair ground that the result, however useful, has the less intrinsic value for others. But the value of the result is evidently quite a different thing from the value of the process. The value of the activities of Newton or Leibnitz or Darwin existed quite apart from the value or import-ance of their work. It is not easy to have a very clear idea of what, in their working hours, they were like, or to be sure whether or not they were worse than Milton or Wordsworth or Velasquez. I myself would rather choose, I feel, to be any of these three than any one of the scientists.

Philosophy, McTaggart always said, was valuable for the comfort it gave. Through philosophy Keynes reconciled himself to his own nature, and to the world. But that he had discovered the rudiments of a 'true ethic' he never seems to have doubted, even though the grandiose project sketched in his 'Miscellanea Ethica' was never achieved.

7 Cambridge and London

THE WRECKAGE

The only break Maynard allowed himself immediately after taking his Tripos was a long weekend at Eton for the Winchester match where 'the number and quality of the beauties', he told Strachey, 'was incredible'. But he was not interested in them. The state of his brain, he explained, was 'so violent and exciting' that he had become 'almost purely intellectual'; a much more comfortable passion than the one he had experienced at Truro with Arthur Hobhouse.[1] He wrote to Swithinbank on 30 June, 'The ease with which one recovers and takes refuge in Political Economy or whatever it may be, is terrifying and humiliating . . . for the last few days a reactionary love of knowledge has entirely engulfed me. It would be a very comfortable altar on which to sacrifice the love of people – don't you think so?'

On 8 July 1905 Maynard went into residence at King's for three weeks, where he led a 'joyless, painless' existence immersed in economics and moral philosophy. He was convinced that Jevons 'was one of *the* minds of the century. He has the curiously exciting style of writing which one gets if one is good enough.'[2] He also re-read and annotated Moore's *Principia Ethica*. His indifference to the affairs of the heart was maintained despite turbulent communications from Northampton, where Lytton Strachey, locked up at Kettering working on his thesis, had fallen violently in love with his cousin Duncan Grant.

If Lytton's news failed to jolt Maynard out of pure cerebration, still less did the Swiss Alps. Geoffrey Winthrop Young, the Eton master and famous mountaineer, had decided that Maynard's outlook needed broadening. So early in August we find him 9000 feet up at Chamonix 'crossing a beastly glacier in the dark', roped to Young, Robin Mayor, and William Slingsby. Maynard was full of admiration for the 'superb' Young who, dressed in green and with single tortoiseshell monocle, had remained imperturbable even as Mayor disappeared down a crevasse. But he railed against the incompetence of the guides; and the scenery failed to move him. 'What rot all this is about nature', he wrote to Strachey on 11 August. Mountaineering was fit only for 'athletic eunuchs'. To Hobhouse he remarked, on 16 August, that 'except as a cleaner and restorer one must put all the exertion and the kind of excitement in nature in the second rank . . . the pleasures of the intellect and of love do seem to me miles first'. Even a conversation with Mary Sheepshanks, the daughter of a bishop, who had turned up at Montanvert, on the subject of Sapphism, failed to compensate for his 'purely animal existence'. He rejoined his family for a week of picture-gazing in Paris, before returning to Cambridge. 'Now I am back,' he wrote to Hobhouse on 3 September from Harvey Road, 'and am very anxious to read philosophy and economics – as usual I am torn now in this direction and now in that.'

At Harvey Road he settled into his work and golf routine. 'Oh that I had two years clear before me with nothing but to work and make love in, and no career or examination,' he wrote to Hobhouse on 5 September. Three weeks of family life had its usual effect of 'calming the nervous system into non-existent',[3] and on 20 September he set off on a round of visits – to Strachey at Kettering, to Hobhouse at Hapsden, to Daniel Macmillan in Sussex. At Kettering his spirits revived under the 'influence of the perpetual gossip which the new method of conversation entirely consists in'.[4] Strachey had at last despatched his two-volume thesis on Warren Hastings for the consideration of the Trinity Electors. In October the blow fell. 'The wicked dons of Trinity have failed to make me a fellow,' he told Duncan Grant on 9 October. 'Poverty, drudgery, etc, must now be faced.' Despondently he moved into a bed-sitting-room in his London home at 69 Lancaster Gate, prepared to earn his living by writing. He would sit by his gas fire reading books for review and sending long gloomy letters to his friends. Maynard now became his main link with the Cambridge world.

Maynard remained at King's for a fourth year, together with Furness and Fay. On 16 July Neville had written in his diary, 'We have not yet decided whether Maynard shall take Part II of the Moral Sciences Tripos or the Economics Tripos.' Fearing the worst, he had also kept open the legal option, making his son a member of the Inner Temple in London. Maynard started weekly supervisions with Alfred Marshall. But he had by no means decided to become an economist. His main intellectual preoccupation was still moral philosophy: this was the period when he was working on his 'Miscellanea Ethica' and writing a long paper on aesthetics. With Strachey's departure he had also become secretary of the Apostles. Reduced to one undergraduate member, Hobhouse, the Society badly needed fresh blood. Maynard made it his business to put it back on its feet again. Much of his postgraduate year was spent in doing so.

October opened with Swithinbank's arrival from Oxford and the first inspection of 'embryos'. 'Never has a term opened with so fair a prospect', Maynard enthused to Lytton. The dazzling vista comprised three freshmen – Henry Norton and Henry Goodhart who had come to Trinity from Eton, and Lytton's own younger brother James, who had come to Trinity from St Paul's. Maynard felt that Norton, a mathematician, had a 'very good logical kind of mind', even if his person was 'girt about by a writhing mass of aesthetic and literary appreciations, which I have – so far – discovered no means of quelling'. His appearance was 'ordinary public school'. Goodhart's presence was 'very apostolic and so is his mind'. James Strachey was always out. 'There was a wonderful interview with Swithin very late on his last evening,' Maynard told Lytton. 'We got as far as it is possible for pure friendship alone without passion.' As Swithin got into the cab taking him to the station, he leant out and smiled. 'I am leaving heaven,' he said.[5]

The trouble was, Maynard soon discovered, that whatever else it might be, heaven was not Cambridge. The party was over. He felt he was living in a world of leftovers. Fay and Furness were amusing enough companions, but neither was tuned into the Moorite wavelength. Sheppard, who in theory was, lacked what H. O. Meredith called a 'serious bottom'. He complicated Maynard's life by never bothering to prepare papers for the Society when it was his turn to read. Worst of all was Hobhouse. Heading steadily towards his third-class honours in the Natural Sciences, Hobby was an unbearable reminder of misplaced hopes. Even the way he ate butter caused Maynard to shiver with horror, 'and that simply because I used to be in love with him altogether and now ... hate him for what he is. ... He never *adds* anything. He lives according to rules and contorts himself trying to discover them, when of course they don't exist. He is always trying to do what he vaguely thinks ought to be done in such circumstances. He never judges anything individual on its own merits. He tries to do his duty. He proceeds from generals to particulars, instead of from particulars to generals.'[6]

The dazzling prospects which had briefly opened out for the Society soon faded. Norton retained his embryonic status by virtue of his mental qualities. Goodhart sank quickly from sight: 'He is a strong churchman. ... Also he shows the most alarming tendency towards the most incredibly long-winded boring speeches'.*[7] Briefly, his place was taken by Ernst Goldschmidt, 'an Austrian Jew of Dutch extraction ... aged seventeen and a half'. But he was no embryo either, though 'something much more romantic. He is the head prostitute of Vienna. ... Heavens! we live leagues from real life where they really do things in style'.[8] James Strachey was promising, but looked incredibly young, and like

---

* Henry Goodhart-Rendel was to become Slade Professor of Fine Art at Oxford.

his brother, was prone to alarming silences. Maynard tried hard to strike up a conversation with him, but all he could get him to say was 'How is Dickinson?'

At Oxford there were at least Swithinbank and Daniel Macmillan, the latter captivating Lytton when he paid a visit early in November. 'As for the general society,' Lytton reported to Maynard,[9] 'I was as usual struck by the extraordinary gentle politeness of it all, and by the high level of intelligence. Don't you think the Society has probably wrecked Cambridge? The Society apart, where can one find a "push" in Cambridge with an even moderate amount of sense, of cultivation, and of impropriety? It's all or nothing with us, Oxford's the glorification of the half-and-half.'

The two friends often discussed Moorism in this way. Its 'nose to nose' ideal seemed to incapacitate them for life outside the confines of the Society. There must be a 'new method, something that will bring ease, that will allow half and halfdom when there are ten, and the whole hog when there are two,' Maynard replied to Strachey.[10] The tone of Grecian suggestiveness which went down so well with the brothers could also suggest to outsiders a wickedness which Maynard at least was far from feeling. A party which he gave for his brother Geoffrey and Rupert Brooke who had come up in December for entrance scholarships (at Pembroke and King's respectively – which they got) left him feeling 'very misanthropic ... the corruption and effeteness of what is supervening; and my utter helplessness and incapacity of creating the impression I wish'. Hobhouse, Norton, Sheppard, Furness and he had floated round the Rugby schoolboys for five hours. 'It seemed to me,' Maynard went on to Lytton

> that we were trying to drag Rupert and my poor brother in and wrap them in our own filth packet; and that there was a kind of fate which completely frustrated us whenever we tried not to. I want to make a move against our methods – for I don't think we're at all corrupt within. As it is we aren't – en bloc – fit company for the youths.
>
> I tried to make Norton see it, but it was no good.
>
> To begin with one must learn to talk football or politics or metaphysics in general conversation and give up trying to make it an imitation of what one says nose to nose. ...
>
> Hobby broke out this afternoon against the Society; his latest instance was poor Greenwood who persecutes him with a weekly letter, describing his 'states of mind' and what time he gets up in the morning at full and maudlin length.
>
> Certainly there is a good deal of wreckage about. Still it was a glorious civilisation in its day.[11]

At other times his crusading zeal returned. 'The world does want a great moral upheaval,' he told Strachey a few months later. 'Let us arise and found monasteries and make people endow us. The new monastic age would be very like the last – its chief features, the exclusion of women and the largeness of its endowments.'[12] But he was away from Cambridge at the time.

Moribund though his emotional life was, Maynard eagerly responded to intellectual challenges. He found his economics for Marshall exciting. Four folders of his notes and essays have survived, on 'Pure Economics', 'Capital', 'Taxation', and 'Trusts and Railways'.[13] For his theory, he studied the two privately printed papers of Marshall, 'The Pure Theory of Foreign Trade' and 'The Pure Theory of Domestic Values', as well as Jevons, Cournot and Edgeworth. Jevons continued to excite him, and in his notes on 'Pure Economics' he summarises the famous passage from Jevons' *Theory of Political Economy* on the origin of value which he was later to cite as 'simple, lucid, chiselled in stone' in his centenary essay on Jevons in 1936:

> It is often asserted that all objects derive their value from the fact that labour has been expended on them: and it is even implied that value will be exactly proportional to labour.
>
> But labour once spent has no influence on the future value of any article. Jevons, therefore, states his doctrine thus:
>
> Value depends solely on the final degree of utility. How can we vary the degree of utility? By having more or less of the commodity to consume. And how shall we get more or less of it? By spending more or less labour in obtaining a supply.
>
> Cost of production determines supply
> Supply determines final degree of utility
> Final degree of utility determines value
>
> The value of labour is so essentially variable, that its value must be determined by the value of the produce, not the value of the produce by that of the labour.

Marshall was impressed by Maynard's work, scrawling remarks in red ink all over his essays in his large loose writing. Although he found a paper on 'Capital' too logomachic for his taste, he thought Keynes had written a 'brilliant answer' to a question on comparative railway systems. For his part Maynard wrote to Lytton Strachey on 15 November 1905:

> I find economics increasingly satisfactory, and I think I am rather good at it. I want to manage a railway or organise a Trust or at least swindle the investing public. It is so easy and fascinating to master the principle of these things.*

* Harrod quotes from this letter (p. 111) leaving out the remark about swindling the investing public. This is a good example of his cleaning-up technique.

And on 23 November:

> Marshall is continually pestering me to turn professional Economist and writes flattering remarks on my papers to help on the good cause. Do you think there is anything in it? I doubt it.
>
> I could probably get employment here if I wanted to. But prolonging my existence in this place would be, I feel sure, death. The only question is whether a government office in London is not death equally.

Strachey replied on 27 November: 'Oh no, it would surely be mad to be a Cambridge economist. Come to London, go to the Treasury, set up house with me. The parties we'd give. . . .' Marshall's pressure fell somewhat flat, not only because Maynard thought him an 'utterly absurd person',[14] but because, with renewed economic prosperity in the 1900s, social issues no longer seemed so urgent. He was attracted by the prospect of endless gossip with Strachey in London. Besides, he probably felt a need to get away from Harvey Road. A visit to London from 14 to 18 December 1905, when he stayed with Lytton at 69 Lancaster Gate, decided him. On his return he informed his parents that he would abandon the Economics Tripos and concentrate on the Civil Service Examination. Marshall regretted his decision. As late as May 1906 he was still urging Maynard to take the Tripos – 'merely re-reading Economics in the few days before it, you would *probably* get a first-class'.[15] But Maynard was adamant. He never did take an economics degree. In fact, his total professional training came to little more than eight weeks. All the rest was learnt on the job.

On his return from London, Maynard was stirred briefly into political activity by the general election which the minority Liberal government of Campbell-Bannerman had called for January 1906, a few weeks after the Conservative Balfour had given up the hopeless task of trying to run the country with a party so badly split on Protection. The fiscal question was the only one capable of bringing Maynard to political life, and he now spent some days on the campaign trail on behalf of Edwin Montagu in Cambridgeshire and Freddie Guest in Staffordshire (responding there to an appeal from his former University Liberal Club colleague Geoffrey Mander), while Sheppard patted the messenger boys' heads at Liberal headquarters in Cambridge. If the Liberal landslide of 12 January 1906 failed to move him to great enthusiasm it did at least stimulate him to get the Society on to a more political tack. He wrote to Strachey on 20 January 1906:

> I tried a novel breakfast party this morning – Keeling* and Fay; and I think it was rather a success. We began with the labour

---

* Frederick 'Ben' Keeling had come up to Trinity College the previous autumn. He restarted the University Fabian Society.

movement and finished up on Ethics. They seem to know as much about productive cooperation as we know about unproductive copulation, and there was a splendid flow of conversation.

The plan to make the Society more political, which included electing Fay, soon petered out. With free trade secure, Maynard's uninvolvement in politics became about as complete as was possible for someone of his temperament.

His labours for the Society took a different form: that of trying to revive his friendship with 'Dilly' Knox. Knox had come up to King's in 1903, but he and Maynard had seen little of each other, moving in quite different circles. Now Knox started to come into the reckoning as a potential Apostle. 'With the least bit more sense he would be obviously superb' Maynard had confided to Strachey on 28 November 1905. But this was Knox's trouble. His brilliant mind was applied to pedantry and trivia: he lacked a 'serious bottom'. Nevertheless, Maynard tried for some months to 'enter Knox's citadel and tear down the grinning mask',[16] not just for the Society's sake but for the sake of their old friendship. 'My dear Adolphe,' he wrote him on Christmas eve, in a letter he never sent, 'You are fond of saying you are an Indifferentist – but you know you aren't really. . . . My dear, you are only as shy about the things that matter, as you used to be about the things that don't. Arise, shine.'[17] But Knox soon faded away again. This left Keynes with his two original embryos – the manic mathematician Henry Norton, and the silent James Strachey. Their 'births' took place on 17 February 1906. Maynard gave an account to Strachey who had gone to stay with his aunt in the South of France. 'Then came the twins – a great success, I think. James's hearth rug manner was very good, but, of course, he didn't say very much. Norton made a long speech, very possessed and fluent, and quite good. The angels were quite carried away by him; the enthusiasm of Trevy [G. M. Trevelyan] and McT. knew no bounds.'

In December 1905 Maynard had started reading Psychology for the Civil Service Examination. In January 1906 he moved to more familiar territory. 'Have you read the Ethics of that superb Aristotle?' he asked Strachey on 23 January. 'There never was such good sense talked – before or since.' On 7 February he wrote:

My dear, I have been deep in Greek philosophy these last few days, Thales and Pythagoras, Zeno and his lover Parmenides: I am sure your sufferings are only due to this prison world, not the particular circumstances in it.

Only when after a thousand existences and a thousand loves we have become purified from Not-Being and are a perfect harmony, we may fly on wings of love into the heaven of Pythagoras and Plato and

McTaggart, where there is the contact of souls. I am sure it must all
be true. We are mystic numbers and the sum is not yet solved. I have
been curiously happy reading about these strange quibblers for
hours together; and I don't wonder Aristotle put this intellectual
activity first. Still I don't agree with him. Love first, philosophy
second, Poetics third, and Politics fourth. I would change with you
– for he [Duncan Grant] seems to love you.

Poetics was chiefly represented in this period of his life by Shakespeare's Sonnets: he had bought the 'most beautiful' forty folio volumes
of his complete works just before Christmas. (Another book purchase
at this time, from Basle 'at incredible expense', was an edition of
Voltaire's poems 'with many prints by Beaumarchais with the types of
Baskerville'.) If Metaphysics entranced him, the Political Science and
Jurisprudence on which he now started filled him with gloom. 'I am
doing hardly any work and shall never be able to pass into that dreadful
Civil Service,' he told Strachey on 8 March. 'You can be idle without it
being paid out so damned soon.'

Maynard was still keeping a protective eye on Swithinbank's doings
at Oxford. At the end of his second year at Balliol, Swithinbank had
fallen unhappily in love with a fellow-undergraduate, John Beazley,
later a world-famous classical archaeologist. Maynard had hastened to
reassure him (30 June 1905): 'But whatever the end, thank heaven that
you can feel.' He found, though, the task of keeping his friendship alive
by correspondence increasingly difficult in face of Swithinbank's failure
to reply to his letters. 'Our correspondence is constipated. There's no
denying it,' he admonished him on 7 January 1906. 'I am prepared to
write once a day or once a week or once a month, but *not* once a year.
. . . By nature I simply ooze letters. Will you do the same?' The chance
for rebuilding bridges came when Maynard spent a long weekend in
Oxford early in March. He reported to Lytton Strachey on 3 March:

> I am in bed utterly exhausted and with a splitting headache after
> 8 hours continuous conversation. . . .
> Oh dear! I've fallen again and helplessly under the domination of
> that wretched Dan. He was radiant – never, never – oh there is
> nothing to say, but I don't think he was ever like this before. And still
> such a silly little boy. . . .
> The disease of this wretched Oxford is that one is never allowed
> a tête-à-tête. . . . I invite myself to breakfast with Proby [Granville
> Hamilton's father had changed his surname to Proby] and write a
> note telling him to ask no-one else; three others get wind of it and
> invite themselves too.
> Swithin, fortunately, I can see – for we sit up late. . . .
> I went to the Jowett this evening and opened a sad discussion after
> a paper called 'Time and the Absolute'.

JMK to Lytton Strachey, 5 March 1906:
... Well, I succeeded yesterday in catching Dan alone – for about an hour ...

We sat on a sofa together and things ended in only a semi-embrace, but I could have done anything – if only I had the nerve. He goes round with the most silly Eton Oppidans and likes to talk theoretically about women. Oh but he is just the same. ...

JMK to Lytton Strachey, 7 March 1906:
I must finish about Oxford; for in spite of my efforts I don't seem to have got to Swithin in the earlier fragments. There is not much to say – he hardly talked about himself at all; but I've never been so unhappy about him. It's not so much that he's depressed (I doubt if he is more than usually so), but I feel as if he were dying – just flickering out, the soul a little way behind the body. ... He has no *flame*. ... Of course he was utterly bankrupt, and I lent him all the money I could – which he immediately spent in presenting me with a book and giving a sumptuous luncheon party for 6 with mulled claret....

The pomp of All Souls is incredible. Everybody, except me, looked like a judge. There were University professors and members of Parliament of the blackest dye (F. E. Smith for instance, do you know him?). The wine was excellent, and Butler* very nice – so I enjoyed myself.

Lytton Strachey to JMK, 7 March 1906, Menton:
You are a lunatic! How you can throw away your opportunities in the way you do I can't conceive. Glances, imaginations, *half* embraces – really. I give you up! When your first Oxford letter left me in suspense as to what was going to happen with Dan, I really did hope there would be something fine; – and then your 'nerves gave way'. Pooh! You're a maniac.

JMK to Lytton Strachey, 11 March 1906:
I think I admit your charge about l'affaire Dan. It *was* mere lack of nerve, but then the situation was very difficult.... I feel that once I attempted rape, he would never sit close to me on a sofa and rub his knee against mine. ...

My dear, I have always suffered and I suppose always will from a most unalterable obsession that I am so physically repulsive that I've no business to hurl my body on anyone else's. The idea is so fixed and constant that I don't think anything – certainly no argument – could ever shake it.

On Monday, 19 March 1906 Maynard left England for Italy. It was his first European holiday without his parents. In *The Economic Consequences*

---

* His Eton friend, H. B. Butler, by this time a Fellow of All Souls.

of the Peace he would later pay his homage to a vanished Europe, 'the internationalisation of which was nearly complete in practice'. His was, above all, the traveller's Europe, knit together as never before or perhaps since by railways, posts, steamships and hotels, all functioning in a completely reliable, predictable, manner: it is small wonder the European bourgeoisie later praised Mussolini for making the trains run on time. The English traveller needed no passport, and his gold sovereigns were everywhere convertible into local currencies at fixed, unchanging, rates of exchange.

He stopped briefly in Paris to see Duncan Grant who had gone there to study painting, spent a couple of days with Lytton in Genoa, 'eating omelettes and discussing ethics and sodomy',[18] and then joined up with Mary Berenson in Florence. The introduction had come through Alys Russell, Mary Berenson's sister. Mary Berenson was a vital, extravagant, flirtatious woman of forty-one. She came from a family of Philadelphia Quakers, the Logan Pearsall Smiths, who had settled in England; had married a Fabian lawyer, Frank Costelloe, by whom she had two daughters, Rachel and Karin; and had then run off to Italy with the art connoisseur Bernard Berenson, to much scandalised comment in staid circles. (A whiff of scandal clung to the whole family: Mary's father had had to give up preaching when his relations with admiring female disciples became too blatantly unspiritual.) Clad in fur coat, Maynard embarked with the mother, two daughters, and an Oxford undergraduate, Geoffrey Scott, for a week's tour of Tuscany by motor.

JMK to Lytton Strachey, 2 April 1906:
The boys vary amazingly from place to place. . . . But throughout the whole length and breadth of Tuscany and Umbria there is not one of more than 17 who is even plain – they are physically repulsive.

We seem to have seen almost every place in the country, and although the week seemed a month I liked the company I kept. Are you surprised? Poor Mary Berenson is grossly slandered; she's simply Alys turned competent and hedonist. They're really extraordinarily alike – just with different twists. . . .

Mary is just the person to travel with in a motor – for her incredible competence as a hostess; all the arrangements for one's comfort were complete. She was full of Italian and money and which hotel was best and what food they could best cook. We must have cost her pints of gold – for everything down to entrance fees to galleries was paid.

The interest I learnt to take in food was almost indecent. . . . One is always hungry in a motor and we ate all day. The last hour or so of each drive was spent in plotting the menu and the first act on reaching the inn was to order it. And she roars with laughter the whole time, allows you to laugh at her, and never worries one. And when she journalised about the pictures, Scott was always there to make the appropriate remark. The Costelloe females, Ray and Karin, don't talk much. But they did very well.*

Mary Berenson and her daughters left Keynes and Scott at Siena where they settled down for ten days of work in a 'pension with eleven spinsters' in the Via Delle Belle Arte.

> Scott [Maynard wrote to Lytton on 2 April] is dreadfully Oxford – a sort of aesthetic person; and of course his point of view always seems to me a trifle shocking; but we are quite happy together. Even in his sodomy, which he takes more solidly than anything else, he seems to want to worship an idealised vision in which he has clothed some good-looking absurdity rather than to come to close quarters. ... I've never seen the aesthetic point of view so close. I find I object to it on high moral grounds – though I hardly know why. It seems to trifle deliberately with sacred reality.
>
> We have here a vast bedroom, a little room and a large balcony looking out over the city – also meals and wine for 5 francs a day.

At Siena Keynes worked six hours a day on history – 'I've never come on any subject that is so easy and cloys so quickly' – the rest of the time taking enormously long meals with the spinsters.

The Italian trip ended with a week with the Berensons at their villa I Tatti in Settignano, just outside Florence. 'The house is packed full of old masters – there are six in my bedroom and study,' Maynard wrote to his parents. He wrote to Lytton on Easter Sunday 15 April 1906:

> I've no news unless I describe our way of life. I seem to have fallen in love with Ray a little bit, but as she isn't male I haven't had to think of any suitable steps to take.
>
> Of course she practically is male – for she obviously practices saphistries. ... But you would really be surprised how nice she is. I would even be quite prepared to elect her at once – without a qualm. Now, don't say I've turned womaniser.
>
> The comfort here is of course incredible; the cypresses and sun and moon and the amazing gardens and villas in which we picnic every day high above Florence have reduced me to a lump of Italian idleness.

---

* Mary Berenson wrote to her mother Hannah Pearsall Smith: 'To them [Keynes and Scott] everything was fun – the scrappy lunches under trees in a drizzle, the arrival at cold carpetless inns, the horrible meals in the mud ... the punctures (we only had two) ... everything was the occasion for laughter and merriment.' (Quoted by Barbara Strachey, *Remarkable Relations*, 232.)

We got to bed later and later and gradually find methods of working fresh meals into the day. Last night it was nearly five before we retired.

Bernard B. is, I am sure rather a bad man, but we've hardly seen him ... and now he's gone off in a motor car to flirt with a foul woman called Lady Sassoon. But Mrs B. I will defend against all. ...

Oh Scott is very amusing but he makes me angry by plotting at the greatest inconvenience to himself never to leave me and Ray alone ....

Donald Tovey is coming to play tunes on the piano.

Ray, a large, handsome, eighteen-year-old, and Karin, at seventeen already going deaf, found the two young men entirely congenial. 'It is hard to say which was the nicer,' Ray wrote to her grandmother. 'They were both utterly unflirtatious, which was an immense boon. They talked to me as if I were a reasonable being ... [and] behaved rationally and naturally just as if they had been clever, well-read girls.' One wonders what Harvey Road would have made of the goings on. They all went on bathing parties at which Scott and Keynes dressed themselves in ladies' knickers and struggled over a pink chemise. On their last night Mary Berenson gave a champagne supper which made them all tipsy. The girls dressed in the men's clothes, Scott wore a dress of Mary's with a gold coronet on his head, and Maynard put on a gown of chiffon, with a headdress of pink ribbons.[19] Mary Berenson was as much taken with her visitors as her daughters had been. She started writing letters to Maynard in which she addressed him as 'My Peerless One', signed herself 'La Mère des Calamités', and hinted at a rapid renewal of revels under the full moon.

While all this was going on, dreadful things were happening in Paris. A post from Lytton brought news that Hobhouse had visited Duncan there, Duncan had fallen in love with him, and he with Duncan. 'Great God,' Maynard wrote back. 'It's more wild and more mad than anything ever happened in the world before. Oh and we have created it. It has sprung and sprouted from the tips of our penes – from yours and mine. And it will spread and grow over the whole world.' He was careful, though, to be suitably sympathetic: 'You know – as always how much I am in love with you and Duncan as a unity – that I can't help feeling that this is only an episode.'

He left I Tatti on 18 April to join his brother Geoffrey in Germany. The visit was not a success:

JMK to Lytton Strachey, 19 April 1906, Feldberghof:
Here I am with my brother – a monument of physical endurance on the top of a high mountain in the midst of snow. I thought I would use this opportunity to make his acquaintance – and I dreamt how

I would worm out of him all his amours, or failing them at least learn all the latest Rugby scandals.

But what a blow! My dear, here he is at nineteen and ... simply uneducated. Oh what's the good of Rugby.

Geoffrey's innocence is not surprising. Rugby, he had told Neville, was 'the cleanest and most moral school in England'.[20] Maynard told Lytton on 31 August that 'the relationship of brother by the flesh is really a ridiculous one. It probably ought to be abolished'.

Recovering from illness and the depression caused by the disastrous turn in his love life, Lytton spent five happy days at Cambridge in May, where he read Jane Austen and found Norton and his brother James 'delightfully gay & youthful', Hobhouse 'a little unhappy', Keynes 'arguing on egoism & working six hours a day', and Walter Lamb 'sucking everyone's blood', but 'principally engaged with Knox – the divine ambiguous Knox . . .'*

Maynard and Neville made their usual thorough preparations for the impending Civil Service Examination. 'Lunch with Maynard,' wrote Neville on 6 June. 'He is now working again at Mathematics and seems to have got into a rather depressed state. His feeling just now is that he will come about 12th.' On 14 June: 'Maynard is back from Oxford & will be at home for a few days. It appears that he has scarcely done any work for the last fortnight.' On 26 June, he and Florence left for their annual Swiss holiday. 'Geoffrey will join us at Freiburg. Maynard will be at home alone for 10 days or a fortnight & will then go into College. He is doing his final preparation for the C. S. Examn.' Maynard wrote to his father on 26 June: 'Never have I had such an infinite sense of time – with fourteen hours a day to work and read Horace Walpole and play the pianola.'

By 2 July he could report that he had 'achieved my 50 hours work last week on Logic and Mathematics so that both are nearly finished. He had been enraged by a book on Logic written by the Oxford philosopher Horace Joseph – 'What a home of diseased thought Oxford is'[21] – but had benefitted from the third edition of his father's book, just going through press. From Pontresina Neville advised him to 'glance at my notes on Bacon'. By 12 July, Psychology had been polished off and Metaphysics and Ethics begun. On 18 July Metaphysics was revised, Ethics begun, with political science, history and economics to follow. Re-reading *Principia Ethica* convinced Maynard all over again that it was 'the greatest work on philosophy ever written'. To Strachey (20 July) he indulged his curious ranking propensity: 'The Bishop [Butler] had to come next after the Yen [Moore]. Then Hume I think; then

---

* Walter Lamb, elder brother of the painter Henry Lamb, later secretary of the Royal Academy. He was one of those who aspired to be an Apostle but was never chosen.

Sidgers [Sidgwick] ipse (but it's a worse book than I remember and he hasn't got the point). Then Shaftesbury. The worst book but one written on the subject is Green's *Prolegomena* [to *Ethics*] and the worst Spencer's *Data of Ethics*. Kant comes into a different category, for he's spinning and is not considering the facts of the case'. The only break was a visit to London with Furness and Fay to see Adeline Genée as Swanilda in *Coppélia* at the Empire. 'It was amazing – one of the most wonderful things I have ever seen,' he told his parents.

To cover the period of the examinations, stretching from 2 to 24 August, Neville had taken a flat at 33 Coleherne Court, London, into which Maynard moved with Florence and Margaret on 1 August. The next day he took his English Composition, selecting as his essay subject 'Drama, Melodrama, and Opera' on which he had already read a paper to the Apostles. To James Strachey he wrote (2 August) of his fellow-examinees, 'They are rather a crew – a few of the more present-able I knew, but good God! I trembled for our Indian Empire when I saw the bulk of them.' In Political Science on Friday, he wrote so fast he got writer's cramp. On Monday, after a day spent revising the papers he did for Marshall, came Political Economy. A break for revision followed, with English History Part I on Saturday 11 August. Florence wrote to Neville: 'Of course it was a bad subject for him, & he did not do well in the Stubbs paper in the afternoon. His family history researches were of use to him in answering the question on chronicles & records.'

After the second History Paper on Monday he went to spend a couple of nights with the Stracheys who had taken a house at Betchworth, near Dorking, for the summer. Here he did his usual six hours a day. He was now almost as friendly with James as he was with Lytton. On Thursday 16 August he faced Metaphysics and Ethics. 'I was so much enraged when I saw the morning paper that I was unable to read it for several minutes,' he angrily told his father. It was not only 'pure ancient, but ancient involving little bits of scholarship rather than metaphysic'. England's future governors were encouraged to discourse on the place of intelligent Creation in Greek cosmology. Logic and Psychology on Saturday 18 August were easy, but 'rather washy, so that I never new whether or not I was gasing [sic] according to their wishes'. On Tuesday and Wednesday came elementary mathematics. Maynard did not like this and had indigestion. Florence sensed that Neville was getting anxious: 'I do not want you to worry about Maynard. I think he is doing quite respectably but has had no special luck.'

The family celebrated the end of the ordeal on Friday 24 August with a visit to Shaw's *You Never Can Tell* at the Royal Court. Then Maynard fled to Surrey to stay the weekend with his Eton friend Humphrey Paul.

'The Maurice Macmillans have taken a house there,' he wrote to Strachey on 28 August, 'so I spent most of yesterday with Dan. His brother Harold who has just got into College is growing up in the Dan style but much more exquisite. . . I played golf with him'. In mid-September he set off for ten days' holiday in the Highlands, staying with James Strachey and Henry Norton in a cottage near Inverness. Here Lytton joined them for 'terrific excursions into the mountains'. Maynard told his father that he had made a start on Probability 'and am rather hopeful. My method is quite new. . .' With the Civil Service Examination out of the way, he had begun working on his fellowship dissertation, just according to his father's schedule, drawn up five years previously.

After going through his papers with his father, Keynes had estimated that he would come in the first ten. This might not be quite good enough as he had determined to take only the Treasury or India Office. However, he came second, with 3498 marks out of a possible 6000. First was Otto Niemeyer, a classical scholar from Balliol College, Oxford, with 3917. The irony is that Niemeyer was later the chief architect, or at least codifier, of the 'Treasury View' which Keynes spent the 1920s attacking. Another irony is that he got his worst marks in economics, 256 out of a possible 600.

JMK to Lytton Strachey, 4 October 1906:

Yes I am a clerk in the India Office – having passed the medical with flying colours, balls and eyesight unusually perfect they said. My marks have arrived and left me enraged. Really knowledge seems an absolute bar to success. I have done worst in the only two subjects of which I possessed a solid knowledge, Mathematics and Economics. My dear, I scored more marks for English history than for mathematics – is it credible? For economics I got a relatively low percentage and was 8th or 9th [in fact he was 7th] in order of merit – whereas I knew the *whole* of both papers in a really elaborate way. On the other hand in Political Science, to which I devoted less than a fortnight in all, I was easily first of everybody. I was first in Logic and Psychology, and in Essay.

II

THE INDIA OFFICE

On 16 October 1906 Maynard started his civil service career as junior clerk in the Military Department of the India Office, at a salary of £200 a year, his first job being to arrange the shipment of ten young Ayrshire bulls to Bombay. The India Office consisted of six Departments run by Secretaries. There were six Assistant Secretaries, eight senior clerks, ten junior clerks and 76 second division clerks. Its main function was pushing paper to and from India, about a hundred thousand pieces of it every year. It was hardly a job to excite Keynes's full interest. One scholar has written, 'The logistics of moving papers to their proper destination was complex, requiring a large subordinate staff. The extensive network of offices and departments – almost $3\frac{1}{2}$ million cubic feet – filled three floors in its half of Whitehall.'[23] Everything had been reduced to routine – a tribute to a vanished world where problems were routine too. This antiquated machine exercised ultimate control over the British Raj. Its Secretary of State, John Morley, was almost an antique himself; the Permanent Under-Secretary, Sir Arthur Godley, was something of a reformer, but he could make little headway against tradition.

Keynes had chosen the India Office because it was one of the two top home departments of state, not because he had any interest in India. Certainly his attitude to British rule was conventional in every sense. He believed the regime protected the poor against the rapacious money-lender, brought justice and material progress, and gave the country a sound monetary system: in short, introduced good government to places which could not develop it on their own. Unlike Leonard Woolf, who saw colonial rule from the lowly position of a district officer in Ceylon, and unlike E. M. Forster and Lowes Dickinson who travelled in Asia, Maynard always saw the Raj from Whitehall: he never considered the human and moral implications of imperial rule or whether the British were exploiting the Indians. Although he was to write and advise extensively on Indian affairs, the furthest east he ever got was Egypt; the only Indians he ever met were at Cambridge or London; the only books he ever read on India were specialised tomes on finance. This was the hallowed tradition set by Macaulay and the Mills in the nineteenth century: the good government of India was a matter not of local knowledge but of applying sound utilitarian principles from London.

One advantage of this approach to policy-making was that it economised enormously on the time that needed to be spent in the office. Civil service life was adapted as far as possible to the habits of the Oxford and Cambridge graduates entering the Administrative Section. Late rising in the mornings was safeguarded by starting work at 11.00 a.m. The day ended at 5.00 p.m. with one hour's break for lunch. There were two months' holiday a year, plus bank holidays and of course Derby Day. Saturday hours were from 11–1.00. 'I am delighted to find that we have shorter hours and longer holidays than any other office,' Maynard informed his father on 17 October. Florence had at first thought he would have no time to work on his fellowship dissertation. She need not have worried. Keynes's speed in emptying his in-tray was always prodigious. He found plenty of time to write his thesis and do his personal correspondence in office hours.

Early in February 1907, Sir Arthur Godley offered him a resident clerkship, with more money – a resident clerk being expected to be on hand to receive telegrams over the weekend. Keynes declined on the ground that the extra work would interfere with the writing of his dissertation. The offer was renewed in October; Maynard's reply makes it clear that it was not just fellowship time he grudged: 'I am still most unwilling,' he wrote to Godley on 3 October 1907, 'to take up the resident clerkship. My fellowship work does not finish until December. But – apart from this special and temporary reason – now that I have settled down in London, I find the idea of sacrificing any of my out of office freedom repellent. I am, for instance, almost always away from London for the weekends; and I should not like to have to give this up.'[24] Not, one would think, the best way of advancing one's career: yet in his attempts to limit his involvement Maynard seems to have had the utmost sympathy and understanding of his superiors. The old tradition of the sinecure died hard; and while it would be quite wrong to say that he, and others, did not do their jobs conscientiously and even with aplomb, at the back of their minds was always the idea that office work was an encroachment on more valuable activities.*

Evidently it occurred to someone that Maynard's talents were being wasted in the Military Department; or it may simply be that a vacancy occurred elsewhere. 'After a state interview of incredible pomp' with Godley[25] he was moved to the Revenue, Statistics and Commerce Department at the beginning of March. It had, he informed his father, 'very little routine work ... and deals with all questions of commerce, Land Revenue, Plague, Famine, Opium Traffic, and so forth'. Installed in a 'charming room to myself overlooking the Park',[26] he was set to work editing the annual report on the Moral and Material Progress of India. 'A special feature of this year's edition,' he gossiped to Lytton, 'is to be an illustrated appendix on Sodomy'. He wrote to him on 7 March:

I like my new department. I haven't much to write at present, but there is an excellent system by which everything comes to me to read and I read it. In fact there is so much to read, that it takes me all my time. Some of it is quite absorbing – Foreign Office commercial negotiations with Germany, quarrels with Russia in the Persian Gulf, the regulation of opium in Central India, the Chinese opium

* Admittedly the argument is not conclusive, because the promotion system was so rigid that it was virtually impossible by extra effort to secure a higher place. Neville was much disappointed to discover, from perusal of the India List, that Maynard's promotion prospects in the Department were poor.

proposals – I have had great files to read on all these in the last two days.

I lunched at the House of Lords to-day, and Gosse was at the next table; really he's purely a figure of fun and the company seemed to realise it. I felt very pompous smoking and drinking coffee in the Library afterwards.

Yesterday I attended my first Committee of Council. The thing is simply government by dotardry; at least half those present showed manifest signs of senile decay, and the rest didn't speak.

Maynard was never one to suffer dotardry gladly. His capacity to get enraged at stupidity, especially when he felt his own expertise was involved, was one of the things that made it so difficult for him to limit his commitments. However, in the India Office there were few outbursts. Early on he clashed with a superior in the Military Department who had questioned the accuracy of his figures, only to be vindicated by higher authority.[27] 'It is absurd to suppose that it is still possible to prepare and present statistics ... without special knowledge,' he minuted to his departmental chief, Sir Thomas Holderness, after reading through one report – and suggested they consult Sanger about appointing a statistician.[28] But most of the time too little was happening to disturb his work on Probability or his correspondence. He got his father to send him learned books by obscure German authors. 'I wish the German word for Probability hadn't 27 letters,'* he wrote to Neville on 8 March. 'I find that my rate of speed with English, French and German is about in the ratio of 1:2:3 – which makes the reading of the 3000 or 4000 pages of German I see ahead of me rather a labour.'[29] At the same time, Maynard was telling Lytton Strachey he was so bored with his dissertation he hardly touched it.[30] The letters were slanted to what he wanted each correspondent to believe. The fact remains that the thesis got written.

Neither London nor the office thus interfered excessively with patterns of life and friendship inherited from Cambridge. There had been talk of sharing with Robin Mayor and Hilton Young, Geoffrey Winthrop Young's younger brother; but eventually he took a service flat – 125b St James's Court, five minutes' walk from his office – on a two-year lease, at a rental of £90 a year. He was soon complaining of an 'epidemic of dinner parties – five in six days'. He saw Strachey regularly for tea or lunch. They talked about Duncan Grant, and Maynard commiserated with him on the death of Thoby Stephen, from typhoid, on 20 November 1906. At this stage, Maynard was not a member of Old Bloomsbury. He had hardly known Clive Bell and Thoby Stephen at Cambridge; he dined occasionally with Vanessa and Clive Bell in

* *Wahrscheinlichkeitsrechnung* – strictly 'calculus of probability'.

London, but was not part of the Bloomsbury At Homes. However, there were many Apostles in London apart from Lytton, of whom the Sangers were special friends. There was the Etonian set based on the two Youngs, Geoffrey and Hilton, Robin Mayor and Ralph Hawtrey.* There were dinners with Mary Sheepshanks. And there was Mary Berenson who had a flat in Victoria where she entertained her 'peerless one' and Geoffrey Scott – the latter often staying overnight with Maynard at St James's Court. Cultural life included *Man and Superman* and *Tristan and Isolde* with The Nose.† From March 1907 dates Maynard's first apparent interest in picture buying. He had been taken by Strachey to a show of Simon Bussy's at Leighton House, Bussy having married Strachey's sister Dorothy. 'It seems to me essential to buy one – the cheapness!' he wrote to Florence.[31] There was even a bit of politics thrown in for good measure. Another of Lytton's sisters, Philippa (Pippa) was active in the Central Society for Women's Suffrage, the constitutional wing of the suffragette movement, founded by Mrs Fawcett, an old friend of Lady Strachey. Votes for women was a political cause which aroused some enthusiasm among the Apostles and their friends: Bertrand Russell even stood for parliament in 1907 in a by-election at Wimbledon as a candidate for women's suffrage. At a procession and meeting organised by the Society for Women's Suffrage Maynard acted as chief steward at Exeter Hall, Pippa writing to him afterwards, 'I don't know what would have happened if you had not been there to hold the staircase.'[32]

Every weekend, as he had indicated to Godley, Maynard fled London. At Oxford in October 1906 he had 'some charming logical conversation' with Bertie.[33] In March 1907 he stayed with Desmond and Molly MacCarthy in Bury St Edmunds. Generally, however, he spent the weekends at Cambridge with his parents, and attending meetings of the Society. Nothing much seemed to have changed:

JMK to Lytton Strachey, 5 November 1906:
We all lost our hearts to Percy Sanger and couldn't think why we hadn't kissed him when he left.
Bertie was up too.
McT. read a paper to the Sunday Essay on Moore's Ethics. It was in the form of an attack but it was really a final capitulation. For after all, McT. is candid. Oh, his physical beauty was astounding.
As for me and Dil – well, I don't know that there's much to tell you.

---

* Robin Mayor and Geoffrey Young were both at the Board of Education, Young having been forced to leave Eton in 1905 for being, as Maynard delicately put it, 'a little careless of appearances'.
† The Nose, also in London, was William Spens, who came up to King's in 1901, became a fellow in 1907, and was later master of Corpus Christi College. He was religious and musical.

The holidays at the India Office, if not fully competitive with those of the universities, were nevertheless ample. December found Maynard, Lytton and Swithin spending a week at the Mermaid Club in Rye, 'a 17th century inn, very pleasant and comfortable'[34] where Maynard worked on Probability; a pursuit which he continued over Christmas at Harvey Road while Neville and Geoffrey wrote up articles on butterflies. In March, holiday time came round again. Maynard, James and Norton crossed over to Paris for a long weekend with Duncan Grant. On his return Maynard joined Moore's reading party assembled at North Molton in Devonshire. This was his first invitation to one of those famous gatherings, regarded as a supreme mark of Moore's favour. Others present were the two Stracheys, Norton, Ainsworth, Bob Trevy and Sanger.[35] The weather was 'quite inconceivable', Strachey wrote to Duncan Grant on 1 April. 'I haven't seen a cloud for the last fortnight.' Ainsworth was lying by him with 'a pair of blue spectacles to keep off the rays of the sun ... reading Plato.' Bob Trevy, the poet, was 'fast asleep and dreaming of his opera on Bacchus and Ariadne, which he has just written for Tovey to set to music, and is the greatest balls you can imagine'. A few feet away under an umbrella sat Maynard reading Galsworthy, with Norton doing mathematics on the grass beside him, and Moore, 'lying full length on a rug, with an umbrella poised over him, making pencil notes in the margin of Locke's *Essay on Human Understanding*'.

In June Maynard was off on his travels again, this time to the French Pyrenees, where he and Fay, now lecturing at Christ's College, joined Neville and Geoffrey.

JMK to Lytton Strachey, 5 July 1907:
I have been walking and climbing immense distances and heights, but as I burnt up my eyes the day before yesterday by spending several hours on the snow without dark specs I have refused to move for the last two days. This has really been pleasant, as I have been able to read a fair amount. I have never found Probability in my bedroom or Miss Austen under a rock more entirely pleasant. I should like to go on doing it here for months. Also it is a very long time since lust has been at so low an ebb (I suppose it is the result of so much walking) . . . .
Fay is only a qualified success, I think. Fortunately we like him, so it is not a failure but (1) . . . Fay, being absolutely the worst walker and mountaineer I have ever seen, either delays us for hours, or has to be left behind; (2) he is *too* ugly. Ugliness of face, hands, body, clothes and manners are not, I find, completely overbalanced by cheerfulness, a good heart, and an average intelligence.
I believe I care very little for anything in the world except a reasonably attractive appearance and a behaviour reasonably friendly to me personally.

Maynard and Fay left Neville and Geoffrey to walk to Biarritz. En route they spent three days in a peasant's hut in Spain, near Torla, in 'the most wonderful valley I have ever seen'.[36] From Biarritz Maynard wrote to his mother on 13 July:

> I breakfast in bed and read a novel for an hour or so; then I get up and work for two hours and food and sun and laziness for the rest of the day. I assure you I am as well as any here with my new clothes, my white shoes, and my tie arranged in folds with an opal pin.

Maynard soon lost all his money at *petits chevaux*, playing his own special system, and was reduced to trying to win some of it back from Fay at piquet in their hotel bedroom.

Despite being congratulated by no less a person than John Morley, the Secretary of State, for a minute of 'admirable promise', Maynard was starting to get bored with his job. He resented having to spend a torridly hot summer in London. First he said there was too much to do. Then there was not enough to do. As an antidote to depression he went on a book-buying spree, one of his acquisitions being 'a most beautiful quarto in a quite magnificent elaborately tooled 17th century contemporary binding' by the Jesuit Father John Keynes.[37] But there is no doubt that it was during this summer that Maynard decided to leave the India Office. He poured out his frustrations to Lytton Strachey on 13 September 1907:

> I'm thoroughly sick of this place and would like to resign. Now the novelty has worn off, I am bored nine tenths of the time and rather unreasonably irritated the other tenth whenever I can't have my own way. It's maddening to have thirty people who can reduce you to impotence when you're quite certain you're right.
>
> Then the preoccupation, which seems characteristic of officials, to save their own skin, is fatal. Drake's* dread of taking any responsibility is almost pathetic. And of course it prevents any original or sporting proposal ever being made. With this machine ... the risk to India of free speech in the India Office is nil ....

It was not till Saturday 12 October 1907 that Maynard came back to Cambridge for a three-week holdiay. 'I have seldom been in Cambridge so long,' he wrote to Strachey on 16 October, 'and had so little to report. I dissert, I play golf daily with Fay and Dil (in his gold rimmers) and that is all.' His correspondence with Lytton covered familiar topics:

JMK to Lytton Strachey, 18 October 1907, Royston Golf Club:
> Dickinson read at his own Society last night on 'Peace or War'. Of course all the world was there. Master R [Rupert Brooke] spoke passably and was a blaze of colour – James dazzled in a solitary chair

* Francis Drake was Assistant Secretary of the Revenue and Statistics Department.

on the far side of the room. But all the world were alas! the oldest of old stagers, except a little board school boy called Cushion.

... Sanger is rumoured for next week as well as you and Hawtrey. James reads. Bell, Vanessa and Virginia have been here this week.

Sheppard read on Saturday, and the Society except me thought it was probably their duty to join the Salvation Army or collect statistics about West Ham,* and that we all live selfish lives.

JMK to Lytton Strachey, 25 October 1907, King's:

I asked Sheppard to get you a room and I think he has got one ... Mr Bernard Shaw converted us all to socialism last night and, of course, millions of rotten embryos float by name and discomfort consciences by the thought that they have not been called on. But I doubt if one is worth anything.

Lytton Strachey to JMK, 28 October 1907:

You've no idea how much I enjoyed myself. It was most charming, and you being there was particularly charming; I wish I always could find you there, and yet also find you at St. James's Court! But I suppose, if it was a question of wishes, you'd only be found at King's. The hopefulness of the general outlook was another cause for enjoyment. It was delightful to feel that people were positively almost beginning to enjoy themselves.

JMK to Lytton Strachey, 30 October 1907, King's:

I do not know what to do about the election of Rupert. James presses for it violently. Norton doesn't know him. Sheppard faintly opposed, I think. So they put it on me, and I'm damned if I know what to say. James's judgments on the subject are very nearly worthless; he is quite crazed. I have been to see R. again. He is all right I suppose and quite affable enough – but yet I feel little enthusiasm.

In the end Rupert Brooke was elected an Apostle in January 1908, the first birth for two years.

Maynard's three weeks of Cambridge life had whetted his appetite for more. His hopes of a rapid release from the India Office rested on getting a prize fellowship at King's. He was now working almost full time on Probability. On 6 December he wrote to Florence: 'I have not averaged an hour's office work a day, so I am well up with the dissertation.' He handed it in on 12 December 1907. The examiners were W. E. Johnson and Alfred North Whitehead.

On 3 February 1908 Neville talked to W. E. Johnson about Maynard's chances. 'On the whole his verdict appears more favourable than Whitehead's.' Neville by no means shared Maynard's enthusiasm

---

* Maynard did not collect statistics about West Ham, but he did a review, in the March 1908 number of the *Journal of the Royal Statistical Society*, of a statistical analysis of the industrial problems of West Ham.

for quitting the India Office. A prize fellowship was for six years only. It offered no career prospects, but could be held concurrently with his India post. On 1 March 1908 father and son had their first and only recorded academic row. 'Maynard wishes to throw up the India Office if he gets a Fellowship at King's. I have argued with him in vain. I think he would give up the idea if I said definitely that I desired him to do so. But I do not think that I ought to take so decided a position as that. He will be throwing up a certainty and taking risks. That fits in with his scheme of life, not mine.'

The next day Maynard told Pigou, one of the electors, that if elected he would come back into residence. The election took place on 17 March. There were four candidates for two places. Only after fifteen votes had been taken did it become clear that Maynard would not be filling one of them. The two new Fellows were Page and Dobbs. 'We feel very much disappointed and depressed,' Neville wrote in his diary. 'I had reconciled myself to Maynard's giving up the India Office, for he seemed so thoroughly to have set his heart on returning to Cambridge and a student's life.' Maynard was not so much disappointed as furious. He was particularly annoyed when told that one reason for turning him down was that he would have another chance next year. He raged against Whitehead's incompetence as a referee, claiming that he had not bothered to try to understand what he was saying.

Keynes's dissertation is essentially the development of ideas in his Apostles' paper of January 1904 (see above p.152). He set out to create a 'new kind of logic' applicable to 'doubtful arguments and uncertain conclusions' which may, nevertheless, be rational and objective. His argument is summed up in these passages from the first chapter:

> In the ordinary course of thought and argument we are constantly asserting that the truth of one statement, while not *proving* another, is nevertheless *some ground* for believing the second. We assert that, with the evidence at our command, we *ought* to hold such and such a belief. We expressly say we have *rational* grounds for assertions which are, in the usual logical sense, unproved. We allow, in fact, that statements may be unproved, without for that reason being unfounded. Nor does reflexion show that it is information of purely psychological import which we wish to convey when we use such expressions as these .... We are in fact claiming to cognize correctly a logical connexion between one set of propositions which we call our evidence and which we take to be true, and another set which we call our conclusions and to which we attach more or less weight according to the grounds supplied by the first. We recognise that *objectively* evidence can be *real* evidence and yet not *conclusive* evidence ... I do not think I am straining the use of words in speaking of this as the probability relation or the relation of probability.

The idea of a premiss's having some weight to establish a conclusion, of its lying somewhere between cogency and irrelevancy, is
altogether foreign to a logic in which the premiss must either prove
or not prove the alleged conclusion. This opinion is, from the nature
of the case, incapable of positive proof. The notion presents itself to
the mind, I feel, as something independent and unique. . . .

Yet that 'probability' is, in the strict sense, indefinable, need not
trouble us much; it is a characteristic which it shares with many of
our most necessary and fundamental ideas. . . .[38]

One of the most striking things about the dissertation was the bold-
ness of Keynes's claims. Implicit in his argument was the view that
probability should be rightly considered as the *general theory* of logic, of
which deductive logic was a special case, applying only to cases of
certainty. Similarly, he was to argue in 1936 that he was producing a
'general theory' of employment, of which the classical theory was a
'special case'. Whether his economic theory in turn is best considered
as a branch of applied probability theory, dealing with rational
economic behaviour under conditions of inescapable uncertainty, has
become one of the central issues in the debate about the status and
intentions of Keynesian economics.

Failure to get elected a Fellow of King's in 1908 was the worst
academic blow Maynard ever suffered. And even then it was merely a
postponement. The chance to resume his student's life came quicker
than he had anticipated. A fortnight after the fellowship debacle, Maynard received a cryptic communication from Marshall. Marshall had
been paying £100 a year for a lectureship in economics out of his own
professorial stipend. The recipient of this bounty had just obtained a
chair at Leeds University. Marshall cautiously suggested to Keynes
that the sum might be made available to him. The caution is understandable. Marshall was about to retire. He could not bind his successor. But he had no doubt that if his own favoured candidate, Pigou,
succeeded him, the offer would become definite. In fact, it was Pigou
who suggested that Marshall write to Maynard.

Maynard showed the letter to his father on Neville's return from the
Riviera on 22 April, saying that he very much wanted to accept:

If I get a fellowship next year and resign this office I am wasting my
time now. This job would give me a raison d'être at Cambridge; if
I refuse, I suppose someone else will accept and it will not be open
to me next year. I am still quite as decided as before that I wish to
leave the India Office. Nothing would suit me better than this; and
even taking into account the fact that I should have at once to begin
to learn a little economics I should have more time for rewriting my
dissertation, with which my mind is much absorbed though not my
time.

Neville replied cautiously next day:

> I am glad we shall see you Saturday. We shall then be able to talk over Marshall's proposal. I may as well, however, at once mention two points that occur to me.
> (i) If you have to prepare a course of lectures on Economics it does not seem to me that you will have more time, or even as much, for your dissertation than if you remain at the India Office.
> (ii) Any stipend that MacGregor has received is a matter of purely private arrangement. Becoming his successor wd not I think give you any University status beyond what you would have as a recognised lecturer....
> Is not Marshall's letter in some respects very vague? I am glad you have not in any way committed yourself at present.

However, Maynard brushed such considerations aside.

On 30 May 1908 the first condition of his return to Cambridge was fulfilled when Pigou was elected to Marshall's chair, over Ashley, Cannan, and Foxwell. On 3 June the Economics and Politics Board, chaired by Neville, authorised two lectureships in Economics, one to be offered to Maynard, the other to Walter Layton, who had just graduated from Trinity with a first in both parts of the Economics Tripos. The understanding was that Pigou would provide them each with £100 a year. Neville immediately offered Maynard an extra £100 as long as he needed it. On 5 June 1908, his twenty-fourth birthday, he resigned from the India Office. He explained to Sir Thomas Holderness:

> For many reasons I am very sorry to do this, and I have only made up my mind after a great deal of doubt and hesitation. But the desire for scientific and theoretical work and for life here is so great that I think I am probably right in giving way to it.
> Please do not think that I have disliked my work in the Revenue Dept. or have been discontented. I have liked it very much and have learnt a great deal from it and from you. But the choice has been between two quite opposed ways of life, and on the whole I think, now at any rate, that the way here is better.

The letter tactfully disguises how uncongenial he had found the experience. To Swithinbank he wrote the same day: 'I hope it isn't madness and that I shall like being up here as much as I think I shall. There will be a dreadful outcry amongst the middle aged. It is heroic of my people to agree.'

His civil service superiors, while greatly regretting his loss, had no doubt that he had made the right choice. 'I personally am one of the last to quarrel with your decision,' wrote Godley. To Holderness Maynard's letter came as a blow: but 'I have never been quite able to satisfy myself that a government office in this country is the best thing for a young man of energy and right ambitions. It is a comfortable means of life and leads by fairly sure, if slow, stages to moderate competence and old age provisions. But it is rarely exciting or strenuous and does not make sufficient call on the combative and self-assertive elements of human nature.'[39] In 1914 Edwin Montagu, then Under-Secretary of State for India, wrote to Holderness, 'I have been often struck by the tedium of life of junior Departmental Officers in the Office. If ... freedom of expression and opportunity had been allowed to Keynes, should we have ever lost him?'[40] The answer is probably yes. Maynard's last day at the India Office was on 20 July. Leaving it, he wrote to his mother on 17 July, was 'quite like dying – initiating stages in pieces of work which move heavily on, knowing that one will never see the outcome .... But I have no regrets – not even now that it has come to it – not one.'

Brief though Maynard's stay at the India Office had been, it had an important effect on his career. The flippant and disgusted tone of his letters to Strachey revealed only part of his attitude, though no doubt a most important one. It left out how good he was at his job, including getting on with his superiors. His secret was genuine ability of a high order, plus what Desmond MacCarthy called 'conversation calculated to impress men of forty'. He was certainly interested in the statistical aspects of his departmental work; and from Lionel Abrahams, head of the Financial Department, he learnt about India's currency arrangements. Godley, in a letter dated 30 March 1909, hoped that Maynard would 'continue to keep an eye on Indian affairs'; Drake had no doubt 'we shall find something to worry you about from time to time'.[41] These proved to be understatements. As Elizabeth Johnson has rightly written, 'Keynes's departure from the India Office did not break his connection with it; indeed, from this time onward the association seems to have expanded.'[42] His expertise on India, supplemented by his study and teaching of economics, and his contacts with civil servants led on quite logically to his writings on India's monetary system and his membership of the Royal Commission on Indian Currency and Finance; these in turn brought further fame at Whitehall and important political contacts. Keynes was summoned to help in his country's crisis in 1914 and to the Treasury in 1915 not just as monetary economist, but as someone who could apply theory to administration. Austin Robinson's claim that Keynes had, at the India Office, learnt to 'see the problems of economics from the angle of the administrator' is thus broadly right, even though the implication that Maynard was already an economist in 1906–8 is partly misleading.

On 21 July 1908 Maynard returned to Harvey Road and moved into King's next day for another bout of student life. He was happier than his parents knew. For not only had he recovered Cambridge; he had gained Duncan Grant.

8 Lytton, Duncan, Maynard

Duncan James Corrowr Grant was twenty-three in 1908, eighteen months younger than Maynard. Born on 21 January 1885 in Scotland at The Doune, Inverness, family home of the Grants of Rothiemurchus, he had spent his early life in India, where his father, Major Bartle Grant, was stationed. From there he was sent to Hillbrow Preparatory School, Rugby and, in 1899, to St Paul's, which he attended as a day boy, living with his cousins the Stracheys at 69 Lancaster Gate or with his parents in Hampstead, when they were in England. At the age of seventeen he had finished his 'rather brief education at St. Paul's school' and had enrolled as a student at the Westminster School of Art. Duncan inherited the beauty of his mother, Ethel McNeill, and his father's musical tastes. They loved their only son, but never quite knew what to make of him. Duncan sometimes felt that his family thought him half-witted.

Maynard had got to know him through Lytton Strachey. In fact for some years he knew more of him than he knew him, since Lytton used Maynard as an outlet for his feelings about his cousin. In turn, Lytton consoled Maynard about Hobhouse. Feeling rejected, they confided in each other – at the rate of almost a letter a day for nearly a year; Strachey's full of romantic but self-mocking passion; Keynes skipping in short, busy paragraphs from love, to Cambridge gossip, to work.

The affair had run into trouble almost from the start. 'There's distinctly something of the lovee about his affection if not about his lust,' Lytton complained to Maynard on 13 October 1905; Maynard in reply commanded him not to think that every kind of disaster was in store. Soon Lytton was lamenting Duncan's indifference, 'an adamantine and irrevocable rock which no power under heaven can move. Shall one dash oneself against it, or shall one turn one's back on it? . . . I generally seem to do both, which is the worst solution.'[1] Maynard wrote back practically that Duncan was probably tired from painting so much at the National Gallery. Keynes, it can be seen, was not entirely satisfactory as an outlet; but to be entirely in tune with Strachey's state of mind would have taxed a more sensitive person than he was. Lytton was both a rationalist and a romantic. He wanted reassurance that his fears were groundless, and also to savour the tragedy of unrequited love; conditions which were difficult to reconcile. Keynes did his best.

Lytton Strachey to JMK, 21 December 1905:
Last night he confessed that there was something wrong – he was, he said, 'a selfish brute'. This means that he occasionally feels absolutely indifferent towards me. It's a little difficult to gather – but I think I understand. He says it's a selfish feeling because it makes him think he's a complete whole in himself. Do you know it? . . . But what distresses him is that it seems to show that he likes me less than I like him – and I suppose this is true. A cynical person would, of course, conclude – not love, but lust. But would anyone say that if he knew all, if he saw all. . . . I'm carried away in dreams of glory when I look at him. . . . The eyes –! no, I want to forget that, to shut that out, to be blinded to such splendours – Ah, can I ever forget the vision of those suffused worlds of blueness, those exquisite revelations of Heaven? It's no good, I'm seized by an excess and agony of love. All the absurdest of the absurdities that one's read or imagined become the commonplaces of life. It is not ridiculous to think of dying to save him a moment's pain. This is raving; but it's raving that can never be expressed to him. He would feel with horror that he could never love *me* as much as that. . . . He cannot look into his own eyes. . . . My nerves have quite gone. I seem to be in direct & mystic contact with the Essence of the World. . . . Even Swithin is dim to me. Adieu!
I'm very glad to be able to write to you. I wonder if you'll be bored.

JMK to Lytton Strachey, 22 December 1905:
Your letters excite me very much, but they seem to come from a strangely different world to that I live in here. I read them first in the buzzing of family conversation; but when everybody has gone to bed and I have read the Sonnets for an hour they seem to come from the world of reality where pleasures and pains are merged and transcended in an almost Hegelian muddle.
Duncan's attitude is much easier to understand; I know well the terror of an affection greater than you can absorb, even when your own affection may appear complete.
Also he probably lacks that obsession which always seems to mark the lover in contradistinction to the loved.
Do you think it will be difficult to accept its absence as irrelevant? I think you will be equal to your fate. It would be a little absurd if you were both to veer about for fear of a greater thing than you could rise to.

Lytton Strachey to JMK, 22 December 1905:
I'm in a wretched state. . . . Have you anything to say that will console me? . . . I was blissfully happy till he said something which brought it over me in a sudden shock that he didn't care for me, &

wanted to escape. He complains of my terrors, and indeed they sometimes strike me as utterly fantastic – especially, oh especially, when he's there before me.

JMK to Lytton Strachey, 24 December 1905:
    If it was any good trying to console people I would try. But of course it isn't, and after all I don't think you are to be altogether pitied. I didn't suffer much pain last week, but I saw no visions and only learnt out of a psychology book that there are three parts of the body that excel all others in ... 'tactile discrimination'....

Lytton Strachey to JMK, 31 December 1905:
    I begin to wonder whether his intellect is satisfying enough.

JMK to Lytton Strachey, 1 January 1906:
    You ask too much. Do you think that you are going to get complete physical, moral, aesthetic, intellectual, passionate, affectionate satisfaction in a lump? But of course one has got to want it.... Do you believe you ever would be in love with someone who was completely intellectually satisfying...?

Lytton Strachey to JMK, 9 January 1906:
    His mind! – I didn't realise before what it was – the audacity, the strength, the amazing subtlety.

JMK to Lytton Strachey, 10 January 1906:
    I was a little sad; partly I suppose envy, but chiefly, I think, because you insist so much he is a genius. I am still afraid that it's all impossible in general.

'Perhaps you can advise something'; 'Please forgive – who else can I speak to?' Lytton's demands for comfort continue; Maynard always responds – it's only a cold in the head; Lytton has nothing to fear from his brother James, etc. Later Lytton was to say that Maynard's commonsense was enough to freeze a volcano. He had had the same feeling about him earlier. 'He is an Apostle without tears,' he had told the assembled brethren soon after Maynard had 'stolen' Hobhouse from him. Perhaps in Maynard's lame responses to his agonies are to be found the seeds of the disintegration of their intimacy. Yet Lytton's fires were partly epistolatory; truth was sacrificed to style. And this Maynard knew well enough.
    In February 1906 Duncan Grant got his chance to study painting in Paris when his aunt Elinor, Lady Colville, gave him £100 for his twenty-first birthday. He enrolled at La Pallette, an art school run by Jacques-Émile Blanche, living at the Hôtel de l'Univers et du Portugal near the Palais Royal. His affair with Hobhouse started up soon afterwards, and continued at intervals till the end of the year: he and Hobhouse spent a holiday together at Rothiemurchus in August. This time

Duncan's feelings were fully engaged. 'My darling,' he wrote to Hobhouse on 10 July 1906, 'if I could only be sure you *really* loved me I should be perfectly happy.... Oh my dearest angel do be able to tell me it's different than it was with Keynes.' Their previous rivalry forgotten, Lytton and Maynard united in deploring Hobhouse's conduct. 'Of all prostitutes, the spiritual ones are the worst,' Strachey declared contemptuously. Under the strain, Lytton's health collapsed – pains in his chest, pains in his balls, and 'wet dreams intolerably frequent . . . I'd give anything to see you, Maynard'. By December the affair was over. 'Arthur told me he had no feelings towards me at all,' Duncan told James on 18 December. At the end of his life Duncan told Paul Roche that Hobhouse was terrified lest his lover's 'passionate remonstrances and expressions of despair' should alert his mother to the nature of their friendship. 'He was full of unnecessary duties,' Duncan said.

In October 1906 Duncan returned to Paris which remained his base till the Summer of 1907, a curiously isolated expatriate figure in the artistic capital of the world. Maynard visited him there in March 1907 in the company of Norton and James Strachey. 'It was charming,' Duncan told Lytton, 'having Keynes and Norton here. I did seem to like Keynes much more than before.... It was curious he should have liked Versailles so much, we spent about an hour there and he talked about nothing except the management of the water works and comparisons to the 'Unter der Linden' in Berlin.'[2] Now it was Strachey's turn to commiserate: 'The number of dim things he must have said. . . .' But Duncan did not mind. 'Dear Duncan, London is almost as empty to me as Paris is to you,' Maynard wrote on his return.[3] Duncan sent back some clothes Maynard had left behind. 'I moved today to my studio which is charming and I hope I shall be able to paint a picture or two in it. Bell, Vanessa and Virginia are here. No news except the sordid [Augustus] John scandals which you may or may not hear from Lytton.'[4]

After the Hobhouse episode, Lytton's affair with his cousin had started up again in a somewhat desultory fashion. He never seems to have seen Maynard as a potential rival in love. He lacked all passion. By 1908 he was starting to wonder what he could have been talking to him about all these years. As compared with his own capacity for the *grand amour* Keynes's feeble lasciviousness seemed to offer no possible threat. He should have been more alerted to those eyes which, as he noted, burnt with an 'ambiguous flame'. And he should have been alerted by what he knew of Duncan's character. Maynard's less passionate personality would make lesser demands on Duncan than Lytton's had made – demands which Duncan could not meet. Lytton's summaries of Maynard left out his capacity for cherishing those he loved – something very reassuring to Duncan, who was too proud and innocent to protect himself from the world. On the other side 'anyone could fall in love with Duncan if he wanted to,' Maynard had written to Lytton as early as April 1906. Of medium height, with dark good looks, he had eyes 'extraordinarily grey and liquid, very pale, with huge irises and long lashes' as well as what Strachey called 'incomparably lascivious lips'.[5] He had an original but completely untrained intelligence. Maynard would have been delighted by the fact that he had never mastered the multiplication table. He loved music and dancing. His visual sense made him 'intensely observant and amused in everything he saw: and the things he saw were especially those to which the majority of people were blind'. He 'responded instantly to the mood of his companion'. He had a 'most charming way of affectionately teasing the people he was fond of'.[6] The very absence of mind which made him seem half-witted to conventional people – his clothes, for example, looked, and often were, other people's cast-offs – was part of his charm for Maynard. Yet he was proud and certain of what he had to do. Duncan, in short, fitted the type whom Maynard was always disposed to worship: the artist with an inner integrity but with an outward need for protection.

Early in June 1908 Lytton went to spend a month in Cambridge, leaving Duncan and Maynard in London. Their affair started as soon as Lytton left. On Sunday 28 June, Florence wrote to Neville in Switzerland: 'John has brought Duncan Grant down with him. This morning we all sat in the garden & read, & this afternoon they two have bicycled to Clayhithe for tea.' This trip to Cambridge must have taken place without Lytton's knowledge. From Fellows Road, Hampstead, Duncan wrote to Maynard on 29 June: 'I know I needn't tell you how much I enjoyed my Cambridge visit ... indeed I don't think I have ever been so completely happy, anyhow since I left school.' They continued to see each other frequently in London: Maynard took Duncan to Eton, where Duncan felt that his friend's past existence was being hurried over for his benefit: 'It rather terrified me to think what a little I should represent to you in 7 years time.'[7] Taking them, on his return to London, to lunch at Simpsons on 14 July, Lytton was alerted to new developments by a whispered aside from Keynes to Duncan, suggesting – as he wrote to his brother James – 'a liaison between Duncan and our dear Detraqué'.[8] Next day he saw Maynard and it all came out.

JMK to Duncan Grant, 15 July 1908:
Dearest Duncan, Lytton has been. He begins 'I hear that you and Duncan are carrying on together'. I feel quite shattered by the interview, but I suppose it wasn't very dreadful really. He takes the cynical line – much interested as a student of human life. But it gave him, as he said, a turn. ... Oh dear, I don't know what to think of the

interview and feel ill and rather distraught. I wish there was no one else in the world but you. Come early to-morrow – as near tea-time as you can. . . .

To his brother, Strachey was far from posing as the detached observer of human life. He wrote to him on 15 July 1908:

I am suffering now too much. I have been through too much. Things are spectral to me now. . . . Oh! There are cruelties in the world. . . .

I do feel though, and write to you, though I told Maynard that I wouldn't until he did, tomorrow, in a wretched agony. It's utterly stupid and absurd, besides being incomprehensible. Ils s'aiment. There can be no comment that I can think of. It's been going on 'for the last five, or five and a half weeks' as that imbecile said. They've kept it horribly secret. He has come to me reeking with that semen, he has never thought that I should know. Ah! but there's only one thing I think – that the nature of Love has been hidden from him, that . . . they are all playing, and taking themselves in.

James tried to comfort Lytton (16 July 1908):

But surely they can't seriously think they're in *love* with one another? If they do, I confess that they appear to me to have got into a quite *filthy* condition. I feel that once – long ago perhaps – even 'he' had a dim idea of what it all meant. And that makes it seem to me incredible that they shouldn't be able to see what they're doing now. Their actual feelings in themselves look to me merely silly. . . . There's hardly any affection. And so irritation's bound to set in – and be fatal too – before long: especially if they attempt a honeymoon. We shall see.

Lytton was working himself up into a fine rage against Maynard. On 17 July 1908 he wrote to James:

What was so shocking about my interview with 'him', when he made the announcement, was the incredible lack of feeling. The famous poem* was the only adequate description. He *was* a safety-bicycle with genitals. It quite gave even me a turn. I believe I might have passed on in the conversation from that, without a visible break, to probability – he would never have noticed. Unfortunately I was too honest, and had a fit, which at least did make him begin very dimly to realise that it was perhaps rather odd and important that he was 'in love'. I think ever since the Hobber days there has been distinct deterioration. Then, there was certainly just a touch of romance; and now the hardness is complete.

* Lytton had written an epitaph on Maynard which was 'too insulting to circulate'.

Of all Strachey's amorous crises, writes his biographer, this was his 'most wretched'.[9] However, a reconciliation of a kind was patched up. Maynard made the first move, writing to Lytton on 20 July:

> I want very much to write and don't know what to say. Has your confusion died away? Do you yet know what you think and feel about us? Please don't be unsympathetic and don't, if you can help it, hate me. Can I come and see you? This is my last minute in this office, but I shall probably be in London until Wednesday.

'The letter seems to me to show affection,' Lytton wrote to his brother on 21 July. 'Friendship has a meaning – don't you really believe that? – and, in this kind of muddle, all that one can do is to act as a friend and be – well, if not "generous" at least decent.' To Maynard he replied:

> My confusion has not died away, and I'm afraid it never will, because, as far as I can see, it was born with me. Such a dazzled and gibbering creature as I am! However, you seem to have put up with that hitherto and I daresay you will in the future. Dear Maynard, I only know that we've been friends for too long to stop being friends now. There are some things that I shall try not to think of, and you must do your best to help me in that; and you must believe that I do sympathise and don't hate you and that if you were here now I should probably kiss you, except then Duncan would be jealous, which would never do!

JMK to Lytton Strachey, 22 July 1908:

> Your letter made me cry but I was very glad to get it. I have decided to linger on until to-morrow and shall come in at or after tea in the hope of seeing you. Would you, perhaps, come and see Isadora Duncan dance afterwards, and forget the real Duncans, with whom no one in the world could help but fall in love, exist?

When he got back to Harvey Road on 22 July Maynard found 'three most lovely books – a present from Lytton. I feel that they are a token of a good deal – it is *too* good of him to behave like this.'[10]

Maynard moved into King's on 25 July, having let his flat to Granville Proby for the balance of his lease. On 27 July Duncan left for the Orkney Islands. He had been invited to stay on Hoy by the millionaire Thomas Middlemore a friend of his mother's, who had bought the island in 1898 for £32,000.

Although Maynard missed Duncan terribly, he adored being in Cambridge again, and regaled his friend with the familiar gossip. 'Nothing could be more peaceful than existence here,' he wrote to Duncan on 26 July. 'My rooms are not very beautifully arranged but they look at the best view in the world – the great green lawns with the river and backs beyond.... With the weather so fine, I should, if you were only here, feel incorrigibly contented.' On 27 July, while Duncan was whirling through the night to Hoy, Maynard listened to a Mr Schloss* reading a paper on 'Relationships' in Ben Keeling's room to the 'Fabian boys':

A dreadful, silly, maundering paper, followed by a blithering speech from Daddy Dalton.† In spite of the serried ranks of females, the paper was chiefly about sodomy which is called 'the passionate love of comrades'. Really James is quite right – these Fabians talk about nothing else.... The thing has grown with leaps and bounds in my two years of absence and practically everybody in Cambridge, except me, is an open and avowed sodomite.

Shove‡ I've now seen twice. He's much the best of them – quite a cut above the other in my opinion. Indeed he's very charming, though not very clever I dare say, and quite nice to look at....

Dear Duncan if I could kiss you and hold your hand I should be perfectly happy, and from wanting to I am discontented and almost, not quite, miserable. Find us a lovely cottage in the North and we will stay there forever....

JMK to Duncan Grant, 29 July 1908:
Today for the first time a little work has been accomplished. I wonder that so many books are written – nothing in the world is such hard work. I hope you don't find it as exhausting to paint a picture, as I do to write a chapter. It seems to be so much more tiring to do part of a big thing, than a little thing equal in size to the part. When one is writing a chapter, one's mind seems vaguely involved in the whole of the rest of the book.

I must go to tea now to meet some bloody working men who will be I expect as ugly as men can be.

JMK to Duncan Grant, 31 July 1908:
... I have been again having tea with working men; I suppose that they're virtuous enough fellows, not as ugly as they might be, and that it amuses them to come to Cambridge and be entertained for a fortnight – but I don't quite know what good it does....

Dearest, dearest Duncan I am in love with Cambridge, but not less in love with you. Write to me often, even if it is a very brief letter.

Meanwhile, Duncan had braved a stormy three-hour sea-journey from Stromness to Hoy, to be received with champagne on his arrival at Melsetter, Middlemore's estate. 'I cannot describe the beauty of these islands, you are going to see them so I won't even try,' he wrote to

* Arthur Schloss had come up to King's in 1907. He later changed his name to Waley, and became famous for his translations of Chinese poetry.
† Hugh Dalton, the Labour politician, had come to King's from Eton in 1906.
‡ Gerald Shove, also an arrival at King's in 1907, became an economist.

Maynard on 29 July. 'They are quite unlike England and have a completely different range of colour from the Highlands and then there is nothing like the soft warm scented air that seems always slightly blowing. The inhabitants are rather beautiful with mild polite manners and musical voices which they evidently admire greatly themselves as one hears them cooing like doves to one another about nothing. They are Scandinavians . . . so you will think I am among my own kith and kin.' The Middlemore house, 'a masterpiece of Celtic art' overlooking the sea, was full of Burne-Jones cartoons, Turner watercolours and Morris tapestries. 'Old Middlemore' was a 'model of true courtesy but talks slower than anyone in the world and thinks even slower'. Duncan painted and read, walked with the women, talked with the men, played cards with both, ate and drank prodigiously, and desperately missed Maynard. 'I would give my soul to the Devil if I could kiss you and be kissed,' he wrote on 29 July.

Duncan Grant to JMK, 2 August 1908:
    Your two letters arrived on Saturday (yesterday) and brought me infinite pleasure. You are the only person I feel I can speak to. You cannot imagine how much I want to scream sometimes here for want of being able to say something that I mean. It's not only that one's a sodomite that one has to hide but one's whole philosophy of life; one's feeling even for inanimate things I feel would shock some people. Here I am surrounded by them, not a soul to speak to. Two more arrived today – old Biddulph and Tom Collins 'a manly old fellow' as the world thinks. Both are quite good, honest sort of people but it's so damnable to think that they can only think me a harmless sort of lunatic or a dangerous criminal whom they wouldn't associate with at any price. I daresay all this is quite exaggerated and absurd and that very soon I shall think nothing of the sort. But I am suffering from acute dyspepsia and a painful abscess in my cheek from this heavy sea air and too much cream. At any rate I wish you were here to stand between me and the world.

Duncan Grant to JMK, 6 August 1908:
    Your letters are like drams of whisky to the frozen explorer. Nearly everyone here seems to have a heart of ice. Except one of the Americans who is extraordinarily stupid. I sometimes feel that a seagull would be the best thing to embrace until you make your appearance. Pretty far gone perhaps, but they really do seem more human than my fellow guests, or rather nearer kin to me. I wonder whether *I* am really something quite different and not a human being at all. I sometimes think so and if it wasn't for you I think I should think so at this moment. However you must not think I am really unhappy, I am only rather astonished. The place is really divine and I don't think anyone notices my peculiarities, in fact I'm becoming

quite intimate with the young ladies and quite friendly with the old men! You can imagine in what a dim way.

Maynard, too, was being driven frantic by Duncan's absence:

JMK to Duncan Grant, 5 August 1908:

Dearest dearest Duncan, I must begin the day with a letter – I'm so delighted to have got yours, the first from Hoy. The hope of one woke me early in the morning and I crept out to look at my table – there was nothing and I was in despair, so I got into bed again quite determined to telegraph. But I had been too early for the post and when I got out again there was your packet for me to kiss and read. Do please arrange for me to come north at the earliest possible moment. The time passes infinitely slowly – never so slowly since I was at school – and there have been a good many black fits lately when I can neither sleep nor work and can only think of you with a kind of heavy despair. Dear Duncan I love you too much and I can't now bear to live without you. Let me have as many letters as possible and charter a cottage or intrigue me into Melsetter as soon as you can.

Between 5 and 10 August, Maynard and his sister Margaret joined a large house-party at Mary Berenson's near Oxford, which greatly cheered him up. To Duncan he explained (9 August):

... We bathe and lie naked in the sun and eat too much and hear conversation on the principles of ART and punt out on the Thames at night with the beautiful body of the punter black against the moon....

I want to see you again dreadfully and find that even in the midst of a crowd of people I am continually sinking into a trance and thinking about you. How dreadful meeting after the first long interval! Shall we be as happy and contented together as ever?

They were reunited at Stromness on 18 August. To Lytton, staying with James at Rothiemurchus, Maynard wrote on 20 August: 'We hired a sailing boat to-day and went over to Hoy, but failed to secure a lodging. There was a very charming farm, but they refused to have us, and another was engaged but we shall try again. It is a most lovely island, one of the loveliest I have ever seen and we approached its rocks most romantically.... I can't write another word with this awful hotel pen.'

'I know we will be happy,' Duncan had written. His expectation was fulfilled. Indeed, the next two months were probably the happiest in Maynard's life. They spent the first fortnight at Stromness, where they lodged in the Mason's Arms Hotel. 'The view above this town,' Maynard wrote to Lytton, 'is of the Bay of Naples and the Island of Capri. We strolled off this evening to have a better look at it and left my rug and papers and Duncan's picture in the field where they were. Imagine our horror on returning to find everything slobbered over . . . by a herd of cows. But the picture was benefited and probability none the worse. . . .' It was in this field, overlooking the harbour, that Maynard wrote a chapter which convinced and converted Whitehead on a fundamental point.[11]

They returned to Hoy and this time persuaded the owners of the farm they had so admired to let them have accommodation there. 'It turned out,' Maynard informed Lytton, 'that they had rooms, but no spare beds and that this was the leading objection. This gave no difficulty and we sailed over in a ship the next day with beds and baggage. The comfort here is complete; our bedroom is on the ground floor next our keeping room and we have a private front door. There are exquisite farm lads like Greeks who flit around and drive us in our gig, and the loveliest schoolboys in Britain called Gillespie who inhabit the lodge. There are cliffs of red sandstone a mile high, black mountains two miles high, golden grass, heather, porpoises and whales. There are also less portentous beauties everywhere, which according to Duncan are suitable to paint.'[12]

At Orgill Farm, they settled down, Maynard told his mother, to 'fixed hours of painting and probability'. The peat fires were always on, and the animals so strange and numerous that even Maynard started to take an interest in them. The only problem was that everyone was suspicious of German spies, so that 'they will have to get used to us before sitting for portraits'. By 13 September, Duncan had started painting Maynard, Probability's back had been broken, and 'Money is beginning to form itself more definitely in my mind.'[13] He wrote to his sister Margaret on 15 September:

> Duncan is sketching the red cliffs. . . . We lead a very peaceable orderly existence with a fair amount of work in it and shall stay here, we hope, for some weeks yet. How awful, if I was still in my office, to have to hurry back to London! There is not a moment when I regret the damned place. . . . We have just finished reading 'Northanger Abbey' out loud. . . . The witch has begun to sing, the wind to rise and the Atlantic rollers to roar, and we must begin our tramp home past a lake along what the guide book calls a dark forbidding valley.

Duncan himself dates Maynard's real appreciation of painting from this time. 'Maynard with his writing board was a good subject, so while he was immersed in the "Theory of Probability" I . . . was immersed in trying to figure out the shape of his face. The result of this I think was that Maynard gradually accepted the fact that painting had its difficulties too, in fact he accepted, without me having to point it out, that the painter had a serious job on hand.'[14]

However, in mid-September, Maynard developed one of his feverish attacks, and he and Duncan invited themselves to Melsetter on 18 September, where they stayed for ten days. 'I am still rather feeble, and glad to lie on the soft sofas and chairs of a luxurious house,' he told Florence on 20 September. Other guests included an admiral, a captain, and a parson, who all 'showed a proper expectation of the forthcoming war with Germany'. In the evening they played 'a quiet rubber of very old-fashioned whist'. Their visit had been a great success, Maynard told his father on 27 September. He had become an indispensable fourth at whist, so that they were being pressed to stay. He had never eaten such delicious food nor drunk such exquisite wines. The house was 'extraordinarily complete with its chapel, museum, theatre, model laundry, farm, golf links and five gardens; and when they go shooting Duncan and I have complete control of it...'. He was doing about three hours' work a day and had begun an article for the *Economic Journal* on Indian prices and currency. 'Probability is well advanced and could be almost finished before I leave the island if I confined my work to it.'

Back at Orgill, Maynard continued to enthuse over the weather, the landscape, and the wild life. 'The prospect of turning out of these accustomed rooms is already gloomy,' he wrote to Lytton on 7 October. 'I don't feel that I much want to see Cambridge again. I don't know why we are leaving here.' Their departure from the Orkneys was postponed, however, when Middlemore invited them to spend a few days at his shooting lodge in the middle of Hoy.

It was not till 22 October that he and Duncan at last tore themselves away, Duncan to go to Rothiemurchus. Maynard arrived back in Cambridge on the evening of the 23rd, his father, as always, being there to meet him at the station. He moved into his new rooms at King's on 24 October. Lytton was his first guest. 'I am so happy to be in Cambridge that I am as cheerful as anyone could wish,' he wrote to Duncan. 'When I have both you and Cambridge, I shall be the most fortunate creature in the world.'[15] Lytton, on the other hand, was far from pleased with the company of his successful rival. 'It was hardly anything but horror,' he told his brother. 'It wasn't only his indelicacy – which was complete, lasting up to the very last, but the sense that it was no good expecting any more to get anything out of that relationship.... It was ashes and dry bones.... In future I shall go to Trinity.'[16] The failure of this reunion was to have bitter consequences for Maynard over the next few months.

The old life reestablished itself. Golf with Neville at Royston in continuous rain reduced him to taking quinine. Dickinson read a paper on Immortality. Rupert Brooke now called Keynes Maynard. There were beauties to be inspected for the Society: George Mallory seemed 'perfectly lovely'.* Duncan came up on 31 October. 'His train was 17½ minutes late. So at least I was informed by Maynard at 1.14,' James Strachey told his brother. 'The general appearance is *extraordinarily married* – If D. comes here to live, however, there'll certainly be flirtations with – oh! anyone. But what I now see is that that won't matter a bit . . . the Machine will merely be amused and exclaim "You always come back to me – to me – to me!" And he always will.'[17]

On 10 November, Maynard went to London to superintend the removal of his things from St James's Court, where he got influenza so badly that he had to spend a couple of days in Hampstead Hospital. Strachey saw him 'rigged out in shetland waistcoats, with long grey arms, fairly beaming with fatuity, for all the world like a gorilla trying to be Mary Moore. It was incredibly shocking! And poor dear Duncan at the end of the bed, sending out oeillades. . . . I fled from the place, howling.'[18] Hospital left Maynard enraged. 'Everything was governed by inflexible rule and regulation, which are the curse of human existence everywhere but particularly in a hospital.'[19] He returned, still weak, to Harvey Road on 16 November, where Probability occupied most of his time, moving back into King's on 20 November.

He and Duncan, who returned to London early in November, now went through a miserable time – partly due to the after effects of the influenza they had both suffered. Duncan, who was searching for a studio in which he could paint and which Keynes could share as a London pied-à-terre, was by 18 November 'extremely depressed and . . . almost in tears, completely unbalanced. Simply because you are not here to right me. I have these sudden fits of depression occasionally merely because someone makes a remark to me which I imagine proves that they have no more idea of what I'm like than a cabbage.' Maynard at first functioned happily in the day but was sad in the evenings because Duncan was not there; his feelings were like 'those of a homesick schoolboy'.[20] By 23 November he was 'excessively miserable during a large part of the day and hardly know how to support existence. . . . If I knew you were coming, I should feel more cheerful in the meantime. . . .' He tempted Duncan for a long visit by the promise of 'millions of people to come and sit for you. . . . If only you come, I shall be happy in body and mind, and really able to do work.' Nor were the freshmen inspiring, the only one of note being a 'Mr [Dennis] Robertson of Eton and Trinity [who] came to lunch and for a walk with me yesterday. There's a good deal in his favour, but a little pudding headed perhaps.'[21] Duncan came on 28 November and stayed till 15 December with Maynard at King's, finishing the portrait he had begun in the

* George Leigh Mallory, who died in the attempt on Everest in 1924, was then in his third year at Magdalene College. He was more Geoffrey's friend than Maynard's.

Orkneys, and starting one of Margaret. His family, who came to inspect the picture, 'all think that the thumb of the left hand is a nobble on the first finger and wonder why my trousers aren't turned up, but the general attitude is one of surprising approval. . . .'[22] Neville bought it for Florence – the first of many sales Duncan made through Maynard.

Duncan's visit revived Maynard's intellectual interests. The revised version of his fellowship dissertation was practically finished by 4 December. [23] A visit from Swithin provided, as always, a welcome, but worrying, experience. Swithinbank, who had gained a disappointing second class in classics at Balliol and had narrowly been dissuaded from embarking forthwith to the Fiji Islands as a sanitary inspector, had surprised everyone by coming third in the Civil Service examination that September. This seemed to ensure a place in the home Civil Service; but, possibly because he never expected to come so high, he had put himself down for the Indian Civil Service only; and was now busy reading books on Burma, preparatory to going out there as district commissioner. Duncan, who had just met Swithin in London at the Stracheys, found him 'the most beautiful person I've ever seen'. At King's, Maynard and Swithin had one of their usual grand conversations lasting most of the night.[24] By contrast, a conversation with another old flame, Hobhouse, left Maynard 'absolutely shattered'. 'He seemed to me awful, horrible, a thing which ought to be put out of the way; and yet I could not forget how much I had been in love with him. I'm sure he was not like this then; it is impossible.'[25] Duncan had rented a studio in St John's Wood, and Maynard spent the first fortnight in January with him. In the mornings, Pernel Strachey would sit for her portrait, and he would study Finance. They prepared their own lunches and spent most of the afternoons washing up. In the evenings they went to the theatre. 'The new studio,' he told his sister Margaret, 'is really a charming place – a fairly large white room with two seat windows to the ground.'[26]

Apart from physical attraction which is indefinable, the attraction between Maynard and Duncan was very much one of opposites: each admired and valued that in the other which he himself lacked. Duncan was beautiful, artistic, unworldly; Maynard was clever, practical, kind. But in this very lack of fit was obvious potential for friction. Maynard liked his life to be well-arranged; Duncan's arrangements were chaotic. Maynard was thoughtful to friends; Duncan was thoughtless.* Maynard began to complain about his failure to write regularly, about his habit of putting off visits. Duncan could not be tied down to a routine

* It was characteristic of Maynard to send a Christmas present of books for the family at whose farm they had stayed in Hoy.

of letters and visits, and disappointed expectations started to prey on Maynard's mind, leading to lovers' tiffs. 'Darling Maynard, what a brute you make me out to be,' wrote Duncan on 29 December, after Maynard had complained of the misery caused by Duncan promising, but failing, to write on a certain day.[27]

'Dearest Maynard, we mustn't often behave like we did today,' wrote Duncan early in 1909. 'It is too exhausting for one's nerves.... You must try – no it's no use.... I must try to behave better, less vaguely & selfishly & then everything ought to go more smoothly.' Maynard's way of showing affection by monetary gifts could also give rise to misunderstanding. Duncan was 'very much enraged' to receive £5 through the post for his twenty-fourth birthday (21 January 1909). 'It's too absurd of you,' Maynard wrote him. 'The thing is good as a means and absolutely unimportant in itself.'[28]

Maynard and Duncan lived very full lives. Maynard had started lecturing, coaching and writing in Cambridge; Duncan had begun to paint professionally in London. Their social lives were also crowded. But whereas Maynard always arranged his life so as to leave room for Duncan, Duncan's arrangements tended to exclude Maynard. Much of Duncan's spare time was spent going to concerts – sometimes with Lytton. On 24 January 1909 he took tickets for Wagner's *Ring* about which he was 'much excited'. Maynard disliked music. He dreaded Duncan drifting into 'all sorts of unnecessary engagements which will make it impossible for us ever to meet again'.[29]

By mid-February 1909 Maynard was reminding Duncan that they had met only three times in the last five weeks. But Duncan's absence was not the only cause of his low spirits at this time. Strachey, as it turned out, had not forgiven him for taking Duncan away from him even though he now found Duncan 'quite singularly unattractive'. He and his brother started a malicious campaign against 'Pozzo di Borgo' as they had taken to calling him among their Cambridge friends – Apostles and embryos – and succeeded in turning opinion against him.* Maynard felt hurt and unloved. Eventually Strachey realised he was going too far. 'I've been feeling rather uneasy about the Pozzo man,' he wrote to James on 14 February. 'On Wednesday night I was at Richmond, and Moore incidentally mentioned him as appearing very depressed and silent – "Looked as if he might be feeling that people didn't like him." I do hope it's nothing definite, or possibly even that it's untrue. But I can't help feeling rather guilty.... Then I suppose there's the possibility that he's beginning to find a coolness in Duncan – or even that he's beginning to think that Duncan hasn't got

* Contrary to what has been said, Lytton Strachey had no one or no thing in mind when he started calling Maynard Pozzo di Borgo. See his letter to James Strachey, 26 November 1908.

much to offer him that he wants. However no doubt the most probable thing is that he's only troubled in a way that's infinitely vague. Only I don't like to imagine it; and if, après tout, il a lu ces lettres!' James replied on 15 February:

I take Pozzo first – as you've enquired about him. I think there can be no doubt Moore's right. Popular opinion seems to be smashing him. Last Saturday, for instance at the Society, Rupert read. Maynard spoke very early – and very ignobly. And everyone thought so & he knew everyone thought so: & simply subsided into his chair & never spoke or was spoken to again the whole evening. His face becomes so thin on these occasions he's quite pathetic; but then he's also ignoble. But also, as a matter of fact, a week ago I had a scene with him. He said it was awful that you hated him. And wiped his eyes a good deal. I think he thought *I* hated him too. I tried to do what I could – not much I fear: somehow I can't feel much affection for him. Well, you may say he's a pathetic figure. But damn it I won't waste tears over him. He has *such* compensations. I'm certain he still feels *quite* fixed about Duncan. He still appears to have not a shadow of doubt. However, if you write him a sentimental letter, I'm sure he'd be delighted.

Lytton Strachey to James Strachey, 19 February 1909:
What you said of Pozzo was very painful. I think I feel about him just as you do – indifference, mingled with a sort of scorn.... Why should [him thinking that we hate him] make so much difference? Does he dimly realise that if we dislike him he ought to be disliked? But then, if Duncan likes him.... The odd thing in it all is that he doesn't seem *really* to care about anything. That eye-wiping! – My God, I too have experienced it. Weeping seems to be fashionable just now.

Lytton Strachey to James Strachey, 11 March 1909:
I've been thinking about Maynard a good deal lately, and he seems to me more and more an almost tragic figure. I'm afraid he must be quite dreadfully in love – how could even he avoid that in the circumstances? The situation's so singularly cramped – no confidants as far, as can be seen, on either side – I believe he's simply living on the accumulations of intensely private passion. Isn't it shocking to think of him so pale and distrait among your unsympathising conversations burning with a desperate inward fire? He's put the whole of his life on a single number. Isn't this true? – If so, imagine the horror when the inevitable happens – because surely it *is* inevitable – and he finds that his one foundation has completely gone – I really shudder at the thought – don't you think he then might actually go? The more I consider this, the more certain it seems to me that I'm the only person who can support him (in one way or another!) and that when the time comes I ought to be

there. . . . I think of taking the opportunity of his fellowship (I suppose on Saturday) to write with some assurance of 'friendship', or as
near that as I can get, merely to keep up some sort of a thread. Do
you agree that decency demands this?

Maynard, as Strachey surmised, was wilting under the force of his
friends' disapproval. Lytton's attitude is easy to understand. In their
friendship he had always been the leader. Now Maynard had become
too successful. Successful in work, while Strachey was still struggling
to make ends meet churning out reviews which he hated, he had proved
successful in love too – and at Lytton's expense. Nor could he help
reducing love to numbers. 'His statistics make me gasp,' James had
written to Lytton, as Maynard revealed the details of his sexual encounters. (He kept count of them in his engagement diary.) The
scatological incidents with which he enlivened his talk now seemed to
Strachey to be merely disgusting – when applied to Duncan. 'His
conversation,' he wrote to James a little later, 'does appear to me
inordinately filthy. I felt as if I was walking in a drain.'

Lytton's attitude to Maynard at this time helped shape Bloomsbury's later attitude to him. His outbursts were not confined to his
brother. On 5 February 1909 he wrote to Leonard Woolf in Ceylon:

> As for poor old Keynes, he's quite absolutely sunk – it's really
> remarkable, the unveiled collapse. If ever a human soul was doomed,
> it's he. And by God I think he deserves his fate. Looking back I see
> him, hideous and meaningless, at every turn and every crisis, a
> malignant goblin gibbering over destinies that are not his own . . . .
> He'll end a spiritual Nixon,* with a whole internal economy of metal
> makeshifts for lungs and lights and heart and genitory organs; but
> he'll never know; he'll never hear the clank.

Virginia Stephen, to whom he proposed at the same time, was the
recipient of similar views. Virginia hardly knew Maynard, and Woolf
had heard little but ill of him from Lytton during his years in Ceylon.
Their critical attitude to Keynes, which was lifelong, may thus have its
roots in Lytton's sexual jealousy.

That jealousy was real enough. But one must also consider these
friends' feelings about each other in the light of Strachey's epistolary
philosophy as set out to John Sheppard on 25 March 1903: 'it is much
easier to say filthy things than charming things, which one may feel just
as much if not more . . . It'd take fourteen years to say everything one

---

*J. E. Nixon (1839–1916) was an eccentric lecturer in classics, parts of whose body
were 'metal makeshifts'. The legend was that two men, Nicholson and Dixon, had been
so dismembered in an accident that only enough was left to rivet together one man –
Nixon.

thought about anyone. So one just says the things which are the amusingest & of course the nastiest as well.'

Once his rival was down, Lytton's own wound began to heal. He could afford to be less venomous. On 16 March 1909 Maynard heard he had been elected to a prize fellowship at King's, all opposition to his thesis having collapsed. From Belsize Park Gardens, his new family home, Lytton wrote to him on 17 March:

Dear Maynard,
I was very glad to hear of the fellowship. One couldn't feel absolutely sure with those devils! I suppose you're now established for the rest of your days, and it seems very clear that you've acted wisely....
I've been wanting to write to you for some time, though really I think it's hardly necessary – only to say that you must always think of me as your friend. I shall think of you in the same way. But I've been rather afraid that lately you may have felt that things had become different. I don't think it's the case. The only thing is that I'm sometimes uneasy and awkward perhaps, partly I suppose because of my nervous organisation which isn't particularly good – but I don't see how it can be helped. I can only beg that you'll attend to it as little as possible, and believe me to be a sensible decent person who remembers and knows.

Maynard was clearly pleased with this delicate apology. But he failed to find the right words in his reply, dated 21 March:

Dear Lytton,
I was *very* glad to get your letter.
Tonight I dined for the second time at their High Table. The food is excellent but, by God, one feels a don. I play the part admirably, perhaps it belongs to me, but I should like to rape an undergraduate in the Combination Room, just to make them see things a little more in their true light.... I hope to be in London sometime this week but the business of rooms for next term and so forth keeps me hanging about.

Lytton complained to his brother that his gesture of reconciliation had been met by a 'sterile letter'. They remained friends; but the best days of their friendship were over.

9 *Economic Orthodoxies*

ATTITUDES TO ECONOMICS

Like most economists at the time, Keynes started teaching economics without having taken a university degree in the subject. His formal training was limited to one term's postgraduate work under Marshall's supervision. His spare time at the India Office had been occupied with Probability. He took the lectureship in economics not because he saw economics as his life's work but because he wanted to get back to Cambridge. Mostly he learnt on the job. Compared with today, there was little to learn, and that was not difficult. Most British economists before Marshall were men reared on a single book – John Stuart Mill's *Principles*. Their successors also tended to be men of a single book – Marshall's *Principles*, supplemented by oral tradition, Marshall's evidence to a couple of Royal Commissions, and privately printed fragments of the Master's thought. Keynes's own copy of Marshall's book was the third edition of 1895. It was comprehensively annotated, showing that he had read it thoroughly, almost certainly in the summer of 1905 (see above, p. 132). In addition, Keynes had soaked up much economics at home; and although he had not been in the Financial Department of the India Office, he left Whitehall with a good working knowledge of India's currency and banking system. But his reading was not extensive. He started on Adam Smith only in 1910, and never became erudite in the literature, as Foxwell was. His grasp of theory came not so much from reading about it as from working out the problems for himself, and discussing them with others. In this way he acquired a firm understanding of a fairly limited range of theory.

Having embarked on economics, Keynes was no less eager than most economists to display his professional competence, seizing such opportunities as his contacts put in his way. His career as an economic journalist started almost immediately on his return to Cambridge. He had the style, lucidity, and above all the quickness to do it. To Duncan Grant he wrote on 6 February 1909:

> Oh, I don't think I told you that I've taken to *Journalism*. Last Tuesday night I received a letter enclosing an article about 'Shippers,

Bankers and Brokers' from the Economist ... and asking if I would write a letter on it 'suggestive and provocative' as soon as possible. I seized my pen and had despatched a reply within an hour and a half of opening the request. Today I open my Economist and find it, a column long, in the leading position, and the Editor [F. W. Hirst] writes to say that he will treat it as a contribution. So I shall get at least a guinea.

When my article, which is now finished appears in the Economic Journal [see below p. 220] I shall send a copy of it to the Editor of the Economist, and offer myself to him as an occasional correspondent on Indian affairs – which would give me an anonymous pulpit for anything on the subject which might come into my head.

A landmark in Keynes's professional involvement in the subject was his appointment as editor of the *Economic Journal* in October 1911 – a post which his father had turned down twenty years earlier. Reading manuscripts played an important part in his economic education. As he was thought, at twenty-eight, to be young for the job, he was given a supervisory editorial committee; but from the start took his own decisions. His first editorial act was to turn down a contribution from the economic historian Archdeacon Cunningham. 'It was the most complete wash and had nothing to do with economics,' he told his father. Everyone agrees that Keynes made an excellent editor, imaginative in soliciting contributions, prompt in his response to them, helpful in his comments. An example of his editorial enterprise (and patience) is the way he coaxed an article out of the reluctant Frenchman Marcel Labordère, a gifted amateur of monetary statistics. Keynes was so impressed with his pamphlet, *Les Migrations de l'Or en 1910*, that he commissioned a contribution from him on French banking, which arrived three years, and many encouraging letters, later. The foundation of Keynes's editorial achievement was the speed with which he got through the work. His professional involvement in economics increased in 1912 when he was elected a member of the select Political Economy Club. He travelled up to London regularly for its Wednesday evening meetings, despatching his *Economic Journal* business on Thursdays at Adelphi Terrace.

Despite these extensions to his education, Keynes's range remained narrower than Marshall's or Pigou's. His main interests in economics spilled over from his work on Probability. Before the war he lectured mainly on the pure and applied theory of money. He had attended Marshall's lectures on money in 1906 and remembered them as being illustrated with 'some very elegant diagrams'. Keynes, as we shall see, did nothing before 1914 to develop monetary theory from the point where Marshall had left it. But he was fascinated by the behaviour of financial markets, as illustrating his theory of rational behaviour under uncertain conditions. In 1908 he told his father: 'I lie in bed for hours in the morning reading treatises on the philosophy of probability by members of the Stock Exchange. The soundest treatment so far is by the owner of a bucket shop.'[1] The investor, he wrote in 1910,

> will be affected, as is obvious, not by the net income which he will actually receive from his investment in the long run, but by his expectations. These will often depend upon fashion, upon advertisement, or upon purely irrational waves of optimism or depression. Similarly by risk we mean not the real risk as measured by the actual average of the class of investment over the period of years to which the expectation refers, but the risk as it is estimated, wisely or foolishly, by the investor. His desire that the net rate of interest shall be as high as possible will be modified by the usually conflicting desire that the rate of risk shall be as low as possible. But no mathematical rule can be laid down respecting the exact compromise which will be struck between the fear of loss and the desire for a high rate of interest ... Since the risk of which we must take account is the subjective risk ... its magnitude very largely depends upon the amount of relevant information regarding the investment that is easily accessible to him. What would be a risky investment for an ignorant speculator may be exceptionally safe for the well-informed expert. The amount of risk to any investor practically depends, in fact, upon the degree of his ignorance respecting the circumstances and prospects of the investment he is considering. It will, however, also depend on what we may term the objective risk, so far as that is known to him, arising, for instance, out of bad and unstable government or the uncertainty of the seasons.[2]

Thus as early as 1910 Keynes was pointing to the part played by 'expectations, ignorance and uncertainty (all left out of the "certainty" models of much conventional ... theory)' in the decisions to invest.[3] In the *General Theory* he would write that 'Money ... is, above all, a subtle device for linking the present to the future'.[4]

His other main intellectual interest stemming from Probability was the problem of causality in economic behaviour – particularly what could and could not be inferred from statistical evidence; this was a continuation of his father's interest in the philosophy of economics. This touched economics at the crucial, and as yet largely undeveloped, intersection between its deductive and inductive approaches. On balance Keynes took the view that the uses of statistics were mainly descriptive. This corresponded with his rejection of statistical theories of Probability. So many possible causes determined events, and the influence of uncertainty was so great, that economics could not be reduced to mere numbers.

Keynes's interest in money fitted the needs of the Cambridge Economics Tripos, following Marshall's retirement and Foxwell's withdrawal. What Marshall called the 'brilliant, compact group of earnest men' whom he joined in Cambridge consisted of the Professor (Arthur Pigou), W. E. Johnson, Lowes Dickinson, John Clapham, C. R. Fay, H. O. Meredith, Walter Layton, and L. Alston. Economics was still a small Tripos – only six candidates took the first Part I in 1905; and by 1910 there were twenty-five. Of the lecturers, Johnson was only marginally an economist, though in 1913 he published an important article in the *Economic Journal* on 'The Pure Theory of Utility Curves', and Lowes Dickinson was not one at all. Clapham, a Fellow of King's College, and Fay, by this time lecturing at Christ's College, were economic historians. So was the Girdler's lecturer, H. O. Meredith, Apostle and friend of G. E. Moore and E. M. Forster. Alston lectured to the poll men – undergraduates reading for a pass degree. Pigou and Keynes were the two main theorists – the real successors of Marshall and Foxwell.

In 1915 Keynes wrote 'The strength of our Economics school in the last few years and its attractiveness to a very able set of men have largely depended in my opinion on a combination in the teachers of a general agreement on principles with much variety of outlook, sympathies, and methods.'[5] The principles were those of Marshall. Keynes was a loyal pupil of the old professor, though he did not share Pigou's veneration of him – he thought him 'rather a silly [man] in his private character'.[6] There was also an important difference of sympathy, for Keynes, unlike Marshall, did not regard economics as a 'handmaiden of ethics' – it was not the activity through which his ethical beliefs found expression. He was a follower of Moore, who had cut the links which for Marshall connected economics to ethics. Indeed, Keynes's social philosophy was already somewhat archaic, if measured by the progressive thought of the time. Like his mother and the Charity Organisation Society, he believed that good character produced good individual material conditions rather than the other way round: anyone of 'capacity or character at all exceeding the average' could escape from poverty, he wrote.[7] As for the economic progress of society as a whole, he believed with Marshall that it could be safely left to market forces operating in the existing framework of law and institutions. The key requirement was the maintenance of free trade. Before the First World War he was not even a monetary reformer, except in the Indian context. These attitudes amounted to the view that no important innovation in economic theory or practice was needed. Keynes was strongly influenced in his attitude by the mood of 'automatic' progress which revived in the 1900s and against which his own experiments in living were undertaken. There is no premonition in his writings of England's economic decay, such as had haunted Joseph Chamberlain.

Although Keynes acknowledged Marshall as his master, in some respects he was personally closer to Foxwell, who wrote little but was immensely erudite in the history of economic thought and institutions. Keynes admired his iconoclasm, his literary style, his bibliomania, his love of fine craftsmanship and of music. Foxwell's sense of values, in short, appealed to him more than did Marshall's. For his part, Foxwell much preferred Keynes to Pigou, and not just because he had lost the professorship to the latter. 'He is such a prig,' Foxwell remarked of Pigou in 1901 – something Foxwell never was.

With 'the Prof' as Pigou was known, Maynard's relations were friendly but not close. They had known each other from Maynard's undergraduate years, when they had played fives and talked economics. But their temperaments and values set them apart. Pigou inherited Marshall's moral authority. 'Tall and handsome as a Viking',[8] a Harrovian and son of an army officer, Pigou carried himself as if on parade. Morals in his mind were inextricably linked with physical exertion, and he was never so happy as when taking parties of handsome, athletic, young men on climbs to Switzerland or the Lake District. His one failing in Marshall's eye was his extreme slovenliness of dress, the old Prof considering Norfolk jackets with holes in both elbows bad for the image of the fledgling Tripos. In other respects Pigou carried on the Marshallian tradition. Economics for him was a moral enterprise. In his Inaugural Lecture in 1908 he welcomed the man who had come to the study of economics because he had 'walked the slums of London'. In his memorial lecture on Marshall in 1923 he repeated that the purpose of economics was to 'furnish for those whom pity drives to action the lamp of assured knowledge and the sharp sword of right analysis' – sentiments whose content, not to mention style, were quite alien to Keynes.

The philosophic difference between the two is neatly pinpointed by Pigou's remark in his first important book, *Wealth and Welfare* (1912), that 'welfare means the same thing as good' – an example of what Moore would have called the naturalistic fallacy. Basing himself on an ethical concept of welfare, Pigou created the subject of 'welfare economics' whose avowed object was to 'make easy practical measures to promote welfare'.[9] Here lies the irony in the careers of the two great Cambridge economists. For it was Keynes whose economics were not derived from his ethics who made the great practical contribution to human welfare; while Pigou was driven to the pessimistic conclusion that 'the hope that an advance in economic knowledge will appreciably affect economic happenings is, I fear, a slender one'.[10]

As colleagues, Keynes and Pigou had their differences. Pigou was appointed professor at the age of thirty, without experience of administration, for which he never developed much aptitude. Though a prolific writer (Pigou's way of learning about a subject was to write a book on it), he disliked lecturing and examining, at least before the First World War, and in 1911 Keynes 'had to give him rather a pi-jaw which he took very well. He said he was quite unaware that he was giving the impression of avoiding duties ...'[11] Keynes's pique with Pigou may have been due to the fact that he had had to take over Pigou's main lecture course on Economic Principles in 1910–11, why it is not clear. At any rate his father wrote in his diary on 8 October 1911 that 'in many ways he [Maynard] seems to be taking Pigou's place as Professor of Political Economy'.

In pre-1914 Cambridge it was Pigou rather than Keynes who provided intellectual leadership in the Faculty. Keynes pursued economics because he was good at it, not because he had a mission to improve the world. He did not rank it very highly, but some parts of the subject gave him real intellectual pleasure without taking up an excessive amount of time: this was important, as his main intellectual interest remained his work on Probability, the long vacations being largely occupied in turning his Fellowship thesis into a book.

II

SELLING ECONOMICS BY THE HOUR

On Tuesday, 19 January 1909 Keynes gave the first of his twice-weekly lectures on Money, Credit and Prices 'before an enormous and cosmopolitan audience – there must have been at least 15, I think'.[12] Given that he was having to 'mug up' the subjects of his lectures his pre-war lecturing load was quite heavy, reaching a hundred hours in his third year, or an average of four hours a week spread over three terms (see Table).

At this period of his life he was an excellent lecturer, not yet having resorted to reading his lectures from the proofs of his books. His special lectures on 'Currency, Finance, and the Level of Prices in India', delivered in both Cambridge and the London School of Economics in the Lent Term of 1911 have, according to Elizabeth Johnson, a 'lively, up-to-date quality about them'. Newspaper clippings provided the latest figures; he would quote from letters he had received; and already he was tossing off the kind of *obiter dicta* that delighted generations of students: 'Leading financiers, being unable to follow an argument, will never admit the feasibility of anything until it has been demonstrated to them by practical experience.'[13] His reward was the gratifying figures of his lecture attendances: 52 at his Stock Exchange lectures in January 1910, with no standing room.[14] His father noted competitively that Maynard's lectures were more popular than Meredith's, or even Pigou's.

TABLE: *Keynes's lecture load, 1908–13.*

Subject	Years taught	Number of terms*	Number of hours per week
Money, credit and prices	1908/9–1909/10	2	2
The Stock Exchange and the money market	1909/10–1913/14	1	1
The theory of money	1910/11–1913/14	1	2
Company finance and the Stock Exchange	1910/11–1912/13	1	1
Currency and banking	1910/11–1913/14	1	2
The currency and finances of India	1910/11	1	1
Money markets and foreign exchanges	1910/11–1912/13	1	1
Principles of economics	1910/11–1913/14	3	2
The monetary affairs of India	1912/13	1	1

* A term lasted eight weeks. SOURCE *CW*, xii, ch. 5.

Maynard did individual coaching mainly for the money. The pay was ten shillings an hour. '[It] is so good', he told Duncan Grant, 'that I could hardly resist it.'[15] By Michaelmas Term 1909 he had twenty-four pupils, bringing in almost £100 a term. He calculated that his income that year would be £700. By December 1910 he had already saved £220. Much of this coaching was hack work which he hated. He felt he was becoming 'little more than a machine for selling economics by the hour'.[16] He particularly disliked teaching women students. 'I seem to hate every movement of their minds,' he told Duncan Grant.[17] Such judgments did not prevent him from recommending Dorothy Jebb of Newnham College for an American job in 1914 as 'amongst the very ablest of the economic students who have taken the Economics Tripos at Cambridge in recent years'.[18] But he was determined to build up an income independent of coaching as quickly as possible, and, in fact, by the end of 1909 was already cutting down on his tutorial work.

Keynes disliked individual coaching because it took up too much time, not because he disliked the company of able students. On 21 October 1909 he started a Political Economy Club for his male economics undergraduates. Over the years it became the most famous institution of the Cambridge Economics Faculty. True to the Cambridge tradition, he turned naturally to the club as his favourite pedagogic instrument. His own creation was modelled on the exclusive discussion societies of King's and Trinity. It met on Monday evenings in his rooms. Membership was by invitation. Each week there would be a paper; all those present would comment on it, in an order determined by lot. Keynes would sum up the discussion. He was at his best when strenuous intellectual activity could be carried out in an intimate atmosphere. He was extremely sensitive to his surroundings. 'The shape of rooms ... seems extraordinarily important to one's calmness and the flow of ideas in work ... It is very difficult to be at ease in a very high room or in one which is crowded with a great variety of objects.'[19]

His own club met in a long room of agreeable proportions, against a background of murals of semi-nude grape-pickers and dancers painted by Duncan Grant. Stretched out in a comfortable armchair, hands tucked up in his sleeves, Maynard gave the appearance of complete relaxation. But the mental machinery was whirring the whole time. His summings-up, interlaced as one pre-war student put it 'with more human and spicy remarks', as well as with flights of fancy, were eagerly awaited by the audience. He was always kind to his students, drawing them out rather than crushing their unformed thoughts. Eminent visitors, on the other hand, could be roughly treated. 'I was on several points taken unawares,' complained Norman Angell (author of *The Great Illusion*), much bruised after one session in 1912.[20]

Many of his students of this period became personal friends; some as colleagues and collaborators were to play an important part in shaping the Keynesian Revolution. Chief of these was Dennis Robertson, son of a clergyman, who went to Eton the year Keynes left, and came up to Trinity College in 1908 to read classics. At first Keynes found him 'pudding-headed'.[21] However, he soon revised his opinion and became Robertson's director of studies when he switched to Part II of the Economics Tripos in 1910. But Robertson's early work on the trade-cycle was influenced more by Pigou than by Keynes.[22] Another important collaborator of the 1920s was Hubert Henderson, a Scotsman from Aberdeen, who came to Emmanuel College in 1909. Frederick Lavington, another student, who died young, was an important name in the development of Cambridge monetary theory. Dudley Ward, an undergraduate at St John's and friend of Rupert Brooke, later joined Keynes at the Treasury in the First World War. Hugh Dalton was also taught by Keynes, but preferred Pigou. Freddie Hardman, killed in the war, and Archibald Rose were students who became close personal friends. Another pre-war student was Claude Guillebaud, Marshall's nephew.

Maynard was fiercely loyal to his students. When Pigou and Edward Cannan wrote dismissive reports on Gerald Shove's dissertation on the Rating System, submitted for a prize fellowship at King's in 1914, Maynard circulated a note of dissent to the Fellowship Electors so hostile to the referees' judgment that Clapham considered it 'insulting'.

It failed to convince the Electors; but Keynes finally succeeded in getting Shove a fellowship in 1926.[23] He used his connections with the India Office to get Indian students – of whom he always had a large number – jobs back in India; he also defended them against a racialist slur in the *Cambridge Reporter*.[24] From one of them, Subba Rau, teaching in Mysore, came a lament which has echoed over the years: 'You will not believe me if I tell you how often I am back at Cambridge in my waking thoughts and my dreams.'[25]

III

THE QUANTITY THEORY OF MONEY

The history of the Keynesian revolution is largely a story of Keynes's escape from the quantity theory of money. What is interesting to the student of Keynes's thought is how little hint of escape there was before the First World War. At Cambridge Keynes expounded the quantity theory with all the fervour of the true believer.

The quantity theory of money was a theory of the price level. It stated, quite simply, that prices vary proportionately with the quantity of money and that the quantity of money determines the price level. The greater the supply of money, the lower its value would be; which is the same thing as saying that the higher the prices would be of the goods and services it buys; and vice versa. The value of money, like that of any other commodity, depended on the laws of supply and demand. But it was a peculiarity of money that there was no demand for it as such – merely a demand for what it could buy. Dalton remembered Keynes saying in his pre-war lectures 'Money is that which one accepts only to get rid of it.' Therefore the value of money depended on its supply – or quantity – only; the demand for it being nothing but the supply of goods available for purchase. Strictly stated, the quantity theory said that, assuming the demand for money is given, the price level will vary proportionately with its supply. Thus quantity theorists explained changes in the price level by changes in the supply of money; which, before the First World War, meant changes in the supply of gold.

Ruled out by assumption was the possibility that changes in the value of money could affect the 'real demand' for goods and services. Money determined only the price level at which transactions took place, not the level of activity itself, which was fixed by the 'real' forces of productivity, thrift, population, etc. This 'classical dichotomy' becomes more understandable in the light of nineteenth-century preoccupations. Not for nothing was economics known as the 'dismal science'. Its great fear was not that the demand for goods and services would fall short of their supply, but that the supply would not suffice to feed hungry mouths called into existence by what the Rev. Malthus called absence of 'moral restraint'. It was assumed that in an impoverished world, all incomes would be spent; the problem was to get enough production or 'wealth' to keep the population alive. This could be done only by increasing the efficiency of production and distribution. That is why saving was regarded as so vital. Saving, or abstention from immediate consumption, was what enabled more goods to be produced per unit of effort in the future. No wonder the Victorians sang hymns to thrift. The problems of rich societies, with static or declining populations, and declining investment opportunities as 'wants' approached satiation, were beyond the nineteenth-century ken.

However, the classical economists did recognise that changes in the value of money could affect the distribution of income in the short-run. This was because some prices were 'stickier' than others, so that changes in the price level could result in transfers of income from one group to another. Such transfers were considered undesirable. Rising prices were unjust, because they tended to transfer wealth from savers, the value of whose savings went down, to borrowers, the burden of whose debts was lightened. Falling prices tended to cause depression because the price of labour was stickier than the price of goods, thus involving entrepreneurs in losses. Hence the main objective of nineteenth-century monetary policy was to maintain long-run stability of prices. This, it was felt, could best be achieved by keeping domestic currencies convertible into gold at fixed rates of exchange. Any tendency for domestic price levels to deviate from the world gold price would set in motion, via exports or imports of gold, offsetting contractions or expansions of domestic currency, before the price deviation had gone too far. The movement towards an international gold standard in the second half of the nineteenth century thus reflected both the middle-class determination to prevent improvident govern-ments from 'over-issuing' notes, and the businessman's fear of business collapses in the wake of such improvidence. Stability of money reinforced belief in God as a guarantee of the social order.*

Keynes inherited the quantity theory as it had been left by Marshall who had worked out his own 'cash balances' version of the theory as early as 1871, and then put it aside in order to concentrate on more important things. Marshall's great contribution to monetary theory was to state it in a way which brought out the unrealistic nature of its key assumption that the demand for money was stable in the short-run and which therefore invited its further investigation. According to

* For a fuller explanation, see Note on the Historical Background to the Quantity Theory, on pp. 230–2.

Marshall individuals keep some constant fraction of their assets in the form of cash or 'ready command' in order to facilitate immediate purchases. The currency of a country consisted of these cash balances. If individuals find themselves with double the cash they had previously required for 'ready command' they spend the excess by buying goods or investments. This increased spending causes prices to double, thus restoring the value of their cash balances to their desired level. The same process will occur in reverse if the quantity of cash is halved. In both cases a demand for 'real balances' is brought into equality with the new supply of money by an adjustment in the price level. Nothing has changed except the value of money.[26]*

In his oral evidence before the Royal Commission on the Value of Gold and Silver (1887) Marshall explained, for the benefit of the chairman Lord Herschel, how an initial increase in the quantity of gold lowered the value of the currency:

> It would act at once on Lombard Street, and make people inclined to lend more; it would swell deposits and book credits, and so enable people to increase their speculation with borrowed capital; it would, therefore, increase the demand for commodities and so raise prices ... It would have the ultimate effect of adding to the volume of currency required for circulation, as I think, because prices having risen, a person who found it answer to his purpose to have an average of £17 in currency in his pocket would now require £18 or £19; and so on for others.... [27]

However, there was another part of Marshall's theory which called into question whether the fraction 'k' – the proportion of their assets which people wanted to keep in cash – was really as constant in the short-run as the above evidence supposed. (Marshall held that in the long-run better banking practices, allowing the development of money substitutes, would lower 'k'.) In his 1871 note he explained that the individual fixed the fraction of his wealth he wished to hold in cash after 'balancing opposing advantages': those of the convenience of holding cash against the interest or income earned by buying investments. This implied that desired money-balances will be influenced by movements in the interest-rate. A lowering of the interest-rate would not necessarily lead to increased investment: it might increase the demand for holding cash by reducing the cost of holding it. It is not

---

* The relationship between the quantity of money and the price level is expressed by the Cambridge monetary equation $M = kPT$, where M is the quantity of money, PT is the volume of transactions multiplied by the average price of each transaction in a unit of time, and k is the fraction of the community's assets held in cash. If this fraction is constant it follows that a change in M will generate a proportional change in PT. The Cambridge 'k' is the reciprocal of V, the velocity of circulation, or rate of turnover of a given stock of money, in Irving Fisher's monetary equation, $MV = PT$.

fanciful to see in this Marshallian formula the germ of what Keynes was later to call the 'speculative' motive for holding money, opening up the possibility that all income received would not be immediately spent, and therefore of using monetary theory to explain fluctuations in business activity.

There are hints in Marshall of new paths of thought, no more. Further monetary investigation into the causes of 'discontinuity in industry' would have required a break with the quantity theory of money for, as Eprime Eshag has explained, 'the quantity theory was primarily concerned with the explanation of price changes when the levels of employment and production were explained in real non-monetary terms'; consequently it 'was found somewhat wanting and to a large extent irrelevant as an instrument of analysis of short-run unemployment and production problems ...'[28]

Two of the surviving sets of Keynes's pre-1914 lecture notes on Money are reprinted in volume xii of his *Collected Writings* – one from his 'Principles of Economics' course, the second from his 'Theory of Money' course. They have been stitched together by the editor from different years, ranging from 1910 to 1914, making it difficult to pinpoint changes in presentation over the period. It is clear that they are heavily Marshallian, though also influenced by Irving Fisher's *The Purchasing Power of Money* which Keynes reviewed for the *Economic Journal* in September 1911. Keynes certainly fleshed out Marshall's skeleton, helped by many conversations with Marshall himself. A student of his, T. T. Williams, wrote to him: 'Your set of lectures are the best complete and concise outline of the theory which I know of – but they are not published.'[29] In fact Keynes published nothing on the pure theory of money till 1923, when he produced a simplified version in chapter 3 of his *Tract on Monetary Reform*. What is interesting about his early lectures is that, lucid and subtle as they often are, he did not develop the Marshallian apparatus of thought in any significant way, and in some respects did not carry it as far as Marshall himself had done.

The topics Keynes dealt with are conveniently divided into four heads: (*a*) causes determining the value of money; (*b*) the mechanism by which changes in the quantity of money affect prices; (*c*) the social and commercial effects of price fluctuations; and (*d*) problems of statistical verification of the quantity theory.

Under the first head Keynes analysed the determinants of the supply of money and the demand for money. He followed Marshall in asserting that the quantity theory in its strict form was true only if the demand for money was taken as given. Nevertheless, he insisted that adherence to the quantity theory was a test of professional competence, citing Lord Goschen to the effect that 'there are many persons who cannot bear the relation of the level of price to the volume of currency affirmed, without a feeling akin to irritation'.[30] At various points in his lectures Keynes castigated 'practical men' and 'bankers and businessmen' who persisted in believing that price fluctuations were caused by trade fluctuations. J. A. Hobson, the theorist of underconsumption, was one person whose 'irritation' with the quantity theory so annoyed Keynes that he refused to review any more of his books, after writing of his *Gold, Prices, and Wages*, 'Mr Hobson has given us the Mythology of Money – intellectualised, brought up to journalistic date, most subtly larded (and this is how it differs from the rest) with temporary concessions to reason.'[31] Authority in economics had come to demand adherence to certain orthodoxies.

In one respect Keynes's account of the demand for money is inferior to Marshall's. There is no reference in the printed extracts of his lectures to Marshall's discussion of the way an individual balances the advantages at the margin of holding money as against income-earning assets. However, he emphasised the role of expectations – 'The fact that money is used not only for immediate purposes of exchange, but also as a store of value and for future exchange, renders its present value dependent, not only upon its present volume, but also upon beliefs which are held respecting its future volume and the future demand for it' – approvingly quoting Marshall's dictum, 'There is, therefore, something fiduciary in the value of gold and silver.'[32]

Keynes gave a Marshallian account of the mechanism by which an addition to the money supply brings about a rise in prices, though bringing in the rate of interest, which had been left out of Marshall's exposition [1913]:

> The new gold in the vaults of the B[ank] of E[ngland] brings about a tendency of the bank rate to fall. This enables speculators and enrepreneurs to increase their purchases. This stimulus gradually spreads through all parts of the community, until the new gold is needed to finance a volume of real trade no larger ... than before.

But his thrust is still towards a long-run statement of the theory:

> It must be noticed that the new money begins by increasing the demand for *some* commodities; but only on the part of the entrepreneur or dealer or middleman; the consumer must *pay* more and must therefore divert some part of his consumption of other things. There is no reason for supposing that in the long run the new gold affects the *total* demand – though of course the money value of the commodities is permanently increased, and the money value of the volume of credit outstanding. Thus if we measured our wealth in

money, the aggregate wealth of the community naturally *appears* to be greater than before.[33]

However, in his specialised lecture course on 'The Theory of Money' Keynes gave a more interesting account [1914]:

> New gold does not, therefore, necessarily lower the bank rate to the full extent which its quantity would justify *at once*. It bides its time until a plentiful harvest or some other ... mysterious agents which influence the cyclical fluctuations of trade set on foot an expansion of commerce and industry ... New gold, therefore, although it may not exert an immediate influence and may wait till other causes have *started* an expansion of trade, assists these causes, accelerates the revival of trade, reduces the period between the old boom and the new one, and eventually serves to keep the bank rate lower than it would have been in the absence of increased gold production.[34]

And a little later:[35]

> New gold raises prices by making borrowers more eager or willing to borrow. It does this for one of two reasons:–
>
> (1) by lowering the rate of discount below the normal
> OR
> (2) by raising the expectation of higher prices in the future more than in proportion to any momentary *rise* in the rate of discount which may take place.

Keynes [1912] grouped the consequences of price fluctuations under four heads: (1) effects on the rate of interest and on anticipated profits; (2) effects on the distribution of wealth; (3) effects on the trade cycle; and (4) political effects. In the printed extracts, there is hardly anything on the first, and nothing on the fourth. The main point to emerge is that Keynes, contrary to Marshall, and to his own view in 1923, concluded that falling prices were somewhat better than rising prices for both social and commercial reasons. Falling prices benefitted the wage-earner and the creditor at the expense of the entrepreneur and the debtor. This made the distribution of wealth more equal and therefore juster.* His solicitude for the wage earner is easy enough to understand; his more surprising concern for the bondholder is explained by his belief that borrowers were rich and lenders 'comparatively poor' –

---

* He cited A. L. Bowley's investigation into the level of wages from the *Economic Journal* of December 1898 which showed that the rise of real wages after 1873 when prices were falling was greater than before 1873 when they were rising. He went on [1914]: 'with the rise of prices since 1900 something similar has happened, and it is commonplace to ascribe the prevailing tendency to strike and industrial unrest as partially due to the effect of rising prices on real wages'. (*CW*, xii, 715–16)

an interesting reflection on his family's circumstances.[36] Although he admitted that falling prices could be bad for business he went on [1912]

> There is no sufficient ground for preferring rising prices to falling prices, and even some reasons for thinking the latter to be preferable. We are misled into the opposite opinion partly because businessmen obtain unusual profits during a period of rising prices, and partly because we have an inveterate habit of measuring industrial progress by the growth of money values. We can never quite clear our heads of the preconception that money is an invariable unit which remains a permanently safe measure of comparison, while commodities change.[37]

Keynes's lectures were sprinkled with historical and statistical illustrations. He saw little prospect of proving the quantity theory by empirical methods, concluding [1912] that 'the inductive verifications of the adherents of the [quantity] theory have been, I think, nearly as fallacious as those of its opponents'.[38] But this was a weakness of statistics, not of the theory. Correlations between gold flows and price movements proved little:

> In the case of the history of gold prices, to which defenders of the Q.T. usually refer with confidence, factors other than gold production have changed and fluctuated so hugely and so notoriously that the use of any apparent close coincidence between the level of prices and gold production in support of the Q.T. is a gross example of a *post hoc, ergo propter hoc* argument. Since other factors have *not* remained constant, the theory would only lead us to anticipate coincidence between prices and gold production if the other factors happened to balance one another; and one cannot easily prove this without assuming the theory itself.[39]

By this time (1912) Keynes was reacting against his own earlier efforts at empirical verification of the quantity theory. In his first article in the *Economic Journal*, 'Recent Economic Events in India', published in March 1909, he had found what Neville Keynes called 'surprising statistical confirmation' of the quantity theory, since he was able to correlate Indian price movements with the inflow and outflow of gold. Producing 'statistics of verification', he wrote to Duncan Grant at the time, threw him into a 'tremendous state of excitement. Here are my theories – will the statistics bear them out? Nothing except copulation is so enthralling and the figures are coming out so much better than anyone could possibly have expected that everybody will believe I have cooked them.'[40] The article itself was considerably more restrained. 'The index number of prices is not well constructed, the volume of currency can only be estimated, and agreement may be due to the fortuitous balancing against one another of causes unconnected with the present discussion.'*

Undoubtedly before the First World War Keynes accepted the quantity theory of money as adequate to the tasks he wanted it to perform. It offered a useful framework for analysing India's banking and currency system, which was his main practical interest. There were no pressing economic problems in England demanding an improved monetary theory. The fact remains that Hawtrey, Pigou, Robertson and Lavington were at this time developing Marshall's ideas in interesting ways while Keynes was not.† His main intellectual interests were elsewhere.

IV

STATISTICAL CONUNDRUMS

The part of economics which interested him at this time had to do with the problem of induction. The hardest part of his Indian article had been the statistical tables. No national accounts were kept in those days, and Keynes was reduced to making inspired guesses at some of the magnitudes involved. In addition, there were conceptual problems with the notion of the 'price level'. It was meant to be an index number expressing the ratio of the average price in any particular year to the average price in a base year. But how was such an 'average price' to be constructed? Here was a new intellectual interest. 'I'm very busy with an abstruse treatise called "The Method of Index Numbers with Special Reference to the Measurement of General Exchange Value",' Keynes informed Strachey on 4 April 1909. He wrote at lightning speed over the Easter vacation, and on 10 May he was able to tell Duncan Grant that he had won the University's Adam Smith prize, worth £60. As usual, his examiners' report infuriated him, particularly Edgeworth's. 'I feel *convinced* that I'm right on almost every point he attacks and where my argument is novel, he simply hasn't attended to it. His criticisms show a *closed* mind ...'.[41]

Since Edgeworth was one of the economists Keynes singled out for

---

* Lytton Strachey read the article with the 'greatest interest' if with some incomprehension. 'For instance, why on earth should it matter two straws whether prices rise if the number of rupees rises at the same time? ... I long to go into the study of economics with the utmost elaboration.' Keynes gave him a lecture on the quantity theory by return of post. 'Prices, by the way, *can't* permanently rise in ordinary circumstances unless the number of rupees rises too.'

† See R. G. Hawtrey, *Good and Bad Trade* (1913); A. C. Pigou, *Wealth and Welfare* (1912). F. Lavington's article, 'Uncertainty in its Relation to the Rate of Interest', was published in the *Economic Journal* (1912); Robertson's *A Study in Industrial Fluctuations* was completed in 1913.

criticism, his reaction to Keynes's argument is not surprising. 'There is no mystery about Index Numbers,' Keynes confidently announced at the start of one of his lectures, and proceeded to show that matters were not simple. The problem was that 'there is no strictly numerical quantity corresponding to the conception of a general level of prices'. The prices of some commodities rose and those of others fell. If the relative importance of the articles being consumed never varied, the problem could be surmounted by correct weighting. But in practice their relative importance was constantly changing with their prices, so that there was nothing constant to compare from one year to another. 'This then is the prime theoretical difficulty and it is one which cannot be surmounted.' The best possible index number of the general price level had to satisfy three criteria: (a) it must include as many commodities as possible both important absolutely and possessing the greatest stability of relative importance; (b) the commodities must be correctly 'weighted'; and (c) the base year must not be too remote.[42]

This was the approach he adopted in his prize essay. In the course of it he made a strong attack on an alternative solution to the conceptual problem proposed by mathematical economists like Jevons and Edgeworth. They had suggested taking an unweighted geometrical mean of a random sample of prices as the required measure, on the assumption that there was a general factor, money, which affects all prices equally in direction and degree; and that variations in relative prices, due to market conditions, cancelled each other out. Thus the geometric average of any random sample in any period would give one a satisfactory index of the residual movement of the price level in that period.[43]

Keynes's attack on the Jevons/Edgeworth approach was in line with his general hostility to the use of mathematical methods in both probability and economics. This has always puzzled observers, given his competence as a mathematician. This hostility did not extend to the actual compilation of statistics. Keynes's 'capacity for observing and assimilating facts was remarkable, and facts for him included numbers. He liked to get a feel of the order of magnitude of the problems with which he was dealing...'.[44] In general, he supported the cause of better statistics, and it was through his efforts that the statistician Udny Yule got a lectureship in Cambridge in 1912.

In the course of his life Keynes was to advance powerful objections to the attempt to establish economics on mathematical foundations, most of them already stated in his work on Probability. He regarded both probability theory and economics as branches of logic, not of mathematics, which should employ methods of reasoning appropriate to the former, including intuition and judgment, and incorporating a wide knowledge of non-numerical facts. In his *Treatise on Probability* he wrote:

The hope, which sustained many investigations in the course of the nineteenth century, of gradually bringing the moral sciences under the sway of mathematical reasoning, steadily recedes ... The old assumptions, that all quantity is numerical and that all quantitative characteristics are additive, can no longer be sustained. Mathematical reasoning now appears as an aid in its symbolic rather than its numerical character. I, at any rate, have not the same lively hope as Condorcet, or even as Edgeworth, 'éclairer les sciences morales et politiques par le flambeau de l'Algèbre'.[45]

Furthermore he held out little hope of verifying particular economic models by statistical methods. The last section of his *Treatise on Probability* argued that most claims on behalf of statistical inference were logically unsound, instances of 'mathematical charlatanry'. He was pessimistic about the possibility of using 'collections of facts for the prediction of future frequencies and associations'.[46]

Keynes's strictures on the use of mathematics are what one might expect from a student of Marshall's.* But they are also of biographical interest. As Sir Roy Harrod pointed out Keynes 'had no specific genius for mathematics ... he did not seek out those abstruse regions which are a joy to the heart of the professional mathematician'.[47] He was not drawn to the Platonic universe of numbers which fired the imagination of his fellow Apostles, Russell and Hardy. The truths which Keynes sought were related to human conduct, which he felt could not be reduced to sets of equations.

One of Keynes's long-standing statistical *bêtes noires* was Karl Pearson, a Kingsman of the 1880s. Leader of the statistical school of probability, he was fired by a passion to apply the calculus of probability to biological data, in order to establish an actuarial basis for eugenic planning. In June 1910, the Galton Laboratory, of which Pearson was director, published a memoir on the influence of parental alcoholism on children. Relying on data collected by the Edinburgh Charity Organisation Society and an account of children in special schools in Manchester, Pearson and his associate Ethel Elderton had divided parents in order of sobriety and examined the reported state of their

---

* Marshall wrote to the statistician A. L. Bowley on 27 November 1906:

> I had a growing feeling in the later years of my work at the subject that a good mathematical theorem dealing with economic hypotheses was very unlikely to be good economics; and I went more and more on the rules – (1) Use mathematics as a shorthand language, rather than as an engine of enquiry. (2) Keep to them till you have done. (3) Translate into English. (4) Then illustrate by examples that are important in real life. (5) Burn the mathematics. (6) If you can't succeed in 4, burn 3. This last I often did.

Quoted in A. C. Pigou (ed.), *Memorials of Alfred Marshall* (1925) p. 427.

children in health, strength and intelligence. The children of the non-drinkers were found to be no better than the children of those who drank. In the Manchester sample both the sober and the drinking families contained at least one feeble-minded parent. This suggested to Pearson that the disabilities of the children were related to hereditary defects rather than to drinking habits. The equality of condition in the children of both non-drinking and drinking parents in Edinburgh was compatible with this hypothesis. The suggestion that parental drinking habits did not harm the children had the Temperance people up in arms. In a sharp review in the July 1910 number of the *Journal of the Royal Statistical Society*, Keynes decided that the Galton memoir was 'almost valueless' and 'actually misleading'. He had two main points. The first was that no general conclusions could be drawn from the studies since their populations were 'unrepresentative' of the whole population. The second was that the Galton memoir had not succeeded in showing that the populations investigated were in fact homogeneous. 'As in the Manchester case, so *on the whole* in the Edinburgh case the authors are comparing drunken stock with *bad* sub-normal sober stock, and find, naturally enough, that there is not much to choose between them.'

The dispute soon spread to the newspapers and the medical profession. Marshall, breaking his rule of not engaging in public controversy, attacked Pearson in what Lytton Strachey called a 'very Marshally' letter to *The Times* of 7 July 1910. Pearson replied to Marshall; Marshall responded to Pearson. 'I thought Marshall's last letter very fine,' wrote Keynes to his parents on 24 August 1910. 'K. P.'s insolence has at last roused the old Prof's blood.' Pearson, unlike Marshall an indefatigable controversialist, rapidly produced a new memoir, in which he dismissed Keynes's point about the unrepresentative character of the two populations studied (in Manchester and Edinburgh) as having 'no logical bearing on the problem in hand'. The sole relevant question was whether the populations studied were themselves random in the technical sense of there having been 'no differential selection' of the drinkers and non-drinkers. Marshall had argued that the fact that drinkers and non-drinkers in Edinburgh earned the same average wages failed to prove that the population studied was homogeneous, since the drinkers might well have earned higher wages had they not drank. Pearson produced figures to show that there was no significant difference between drinkers and non-drinkers in the grade of trade they followed. This, he thought, undermined Marshall's contention, since a trade was, as a rule, chosen early in life.

In what he considered a 'smashing reply', published in the December number of the *Journal of the Royal Statistical Society*, Keynes ignored this point about the grade of trade, insisting that Pearson's hypothesis that drinking did not depress the social and economic status of the drinkers (and hence the performance of their children) would be plausible only had he shown that the 'Edinburgh drunkards were on a par with the other inhabitants of the district *before they* drank'. This he had not done. Keynes's style as a controversialist is captured in the following passage:

> But let us apply his [Pearson's] method in detail to the example, suggested by Professor Marshall, of the patients who come for treatment to a hospital. They are divided into two classes – those who are suffering from *delirium tremens* and the rest. We find that since they contracted their diseases they have lived in the same neighbourhood, have paid about the same rent, have received an equal amount of charitable aid, and have succeeded in earning about the same wages. Thus the sample is, in Professor Pearson's 'technical sense', random within the field of investigation. We reach, therefore, on Professor Pearson's principles, the interesting and important conclusion that *delirium tremens* prolongs life, or – if we are in a cautious mood and the death rate from it is not much below the average of the hospital – that it does not perceptibly shorten it.

Unabashed, Pearson returned to the fray with a long letter published in the January 1911 number of the *Journal*. Keynes signed off with a rejoinder in the February 1911 issue, in which he denied once more that Pearson's statistical methods could throw any light on the question at issue:

> I can imagine only one set of circumstances in which they could be used with real hope of success; – namely, if we had a numerous set of parents who, beginning married life as teetotallers, had some children, and after taking to drink later, then had some more. We could then compare those who were conceived and brought up in temperance with those, born of the same parents, who were conceived and brought up in drunkenness. Unless a band of teetotal parents, who already fulfil the first condition, will submit, in the paramount interests of science, to qualify themselves for the second, the statistical method is unlikely to find a proper field for the exercise of its operations.

Keynes's antagonism to Pearson's statistical ambitions throws light on his own social and personal values. He appears in this controversy first and foremost as the son of Florence Keynes, upholding a traditional Victorian attitude that regarded drink as a significant cause of social misery. This comes out strikingly in his notion of drink as setting off initially superior stock down a Skid Row which ends in the slums – a proposition which, he says, has the support of 'general experience'. This conclusion is in line with his conviction that the distribution of social and economic advantages reflects in general the distribution of character in the population. He also appears as the upholder of the medical doctrine that the influence of parental drinking is transmitted to the children via 'prenatal toxic effects' (though in this case, surely only the mother's drinking habits are relevant*). Keynes was also hostile to the provenance of Pearson's efforts. Pearson was heir to the eugenics programme of Francis Galton who, in his *Hereditary Genius* published in 1869, had condemned the celibacy of the intellectual classes as destructive of human progress. The Galton–Pearson ideal of a *fecund* intellectual class was at variance with the *sterile* ideal which Keynes, Marshall, and the generality of emancipated opinion had then adopted as the means to the good life (however that was defined). Having families interfered with intellectuals either being good or doing good. On this, at least, Moorites and Marshallians could agree.

Keynes's hostility to Pearson also reflects his hostility to the use of mathematical methods in social science. He called the first Galton memoir 'a salient example of the application of a needlessly complex mathematical apparatus to initial data, of which the true character is insufficiently explained, and which are in fact unsuited to the problem in hand'.[48] His statistical criticisms

> all amount, in effect, to the contention that Professor Pearson's assumption of an initial equality (i.e., if alcoholic habits had not been contracted) between his alcoholic and non-alcoholic parents is unjustifiable. Hence an eventual equality amongst the offspring is no disproof of the injurious effects of alcohol. This is a most fundamental criticism, because [it] applies . . . to almost all possible investigations on these lines.

The question of whether 'alcoholic homes exert in general an evil environmental influence upon children' could be investigated only by experimental, not statistical, methods.[49]

It is not at all clear that Keynes got the better of the statistical argument. He misunderstood that part of Pearson's case resting on the grade of job. More fundamentally, he seemed to deny any possibility of establishing *ceteris paribus* conditions. Had his criticisms been ac-

* Marshall's medical theory allowed for the influence of the father's drinking habits as well. He wrote to the Cambridge geneticist W. H. Bateson on 26 October 1908:

> I cannot – to be frank – see that your facts are inconsistent with the belief that the *quality* of life of the parents affects every juice and every fibre and every cell inside the genital organs as well as outside . . . Why should it not be true that the social life of many generations of parents – quite independent of selection – affects the nerves, i.e., the quality of character of later generations?

See Marshall Library, Marshall Papers, Box 3, item 2.

cepted by investigators as valid, practically all statistical investigation of social problems would have been ruled out of court.

v

FREE TRADE

Keynes's commitment to free trade was no less firm than was his commitment to the quantity theory. He regarded the case for free trade as scientifically established; denial of it was evidence of incompetence in economic reasoning. (To Keynes unsound views on the quantity theory, free trade, and marginalist analysis were expressive of some 'natural malformation of the mind' to which 'practical men' were particularly prone.) The most extensive surviving record of the way he defended free trade before 1914 comes from some notes he made for his speech to the Cambridge Union on 8 November 1910.

In these notes Keynes concentrated on refuting the employment argument for Protection. The Protectionists said

> These goods are coming in. If we keep them out someone will have to make them. Perhaps it will be us or our friends. What is the answer to this? International Trade ...
>
> If they can be made in this country as cheaply as abroad, they will be made now. They will only be made here after the duty if the price is raised. Thus those who buy them will have to restrict their purchases in some other direction; and thus reduce employment there. The amount of goods which can be earned by a week's labour will be reduced and you cannot hope permanently to cure unemployment by diminishing, on the average, the productiveness of labour. And the level of comfort of the working classes all round will be lowered.
>
> The Tariff Reform case rests on the principle of making things relatively scarce. To those who are concerned with making these things, this is no doubt advantageous. But it causes an amount of distress more than equivalent elsewhere. The community as a whole cannot hope to gain by making artificially scarce what the country wants.

Keynes gave as an example of the advantages of the policy of free imports the import of soya beans from Manchuria which had started in 1906; these had been excluded by high tariffs from Germany, France and other Continental countries. They now constituted an important part of the import trade of Hull, providing a new source of revenue for the shipping industry. They were reducing agricultural costs by providing cheaper cattle feed; also soap would be cheaper. The beginning of an export trade from Hull to the Continent was evident – soya cake was going to Europe, manufactured in Hull mills.

Keynes concluded that Protection could not increase employment. He emphasised the impossibility of general overproduction. Unemployment occurred only as a result of miscalculation of one sort or another. The first effect of a tariff would be to increase miscalculation. His notes ended:

I have said nothing of the positive arguments for F.T.

International Relations
Internal Corruption
Trusts
Raising of Cost of Living
Undesirable Redistribution of Wealth
Increased costs of production limiting competition in neutral markets.

Equally orthodox was an article Keynes contributed to the *New Quarterly* in February 1910 in defence of unlimited capital mobility. There were no new paths of thought here.

One must remember that ever since the 1880s 'irregularity of employment' had been increasingly recognised as a grave social evil. In his Tariff Reform campaign which started in 1903 Joseph Chamberlain had specifically advanced Protection as a remedy for unemployment. No doubt many of his arguments were bad ones; in particular he failed to deal adequately with the relationship between foreign trade and employment. Keynes's attitude now seems unduly complacent. But events provided no stimulus to rethink old orthodoxies. Between 1900 and 1914 British exports revived; free trade seemed adequate to sustain British prosperity. Given all its other advantages, as well as the fact that Protection had become the creed – from Keynes's point of view – of the least progressive, most economically illiterate, section of the Conservative Party, there was no call on him to shift from his inherited professional and political position.

What is striking about Keynes before 1914 is how little he was involved in the Marshallian research programme of making economics into an instrument of social reform – especially for Britain. He made little contribution to monetary theory, and had no new suggestions to offer on policy. The whole Edwardian debate on the reform of the Poor Law and its bearing on the problem of cyclical unemployment passed him by. His views on the use of mathematical and statistical methods were mainly critical and destructive. This is not to denigrate his later achievement, or even to criticise his lack of achievement before 1914, but merely to draw attention to the conditions of his economic creativity. He was not an instinctively original economist, like an economic theorist who is fascinated by intellectual puzzles, regardless of whether they have any practical importance. His attitude to the subject did not, in itself, stimulate him to original work. He regarded it as an inferior branch of knowledge – inferior to philosophy in which he still hoped to make an original contribution to thought. Nor, unlike Marshall and Pigou, did he have any strong ethical stimulus to improve the 'organon' for the purpose of attacking poverty. His ethical ambitions, as we have seen, lay elsewhere.

Without a strong intellectual or ethical stimulus, Keynes's capacity for original economic thought had to be evoked by some practical problem. But at that time there was no sufficiently important practical issue to cause him to question established theory. The existing corpus of knowledge was adequate, *provided* it was adhered to. Hence his defence of orthodoxy was not just mental laziness, or a narrow concern with professional standards, but was part of what he called his 'meliorism'. The quantity theory, like the theory of comparative advantage, was part of the intellectual equipment of progress. It was the challengers, not the defenders, of orthodoxy who were the enemies of progress. The economists were its custodians. It has been fashionable since the Keynesian Revolution to say that this view of the matter depended on a 'full employment assumption'. But events had not decisively challenged the view that an economy left free to find its own level tended naturally towards full employment.*

These attitudes led naturally enough to political indifference as well. Before 1914 Keynes was not an innovator of policy. Progress demanded the steadfast application of existing principles by the Liberal Party. Keynes's occasional political interventions before 1914 were nearly all prompted by attacks on free trade. He was in political demand by his Liberal friends as someone who could readily expose the fallacies of Protection; and he was happy to oblige from time to time.

Given Keynes's values and priorities it made little sense for him to invest much intellectual effort in economics before 1914; and the results showed it. But his very limitations before 1914 were to become a source of strength later. His low ranking of economics as an intellectual pursuit protected him from theoretical superfluity, always a great temptation for the brilliant puzzle-solver; his lack of ethical ambitions in the subject helped to ensure that his later interests were narrowly focussed on problems of statecraft rather than being dissipated over the whole field of social reform. Many theorists have been more elegant; many economists have had higher ethical ideals; none have achieved so much practical good.

*Consideration of Keynes's unpublished paper 'How Far are Bankers Responsible for the Alteration of Crisis and Depression?', read to the Political Economy Club in London on 3 December 1913, is best postponed till volume two. A response to the work of Hawtrey and Robertson, it is Keynes's one pre-war foray into the theory of the business-cycle.

The monetary theory of the classical economists was a reaction against the doctrines of the eighteenth-century mercantilists who thought that an increase in money had a directly stimulating effect on economic activity. Their aim was, therefore, to increase their own country's share of the precious metals – by plunder or by a policy of running an export surplus. Adam Smith in *The Wealth of Nations* (1776) accused the mercantilists of confusing money with wealth. His contemporary, David Hume, showed, further, that a country's attempt to accumulate gold (by restricting its imports) was self-defeating, since the inflow of gold would cause its prices to rise, making its exports less competitive, and thus causing gold to flow out again. Finally, David Ricardo showed that each country will tend to hold gold in proportion to its real income, because it is that particular distribution of gold which equates the gold price level between different countries. The defeat of the intellectual structure of mercantilism – such as it was – was completed by the promulgation of Say's Law, which denied that there could be any shortage of total demand for goods and services, since 'supply creates its own demand'. In pursuing their goal of accumulating treasure by plunder or trade restrictions the mercantilists were diminishing the growth of wealth by making the allocation of resources less efficient than it would have been, since their policies tended to diminish the size of the market and hinder the international division of labour.

The quantity theory, and the accompanying *laissez-faire* attitude to the distribution of the precious metals, was not accepted without fierce controversy. There were what Keynes called 'three grand discussions' of monetary policy in Britain in the nineteenth century: the bullionist controversy of 1796–1821, following the suspension of specie payments during the Napoleonic wars; the Currency versus Banking School debate of the 1840s; and the Bimetallist controversy of the 1880s. The first two involved monetary theory as well as policy. They revolved round the question of the over-issue of notes, and how to prevent it. The banking school denied that there could be any 'over-issue' of notes since the amount of a country's currency at any time supported the actual value of business being done. Against this the currency school pointed out that the prices of all transactions could be halved or doubled without the amount of real wealth exchanged being any different. It was the quantity of money, and nothing else, which explained the price level. The banking school raised a theoretical issue central to today's debate about monetary policy: whether a change in the money supply is the cause or merely the consequence of changes in the price level.

In the nineteenth century the banking school were thought to have had the worst of the theoretical exchanges, being convicted of having confused nominal with real income. The way to prevent over-issue of notes was rigid adherence to the gold standard. The Bank Charter Act of 1844 gave the Bank of England a legal monopoly of the note-issue; laid down that the amount of legal tender currency in excess of a certain sum, the 'fiduciary issue', should be fully backed by gold; and imposed on the Bank the obligation to convert notes into gold on demand at a fixed rate.

The third great monetary discussion, which took place while Keynes was growing up, was provoked by the fall in prices in the 1880s and the accompanying trade depression. Observers not unnaturally linked these two things together, attributing both to the contraction in the world money supply due to the exhaustion of existing gold stocks and an increase in hoarding by countries like India. (This was explained by the rise in the price of gold relative to silver, India then being on a bimetallic standard.)

These linkages were brought out by Neville Keynes in his evidence to the Royal Commission on the Depression of Trade and Industry (1886). The depression in trade was 'partly but not wholly due' to the rise in the value of gold relative to other commodities. This discouraged enterprise for five reasons: (a) because a fall in price between the start and the completion of a transaction involved the trader in loss; (b) because the trader tended to exaggerate his own loss by not taking sufficient account of the general fall in prices, (c) because the profits of enterprise were temporarily diminished on account of increased depreciation of fixed capital; (d) because the ratio of profits to wages fell as a result of the fall in money wages lagging behind the fall in prices, and (e) because the fall in prices increased the burden of debt, transferring wealth from borrowers to lenders. Such evidence was not intended to challenge the now orthodox quantity theory, merely to point to the difficulties of adjusting from one price level to another. Its implication was that monetary policy should be used to raise prices, and thereafter stabilise the price level. Out of such considerations developed the movement for bimetallism, which was an attempt to increase the amount of legal tender money by obliging the central bank to mint both gold and silver on demand at a fixed ratio.

However, bimetallism made little headway. Despite the complaint of William Jennings Bryan that the American economy was being 'crucified on a cross of gold', the international trend was towards the adoption of monometallic (or gold) standards, and the 'sound money' policies which they entailed. The distress caused by what Marshall called 'discontinuity of industry' gave rise to much theorizing (mainly on the Continent) about the causes of business fluctuations, but most of it was concerned with 'real' and not 'monetary' factors. The theory of money remained a theory of the price level and nothing else.

Historical circumstances favoured the success of the quantity theory. Those opponents who advocated a more accommodating monetary policy were up against powerful vested interests, who were in control of politics, and who saw in an independent central bank tied to the gold standard an essential safeguard against the extravagance of governments. Domestic economies were still sufficiently flexible to prevent business fluctuations from degenerating into permanent depressions, thus making it possible for economists to 'abstract' the trade cycle from normal (or long-run) theories of economic behaviour. Britain's structural role in the world economy as chief exporter of capital and 'lender of the last resort' prevented major changes in the international distribution of the precious metals, thus damping down both inflationary and deflationary pressures on domestic economies. The result was that the quantity theory of money was not undermined by intolerable events.

10 Private Lives

PRIORITIES

In the years following his return to Cambridge, the tempo of Maynard's life accelerated. The semi-idle junior clerk at the India Office became the hard-working Cambridge economics don, journalist, editor and author. His first book, on India's monetary system, appeared in 1913. Over four successive long vacations in England, from 1909 to 1912, he worked on turning his thesis on Probability into a book – a task which dragged on as he rewrote and added new chapters. But Probability also accompanied him to the Pyrenees, Greece and Sicily; he took Index Numbers to Versailles; and Indian currency to Egypt. Unlike his father, he could combine his intellectual work with involvement in practical affairs. He interested himself in the management of his college's finances; his career of public service started with his appointment to the Royal Commission on Indian Currency and Finance in 1913. His hobbies blossomed too. Golf was in retreat, but he went on adding to his book collection; in 1911 he bought his first important works of art; he gambled at Monte Carlo, and from 1913 on the Stock Exchange as well. As he was to do all his life, he still found time to pursue intellectual hobbies.

In the midst of this activity only politics languished. If Liberal England was dying, Maynard and his friends were extraordinarily unaware of it. The Fabians had reached Cambridge, the Suffragettes marched and chained themselves to railings, Lloyd George's budget of 1909 and the House of Lords' reaction to it provoked a constitutional crisis, the class war intensified, Ireland was in uproar, one international crisis followed another. Maynard was aware of these things, tangentially involved in some of them, but was basically indifferent to them, and hardly conscious of their longer-term implications. The way in which he wrote of Europe after the First World War reflected a different perspective – that of his travels, the freedom of exchange, the stability of currencies, the sense of progress, the ordered conditions of life. The 'extraordinary bitterness of political and social controversy' recalled by Esmé Wingfield-Stratford hardly found an echo in his world.

Partly this was because he was still under the spell of *Principia Ethica*. But one must not forget that it was genuinely possible to indulge a different kind of hope at that time, one which was cut off by the war. In his influential book *The Great Illusion*, published in 1911, Norman Angell came close to arguing that a major war was an economic impossibility as well as an absurdity. The world had become too interdependent; there could be no 'victors' in any rational sense. Keynes and his friends, like Angell, were rationalists and meliorists. They were aware of dark forces lying in wait to ambush civilisation; but believed they would be scattered by 'automatic' economic progress. The changes which economic improvement was bringing about would leave society more, not less, settled. In the years before the war Keynes and his friends were caught up in a cultural renaissance which to them heralded a major advance in civilisation. These things occupied the foreground of their consciousness; the atavistic posturings of the statesmen they dismissed as 'the amusements of the daily newspaper' as Keynes later put it.

To be in love with one's friends, with beauty, with knowledge; these remained Maynard's lodestars. Duncan Grant and Probability were the fixed points in his life; elections to the Apostles caused him more excitement than general elections. His London life came to be based on the Bloomsbury Group. He shared its intellectual values and its artistic enthusiasms, and participated in its wild fancy dress parties. Bloomsbury accepted him with some reservations. The events of 1908–9 had opened up a breach between him and Lytton Strachey which was never entirely closed. Maynard's intellectual brilliance was admired; his crudity and worldliness were often deplored.

II

CAMBRIDGE CONNECTIONS

In the summer of 1909 Maynard moved into the suite of rooms over the gatehouse leading from King's Lane to Webb's Court which he occupied till he died. He never became a 'College' character like the O. B., Sheppard, or Pigou, parading his eccentricities to the delight of the undergraduates. To all but a tiny circle he was the don 'who can quote figures at you'.[1] That circle still consisted of the Apostles and their friends. Here nothing much seemed to have changed. 'Even the womanisers pretend to be sods, lest they shouldn't be thought respectable' Maynard informed Duncan soon after his return.[2] The great event of his first term as a lecturer was the 'birth' of Gerald Shove, after great opposition from Lytton. 'An election is an awful and terrifying thing,' Maynard told Duncan. 'I slept for less than three hours on

Saturday night; and I gather that Rupert and James were scarcely
more fortunate . . . The exhaustion was made no better by golf with Fay
and a boring dinner party at the Whiteheads', where even Bertie's
sallies seemed flat.'[3] Conversation was still mainly about ethics and
love. At Sheppard's Sunday evening salon, which continued till 2 a.m.,
Rupert Brooke attacked Shove for calling himself a Christian when he
wasn't one. 'Master B[irrell]* had never seen a real set-to before and
loved it, screaming with excitement'.[4] At the annual dinner of the Carbonari, the radical King's College society founded by Rupert Brooke,
a drunken evening, so Maynard informed Duncan on 7 February 1909,
was had by all – 'the leading drunkard being Mr. Schloss, poor Master
Birrell ill over the dinner table, Gerald unable to walk, and Daddy
mellifluously boozed'. The intrigues continued unabated. 'James
[Strachey] and George [Mallory] now stroke one another's faces in
public.'[5] Gerald Shove and Master Birrell seemed to be falling in love
with each other; Shove was trying to repel the advances of 'Daddy'
Dalton; while the comely Rupert Brooke was still being hopelessly
serenaded by James. Behaviour at King's was growing less and less
restrained. The day after Founder's Feast on 5 December 1909, Maynard wrote to Duncan:

> Yesterday evening will always mark an epoch, I think, in the history
> of King's manners. If there was debauchery, it was private. Manners
> not morals gave way. Quite suddenly our rigid rules of convention
> that one kisses no one in public utterly collapsed – and we all kissed!
> The scene really can't be described. Alfred [Brooke], Frankie [Bir-
> rell], Gerald, Mr. Hardman (Freddy), Sheppard – and many others
> . . . everybody was there. What our reppers [reputations] will be,
> heaven knows . . . We've never behaved like this before – I wonder
> if we ever shall again. . . .

No doubt Maynard embroidered for the benefit of Duncan in London;
yet the historian of King's College, Patrick Wilkinson, records that a
visitor to the College in 1908 was surprised at 'the openness of the
display of affection between [male] couples'.[6]

Family life provided a staid contrast. Each Sunday, when in Cambridge, Maynard came to Harvey Road for lunch or supper. There was
a family holiday in March 1909 at Whitchurch, near Tavistock. In the
mornings Maynard worked on Index Numbers, in the afternoons he
played golf with Neville, in the evenings he played patience with Margaret. The only distraction was a trip across the moors to visit Rupert
Brooke whom they found clad in football shorts, breaking eggs on his
knees, and reading the Minority Report of the Poor Law Commission.

---

* Francis Birrell, the son of the Liberal politician Augustine Birrell. He had come to
King's from Eton to read history in 1908, and was an 'embryo'.

On 7 April 1909 Maynard and Duncan left for a fortnight's holiday in Versailles, Maynard taking Index Numbers with him. It brought about the first crisis in their relationship. Indeed, by the time they got back the affair seemed to be over, Duncan writing to James, 'I've told him that I'm no longer in love with him.'[7] Lytton noted this development with grim satisfaction. The report, however, was premature. 'I wonder if you will allow *me* to be fond of Maynard,' Duncan wrote to Lytton after seeing him on 3 May. 'It seemed as if you would put it down to my not seeing him as he is ... and not thinking that I could have different feelings because I am different to you ... In fact I feel distinctly ... that you would go on always finding fault with me until I became a second you ... I do sometimes feel that I should like the searchlight of your criticism to play on me occasionally ... but not always'. Lytton was forced to conclude that 'the Pozzo affair is not quite as dead as I'd thought'. The circumstances which led to the breach are not known. It is clear, though, that while Maynard was as much in love with Duncan as ever ('I still reckon everything here with reference to when I shall see you again,' he wrote him forlornly from King's on 26 April), Duncan refused to be locked into a single relationship. A reconciliation was patched up, and they drifted on. As for Lytton, 'I find that I'm not at all in love with Duncan – but my rage against Pozzo only seems to have increased.'[8]

At Cambridge, the most memorable event of the summer term was staged by Geoffrey, now in his final year at Pembroke. He and two friends had invited the novelist Henry James to visit Cambridge, Henry James accepting, so Maynard informed Duncan, 'in an enormous letter even more complicated than a novel ...' On Sunday 13 June 1909 Maynard gave a breakfast party for Henry James at King's. It was not a success. He had invited, among others, Harry Norton, who responded to each remark with manic laughter. Henry James was not amused. Desmond MacCarthy found him sitting disconsolately over 'a cold poached egg bleeding to death' surrounded by a respectful circle of silent undergraduates. However, the visit did produce a classic James remark. Told that the youth with fair hair who sometimes smiled was called Rupert Brooke, who also wrote poetry which was no good, Henry James replied, 'Well, I must say I am *relieved*, for with *that* appearance if he had also talent it would be too unfair.'[9]

Geoffrey followed his Henry James coup by landing a first in the Natural Sciences Tripos. The family celebrated with a holiday in the Pyrenees, where they had been two years before. Maynard found his brother's company a great disappointment. 'Geoffrey is *hopeless*,' he complained to Duncan from Lychon on 28 June. 'I don't quite know what I am doing here.' They drove and walked in the mountains. Soon Maynard was able to report that he was doing 'a moderate amount of work with a good deal of pleasure'. But he found a 'dreadful lack of excitement'. Moreover, his 'lynx-eyed' parents prevented any possibility of an 'adventure'. By 8 July they had moved on to Gavarnie, where Maynard worked on Probability, the theory of heredity ('I think I may have got some results which will be worth sending to the Professor of Biology [William Bateson],' he informed Duncan), and read Conrad's novels. From Gavarnie he was able to make a brief trip, alone to 'his' valley in Aragon. 'It seemed to me even fuller of emotional beauty than before. It must be the loveliest spot in Europe, full of a kind of enchantment and imagination which is extraordinarily definite, and one lives in it in a trance. I was perfectly happy there. When I have to flee the country, it will be to this valley that I shall retire, to live amongst trout and strawberries and Spanish shepherd boys....' His romantic mood was not even disturbed by the presence of a grim Russian count with six attendants and endless pots of Dundee marmalade. 'Your valley sounds enchanting,' Duncan replied. 'I wonder whether it is all in your imagination – I expect so. I mean you have found *your* valley. Perhaps mine would be different.' Biarritz, as before, was 'charming'. But on balance the holiday had not been a success. 'I felt, somehow, extraordinarily lonely. For a whole month every thought and feeling was locked up inside me.'[10] It was to be his last Continental holiday with his parents.

He spent only four days in Cambridge – long enough to catch a glimpse of Augustus John encamped at Grantchester 'with two wives and ten naked children' – before rushing off, on 26 July, to Burford, in the Cotswolds, where he had rented a house for the summer. He busied himself with arrangements to receive his guests. A studio was prepared for Duncan. A housekeeper was engaged, a nervous, lugubrious lady, but very economical. 'Food doesn't agree with her – so she doesn't have any meals,' he informed his mother. The only problem was local society. The Vicar had called. The 'abominable' Mrs Percival had asked him to a dance. He had been forced to accept dinner from Mrs Williams, who was 'stone deaf'. 'The privacy of my quiet country house is being destroyed and my peace of mind disturbed. It is intolerable,' he wrote to Florence.

Throughout the summer there was a stream of visitors. Swithinbank was the first to come, full of Burmese words, scandals about Eton and Dan ('inordinate wine and women'), and complaining that he had 'never copulated and so far as he can see never will'. On 31 July, James Strachey appeared; on 2 August Swithin left to coach Harold Macmillan, Dan's younger brother, now an Eton Colleger. On 3 August Sheppard turned up with Cecil Taylor (known as 'Madame'). Duncan came on 5 August and resumed his portrait of Taylor. 'The menage was of two married couples and myself,' James reported to Lytton.[11] Sheppard was edgy at the prospect of Madame's impending departure for a year in Germany and suspected that Duncan was flirting with 'her'. Maynard was 'rigid'. Duncan was angry with Maynard; Taylor smiled enigmatically. 'How scandalous', James wrote to Lytton, 'that two people (in modern life) should live in such undetermined relations [as Maynard and Duncan]. It's evident that the reason *we* don't understand them is that *they* don't . . . And poor Duncan. "I'm sorry, Duncan, but you really mustn't put that cup there." "Replace that volume, *please*, if you don't require it any longer."[12]

The company of his moody and critical friends left Maynard depressed. Unexpectedly he turned for reassurance to Lytton, who had been improbably banished by Lady Strachey to a Swedish sanatorium to recover his health. '[I] should very much like to be able to talk to you again, if it ever became possible,' he wrote to Lytton on 11 August. Strachey replied sympathetically. 'I wish you weren't unhappy. I think you have two things which in the long run ought to give you happiness – a decent competency, and the capacity and desire for doing important work. Love's the very devil. But it *is* Time's fool; and my experience is that when it's once flown finally out of the window, one's astonished to find how well one can get on without it.'[13]

Except for a brief visit from Florence and Margaret in mid-month, Maynard spent September at Burford alone with Duncan. This cheered him up considerably. He resumed his work on Probability; Duncan painted still lifes in the mornings and landscapes in the afternoons. They took long bicycle rides, recapturing the contentment and companionship they had found at Hoy. Whitehead had told Maynard to publish his dissertation right away. But Maynard was dissatisfied with it. 'It wants a good deal of alteration,' he told Lytton on 23 August. 'Part I will soon be finished . . . After every retouch it seems to me more trifling and platitudinous. All that is startling is gradually cut out as untrue, and what remains is a rather obscure and pompous exposition of what no human being can ever have doubted.' As for Lytton's new philosophy – 'A competence! A job! ∴ happiness' – only someone exiled to a hydropathic limbo could believe that. 'I shall soon be laying Probability aside until the Easter vacation,' Maynard told his father on 3 October. He had finished sixteen chapters of a projected twenty-six covering the fundamental ideas and their mathematical statement. He still hoped for early publication.

III

POLITICS

On 7 November 1909 Maynard visited Rupert Brooke at Grantchester and found him sitting in the midst of admiring female Fabians with nothing on but an embroidered sweater. That evening he entertained two 'embryos' to dinner – E. A. Kann, an undergraduate at Emmanuel College, and Alfred Brooke, Rupert's younger brother from King's. 'I trust Alfred to carry the party off,' Maynard wrote to Duncan beforehand. 'But he talks of nothing but Sodomy and the Budget, and Mr. Kann talks of nothing at all, So I fear that with my sense of propriety looming, it may be the Budget.' Women and politics had hit undergraduate life. Their meeting ground was the Cambridge University Fabian Society. Restarted in 1906 by 'Ben' Keeling, as the first undergraduate club open to both sexes, it claimed a hundred members a year later. Radicalism at Cambridge now meant Socialism and the Women's Vote more than Sodomy and Atheism. Undoubtedly the success of the newly-formed Labour Party in the 1906 election had something to do with the change. Keir Hardie and Ramsay MacDonald came to Cambridge and had their meetings wrecked. Nationally, the women's movement had taken a militant turn with the establishment of the Suffragettes. On 29 April 1909 Lloyd George infuriated the Right with a 'class war' budget which proposed a modest 'supertax' and a tax on land values to help pay for Dreadnoughts and social insurance. In England, as indeed on the Continent, Radicalism and Reaction seemed to be shaping up for a fight, thus forcing politics on the attention of the least politically attentive.

The change in sexual atmosphere had a number of causes. Among them was the strong heterosexual lead given by Rupert Brooke, Cambridge's outstanding undergraduate of his generation. As Hilton Young noted, Brooke, despite his beauty, was 'beef and beer, not nectar and ambrosia';[14] Fabian and womaniser rather than philosopher and aesthete; hearty, rather than shrinking in the style of the Strachey brothers. There were also coeducational influences from Bedales. Then there was the presence of a group of clever, attractive and rebellious women students. Apart from Ka Cox, three families did much to put women on the map at Cambridge, at least as far as the élite of undergraduates was concerned: the Costelloes, the Oliviers, and the Darwins, the first two with Fabian fathers. Although Moore returned to Cambridge in 1911, his glory, according to Keynes, undimmed, he seemed less relevant to the new generation of students than Mr and Mrs Webb, Bernard Shaw, H. G. Wells, and even William Morris. All-male reading parties in country inns gave way to camping, hiking and mixed bathing, as the older ideals of a simplified life, with unstuffy clothes and wholesome food, re-emerged in a heterosexual setting. 'Ka [Cox] came striding along the road in time for lunch yesterday,' Virginia Woolf wrote to her sister in 1911 'with a knapsack on her back, a row of red beads, and daisies stuck in her coat.'[15] The 'neo-pagans' as she called the circle round Rupert Brooke flocked to the Fabian summer schools in Wales, where they slept on the beach, and alarmed the prim Beatrice Webb with 'their anarchic ways in sexual questions'.

With the Fabians as the new centre of attraction, the Apostles lost something of their *éclat*. There was an overlap, of course. Rupert Brooke was the socialist crusader in the land of sods; James Strachey preached the doctrine according to Moore at the Fabian summer camps. Harry Norton reported to Maynard on 26 August 1908:

> James ... has gone to a cottage next door to the Sidney Webbs, whom he has battered, – so he & Daddy & Gerald think – into dust with *Principia Ethica*, and is going, or, by now, may have gone, to the Summer School at Barmouth. There's only one bed, & one arm chair, so Ben-Hadad [Keeling] tells me, in the School, (The other socialists sleep on the grass). These have been placed at high water mark, and James is to glide from one to the other, smoking his pipe & reading the works of the Yen [Moore] aloud, while Mr. Wells, Mr. Bernard Shaw, Mr. Granville Barker, Mr. Graham Wallas et plusieurs autres build sandcastles round him & Ben copulates furiously with a jellyfish.[16]

The Society resisted the socialist onslaught by the well-tried tradition of sterility: there was one election only between 1909 and 1912, by which time the socialist tide had largely spent itself. The gravamen of the old guard's charge against the Fabians was that their beliefs were irrationally held, like those of Christians. This is made plain in a letter Gerald Shove, fresh from a Fabian summer camp, wrote to Maynard on 15 September 1910:

> James and I nearly fought on the way back to Oxford – about Socialism. It *is* extraordinary to see how even the most apostolic of socialists gets hot and dishonest as soon as one dares criticise his views. It's more difficult to understand than the Christian's attitude: the beastly emotions *he* gets out of his belief do afford some reason for his *wishing* to hold it, and consequently getting angry when anyone throws doubt on it, but I can't believe that sensible people like James – or even people like Rupert – really get any 'spiritual comfort' out of believing in Socialism; yet they seemed *determined* to believe in it at all costs – just as the Christians are determined to cling to the cross. Do you think it's merely pride? – that they don't want to admit that a position they've once taken up with confidence is untenable? I feel somehow that the *nature* of the belief has got something to do

with it: I don't believe they'd be the same, for instance about free
trade . . . A good many people, I suppose, hold *all* their important
beliefs in a religious way: but they're mostly quite stupid: they form,
of course, the bulk of the socialist party. Ben [Keeling] was like that
tho' he had a certain amount of intelligence, but I should have
thought that James certainly and Rupert probably wasn't.[17]

Maynard's pattern of life was not uninfluenced by these new currents.
Women younger than himself – notably Ka Cox and Daphne and
Brynhild Olivier – became part of his circle of friends, though there is
no evidence that his ways had become any less unflirtatious than those
noticed by Ray Costelloe in 1906.

Peter Clarke has written of Maynard's political position at this time:
'There is, in short, unmistakeable evidence of an earnest political commitment to the new Liberalism'.[18] The evidence is that he spoke, in
February 1911, with Sidney Webb, in support of a motion at the Cambridge Union 'That the progressive reorganisation of Society along the
lines of Collectivist Socialism is both inevitable and desirable.'[19] One
could add that a few months later he announced to his surprised father
that he was 'in favour of the confiscation of wealth', and that in 1913
he had lunch with Beatrice Webb at Newnham, which he found a 'deep
spiritual experience'. As the basis for a claim of 'earnest political commitment' to anything, such evidence is extremely flimsy. Whatever
Keynes's political views, his *commitment* to doing anything about them
was very weak.

In his Cambridge Union speech Keynes defended the public service
motive for action. Nelson was a 'servant of the State, and he was not
efficient from motives of material self-interest, but because it pleased
him to do his "job" as well as possible'. More generally his political
views at this time were conditioned by the fiscal debate in which
progressive or 'confiscatory' taxes were seen as the main alternative to
Protection. Keynes's support for increased direct taxation stemmed
more from his commitment to free trade than from any enthusiasm for
'redistribution'. It was the threat to the 'old' not the attraction of the
'new' Liberalism which stirred him to intermittent political activity in
these years. As secretary of the Cambridge University Free Trade
Association he presided at a big free trade meeting at the Cambridge
Guildhall on 30 April 1909, the day after Lloyd George's budget
speech. In the summer of 1909 he took time off from Probability to
write an article for the *New Quarterly*, edited by his friend Desmond
MacCarthy, rebutting the Protectionist charge that the Budget would
cause a flight of capital (see above p. 228). When the House of Lords
threw out Lloyd George's budget on 30 November 1909, provoking a
general election, Keynes wrote an article in the *Cambridge Daily News*
of 29 December 1909 advising his readers to vote Liberal on the

grounds that a Conservative victory would cause a constitutional crisis. He then trundled across to Birmingham for some electioneering on behalf of Hilton Young who was fighting Austen Chamberlain at East Worcester. 'Life without a howling audience to address every evening will seem very dull', he wrote to Lytton Strachey from the Queen's Hotel, Birmingham, on 14 January 1910. 'What an abominably bad state of mind you must have got into', replied Lytton cheerfully. On 8 November 1910 Maynard spoke once more in defence of Free Trade at the Cambridge Union. 'His cold, intellectual style is well suited to destructive criticism of economic fallacies and he was delightfully crushing', noted *Granta*. He campaigned again on behalf of Edwin Montagu at Histon in the December general election. These were the high points of Keynes's pre-war political involvements.

His interests at this stage of his life carried him not to Westminster, Whitehall, or the City but to Bloomsbury. In December 1909 Duncan took the lease of a ground floor flat at 21 Fitzroy Square. The front room was to be his studio: Maynard had a bedroom at the back. Maynard was in London in December to examine for the Locals at the Mercers' Grammar School, Holborn. He took time off to go dressed as a cook to the Slade School's fancy dress ball. To Florence he wrote: 'Who, to my immense surprise, should enter but Geoffrey! – clad as an ancient Briton. Then on top of Max Beerbohm, Will Rothenstein, Wilson Steer and all the other artists, in came a whole train of them – Gwen and Margaret Darwin, K. Cox, Karin Costelloe, Justin, Rupert, Jacques.' At two in the morning they were all 'gallivanting in the streets of London as dead leaves before the West Wind'.* Virginia and Adrian Stephen's At Home on 23 December was a less liberated occasion. Lytton and James Strachey, Frankie Birrell, Duncan Grant, Harry Norton, Horace Cole [a friend of Adrian's] 'sat round most silent, and I wished for any woman', Virginia wrote to her sister. 'I talked to Frankie and Keynes most of the time, but it was desperate work'.[20]

IV

BLOOMSBURY

With his bedroom at Fitzroy Square, Maynard established a physical presence in the Bloomsbury district of London. The Bloomsbury

---

*Jacques Raverat, a Frenchman, was educated at Bedales and Emmanuel College, Cambridge. He studied mathematics, but took up painting. Gwen Darwin, a granddaughter of Charles Darwin, who later married Raverat, was studying at the Slade Art School. Her sister Margaret later married Geoffrey Keynes. Justin Brooke, Rupert's namesake, not relation, was at King's. He had founded the Marlowe Dramatic Society. Rupert Brooke was dressed as the West Wind.

Group – 'Old Bloomsbury' as Virginia Woolf and Vanessa Bell later called it – had already come into existence, drawing its name from a particular kind of social and cultural life which grew up among a group of friends in a couple of adjacent Georgian squares in that unfashionable part of London. The most convenient starting date is March 1905 when the Stephen children – Vanessa, Thoby, Virginia and Adrian – launched their Thursday evenings' At Homes at 46 Gordon Square, to which Thoby's friends, down from Cambridge, started to come: notably Saxon Sydney-Turner, Clive Bell, Lytton Strachey, and Desmond MacCarthy. 'These Thursday evenings' Virginia Woolf recalled in 1922, 'were, as far as I am concerned, the germ from which sprang all that has since come to be called ... Bloomsbury'. Thoby Stephen ('the Goth') with his Apostolic connections was, as we have seen, the key link between the Cambridge and London worlds. But the common ground of their intercourse had already been prepared. For at almost the exact moment when the Strachey generation of Apostles was working out, under Moore's influence, a philosophy of life which scorned worldly values and conventional duties, the Stephen children had fled the stuffy respectability of the dead Sir Leslie Stephen's South Kensington house, with its encumbrance of smart relations, for what Virginia called the 'crude and impertinent' life of Bloomsbury; perhaps with the idea of establishing a salon for Thoby's friends already in their minds. According to Quentin Bell,[21] the 'essential element in the situation ... was the sense of liberation at 46, Gordon Square. The Stephen children were orphans. They had escaped from an extremely depressing Victorian home. They were young. In that uncontrolled, unchaperoned environment Thoby Stephen's friends might continue the conversation which had begun at Cambridge'. The conversation on Beauty, Love, Philosophy may have been liberating, but it was far from vivacious. Except when Clive Bell was there to add a flow of chatter it was marked by huge silences which would have done credit to McTaggart. The other essential feature of the situation was that the Bloomsbury At Homes offered an opportunity for unflirtatious contact between the sexes. Vanessa and Virginia, though both extremely beautiful, had fled the marriage market which passed for ordinary social life. Thoby's friends were either not interested in women, or sexually inhibited in their presence. There was a certain security in this situation for both sides. They also lacked what Virginia called 'physical splendour'. As she remarked: 'The society of buggers has many advantages – if you are a woman. It is simple, it is honest, it makes one feel ... in some respects at one's ease'.[22] In this company Clive Bell's 'special charm of normality'[23] stood out as a disturbing factor.

In 1907, following Thoby's tragic death from typhoid – an event which linked the two sides in a common sorrow – Clive Bell married

Vanessa Stephen. There were now two Bloomsbury salons – the Bells' at 46 Gordon Square, and that of Virginia and Adrian who took over 29 Fitzroy Square. Vanessa Bell, with her beautiful Pre-Raphaelite face, but down to earth manner and bawdy tongue, was determined to make her career as a painter. Her Friday Club became a centre for the discussion of the visual arts. Virginia, ethereally beautiful, but socially awkward and frightened of men, and already showing signs of mental breakdown, had started working on her first novel, *The Voyage Out*. Their younger brother Adrian was an amiable, ineffective giant. At Cambridge he had been (in Quentin Bell's phrase) an 'evening shadow' of Thoby; but he was clever, ironic and occasionally alarmingly high-spirited. Virginia and Adrian resumed the Thursday evenings at Fitzroy Square, which were frequented by a new generation of Apostles and their friends – Harry Norton, James Strachey, Gerald Shove, Francis Birrell. The characteristic Bloomsbury mode was establishing itself – unadorned honesty in conversation and personal relationships, a passion for literature and the visual arts. Politics, together with bourgeois sexual conventions, were damned as prime examples of cant; but there was a profound insight into the niceties of intellectual and cultural rank, and a constant concern with the problems of domestic servants.

What had not yet started was the debate about what Bloomsbury stood for, who was in it, whether it was good or bad, subsequently subjects of absorbing interest to both its admirers and detractors. Nor could it start until the circle had attained, through the achievements of its individual members, and their public support for each other, the status of an influential cultural coterie. This position was reached in stages. The public image of Bloomsbury was already forming just before the First World War, mainly in connection with a new attitude to the visual arts and design. It was sharpened by Bloomsbury's general hostility to the First World War. It became fixed with Lytton Strachey's disparagement of the achievements of 'Eminent Victorians'. By the 1920s the main lines of criticism had become clear. According to Arnold Lunn, in a letter to Clive Bell dated 16 January 1957, Bloomsbury 'made fashionable a new attitude to religion. They dismissed it with a raised eye-brow [as] something not worth taking seriously. You find this attitude among undergraduates but not as a rule among people of adult intelligence'. There was a lack of intellectual integrity, of which the main example was the writing of Lytton Strachey. 'His fundamental fault was a moral one: in the last resort he did not care enough for the truth. Where his portraits are false they are not merely false but falsified.' Bloomsbury's third failing was what Lunn called 'fake objectivity'; they dressed up their contempt for conventional standards in a philosophic language derived from Moore.

Finally, Bloomsbury exhibited a 'flight from asceticism, a certain soft-ness'. It dismissed the asceticism of chastity, of duty, of the trenches with a snigger.[24] It is noticeable in this critique that the 'tone' of Bloomsbury's disparagement of sacred belief is disliked as much as the substance. Much, though not all, of this criticism is echoed by Roy Harrod in his biography of Keynes, with the implication that Keynes somehow escaped from these limitations. Defenders and admirers of Bloomsbury argue, on the whole, that what critics perceived as faults were not faults at all but expressions of a more civilised, more enlight-ened attitude to life.

In 1965, the publication of Michael Holroyd's biography of Lytton Strachey revealed another aspect of Bloomsbury's collective life: not just the widespread homosexuality and bisexuality, but the sexual merry-go-round, as friends became lovers and then went back to being friends. These revelations have produced an ambivalent attitude to Bloomsbury: they fascinate, but they repel. Can such people ever have felt deeply about anyone or anything? Was not every human emotion to them a subject for jokes, dissection, manipulation? Their very vocabulary seems insipid: people and opinions were always 'charm-ing', or 'amusing', or 'absurd'. Against this, cannot it be claimed that they had discovered a more civilised principle of sexual and emotional order than the artificial restrictions, endless deceits, and unnecessary separations attached to the monogamous ideal? Did they not at least have the virtue of honesty? And were they not redeemed, despite every-thing, by their genuine love and championship of the arts?

Once the debate is launched along these lines, it is impossible to get away from the question of G. E. Moore and the influence of *Principia Ethica* on Bloomsbury. This is quite distinct from the trivial question of who in Bloomsbury actually read the book: enough did for its flavour to be common property. For it was Moore who tried to redefine the content of ethical discussion by insisting that the primary question was not 'what ought I to do' but 'what is good'; and that the primary question could be answered only by reference to some conception of the good life. The virtues, Moore said, have no value in themselves. They are valuable only as a means to what is good, and must be rationally proportioned to it. If Bloomsbury can be defined by a common attitude of mind – as it surely can – this is it. Members of Bloomsbury were uncommonly interested in the question of what constitutes a good life, and their preoccupation with this question shaped to an unusual extent the kind of lives they actually led, and their valuation of people and activities. Moore was not the unique or original begetter of this pre-occupation. What he did was to draw attention, in precise philosophic form, and for a certain group of people, to the question of what is meant by being civilised, or, in his own language, what it means to 'be good'.

He did this against the background of widespread dissatisfaction with certain ideals of conduct held up for admiration by the Victorians, including conventional sexual morality, but also the pursuit of material success, the exaltation of activities which were useful, and so on; as well as with the philistine attitude to the arts which accompanied them.

Bloomsbury, it is true, was devoid of Christian belief. But in this there was nothing distinctive, and its atheism was not derived from Moore. What Moore said was that, even if God existed, his existence would not answer the primary ethical question, for of any state of affairs deemed by God to be good, it would still be meaningful to ask: is it good? More distinctive was Bloomsbury's hostility to beliefs *religiously* held. For all beliefs, one must be able to produce arguments commanding the assent of reason. If Christianity was not such a belief, then so much the worse for Christianity. But the same applied to Marxism and to what Keynes called the 'pseudo social service' religions. In the interwar years, the Bloomsbury attitude of scepticism to all political dogmas came equally under attack from Right and Left. And there is no doubt it encouraged, though it did not entail, political passivity. Political activity could certainly be justified on Moorite grounds if there was an immediate political threat to civilised values – for example, the threat of war. Whether a life *wholly* devoted to politics was compatible with a good state of mind was far more doubtful. One must always remember that the apolitical stance of Bloomsbury reflects the fact that it was a time when the threat of social upheaval had receded and the threat of war had not yet materialised. This partly accounts for the attraction to them of Moore's philosophy, and perhaps partly explains the appearance of the philosophy itself at that juncture.

None of this is to deny the existence of a tension between Cambridge rationality and Bloomsbury sensibility. Virginia Woolf was struck by the 'crippling effect' of Cambridge's *analytical* spirit' on her father, unrelieved by any 'distracting interests – music, art, the theatre, travel'.[25] Bloomsbury's outlook represents an attempt to marry Cambridge rationalism to aesthetic and sexual emotion. The way it did so was to apply the analytical method to love and the arts. The marriage was made easier by Moore's doctrine that 'good' itself was unanalysable.

A second way to think of Bloomsbury is as a group of friends, but with the proviso that they 'found' each other because it was very easy for them to do so. Of course, one cannot ignore elements of accident and individual choice in bringing the group together. Nevertheless, the fact remains that Bloomsbury was formed out of a few pre-existing and overlapping family and cultural connections: the Cambridge Apostles on the one hand, and the two family clans of Stracheys and Stephens on the other. Once this institutional nexus is understood, the question of where the exact frontiers of Bloomsbury lay, who was in it at any one time, becomes a secondary matter, a pastime for cultural snobs.

Quentin Bell lists twenty members of Bloomsbury in 1913. Their interconnections can be exhibited most plainly in the following table:

BLOOMSBURY GROUP, 1913

	Cambridge	College	Apostle	Strachey	Stephen
E. M. Forster	×	King's	×		
David Garnett					
Sydney Waterlow	×	Trinity			
Desmond MacCarthy	×	Trinity	×		
Molly MacCarthy					
Roger Fry	×	Trinity	×		
Vanessa Bell					×
Virginia Woolf					×
Duncan Grant				×	
Clive Bell	×	Trinity			
Saxon Sydney-Turner	×	Trinity	×		
Leonard Woolf	×	Trinity	×		
Lytton Strachey	×	Trinity	×	×	
Adrian Stephen	×	Trinity			×
Maynard Keynes	×	King's	×		
Gerald Shove	×	King's	×		
James Strachey	×	Trinity	×	×	
Marjorie Strachey	×	Newnham		×	
H. J. Norton	×	King's	×		
Francis Birrell	×	King's			

Of the twenty, ten were Apostles and fifteen had been to Cambridge. Of the two without a cross, Molly MacCarthy was the wife of Desmond MacCarthy, and David Garnett came from a well-established literary family, and was a childhood friend of the Olivier sisters. The Stephens, though unrepresented in the Apostles of this period, had a strong nineteenth-century connection with The Society; Clive and Vanessa Bell's son Julian was to become an Apostle in his turn, as was Waterlow's son John.

These strong inherited connections go some way to explain Bloomsbury's exclusiveness. It was curious about outsiders 'rather one might say as a collector of beetles, for instance, is interested in the world of beetles. They were glad that some selected beetles should come into the enclosure for them to find out what was going on there outside . . .' The commentator, Hilton Young, who considered himself one of the favoured beetles, went on to remark that 'a common-place opinion astonished them all, but provoked in them different reactions. It moved Virginia to silence, Vanessa to a sympathetic effort to give it meaning,

Lytton to change the subject, and Clive to genial but explosive laughter.'[26]

Bloomsberries, as they called themselves, might be curious about outsiders. They were also frightened of them, and could be chilling to them. Bloomsbury provided a retreat for people, some of whom had been scarred early in life by their contact with the outside world. Within the circle of intimacy they developed opinions, styles of conversation, behaviour, even dress, which shocked outsiders. Blasphemy was a credo going back to Cambridge days; bawdiness was almost *de rigueur*. The characters and sexual tastes of their friends, the continual rearrangement of their affairs, were topics of absorbing interest. The peculiar flavour of Bloomsbury depended not just on leisure but on keeping a sharp division between insiders and outsiders. Keynes fitted in well enough. He was unshockable; and the indelicacy to which he gave free rein with his friends was usually regarded as a social asset. 'You are rather like a Chinese Buddha as a host' Vanessa Bell wrote to him on 16 April 1914 after one week-end house party.'You are silent but not so silent as Saxon & manage to create an atmosphere in which all is possible. Perhaps you talk more than a Buddha would though. Anyhow the result is what I imagine it would be with a Buddha. One can talk of fucking & sodomy & sucking & bushes all without turning a hair.'[27]

A third aspect of Bloomsbury is that it was a cultural, not an academic, coterie. Of the members listed above, only three – Maynard Keynes, Gerald Shove and Harry Norton – held academic jobs. Perhaps this was the last period in English history when a group of such intellectual excellence could have assembled in London outside the university system. It was this assimilation of fine intellects to the tradition of the salon rather than the common room which made Bloomsbury such a formidable cultural force. Bloomsbury consisted of both creators *and* publicists. On balance, the achievement of the latter was greater than that of the former. By international standards the Bloomsbury painters – Vanessa Bell, Duncan Grant, Roger Fry – were not in the front rank. Likewise, in literature only Virginia Woolf is indisputably in the highest class. But in the way they set about redefining the relationship between culture and society, and in their advocacy of specific theories, the Bloomsbury publicists were first-class.

That the opportunity was there for any clever and strongly-motivated cultural coterie to seize is plain in retrospect. Bloomsbury was a particular expression of, and gave direction to, the 'revolt against the Victorians'. The rejection of conventional sexual morality was one facet, but only one, of the revolt against 'false values' in the name of which Victorians had sacrificed the possibility of leading a good life.

Members of Bloomsbury were generally exceptional children of exceptional parents, who had seen their parents' lives being cluttered up and strangled by unnecessary duties. In place of these, Bloomsbury substituted the ideal, not of doing what one liked, but of doing what was good. Cultural enjoyments were placed at the centre of the good life. Instead of culture being an aid to good conduct, good conduct was redefined as the means to culture. This in turn led to a change in cultural theory and practice. An attempt was made to detach the cultural object from conventional associations. Already before 1914 Roger Fry and Clive Bell, Bloomsbury's two main art publicists, were insisting that aesthetic enjoyment derived from 'significant form' in the pictures themselves rather than from associations in the viewer's mind. In Virginia Woolf's novels, too, story-telling is sacrificed to form. As Nigel Nicolson puts it: 'As one might return from a country walk with a handful of wild flowers and arrange them in a vase, neatly, to create something beautiful and significant out of a jumble, so Virginia Woolf would collect sights, smells and snatches of talk, and put them on a page before they died.' In his biographies Lytton Strachey deliberately distorted his portraits to shock his readers into seeing familiar things in new ways. As in their art, so in their lives members of Bloomsbury refused to allow feelings to be cramped by conventional associations. They were not sexual anarchists but rather creators of a new kind of sexual order inherent in a proper concept of the good life. That is why Bloomsbury was able to undertake the frequent rearrangement of its emotional affairs while remaining so (comparatively) free from sexual jealousy.

In these ways, Bloomsberries were cultural and sexual revolutionaries. In other ways they remained rooted in the assumptions of their times. Indeed, the particular form of their 'revolt against the Victorians' depended on other aspects of Victorian life remaining in place. Culture was not regarded as a force to reshape social relations, but to reorient the élite to 'what is good'. Bloomsbury was as hostile to any notion of a 'proletarian culture' as it was to 'capitalist culture'. Both were symptoms of a degraded industrial system. There was little desire in Bloomsbury to make contact with the 'mass mind', little faith in the possibility of a 'common culture'. Bloomsbury's cultural artefacts were highbrow; its propaganda aimed entirely at the (highly) educated middle classes. There was always a clear tension between its cultural ideals and democratic sentiment: civilisation, as Clive Bell put it, always rested on having someone to do the dirty work. Maynard Keynes, as we shall see, attempted to go beyond this contradiction; but it cannot be claimed he got very far. And he, like the rest of the Bloomsberries, depended completely on domestic servants to sustain their own lives. In these ways Bloomsbury was rooted in the class assumptions of

the Victorians. Their revision of the Victorian scheme of life tended to
take them back to the eighteenth century idea of a cultured aristocracy
rather than towards the ideal of a civilized democracy; or rather they
could not conceive of a civilized democracy which lacked an endowed
aristocracy of talent, with all its inegalitarian implications; while their
own experience seemed proof that such an aristocracy could not come
out of 'nowhere'.

The cultural influence which Bloomsbury eventually acquired was
based on the clarity of vision of its publicists and the mutually supporting achievements of its members. But two further ingredients must be
added: its relative financial independence and its power of patronage.
Bloomsberries were not rich. But they were never forced into dependence on institutions alien to their spirit. There was just enough inherited wealth to go round to enable them to lead their preferred lives
until their own talents could give them an earned independence. No
Bloomsbury group would have been possible had people like Strachey
and Bell, Virginia and Vanessa, been dispersed round the provincial
universities. Equally important, Bloomsbury over the years was able
to find outlets and platforms for its work and theories in influential
journals and art galleries and thus, to some extent, become an arbiter
of taste. Through this position members were able to get their younger
friends jobs, commissions and shows. None of this would have been
possible had they not, in fact, wielded the power of the pen and the
brush to great effect. But it was not enough. Financial backing was
needed. Here the role of Maynard Keynes became crucial. He came to
give Bloomsbury financial muscle, not just by making a great deal of
money himself, which he spent lavishly on Bloomsbury causes, but by
his ability to organize financial backing for their enterprises. (Before
1914 he had already started managing some of his friends' money for
them.) Indeed, from the First World War onwards it is almost impossible to find any enterprise, cultural or domestic, in which members of
Bloomsbury were involved, which did not benefit in some way from his
largesse, his financial acumen, or his contacts. Condemned, or selected,
by aptitude and disposition to work largely in the world of means rather
than ends, this was his way of promoting and paying homage to the
vision of the good life which he shared with his friends.

It was in the winter of 1910–11 that the world first discovered the
existence of Bloomsbury. On 5 November 1910, Roger Fry, an old
Apostle, who had just resigned a lucrative job with the Metropolitan
Museum of Art in New York, put on an exhibition called 'Manet and
the Post-Impressionists' at the Grafton Galleries. It was an event of
momentous importance in the history of British taste. Its core consisted
of 21 Cézannes, 37 Gauguins, and 20 Van Goghs which Fry and Desmond MacCarthy had selected from dealers and private collectors in

Paris. Although most of the paintings were twenty or thirty years old they horrified a British public which had missed out on Impressionism itself (represented in England only by the anaemic productions of the New English Art Club) and which was therefore still habituated to what Frances Spalding has called 'story-telling in paint'. Critics dismissed the French paintings as 'the output of a lunatic asylum'. To some of them brash colour, broken brushwork, and distorted shapes portended the dissolution of the social order. Roger Fry was by this time intimate with the Bells; and Bloomsbury took up the cause of Post-Impressionism with enthusiasm. Vanessa and Clive Bell, Virginia, Adrian, Roger Fry and Duncan Grant all went to the Post-Impressionist ball in March 1911, the women scandalising the press and the other guests by appearing as Gauguin-like savages, draped in African cloth. Fry put on a second Post-Impressionist exhibition, more professionally organised, in October 1912, dominated by the works of Picasso and Matisse, but in which Duncan Grant was also represented together with other modern English painters. Less revolutionary, but more dramatic, in its impact on London's artistic life, was the first season of the Ballets Russes in June 1911, in which Diaghilev introduced to London audiences the fabulous Nijinsky in Schumann's *Carnaval* and Weber's *Le Spectre de la Rose*, both choreographed by Michel Fokine. In the latter, Nijinsky's leap through the open French window, light as a petal in the breeze, to alight beside the sleeping Karsavina, electrified London audiences.

Leonard Woolf, returning from seven years in Ceylon, strongly felt that exhilaration of life in 1911, when it seemed as if the world was on the brink of becoming civilised. It was a wonderfully sunny summer. In politics it looked 'as if militarism, imperialism, and antisemitism were on the run'. The revolution of the motor car and aeroplane had started; Freud, Rutherford and Einstein had begun their work. 'Equally exciting things were happening in the arts. On the stage the shattering impact of Ibsen was still belatedly powerful and we felt that Ibsen had a worthy successor in Shaw as a revolutionary ... In painting we were in the middle of the revolution of Cézanne, Matisse, and Picasso ... And to crown all, night after night we flocked to Covent Garden, entranced by a new art, a revelation to us benighted British, the Russian ballet in the greatest days of Diaghilev and Nijinsky'.[28] Bloomsbury felt no premonition of disaster; only a joyful sense of awakening after the long Victorian night.

V

THE END OF THE AFFAIR

Considering how many values and friendships he shared with Bloomsbury, Maynard's entry into the charmed circle was surprisingly
delayed. Bloomsbury was not the centre of his social or intellectual set
during his years at the India Office, though he saw something of the
Bells. In 1909 he was still Keynes, not Maynard, to both Vanessa and
Virginia. Lytton's hostility probably explains why Bloomsbury was so
tardy in accepting Maynard as a member, as well as his own reluctance
to base his London life on the group. It was now Duncan who eased
Maynard's passage into Bloomsbury, Duncan's charm winning much
readier acceptance than Maynard's frightening, and occasionally
gloating, brilliance.

For Duncan Grant, the move to Bloomsbury in 1909 proved as
liberating and exhilarating as it had been for the Stephen sisters five
years previously. 'Fitzrovia' was then the home of the artistic *avant-
garde*. The fashionably-dressed Walter Sickert, doyen of the New English Art Club, had his studio at 19 Fitzroy Square, where he played host
to a Fitzroy Group which included painters like Spencer Gore, Augustus John, Robert Bevan and Harold Gilman. Henry Lamb had taken
over Augustus John's studio at 8 Fitzroy Street. The young Slade
School painters Gwen Darwin and Stanley Spencer came to Vanessa
Bell's Friday Club. Here, on 21 February 1910, Duncan heard Roger
Fry on 'Representation as a means of Expression'.[29] Fry was in the
throes of the life-change which would turn him from a painter of mock
seventeenth-century landscapes and authority on Old Masters into an
intimate of Bloomsbury and a revolutionary protagonist and theorist
of modern art. Duncan's friendship with Vanessa and Clive and Roger
developed rapidly in his new surroundings. 'Duncan may be going to
be a great painter' Vanessa wrote to Clive in 1910. 'There seems to me
to be something remarkably fine in his work & in the grand manner.
He is certainly much the most interesting of the young painters'.[30]

In February 1910, Duncan had his first dinner at 44 Bedford Square,
home of the exotic, much discussed Lady Ottoline Morrell. She found
him shy, vague, elusive and bewitching; he was readily absorbed into
her world of lustre and illusion, fascinated by her extraordinary face
with its jutting jaw, and by her fantastic clothes. Ottoline was not part
of Bloomsbury, but she provided a welcome relief from its austerities,
and was a perfect foil for its malice and cultural snobbery. A generous,
perceptive, clever, though absurd, aristocratic groupie of the arts, she
felt it her mission to inspire and promote writers and artists, which she

did to great effect; without, of course, receiving the gratitude she deserved. Duncan became a regular *habitué* at her salon. In 1912 he met Nijinsky there, playing tennis in Bedford Square, while Nijinsky and Diaghilev's designer Leon Bakst looked on. Maynard's first recorded dinner party at Ottoline's did not take place till Thursday, 15 June 1911.

Duncan's absorption in his new life inevitably made Maynard and Cambridge seem more remote. He took to wandering into 29 Fitzroy Square, home of Virginia and Adrian, in his borrowed, oversize trousers, vague and charming. His intimacy with them was fortified by the famous 'Dreadnought Hoax' of 20 February 1910 when he was commandeered by Adrian and his friends to join in impersonating the Emperor of Abyssinia and his family. Dressed in exotic clothes and jewels as princes of the blood, he and Virginia visited the British fleet anchored at Weymouth with their 'father' and were received with royal honours on the flagship by the Admiral, Sir William Fisher, Adrian's cousin, who was completely taken in by his six-foot five-inch relative disguised as an interpreter. 'What a lunatic affair! Are you going to jail for it?' enquired Maynard anxiously, after news of the hoax, released by one of the hoaxers, was splashed across the front pages of the newspapers. (Duncan was temporarily abducted by some hearties, but all he got in the way of official reprimand was a mild ticking off from Reginald McKenna, First Lord of the Admiralty.)

On 28 February 1910, Duncan confessed to Maynard that he was falling in love with Adrian Stephen. 'Adrian', wrote David Garnett, 'had extraordinarily innocent eyes: he looked through them at the passing scene like the child in Hans Andersen's story of the Emperor's new clothes – as though he could not believe what they saw. Then, aware of the inadequacy of words, he caught one's eye and either made a most horrific comic grimace, or laughed.'[31] One can see why Duncan, with his painter's eye for the absurd and incongruous, and with his suspicion that clever people thought him little better than a half-wit, should feel at ease in Adrian's company. Maynard professed to take his infatuation lightly. 'It sounds perfect from the point of view of pleasure' he wrote back on 3 March. This seems an inadequate response. But perhaps Maynard realised that Strachey-like outbreaks of recrimination and despair would only destroy their friendship. He adapted himself to the new situation as best as he could. Duncan did not give up Maynard; he simply added Adrian. Maynard's love for Duncan did not die. But he accepted that his place in Duncan's life would become progressively smaller. And this helped him accept, and be accepted by, Duncan's new friends.

On 17 March 1910, Maynard and Duncan left London for Marseilles, where they boarded the *S.S. Danube* for a seven-week holiday in

Greece and Asia Minor. Duncan had hesitated before agreeing to come. 'It is a *great* weight off my mind . . . that you have made up your mind,' Maynard wrote to him on 3 March. 'I am sure it will be delightful and I don't see why we should lose our tempers with each other.' They shared a large cabin on the deck. By 22 March Maynard had read 'nearly half of Adam Smith. It is a wonderful book.' In Athens, they established themselves in a hotel overlooking the Parthenon; and then started on a week's tour, by horse, of the Peloponnese. To his parents Maynard extolled the 'wonderful Hermes of Praxiteles' and 'the most perfect temple' at Bassae. The pain of travelling in a primitive country could be wonderfully eased by the personal services available to the moderately affluent visitor:

> The comfort of travelling with a dragoman is very great [he wrote to his father on 2 April 1910]. He has to take nearly all our food with him as one can get nothing in these mountain villages – and did all our cooking. But he is an excellent cook and is ready to produce a complete table d'hote meal at any time or place out of a great basket which he carries round with him. He also makes all the arrangements, does all the bargaining, and pays the bills and the tips and takes the tickets – so that we have all the care taken off our shoulders. He is an elderly Venetian, charming to us, but a little too gentle, perhaps, to be equal always to meeting the world as fiercely as a dragoman should.

Back in Athens an unexpected strike delayed their departure for Smyrna in Turkey. Keynes found the Smyrna bazaar 'more like the Arabian nights than one would have believed possible', but the place that impressed the travellers most was Brousse, the ancient Ottoman capital, where they spent a week in a town 'crowded with mosques and baths and mausoleums'. Here Maynard had Turkish baths in a bath house built by Murad II. At Troy they stayed with an English couple, the Calverts, who owned a farm: with typical consideration Maynard sent them, on his return, two valuable old books on the topography of Troy. They returned via Constantinople and Berlin, reaching England on 8 May.

That summer Maynard made a determined effort to finish Probability. Having rewritten Parts I and II, covering the ground of his fellowship dissertation, the previous year, he was embarking on a new section – Part III of the published book – dealing with the logic and justification of inductive methods, on which probability arguments rest. 'No clear or satisfactory account of them is to be found anywhere,' he wrote.[32] On 7 June 1910, Lytton, who was staying at Cambridge, found 'The Society . . . incredibly stiff and metaphysical. Pozzo on Induction – so solid and bulky with Hawtrey, poor old Dickinson, Robin Mayor,

Hardy and the rest *en suite*.' Maynard went on working on Probability at King's over the Long Vacation term. To Lytton, about to return to Stockholm, he wrote on 10 July: 'Scarcely anyone is up yet and one lives, rather pleasantly, the life of a recluse whose main interest is Analogy. Norton has lately come, and Furness from Egypt, quite unchanged, is here. Sheppard disappeared after a day or two; Gerald and Frankie [Birrell] are still away. There is Alfred but not Rupert.' He found the work very difficult. 'I've had to rewrite what I've been doing over and over again,' he told Duncan on 10 July, 'but I think I've really made some progress and that my final account of the nature of scientific argument is better than anyone else's. But there is still time for it to break down.' The first chapter on Induction was finished on 27 July.

Probability went back with him to the Little House, Burford, which he had once again rented for the summer. On arriving there on Saturday, 6 August, he was shocked to discover that that 'devil Kann' had failed to show up, leaving him alone for three days. To Duncan he complained, 'I find that I don't, on the whole, like to be quite alone. I can't do any more work than usual and my mind preys on itself in the most dreadful way.'[33] From this unnatural solitude he was rescued by the arrival of Sheppard and Madame (Cecil Taylor), the former in a much better mood than the previous year, since Maynard had managed to secure money from Emmanuel College for Taylor's return to Cambridge. ('You are really awfully like God,' Taylor wrote to him.) While Sheppard wrote his book on Greek tragedy, Maynard and Taylor cycled affably in the afternoons. Gordon Hannington Luce, also an undergraduate from Emmanuel, came next, followed by Daniel Macmillan, Frankie Birrell and Gerald Shove. Macmillan's condition was truly deplorable: 'verging on melancholia ... thinking himself an utterly worthless creature. ... Isn't it dreadful? ... He seems to have no intimate friends, practically no interest in life, and a bad liver. He ought to have a little work, plenty of exercise, and troops of lovers ... What's to be done?'[34] Daniel Macmillan was about to find 'a little work' in his family's publishing firm. James Strachey arrived on 3 September from his Fabian summer school to find Maynard and Gerald discussing Probability. 'I must say that I require a *touch* of the Artistic Temperament' he told his brother Lytton. 'They weren't very sympathetic. In the evenings Pozzo plays patience nowadays.'[35] When Strachey left, Maynard took off on a solo bicycle trip in Berkshire, Hardy's *The Dynasts* in his pocket. He returned three days and twenty punctures later. Probability made better progress. On 19 August he felt that 'the end really seems to be in sight now'. By 29 August he had finished Part III comprising six chapters on Induction and Analogy, and was starting on Part IV, Applications. By 25 September he had a complete first draft, and looked forward to giving the book to the

Cambridge University Press that Autumn. But this proved yet another false hope.

It was not till 14 September that Duncan had finally arrived for a fortnight. He had stayed briefly with Maynard at Cambridge at the end of July, but the visit had not been a success. 'I only hope I did not behave so unbearably as to make it too unbearable for you' he had written after he left. Instead of coming to Burford in August he had gone to stay with Adrian at Skegness. For consolation Maynard turned to the 'frivolous young butterfly' Frankie Birrell. 'I must try, if I can, to fall in love with someone besides you,' he wrote to Duncan.

Although he and Duncan still made love occasionally, the sand of their affair was running out. Duncan took to jogging with Adrian before breakfast; he was now frequently away for week-ends with Roger Fry at his house, Durbins, near Guildford. On 17 December 1910 Maynard wrote a note from 21 Fitzroy Square:

Dearest Duncan.

It makes me miserable not to find you here – though I expected that you would in the end stay at 29. I don't know what to do about staying in London. You're married to Adrian now, which you weren't before. So you naturally want always to be with him, when you haven't got any necessary engagements. So I shall hardly ever see you except when out of kindness you think you ought to try and make some arrangements. Thus I'm always in the position of pressing you to do what you'd rather not, and you of wondering how much your fondness for me demands of you. I can't bear such a state of affairs. It's wretched to be trading on your kindness, and I'm always in a state of uncertainty as to whether you will in the end turn up.

What do you think? It seems to me that when you're alone with me, it's all right. But when Adrian is in the next house, whenever you're with me it's being away from him, and you see me because I want it, not because you do. Please don't misunderstand this letter. It's the fault of fate and not at all of yours. But I'm feeling very wretched and don't know what I ought to do. Your ever loving,

JMK

PS. Please when you read this letter try and decide exactly what your feelings are about it.

Duncan replied next day in terms which were far from reassuring, although perhaps meant to be:

Dearest Maynard,

Please do not be so depressed. I hope most of your depression is the result of severe tiredness and overwork, because I don't honestly think things have changed as much as you think. I certainly am not always wishing to be with Adrian when I am with you. For one thing it is not always possible to be with him & when I am as certain as I

am of Adrian's affection for me, I can afford to be much 'kinder' as
you call it than the case when I was uncertain about it. I simply mean
that I have none of the anxieties that I used to have & can therefore
enjoy myself in every way more than I used to including being with
people I like.

To be quite practical I should probably be in the studio in any case
... for nearly all day every day. I might want to be with Adrian in
the evening but there do occur occasions when I cannot. I don't know
how you would like this state of affairs – but it would mean seeing you
a good deal ...

Yrs,   Duncan Grant

Maynard found some compensation with St George. St George (as
Maynard and Duncan always called him) was a 'lovely' Cockney lad,
Francis St George Nelson, seventeen years old in 1909 when Duncan
first engaged him as a model. He was employed in the pantomime, and
would disappear for long intervals on tours with collapsing theatrical
companies, who left him stranded in a succession of seaside towns,
Maynard having to organise hurried rescue operations. Maynard and
Duncan were genuinely fond of St George. He was a vicarious source
of low-life adventures. St George was by no means averse to 'fun and
games', though he was basically a womaniser. Maynard first slept with
him in December 1909; a year later they had an improbable reunion.

JMK to Duncan Grant, 24 December 1910:

What do you think I'm doing at the Victoria Commercial
Hotel, Ramsgate? A letter came from St George yesterday asking
me to come here and stay with him. So I came, and spend my
evenings in the basement of a lodging house chatting with low
comedians – whose chief characteristic seems to be their extraordinary kindness ...

Poor St George I found in rather a bad way. He has had the clap,
from which he's only just recovered, and weakened by that he's
suffering a great deal from toothache and a bad throat. In addition
his mother has gone bankrupt and been sold up, and so instead of
getting money from her he has to send her 5/- when he can. He's
really very much overworked. After touring Wales, where he was
always cold and wet and stopt at a different place every night, he had
to hurry here where he rehearsed the pantomime from 9 to 6 without
meals ... So his spirits are rather low. However he's in very good
looks, with long hair and handsomely dressed (in complete taste) ...
He's really quite unchanged after a year's adventures. His companions seem very fond of him and call him Bubbles (or Bubs). ...

This is a most remarkable place. Lodging houses and hotels tower
one above another to an incredible height against a lurid sky, and
below long empty esplanades above chalk cliffs and a muddy sea.

The streets are full of sailors home for Christmas. Everything is second or third class.

JMK to Duncan Grant 3 February 1911, King's College:
When I got back here on Tuesday evening, what should I find but another telegram of despair from St George – so he's not dead after all – this time at Todmorden (wherever that may be), announcing that he'd had no food since Friday, but giving no address. However I thought he might be sitting in the Post Office, clothed in rags waiting for some money, and so sent it there. Two letters have since arrived, giving details. It seems that ever after Ramsgate the company has been a fearful failure. The managers have got to the end of their money, and St George's salary has dropt to 5/- a week. 'I am not the only one who is treated in this way; we all have to share alike, but we give in to the girls' ... The poor boy had written home in vain; but he was driven, I gather, to the last appeal to me not so much by hunger as because he had had to pawn his beautiful blue suit, and was becoming terrified lest he should have to leave it behind for ever at Todmorden. However his first act has been to redeem it.

While St George vanished again to some remote place, Maynard and Duncan took their last pre-war foreign holiday together – to Morocco and Sicily in March–April 1911. Once again, there was trouble over the arrangements, Duncan insisting on meeting Adrian in Italy. After spending a few days in Tunis ('The Arabs are wonderful – very beautiful and the first race of buggers I've seen', Maynard informed Lytton) they crossed to Palermo, where they went to the opera. At Taormina, they stayed at a hotel improbably kept by a Dr and Mrs Dashwood, where all the guests dressed for dinner as in an English country house. At Segesta they admired 'one of the finest [Greek] temples in Sicily'. At Monreale they saw the magnificent cathedral 'entirely clothed with pictures and mosaic' before going on to Syracuse. Duncan was much impressed by the Byzantine remains which soon started to influence his painting; Maynard by Duncan's Italian. The holiday ended badly. Duncan left Sicily on 9 April, leaving Maynard in the company of Lytton's sister Dorothy, who had married the painter Simon Bussy. On 15 April Duncan and Maynard had a painful reunion at Naples:

I only sent you away to-night [Maynard wrote] when, being tired, my nerves and feelings had been too much strained by the course of the day. You tried to hush up the fact that I had any feelings, and I thought that alone I might get well sooner. But it hasn't been so, and I have to write a letter because in this wretched town I feel miserable and lonely. You could have made me much happier if only your feelings had allowed you to speak one kind word openly. Dearest Duncan, I came deeply needing some open sign of affection, and although I felt you had affection for me underneath, you seemed sodden and had none to give away to me.

The wound of Duncan's coldness was only partly healed by three days at I Tatti, where he discovered Geoffrey Scott, and allowed his moral fibre to be sapped by the tremendous luxury generated by B. B.'s increasingly profitable art partnership with Joseph Duveen.

The months which followed were not a particularly happy period in Maynard's life. Duncan had given it an emotional centre, which was now crumbling. For someone whose need for affection was as great as Maynard's, to be deprived of it was to rob life of much of its savour. Nor could the spate of marriages going on around him fail to remind him of his own uncertain emotional prospects. Jacques Raverat and Gwen Darwin, Oliver Strachey and Ray Costelloe, Fay: they all succumbed in the summer of 1911. Even Furness, back on leave, announced marital plans.

However, Maynard was more resilient than Lytton had feared. Probability remained unfinished. As a result of his controversy with Karl Pearson (see above p. 223) he had decided to add yet another section, on the logical foundations of statistics.[36] He spent much of July and August 1911 at King's working on the extra chapters, although he kept having dreadful dreams about Duncan which woke him up in tears. There were the usual distractions. Rupert Brooke was visited at Grantchester, where Geoffrey appeared 'looking more like a tree or some natural object than ever'.[37] There was a mild flirtation with Justin Brooke, who reminded Maynard of a 'faun or some creature of the wood'. When statistics palled, he slipped up to London to 'view Mr Nijinsky's legs'.[38] There was a brief excursion to Court Place to stay with Mary Berenson. From there he wrote to Duncan on 29 July: 'We are going out for a picnic with the entire bunch of Oliviers. What will poor I do amongst so much female beauty?' By 22 August he was (he told Lytton) 'absolutely alone reading endless and appalling books in German and would be fairly contented if it weren't for an angry member vainly demanding a little excitement'.

The member was quelled by a few days camping at the end of August, in Devon with assorted women – Virginia Stephen, Ka Cox, and Daphne Olivier. To his father Maynard wrote that 'camp life suits me very well. The hard ground, a morning bathe, the absence of flesh food, and no chairs, don't make one nearly so ill as one would suppose'. But Duncan had refused to come. He had spent the earlier part of the summer at Durbins, with Roger Fry and Vanessa Bell, who had just become lovers. Now he stayed in London painting murals of bathers and footballers at the Borough Polytechnic at the Elephant and Castle, which reminded *The Times* reviewer more of 'primitive Mediterraneans in the morning of the world' than of 'Cockney bathers in the Serpentine'. Back in Cambridge, Maynard was 'all solitude and heat. It is one of my consolations to pick up each afternoon a few books from my shelves, take them to Mr Stoakley and choose a binding. Then I get shaved'.[39] A visit to Duncan in London early in September was a failure, leaving him depressed. 'I always want so much to see you that I am easily disappointed if, when I can see you only for a short time, something in your state of mind interferes between us.' In desperation, he brought a boy back to 21 Fitzroy Square. 'He told me that there are many fewer of them about this week because last week the police were active and locked two up.'[40] Despite episodes of this kind Maynard was never, as he told Duncan, 'much affected . . . by *mechanical* randiness'.[41] It was affection he chiefly wanted, and he was failing to get it any more from Duncan.

On his return from London he was diverted from Probability by a new adventure, involving an Indian called Bimla Sarkar (Bridegroom of the Goddess of Purity) who had arrived in Cambridge the previous autumn to prepare himself for entry into one of the Colleges. Instead he had succeeded only in accumulating debts, which his father refused to pay. How Maynard first got involved with him is unknown. At any rate he set to work to clear up the mess; by 16 March 1911 Sarkar was writing to him that 'so long as I live I shall bear the most grateful memory of your kindness to me'. On 17 July 1911 Sarkar came to lunch. 'He told me' Maynard informed Duncan next day:

> how he had run away from India, though his father has now forgiven him. Being the only son of a Brahmin of the highest caste and girt with the sacred thread, he has certain duties to perform to the soul of his dead mother. If he left India he became impure and unable to perform these duties – so that his father would never have consented voluntarily to his coming here.
>
> He is so dreadfully nervous and highly strung and full of emotions that it is very difficult to deal with him. He has written me a long essay on Marlowe and Shakespeare.

Though Sarkar's interests were entirely literary, he decided he wanted to read economics under Keynes. When Maynard got back to King's in September 1911 after his summer camp with the neo-pagans, he found Sarkar in attendance. 'I've spent much of to-day attending to his affairs and trying to console and divert his mind' Maynard explained to Duncan on 7 September.

> He is a strange and charming creature. I don't know how our relationship is going to end. I have had all to-day the most violent sexual feelings towards him; and he on his part has paid me four or five visits on one pretext or another, finally saying that he came

Maynard Keynes, portrait by
Gwen Raverat, 1908

Vanessa Bell, on the terrace at
Asheham, 1913

David Garnett, portrait by Dora Carrington

Gordon Hannington Luce, portrait by
Duncan Grant

Francis Birrell in France, 1915

Bertrand Russell,
Maynard Keynes,
Lytton Strachey, at
Garsington, circa 1915

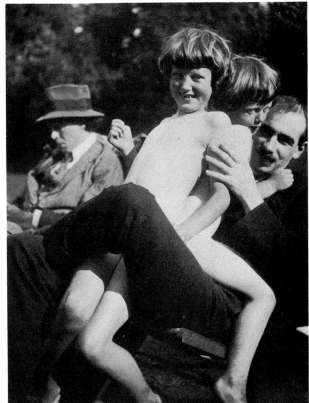

Maynard Keynes with
Julian and Quentin Bell,
Clive Bell in
background, West
Wittering, 1915

Sir Austen Chamberlain

Reginald McKenna

Andrew Bonar Law

The Asquiths on a visit to Ireland, 1912

Front row: Lady Rachel Verney, H. H. Asquith, Margot Asquith, Augustine Birrell, Violet Asquith
Back row: Sir Harry Verney, Arthur Asquith, The Master of Elibank, Elizabeth Asquith, Cyril Asquith, Maurice Bonham-Carter.

Signing the American Loan, May 1917

rd Cunliffe, Sir Cecil Spring-Rice, William McAdoo, Sir Samuel Hardman Lever, Sir Richard Crawford, Oscar T. Crosby.

Dr Carl Melchior

The German Delegation, May 1919
Melchior second from the left

Clemenceau, Wilson and Lloyd George after the signing of the Treaty,
28 June 1919

Louis-Lucien Klotz
French Minister of Finance

W. M. Hughes
Prime Minister of Australia

Maynard Keynes at Charleston, where he wrote *The Economic Consequences of the Peace*

Daniel Macmillan, who published the book

because he was so miserable when he was anywhere else. When he is away he writes me long letters to the effect that I am the only person on earth to whom he can open his thoughts freely and that he must come to King's for the sake of my 'blissful company'. And yet I don't feel at all certain what feelings there are in his odd Indian head. What will happen to-morrow if he again wants to spend the day here?

Sarkar became another of Maynard's protégés. He got him into Clare College, but he soon had to withdraw, as his father refused to send money. Maynard supported him for several months, but in the end threatened to have him repatriated. Sarkar refused to go: the shame would be too great. His letters to Maynard are rambling, but often sensitive to the nuances of their relationship: 'Did you do all these [things] for me out of affection or out of pity?' he wrote on 8 February 1912. 'If the former, would it cease from this time, or would it continue at least as long as I live? If I have forfeited your affection may I know of it?' To Duncan Maynard reported a day later:

The Sarkar affair is, I hope, over for the present. Some very troublesome things have happened. But on Wednesday I wrote to say that I could no longer support him, and offering to assist him with a passage if he would go back to India this Saturday. He refuses to go back, but accepts the fact that I disclaim all further responsibility; and writes a much more decent letter than I've had from him for a long time. What will happen to the poor creature, I can't conceive.

Gradually Sarkar's position improved. He found an uncle to support him in Tufnell Park, London. Maynard went on seeing him, giving him presents, and bailing him out in emergencies.[42]

The final diversion of this lonely summer was provided by politics. In the middle of September 1911 Maynard set off with Gerald Shove for a fortnight's tour of Ireland with a group of fifty Liberal M.P.s – members of the 80 Club, of which he was a member. The company of the politicians was a wonderful restorer of self-confidence. 'You haven't, I suppose, ever mixed with politicians at close quarters' he wrote to Duncan on 3 October. 'They're *awful*. I think some of these must have been the dregs anyhow, but I've discovered, what previously I didn't believe possible, that politicians behave in private life and say exactly the same things as they do in public. Their stupidity is inhuman'. Maynard eventually managed to break free from his '50 pomposities' and spend a week by himself. Except for Galway, he found Ireland sadly lacking in mystery. The country round Glengariff, he felt, was exactly what a hotel keeper, having the best taste of his class, would have created. 'Although [it] is wild and almost uninhabited, I feel as if Queen Victoria and the Prince Consort must some time about 1850 have unveiled it and declared it open'. The visit, he told his mother, had converted him to Home Rule, though 'It is perfectly plain that the people are now on the whole prosperous and that the conditions and feelings of twenty years ago have gone away completely'.[43] The comment is another example of Keynes's political complacency before the First World War.

He returned to Cambridge in a much better state of mind. To Duncan he wrote on 31 October 1911: 'To-night I feel extraordinarily happy and very much in love with you and as if whatever you did and whomever you might love didn't matter in the least. But I suppose it's a temporary madness'.

11 An Indian Summer

CHANGING PATTERNS

Keynes was one of those rare persons who could both think and act at the highest level. His life falls into cycles or phases, in which the emphasis shifts from one to the other. There is no doubt that these shifts are related to what was happening in the world. At some times, particularly during the two World Wars, there was a greater demand for Keynes's practical genius, and a greater satisfaction to be had from exercising it. But the cycles can also be seen in terms of action and reaction. Periods of great intellectual effort demand their release in practical activity; while practical activity prompts, sooner or later, a yearning for the cloister. Before 1914, Keynes's desire for the cloister was uppermost; partly because he was at this period most under the immediate influence of Moore's philosophy; partly because the nature of his sexual relations fitted private life better than public life – a point of considerable importance even today, but more so then, when homosexual acts were illegal, and the danger of blackmail much greater.

As he approached thirty, the practical, administrative, worldly side of his nature began to assert itself. The back of Probability was finally broken in 1912. By then, too, his affair with Duncan had petered out. He needed more work, more 'amusement', to fill the empty hours. Once drawn into something, the desire to do it thoroughly, as well as his speed in the despatch of business, would ensure that his involvement expanded.

The start of this changeover can be seen in his Cambridge life in the years leading up to the First World War. A letter he wrote to Duncan on 24 November 1910 gives a good indication of his state of mind at this time:

> I've got very little news, for I've been very busy and seem to have more and more purely business engagements – which leave me, when I've finished them, feeling dissatisfied with existence. I am going to do some electioneering. And at other times I'm apt to be playing bridge. These things amuse me at the time, but one's not, as St.

George says, best pleased with oneself in the long run. And the future doesn't seem any better, for I wretchedly want, at the same time that I do not want, to do these things. The Provost sent for me the other day, and I went feeling as if the headmaster had sent for me for goodness knows what. But he only wanted to know whether I should like before very long to become a Bursar for the College (i.e. manage the College Estates). I said I would if it did not mean so much work as to interfere with more serious occupations – for it makes my fellowship permanent and will, of course, some of it, amuse me. Also Meredith has been made a Professor at Belfast, and I shall probably succeed to the University lectureship he gives up. [Maynard was appointed to the five-year Girdler's Lectureship in Economics in December 1910.] Why is it so difficult to draw the line between doing no routine work and doing too much?

Maynard's fellowship in fact became permanent the following June, when he was appointed College Lecturer in Economics. But the Provost's approach indicates the area of college life in which he had started to make an impact. Anything to do with financial administration 'amused' him, and he had already begun to run a critical eye over the college accounts, having been appointed an inspector of them in 1909. In 1911 he graduated to the Estates Committee, from which position he planned a campaign against the conservative administration of the bursars, Grant and Corbett, who believed in starving college services and investments in order to maintain large cash balances. Mobilising the younger Fellows – who now included Dilwyn Knox – he succeeded in getting the bursars' policy defeated at the college's annual congregation on 11 May 1912. As a successful rebel, he was naturally co-opted onto the Bursarial Committee. His ascent to the Bursarship itself was now a foregone conclusion. In 1912 he became a Fellowship Elector, which meant that every year he had to read several enormous theses on any subject under the sun. These growing college responsibilities were added to old university chores never relinquished. He continued to serve on the committees of the Union and the Liberal Club. He kept up his attendance at most of the old societies, and in 1911 was invited by McTaggart to join a new one – the Eranus. He developed a curious interest in psychic phenomena, going regularly to meetings of the University's Society for Psychical Research, and joining its committee in 1911. Whether he had any psychic experiences himself is not recorded. But it was an interesting throwback to Henry Sidgwick, whose efforts to establish the immortality of the soul by empirical methods Keynes had so derided in 1906.

Keynes's 'amusements' by no means replaced the serious aspects of his Cambridge life, particularly the quest for friendship. Although he 'took wing' from the Apostles in November 1910, having read the

Society twenty papers in nearly eight years, his friends were still mainly Apostles, while the inspection of 'embryos' continued to provide new, though increasingly less intense, emotional satisfactions. By 1911 his closest Cambridge friend was Gerald Shove – the 'silent Shove' as Rupert Brooke called him – a man subject to black moods but with a vehement, biting edge and a blasphemous, dare-devil side which Maynard found attractive. Together they would go to inspect university athletes at sporting events, Shove being quite overcome by the beauty of Philip [later Noel] Baker, a King's undergraduate, as he ran in the half-mile – and surmising that the Prof's fainting fits were occasioned by the same stimulus. In March 1912 he and Maynard took an 'eating and gambling' holiday in Monte Carlo, Maynard's first Easter holiday for three years without Duncan. 'We both enjoy the tables inordinately and play for hours,' he reported to Duncan on 28 March, 'Gerald creating a dreadful scandal by the loudness of his oaths when he loses.'

Maynard's romantic interests, however, lay elsewhere. In the spring of 1912 there was a brief 'adventure' with a King's College undergraduate called Chester Purves. But that summer he fell more substantially in love with Gordon Hannington Luce of Emmanuel College (one of the exceptional undergraduates attracted to that college in that period), who had become an Apostle in January 1912. Lucy, as his friends called him, was the thirteenth son of an impecunious vicar, fair and stocky, with poetic ambitions. Maynard became very fond of him, falling into his usual protective role by advancing him money to continue his studies in English literature. Luce returned his affection, and an affair between the two men flowered briefly in the summer of 1912. But there were few prospects in England for aspiring poets without private means, and, like Swithinbank, Luce decided to go East, Maynard using his India Office connections to get him a job teaching English literature at the Government College, Rangoon. He embarked in September 1912, accompanied by Furness who was returning to Egypt, and E. M. Forster and Lowes Dickinson who were going out to India. In Burma he made contact with Swithinbank, looking gauntly beautiful, but pale, 'gentle, but administrative ... not cold, but somewhat closeted'.[1] Luce, much to Maynard's dismay, soon married a Burmese girl, Teetee Moung Tin. But their friendship survived.

A few days after Luce sailed for Burma, Maynard was off to Hungary to visit another Apostle called Ferenc Békássy, an aristocratic friend of Noel Olivier's from Bedales, who had come to King's in October 1911 to read history. He was far from being standard Apostolic Man, preferring Nietzsche to Moore, and action to contemplation, though he too had poetic leanings. Maynard spent a fortnight in September at his ancestral home, Kis Sennye, Rum, in a mediaeval splendour which conjured up Tolstoy's Russia, before returning via Vienna, whose 'many new buildings in the flat style' and 'astounding' Breughels great-ly impressed him.[2]

It was on his return from Vienna that he met one of the most brilliant products of that brilliant culture – a slender young man of twenty-three with fair hair, blue staring eyes, and a passion for philosophy called Ludwig Wittgenstein. The son of a Viennese millionaire industrialist, Wittgenstein had, according to Sydney Waterlow who was in Cambridge at the time, come to England in order to learn to fly; 'that on this quest he had gone to Manchester, where he had been told that he had better first go to Cambridge and learn mathematics'; that at Cambridge he had drifted to Russell's lectures, and Moore's, and decided that his vocation was philosophy, not aviation. Waterlow remembered him 'as a creature from another world, unversed in any routine of knowledge, but with a demonic gift of seeing round all subjects'. Maynard, who was introduced to him by Russell on 30 October 1912, immediately recognised him as a man of genius, and a fortnight later had engineered his election to the Apostles, ignoring Russell's warning that Wittgenstein would not thank him for it. Russell was right. Wittgenstein was appalled at the thought of having to spend his evenings in the company of Békássy – whom he detested as a Hungarian aristocrat – and a King's freshman called Francis Bliss, who did not number philosophical acumen among his accomplishments. After one meeting, Wittgenstein resigned, complaining to Keynes that the brethren had not yet learnt their toilets, a process which, though necessary, was indecent to observe.[3] Lytton Strachey persuaded him to withdraw his resignation, but Wittgenstein stopped attending. Keynes thought him 'a most wonderful character . . . I like enormously to be with him.'[4] Wittgenstein showed his generosity when he put up £200 a year to relieve W. E. Johnson of his teaching responsibilities. But relations were never easy with this prickly genius. The misunderstand-ings which marked everyone's dealings with him come out in a note he wrote to Maynard, who handled the details of the Johnson bequest. 'Thanks very much for the trouble you take over my business. *My* reason for not seeing you oftener last term was that I did not wish our intercourse to continue without any sign that *you* wished to continue it.'[5]

Two of Maynard's students who did not become economists but became close personal friends were Sydney Russell-Cooke, later a stockbroker, and Archibald Rose, already a diplomat. Maynard had an affair with 'Cookie' which went on for some months in 1913–14; they gambled together modestly on the Stock Exchange. Archibald Rose was an advanced student with thirteen years in the consular service in China behind him – a very small, fastidious man, with a droll manner, who had learnt Mandarin and become a good amateur jockey. Maynard introduced him to economics, and he introduced Maynard to riding. Maynard detested most physical activity; but he had a vague yearning for country squiredom and its sartorial accompaniments, which riding satisfied. He and Rose would go riding most Saturday afternoons in 1912 when Maynard was in Cambridge. In April 1912 they took a riding holiday together through Wiltshire and the New Forest. Rose, who went back East again in 1913, was one of Maynard's few close friends who understood the active side of his nature, and sympathised with it. 'I want you to have a "middle-period" – somewhere out of Cambridge. It seems to me necessary if you are really to fulfill yourself,' he wrote to him from Delhi on 4 February 1914. On 24 July of that year he urged him to do 'something which would be primarily practical'. His wish was granted sooner than he expected.[6]

Russell-Cooke and Rose were friends from outside Maynard's usual world. They had no entry into his general Cambridge set of Apostles, embryos, and neo-pagan women who still assembled at country inns for leisurely holidays, spiced with intrigue and gossip. Maynard was present at the New Year's reading party of 1912, which Rupert Brooke got together in West Lulworth, Dorset. While Maynard wrote his next term's lectures, Ka Cox flirted with the painter Henry Lamb to Rupert's fury, as did Lytton Strachey, though to less effect. This was a holiday of some importance in the cultural history of the time, since it marked the start of Brooke's estrangement from Bloomsbury, and his transformation from 'the Fabian intellectual to the chauvinistic fugleman of 1914'.[7]

Maynard himself rented the Crown Inn, Everleigh, near Marlborough in July and August 1912, to which his friends came in relays. This was another neo-pagan occasion, with three of the Olivier sisters turning up, as well as Ka Cox, smarting from her rejection by Rupert. Brynhild, the most beautiful, though not the cleverest, of the Olivier girls, was at this time very attracted to Maynard. He was happy enough to take her riding; but she made no progress with him, and soon married a Kingsman, A. E. Popham. Maynard still felt that women were intruders into the cloister, unless like Vanessa and Virginia they posed no threat of emotional entanglements. From the Crown Inn he wrote to Duncan on 26 July:

> I don't much care for the atmosphere these women breed and haven't liked this party nearly as much as my last week's. Noel is very nice and Daphne very innocent. But Bryn is too stupid – and I begin to take an active dislike to her. Out of the window I see Rupert making love to her – ... taking her hand, sitting at her feet, gazing at her eyes. Oh these womanisers. How on earth and what for can he do it.
> Lucy remains charming but *his* atmosphere is [sub]merged[?]

Maynard's relations with his family, too, were changing in the years before the war. He was becoming less dependent on his father, more on his mother. In October 1910, at the age of fifty-eight, John Neville Keynes became Registrary – or administrative head – of the university, a post he filled with exemplary tact and good sense for fifteen years. Six months later he was made an honorary Fellow of his old college, Pembroke. At last the iron grip of duty started to relax. His hours of work dropped from 2,000 in 1910 to 1,500 in 1913. By contrast Florence's energy continued to expand. Her appetite for business was voracious. In 1911 she was elected a Cambridge town councillor; she joined the Committee of the National Council of Women. She travelled all over England attending conferences; at Cambridge she became a familiar, if unsafe, figure on her bicycle, rushing from one good cause to another – now stirring up the Public Health Committee on sanitary arrangements, now agitating about juvenile unemployment. To Maynard's friends she was the 'good Mother Keynes'.

No more than before did her public work exclude family concerns. Indeed, as Neville withdrew from the active management of family affairs into his private world of hobbies – collecting butterflies, philately, golf, bridge – Florence took his place as the family's mainstay. Increasingly Maynard wrote to her and consulted her rather than Neville – a dramatic reversal of previous practice. It was through Florence's continued interest in her children's doings that 6 Harvey Road retained its place in their lives as their home from home, to which they would return at week-ends to deliver up their news, while Neville, dignified, benign, increasingly silent, expertly carved the Sunday joint and uncorked his choice wines. At Harvey Road the Victorian conventions showed a surprising power of assimilating some of the currents of modernity. Possibly under their children's free-thinking influence, Neville and Florence had given up going to church. They made an effort to come to terms with Post-Impressionism; Neville developed a love of the ballet. It is not clear how much, if anything, Florence knew of Maynard's sexual tastes. 'I had a dreadful conversation with my mother and Margaret about marriage,' he wrote to Duncan Grant on 11 October 1910, 'and practically had to admit what I was. How much they grasped I don't know.' Whatever Florence may have suspected, she remained devoted to him, and proud of his successes. He returned her devotion. There was no break or quarrel, just development and change.

Maynard was less successful in his relations with Geoffrey. He was pleased enough when he heard that he had won the first prize in the scholarship examination at St Bartholomew's Hospital, the first step in his career as a surgeon. 'Please give him my congratulations,' he wrote to Neville on 30 September 1910. 'We're really a wonderful family, take us all round, at examinations. Probably the finest in the kingdom, I expect. If only the examination system lasts, another two or three hundred years, we shall end, I'm sure, by being the Royal Family.' Geoffrey had very much Maynard's double character, that of the scientist who valued, above all, the arts. By 1911 he had submitted his first Blake bibliography to the Cambridge University Press. (It was turned down.) He collected antiquarian books, loved the ballet, was a friend of Rupert Brooke and the sculptor Eric Gill (a couple of whose sculptures Maynard bought). But he lacked poetry. He was a crafts-man, who proved that genius is the art of taking infinite pains. May-nard required a touch of fancy in his intimates. Geoffrey was cruelly hurt by his brother's indifference, and by his parents' obvious preference for Maynard. His father's refusal to lend Geoffrey £350 to buy a Blake masterpiece was a bitter blow. 'Blake is a cult,' Neville told him dismissively. By contrast, Neville showed increasing confidence in Maynard's financial judgment, transferring to him the management of Florence's dowry, worth £5,000. But mainly Geoffrey kept his frustra-tions to himself; they emerged only by omission in his autobiography seventy years later. The surface of family life remained unruffled.

Maynard remained much closer to Margaret. 'Yesterday Margaret came to lunch with me and we got on very well together,' he told Duncan on 1 July 1910. 'She's charming, I think – much nicer than your horrid Geoffrey.' Margaret's competitive successes were modest by Keynes standards – 'two second prizes for her annuals and a third for beans', Maynard informed his parents the same month. However, in February 1911 he found her pamphlet on *The Problem of Boy Labour* 'extraordinarily good – so written as to be a most interesting and even moving document'.[8] The great love of Margaret's life before her marriage was Eglantyne Jebb, whose sister, Dorothy, had been at Newnham. The intimacy between Maynard and Margaret was deepened by his knowledge of this relationship. In February 1913, after a short courtship which involved joint committee work, Margaret became engaged to A. V. Hill, a physiologist who was Fellow and Junior Dean of Trinity College, Cambridge. They were married by Dr John Brown, on 18 June 1913, and on 10 June 1914 they had a daughter – christened Mary Eglantyne, but always called Polly. Hill is 'fright-fully puritanical – but then that suits her', Maynard told Duncan.[9]

Thus Keynes fleshed out his Cambridge life in the years before 1914, expanding his worldly concerns within a framework which remained Moorite. Lytton Strachey imagined him in 1912 'with infinite exac-titude – the green baize board, pupils in the inner room, toasted buns, the reporter [to take down dictation], bridge with Dilly, a sticky walk with an impossible embryo.'[10] Maynard's own view of his existence can be gathered from a letter he wrote to Duncan on 30 January 1912:

As for the young men here, I lose more interest in them every day; – and indeed seldom speak to them. There are one or two who row on the river and whom Gerald and I go to look at. But a duller collection, on the whole, I've seldom seen. Or is it that I no longer care? Anyhow Cambridge presents itself to me more and more as a sort of machine, like the India Office or anything else, and hardly at all as – whatever it was I sometimes used to think it ... Meanwhile I improve the machinery. A young man shaves me in my sleep so that I awake smooth and as free from anxieties as the bearded. Another young man comes round after hall to take down my words by short-hand. And I am playing bridge better than ever. So I shall, I suppose, inevitably go on and on improving it.

In 1908 Maynard had fled London for Cambridge; now he was drawn increasingly to London. From the autumn of 1911, when he started editing the *Economic Journal*, he took to spending the middle of each week in term-time in the capital – a pattern which continued until 1937. The new regularity of his visits coincided with the general demand for the revision of Bloomsbury's living arrangements. As Quentin Bell describes it:

> The lease of 29 Fitzroy Square was coming to an end; Virginia and Adrian, tired perhaps of their quarrelsome tête-à-tête, proposed a domestic revolution: they would share their home – it would have to be a large home – with other friends; for this purpose they considered a house in Bedford Square, but it was at 38 Brunswick Square that in October [1911] they found what they wanted.[11]

This revolution suited Maynard who was physically cramped and emotionally frustrated in his back room at Duncan's. The lease of 38 Brunswick Square was taken in his name. He had the ground-floor room, running the length of the house, Adrian had the first floor, Virginia the second. A couple of months later, Leonard Woolf, back from Ceylon, moved into the top floor; Vanessa decided that she liked him 'very much ... He is of course very clever & from living in the wilds seems to me to have a more interesting point of view than most of the "set"'.[12] Virginia was put in charge of the domestic arrangements. Living was collective, but feeding was individual, each 'inmate', as Virginia called them, picking up his tray from the hall, and returning it when his repast was finished. Rents, which Virginia collected, varied from 35s to £2 a week. 'The only thing that seems certain,' Virginia wrote to Ottoline Morrell, 'is that a house is the cheapest way of living and if you have a house you must have servants.'[13] This plan was to be the basis of the collective living arrangements of the Bloomsbury un-marrieds for the next ten years or so. It was not without frictions, but worked reasonably well. There were, of course, no arguments about who did the washing up. 'I am getting, through this house, a complete

London life,' Maynard told his mother on 23 December 1911. 'The worst of [it] is that there are so many people to attract callers that callers come in rather a thick stream. Woolf and I are just starting out for Selfridge's to buy presents for the servants with whom we wish to curry favour.'

Maynard remained at 38 Brunswick Square for the next three years. During that time there were changes. Leonard Woolf married Virginia Stephen in August 1912, and they both moved out in October. Leonard's place on the top floor was taken by Maynard's brother Geoffrey in January 1913. In his autobiography, Geoffrey made a point of emphasising that he was never a member of the Bloomsbury Group, for some of whose members – notably Clive Bell and Harry Norton – he developed considerable antipathy.[14] The closest he got to Virginia was when he saved her life in September 1913, after she had taken an overdose of veronal in Adrian's room. Not that Virginia was particularly fond of Maynard: 'No: being in Spain does not make me love him better,' she wrote to Ka Cox on her honeymoon.[15] Gerald Shove and Henry Norton occupied Virginia's old rooms at various times. The appearance of Maynard's room, too, changed considerably in these years, as Duncan and Frederick Etchells painted its walls with a continuous street scene, in a spotted style reminiscent of Signac. It was dominated by a collision between two hansom cabs. Whether Maynard found it calmed his nerves may be doubted. But his London life was intended for excitement, not calm.

There were hints, no more, of the more substantial London existence he was to create for himself in the 1920s. There was talk of a City editorship of the *Morning Post* which came to nothing.[16] He was almost made chairman of the Gilchrist Trust, but the Trustees eventually decided in favour of 'past experience' rather than 'young blood'.[17] He turned down a consultancy worth £200 a year.[18] Through his membership of an economics dining club which met alternately in Cambridge and London, as well as through the Political Economy Club, he started to make contacts with financial journalists like F. W. Hirst, editor of the *Economist*, and with bankers and businessmen who would be useful to him later. He began investing on the stock market, with the proceeds of his own savings, as well as Neville's 'birthday money'. In 1914 he also started speculating with the help of a £1,000 overdraft facility from his bank, Barclays, and the proceeds of a £1,000 loan from Roger Fry. The picture he gave in 1919 of the pre-war 'inhabitant of London', lifting up his telephone – as he sipped his morning tea in bed – to invest his money all over the world, is already recognisably himself.*

---

* For a note on Keynes's pre-1914 investments see appendix on p. 286.

Keynes's continuing interest in Indian finance went beyond the affairs of Bimla Sarkar. Following his retirement from the India Office he played a delicate part, acting as public defender and private critic, of India's evolving financial system. In the Lent Term of 1911 he gave six lectures at the London School of Economics and at Cambridge on 'Currency, Finance and the Level of Prices in India'. These lectures formed the basis of a paper 'Recent Developments of the India Currency Question' which he read to the Royal Economic Society on 9 May 1911. As usual, he showed a draft to Lionel Abrahams, the Financial Secretary at the India Office, whose reply showed that Maynard was accepted as a licensed critic:

> I am sure we have much to learn from you. Our official discussions are sometimes narrow; and outside criticism is often dogmatic and impractical, like that of a German pamphlet that I was looking at the other day, which said that we had on the whole done the right thing, but with no proper knowledge of the metaphysical and world-historical significance of our action. Your knowledge of both the practical official's and economist's standpoint will enable you to say much more helpful things.[19]

In fact, Maynard had already grasped, or discovered, the world-historical significance of India's monetary arrangements, though in language evidently acceptable to the official mind – namely, that they represented not an imperfect or limping gold standard but 'a more scientific and economic system' in the forefront of monetary progress, which he called the Gold-Exchange Standard. 'If the gold is only required for foreign payments and not for internal circulation,' he wrote in February 1910, 'it is cheaper to maintain a credit at one of the great financial centres of the world, which can be converted with great readiness to gold when it is required, and which earns a small rate of interest when it is not required.'[20] The vision had come long before he was ready to work out all its practical consequences. But he was convinced, as he said in his paper to the Royal Economic Society, that out of this system would evolve 'the ideal currency of the future'. His audience heard an expert account of how the system was operated by the Indian government, with suggestions for improvement.[21] Even before he delivered his L.S.E. lectures he had had the idea of turning them into a 'small book'.[22]

The decision to break off from Probability to write a book on India was taken suddenly early in November 1912. India's monetary arrangements had briefly become a matter of public interest as a result of the Indian 'silver scandal' which broke at the beginning of the month. Messrs Samuel Montagu & Co., a firm of bullion-brokers, had been purchasing silver on behalf of the Indian government for its gold standard reserve – secretly, so as to avoid speculation. However, the firm was too well-connected politically. Herbert Samuel, the Postmaster-General in Asquith's government was the younger brother of Sir Stuart Samuel, a partner in the firm; Samuel's uncle, Lord Swaythling, a senior partner, was the father of Edwin Montagu, who was Under-Secretary of State for India. The Indian silver scandal was an offshoot of the far greater Marconi scandal raging at the same time, and also involving members of the government. The thread linking the two was the suggestion that public men, some of whom happened to be Jews, were using their political positions to enrich themselves by diverting government contracts to firms in which they had a financial stake. As rumours of corruption spread, *The Times* ran five long articles by 'An Indian Correspondent' calling for a thorough investigation of India's monetary arrangements. 'A rash of questions erupted in the House of Commons concerning the cash balances of India, the selling prices of the securities held in the Indian gold standard reserve, the market price for silver, the approved list of borrowers from the India Office balances, etc.'[23]

This was the background against which Maynard decided to turn his lectures quickly into a book. What was needed was an authoritative account of how India's system worked. Keynes, with his combination of inside knowledge and outside position, was uniquely placed to be 'helpful'. As he wrote to Foxwell on 18 November 1912:

> I quite agree with you that there is no reason in the world why the India Office should make such a mystery of their currency. But their difficulty is that none of them connected with the place who make speeches understand the currency, so that they are very short of spokesmen in these matters.[24]

An official of the India Office commented in turn that Keynes's letter to *The Times* of 24 November, confuting the arguments of 'An Indian Correspondent', was 'the best statement on our side that has yet appeared'. Keynes may have also wanted to help clear the name of Edwin Montagu, who had given him his first paper speech at the Cambridge Union and who was now under attack for his alleged involvement in the silver scandal. A contract with Macmillan to write a book on 'The Monetary Affairs of India' was signed on 15 December; at the same time he decided that his book on Probability should also be published by Macmillan, instead of by the Cambridge University Press who had been making difficulties about setting the book up in print before he had finished writing it. Both Macmillan's contracts were on a half-profits basis. A great attraction of the new publishing connection was that he would be dealing with his old Eton friend, Daniel Macmillan.

The book (whose title was changed to *Indian Currency and Finance*) was written astonishingly quickly, mainly over the Christmas vacation. By 6 March 1913 Neville was already starting to read proofs of it, two days before Maynard left for Egypt to stay with Furness, now a high official in the Egyptian ministry of the interior, who had promised him 'all the attractions which made Gomorrah such a popular resort in the good old days'. Maynard travelled 'de luxe' from Calais to Milan in the same train as Nijinsky, and then took a boat to Cairo. By 20 March he and Furness were ensconced in the Savoy Hotel, Luxor, looking out onto 'charming gardens of orange trees and nameless flowers descending in a terrrace to the Nile . . . and across the river to the red hills of the desert opposite'. He found some of the Egyptian temples rather boring though.[25] Back in Cairo, he spent four days with Maurice Amos, a judge in Egypt's Court of Appeal and formerly a philosopher friend of Moore and Russell from Trinity College, Cambridge. From Cairo Maynard went to Alexandria to spend the rest of his time with Furness: they took a two-day trip into the Libyan desert where 'the brilliant blue sky, the white sands of the desert and the red Roman ruins make one of the most amazing views I've ever seen.'[26] In Alexandria, he enjoyed the services of Furness's house-boys Salem and Mustapha, 'had a w–m–n' as he told Duncan,[27] and revised proofs of his Indian book in the light of comments. ('I have rewritten several passages you object to,' he informed his father, 'and (with the exception of *shew*) have adopted about 90 per cent of your minor criticisms'.)

He was by no means finished with India. Bowing to pressure from critics of India's monetary system – both the scandal-mongers and those who wanted India to be placed on a full gold standard as recommended by the Fowler Committee of 1898 – the government had agreed to set up a Royal Commission on Indian Finance and Currency. A few days after arriving in Egypt, Maynard got a letter from his old chief, Sir Thomas Holderness, offering him the secretaryship of the Commission, a full-time appointment starting at the beginning of April. Maynard was in a quandary. The offer was a compliment, but he had no wish to break off his holiday so soon: he had two courses of lectures to give in Cambridge and, as he cabled back to Holderness, he wanted freedom to publish his book. After seeing the proofs of the book, which Maynard had left with Abrahams, and assuring his political superiors that their contents were both expert and respectable, Holderness cabled back on 3 April: 'Am instructed to offer you seat on commission. This is considered in view of book more suitable than secretaryship and will give greater scope. Hope you will accept.'[28] To his father Maynard wrote that he was 'delighted at the change. It's a much better plan, and

I feel myself by contrast left in prospective leisure.'[29] The high honour had come to Maynard just two months before his thirtieth birthday. The instructions to which Holderness alluded were issued by Edwin Montagu who thus gave Maynard's career another helpful boost.[30]

Indian Currency and Finance was published on 9 June 1913. It is the first of Maynard's short books (the others were *The Economic Consequences of the Peace, A Revision of the Treaty*, and *A Tract on Monetary Reform*), all written very quickly, in response to immediate events, and utilising material Keynes had readily to hand, such as unpublished lecture notes, memoranda, papers, and so on. The first two were based on Keynes's experience as a government official, though the tone of each was very different, Maynard using his inside knowledge to defend government performance in the first book, and to attack it in the second. The structure of the four books also exhibits a strong family resemblance, a central technical discussion being set in a historical or political frame, and rounded off with constructive suggestions for policy. Maynard never solved the problem of bringing these discussions properly together. His historical vision, his technical expertise, his civil servant's concern for what was practical were expressions of three different aspects of his mind. They remained largely unintegrated, like the three voices of Maria Callas.

The book opened with an account of the evolution, and a parade of the virtues, of the gold-exchange standard, a system based on a paper currency maintained artificially at par with gold by means of credits abroad in sterling, as opposed to the gold standard proper, one in which there was a gold currency for internal circulation and gold reserves for settling international debts. Far from being a sign of second-class status, the former system, Keynes maintained in his justly well-known second chapter, was in the 'mainstream of currency evolution', because it economised on the use of gold internally and internationally, thus allowing greater 'elasticity' of money in response to business needs. Looking beyond India, Keynes foresaw the international gold standard giving way to a more scientific system based on one or two currency reserve centres. 'A preference for a tangible reserve currency', he declared confidently, 'is ... a relic of a time when governments were less trustworthy in these matters than they are now'.[31] International monetary reform, based on the gradual elimination of gold, was thus a constant in Keynes's thought. So also was his belief that Britain was the natural energiser, and centre, of a reformed monetary order. Of the prospective benefits of an international gold-exchange standard, he took, like its British advocates in the 1920s, an unduly rosy view. He assumed there were no costs for the currency reserve centre. He never considered the possibility of a loss of confidence in the reserve currency, and what its consequences would be for the system as a whole. He

assumed a world without wars, and with very little national feeling –
at least in the dependent parts of European empires. There was little
need to worry about such things before 1914, though some did.

The core of the book is a description of the interlocking mechanisms
– the purchase and sale of Council bills in London, the regulation of the
note issue, and the management of the government's reserves and cash
balances – by which the Secretary of State supported the exchange
value of the rupee. Here Maynard was able to show his mastery of the
working of financial institutions. His purpose was to refute ignorant
criticism, British as well as Indian. Thus he showed how, contrary to
nationalist assertion, India benefited from holding its reserves in London.[32] He also refuted the scandal-mongers by demonstrating that it
was rational for the government of India to buy its silver from Messrs
Samuel Montagu. The mistake of the India Office had been to underestimate 'the deep interest which the House of Commons takes in
suggestions of personal scandal', a situation bound to continue 'so long
as the relations of the House of Commons to India combine in high
degree responsibility and ignorance'.[33]

However, the book was not intended to be merely descriptive and
apologetic. There was criticism, too. If in the management of its external exchange India was in the forefront of monetary progress, the same
could not be said of its banking system. The absence of a central bank
was a major weakness. Government reserves for maintaining the exchange were not part of bankers' reserves. This meant that the Indian
money-market was starved of funds during the busy season when gold
and silver had to be imported from London, raising the discount rate
unduly to cover the cost of remittance. Also, part of the imported metals
went into hoards. If the government's reserves could be added to the
bankers' reserves, the note issue could be expanded, allowing lower
interest rates and inhibiting hoarding. On the practicability of
establishing a central bank, Keynes was non-committal, his caution
enhanced by his foreknowledge of his appointment to the Royal Commission.

As always with Keynes, the general tone of technical mastery and
gravitas is enlivened by passages of fancy and spiced by bantering asides
at the expense of figures in authority. Gambling and hoarding always
excited his psychological and historical fancy, and he rarely touched
upon them without being stimulated to a piece of bravura writing. In
this book he quoted Jevons's remark about India being the 'sink of the
precious metals', always ready to absorb Europe's redundant gold and
save it from inflation, 'ruinous though it has been to her own economic
development'.[34]

Quoting the words of a secretary of state who had vetoed a proposal
to set up a central bank in 1867, he commented: 'no need to name him,

it is the eternal secretary of state speaking, not a transient individual'. A rational project had been 'smothered in the magnificent and empty rhetoric of political wisdom'.[35] Discovering the 'shocking' fact that the Indian government's stockbroker was paid more than any other official except the viceroy, he wondered 'how long it will be found necessary to pay City men so entirely out of proportion to what other servants of society commonly receive for performing social services not less useful or difficult'.[36] It was the subversiveness of tone more than of thought which gave Maynard some of his reputation for radicalism.

Although one or two of the reviewers thought *Indian Currency and Finance* too close to the 'official apologists' of the Indian system, the book's notices were mainly enthusiastic. The *Transvaal Leader* of 8 September 1913, taking an unusually tolerant view of Maynard's hint that South Africa's gold would one day be required only for stopping teeth or making jewellery, saw him as 'one of the modern type of university don – a man who combines deep knowledge of the theory of his subject with an intimate acquaintance with business affairs and a grasp of the problems that "practical" men have to meet'. In the *Economic Journal* of December 1913, Foxwell, while praising Maynard's statistics, welcomed the fact that he had kept his 'technical apparatus . . . behind the scenes' where it belonged. He found the book rivalled Bagehot in usefulness and Jevons in style. From today's perspective Keynes's account seems rather old-fashioned in its assumption that the sole criterion of policy was the maintenance of the international reserves, and in its view that gold hoarding could be reduced by deliberately curtailing the monetary use of gold.[37] In terms of sales it was the least successful of Keynes's books, only 946 copies having been sold a year after publication. His share of the profits was just £30.

By the time *Indian Currency and Finance* appeared, the Royal Commission had already been taking evidence for a month. It held its first meeting on 5 May and adjourned for the summer on 6 August. Its chairman, Austen Chamberlain, son of Joseph Chamberlain, who read Maynard's book in August for the first time, did not know 'whether to congratulate you on it or console myself' since Maynard would certainly be considered 'the author of the Commission's report'.[38] Maynard had taken a vigorous part in the cross-examination of witnesses, being especially sharp with advocates of a full gold standard for India, and with critics of the idea of a central bank. To Foxwell he wrote a little later:

It has been very interesting at the Commission how many of our best and (on other points) most intelligent witnesses have stuck up for a gold *currency*. But they can never stand up to cross-examination with any sort of success; and their position is usually due, I think, to sheer ignorance of the facts and arguments on the other side.[39]

The following excerpt shows him in the unfamiliar role of an advocate of City interests against the more cautious line taken by the ex-Governor of the Bank of England, who was worried about increasing sterling's liabilities:

> Mr. Keynes: But you would not deprecate the extension of England's liabilities in that way would you? You would not wish London to be less an international money market, would you?
> Mr. Cole: No: I want to see England maintained as the international money market, and that it should have the position it holds today.
> Mr. Keynes: Then you would be sorry rather than glad if India was to give up holding its balances here?
> Mr. Cole: From the point of view of the Bank of England I would rather they were what I call kept within more moderate limits; that is all.[40]*

On the central question of whether India should aim for a gold currency, it transpired that the Commission, with one exception, favoured Keynes's view that the existing gold exchange standard should be maintained. But a split was apparent on the banking question. Lionel Abrahams of the India Office had prepared a memorandum for the Commission in June, arguing that the main advantage of having a State Bank would be 'the deposit with the Bank of money now in the Reserve Treasuries which could be placed at the disposal of trade with a beneficial effect on the rate of discount and on business generally'. A State Bank would also be the best agent for 'lending from the paper currency reserve, if the practice was introduced'.[41]† However, the Commission refused to commit itself in favour of this proposal. Instead it asked two of its members, Keynes and Sir Ernest Cable, to draw up a scheme for a State Bank over the summer.

Maynard had been enjoying his London life. On duty he presented a picture of perfect bureaucratic respectability, appearing at the Com-

---

* India's sterling balances in 1912 amounted to £18.4m.
† The terms used need explanation. In the absence of a central bank, the Indian Government's cash reserves were held in Reserve Treasuries all over the country, mainly in the form of notes. The Paper Currency Reserve provided a 100 per cent gold and silver backing for the note issue. However, the government was empowered to make a 'fiduciary issue' of up to 20 per cent of the note issue from the Paper Currency Reserve by buying securities. This was the 'unbacked' part of the paper currency designed to allow for a certain elasticity in the money supply in response to seasonal variations in the demand for money or to mitigate the effects of a commercial or banking crisis. In practice there was no elasticity since the fiduciary issue remained fixed at 20 per cent.

mission 'bald and top-hatted', hobnobbing with civil servants and politicians. He met Asquith for the first time.[42] His social life was filled with another cast of characters, whom he was no doubt starting to titillate with spicy gossip from high places. Evenings at 38 Brunswick Square would often be spent playing poker with Adrian, Gerald Shove, and Saxon Sydney-Turner. Sometimes Noel Olivier and Karin Costelloe would drop in; also a gauche young friend of Adrian's called David Garnett, then a biology student at the Royal College of Science, and known as Bunny because of a rabbit-skin cap he had had as a boy. Bloomsbury parties were getting wilder. Karin wrote of one, in late June 1913, to her mother Mary Berenson:

Oliver [Strachey] and I went as Karsavina and Nijinsky (he in a red ballet costume and I in a piece of purple satin and a wreath). We enacted Spectre de la Rose with much success. We followed that by the ballet of Job, in which Keynes, as the devil, poured boils in the shape of cherries upon the writhing Roger Fry. Then came Lytton's play acted by Clive, Marjorie, Vanessa and Duncan. It was a wildly twisted take-off of the actors themselves, exquisitely finished, very witty, and not exactly proper . . . .[43]

There were more serious cultural events. That summer Diaghilev brought two 'firsts' to London: Chaliapin in *Boris Godunov* and Stravinsky's *The Rite of Spring*. On 8 July 1913 Roger Fry's Omega Workshops opened at 33 Fitzroy Square, a venture designed to turn the talents of Bloomsbury painters and their friends to decorative art. Maynard was an early customer, though not apparently a financial backer. 'The Omega stuffs look very fine on my chairs', he told Duncan on 25 September. 'Unfortunately the upholsterer has stuck them on what is, to my thinking, upside down.' In the row which led to the withdrawal of Wyndham Lewis, Frederick Etchells and two others from Omega in October he sided completely with Roger Fry. 'I received yesterday a letter of a disgraceful character signed by Etchells, Lewis and others', he told Duncan on 13 October. 'Such people must obviously work by themselves.' He would not countenance attacks on his friends.

He managed to snatch a few holidays. In July he spent some days with Sydney Russell-Cooke and his family on the Isle of Wight, going on to stay with the Macmillans at Birch Grove in Sussex. (Perhaps it was on this occasion that Harold Macmillan remembers his parents being annoyed with Keynes for appearing at breakfast in slippers.) In mid-August there was a brief interlude of camping with Duncan, Vanessa, Adrian, Roger, Gerald and Daphne Olivier in Norfolk. On 10 September he joined Clive and Vanessa and a large Bloomsbury weekend house-party at Asheham, the Woolf's country house in Sussex, before rushing off to Birmingham for a meeting of the British

Association for the Advancement of Science. All the decent hotels in Birmingham were full, so he stayed in a kind of superior pub. To Duncan he wrote on 11 September: 'I found St. George last night (cured, thank God, of his disease) and he is living with me at this quasi-hotel, – though, in effect, only at night as I desert him all day for my scientific friends.' In addition to nights with St George, and learned daytime discussions with Fay and Meredith, Maynard went to a football match which reminded him of a Roman amphitheatre – 'The crowd makes a dull roar nearly all the time, rising to a frenzy of excitement and rage when the slightest thing happened' – and visited the Birmingham Repertory Theatre. It was, he told Duncan, 'exactly what we ought to have in Cambridge'. This thought lodged in his mind, long after St George had vanished from his life.

Indian business, meanwhile, had resumed when he went to stay with Sir Ernest Cable in Devon on 27 August. Cable, the owner of a big jute business in India, and a former member of the Bengal Chamber of Commerce, had written a skeleton memorandum dealing with the capitalisation of the proposed State Bank. He invited Maynard to stay with him to discuss it and have 'a day or so at the partridges'. Maynard went back to King's to write the final memorandum which, he said, 'ought to make any banker's mouth water'. It was circulated to the Commission over his sole signature on 6 October 1913.

The memorandum contained a number of sections dealing with the Bank's constitution, capitalisation, functions, etc. Keynes rejected the model of the Bank of England as unsuited to Indian conditions. In his scheme, tailored to meet inherited arrangements, the three existing 'Presidency Banks' at Calcutta, Bombay, and Madras would form the 'head offices' of a federal system over which a Central Board would preside at Delhi: a model adapted from Germany, and similar to the Federal Reserve System currently being established in the United States. Perhaps of most interest to the student of Keynes's thought is the contention that certain public functions are best performed by semi-autonomous bodies rather than directly by the state – which foreshadows the argument in his well-known essay of 1925, 'Am I a Liberal?' On the one hand the new State Bank would act as a 'buffer' between the Secretary of State and political criticism: in reply to 'questions in Parliament on details of executive authority' the Secretary of State could reply quite properly that 'it was entirely a matter for the Bank'.[44] On the other hand, it would give discretion to banking experts which public officials could never allow themselves. Keynes's characteristic preference for discretionary arrangements as opposed to fixed rules emerges very clearly, as does its condition: expert management shielded from political interference.

He was equally emphatic about the economic advantages. The capacity of a central bank to mobilise the reserves now scattered through the banking and treasury systems would make India much better able to meet a banking crisis.* By holding the balances of the government and as manager of the Paper Currency Reserve, the Bank would have both more resources, and more discretion, to expand credit money.[45]

More witnesses were seen from 23 October to 14 November. Then Chamberlain and Basil Blackett, the Commission's secretary, drew up a draft report, which was circulated for comments. By this time clear areas of agreement and disagreement had emerged. The gold standard was definitely rejected. There were too many doubters and vested interests for the State Bank proposal to go through. A compromise was patched up whereby Keynes's memorandum would appear as an annexe to the Report, with a recommendation that an expert committee be set up to study it. The Commission would make its proposals for giving more elasticity to the currency on the assumption that there would be no Central Bank.

It was now that a row blew up over what Chamberlain was to call 'a minor point of note issue management'. The point of dispute was highly technical. The draft report had gone some way to meeting Keynes's demand for greater seasonal elasticity in the note issue by providing for an increase in the fiduciary issue up to one-third of the note issue. Keynes, on the other hand, was determined to establish the principle that the various reserve funds – the gold standard reserve, the paper currency reserve, and the government's cash balances in the reserve treasuries – should be treated as a single reserve from the point of view of lending, with discretion given to the officials to decide from which fund to make temporary loans to the public at any particular time. A consistent purpose runs through his proposals on both external and domestic banking: namely, to increase the efficiency of monetary response to business demand by centralising reserve management in the hands of experts prepared to follow an active, or discretionary, lending policy rather than rely on ultra-cautious 'rules of thumb'.

However, this purpose of Keynes was beyond the grasp of his more prosaic colleagues; and the technical reforms which he and another Commissioner, R.W. Gillam, proposed in the management of the note issue, in two memoranda fired off early in December, were considered

---

*'With no central reserve, no elasticity of credit currency, hardly a rediscount market, and hardly a bank rate policy, with the growth of small and daring banks, great increase of deposits and a community unhabituated to banking and ready at the least alarm to revert to hoarding . . . there are to be found most elements of weakness and few elements of strength.' (*CW*, xv, p. 197)

too clever by half. The Commission met for three days before Christmas to discuss the draft report and its amendments. Maynard wrote to Florence (20 December 1913):

> The Commission is very nearly finished now, and most of the Report is in its final form. The last three days have been about the most exacting to character and intellect that I have ever been through and I feel rather a wreck – wishing very much that I was off to the South of France for an immediate holiday. We sat for seven hours a day, and one had to be drafting amendments at top speed and perpetually deciding within 30 seconds whether other people's amendments were verbal and innocent or substantial and to be rejected. I must say that Austen came out of the ordeal very well, and I believe he may yet be Prime Minister – I don't suppose in the purely intellectual sense that he's any stupider than Campbell-Bannerman was.

Maynard regarded Chamberlain with a mixture of affection, respect and amusement. 'Your description of the chairman's brain makes me shriek with laughter,' Cable wrote to him early in December.[46] On the other hand, Russell-Cooke wrote on 21 December; 'I hope your admiration for Austen Chamberlain will not lead you to accept office in the next Tory government... You would become a bigoted Tory within five years, and prostitute your expert knowledge of Economics as Sir William Anson and Prof. Dicey have sacrificed their "Constitutional" judgment.'[47]

The Commission had broken up for Christmas without having come to Keynes's notes of dissent. At the beginning of January he left England for Roquebrune on the Riviera – although without Russell-Cooke whom he had hoped would come with him – intending to return in time for the Commission's next meeting, fixed on 12 January. But just as he was about to set off back home he was 'smitten down by a somewhat bad attack of tonsillitis – temperature 103'.[48] He was being nursed, he reported, by Dorothy Bussy's sister, Mrs Rendel. An hour after receiving a telegram that his illness had been rediagnosed as diphtheria, Florence left Cambridge, crossing the Channel on 14 January. At midnight of the 15th she reached Menton, where Maynard was now in a nursing home feeling better. 'There is still some disease in my throat,' he wrote to his father the same day, 'though I think I have got benefit from the gallons of serum they pumped into me yesterday and the day before.' He was cheered up not just by Florence's arrival, but by that of Duncan, who had come out to stay with his mother. As Maynard continued in a highly infectious state, Florence improbably took to the tables at Monte Carlo in Duncan's company. 'My companion won rather more than I lost and remonstrated at being dragged away,' she recalled many years later.[49] Maynard's departure was delayed till the end of the month; he was still being prescribed strychnine for 'paralysis of the soft palate' in March. Meanwhile his father noted (22 January 1914) that 'Maynard is afraid that in his absence the reactionary party got too much their own way on the Commission'.

In his absence the Commissioners, trying to make sense of his notes, had managed to hit on a formula which was somewhat more restrictive than their original one. Angered, Maynard fired off a letter from Menton on 23 January saying that if the new draft stood he would have to write a note of dissent to the Report. Back in England, he sent Chamberlain a cogent letter on 3 February. The basic failure of the new formula, he wrote, was its inability to think of the various funds as other than in watertight compartments. 'The Government's real capacity to make temporary loans depends on the sums in their paper currency reserve and in their balances regarded jointly . . . . In fact, the proposed scheme extends and perpetuates the multiple reserve system which is anyhow a great defect in the Indian system.'[50] He proposed new drafting amendments. Before this onslaught, Chamberlain gave way and, on his own authority, authorised the changes. Whether he understood what he was doing is doubtful. He regarded the issue as of little practical importance. It is hard to agree with Elizabeth Johnson that 'it was in his treatment of the paper currency reserve that [Keynes] left his mark on the Report.'[51] Much more important were his annexe on the State Bank and his part in getting the Commission to endorse the gold-exchange standard. Marshall, who read the Report when it came out, was 'entranced by [Keynes's State Bank memorandum] as a prodigy of constructive work. Verily we old men will have to hang ourselves, if young people can cut their way so straight and with such apparent ease through such great difficulties.'[52]

III

ON THE BRINK OF CIVILISATION

Vanished worlds always seem different in retrospect from what they were like at the time; more golden, or blacker. Joys and sufferings are never so intense as recollection or history makes them. In particular, a great foreclosure always makes the preceding prospect seem rosier than it was. So it is not surprising that Keynes and his friends looking back on the world before 1914 thought that it was on the point of coming right for them, would have come right for them had it not been for the war. They were, of course, a highly privileged group, and the golden age they looked back on was very much that of their world. Nevertheless, they were not wholly wrong, either about their prospects or about possibilities in general; and even if they were wrong this would not matter from the biographical point of view, for it was their own interpretation of past experience which influenced their subsequent lives and future efforts.

In his essay 'Before the War', dated 1917, Clive Bell wrote,

> In the spring of 1914 Society offered the new-comer precisely what the new-comer wanted, not cut-and-dried ideas, still less a perfect civilization, but an intellectual flutter, faint and feverish no doubt, a certain receptivity to new ways of thinking and feeling, a mind at least ajar, and the luxurious tolerance of inherited wealth. Not, I suppose, since 1789 have days seemed more full of promise than those spring days of 1914.[53]

For Bloomsbury, promise meant chiefly culture; culture in 1914 meant to them, above all, ballet. Ballet was the art form which defined the age, just as thirty years previously it had been Wagnerian opera. It owed its ascendancy mainly to Diaghilev, the greatest of the twentiety-century impresarios. Diaghilev not only introduced to the West the genius of the singer Chaliapin and the dancers Karsavina and Nijinsky, but he was determined to make the ballet a catalyst for all that was modern and exciting in the arts. He coaxed miraculous scores out of Ravel, Stravinsky, Strauss and Debussy; the visual impact of his productions – with scenery and costumes designed by Benois and Bakst and Nijinsky's miraculous elevation – was profound. As Richard Shone writes, 'Its influence was widespread in the theatre, in interior decoration and fashion, and painting . . . It was not simply the revelation of colour that astonished the painters but the dancers' command of space and the movement of bodies in a way never seen before.'[54] The contrast between this pre-war impact of Russia on the West ('They, if anything can, redeem our civilisation,' Rupert Brooke wrote to Eddie Marsh after seeing the Russian Ballet) and that of 1917 is almost too painful to dwell on.

But the effect of the Ballets Russes was not just confined to the arts. It brought Society and the arts into contact in a way which Post-Impressionism had not, and in this Bloomsbury, naïvely no doubt, saw a great hope: the governing class was becoming civilised at last. As Lydia Lopokova later put it, Diaghilev 'had the cunning . . . to combine the excellent with the chic, and revolutionary art with the atmosphere of the old regime'.[55] Ottoline Morrell and Lady Cunard led the way. According to Osbert Sitwell, Margot Asquith made No. 10 Downing Street 'a centre of such an abundance and intensity of life as it had not seen for a hundred years and is never likely to see again'.[56] The civilising and elevating mission of the arts was taken seriously by Bloomsbury. It was bound up with their optimism about the future. There is no hint in pre-war London of aestheticism as an escape from a crumbling society, which is said to have dominated the cultural consciousness of pre-1914 Vienna. Rather the arts, 'progressive' politics, economic improvement seemed to be marching hand in hand towards a better future. The political vocation itself might be held in low esteem; certainly the Bloomsbury publicists had only the haziest notion of where or how the masses were to fit into this newly civilised world; but that things were getting better they had no doubt. Hence the profound shock of the events of August 1914. That these archaic, opera-bouffe figures in their uniforms and top hats would be able to close down civilisation was simply not a thought which had occurred to them.

Keynes was too much preoccupied with the final stages of Probability to take much notice of Diaghilev's last triumphal pre-war London season, featuring Ravel's *Daphnis and Chloe* and the apotheosis of Chaliapin. On 7 March 1914, Neville had started reading the proofs, which he found 'very difficult'. Maynard took a reading party to Asheham for Easter (to which he invited Bimla Sarkar), but was soon back at work. To his parents, on holiday in France, he wrote from Cambridge on 17 July,

> I am now very deep in Probability and enjoying myself. I had 5 hours with Johnson on Friday and got some most useful criticisms and suggestions. From conversations with Russell and Broad I have got less. I have been much encouraged by Johnson's and Russell's reception of my Theory of Induction ... I finished this two or three years ago, but no one has read it till now.

Towards the end of July he spent three pleasant days with the Oliver Stracheys at their house near Pangbourne. Moore was one of the party, losing 16s 6d to Maynard at bridge, and going through a good part of his proofs with him.

Although the Archduke Franz Ferdinand had been assassinated on 28 June, only a month later was there a first reference to the worsening international situation. Characteristically it was in the context of Stock Exchange speculation. Maynard had put in an order for Canadian Pacific and Rio Tinto, 'which is courageous of me ... The odds appear to me *slightly* against Russia and Germany joining in.'[57] On 30 July he was still gossiping to Neville by letter about his rooms which he had just had redecorated ('I can't make up my mind about the carpeting of the big room') and about his plans to go into camp in Cornwall with Geoffrey and Margery and Brynhild Olivier. On 31 July Maynard wrote to his father that the war news 'interferes dreadfully with my work – I cannot keep my mind quiet enough'. Next day Germany invaded Belgium. On 4 August 1914 England declared war on Germany, and Bloomsbury's – and Maynard's – world collapsed.

APPENDIX TO CHAPTER 11

KEYNES'S SPECULATIONS BEFORE THE FIRST WORLD WAR

As part of his 'clean-up' job on Keynes, Sir Roy Harrod denied that Keynes had speculated on the Stock Exchange before 1919. His most explicit statement on the subject comes not in his biography of Keynes but in a review article he wrote on Clive Bell's *Old Friends* in the *Economic Journal* of December 1957, pp. 693–9. Clive Bell had written, 'I fancy it was about this time [summer of 1914] or a little earlier that he [Keynes] took to speculating'. Roy Harrod commented:

> [This] antedates his speculation by more than five years. He took to speculation in September 1919 ... When writing his life, I went in some detail into his financial affairs. In 1919 he still had no capital, save for a few pounds in the bank ... If he had had some flutters at an earlier date, they could only have been occasional, and they led to nothing.

Harrod's reason for emphasising this latter date is made clear by his continuation:

> It is important that this should be clearly understood, since there were many ill-wishers in his middle period who asserted that he took advantage of inside information when in the Treasury (1915–June 1919) in order to carry out successful speculations. This allegation is entirely without foundation, and it is accordingly desirable that Mr. Bell's wrong dating should be corrected.

To Clive Bell himself, Sir Roy had written a little earlier (13 January 1957):

> all the evidence I have seen is that he did no more than an occasional flutter such as anyone might do, but nothing regular or systematic, until September 1919. The point is important because of the beastly stories, which are very widespread ... about his having made money dishonourably by taking advantage of his Treasury position. (King's College, Charleston Papers, Box 3)

The facts are rather different. Professor Donald Moggridge, who went through the same sources as Harrod did, provides details of Keynes's pre-war financial position in his introductory chapter to Vol. XII of the *Collected Writings*. They are summarised in the Table, which shows that Harrod's statement that 'In 1919 he [Keynes] still had no capital, save for a few pounds in the bank' is not true.

Professor Moggridge explains:

> Keynes's career as an investor began with what he, in his records, referred to as his 'special fund' or 'special account'. This was the repository for his birthday money, various academic prizes and the

like which J. N. Keynes had kept for his son. Keynes used the proceeds for loans to his friends (Bernard Swithinbank, Lytton Strachey, John Strachey, J. T. Sheppard, H. J. Norton and George Mallory), for furniture and for books on probability, but from July 1905 its major role was as the basis for his investments. At the time of his first transaction, the fund stood at just over £181.

Keynes's first purchase occurred on 6 July 1905 when he bought 4 shares of the Marine Insurance Company for £160 16s.0d. His next came just under six months later when he bought 4 shares in the engineering firm Mather and Platt for £49 7s.9d. He made no further investments until 1910. From the records that survive in the Keynes Papers, it would seem that this reflected the fact that he was living up to his income and saving no more than a few pounds a year. Once his income rose to a level that permitted larger savings, Keynes expanded his portfolio by buying shares in Horden Collieries and Eastern Bank in 1910. The next year saw his first switches in the market, while in 1913 he was involved in a brief speculation in shares of U.S. Steel which netted him £5 15s. Generally during this period Keynes's dealing activities were limited and purchases of additional securities were the order of the day. (*CW*, xii, p.3)

TABLE *Keynes's financial position, 1908–20*

	Income (£)				Assets (£)		
Year	Academic	Allowance from JNK	Other	Total	Securities	Other[a]	Net
1905–09	115	180	85	380	(1908) 197	120	317
1909–10	580	110	15	705	(1909) 218	246	464
1910–11	575	135	20	730	(1910) 539	66	605
1911–12	623	105	41	769	(1911) 940	87	1,027
1912–13	726	95	89	910	(1912) 1,463	23	1,486
1913–14	741	85	165	991	(1913) 1,691	254	1,945
1914–15	702	80	290	1,072	(1914) 4,617	−115	4,502
1919–20	3,819		1,337	5,156	(1919) 14,453		16,431

[a] Bank balance

There is little hint of speculation here, and Professor Moggridge appears to endorse Harrod's position (though not his exact dating) when he writes that 'he [Keynes] began his career as a speculator in August 1919' (*CW*, xii, p.4).

However, he admits as 'exceptions' to this view the speculation in U.S. Steel already mentioned and, much more important, an arrangement he made with Roger Fry on 3 April 1914 'whereby Fry loaned Keynes £1000, repayable at six months' notice on either side, at 4½ per cent per annum. Any profits or losses on the Fund, after payment of the 4½ per cent, were to be shared equally.' That this loan was for speculative purposes is clear from a letter Fry wrote to Keynes on 5 March 1914, enclosing a list of his shares on which he sought Keynes's advice, and going on, 'I might realize some of the less desirable invest-ments . . . & let you play with some of it sharing profits'. (KP, KC, Box 20 F). Keynes clearly grasped at the opportunity. Another 'exception', which is omitted by Moggridge, is that Keynes obtained an overdraft of £1,000 from his bankers, Barclays, in July 1914 for speculative pur-poses. Of this he had drawn £467 by October (JMK to JNK 30 July, 3 October 1914), mainly, it seems, to purchase shares in Canadian Pacific and Rio Tinto on 28 July 1914. This was an (unsuccessful) speculation against war breaking out.

The following conclusions seem justified:

1. Keynes already had a substantial capital in 1914 which, in today's values, amounted to over £100,000.
2. By the time war broke out he had borrowed today's equivalent of over £50,000 to finance his speculative ventures.

Whether all this just adds up to an 'occasional flutter such as anyone might do' which 'led to nothing', the reader must judge.*

* £1 in 1914 was worth £28.86 in 1982 values.

12 Adapting to War

WAITING FOR EMPLOYMENT

Keynes was not allowed to remain in distracted idleness at Cambridge. On Sunday, 2 August (post was delivered on Sundays in those days) he received a letter from Basil Blackett, who had returned to the Treasury after his stint on the Indian Commission. Blackett wrote:

> I wanted to pick your brains for your country's benefit and thought you might enjoy the process. If by any chance you could spare time to see me on Monday I should be grateful, but I fear the decisions will all have been taken by then. The Joint Stock banks have made absolute fools of themselves and behaved very badly.[1]

Keynes did not tarry. He persuaded his brother-in-law A. V. Hill to drive him up to London the same day in the side-car of his motorcycle, and went straight to work at the Treasury. In the next few days he supplied it with ammunition in its battle for the mind of the Chancellor of the Exchequer, Lloyd George. On 6 August he was able to write from Treasury Chambers to his father (safely back from France):

> The pressure of the financial crisis ought to be over by tomorrow. In the meantime I am living chiefly here with excursions to the India Office and the City.
> The Bankers completely lost their heads and have been simply dazed and unable to think two consecutive thoughts.
> Specie payments by the Bank of England have now been saved – by the skin of its teeth. The points now to concentrate on are the saving of the acceptance houses (I doubt if a single Director of the Bank of England is solvent today) and the settling of the £1 note issue. I've just heard that they consider I played an important part in preventing the suspension of specie payments, as it was my memorandum [which] converted Lloyd George.

Keynes published three lengthy accounts of the crisis, which he intended to use for a short book which never materialised. Essentially it arose from the inability of foreigners to remit money to London, or to obtain further credits there, to pay their debts. This threatened to produce two sets of chain reactions, whose ultimate result would be to deprive the Bank of England of the gold it needed to defend the gold standard – even though the exchanges were turning in sterling's favour.

According to E. V. Morgan's standard account, the proximate cause was a breakdown in the mechanism of international payments. Half of the world's trade was financed by British short-term credits. At the end of July £350m worth of bills of exchange – debts by foreigners to British joint stock banks and discount houses which had been 'accepted' by the London merchant banks – were outstanding. The inability of foreigners, in the run-up to the war, to remit funds to London as the bills matured threatened the solvency of the holders of this debt. As Keynes wrote, 'Such a failure of the remittance system . . . must have the most far-reaching consequences. The banks . . . are depending on the accepting houses and on the discount houses; the discount houses are depending on the accepting houses; and the accepting houses are depending on foreign clients who are unable to remit'. When foreigners defaulted, the banks, claiming fears for their solvency, called in loans from the discount houses, who were forced to go to the Bank of England to get their bills re-discounted at rising interest rates; cashed their notes for gold at the Bank of England; and – most notoriously on 31 July – refused their customers gold. (This 'internal run' cost the Bank of England £12m of its £27m gold reserve.)

The second cause of trouble, emphasised by Keynes, stemmed from the inability of foreigners to pay up on settlement date to the City stockbrokers through whom they had bought shares on the London Stock Exchange. To pay back their loans to the banks, the brokers had to sell the securities they held for their foreign clients. The resulting fall in the value of shares caused some banks to cancel loans to, or demand extra cover from, customers to whom they had made or promised collateral loans. Thus both chains of failure converged on the joint stock banks who found part of their assets frozen with unchanged liabilities; while the actions of the joint stock banks and discount houses threatened the Bank of England as 'lender of last resort' with the loss of its gold.

The authorities moved fast. The Stock Exchange was closed on 31 July to prevent, it was said, the banks from dumping shares on the market. To protect their position, the bank chairmen went to the Prime Minister and Chancellor of the Exchequer on 1 August with a request to be relieved of their obligation to pay gold on demand. Lloyd George tended to side with them. Pending a decision the Bank Rate was raised to 10 per cent on 1 August to protect the Bank of England's gold reserves; on 3 August the government declared a month's moratorium on payment of bills of exchange: this relieved the accepting houses. Bank Holiday was extended by three days.

In this crisis Keynes gave the advice he was to continue to give throughout the war. In a crucial memorandum of 3 August, which converted Lloyd George, he argued against suspending specie payments 'before it is *absolutely* necessary'. He took Bagehot's position that the gold reserves were there to be used, not 'hoarded'. He used the confidence argument. The future position of the City would be jeopardised if it suspended specie payments at the first sign of emergency. This was particularly so in view of the growth of London as banker for others' reserves which is 'profitable and enormously enhances London's position as a monetary centre'. Keynes suggested that gold payments be restricted internally, but retained for international transactions.[3] This was the opinion which, more or less, carried the day. The banks' gold reserves were centralised in the Bank of England. The Treasury was empowered to issue emergency currency notes of £1 and 10s, or 'Bradburies' as they were named, since they were signed by Sir John Bradbury, joint permanent secretary of the Treasury. Gold payments for external debts were kept. Bank Rate was back to 5 per cent on 8 August. The banking crisis, which had been largely a figment (or creation) of the bankers' imagination, was over.

There remained the problem of restarting the City. Foreign trade required the reopening of the discount business. Keynes argued that all that was necessary was for the Bank of England to guarantee new engagements by the accepting houses, combined with a moratorium on past acceptances, leaving the banks and discount houses to hold some bad debts for the time being. (No one, it must be emphasised, expected the war to go on for long.)[4] However, the government instead instituted a package of rescue operations which Keynes considered grossly extravagant. On 13 August Lloyd George, on the advice of his special assistant, Sir George Paish, empowered the Bank of England to re-discount at 5 per cent all bills accepted before 4 August, the government guaranteeing the Bank against bad debts. Even Sir John Bradbury wished the Chancellor had managed to obtain some assurance from the banks of restraint in cashing bills.[5] By the end of November the Bank of England had re-discounted £120m worth of bills. On 5 September the government announced that the Bank of England would advance funds to the acceptors to pay pre-moratorium bills on maturity, the Bank undertaking not to claim repayment till one year after the war. Just over £60m was advanced. The banks and the City were thus relieved at the expense of the taxpayer. Immediately, the money-market was awash with liquid funds which drove down the rate of interest and provided the basis for the inflationary finance of the early months of the war.[6]

What emerges from Keynes's published accounts in the *Economic Journal* and elsewhere is a profound antipathy towards the joint stock bankers. He criticised them for unduly restricting loans to the Stock Exchange, for calling in an unnecessary amount of loans from the discount market, for drawing gold from the Bank of England and hoarding it, and for refusing to pay customers gold when requested. 'Our system', he wrote, 'was endangered, not by the public running on the banks, but by the banks running on the Bank of England.'[7] To Marshall he complained on 10 October that Sir Felix Schuster, Governor of the Union Bank, was cowardly, and Sir Edward Holden, Chairman of the Midland Bank, was selfish; the rest were 'timid, voiceless and leaderless'. He blamed the low calibre of directors and bank managers.[8] However, a recent writer, Marcello de Cecco, sees the actions of the bankers, as well as of other actors, as part of an ongoing power struggle in the City, with the joint stock banks, essentially, trying to take over the control of the gold reserve from the Bank of England, and lucrative business from the merchant banks. The damp basement of the Marshall Library at Cambridge has recently disgorged a letter to Keynes from Sir Felix Schuster, dated 9 October 1914, in which the head of the Union Bank, rejecting Keynes's strictures, blamed the fall in share prices and the 'internal run' largely on the discount houses. Insofar as the banks contributed to the latter, it was because the Bank of England failed to supply them with the £5 and £10 notes being demanded by customers for their summer holidays, having run out of the paper on which to print them. More importantly, it was not the bank chairmen who were urging suspension of specie payments: it was Lord Cunliffe, Governor of the Bank of England. Keynes retracted some of his criticisms.

In his *Economic Journal* article of December 1914 Keynes poked fun at the idea that a gold reserve was for display only: if it were so one might just as well 'melt the reserve into a great golden image of the chief cashier and place it on a monument so high that it could never be got down again'. A more important pointer to the future is his view that the gold standard was an interference with the task of currency management, 'the intellectual and scientific part of the problem [of which] is solved already'. He feared that the influx of gold, which had followed Britain's success, alone among the allies, in preserving specie payments, would produce inflation.

> If it proves one of the after effects of the present struggle, that gold is at last deposed from its despotic control over us and reduced to the position of a constitutional monarch, a new chapter of history will be opened. Man will have made another step forward in the attainment of self-government ....[9]

There was a personal side to the banking crisis. Keynes and his father had lent money to the discount market. Like others in the same position, they feared a default. In urging the government, in his memorandum of 5 August, not to guarantee the bills held by the discount houses, Keynes was giving advice directly contrary to his own interests. As he informed his father on 28 August,

> Lloyd George's action ... in guaranteeing pre-moratorium bills, though it was not the best course and I argued against it all I could ... has probably had the effect of saving you and me several hundred pounds at the expense of the general taxpayer. It means that the National Discount Company is absolutely guaranteed against bad debts and can turn all its assets into money ...

The only bankers who emerged well from the crisis, Keynes thought, were his own, Barclays. They had taken no action to curtail his £1000 overdraft facility.

Keynes's memorandum of 3 August 1914 may have helped to change Lloyd George's mind. It did not lead to a partnership between the two men. Lloyd George, who took credit for ending the crisis, was quite happy to bring in his own advisers to shoot down the Treasury's arguments; he resented the Treasury bringing in theirs to shoot down his opinions.[10] (He does not mention Keynes in his account of the crisis in his *War Memoirs*.) Thus Keynes's intervention did not secure him an immediate Whitehall appointment. Basil Blackett wrote to him apologetically on 13 August:

> I am afraid Paish has rather queered the pitch here. I should not dream of saying ... that there's nothing you could usefully do here, but the position is that there is nothing we can usefully do to rope you ... in. You must rest content with the knowledge that you ... have written a Memo[m.] which converted Lloyd George from a Holdenite into a Currency Expert.[11]

To his father Keynes wrote the next day: 'The War Com[mittee] was finally constituted on lines which precluded my inclusion. The job I might have got they've given to [Sir George] Paish [who was made Special Adviser to the Chancellor] and he got it through being in with Lloyd George from the beginning'.

Business at the Treasury being over, Keynes tried to slip back into the old routine. He resumed work on the proofs of Probability. On 23 August he went camping in Cornwall for a few days with the Olivier sisters. But he was restless. He wanted an occupation connected with the war. This he found in writing. His article on 'Currency Measures Abroad' had already appeared in the *Morning Post* on 11 August. From Asheham, where he stayed from 28 August to 7 September, he conducted a correspondence in the *Economist* about the gold holdings of the joint stock banks. (Its editor, Hirst, he wrote was 'in a dreadful state ... He is a violent pacifist, passionately incensed at our being in the war, and far more interested in these political questions than in finance.')[12] He finished his account of the financial crisis for the *Economic Journal*. Short of being in the war machine itself, the best he could do was to offer his advice from the outside. One man happy to listen was Edwin Montagu, since February Financial Secretary to the Treasury. In a letter of 4 September Keynes warned Montagu of the dangers of inflation and expressed mistrust of Lloyd George. 'As one of the few people who combine special knowledge of these things with *not* having their personal future at stake, I chafe at being a purely passive observer,' he wrote.[13] He lunched with Montagu on 12 October, and sent him several memoranda, slipping over to Paris in mid-December to compile 'Notes on French Finance'. He wrote newspaper articles on the financing of Germany's war effort, condemning the censor's policy of limiting access to the German press.[14] Hilton Young, who was City Editor of the *Morning Post*, remembers him at this time canvassing leading papers in support of his view that 'the government should collect all free cash and credit into its own hands by issues of Treasury Bills'.[15] In these ways he was staking his claim for future employment.

On 10 October 1914 he returned to a Cambridge depopulated of undergraduates, and with the Backs behind King's occupied by a military hospital. He now lectured to 'blacks and women', comforted the 'wounded Tommies ... Some of them look very nice', and helped Sheppard look after Belgian refugees – 'ugly, bourgeois, and bores'.[16] London living arrangements had changed too. At the end of September, the lease of 38 Brunswick Square expired. Keynes moved into rooms in 10 Ormond Street. Bloomsbury was once again rearranging its emotional affairs. Adrian Stephen had just got engaged to Karin Costelloe. His affair with Duncan was over. Meanwhile Duncan had replaced Roger Fry as the object of Vanessa's love. Duncan was not in love with her, but their painting drew them together, and when the Brunswick Square ménage broke up, he went to live at 46 Gordon Square, taking a studio at 22 Fitzroy Street. Vanessa found Maynard very gloomy at the beginning of October:

> [He] seems to be fearfully lonely in his rooms. He talked a great deal about Duncan & said rather bitterly I thought that it was strange that the effect of Adrian's marriage should be to separate him from Duncan – they had lived together now for 6 years off & on. I think he suggested to Duncan that they should share rooms together but didnt press it as he saw that Duncan didnt want to. But I think he is rather upset that D. should not want it.[17]

On the credit side was Maynard's growing friendship with Vanessa herself, which started from their time in camp together in Norfolk in 1913, and ripened in April 1914, when Vanessa had joined Maynard's house party at Asheham, which he had rented from the Woolfs. May-

nard's lack of delicacy, which offended even Lytton, excited the bawdy
Vanessa, who wanted to be one of the boys. By the autumn of 1914 their
intimacy was cemented by their unavailing love for Duncan. Vanessa
offered to take Maynard as a lodger at 46 Gordon Square; but he,
sensing perhaps that the situation might become too emotionally
fraught, decided to stay put at Ormond Street.

Keynes, writes Terence Hutchison, 'eager, apparently, as any young
patriot of those days – such as Rupert Brooke – to join the war effort,
had to return impatient and restless, for the Michaelmas Term at
Cambridge'.[18] This is not quite accurate. For one thing, unlike Rupert
Brooke, he did not enlist, and never considered it. This is not just
because he thought he could help the war effort more by doing something else, but because fighting lacked for him any romantic appeal.
His attitude was completely different from that of bored aristocrats like
Julian Grenfell who saw in war an escape from uselessness. Grenfell's
attitude was shared by Maynard's friend Ferenc Békássy, and it greatly
distressed him. In early August he did his best to dissuade him from
returning home to enlist in the Hungarian army. When Békássy insisted, he agreed, with a heavy heart, to pay for his journey back home.
Challenged by David Garnett that he should have refused on the
double ground that he might be sending Békássy to his death and also
helping the enemy, 'Maynard disagreed violently. He said he had used
every argument to persuade Békássy not to go – but having failed to
persuade him, it was not the part of a friend to impose his views by
force, or by refusing to help.' In his memoirs Garnett commented:
'Maynard's high ideal of friendship in fact cost his friend his life.'[19] He
also did his best to stop his brother Geoffrey from enlisting in the Royal
Army Medical Corps, again unavailingly. He was terrified lest Duncan, pressurised by his family's military tradition, should volunteer.

On the other hand, Maynard, at first, had no great anti-war feeling.
He was not a pacifist, and was not interested in the political origins of
the war. For example, he had nothing to do with the Union of
Democratic Control, started by left-wing Liberals and liberal-minded
Socialists who attributed the war to Britain's secret military commitments to France. His instinctive attitude was that of the economist and
civil servant. The war was a fact of life. It should be run as efficiently
as possible while it lasted, and he felt (rightly) that he had a
contribution to make to that end. He also shared the common view that
the war would end quickly – not because he believed that the Entente's
forces would soon be in Berlin, but because he thought, like Norman
Angell, that the modern world was organised for peace, and could not
readily be put on a war footing.[20] His initial attitude to the war was thus
fairly cool because both its appeal and its horror lay outside the limits
of his imagination. Florence, too, took a businesslike approach, busying

herself with local war work.[21] Of all the family it was Neville who understood the meaning of the war soonest and felt it most vividly. It was, he wrote in his diary on 23 August, 'a constant nightmare, day and night; but especially in the early morning'.

Maynard's friends were divided in their response. Békássy, as we have seen, returned to fight for the Central Powers. 'It's a part of "the good life" just now', he wrote to Noel Olivier.[22] On the other hand, Luce wrote from Rangoon that 'Feri [Békássy] is the chief argument that keeps me pacifist.' Another close friend of Maynard, F. L. ('Peter') Lucas, a Trinity classicist who had recently been elected an Apostle, also joined up. So did Rupert Brooke. Desmond MacCarthy volunteered for the Red Cross. But most of Bloomsbury and their friends resisted the call to arms. In his biographer's words, 'Lytton himself seems to have believed that all physically fit intellectuals should be prepared to defend the shores of England, but with this reservation: no intellectuals were in fact physically fit.'[23] In intervals of reading Maynard's article on the Financial Crisis at The Lacket, near Marlborough, which he had rented from Hilton Young, Lytton 'knit a muffler in navy blue wool for the neck of one of our sailor-lads. I don't know which but I have my visions.'[24] Basically, Bloomsbury just wanted to be left alone. Unwillingness to fight did not as yet extend to active opposition to the war. In this respect it was unlike Bertrand Russell who from the start opposed it on political grounds. In the Russell generation of Apostles there was a considerable reserve of pro-German, anti-Russian, feeling, to which Maynard himself was not immune. The war, he told Moore on 24 October, had 'destroyed his opinion of Germans; he didn't think they would seriously believe and act on such absurd principles, as war had shown they do'. Levy, who quotes this remark from Moore's diary, comments: 'This statement by Keynes nicely captures the pro-German background against which such points were argued.'[25]

It was only as reports of casualties started to come that the horror of what was happening dawned on Maynard. Geoffrey, operating at the makeshift British Military Hospital, wrote to him from Versailles on 20 September 1914: 'One boy, a Seaforth Highlander, suffered more than I have ever seen any human being suffer before he died.' On 15 August, Maynard had had a cheerful letter from Freddie Hardman: 'Is there anything particular you would like me to bring you back from Berlin – a little etching or so?' Maynard wrote back, on 25 October, a letter full of Cambridge gossip. It was returned with the word 'Killed' scrawled across it. Hardman had died leading his men in hand-to-hand fighting. 'It is too awful that such things should happen,' Maynard wrote to Duncan on 4 November. 'It makes one bitterly miserable and long that the war should stop quickly on almost any terms. I can't bear that he should have died.' On 9 November he reported that Lucas had come to say goodbye. 'It is dreadful that he should go. All my sub-conscious feelings about things are now deeply depressed, which they weren't before. It seems to make it hardly any better that we should be winning.' His father's misery, too, started to affect him. Geoffrey, from Versailles, attributed it to 'a tiredness of the brain cells . . .' (25 November 1914), but Neville's diary reveals the true cause: 'I am 62 today,' he wrote on 31 August. 'Earnestly I trust that by the time my next birthday comes round this terrible war will be over, & that I shall be able to look forward to the future with less anxiety.' Almost the only thing which could stir him out of his apathy was golf; and he and Maynard, both with time on their hands, spent much of their Christmas on the golf links at Royston, as the guns on the Western Front fell briefly silent.

II

TREASURY OFFICIAL

On 6 January 1915 Keynes at last got a job in Whitehall as assistant to Sir George Paish, at a salary of £600 a year. The appointment was temporary, for the duration of the war, and Keynes was allowed to continue editing the *Economic Journal*, and writing, provided he did not use official materials. He started work on 18 January. Harrod attributed the appointment to pressure from Blackett,[26] but Keynes himself believed that Montagu was the moving force. Looking back in 1924, he felt that he owed Montagu 'nearly all my steps up in life':

> In 1913 when he was at the India Office, it was he who got me put on the Royal Commission on Indian Currency, which was my first step into publicity (my name was known to no one outside Cam-bridge before then). It was he who got me called to the Treasury in 1915 during the War. It was he who got me taken to Paris in Febru-ary of that year for the first inter-Ally Conference and so established me in my war work. It was he who introduced me to the great ones (I first met Lloyd George in a famous dinner party of 4 at his house; I first met McKenna through him; I first met Margot [Asquith] sitting next to her at dinner in his house). It was he who got me invited to the dinners of the inner-secretaries during the early part of the war (private gatherings of the secretaries of the Cabinet and of the chief ministers who exchanged the secret news and discussed after dinner the big problems of the war).[27]

On 21 January Keynes wrote to his father: 'After a slack beginning I am now very busy, having become Secretary of a Secret Committee of the Cabinet presided over by the Prime Minister. First meeting this morning. So I know exactly what a cabinet meeting is like. This is of course absolutely private.'[28] (Asquith told Venetia Stanley that the Secretary of the Committee was 'a clever young Cambridge don called Keynes'.) The Committee was to enquire into rising food prices. By 25 January Keynes had produced a memorandum on the problem which 'has the same air of dashing into things as those early papers he wrote for the India Office'.[29] Over the next couple of months, as Secretary of the Cabinet's Wheat Committee, he was active in organising government purchases of Indian wheat at below the world market price – a policy made possible by the embargo on private Indian wheat exports, suggested by Keynes's old boss Sir William Holderness.[30]

On 30 January his father received more news: 'I *am* going to Paris, – and we start Sunday or Monday. It's a most select party: Lloyd George, Montagu, the Governor of the Bank of England [Lord Cunliffe], and me, together with a private secretary. We are to be guests of the French Govt.'[31] Keynes's chance came because Lloyd George had 'no use', he told Montagu, for his two permanent secretaries, Bradbury and Ramsay. Bradbury was suffering from a 'swelled head' as a result of his 'Bradburies', while Ramsay was 'the kind of slow-witted person who after a prolonged consultation can tell you in two days time that you have taken the wrong turning. I have no use for such men in a conference.'[32] Montagu suggested Keynes, and so he was chosen as Treasury representative, together with Blackett. His friends found him 'happy and excited' at the prospect of the trip. Britain, he told them, was to lend Russia between £60m and £100m, and Italy a 'large sum which simply means bribing [it] to come in [to the war] . . . fearfully immoral'.[33] (Asquith, it is clear, was not the only leaky member in Whitehall at this time.)

The conference which Keynes attended in Paris from 2 to 5 February was the first inter-Ally conference. It inaugurated the whole complex system of inter-Ally war credits. Russia, and to a lesser extent France, could no longer export enough goods or gold to pay for their purchases abroad of essential war materials. Britain, whose international financial position was much stronger, had to start financing them. Britain and France agreed to make a joint loan to Russia; Russia agreed to increase its wheat exports as soon as the Dardanelles was open. Russia and France also agreed to transfer gold to the Bank of England. Britain's first credit to France followed in April. From the decisions taken at the conference stemmed the whole post-war debt problem, since it was decided that transfers were to take the form of loans, not grants. Once Britain started to finance its allies, it was inevitable that it would seek to control their foreign spending, so as to make sure that the money was not frittered away or simply used to support the exchange value of their currencies. Financial control led, by stages, to a centralised buying system, with Allied orders abroad placed through Britain, and paid for by British credits earmarked for Allied accounts at the Bank of England. This was the system which Keynes helped to build up over the next two years, and over which he came to preside. Its evolution can be traced in the Anglo-French agreement of April 1915, the Anglo-Russian agreement of September 1915, the Anglo-Italian agreements of June and November 1915 and the Four Power Protocol of July 1916. Britain would advance its allies credits for their purchase of war materials in return for some control over their buying, and the deposit of gold in London as partial collateral. Purchasing Committees were set up in London to handle the orders. Keynes played a prominent part in the negotiation of these agreements. His influence on the initial decisions taken in Paris comes out most strongly in his insistence that Russia be obliged to hold some portion of its gold reserves in London. 'Only the English,' he minuted characteristically, 'have realised that the main use of gold reserves is to be *used*.'[34] In Paris Keynes met Alexandre Ribot, the French Finance Minister, and attended a reception given by President Poincaré. The newspapers registered a new arrival on the Allied scene: Professor Kains of the London School of Economics.

At this stage Keynes was simply a junior adviser among many. But he was quick to make his mark at the Treasury, helped in this by the rapid eclipse of Sir George Paish. On the outbreak of the war, he later recalled, Paish

> was sent for by Mr. Lloyd George to go to the Treasury as his leading financial expert, and for about a day and a half in August 1914 he was very important at the Treasury. As usual, however, Mr. Lloyd George soon got bored with him and stopped reading his lengthy memoranda. He was, however, given a good salary and an exalted title ... and ... a room at a considerable distance, over at the Road Board in Caxton House.
>
> When I first came to the Treasury in January 1915 I was nominally appointed Paish's assistant. But I was given a seat in Blackett's room, as well as with Paish at the Road Board. After a few days I came to the conclusion that Paish was barely in his right mind and before long I ceased going over to the rooms at the Road Board. Not long afterwards he had a complete nervous breakdown.[35]

As Elizabeth Johnson rightly says Keynes 'seems to have possessed a Treasury eye from the start'.[36] He was quick to relate individual spending proposals to overall principles of financial policy, and to appreciate the connection between internal and external finance. He had the indispensable civil servant's gift of producing crisp, lucid memoranda at a moment's notice. He enjoyed the atmosphere of the Treasury – 'very clever, very dry and in a certain sense very cynical;

intellectually very self-confident and not subject to the whims of people who feel that they are less hidden, and are not quite sure that they know their case'. He appreciated that its aesthetic – the very form of a Treasury draft – was an indispensable ingredient of its prestige. Here was one source of his lack of rapport with Lloyd George. The Chancellor, he wrote later, 'had no aesthetic sense of the formalisms'. He also 'never had the faintest idea of the meaning of money'.[37] On his first trip to Paris, Keynes did not hesitate to tell Lloyd George to his face that his views on French finance were 'rubbish'.[38] It was against spendthrifts like Lloyd George that the system of Treasury control had been invented. Keynes later compared it to conventional morality. 'There is a great deal of it rather tiresome and absurd once you begin to look into it, yet nevertheless it is an essential bulwark against overwhelming wickedness.'[39]

Maynard celebrated his appointment at the Treasury by giving a party for seventeen on 6 January 1915 at the Café Royal. Guests included the Bells, Sheppard, Cecil Taylor, Frankie Birrell, Duncan Grant, David Garnett, assorted Oliviers and Stracheys, and Desmond MacCarthy. Afterwards they went back to 46 Gordon Square for Clive's and Vanessa's party. There they listened to a Mozart trio, played by the three D'Aranyi sisters (old Bedalians), and then went upstairs for the last scene of a Racine play, performed by three puppets made by Duncan, with words spoken by the weird-voiced Stracheys. 'The evening ended with Gerald Shove enthroned in the centre of the room, crowned with roses . . .'[40] Bloomsbury was recovering its nerve after the initial shock of war. Bunny Garnett and Frankie Birrell had started a Caroline Club which met on Tuesdays at Hugh and Bryn Popham's house in Caroline Place to read plays. Maynard would sometimes drop in after work. At other times he could be found at the Café Royal with friends like Birrell, Garnett, Shove, one or other of the unmarried Oliviers, and occasionally Molly Hamilton, an ex-Newnham woman who was active in the anti-war movement. Ottoline Morrell had resumed her Thursday evening dinner parties, where much drink was consumed, and dancing became wild to Philip Morrell's accompaniment on the pianola. The gaiety of those who fought and those who stayed behind had not yet been much dimmed: the ghastly slaughter was still largely in the future.

At his dinner party of 6 January, Maynard had put David Garnett between Vanessa and Duncan and that, figuratively, was where he was to remain for the next four years. Duncan fell passionately, and jealously, in love with Bunny, whose own animal spirits were, as Michael Holroyd writes, 'strong and surprisingly various'.[41] Vanessa, who loved Duncan, realized that the only way she could hold him was to allow Bunny to share their lives. A *ménage-à-trois* soon developed, based on a succession of rented farmhouses. In the spring of 1915 they took Eleanor, near West Wittering, Sussex, from the St John Hutchinsons. Maynard would visit them at weekends, a semi-avuncular fourth. 'Till this morning', Duncan wrote to Hilton Young from Eleanor in April 1915,

> there was a house party of sorts consisting of Lytton Strachey and Keynes. Maynard is a very grand person now .... He goes to the Treasury every day and works very hard and he told me he had saved the Government £1,000,000 in a morning .... Lytton is getting very benign and is writing I'm told a very good book consisting of short lives of eminently disagreeable Victorians ....[42]

Maynard found no one to take Duncan's place in his life. Frankie Birrell slept with him 'for old time's sake'; and there were pick-ups. These casual adventures were not without danger. His landlady at 10 Great Ormond Street, her interest aroused by the odd sexual goings-on, hinted at blackmail.[43] Maynard decamped in February 1915, renting 3 Gower Street. Here he let upper rooms to Gerald Shove and John Sheppard, who was working as a translator at the War Office. The attics were taken by Katherine Mansfield and Middleton Murry, who later married. Maynard engaged a 'formidably ugly and genteel' housekeeper, Miss Chapman, daughter of a bank manager, with whose aid he gave a 'series of gay parties'.[44]

With so many relationships precariously poised, Bunny's thoughtless behaviour produced storms. After one Thursday evening at Ottoline's, on 25 March, Maynard, Duncan, Gerald and Bunny returned to Gower Street. Bunny wrote in his diary: 'I went upstairs the worse for whisky and ... kissed Maynard in bed and heard a noise. Duncan was in a most awful state about it and I wasn't very nice really – Duncan wept – I consoled him and went to sleep alone ...'. Next day Maynard wrote to Duncan contritely:

> I wish you had not gone away this morning without coming to see me. I spent a miserable night, because I felt to blame. I was taken by surprise and it took me a few minutes to see quite clearly what was happening. But I really knew in my bones all the time, and why you had come up to bed and what you felt. Whereas Bunny is such a silly fool that he had no conception of that, and simply thought, as far as I could make out, that he'd done me a good turn.
>
> The whole episode meant nothing, except that I'm not perfectly reliable in some circumstances ...
>
> But it's only you I care about above everything, and I'm miserable to have been so weak.

Absorption in Whitehall and Bloomsbury helped keep Keynes's mind off the fate of his fighting friends as well as the larger issues which

preoccupied some of his anti-war ones. But to the latter his gaiety
seemed forced, his arguments insincere. He was good at his work –
tossing off elegant memoranda at twenty-four hours' notice – and enjoyed it. Moreover, pardonably identifying the public interest with his
own employment, he convinced himself that the conduct of the war was
at last in capable hands. 'We are bound to win – & in great style too,
having at the last minute applied all our brains & all our wealth to the
problem,' he told the Woolfs over oysters at Richmond on 20 January
1915. But he was uncomfortable when asked why he had allowed *his*
brain to be mobilized. His standard answer was that he worked only for
pleasure – and war work gave him pleasure. Bertrand Russell and
D. H. Lawrence, with whom Maynard dined in Cambridge on 7 March
1915, were not alone in finding this answer an evasion. 'Keynes,'
Russell wrote to Ottoline Morrell, 'was hard, intellectual, insincere,
using his intellect to hide the torment in his soul . . . he spoke as tho' he
only wanted a succession of pleasant moments, which of course is not
really true'. Both Russell and Lawrence attributed Keynes's frivolity
to the 'sterilizing' effect of homosexuality; Lawrence went as far as to
find Keynes 'corrupt and unclean'.[45] Yet there was truth in Keynes's
reply, though it does not entirely reflect credit on him. He had not
begun to think seriously about his own relationship to the war. He was
fascinated by his work – that was justification enough. More disturbing
thoughts he brushed aside with the reflection that the war was bound
to end soon. 'German finance is crumbling,' he told the Woolfs in
January.[46]

Yet depression was never far below the surface of his buoyancy.

JMK to Duncan Grant, 25 April 1915:
   This has been a horrible weekend, and I feel again, although I
thought I would not, as I did after Freddie's death. Yesterday came
news that two of our undergraduates were killed, both of whom I
knew, though not very well, and was fond of. And to-day Rupert's
death. In spite of all one has ever said I find myself crying for him.
It is too horrible, a nightmare to be stopt anyhow. May no other
generation live under the cloud we have to live under.

On 25 June 1915 Békássy was killed in Bukovina.

JMK to Duncan Grant, 24 July 1915:
   I don't believe I have any photograph at all of Feri; but somebody
must have one, I should think, taken at a camp. I have heard from
Noel that she has just got a letter from him written five days before
starting for the front. It seems now an extraordinarily short time ago
that he came rushing back for his sister, and how walking through
Leicester Square after going to the Picture Palace near there on
Sunday night when war was certain, I was very depressed but he

excited and not very depressed ... said 'It will be a very wonderful experience for those of us who live through it'. He was certain to be killed. When one thinks of him it is his *goodness*, I think, one seems to remember. But it's no use talking about him. I think it's better to forget these things as quickly as possible.

The change of government in May 1915 brought Keynes new responsibilities. On 19 May 1915 Asquith formed a coalition with the Conservatives. Two things brought it about. 'The dearth of munitions had become a public scandal. And Lord Fisher [the First Sea Lord], after "anxious reflection", had come to the conclusion that he could no longer continue as the colleague of Churchill at the Admiralty.'[47] In the background was the failure of the Anglo-French spring offensives on the Western Front – beaten back it was alleged because the artillery ran out of shells – and the setback at the Dardanelles. Lloyd George was made the first Minister of Munitions; Reginald McKenna went to the Treasury, 'holding the Exchequer as a seat-warmer for Lloyd George'.[48] Maynard became a member of the Treasury's No. 1 Division, centrally concerned with the financial direction of the war. Early in June he accompanied the new Chancellor to Nice for a day's conference with the Finance Minister of Italy, Britain's newest ally. Crossing the Channel in a battleship and returning in a destroyer filled him with childlike excitement.

No sooner had he started on his new duties than he was obliged to take an enforced rest of almost two months. A couple of days after getting back from Nice he caught what his father called 'a severe internal chill'. Florence came up to London straightaway. On 12 June he underwent an emergency operation for appendicitis at his house. 'It was very necessary,' his father wrote, 'as there was in the appendix a hard formation of the size of a cherrystone and perforation had begun. I did not see much of him, but I was the first person he recognised when he came to after the anaesthetics.' Recovery was quick. By 15 June, Maynard was attending to his correspondence, his mother acting as his secretary. On 17 June Blackett was in to see him. But on 22 June he reported pain. The surgeon, George Gask of Bart's, 'says that this rheumatic sort of pain that Maynard has is not unusual after a septic operation – some of the poison gets into the system.'[49] But a day later he was diagnosed as suffering from pneumonia. The crisis came that night, and by the morning he was on the mend. Florence nursed him at Gower Street, with the help of two nurses. He 'keeps calm and cheerful, but his breathing has been very bad', Neville noted.

It was not till 9 July that Maynard returned to Cambridge, by motorcar, with his parents. On 14 July he was able to dine at King's. A couple of days later he continued his convalescence at Garsington, near Oxford, which Ottoline Morrell had just transformed from a rather run-down Tudor manor house into a lush, perfumed, oasis for her writer and painter friends. 'I was very happy there and got on very well with the inmates of that household,' he told Duncan. 'Ott. tried to get up an affair (with a certain amount of success) between me and Julian [her nine-year-old daughter] by putting up Julian to be pretending to be a boy (unless this was simply natural instinct on Julian's part).' To his mother he wrote that 'this is a most lovely place, but the weather is dreadful'. He added, 'I couldn't say to you all I felt of gratitude and deep affection. It has really been nice, in spite of the circumstances, to spend five weeks together.'[50]*

Ottoline 'liked Keynes immensely' – better than in the very first days of the war, when he had stayed overnight at Bedford Square. Then she saw him as 'that satyr Keynes, greedy for work, fame, influence, domination, admiration', with a manner which, except to a few intimate friends, 'borders on the insolent'. Under the more relaxed conditions at Garsington she started to appreciate 'the atmosphere of his personality – a detached, meditating and yet half-caressing interest in those he is speaking to, head on one side, a kindly yet tolerant smile and very charming eyes wandering, searching and speculating, then probably a frank, intimate, and perhaps laughing home-thrust ...'.[51] In the following months, Maynard frequently made up house-parties at Garsington, mingling with Bloomsbury friends and a sprinkling of Liberal politicians. On this occasion he went on for a weekend with Lord Cunliffe, the Governor of the Bank of England, on the Isle of Wight, before returning to the Treasury at the beginning of August.

---

* Julian Vinogradoff writes: 'The reason I wore [boys' clothes] was Freudian – my father was always complaining that he had no son, so I was trying to fill that need! My mother had nothing to do with it, nor indeed had I any feelings for Maynard, in fact I was rather frightened of him'. Letter to author, 27 October 1983.

13   Keynes and the First World War

I

WHAT KIND OF WAR?

No sooner had Keynes returned to active duty than he found himself involved in a big row between McKenna and Lloyd George about the shape of the British war effort. The Treasury had a well-defined position, which it called 'discrimination'. There were not enough resources to go round. Therefore one had to choose where to put them – raising large armies, producing shells, or producing goods for exports. As Chancellor, Lloyd George had accepted this logic.[1] But a change of office brought a change of view. As Minister of Munitions Lloyd George now expected the Treasury to give him all the money he needed to produce enough shells for a 70-division field army. McKenna, however, inherited Lloyd George's previous programme of 'discrimination' – which he interpreted as discriminating against great armies and munitions in favour of the export trade. The Treasury's argument was simple. The financial structure of the Alliance depended on Britain's being able to export or borrow enough to pay for the Alliance's external spending. So the export industries had to be kept going at all costs; and Britain must maintain its creditworthiness with the United States by not allowing its exchange rate to fall. Lloyd George tended to pooh-pooh such arguments. There were more resources available, he claimed, than the Treasury believed. For example, women could be drawn into war work; and the Americans would always provide credit in their own interest.

In the event, Lloyd George was usually proved right and the Treasury wrong. The Treasury's calculations were all based on what would now be called a 'full employment' assumption. Both internal and external resources available to Britain to fight the war were regarded as 'given'. There was so much productive capacity, so much gold, so many foreign securities. If you tried to do more of one thing, you had to do less of another. This way of looking at things was deeply ingrained in the Treasury's thinking. Government spending was always alternative to something else – usually something more desirable.

In McKenna the Treasury had got a Chancellor after its own heart. Lloyd George and he were temperamentally poles apart. 'A mind that saw everything in pictures clashed with one that saw everything in figures; emotion was brought daily to earth by calculation.'[2] Margot Asquith, a great admirer of McKenna, nevertheless found his mind 'dapper' like his clothes, 'cocky and cocksure to an irritating degree'. Lord Beaverbrook wrote of him: 'He likes to assert his view, and if you run up against some projecting bump in his opinions you must merely nurse a bruise.'[3] He and Lloyd George would have irritated each other at the best of times. Now they were also on opposite sides of the political argument. Lloyd George, together with most Conservative members of the Coalition, was in favour of conscription. McKenna, Grey, Runciman, Crewe, and most of the old Liberals round Asquith opposed it. McKenna, always prone to see plots, suspected Lloyd George of stirring up Northcliffe and the press in favour of conscription. He had good reason. He had opened a letter to Lloyd George, wrongly addressed to the Treasury, discussing a conscriptionist conspiracy.[4] Relations between the two men sharply worsened.

It was in relation to conscription that the economic arguments became politically relevant. That there was nothing so desirable as winning the war was generally agreed. But there was room for much debate about what kind of war Britain should be fighting. The Treasury line gave comfort to all those who believed that Britain should fight a war which interfered as little as possible with 'business as usual'. This was basically the position of the Asquithians. They accepted the war as a necessary evil, but feared its consequences and tried to limit its damage. The weakness in the Asquithian position was Asquith himself. He was against conscription; but favoured the massive British military build-up which made it inevitable. Asquith did not realise this. He and his Secretary of State for War, Lord Kitchener, supported the generals' strategy of massing guns and men for a breakthrough on the Western front in order to avoid conscription, not to promote it. But their policy depended on the generals winning the quick victories which they promised but failed to achieve. Lloyd George did not suffer from this inconsistency. He wanted Britain to fight the total war which would give scope for his organizing and political genius. But his instinctive mistrust of all experts extended to the generals and their promises of military breakthrough in Flanders. He wanted great armies – but to use them elsewhere.

McKenna at the Treasury was clearly in a key position to influence this debate, which meant that Keynes, who soon became his favourite adviser, was drawn into it too. The two men got on excellently. Many years later Keynes recalled the 'immense kindness and true intimacy' he received from McKenna at the Treasury in 1915; his 'confident, optimistic, and yet sceptical mind ... always passionately devoted to the public good'; the weekends he spent at the McKennas' country house at Munstead where Pamela McKenna's 'personal attention to the happiness of her guests raised bodily comfort above itself to become the gentlest of muses'.[5] They came from very much the same background: McKenna, the son of a civil servant, had read mathematics at Cambridge; he was staunch in defence of free trade and civil liberties. Moreover, Keynes's economics and sympathies both inclined him to the Asquithian side. He too, at this stage, was not against the war, but for limiting its effects. He was well placed to appreciate the impact of domestic policy on external finance; and to understand how the external constraint might be used to influence domestic policy. Above all, he was desperately anxious that the state should not interfere with the lives of his friends. All his instincts, therefore, favoured Britain fighting a war of subsidies, not of great armies. This was traditional British policy, and made economic sense. Its morality is questionable. It suggested that British liberals were indifferent to people being killed, provided they were foreigners. Keynes soon realised this, and from 1916 onwards he wanted to end the war by a compromise peace.

These issues crystallised in the last six months of 1915. Initially much of Keynes's work for McKenna was taken up with budgetary problems. The technique of transferring resources to the war effort was not well understood; Keynes himself had to learn on the job. At first the government saw the problem as simply one of raising money to pay for its expenditure, assuming that, by doing so, other people's spending would fall off by the same amount. Instead prices started rising. The reason is obvious in retrospect. The government had been paying off the bad debts of the City, thus putting extra cash into private hands. Relying on a short war it decided not to raise taxes by much. Instead it borrowed the money by the issue of a war loan of £350m in November 1914. However, the loan had been largely taken up by the banks, who simply counted the Treasury bonds as part of their reserves and lent just as much as before to private customers. So private spending had gone up as well as public spending. The trouble was, Keynes minuted on 14 May 1915, that the war loan had failed to diminish private purchasing power by the amount the government was spending on war purchases. 'The public is the only ultimate source of command over the material resources of the country; and direct application to them is the only safe way of securing command over these resources, except for temporary periods for amounts which are not too large.'[6]

In 1915 Keynes was mainly worried about the effects of inflation on the balance of payments, and thus on the sterling–dollar exchange. In a paper entitled 'The Meaning of Inflation' which he wrote on 15 September as part of the preparation for McKenna's first budget, he showed how an increase in the money supply could worsen the balance of payments, via differences in the propensity to consume. If the 'new money' went mainly to the working class, most of it would be spent rather than returned to the government in the form of taxes or loans. 'If they buy more ... our imports are increased and our surplus available for export is diminished.' If they merely pay higher prices for what they previously bought 'there is a concealed tax'. But 'in a country ... which depends on international trade, the influence in the direction of higher prices is in part just as bad as its influence in the direction of increased consumption: for we have to pay higher prices over the whole of our imports and not only over the increase in them ... The effect of inflation, therefore, ... must necessarily be to increase our adverse balance of trade. But foreigners are under no obligation to accept our bank-money in payment. The "promises to pay" materialise into "demands to pay", which cannot be met. When this happens in Brazil, Brazil is said to be bankrupt.'[7]

The moral Keynes drew was unequivocal. Given the desirability of maintaining the existing exchange rate, the government faced the choice either of conscripting wealth on a much greater scale than it had hitherto done, or reducing the rate of increase of its war spending. McKenna decided to pursue both strategies simultaneously. In his budget of 21 September 1915 he increased income tax and imposed an excess profits tax and also the McKenna duties on certain imports. At the same time he started arguing the case for moderating Lloyd George's great gun programme.*

E. V. Morgan writes that from the point of view of the British government 'the dollar exchange was the crux of the problem, for upon the maintenance of an adequate supply of dollars at a reasonable price, depended the whole vast purchasing programme of food, materials and munitions for ourselves and our Allies'.[8] By the spring of 1915 the dollar exchange had turned adverse – that is, American exporters held more claims on sterling than British exporters held claims on dollars. As a result the price of obtaining dollars started to go up. In April 1915 the Bank of England began shipping gold from Ottawa to the British

---

* Looking back after the war, Keynes took a more benign view of wartime inflation, seeing it as a mechanism for reducing working class consumption and thus transferring resources to the war effort. As he told the story in *A Treatise on Money*, ii, 170–6, higher prices led, via a fall in real-wages, to a 'profit inflation'. 'The booty having fallen into the laps of entrepreneurs, the Government would have the choice of taking it from them by loans or by taxation ... in the forms of income-tax, super-tax, and excess-profits tax ... To let prices rise relatively to earnings and then tax entrepreneurs to the utmost is the right procedure for "virtuous" war finance'. He concluded that 'this is very nearly the system which the British Treasury had actually evolved by the method of trial-and-error towards the end of the war'.

government's New York purchasing agent, J. P. Morgan, and buying dollar securities held by British subjects. (In July McKenna saved one desperate situation by commandeering $40m worth of Prudential Assurance's American securities to pay the advance on a munitions contract.) At the same time, Britain put pressure on its Allies to centralise their gold holdings at the Bank of England, in return for British credits. Anglo-French financial diplomacy gave rise to much friction which was to sour Keynes's attitude to the French. The British refused to allow French importers to borrow privately in London, instead advancing the French government official credits. The double object of this was to centralise the management of Allied purchases in London, and to force the French to disgorge gold. The French were convinced that the British were trying to engineer a fall in the franc. Keynes, who emerged as one of the architects of the British policy, had no doubt that the French banking system was corrupt.

These measures could not avert an exchange crisis in August 1915. By 1 September, sterling was selling at a discount of 7 per cent in New York (a pound was fetching $4.47 instead of the official rate of $4.80). To restore the position the Bank shipped more gold to New York; the Treasury also opened its own account at J. P. Morgan, into which it paid the proceeds of sales of dollar securities, collateral and gold. (Remedial measures were hampered by the friction which developed between McKenna and the autocratic Governor of the Bank of England, Lord Cunliffe.) On 20 August 1915 Keynes attended an inter-Ally financial conference at Boulogne, at which it was agreed to seek an American loan, and at which France and Russia agreed to earmark more of their gold for the use of the Bank of England. The dollar exchange was temporarily stabilised at a little below the pre-war parity. But the American loan, negotiated in September by Lord Reading, was disappointing, only £100m being obtained instead of the hoped-for £200m, and of that only £33m was taken up by the American public. It was clear that, outside the New York financial community, and its associated munitions interests, there was little enthusiasm for lending money to the Allies. The route of borrowing direct from the American public was barred.

The crisis in external finance coincided with a crisis in military strategy. With the failure of the Gallipoli expedition to open the road to Constantinople, the French were pressing for a resumption of big offensives on the Western Front. Thus financial and strategic issues became closely interlocked. Was the best policy to commit all Britain's resources recklessly to a gamble on quick military victory or to harness them for a long war? And this issue was bound up with the domestic debate over conscription. The commitment by Britain to an offensive strategy, given the demands of the military, implied conscription; a strategy of attrition gave a chance of avoiding it. Edwin Montagu expressed the Liberal view in a letter he wrote to Asquith on 3 July 1915:

> I cannot understand how the Government is content to go on recruiting and recruiting men of all ages and employments. We must increase our export trade and we can only increase our export trade by the employment of more men than at present, not only on munitions but on their normal avocations.
>
> I am perfectly certain that if we had been content with a smaller Army at the start of the War and refused to enlarge it beyond a certain definite figure, we should have now an Army smaller but better equipped; we should have been able to make munitions for the Russians, which would pay us better, and we should have been more use to our Allies. Let us for Heaven's sake stop now.[9]

On 23 August 1915, McKenna presented his case to a new Committee on War Policy, primed by a memorandum from Keynes. His chief argument was that 'the labour forces of the United Kingdom are so fully engaged in useful occupations that any further diversion of them to military uses is *alternative* and not *additional* to the other means by which the United Kingdom is assisting the Allied cause'. Walter Runciman, the President of the Board of Trade, had estimated that 840,000 men could be spared from civilian occupations; but as he told Margot Asquith, even if it were possible to equip them as soldiers

> there wd be a fiendish outcry – that in none of the [e]xempt industries miners engineers or railway men wd be bought off; that they would stand by their forced fellows & cry out as loud as the rest – That *no* compulsion for foreign service was feasible – that voluntary heroes & conscripts cd not & wd not fight side by side ... and most important of all there wd be strikes all over the country.[10]

This comment shows how remote the anti-conscriptionists were from the national mood. Conscription, like rationing later, was welcomed as providing for 'equality of sacrifice'.

Keynes's memorandum emphasized the economic choice. The 'vital question', he insisted, was 'how far the compulsory depletion of men from the less necessary industries leaves things in other respects as they were'. There would be economic repercussions:

> The labour of these men, since they are employed, satisfies a part of the consuming power of the community. Unless this consuming power is *confiscated*, it will find an outlet elsewhere, either by drawing men from the more necessary industries into the now depleted less necessary, or by increasing civilian demands from the more necessary industries, or by increasing the purchases of imports.

It was not possible to control production, Keynes màintained, without controlling consumption in an equally drastic manner. Hence 'without a policy for the confiscation of private income, a considerably increased army and a continuance of subsidies to allies are *alternative*'.[11] Although the memorandum was careful not to choose between these alternatives, the choice as presented was weighted in such a way as to incline liberal-minded ministers to favour the last. McKenna and Runciman, in fact, argued explicitly for the policy of subsidies.

'The Committee found his arguments ingenious but unconvincing', Lloyd George wrote later about McKenna's presentation; a verdict endorsed by Asquith's biographer Roy Jenkins:

> McKenna presented his argument in too intelligent a way. He was asked whether it meant that, as Chancellor, he could not afford to pay for 70 divisions. Had he returned a firm *ex cathedra* affirmative, both Kitchener and Austen Chamberlain (a strange couple of Gladstonians) might have bowed to the mystique of the Treasury. But when he patiently explained that it was not so much money as the physical allocation of resources, or the 'depletion of industry' as it was then called, which was the trouble, they became mystified and unconvinced.[12]

Although this may well have been true, the over-ingenuity of McKenna's arguments was not the decisive factor in his failure to win over his colleagues. An important decision in favour of the Western strategy had already been taken. On 20 August – three days before McKenna addressed the special Cabinet Committee – Kitchener told the Cabinet he had been forced to agree to the French demand for a renewed autumn offensive. Joffre, the French Commander-in-Chief, was convinced he could win a great victory. For the British the result of the Battle of Loos – which opened on 25 September and was called off a fortnight later, without gaining any ground – was 60,000 casualties; the French lost 150,000.* The generals' response was to plan bigger offensives for 1916. Roy Jenkins writes, 'So long as the Government permitted the generals to engage in frontal attacks on heavily fortified positions, with the frightful losses which were inevitably involved, they left themselves no ultimate alternative to conscription.'[13] This leaves out the fact that a quick military breakthrough in 1915 offered Asquith his best chance of avoiding conscription of both wealth and manpower.

As Zeppelin bombs fell round him in Gower Street, Maynard wrote to his mother (8 September), 'I'm extremely busy at the Treasury, but

---

* On 28 September Kitchener had told Margot Asquith, 'If we push on we can get into Brussels and in any case Lille is certain.'

am enjoying the work. Today I have been commissioned by the Chancellor to write an important memorandum; and, as usual, have only a day to do it.' Keynes's memorandum of 9 September 'The Financial Prospects of this Financial Year', which was circulated to the Cabinet, formed the basis of McKenna's statement to the Cabinet on 13 September 1915 in preparation for his emergency autumn budget. McKenna said he could keep things going till 31 March 1916 with the aid of familiar expedients; but reverted to his argument that, beyond that, Britain must conserve resources to outlast Germany financially. Keynes's note took an extremely gloomy view of the financial prospect. He calculated the deficit for the current year at £700m and growing rapidly. About £500m of this deficiency could be met, he thought, from 'real' resources – the proceeds from taxes and loans, the sale or liquidation of capital assets, and the proceeds of loans from abroad. The balance would have to be met by 'inflationism' – by printing money. 'We ought to be able to do this without producing a catastrophe in the current financial year, provided peace puts us in a position to cancel this inflationism immediately afterwards. Otherwise the expenditure of the succeeding months will rapidly render our difficulties insupportable.' The reason was that inflation would bring about a collapse of the exchange and with it the ability to pay for imports from the U.S.A. Keynes concluded:

> The alternatives presented to us are, therefore, alternatives of degree. If by flinging out our resources lavishly we could be sure of finishing the war early next spring, I estimate that they might be about equal to our needs. If, on the other hand, it would be oversanguine to anticipate this, it must be considered whether it is more desirable to average our expenditure, or, alternatively, to be lavish until about next January, ... and then, having regard to the near future, to curtail rigorously and tell our Allies that for the future they must look to themselves.
> It is certain that our present scale of expenditure is only possible as a violent spurt to be followed by a strong reaction, that the limitations of our resources are in sight; and that, in the case of any expenditure, we must consider not only, as heretofore, whether it would be useful, but also whether we can afford it.[14]

According to one commentator, 'McKenna's report and Keynes's memorandum marked the emergence of the Chancellor and his brilliant young aide as the Laocoon and Cassandra of the British Government.'[15] Keynes's alarmist assessment infuriated Lloyd George. In his *War Memoirs* he wrote that

> Mr. McKenna's nerve was shaken by these vaticinations of his chief adviser Mr. J. M. Keynes. The latter was much too mercurial and

impulsive a counsellor for a great emergency. He dashed at conclusions with acrobatic ease. It made things no better that he rushed
into opposite conclusions with the same agility ... When the hour of
impending doom struck and we still bought greater quantities than
ever of food, raw material and munitions from abroad and were
paying for them and our credit was still high, the date of the impending collapse was postponed until the autumn.[16]

Such derision was easy in the light of later events. Keynes was making
an intelligent inference on the basis of the evidence available: he was
not banking on 'something turning up'. In particular, President Wilson's 'too proud to fight' speech after the sinking of the *Lusitania* gave
little assurance of America's eventual entry into the war, which finally
solved the financial problems that Lloyd George dismissed as irrelevant.

A more interesting point is that the McKenna–Keynes line was
counter-productive in terms of its avowed objective. What these
Liberals were aiming for was a greater emphasis on subsidy and less on
fighting, in an effort to avoid military conscription. Yet their very
financial pessimism encouraged Asquith to gamble on a quick military
victory as a way of evading his growing political dilemmas. Thus,
paradoxically, they encouraged commitment to the Western strategy
which, in the long-run, required conscription.

On 17 September 1915 Keynes wrote to his father:

I doubt if I've ever worked harder than during the last two weeks;
but I'm wonderfully well all the same. The work has been as interesting as it could be. I've written three major memoranda, one of which
has been circulated to the Cabinet, and about a dozen minor ones on
all kinds of subjects, as well as helping Ramsay [at the Treasury]
with the vote of Credit and the Budget, and keeping going with
routine, and the Ec. J. in the evenings. I spent most of Wednesday
in the H. of C. at the Vote of Credit debate. The P. M. was splendid.

This was one of the most hectic periods of Keynes's life. 'I'm desperately busy as the brunt of the Russian negotiations has fallen on me.
I had to do 12¾ hours at a stretch yesterday', he informed Florence on
30 September. (In the agreement between the two governments, signed
that day, McKenna agreed to extend monthly credits to the Russians
in exchange for the loan of Russian gold and control of Russian purchases, something Keynes had been pushing.) On 13 October 1915,
Balfour, the leading Tory anti-conscriptionist, summoned him for a
briefing on the Treasury objections to conscription. A couple of days
later he had to write a memorandum, for circulation to the Cabinet, on
details of Britain's subsidies to its allies. To his father he wrote on 15
October that he was 'exceedingly done up ... it was a combination of

work and excitement . . . I've been moving in very high life most of the week . . . and I am spending the weekend with the Prime Minister'.

In her diary for Saturday, 16 October, Margot Asquith wrote that she and a 'Treasury man Keynes' had won nine pounds at bridge off Lady de Trafford and Edwin Montagu. This weekend was the start of Maynard's friendship with the Asquiths. The Prime Minister liked to spend the weekends away from London at his country house, The Wharf, in Sutton Courtenay, Berkshire, relaxing with friends over a game of bridge. He and his daughter Violet would sometimes motor over for Sunday lunch to Ottoline's at Garsington, where the mandarin liberalism of Balliol College, Oxford, mingled warily with the subversive culture of Apostolic Cambridge. Maynard was not a great bridge player; but he was better than Margot, who played with ardent incompetence; and he won large sums of money at The Wharf and at No. 10 Downing Street, despite the distracting attentions of Margot's flirtatious stepdaughter, Elizabeth Asquith (later Princess Bibesco). Margot, whose insomniac nights were spent in writing acute character sketches of her prominent friends, left none of Maynard. Was he still too junior to engage the full attention of a prime minister's wife? By the time he became a great man, Margot Asquith's diary had stopped.

The coalition government was being driven steadily to military conscription, despite Asquith's apparent conviction that it would mean revolution. In a last effort to preserve the voluntary system, Lord Derby was made director-general of recruiting in October 1915, with the promise that if his recruiting campaign failed, the government would introduce compulsion. (Derby's brief was to get single men between 18 and 41 to 'attest' their readiness to serve if called upon to do so.) By this time the early enthusiasm for volunteering had disappeared: half the eligible bachelors failed to attest, including Maynard. He was still predicting financial collapse, if not in April, by October of the following year.[17] November saw him engaged in long negotiations with the Italians: they agreed to limited British controls over their external spending, and to ship gold in return for a British credit. On 8 November, as if his war work were not enough, he gave the first of six public lectures at University College, London, on the war finance of the Central Powers. On 10 December he wrote to Florence:

> It has been a very hard week – breakfast to bedtime every day except Monday when I stopt at 8 p.m. Ordinary work was held back by one of those awful battles over a big wheat contract which lasted a day and a half and which wear one out more than anything. I finally also got rid of the Dec. Journal this evening. I am on a new . . . War Office Com[ee] for looking after the remnant of the Serbian Army in Albania. It's very interesting as it brings me for the first time into direct touch with military affairs.

In December 1915 the strain on external finance was temporarily relieved by a shortage of freight. As a result, France and Italy could not spend their permissible drawings on the British account – chiefly for the purchase of Canadian wheat – because they could not obtain the shipping. From the financial point of view this was satisfactory. 'But,' Keynes wrote on 18 December 1915, in a note circulated to the Cabinet over McKenna's initials, 'it is exactly the same sort of relief which our blockade of Germany affords to Dr. Helfferich [the German Secretary of the Treasury].' He used the freight shortage to draw attention once more to the problem of resource allocation:

> To carry overseas each new division of an expeditionary force is *alternative* to carrying food, munitions or other necessary commodities to the allies or to ourselves. We have to decide not merely that one more division would be useful, but that it would be so useful that it is worth while to incur a deficiency in one of these other directions.[18]

However, such arguments made no impression on the course of events. Asquith agreed with them;[19] but he would not go against the advice of the generals, and by the end of 1915 the Army was firmly in the hands of the 'Westerners'. Both Haig, the new Commander-in-Chief, and Robertson, the new C.I.G.S., were 'unswerving in their belief that the war could only be won by killing Germans in Flanders. And they were both prepared to accept without flinching the British share of the casualties which this must involve.' On 28 December the War Cabinet approved of Robertson's plan for a vast new Allied offensive in the spring of 1916. 'In these circumstances,' writes Mr Jenkins, 'the job of the politicians ceased to be that of looking for strategic alternatives and became concentrated upon supplying men and munitions for the slaughter.'[20] The same day, 28 December 1915, the Cabinet accepted the principle of military conscription. On 27 January 1916 the Military Service Act, providing for the enlistment of all single men between the ages of eighteen and forty-one, received the Royal Assent. The question of what kind of war Britain should fight had been settled.

II

CONSCIENTIOUS OBJECTION TO CONSCRIPTION?

Under the Military Service Act all bachelors and childless widowers between eighteen and forty-one were 'deemed ... to have been duly enlisted'. Certificates of exemption could be granted by government departments to those of their officials who were doing work of 'national importance'. Others could apply for exemption to local tribunals on grounds of (a) the national importance of their work, (b) hardship, (c) ill-health, and (d) 'a conscientious objection to the undertaking of combatant service'. A tribunal could either reject such an application outright or give an exemption on one of the four grounds. An exemption could be absolute, conditional or temporary. A conscientious objector could be given an exemption outright or 'from combatant service only or may be given [it] on condition that [he] is or will be engaged on some work which in the opinion of the Tribunal is of national importance'. The act provided an appeals procedure from the decisions of the local tribunal.

In his biography of Keynes, Roy Harrod wrote (p. 213); 'It has to be recorded that many of Keynes's most intimate friends of the Bloomsbury circle were Conscientious Objectors'. He went on (p. 214):

> Keynes himself did not share their view. But it inevitably had an important influence on him ... They pressed him in argument, and, to meet their case, he made two gestures of appeasement. Of these, the first was a trivial one, which need not be taken very seriously. He announced for their benefit that, although he was not a Conscientious Objector, he would conscientiously object to compulsory service. Accordingly, when he received his calling-up notice, he replied on Treasury writing-paper that he was too busy to attend the summons. This appears to have quelled the authorities, for he was troubled by them no more.

His second method, Harrod records (p.215), was 'a far more serious matter'. While arguing that 'we must go through' with the war, he pledged to do his best to 'establish world affairs on a new and better basis, so that this shall not happen again'. This 'implicit pledge' contributed to the 'passion and venom' with which he penned *The Economic Consequences of the Peace*.

In 1957, Clive Bell published a volume of personal reminiscences called *Old Friends*. It contained a – partly unflattering – portrait of Keynes whom, he admitted, he did not 'love'. In the course of it, Clive Bell wrote:

> It seems not generally to be known ... that ... Keynes was a conscientious objector ... To be sure he was an objector of a peculiar and, as I think, most reasonable kind. He was not a pacifist; he did not object to fighting in any circumstances; he objected to being made to fight. Good liberal that he was, he objected to conscription. He would not fight because Lloyd George, Horatio Bottomley and Lord Northcliffe told him to ... As for his conscientious objection, he was duly summoned to a tribunal and sent word that he was much too busy to attend.[21]

After reading *Old Friends* Harrod wrote to Bell on 13 January 1957 that he intended to take him up on a couple of points, one of which was 'about conscientious objection. I cannot agree with even the very modified version you give of it.' Harrod was clearly worried by the suggestion that he had misrepresented Keynes's attitude to conscription.[22]

Harrod dealt with Clive Bell's assertion in a note published in the *Economic Journal* in December 1957. He wrote:

> I submit that there was not any sense, peculiar or other, in which Keynes was a Conscientious Objector in the First World War ... He held that it was the duty of Britain to intervene in 1914; that granted, there was nothing more to be said about 'objection'. I submit that, had Keynes not been doing work of supreme national importance, and had he been physically capable of being an efficient soldier, he would have answered the call when it came to him.

As for Keynes's being summoned to appear before a tribunal, 'the explanation is really quite simple. When he received the tiresome calling-up paper he was doubtless irritated and answered as Mr. Bell described. And then having done that, he made the most of it with his Bloomsbury friends. Surely a harmless ruse!'

Both in this riposte, and in his book, Harrod omitted to say, or register, that Keynes's letter saying he was 'too busy to attend' was sent not in reply to his 'calling-up notice' but in reply to a summons to appear before a local tribunal – that is, that he must have written a previous letter applying for exemption.

The contents of this letter were revealed by Elizabeth Johnson in a rejoinder to Harrod published in the *Economic Journal* of March 1960. Mrs Johnson had been working on Keynes's economic papers as the first editor of his *Collected Writings*. She had discovered 'a small file among his papers which contains the documents concerning both his exemption and his application to the Holborn Local Tribunal'. It starts with a standard letter from Sir Thomas Heath, joint Permanent Secretary to the Treasury, dated 23 February 1916, enclosing a certificate of that date exempting Keynes from combatant service 'on the ground that you are engaged on work of national importance'. This was all that Keynes required to exempt him from call-up. Nevertheless, he took the further step of writing out an application for exemption on grounds of conscientious objection. A draft of this letter exists, written on King's College writing paper, dated 28 February 1916. It is addressed to 'The Tribunal', and signed 'J. M. Keynes'.

> I claim complete exemption because I have a conscientious objection to surrendering my liberty of judgment on so vital a question as

undertaking military service. I do not say that there are not conceivable circumstances in which I should voluntarily offer myself for military service. But after having regard to all the actually existing circumstances, I am certain that it is not my duty so to offer myself, and I solemnly assert to the Tribunal that my objection to submit to authority in this matter is truly conscientious. I am not prepared on such an issue as this to surrender my right of decision, as to what is or is not my duty, to any other person, and I should think it morally wrong to do so.

Mrs Johnson suggested that this letter shows that Keynes objected to conscription on the classical liberal ground that the state had no right to compel its citizens to fight. However, this, I think, is a misinterpretation. It is quite out of character for Keynes to take a stand on abstract right. He was too much of a political utilitarian to deny that government had the right to do anything which would increase the social advantage. His objection to being conscripted was more concrete and more personal. He did not consider that he should volunteer for military service in the existing circumstances; it was his right to resist the state's attempt to make him to do something contrary to his convictions. Although Keynes's language is not ideally clear, the letter sought to draw attention to a conflict of rights rather than to deny that the state had any rights in the matter. Otherwise, what was the point of dragging in his own attitude to volunteering, which was, strictly speaking, irrelevant to the question of the state's right to conscript?

If we adopt this interpretation, the question of why he objected to volunteering for military service becomes relevant. He makes it clear that it was not for pacifist reasons. We must also assume that he was not making the trivial point that he could serve the nation better where he was. This was, after all, up to his superiors to decide, and they had already done so by exempting him from military service. The supposition must be, I think, that he was making a political point about the war. Keynes's attitude to the war has to be taken in conjunction with that of his Bloomsbury friends. By the beginning of 1916 most of them had come to believe that it should be ended as quickly as possible by negotiations leading to a compromise peace. They rejected, in other words, the official war aim of a fight to the finish. This was the political root of their resistance to being conscripted; and it was Keynes's also. He objected to being drafted for a war whose continuation he believed to be wrong.

The evidence that Keynes did think the war was futile cannot be neatly summarised in one quotation. But there is certainly plenty of it, as we shall see. Moreover, his arguments with his Bloomsbury friends early in 1916 make sense only on this hypothesis. For the question they asked him was how could he justify remaining at the Treasury if he agreed with them that the war was immoral. He could never give an answer which satisfied them.

Elizabeth Johnson points out that there is no absolute certainty that Keynes sent 'precisely this statement' to the Holborn Tribunal. But from the fact that he was summoned to appear before the Tribunal it is clear that he must have made an application to do so. A postcard, postmarked 23 March 1916, and addressed to him at 3 Gower Street, from the Clerk to the Holborn Local Tribunal, notified him that his case would be considered on 28 March 1916. Keynes wrote from the Treasury on 27 March 1916 that he was too busy to attend this hearing. On 29 March 1916 the Clerk of the Holborn Local Tribunal sent him a letter, addressed to Treasury Chambers, informing him that his application for exemption had been dismissed because 'you have already been exempted for six months by the Treasury'. He could, however, apply for further exemption after six months. In fact, the Treasury renewed his exemption, without time limit, on 18 August 1916, and he never renewed his application to the Tribunal.

Harrod's reply appeared as 'A Comment' in the same issue of the *Economic Journal*.

Gratitude is due to Mrs. Johnson [he wrote] for her diligent research. She has convicted me of two or three inaccuracies in my text, and more important, of not sufficiently bringing out the passionate fervour of Keynes's objection to conscription. Evidence for this is supplied, *inter alia*, by his draft statement for the Local Tribunal. Whether I missed this, when going through his mountainous files, or saw it, but gave it insufficient weight, I cannot now be sure.

Harrod promised to 'rectify these matters' in any new impression of his book.* However, he refused to budge from his main position that Keynes could not be considered a 'Conscientious Objector to Conscription'. His failure to appear before the Tribunal, Harrod argued, only made sense on the assumption that he had withdrawn his 'conscientious objection'.

What is one to make of all this? No one will deny that there were inconsistencies in Keynes's attitude to the war, rooted in inconsistencies – very human ones – in his own character. The pleasure which his war work gave him, his delight at being at the centre of things, only gradually gave way to the conviction that, as he put it to Duncan Grant in December 1917, 'I work for a government I despise for ends I think criminal.' But what cannot be sustained is Harrod's interpretation of Keynes's conduct, either as regards the conscription issue, or the war

* A Penguin edition was published in 1972, six years before Harrod died, in which nothing was altered.

itself. He not only omits the great battle of 1915 between McKenna and Lloyd George, including Keynes's crucial memorandum of 9 September 1915 which so enraged the latter, but writes of this period (p.206): '[Keynes's] work was extremely exacting. It does not seem to have given rise to major political or inter-departmental crises. All went forward smoothly. It is a happy nation that has no history.' Harrod must have known from Lloyd George's *Memoirs* – if from no other source – that this was not true. On the conscription issue itself, it is not credible that he 'missed' Keynes's draft letter of 28 February 1916 to the Holborn Tribunal. And surely he must have known that Keynes could only have been 'summoned' had he lodged an objection. One gets the distinct impression that Harrod knew the facts but was covering them up. His motives can only be guessed at. My own view is that he thought Keynes's conscientious objection was dishonourable, and tried to cover up the traces.*

Elizabeth Johnson's publication of the true facts left one important question unanswered. Why did Keynes not appear at his own exemption hearing on 28 March? Harrod's suggestion that Keynes had withdrawn his 'conscientious objection' is clearly untrue. He did not withdraw his application, as he might have done. The case was heard and dismissed. But equally one cannot accept at face value Keynes's explanation to the Tribunal that he was 'too busy' to attend, since he could easily have got the hearing changed by pleading Treasury business. Mrs Johnson assumes that Keynes's application was a symbolic gesture only: therefore there was no point in turning up. But there is another possibility: that it was intended for use. Since, when he made it, Keynes had already been exempted by the Treasury, this must mean that on 28 February 1916 he was thinking of *resigning* from the Treasury. On this hypothesis his non-appearance at the Tribunal a month later can be explained by the fact that he no longer intended to resign, and was therefore no longer bothered about the verdict.

How close did Keynes come to resignation in January–February 1916? Michael Holroyd takes the view that there was 'no chance of

---

* Harrod was successful, however, in planting a false trail which has been followed by many other writers, though he was not the first in the field. E. A. G. Robinson's long obituary notice, first published in the *Economic Journal* of March 1947, and since reprinted unchanged many times, gives no hint of ambiguity in Keynes's attitude to the war. Robert Lekachman, *The Age of Keynes: A Biographical Study* (1966) reproduces the original Robinson–Harrod version; as does Michael Stewart in his chapter on 'Keynes the Man' in his Pelican Original, *Keynes and After* (1967). Michael Holroyd is also misled by Harrod in his *Lytton Strachey*, ii 172 (1968). Paul Levy is misled by Harrod into remarking that 'Keynes did not apply for exemption at all' (in Milo Keynes (ed.), *Essays on John Maynard Keynes* (1975) p.69). D. E. Moggridge, *Keynes* (1976), pp.18–19, is the first biographer to have broken free from the Harrod version.

resignation'.[23] However, there is important contrary evidence which needs to be set out to give a picture of his state of mind in the circumstances in which he found himself.

Conscription cast its shadow before it. From the autumn of 1915 Keynes's involvement in the war effort came under increasing criticism from his friends, some of whom were beginning to suffer. In October 1915, Duncan Grant and David Garnett had left for Paris, where Duncan had been commissioned to design costumes for a play. At Folkestone, Duncan was abused by an English officer for being a pacifist; and, on arrival in France, refused admittance; and deported as an undesirable alien. Keynes succeeded in getting the officer reprimanded; but Bunny, who had been allowed to proceed to Paris, wrote him an angry letter on 15 November 1915:

What are you? Only an intelligence that they need in their extremity ... A genie taken incautiously out of King's ... by savages to serve them faithfully for their savage ends, and then – back you go into the bottle. Probably you won't make any difficulty about that – you probably long to be back in it – but don't be too good-natured. Don't believe the savages are anything but savages. Oh there are a sprinkling of genii with whom you work – and our savages are better than other savages – but never believe in these savages with their human sacrifices.

You pull the strings and the idol Juggernaut opens its mouth & shuts its eyes ... But don't believe in the profane abomination.[24]

David Garnett felt ashamed of this letter, but to his surprise Maynard 'agreed that there was a great deal of truth in what I had said'.[25]

Throughout January 1916, Keynes's attitude fluctuated. On 6 January he told his father he wanted to resign. On 13 January he wrote to Florence that he would stay on 'until they actually begin to torture my friends'. A real split, he thought, would 'bring peace nearer'. On 16 January Neville reported Maynard taking an 'extreme view' on conscription. On 28 January Florence reported that he was still 'thoroughly interested' in his work. Most indicative is his outburst to Ottoline Morrell on 4 January: ' "I wish the press-gang or the drum/With its tantara sound would come" and deal with all these bloody men who enrage and humiliate us. I still think that not quite all is lost, and the strength of true feeling left in England is being underestimated. But we are entirely in the hands of the working classes . . . Oh for a general strike and a real uprising to teach them.'

These excerpts have to be set in context. On 29 December, five of

Asquith's ministers – Simon, McKenna, Runciman, Grey and Augustine Birrell – submitted their resignations. Asquith gave the background in a letter he wrote to Edwin Montagu the previous day:

> The ground they [McKenna and Runciman] put forward is not the actual decision of the Cabinet: indeed they both say they will not oppose the proposed Bill. The ground is that the reasons given for the decision involved the raising of men for 67 Divisions, and that in their view such men are not forthcoming, without fatal injury to our other resources & obligations. I told them that no such conclusion was implied in to-day's decision: that on the contrary A. J. B. & Grey and I had expressly reserved all such questions. I made no impression on them, & I am afraid that this is the climax of 6 months of discontent & protest on their part. Can you and Rufus [Isaacs, later Lord Reading] do anything with them to-day?[26]

This letter indicates the kind of compromise Asquith was offering. In selling it to the dissident ministers he was helped by Sir Maurice Hankey, secretary of the War Committee, and by Montagu, who had switched to the line that would later enable him to serve under Lloyd George: on 30 December Montagu urged Grey to stay in the Cabinet and 'make the best of it rather than help the Germans'.[27] Asquith proposed to set up a Cabinet Committee to 'investigate, over a period of a month, the competing military and economic claims'.[28] This satisfied McKenna and Runciman, who decided to carry their fight to the Committee. Without them Birrell would not go. Grey was sharply reminded by the Prime Minister that it was he who had got Britain into the war in the first place. As a result, the government got through the first reading of the Military Service Bill of 6 January 1916 with only Sir John Simon's resignation.

What would Keynes have done had McKenna and Runciman gone? There is important evidence on this point. On 31 December 1915 Lytton Strachey wrote to Ottoline Morrell:

> I went to see [Bertrand Russell] this morning and we had lunch with Maynard in an extraordinary underground tunnel, with city gents sitting on high stools like parrots on perches, somewhere near Trafalgar Square. Maynard . . . couldn't tell us much – except that McKenna is still wobbling; but he seemed to think it not unlikely that he and Runciman would resign – in which case he would resign too, and help them fight it.[29]

When McKenna decided to stay, Maynard stayed on to help his chief fight for the Treasury position. The Treasury section of the Committee's report was drafted by Keynes in late January – this was when

Florence reports that he was 'still thoroughly interested in his work'. The key argument was that the Chancellor attached decisive importance to the maintenance of specie payments, and that this was inconsistent with the policy of 'raising great armies'. The Committee's report was signed by Asquith, Austen Chamberlain and McKenna on 4 February 1916. It concluded that the risks of maintaining a 62-division army in the field could be contemplated for a short period, but only with the help of underspending by the Allies. It was, in effect, a gamble on a quick victory. Throughout January McKenna hovered on the brink of resignation. But eventually he signed the report on 4 February.* So why should Keynes have still been contemplating resignation on 28 February? Here we must introduce another factor: the pressure on him to do so by his Bloomsbury friends, and particularly by Lytton Strachey, which reached its maximum shortly before Keynes sent off his letter to the Tribunal.

Applications for exemption had to be in by 2 March. Practically all the male members of Bloomsbury decided to claim exemption as conscientious objectors. It is too sweeping to call them all pacifists. Gerald Shove was. But in the early days of the war it would have been hard to find any member of Bloomsbury who would not have been prepared to fight – in principle. It was the progress of the war itself that changed attitudes. By 1916 no one in Bloomsbury believed any longer that the objects and possibilities of the war justified the sacrifices being demanded in its name – sacrifices of lives and liberties. Maynard shared the political and ethical positions taken up by his friends. He had come to the conclusion that it was wrong to continue the war. He wanted a 'peace without victory'. He knew this was the view of some members of the Cabinet, notably Lord Lansdowne. He would have preferred them to resign and lead a campaign for the opening of peace negotiations.

But, as Paul Levy rightly points out,[30] the very fact that this was his position demanded some sort of response from him. How could he justify his own war work if he disagreed with the objects and methods of the war? Keynes could hardly have replied that it was his 'duty' since, as he wrote in 1938, 'we entirely repudiated a personal liability on us to obey general rules'. He had promised to resign if McKenna did; but what, in the end, did McKenna's conscience have to do with his? 'Certainly', writes Michael Holroyd, 'both Lytton and Russell felt

---

* On 23 January 1916 Runciman wrote to McKenna that the War Office's undertakings were 'worthless'. He went on, 'What guarantee is given or can be given that in July we are not once more manoeuvred into the replenishing of the 70 divisions. . . . It must be 54 or 57 [divisions] now – *or we have failed*'. The 'guarantee was the generals' promise of a victory in the spring offensive. (McKenna Papers 5/9)

he had "ratted", and, individually, they both pressed him to quit the Treasury, reasoning that it must be impossible to reconcile his avowed sympathy for conscientious objectors with the job of demonstrating how to kill Germans as cheaply as possible'.[31] The climax of this pressure came on 20 February 1916, when Lytton Strachey 'put the conscientious objector's equivalent to the white feather on Keynes's dinner plate'.[32] Strachey had cut out a newspaper report of a vehement-ly militaristic speech by Edwin Montagu* ('it had every horror – not only protection but the necessity for smashing Germany etc' he repor-ted to his brother James) and enclosed it with a single-line letter to Keynes: 'Dear Maynard, Why are you still in the Treasury? yours, Lytton.' Strachey's letter goes on:

> I was going to post it to him, but he happened to be dining at Gordon Square where I also was. So I put the letter on his plate. He really *was* rather put out when he read the extract ... He said that 2 days before he had a long conversation with Montague [*sic*] in which that personage had talked violently in exactly the opposite way. He said the explanation was cowardice. I said that if their cowardice went as far as that there was no hope. And what was the use of his going on imagining that he was doing any good with such people? I went on for a long time with considerable virulence, Nessa, Duncan and Bunny sitting round in approving silence ... The poor fellow seemed very decent about it, and admitted that *part* of his reason for staying was the pleasure he got from his being able to do the work so well. He also seemed to think he was doing a great service to the country by saving some millions per week ... He at last admitted that there *was* a point at which he *would* think it necessary to leave – but what that point was he couldn't say.[33]

The next day Keynes sent off a cheque for £50 to the National Council against Conscription. He got the Treasury six-month cer-tificate of exemption on 23 February. Five days later he applied for exemption on the grounds of conscientious objection to meet the 2 March deadline. Was it a gesture of appeasement or a contingency plan? The most probable answer is that he was keeping his options open. He had not decided to resign, but he might. He had indicated to his mother the circumstances in which he would: if they started 'tortur-ing my friends'. No one knew yet how the appeal system would work out in practice. The general expectation in Bloomsbury was that many of them would go to prison. If Maynard resigned, he would refuse to

---

* Edwin Montagu, the politician, not C. E. Montague 'the liberal journalist who had dyed his hair grey', as Paul Levy says.

volunteer or be drafted. His position would then be exactly the same as that of his Bloomsbury friends.*

If Keynes was wobbling in the last week in February, by 28 March, the day fixed for the Tribunal's hearing, he had clearly decided to stay put. Several factors influenced him. We must remember that throughout this period he was under great pressure from his parents not to 'throw everything up'. There were claims of affection here as strong as those which bound him to his friends. A second factor was that Keynes really hoped the war might soon be coming to an end. In January and February 1916, President Wilson's special envoy, Colonel House, had been on a tour of belligerent capitals urging a peace conference. On 6 March 1916, the British and American governments reached an understanding that when 'the moment was opportune' the European Allies would invite Wilson to summon a peace conference.[34] Keynes would undoubtedly have heard of this agreement from his Cabinet contacts. He felt that the opportune moment could not be long delayed. Money was running out fast – he had fixed 31 March 1916 for the end of the world, though this had been postponed by a few months. He was probably the author (under the pseudonym 'Politicus') of an article in the April number of Gerald Shove's pacifist monthly *Face the Facts* which said that the stalemate on the Western Front was 'speedily making the case for immediate negotiations unanswerable'. He expressed similar views in an address to the Admiralty on 15 March. There was no point in resigning if peace was coming soon anyway.†
Once more he found himself caught up in the giddy social whirl which so enhanced the pleasures of Whitehall existence:

This weekend [he wrote to Florence on 26 March] I am staying with Lady Jekyll, the other guests being Mr and Mrs McKenna and Mr

* In clearing up one set of confusions, Elizabeth Johnson unfortunately introduced another (*CW*, xvi, p. 157). Discussing Keynes's state of mind in this period she says his attitude was nearer that of Sir John Simon than to that of his 'pacifist' Bloomsbury friends. But his friends were not pacifist. They objected to being conscripted because they would not have volunteered under the circumstances; and they would not have volunteered because they no longer approved of the war. This was exactly Keynes's position. Sir John Simon resigned from the government and then *volunteered for military service*, serving as a major in the RAF. Moggridge (in his *Keynes*, pp. 17–18) follows Elizabeth Johnson. In fairness to Mrs Johnson, Sir Roy Harrod once more appears to be the source of confusion (*Economic Journal*, March 1960).
† Wilson's peace initiatives were invariably mistimed. Both now and a year later they came *after* the generals on both sides had made their plans for the next round of offensives designed to bring them victory, instead of immediately after the *failure* of those offensives, when they might have done more good. It seems incredible that Wilson did not realise this. Nothing more was heard of the plan to call a peace conference. Keynes's disenchantment with the President's diplomacy, one suspects, dates from long before he personally experienced it at Versailles in 1919.

and Mrs Runciman ... Last weekend I went to Ottoline's at Garsington. Sir John Simon came to tea on Sunday – I wish he wasn't such a desperately dull man. I've dined twice at Downing Street in the last fortnight ... Lord and Lady Waldstein asked me to dine to meet the American Ambassador. I dined with Violet Asquith and her new husband [Maurice Bonham-Carter] in her new house, her first party in honour of Margot; I have delivered my evening lecture at the Admiralty; and I have testified before the wicked leering faces of the Hampstead Tribunal to the genuineness of James's conscientious objections. Oh, and I've brought out the March E. J. and entertained a Swedish Professor [Knut Wicksell].

In his reply to Elizabeth Johnson in the *Economic Journal* of March 1960 Harrod suggested that Keynes had given up his 'conscientious objection' because he realised that his friends were not going to be tortured. The opposite seems nearer the truth: Keynes had come to realise that he might use his official position to *save* his friends from imprisonment.[35]

Naturally enough the case that concerned him most was Duncan's. Early in 1916 he advised him and David Garnett that it would strengthen their claim for exemption on conscientious grounds if they were seen to be engaged on 'work of national importance' before their cases came up. A cousin of Duncan's had recently died, leaving a neglected house and orchard in Wissett, a village in Suffolk, where Duncan and Bunny set up as fruit farmers, Vanessa looking after them. From Wissett, Duncan Grant wrote to his father, Major Bartle Grant, trying to explain why he was a conscientious objector:

I never considered the possibility of a great European war. It seemed such an absolutely mad thing for a civilised people to do. I had become I suppose in a sense unpatriotic, as most artists must do. I began to see that one's enemies were not vague masses of foreign people, but the mass of people in one's own country and the mass of people in the enemy country, and that one's friends were people of true ideas that one might and did meet in every country one visited. I still think this and I still think the war utter madness and folly.[36]

Duncan's and Bunny's applications were heard on 4 May before the local tribunal at Blymouth, Maynard coming up to give evidence on their behalf. Adrian Stephen presented their case very badly, 'as though he was addressing a Judge in Chancery'. The chairman, thinking Tolstoy was a town in Russia, was unimpressed when told that Garnett's mother Constance, a lifelong pacifist, had visited the pacifist sage there.[37] They were refused exemption. Later that month their appeal was heard at Ipswich. By this time Maynard had taken charge, arriving for the hearing full of Treasury briskness. 'Carrying a large locked bag with a Royal cipher on it, he demanded that our cases should be heard as expeditiously as possible, as he had left work of utmost national importance to attend.'[38] This time they were awarded non-combatant service (that is, in the army, but not fighting) against which Maynard immediately appealed. In mid-July 1916, both Duncan and Bunny were exempted from military service on condition that they did work of 'national importance'; but their existing work at Wissett did not qualify because they were self-employed. On 11 August Maynard put the case for their being allowed to stay on at Wissett before the Central Tribunal. But by this time they had already decided to seek employment elsewhere.

This was only one of a number of cases in which he was involved that summer. He appeared in June on behalf of Gerald Shove; he helped the appeal of an undergraduate from Pembroke; he got McKenna to write a letter on behalf of the novelist Gilbert Cannan. On 18 June 1916 he wrote to Dennis Robertson: 'The Tribunal crisis is getting over now as concessions to the C.O.s are impending. But it has been a foul business, and I spend half of my time on the boring business of testifying to the sincerity, virtue and truthfulness of my friends.' In this activity he was able to find a moral justification for staying on at the Treasury.

14 Touch and Go

The pattern of Maynard's wartime life was now established. He spent his days working at the Treasury. The evenings he would spend with others – either with the great and the good or with such friends as remained in London. He took as many week-ends as he could in the country or with his parents at Cambridge. A noticeable change came over his social life. Put bluntly, the supply of young men had dried up. Cambridge was no longer available to replenish his friendships; existing friends were at the Front or scattered round the countryside doing agricultural work.

For the first time in his life Maynard had to console himself with female companions. Women, too, felt a dearth of eligible men. A group of them, known as the 'Cropheads' or 'Bunnies' because they wore their hair short, attached themselves to the Bloomsbury men. They included three ex-Slade students, Dorothy Brett, Dora Carrington, and Barbara Hiles, and the Newnham graduates Fredegond Maitland, Faith Bagenal, and Alix Sargant-Florence. It was the war, in fact, which enabled Bloomsbury to catch up with heterosexuality. The 'buggers' belatedly discovered the joys of domesticity. Adrian Stephen had led the way by marrying Karin Costelloe; now Gerald Shove confessed that he wanted, above all, to be looked after – in 1915 he married Fredegond Maitland, a niece of Virginia Woolf. James Strachey capitulated in 1920, after a long siege, to Alix Sargant-Florence. With Bunny Garnett away in France for much of 1915, Duncan and Vanessa became lovers. Most amazing of all in 1916 Lytton Strachey found himself – in Clive Bell's words – 'distinctly épris of [Dora] Carrington ... he discovered suddenly that he was profoundly moved by her legs. I suppose he will soon discover that she has an amazing soul'.[1] In December 1917 he settled down with her at the Mill House, Tidmarsh, near Pangbourne, Maynard contributing twenty pounds a year to the rent.

Maynard himself was attracted to Barbara Hiles, a vivacious, doll-like creature, with red cheeks, blue eyes, and curly hair. But there was, as yet, no question of his 'settling down', unlike his brother Geoffrey who married Margaret Darwin in 1917. His life was much fuller, more exciting, than that of his Bloomsbury friends. On his Treasury income (now £700 a year) he could run a bachelor establishment. And 'home life' was provided by his parents at Cambridge, as well as by Vanessa, Duncan and Garnett at Wissett, and later at Charleston.

Not that he spent all his free weekends with these two 'families'. In 1916 his friendship with Lady Ottoline Morrell was at its height, and he was frequently at Garsington. The Morrells' Tudor manor house continued to provide an uneasy meeting ground between the war's opponents and the Liberal establishment. On one occasion, Asquith's daughter, Violet Bonham-Carter, and Lytton Strachey had such a violent argument about conscientious objectors that all Maynard's wit and Desmond MacCarthy's anecdotage were needed to salvage the weekend.[2]

Garsington was filling up with 'honorary gardeners' – conscientious objectors employed by Phillip Morrell to do 'work of national importance'. That summer Aldous Huxley, Gerald and Fredegond Shove, Clive Bell and others took up residence in the main house or nearby cottages, occasionally bestirring themselves to cut wood, prune hedges, or mind the hens. (The supply of eggs fell off suddenly after Gerald had been put in charge of the poultry.) Ottoline's reputation never recovered from the influx of articulate, witty, and alarmingly gossipy writers and intellectuals, who included D. H. Lawrence and his wife Frieda. Devoted to the encouragement of Art and Beauty, the Art she made of herself was too flawed to survive continuous exposure to the connoisseurs of human nature with whom she liked to surround herself. Her hospitality was rewarded with merciless lampoons in conversation, letters and novels. Maynard was happy to accept Ottoline's hospitality without malice, though he enjoyed the spiteful stories his friends spread about her. At Garsington, he struck Aldous Huxley as 'fascinating – he had this immense range of knowledge, and he would come out with these *curiously* elliptical remarks about things ...'[3]

On 6 June 1916, Kitchener was drowned off the Orkneys when the ship taking him to Russia on a mission to discuss military and financial strategy hit a mine. Maynard had been excluded from the party only at the last moment. The thought of how nearly he had been with Kitchener was enough to give Neville headaches. 'I wonder what it would have given him to think you were,' Margaret wrote to her brother. Instead, Maynard stayed in London receiving deputations from the Holy Synod of Russia and the government of Serbia to whom, as he told his father, he 'doled out presents I should have liked myself'.[4] (He initialled chits for the purchase of beeswax for the Russian Church and underwear for a Grand Duchess.)[5] His memoranda continued to rile Lloyd George, who succeeded Kitchener as Secretary of State for

War. In a note of May 1916, Lloyd George had called the Treasury's attempts to ration Russian buying the 'height of stupidity', suggesting that American contractors would be willing to provide credits directly to the Russians, without charge to the British Exchequer, rather than see their industries collapse for want of foreign orders. McKenna's reply of 5 July 1916, drafted by Keynes, and circulated to the Cabinet, entered into detailed criticisms of Lloyd George's logic and facts, rather in the manner of a tutor reproving the efforts of a backward student.[6] Lloyd George notched up another grievance against Keynes.* July sped by in conference with the French and Italian finance ministers. Maynard wrote to Florence on 24 July: 'I have a vague memory of several official banquets, dinner at the Italian Embassy and the like; but otherwise everything has slipt away. Three weeks ago I went to the McKennas for the weekend and yesterday I was at Ottoline's. To-morrow I dine at the P.M.'s.'

Social life continued in August with one week-end with the Asquiths and another with Oliver and Ray Strachey at Durbins, which Lady Strachey had rented from Roger Fry. His brain 'weak with work', Maynard wrote an account of his doings to Vanessa Bell on 21 August 1916:

> Moore was there [at Durbins] as charming as ever, and Marjorie Strachey . . . also rather charming. Moore and Oliver played Brahms duets when they weren't playing bridge. Adrian and Karin turned up on Sunday morning, having not yet gone milking.†
>
> The weekend before that I spent with Margot at Bognor and won £25 off her at bridge which was rather scandalous. There was an enormous party. Just after we had sat down eighteen to lunch, Margot explained to me that she had come down to Bognor because she was so tired of seeing people. It was chiefly a youthful party – Nancy Cunard and her young man, Lady Diana Manners, etc., etc., mostly followers of 'the fun life' as it's called. I believe that, with my physical eye I saw the moment of the P.M.'s conversion to the [woman's] suffrage.
>
> This evening Ka called at the Treasury, very blooming and also, I suspect, in a very managing mood. She carried Saxon off to supper.

---

* It is difficult at this period to distinguish McKenna's tone from Keynes's. Neither pleased Lloyd George. As Montagu wrote to Margot Asquith on 8 August 1916: 'It is well-known that [Lloyd George and McKenna] dislike each other; it is well-known that they make the fatal error of doing their work surrounded by their own particular choice of press-man: but McKenna shows himself small in his everlasting objections, often petty and always badly stage-managed, to anything that Lloyd George proposes'. (Quoted in S. D. Waley, *Edwin Montagu, A Memoir*, p. 100.)
† Adrian Stephen was a conscientious objector.

There was a one-day trip to Calais on 24 August – 'interesting but very exhausting, as everything had to be rushed, we crossing the channel twice in the day and getting only five hours sleep in 40'[7] – then another weekend in 'Circe's cave' as Lytton called Garsington, before Maynard slipped away for a week's holiday to Wissett.

10 September 1916 found him at Munstead House, Godalming where, Maynard informed his mother,

> the C[hancellor] of [the] E[xchequer] is taking an intermittent holiday and where we mix up talk about the nation with walks over the hills. We are on very intimate terms now and I have got extremely fond of him. I'm living in extreme luxury here, in bed till lunchtime and much pampered. Before I took my holiday I was feeling more used up than I have been for a long time.

With Bloomsbury now virtually emptied of Bloomsberries, the question arose what to do about 46 Gordon Square. Clive Bell hoped Maynard would take it over. He had a personal motive, requiring a London bedroom for his fortnightly tryst with his mistress Mary Hutchinson, the wife of the lawyer St John Hutchinson, and a cousin of the Stracheys. Maynard foresaw problems. The lease of Gower Street still had nine months to run. He wrote to Vanessa:

> Clive whom I've just been talking to may be rather a difficulty I think. He evidently means to be in London a fair amount and also to be an inhabitant of Gordon Square; and there isn't really room for him. I feel a little in danger of becoming, by virtue of the change, instead of a householder the rather insecure tenant of two rooms. It isn't possible, it seems to me, for Gordon Square to be occupied by the Bell family as heretofore, plus Mary on occasions, and for Sheppard and me to be superimposed on it. Then there's Bunny and Duncan whom we want to be in a position to put up. Clive wants some status and security in the house. Particularly when peace comes I foresee difficulty, if the house is his in any sense as well as yours and mine and the [Bell's] children's.[8]

Maynard's misgivings turned out to be justified; however, there were advantages, and he moved in at the end of September 1916, taking Sheppard with him from Gower Street. He paid the rates and the two servants, Blanche and Jessie; the Bells continued to pay the rent, keeping four rooms for their own use. Harry Norton joined them in March 1917. Dorothy Brett, Dora Carrington and Barbara Hiles moved into 3 Gower Street, to be looked after by 'Chappers'.

Wissett was abandoned at the same time, following the Central Tribunal's ruling that Duncan and Bunny could not remain self-employed. The first plan was for them to join the honorary gardeners at Garsington. But this would have left out Vanessa. Virginia had meanwhile discovered a farmhouse, a mile from Firle, and four miles from Asheham, which she urged Vanessa to take. 'It has a charming garden, with a pond, and fruit trees, and vegetables, all now rather run wild, but you could make it lovely. The house is very nice, with large rooms, and one room with big windows fit for a studio.'[9] It became vacant in September; Vanessa, in 'one breathlessly efficient day' at Lewes, rented it from James Stacey who held a lease from Lord Gage, the owner, and persuaded a young farmer, Mr Hecks, to employ Duncan and Bunny as labourers on his farm. Maynard paid his first visit to 'Duncan's new country house' as he called Charleston at the end of October.[10] It soon became his favourite weekend retreat.

The double rearrangement consolidated Maynard's position in the Bloomsbury Group. 46 Gordon Square was, in Clive Bell's words, Bloomsbury's *'monument historique'*, and now Maynard was left in effective possession. Most of the practical arrangements for Bloomsbury's collective London life were concentrated in his hands. The move to Charleston gave him a secure foothold in what was to become Bloomsbury's chief rural outpost. It was an ideal weekend place – only an hour by train from London. It was four miles from Asheham. And at Charleston he could relax in a way which was impossible with the more rigid Woolfs and Stracheys. Here he was accepted for what he was. He could bask in a warm glow of approval and affection, unchilled by the Cambridge habit of relentlessly dissecting character and analysing motives, from which he rarely emerged unscathed. Charleston was more a world unto itself than the other Bloomsbury establishments. The lives of Lytton Strachey, the Woolfs, even Clive Bell, for all their commitment to unworldly values, overlapped too much with Maynard's for them not to feel threatened by his successes. Jealousy tended to take the self-protecting form of disapproval. With Vanessa, Duncan and Bunny, Maynard's relationships were completely non-competitive. They could much more easily accept him as an authority on matters outside their range. They regarded his sorties into high society as sources of amusing gossip rather than as subjects for moral sermons. They were not always questioning his sense of values. Even Maynard's grossness, which offended Lytton Strachey, was less out of place in Charleston's earthy, bawdy atmosphere. There was occasional friction, of course. Maynard would often pronounce emphatically on matters about which he knew nothing. Once he and Bunny were walking on Firle Beacon when they heard the distant sound of gunfire from across the Channel. Garnett, who had had a scientific education, remarked that it was being carried by the wind. Maynard said the wind could make no difference, as sound travelled through the ether. When Garnett persisted, Maynard turned in his most superior manner to Clive: 'Bunny says the Cambridge physicists are wrong about the diffusion of sound.' Such remarks, however, were accepted as amiable foibles, rather than as signs of profound character defects.

Charleston became Maynard's chief wartime family. He would arrive on a Friday or Saturday evening, recount his war news, and then stay in bed till lunch the following morning, by which time he would have worked through his files, leaving a wastepaper-basket full of torn-up paper. After that he was a free man. There would be gossip and walks on the Downs. He even became an honorary gardener in a small way, weeding the gravel-path methodically with his pocket-knife while kneeling on a small piece of carpet. 'It would have been easy to tell the length of his visits by the state of the path,' recalled David Garnett. Maynard infected them all with his buoyancy.[11]

II

FINANCIAL CRISIS AND CHANGE OF GOVERNMENT

As the third winter of the war approached, the crisis which the Treasury had for so long predicted seemed finally upon them. By that time Britain had become completely dependent on the United States for fighting a continental war. The stability of the Allied exchanges, and the whole structure of inter-Ally finance, depended on Britain being able to borrow enough dollars in the United States to pay for Allied spending. By September 1916 it was paying out over $200m a month in the U.S.A. (about two-fifths of its total war expenditure). Of this about one half was being paid for by dwindling reserves of gold and the sale of British-owned American and Canadian securities. The rest was being borrowed by the sale of Treasury bills, public issues of U.K. bonds, and collateral loans.

On 3 October 1916, at the suggestion of a Foreign Office clerk, Richard Sperling, an Inter-Departmental Committee was set up under Lord Eustace Percy to review the position. Keynes was the Treasury representative. In two trenchant memoranda he spelt out the details and implications of Britain's growing dependence. He estimated that over the coming six months Britain would need to spend at least $250m monthly in the United States, of which it would have to borrow at least $200m. It was on Britain's ability to raise these sums that the Allies relied to buy their munitions, metals, oil and wheat. By mid-1916 Britain was paying for the whole of Italy's foreign war spending, most of Russia's, two-thirds of France's, half of Belgium's and Serbia's. As Keynes put it: 'We have one ally, France. The rest [are] mercenaries.'[12]. He doubted whether private American banks would go on lending on the scale required. Over McKenna's initials appear the ominous words, 'If things go on at present, I venture to say with certainty that by next June or earlier the President of the American Republic will be in a position, if he wishes, to dictate his own terms to us.'[13] In Cabinet, Lloyd George once more attacked this despondent conclusion. 'If victory shone on our banners,' he said, 'our difficulties would disappear. Success means credit: financiers never hesitate to lend to a prosperous concern.' The revelation of British dependence on the United States (Lord Eustace Percy wrote that 'our job is . . . to keep sentiment in America so sweet that it will lend us practically unlimited money') had its impact on the review of British war aims taking place at the same time, out of which emerged Lord Lansdowne's memorandum of 13 November 1916 calling for immediate peace negotiations.[14]

Except for bankers of German origin like Paul Warburg, the American financial establishment was pro-Ally, as was the U.S. Treasury. American farmers and manufacturers, too, had a vested interest in maintaining a high level of Allied buying – which was on a much larger scale than Germany's. New York was also eager to take London's place as the world's financial centre. But political relations between America and Britain were bad for much of 1916. Britain's use of its naval supremacy to prevent American supplies from reaching Germany – it also started black-listing American firms which traded with the enemy – aroused great anger at a time when Germany, behaving with unusual circumspection, had reduced its submarine campaign. The execution of the leaders of the Easter Rebellion in Dublin angered Irish–American opinion. With the presidential election approaching, Wilson was anxious to conciliate American voters of Irish and German descent, who were anti-British, and of Polish and Jewish descent, who were anti-Tsarist. Also Wilson wanted to stop the war, and whereas Germany was proving relatively amenable to his peace moves (at least verbally), Lloyd George, in a well-publicised interview on 22 September 1916 with an American journalist, enunciated the policy of the 'knock-out blow'.[15]

Britain's reliance on J. P. Morgan as its American financial agent was also politically counter-productive, since it saddled the Allied cause with the opprobrium traditionally attaching to Wall Street bankers. J. P. Morgan & Co. of New York stood at the head of a powerful banking group with extensive interests in the steel, construction and munitions industries. It did practically all the Allied financing and purveying before America came into the war, Allied requests being transmitted through its subsidiaries, Morgan, Grenfell & Co. of London and Morgan, Harges & Co. of Paris. The commitment of this block of private financial and industrial power to the allied cause convinced radicals and progressives that the U.S. was being dragged into a 'war for Wall Street'. The fact that Morgan's backed the Republican candidate, Charles Evans Hughes, against Wilson in the presidential election of 4 November 1916 did not help matters.

Thus as Britain grew more financially dependent on the United States, its political relations with America deteriorated. In his memorandum of 10 October, Keynes drew the sensible conclusion that 'the policy of this country towards the U.S.A. should be so directed as not only to avoid any form of reprisal or active irritation but also to conciliate and please'.[16] These words fix the moment when financial hegemony passed irrevocably across the Atlantic.

On 27 November 1916 the U.S. Federal Reserve Board brought on the worst British financial crisis in the war by telling its member banks to cut down their credit to foreign borrowers, and warning private investors against giving loans on the security of Allied Treasury bills. There were genuine financial fears behind this warning (H. P. Davison, a partner in Morgan's, had said he would flood the U.S. money market with one billion dollars of Allied Treasury bills), but the main motive of W. P. Harding, acting governor of the Federal Reserve Board in the absence of the pro-British Benjamin Strong who was away ill, was the desire to bring financial pressure on the Allies to end the war. President Wilson strengthened the Board's warning for the same reason. There was nothing for it but to pay up. For three weeks Britain lost gold at an average of over $5m a day, 'which in those days', Keynes recalled, 'we considered simply terrific'. He recalled the emergency in 1939:

> Chalmers and Bradbury [Joint Permanent Secretaries to the Treasury] never fully confessed to ministers the extent of our extremity when it was actually upon us, though of course they had warned them, fully but unavailingly, months beforehand of what was coming. This was because they feared that, if they emphasised the real position, the policy of the peg might be abandoned, which, they thought, would be disastrous. They had been brought up in the doctrine that in a run one must pay out one's gold reserves to the last bean. I thought then, and I still think, that in the circumstances they were right. To have abandoned the peg would have destroyed our credit and brought chaos to business; and would have done no real good.[17]

By mid-December the crisis had eased, with the help of underspending by the Allies, and generous overdraft facilities made available by Morgan.

Keynes's loyalties were again being cruelly torn. On the one hand he was working feverishly to get Britain through the financial crisis; on the other hand he hoped the crisis itself would bring the war to an end. His hopes rested once more on President Wilson who had launched another peace initiative on December 18, calling on the belligerents to state their peace terms. On 29 December Virginia Woolf wrote to her friend Margaret Llewelyn Davies: 'Maynard thinks we may be on the verge of ruin, and thus of peace; and possibly Wilson intends to cut off our supplies and altogether quite hopeful.'[18] By this time he was having to carry on his work under a new, and much less welcome, political chief. On 6 December 1916, Lloyd George replaced Asquith as Prime Minister, the Conservative Bonar Law succeeding McKenna as Chancellor of the Exchequer. Keynes's depression at this turn of events was not improved by his indifferent health. He had three bad attacks of influenza in the winter of 1916–17, and was generally run down.

On the other hand, the financial situation seemed to favour the President's call, on 22 January 1917, for a 'peace without victory'. The drain of gold still continued. On 22 February Keynes calculated that available resources would not last 'for more than four weeks from today'. His view was shared by Walter Page, the American Ambassador in London, who cabled his government on 5 March:

> The pressure of this approaching [financial] crisis, I am certain, has gone beyond the ability of the Morgan financial agency for the British and French Governments ... It is not improbable that the only way of maintaining our preeminent trade position and averting a panic is by declaring war on Germany.'[19]

The British were, in fact, saved by the Germans, who had no idea of the desperate straits to which their enemy had been reduced; something which would have been signalled had Britain suspended convertibility, against which Keynes continued to argue vigorously and successfully.[20] They launched unrestricted submarine warfare on 1 February, in order to cut off Allied supplies from the United States, not realizing that 'finance was about to accomplish the same result'. On 21 February Richard Sperling of the Foreign Office minuted that 'we should have found it impossible to get the action of the Federal Reserve Board reversed if the German Govt. had not, as usual, been more stupid than ourselves in our dealings with the U.S.'.[21] As President Wilson himself realised, the German action killed off the last hope of 'peace without victory'. On 6 April 1917 America declared war on Germany. Keynes's skill in controlling Britain's overseas spending, by helping to stave off financial collapse, had the paradoxical result of delivering the President to Lloyd George and to the policy of the knockout blow.

This time there was no serious thought of resignation. Lloyd George cordially reciprocated Keynes's mistrust. Maynard explained to his mother on 11 February that

> I was approved and included in the final list to get a C.B. this honours list. But when Lloyd George saw it he took his pen and

struck my name out – an unheard of proceeding. Partly revenge for the McKenna War Council Memorandum against him, of which he knows I was the author.

But in compensation he had got

a more solid advantage in the last few days, having been properly constituted head of a new Dept. with a staff behind me, to deal with all questions of External Finance. It will be an enormous advantage to have a staff of my own, whom I can organise according to my ideas. I have been given some very good men ... I was told I could have some more pay if I asked for it. But I didn't.

Keynes was named head of 'A' division reporting directly to Sir Robert Chalmers and the Chancellor. By the end of the war his staff numbered seventeen, mostly temporary civil servants. They included his old student Dudley Ward, a clever young man of eighteen called Rupert Trouton, who became his student after the war, and Oswald Toynbee Falk, a partner in the stockbroking firm of Buckmaster and Moore. An actuary who was passionate about ballet, Falk joined the Treasury team in October 1917, soon after Keynes had become a founder-member of a small dining club which Falk started – known as the Tuesday Club – which met at the Café Royal to discuss post-war financial problems.* Andrew McFadyean, who was transferred to Keynes from another division at the Treasury, recalls the exhilaration felt by

a younger man to see that razor-sharp mind dissecting a problem and stating it in terms which made it look simple, and in language which it was a joy to read ... Keynes would rarely – that at any rate is the impression left on my mind – reach the Treasury before midday and he would leave it about eight. He was a prodigiously fast worker, and there was never much in his in-tray at the end of the day.[22]

Keynes's promotion locked him even more closely into his Treasury work. Soon he was able to draw comfort from events in Russia. The revolution of 12 March 1917, leading to the abdication of the Tsar, had 'immensely cheered and excited him', he told Florence. 'It's the sole result of the war so far worth having'.[23] The anti-Tsarist attitude of Maynard's generation died hard.

Both America's entry, and Russia's gradual retirement, from the war promised to ease the financial strain of the previous few months.

* Those present at the first dinner at the Café Royal on 19 June 1917 were Sir Charles Addis, O. T. Falk, H. S. Foxwell, J. M. Keynes, A. W. Kiddy, Geoffrey Marks, F. E. Steele, and Hartley Withers. On 20 November 1917 Falk opened a discussion on 'Currency and International Trade and Finance: England's Position Now and after the War'; on 11 July 1918 Kiddy's subject was 'Shall we retain our position as the leading monetary centre after the war?' The banker R. H. Brand opened a discussion on the post-war debt problem in October 1918.

Work has not been overwhelmingly heavy [Maynard wrote to his mother on 6 May 1917] and the negotiations with the U.S. which occupy a good deal of my time are going extremely well. If all happens as we wish, the Yanks ought to relieve me of some of the most troublesome of my work for the future. Relations with Russia on the other hand are not as they should be.

(After July Keynes refused any more credits to Russia.[24]) But the strain under which he had been working left him with little patience for the continued needling of his Bloomsbury friends. 'Did you hear of Maynard's terrible outburst at Easter, when he said that Asquith is more intelligent than Lytton?' wrote Virginia Woolf to her sister on 26 April 1917. 'Lytton,' she added, 'thinks this a very serious symptom.'

III

THE FINANCIAL DIPLOMACY OF WAR

At the end of May 1917 Keynes was made Companion of the Bath, Third Class 'through the kindness of Chalmers who exerted the strongest possible pressure through the Chancellor of the Exchequer and made mine the sole name put forward by the Treasury'.[25] Unexpectedly he got on excellently with the new Chancellor, Bonar Law. Cautious and pessimistic, Law was no intellectual like McKenna, but he was extremely quick to grasp, and remember, a point put to him 'in those hurried moments which a civil servant gets with his chief before a conference'.[26] Law came to rely on Keynes's advice in all matters of external finance. Keynes became genuinely fond of Law, a sad man, whose sadness was increased by the death of two of his sons on active service. He was soon making up bridge fours at 11 Downing Street.

Once America entered the war on the Allied side, the game of international finance changed, and with it Keynes's role. Funds were now assured. The question was the terms on which they could be obtained, and the implications of the new relationship for the conduct of the war, war aims, and the balance of post-war power. America would back the Alliance till it won; but with a view to playing a dominant part in the peace settlement and post-war trade and finance. Britain had to contrive to manage its affairs so as to limit the scale of its liabilities and keep the maximum room for post-war manoeuvre. As was to happen much more obviously in the Second World War, British brains were matched against U.S. money – or that is how the British saw it. One of those brains was Keynes's.

Admittedly the plot was not clearcut. There were internal frictions on both sides. In the United States there were four centres of financial power: the Treasury, the Federal Reserve Board, Wall Street and Congress. William Gibbes McAdoo, the Secretary of the Treasury and Wilson's son-in-law, combined, on one hand, a somewhat desperate ambition to bring the other three under his control with, on the other, considerable ignorance of finance, and considerable fear of Congress in practice. His policy in 1917 was partly governed by a determination not to allow U.S. Treasury funds to be used to pay off British debts to the New York bankers. Benjamin Strong, the leading force in the Federal Reserve Board, wanted both to establish the Board's independence of the Treasury and to see his own bank, the Federal Reserve Bank of New York, supplant the Bank of England as manager of the world's monetary system. Leading New York bankers like the Anglophile Thomas W. Lamont saw private loans to Europe as the best way of establishing New York's financial hegemony; they disliked official interference in the lending business. Many Congressmen disliked the New York bankers as much as they mistrusted the British; they would have preferred America to stay out of the war.

Britain's financial policy was under better control, but British authorities had to tread a wary course between the conflicting U.S. interests, and there were elements of divided jurisdiction here, too. The Treasury's old hankering for limited financial commitments ran up against the insatiable demands of the war departments both in Britain and its European allies. Such control as it was able to retain over total spending rested on the sanctity of the sterling–dollar exchange and the limitation of shipping space. But it had to share management of the exchange rate with the Bank of England, whose Governor, Lord Cunliffe, resented the meddling of Treasury officials in the Bank's traditional preserve. In 1915, taking advantage of his friendship with Lloyd George, Cunliffe managed to get McKenna to agree to centralise the management of the exchange in a London Exchange Committee – a consortium of bankers, of which he was chairman. However, the Treasury, notably Sir Robert Chalmers and Keynes, chipped away at the Committee's functions, and by the summer of 1917 Cunliffe was ready for a showdown.

The third force in Britain's U.S. financial diplomacy, the Washington Embassy, was more of a hindrance than a help. The Ambassador, Sir Cecil Spring-Rice, a diplomat of the old school, and a friend of Theodore Roosevelt, was on bad terms with the Democratic Administration. A man of wit, as well as of biblical turn of phrase (he wrote the hymn 'I vow to thee my country'), he did the British cause little good with his party joke that 'Wilson is the nation's shepherd and McAdoo his crook'. The Embassy was also woefully lacking in financial expertise. Until the able and diplomatic Lord Reading was appointed Ambassador, in January 1918, Britain had to rely on high-powered *ad hoc* missions to advance its financial interests in the United States; but these tended to create further jurisdictional and personal disputes.

Keynes's hope that America would take care of his problems was not realised; the problems just changed. In January 1917, the Treasury, in an effort to distance itself both from J. P. Morgan and from the Bank of England, had sent out its new Financial Secretary, Sir Samuel Hardman Lever, to New York to raise money and take over the management of the Morgan account. Lever, a chartered accountant with New York connections, succeeded in swelling the British government's debt to Morgan's to $400m by the time America entered the war; but when he asked McAdoo, on 9 April, for $1,500m for six months, he was met with astonishment and annoyance. McAdoo was suspicious that the money would be used to pay back Morgan's and support the sterling–dollar exchange rather than to buy American goods; also no machinery for allocating the proceeds of the $2,000m Liberty Loan, authorised by Congress, among the various Allied claimants had yet been worked out. Lever, a morose man, did not help matters by his secretiveness; nor did successive missions to the United States headed by Balfour and Northcliffe bring about any large-scale release of funds. McAdoo, 'a Wall Street failure with designs on the Presidency', as McFadyean acidly described him, was content to advance the begging British money in weekly dribs and drabs, using the Allied penury to concentrate control of purchasing in U.S. Treasury hands.[27]

In June the situation got worse as heavy British demands for wheat, coinciding with the withdrawal of U.S. funds from London to invest in the Liberty Loan, weakened sterling. In London, Keynes masterminded the Treasury's campaign to keep the U.S. money flowing, drafting the crucial memoranda and telegrams explaining the British government's position to the Americans, as well as the instructions Bonar Law was sending to Lever. Last-minute American advances just enabled the British to get through June. However, on 20 July, Bonar Law transmitted to McAdoo a message drafted by Keynes that 'our resources available for payments in America are exhausted. Unless the United States government can meet in full our expenses in America, *including exchange*, the whole financial fabric of the alliance will collapse. This conclusion will be a matter not of months but of days.'[28]

On 28 July Lever was instructed, on Keynes's advice, to support the sterling–dollar exchange as long as he had any dollars left, and then suspend convertibility. The Bank's remaining gold was to be protected as the ultimate liquid reserve.[29] Kathleen Burk writes that Keynes 'grasped the nettle and suggested the heretofore unthinkable: in a choice between the rate of exchange and the remaining gold, the rate would have to give way'.[30] That this was the start of Keynesian economics, as she seems to believe, is far from obvious. A telegram drafted by Keynes to McAdoo, explaining the exchange situation, brought about a further release of U.S. funds at the eleventh hour, saving the position.[31]

The government's ability to contain the crisis was hampered throughout this period by friction between the Treasury and the Bank of England. On 3 July 1917 Cunliffe complained to Bonar Law that Chalmers and Keynes between them were reducing his Exchange Committee to a 'cypher' by withholding from it information and assets. In retaliation he gave instructions to withhold the Bank's gold at Ottawa from Sir Hardman Lever in New York. He also demanded that Chalmers and Keynes be dismissed. Bonar Law retaliated by forcing the resignation of the megalomaniac governor.[32] It is easy to see why his Treasury officials loved him.

The crisis – 'the worst ... I can remember since the war began'[33] – left Keynes shattered. For five weeks he had worked nine to thirteen hours a day 'of the hardest possible exertion'. Matters were made worse by German air-raids which forced him to flee to the basement of Gordon Square. His only relief had been six hours of strenuous weeding at Charleston. Florence swelled with pride at Maynard's importance. 'How exciting it must be for you to attend the Cabinet meetings. Indeed, it seems to me that you are having such experiences as will make the whole of life pale afterwards.'[34]

At the beginning of August the French and Italian finance ministers inconveniently turned up in London. But on 8 August Maynard at last managed to get a week off, which he spent at Charleston, slowly recovering on a daily routine of lying in bed in the morning, gardening in the afternoon, and retiring promptly at 10.30 p.m. Having got the weeding under control, he graduated to planting cauliflowers and digging potatoes. There was another heavy London weekend on 18–19 August, when he brought home eighty-nine papers from the Treasury on Saturday, which he polished off on Sunday. The effect of his holiday was 'wearing off dreadfully quickly and I must try to get some more if I am to keep well'.[35] The holiday came in the unexpected form of a trip to the United States with Lord Reading – a month away with almost nothing to do, he informed Vanessa from The Wharf on 3 September, the eve of his departure.

Reading was sent to America to try to resolve the impasse between Hardman Lever and the U.S. Treasury (McAdoo was now refusing to see Lever). Keynes's voyage out, on the SS *Louis*, took a week, of which he spent three days seasick. There were daily two-hour conferences with Reading and Colonel Ernest Swinton, Assistant Secretary to the War Cabinet. For the rest Keynes sat on deck or played piquet, winning twenty pounds off a Polish count. In Washington he stayed in a 'small and comfortable house' with the Readings, both of whom he 'liked immensely'[36], despite Lady Reading's deafness. Reading's job, like that of all previous special commissioners, was to squeeze more money out of McAdoo. He finally succeeded in getting McAdoo's agreement for a proper schedule of monthly loans. In addition, with Keynes's help, he arranged a $50m loan for British purchase of Canadian wheat, a considerable concession, since U.S. policy was to provide dollars only for things bought in the United States. Reading, who thought very highly of Keynes,[37] wanted him to stay an extra ten days, but Bonar Law refused. Keynes made a less favourable impression on the British Ambassador. Spring-Rice wrote to his wife Florence:

> This morning we got a visit from Reading's Treasury clerk who was very Treasuriclarkacious and reduced Dicky [Sir Richard Crawford, his economic adviser] to silentious rage and Malcolm [Robertson, a counsellor] to a high treble. He was really too offensive for words and I shall have to take measures. He is also a Don and the combination is not pleasing. He is also a young man of talent and I presume the rule for such nowadays is to show his immense superiority by crushing the contemptible insignificance of the unworthy outside. He does it hard. Lord Reading himself is most agreeable and pleasant to deal with.[38]

Keynes reported back to London that the Ambassador was mentally unhinged; soon afterwards he was retired.[39]

Keynes was not a success with the Americans either. 'Rude, dogmatic, and disobliging' to them in London, he made a 'terrible impression for his rudeness out here', Blackett wrote from Washington.[40] Again the feeling was reciprocated. 'The only really sympathetic and original thing in America is the niggers, who are charming,' Keynes informed Duncan Grant.

He returned to Britain on the SS *Aurania*, converted into an American troopship, in a two-week zigzag across the Atlantic to avoid German submarines, landing at Liverpool on 22 October 1917.

> It's a most beautiful sight [he wrote to Duncan at sea on 10 October] – seven great liners travelling in formation led by a cruiser and flanked by two destroyers. When we reach the danger zone, which is not yet, we hope to be picked up by another fleet of destroyers and hydroplanes ... Our cruiser, by the way, is camouflaged in the best Omega style. The painted abstract design which covers her is intended to destroy in the observer all sense of the vertical ...

So far the weather has been very good and I've hardly felt a qualm. The mornings I spend in bed reading Lockhart's life of Scott which is extraordinarily good ... Then I lunch at the Captain's table with the American colonels, innocent middle-aged gentlemen from the Mexican border. The great amusement of the afternoon is boxing matches got up by the Yank Tommies, with whom one also chats. One young fighter who must have Red Indian blood in him is my favourite. After dinner, which is at six, I play bridge with the subalterns or poker with the colonels.

It's too much of a business to tell you anything about America until I come to Charleston which I hope will be soon ... But I'll tell you this, – that the Americans are furiously for war and, unless the secret despatches in my bag hold something from far up the sleeve of President Wilson, all prospects of peace seem to me to be disappearing until Germany is *beaten*.

The character of Keynes's work now changed. 'A' Division was so well organised that he had practically no drafting to do any more, which was a great relief.[41] The era of exchange crises was over. Worries about maintaining the sterling–dollar exchange – hitherto the pivot of inter-Ally finance – gave way to the worries of bargaining with Allied and American officials over the distribution of American largesse, a process involving different rituals, skills and techniques. Political and diplomatic factors came to the fore, technical economic considerations retreated. Politics were now as rampant in the sphere of external finance as they had long been in the sphere of domestic finance. On the whole Keynes did not welcome this change, though it lightened his burden. His whole training as an economist and Treasury official rebelled against such blatant political interference with the allocation of resources. Personally he lacked the emollient skills of a Lord Reading. Intellectually he felt himself, and the tradition he represented, to be far superior to anything the Americans could put up against him, and resented the change in Britain's circumstances which separated the brains from the money.

The bulk of his time was now spent in negotiations at innumerable inter-Ally conferences. In November 1917 he was over in Paris for one such jamboree, sitting with Balfour, Reading and Northcliffe as part of the British delegation.[42] In December 1917 he wasted days on 'a newly established monkey-house called the Inter-Ally Council for War Purchases and Finance',[43] where he had to listen to 'vain, mendacious and interminable French and hateful Yank twang'.[44] Set up at the insistence of the Americans and under an American chairman, the Assistant Secretary to the Treasury, Oscar T. Crosby, an ex-director of a street-car company, to scrutinise competing Allied claims for American money, it met monthly, alternately in London

and Paris. British estimates of what they would require in America
in the coming month were worked out by an American Board in
Whitehall, of which Austen Chamberlain was chairman, and Keynes
Treasury representative. They were then taken to the Inter-Ally
Council. Keynes described its second meeting in Paris at the end of
January to Basil Blackett in America: 'A vast number of us sit round
a table in a gilded palace to listen to the eloquence of Crosby – equally
torrential in either language.' Tiresome as the business was, Keynes
conceded it had its uses. Treasury control over Britain's external
spending could be reinforced by 'flourishing the name of Crosby with
great effect in the faces of recalcitrant departments'.[45] To his Charleston friends he retailed more intimate gossip about his Paris jaunt. He
had dined at the Ritz with Lord Beaverbrook, 'hideously ugly and
utterly debauched'. His company had been sought by Count Horodin-
sky, a Polish intriguer, 'enormously fat, scented, pomaded, powdered'.
At the Hotel Crillon he had been accosted by an 'elegant young man'
dressed as a French airman who invited him to his bedroom. Wisely
Maynard had refused, as he turned out to be a German spy. The head
of the British Secret Service in Paris had told him that the British
employed hundreds of French whores whose job it was to detect
Germans masquerading in British uniforms, and suborn neutral
statesmen for the Allied cause.[46]

The last big battle he waged on behalf of the Treasury was the
attempt to get America to take over the financing of France and Italy,
thus reducing the rate of increase in Britain's debt to the United
States. Under the previous division of labour agreed with McAdoo,
America was to supply dollar credits directly to each Ally for its
purchases in the American market, Britain financing all its European
Allies' other purchases. But Britain could no longer do even this
reduced job out of its own resources. Consequently it was still having
to borrow big sums in the United States, on its Allies' behalf. As the
British Treasury saw it – accurately, as it turned out – Britain was
accumulating liabilities to the United States which it would have to
pay back, in order to lend money to its Allies, much of which it would
never see again. The Americans, of course, preferred to accumulate
superior British obligations to inferior French and Italian ones.

In a telegram which went from Bonar Law to Lord Reading at the
end of March 1918 Keynes insisted that 'the U.S. Treasury should
take over all the future obligations of France and Italy ...'. Britain
would continue to procure supplies for its European Allies outside
America, being paid in dollars obtained from the American Treasury
rather than in European IOUs.[47] Implicit in this proposal was continued British Treasury control over the non-American buying of its
Allies. Keynes was not unaware of the advantages to Britain, made

possible by a combination of naval and financial power, of cornering major world commodity markets, since, to the extent that Britain could establish itself as sole supplier to neutrals, it would gain much-needed supplies of European currencies, thus lessening its dependence on dollar borrowings. Thus his demand that Britain should retain control over the non-American purchases of the European Allies coincided with his scheme for buying up the world wheat crop.[48] The French and Italians naturally resisted this part of the British plan. They proposed that their non-American purchases be placed in the hands of an inter-Ally executive committee. Keynes did not find this at all welcome. However, he reluctantly had to concede that 'if Mr McAdoo accepts our proposals for taking off our shoulders the burden of French and Italian finance ... the Americans can justly ask for an inter-ally body to pronounce on the propriety of allocations they are expected to finance'.[49] Britain's financial dependence on the United States was the rock on which Keynes's ingenious plan foundered. It was unrealistic to expect that the Americans would allow their money to be used to bolster Britain's competitive position in world markets. The Americans, Keynes exploded, seemed to take pleasure 'in reducing us to a position of complete financial helplessness and dependence'.[50] This was the new reality which all Keynes's future economic plans had to take into account. It was part of the passing of the old conditions brought about by a war which he hated.

If the management of Britain's external finance no longer gave him much intellectual or emotional satisfaction, contemplation of domestic politics induced a feeling of black despair. 'I work for a government I despise for ends I think criminal', he told Duncan Grant on 15 December 1917. Maynard rejected Lloyd George's commitment to total victory, and feared its consequences. The Prime Minister's remarkable political skills aroused in him only aesthetic and moral repugnance. He lived in the hope that Lloyd George's deviousness would prove his undoing. He fantasised about the downfall of his class which had so nervelessly placed supreme power in the hands of an adventurer. Maynard's political understanding was not the most conspicuous of his qualities at this period of his life. He was taking too many political lessons from the Asquithians whose failures had opened up the path for Lloyd George. He failed to give Lloyd George credit for his courage and resourcefulness in adversity, and for his determination to keep British lives out of the generals' maw. All he could see was that he was playing the part of a 'dirty scoundrel' with the generals – an ironic identification with the generals' own view.[51] He failed to realize that Asquith, McKenna and the others did not want a negotiated peace any more than Lloyd George did, and failed to explain anyway how the Germans were to be brought to a conference except on their own or on the Allied terms. Indeed, a gross overestimate of the strength of the German moderates, as well as a misunderstanding of their aims, was characteristic of the whole of the British middle-class peace movement.*

From Charleston, where he spent the Christmas of 1917, Maynard sounded off to his mother about the prospects for the future:

> My Christmas thoughts are that a further prolongation of the war, with the turn things have now taken, probably means the disappearance of the social order we have known hitherto. With some regrets I think I am not on the whole sorry. The abolition of the rich will be rather a comfort and serve them right anyhow. What frightens me is the prospect of *general* impoverishment. In another year's time we shall have forfeited the claim we had staked out in the New World and in exchange this country will be mortgaged to America.
>
> Well, the only course open to me is to be buoyantly bolshevik; and as I lie in bed in the morning I reflect with a good deal of satisfaction that, because our rulers are as incompetent as they are mad and wicked, one particular era of a particular kind of civilisation is very nearly over.[52]

The proximate cause of this gloomy epistle was the government's announcement of food rationing. Like other less reflective members of the middle classes Keynes tended to equate social order with the continuance of his own customary standard of comfort, and take an exaggerated view of the consequences of any diminution in it. To Florence his Christmas visions suggested communal kitchens and the drying up of the supply of domestic servants.[53] Maynard's incipient bolshevism stopped well short of food rationing, which filled him with horror. He feared he would have to take frequent trips abroad to get a square meal. 'The proposed [rationing] rules seem to me appalling – calculated to dry up the food supply on the one side and starve me on the other.'[54] In fact, food rationing worked perfectly well in both world wars, and posed no permanent threat to the social order.

There was still the hope that the war would end before the expropriation or starvation of the rich took place. On 29 November 1917 the *Daily Telegraph* published Lord Lansdowne's Peace Letter calling for renewed efforts to end the war by negotiation. Keynes immediately perked up. 'Maynard says that Bonar Law has dished the Government; the country entirely with Lansdowne ... This was

---

* In an article in the *Economic Journal* of September 1915, Keynes concluded a review of wartime German economic literature by saying that the general note 'is of moderation, sobriety, accuracy, reasonableness, and truth'.

from Lord Reading.'[55] But Virginia Woolf had learned to distrust Keynes's Christmas prophecies. His hopes of an early peace were kept alive by the proclamation of Wilson's Fourteen Points for ending the war, and Lloyd George's speech to the Trade Union Congress setting out the Allied peace terms. 'I am not sure that [Lloyd] George's speech was quite as satisfactory as it seemed at first blush', Maynard wrote to Florence on 13 January 1918. But he still thought that 'peace really seems a little nearer'. Soon he was reduced once more to seeking relief through a change of government. The Prime Minister was in great trouble following his dismissal of Sir William Robertson, Chief of the Imperial General Staff. But he struggled on. Maynard wrote to Florence on 22 February 1918:

> The course of politics at the beginning of the week was deeply shocking. Bonar could have become prime minister if he had liked, but he funked it; and as no one else seemed inclined to take the job, the goat* struggled through ... his method of disposing of Robertson was an extraordinarily characteristic compound of humbug, chicane and straightforward lying.

Contrary to his hopes, the Goat overcame yet another – and the last – challenge to his leadership in the Maurice debate of 9 May 1918.[56] As Ludendorff launched a desperate German offensive on the Western Front Keynes reflected on the state of the nation from the congenial surroundings of The Wharf:

> Politics and War are just as depressing, or even more so than they seem to be. If this Gov^t were to beat the Germans, I should lose all faith for the future in the efficacy of intellectual processes: – but there doesn't seem to be much risk of it. Everything is always decided for some reason other than the real merits of the case, in the sphere with which I have contact. And I have no doubt that it is just the same with everything else.
>
> Still and even more confidently I attribute our misfortunes to George. We are governed by a crook and the results are natural. In the meantime old Asquith who I believe might yet save us is more and more of a student and lover of slack country life and less and less inclined for the turmoil. Here he is extremely well in health and full of wisdom and fit for anything in the world – except controversy. He finds, therefore, in patriotism easy excuse for his natural disinclination to attack the Gov^t People say that the politician would attack, but the patriot refrain. I believe the opposite is true. The patriot would attack but the politician (and sluggard) refrain.[57]

---

* Lloyd George was generally called 'George' or 'the Goat' by his political opponents. He was known to dislike being called plain Mr George; the second suggested a propensity to play around – with women and truth.

This letter should be set by the side of another he wrote to Beatrice Webb on 11 March giving his reasons for the loss of Treasury control over expenditure. Beatrice Webb had requested his comments on a draft Report which she had written for Lord Haldane's Committee on the Machinery of Government.* Maynard never deviated from these views, despite his later attacks on the 'Treasury View':

> My own opinion is [he wrote] that, given a strong Chancellor of the Exchequer and given a Cabinet which desires strict control of expenditure, the present system is well adapted to do its work. The breakdown of Treasury control on important matters which has taken place to a large degree during the war is due, I strongly affirm, neither to any intrinsic impossibility in the task nor to any intrinsic inefficiency in the present system of control. The explanation is to be sought rather in a Government which habitually put finance last of all relevant considerations and believed that action however wasteful is preferable to caution and criticism however justified. My official superiors often remind me of the maxim traditional in the Treasury that no subordinate official can hope in the long run to be stronger than the Chancellor of the Exchequer. And in turn I suppose it is true that no Chancellor of the Exchequer can in the long run enforce a policy which is opposite to the prevailing current in the Cabinet or contrary to the temperament of an autocratic Prime Minister.[58]

IV

'HE MUST BE TALKED TO'

If Keynes despaired about the government, his Bloomsbury friends were starting to despair about him. It was no longer primarily his war work to which they objected; but the effect of that work, and of its accompanying social life, on his character. Virginia Woolf forecast that if he remained much longer at the Treasury he would be lost to humanity, as perhaps he already was.[59] To be sure, he was still very much a part of both London and rural Bloomsbury. He was regularly to be seen at the 1917 Club, a Soho meeting place for radical and anti-war intellectuals, often in the company of Barbara Hiles. It was with Barbara – chastely loved by Saxon Sydney-Turner, more vigorously by David Garnett, and about to marry Nicholas Bagenal – that Maynard made his first modest forays into heterosexuality.[60] Such frolics were regarded with indulgent amusement by his friends. But the weekends

---

* Sidney Webb had asked him earlier in the year to stand as Labour parliamentary candidate for Cambridge University. Keynes turned it down. He also refused both a Russian and Belgian decoration at this time, explaining to Florence: 'If people come to you with a decoration in one hand and a request for a million pounds in the other, the position is a little delicate.'

at The Wharf, the dinner-parties and receptions of Allied and parliamentary big-wigs, the bridge parties with Bonar Law, from all of
which he would return full of self-importance and authoritative
pronouncements – that was another matter.

Not that his connections and salary were not useful. He intervened
with Max Beaverbrook, the new Minister of Information, to get commissions for Duncan and other painters under the Ministry's War
Artists Scheme.[61] He provided Bunny with money for his bees at Charleston. The most stunning of his coups occurred in March 1918. Duncan had found out that the contents of Degas's studio were about to be
auctioned off in Paris. Couldn't Maynard persuade the government to
buy some of them for the National Gallery? Maynard, who was due to
go to Paris himself for a meeting of the Inter-Ally Council, promised to
approach Bonar Law. On 21 March 1918 Duncan received a telegram
at Charleston: 'Money secured for pictures'. Maynard explained to
Vanessa two days later: 'My picture coup was a whirlwind affair –
carried through in a day and a half before anyone had time to reflect
what they were doing. I have secured 550,000 francs to play with [equal
to about £20,000]; Holmes [Sir Charles Holmes, the Keeper of the
National Gallery] is travelling out with us; and I hope we shall be able
to attend the sale together.' He added, 'Bonar Law was much amused
at my wanting to buy pictures and eventually let me have my way as
a sort of joke.'[62] Vanessa replied excitedly, 'We have great hopes for
you & consider that your existence at the Treasury is at last justified.'
David Garnett added, 'You have been given complete absolution &
future crimes also forgiven.'

Maynard attended the sale wth Holmes on 26–7 March. Prices were
depressed as the German bombardment could be heard fifty miles
away. The following evening Austen Chamberlain who was driving
back to London dropped Keynes off at the bottom of the lane leading
to Charleston. He arrived at the farmhouse just as Vanessa, Duncan
and David Garnett were finishing supper, informing them that he had
left a Cézanne in a haystack. While Holmes had bought a Corot, a
Gauguin, and several paintings and drawings by Delacroix, Ingres and
Manet for the nation, Maynard had helped himself to one of the plums
of the collection, Cézanne's *Apples*, for £327, as well as two pictures by
Delacroix and an Ingres drawing. This was the start of his career as a
serious collector. As Holmes had a prejudice against Cézanne, no conflict of interest had arisen. In fact, £5000 of Bonar Law's donation
remained unspent.

Maynard's absolution was short-lived. What he called his 'experiments in High Life' continued through the spring and summer –
dinners with a Rumanian Prince, with the Princess of Monaco, and, to
cap it all, with the Duke of Connaught, George III's great-grandson.

In mid-May he was able to take a week off at Charleston, where the weather was perfect. 'I sit out or weed all my working hours and my daily bag from the Treasury doesn't mean more than one or two hours of work a day'.[63] His portrait was painted by Duncan, Vanessa and Roger Fry. Less perfect was Maynard's character, in the opinion of his friends. David Garnett has described Bloomsbury's cogitations on this absorbing subject in a long diary entry dated 28 May 1918:

> *Maynard*. There has been a general alarm that he is going rapidly to the devil. Nessa told me about a scene when she was in London. Harry, Sheppard & she were talking. Maynard came in, contradicted everyone, and refused to go into anything. The subject was whether one could have any feeling at all about England after the refusal of Emperor Karl's overtures . . .* Maynard treated them with contempt & behaved like a public-schoolboy of the worst kind & said several times 'Go to bed, Go to bed'. Sheppard got very angry & said – 'Maynard you will find it a mistake to despise your old friends'.
>
> Nessa . . . suggests that Maynard is now possibly so far on the downhill path that nothing will save him. Harry thinks it is not at all simple – That M. is aware of many of his habits being disgusting to other people – such as helping himself with his own spoon or fork instead of passing his plate, and persists in doing them because it flatters him that people like him so much they don't mind what he does. (This is often my own feeling but not about table manners – but in complete unreserve of all baseness with Duncan.)
>
> Sheppard says Maynard is . . . a bit mad on the subject of his own importance. He had heard him say the other day to Jessie [the parlourmaid at No. 46] 'I'm going to dine tonight with the Duke of Connaught. Isn't that grand?' – 'Yes Sir that is grand'. Sheppard refuses to regard this as the obvious thing it would be in 99 cases out of 100 – a joke. He says Maynard really thinks it is grand – knowing he couldn't impress Harry & Sheppard with the Dk of Connaught he had to tell Jessie. 'Nonconformist snobbery. I know all about it – they're like bugs in the rug. Bugs in a rug'.
>
> General conclusions were that Maynard has a lot of low blood in him – Sheppard . . . says from his nonconformist snobbish ancestry. That he is at a critical point in his life, that it may be fatigue [or] deterioration of his brain which is the only thing that ever made him remarkable . . . Duncan has been asked to give him a lecture . . .

* Emperor Charles of Austria had approached Poincaré, the French President, on 20 March 1917 with a peace offer, accepting the return of Alsace-Lorraine to France, and all the open Allied demands. However, the Allies were tied by their secret commitments to give Constantinople to Russia and the Tyrol, Trentino, and Istria to Italy, and so rejected this opportunity of shortening the war by detaching Austro-Hungary from Germany. Clemenceau made public Charles's letter in April 1918.

Maynard was so delightful that I fancy he was given his lecture early in his visit – none of the vices remarked on was noticeable after the first evening.

Bunny's own attitude to Maynard was more generous and better balanced:

> My own view of the whole thing is that it is one of their periodic alarms ... Maynard is always very tired. He works too much. He then wants something he can do with one tenth of his attention – which is to talk to the inane about the inane. Anything requiring him to think new thoughts or follow new arguments produces violent irritation in self-protection. His character is not entirely dependent on brain. He has a great deal of *love* & capacity for love. That will keep him if not straight at least capable of zigzagging back.*

Soon Clive Bell was adding his voice to the chorus of complaints. He had lent his room at 46 Gordon Square to a friend of his '*emballé* of a young woman'. Unfortunately they had used Sheppard's room by mistake. 'We were given no warning of this', Maynard explained to Duncan on 16 June 1918, 'and it was very embarrassing to the regular inhabitants all of whom happened to be at home: poor Sheppard was too nervous to ... go to bed until 3.30 when the lovers disappeared. We are sending a protest to Clive that he must restrain his good nature more narrowly.' Maynard's letter to Clive was not well received. He 'took it upon himself to write me the sort of letter an ill-bred millionaire might write to a defaulting office boy' he complained to Vanessa. He found it hard to restrain his sense of grievance. 'I am to pay £125 a year for bed and breakfast three days a fortnight ... while the others pay £150 for everything all the year round, I am stuffed into the two worst rooms in the house for my money, everything is organized for Maynard's convenience so that I am made to feel more like an unwelcome guest than a tenant, and now my friends are to be chosen for me ...' He decided on counter-measures. 'If Maynard can behave like an old virgin Jewess I can behave like a British businessman. The house is ours, stands in my name ... I say – denounce the treaty.'[64] However, actual possession and a Treasury salary increased to £1000 a year proved stronger than Clive's resentment. The lease of 46 Gordon Square was renewed in September 1918 – in Maynard's name. Clive retained his two attic rooms. But there was still friction. Maynard had commandeered Clive's bed, substituting one that felt 'more like the seat of a third-class railway carriage'. As the war's end approached, Clive wrote to Maynard, 'I must have my bed

---

* I have slightly rearranged the order of this entry to make it more coherent. David Garnett jotted down Vanessa's report as he remembered it, without regard to sequence of ideas or observations. The Sheppard and Norton remarks were evidently made to Vanessa at 46 Gordon Square. Maynard's visit to Charleston was the one in May 1918 referred to above.

back ... Nothing could be more easy for you than to get a new one for yourself.' Since Maynard proved in no hurry to oblige, Clive had his own bed moved upstairs. 'Dear Maynard,' he wrote from Garsington, 'I had no notion of leaving you to sleep on the floor.' He was sending down his third-class railway carriage. 'As you appear to fuck less than I do it may serve well enough'.[65]*

By August 1918 it was clear that Germany's last fling had failed. The British counter-attack breached the Hindenburg line on 29 September. The same day Ludendorff insisted that the war must end to save his armies. On 4 October the new German government of Prince Max of Baden asked for an armistice on the basis of Wilson's Fourteen Points. 'What an astonishing fortnight this has been in the history of the world!' Maynard wrote to his mother on 13 October. 'Six months from now expect me back at Cambridge quite quit of the Treasury.' Twelve days later doubts had returned. 'I still think the prospects of peace good. But I suspect a possibility of wickedness on our part and an unwillingness to subscribe to the whole of Wilson's fourteen commandments.'

The war ended for Maynard in an unceasing social whirl: weekends with the Asquiths, the McKennas, Maud Cunard and Sir Thomas Beecham; dining out every evening with politicians, diplomats and society hostesses. On top of this Duncan and Vanessa had been staying at 46 Gordon Square decorating Maynard's drawing room, and the Diaghilev Ballet had returned to London. Oswald Falk took Maynard to see it. 'There's no genius in it this year, but all the same it is most enjoyable,' Maynard wrote to Duncan on 17 September. 'The lady, Lupokova, is poor. But the new Nijinski – Mr. [Stanislav] Idzikovsky – , although no replacer and just an ordinary well trained youth, has a charm or two. At least I think so.'† On 10 October Maynard met Lopokova at a party given by the Sitwells in Chelsea, possibly for the first time. On 19 October, after having been to the ballet again with his young friend the painter Edward Wolfe, he was writing about her quite familiarly to Duncan, though his interest was clearly elsewhere:

> We went round afterwards to Lupokova who was as usual charming (making us pinch her legs to see how strong she was – which we did

---

* Maynard's was not the only character to wilt under the strain of war. Clive Bell withheld from his parents the knowledge that he was a conscientious objector, preferring them to believe he was medically unfit, in order, as he put it to Vanessa, 'to preserve our lien on the Bell millions'. Vanessa tried to hush up the fact that the daughter she had early in 1919 was by Duncan and not Clive, probably for the same reason. Honesty had its limitations for everyone.

† On 16 September the Diaghilev Ballet had danced *Prince Igor* and *La Princesse enchantée* at the Coliseum. However, Lydia had previously 'captured the heart of London' as Mariuccia in Massine's *The Good Humoured Ladies* (Buckle, *Diaghilev*, p. 348). Oswald Falk recalled that after Maynard had seen Lydia for the first time he remarked, 'She is a rotten dancer – she has such a stiff bottom'.

very shyly; Clive should have been there). But why I mention this is to lead up to Idzikovsky whose acquaintance at last we've made. The Ballet had been Enchanted Princess and [Prince] Igor and Wolfe had been rapturous over Idzi's body. So on visiting Lupokova we enquired after him. 'I hear his voice in the passage outside,' cried Lydia. 'Call him in.' Which done, in stepped the most ridiculous little creature you ever saw. Very tiny (which we expected) but with white flaxen hair brushed back from his forehead, a pasty face with ridiculous little peaked features, the whole crowned by pince nez with no rims to them ... The others didn't seem to take him at all seriously and Mr. Baroque [Lydia's husband Randolfo Barocchi] gently ragged him, throwing his arms round him and crying out 'Good night, my love' as he went away. 'I don't like dancing with him,' said Lydia. 'It is not nice to dance with something only up to your breasts and I am always afraid he will drop me'.

Maynard's days were spent in exhausting negotiations with the French. Early in November he was 'writing a Memorandum on Indemnities at top speed for an airman to fly to Versailles with'.[66] On 21 November 1918, ten days after Germany's surrender, he wrote to his mother, 'I have been put in principal charge of financial matters for the Peace Conference'.

One nightmare was over; another was about to start. Less than a year later Maynard had quit the Treasury and was penning his passionate denunciations of the Peace Treaty. Yet it is clear that the fury which went into The Economic Consequences of the Peace was not the product of the Peace Conference alone but had been building up throughout the war. The attitudes he displayed in that book – mistrust of Lloyd George, contempt for the Americans, anger that politics had ousted reason, fear of general impoverishment – had all poured out in his wartime letters. The monkey-house of Versailles was merely the monkey-house of the Inter-Ally Council writ large. It is wrong to portray Keynes, as Harrod does, as having gone to Versailles with high hopes, only to feel betrayed. He suspected 'wickedness' even before the war ended; Versailles confirmed it. Another point must be borne in mind. Keynes carried to the conference a burden not just of collective guilt but of personal guilt for his part in the war. He was looking for a way of making an act of personal reparation. Versailles provided him with the issue he needed, as, in the nature of things, it was bound to do.

15   Zigzagging: Keynes at the Paris Peace Conference

THE COST OF THE WAR

The Paris Peace Conference opened in January 1919. Keynes's main job in the two months preceding it was to prepare the Treasury's position on the question of a German indemnity. He and the economic historian W. J. Ashley had produced a paper on the historical experience of collecting indemnities as early as 2 December 1916.[1] Basing themselves mainly on the indemnity which Germany imposed on France in 1871, they concluded that payments from losers to victors would be favourable to victors provided they took place over a period of years rather than all at once. That some payment would be required from Germany was clear from the terms of the armistice agreement.

Wilson's Fourteen Points (7, 8, 11) had talked only about Germany 'restoring' the invaded territories. But the armistice agreement which the Germans signed contained a rider, inserted by Britain and France, to the effect that by 'restoration' the Allies understood that 'compensation will be made by Germany for all damage done to the civilian population of the Allies and to their property by the aggression of Germany by land, sea, and from the air'. (The British had changed 'invasion' to 'aggression' in order to get a larger share of the spoils.) Although this formula ruled out charging Germany for the costs of the war it left plenty of scope for the Allies to bid up their competing claims for 'compensation'.

Treasury planning for reparations took place within the framework of Wilson's Fourteen Points as modified by the rider. In Keynes's first memorandum on the subject, dated 31 October 1918, a further point emerged: any reparation demanded of Germany for the damage she had caused must take into account her capacity to pay. It must not be so severe as to crush Germany's productive power; for, in the end, moveable property, gold, and foreign securities apart, Germany could pay only by exporting goods to earn foreign currency.[2] There were thus two sets of figures involved: the damage Germany had done by its 'aggression', and the probable size of its 'capacity'. The first was actual, the second hypothetical. There was no reason why they should match.

In the main Treasury memorandum of 26 November 1918, largely based on Keynes's 31 October draft, they did not. It was estimated that a round figure of £4000m might be taken as representing the preliminary claim of the Allies under the head of 'reparation'. The Treasury document emphasised that this represented damage 'done *directly*' to the civilian population – mainly destruction of civilian life and property through enemy action. It excluded indirect damage – for example, the Allies would not be entitled to claim the costs of pensions paid to widows of soldiers killed in action. Britain, it was suggested, could legitimately claim 15 per cent of the total damages. However, the maximum Germany could pay was estimated at £3000m; and an actual payment of £2000m would be 'a very satisfactory achievement in all the circumstances'. This figure was reached by estimating the export surplus which a post-war Germany could be expected to generate, based on pre-war figures, and modified by loss of territory, moveable property, etc. The assumption was that Germany would pay this over a number of years in the form of an annual tribute. 'If Germany is to be "milked", she must not first of all be ruined', the memorandum concluded.[3]

The Treasury was not the only agency concerned with working out the sums of German payments. A powerful lobby had grown up outside Whitehall dedicated to the proposition that Germany must be charged the 'whole costs of the war'. It was composed, on the one hand, of business interests who wanted German rather than British industry taxed to finance the huge National Debt which the war had created and, on the other hand, of representatives of the British Dominions, who wanted compensation for the Empire's sacrifices, which the formula of 'reparation' excluded. (As Robert E. Bunselmeyer suggests, the argument between those who wanted an 'indemnity' and those who were prepared to settle for 'reparation' broadly followed the pre-war Protection-versus-Free-Trade debate). Lloyd George was a 'Jekyll and Hyde', sometimes breathing fire against Germany, at other times recognising the need for moderation and worried by the effect which large German transfers would have on Britain's export industries. However, he had to pay attention to the opinions of the Conservatives, who provided him with his parliamentary majority, and to the Dominion leaders gathered in London in the Imperial War Cabinet. The balance of opinion in the political combinations he had conjured up to fight the war was thus much less liberal than he, perhaps, would have liked to be.

The General Election of 14 December 1918 provided the link between 'the mentality of war, especially economic war, and the making of peace'.[4] The Australian prime minister, William Morris Hughes, was enraged by the Wilsonian formula, and the Treasury estimates based on it. On 7 November he publicly demanded that Germany be made to pay the costs of the war; his cry was taken up by leading newspapers. Hughes's outburst, repeated a few days later, frightened Lloyd George, as the Dominions were to be directly represented at the Paris peace talks and Lloyd George had to carry them with him. On 26 November 1918, the day after the dissolution of Parliament, the Imperial War Cabinet decided to appoint a Committee of its own to determine how much Germany should and could pay. Hughes was made chairman to muzzle him; the Committee was stuffed with Conservative Protectionists; Lord Cunliffe was included to add the authority of an ex-governor of the Bank of England. Keynes and Llewellyn Smith of 'A' Division attended the first few hearings. They warned of the effects of large German exports on British trade. In that case, Hughes argued, Britain and the Allies could raise tariffs against Germany. 'Yet he made no effort to discover how Germany could pay the entire costs of the War except through an export surplus.'[5]

The Committee's final report of 10 December put the total cost of the war at £24,000m (which is roughly what the Treasury had estimated), and claimed that Germany could and should pay the whole amount in annual instalments of £1200m. The War Cabinet rejected this conclusion as a 'wild and fantastic chimera', but not before Lloyd George had promised at Bristol on 11 December that if re-elected he would charge Germany the whole cost of the war, an 'expert' Committee having told him Germany could pay it. In his election campaign, Lloyd George had yielded to popular clamour as well as to the pessimistic forecasts of his campaign managers. Fighting on a Coalition programme of reconstruction, he found that his speeches fell flat unless he talked about punishing Germany. Other ministers used more extreme language. At Cambridge, Sir Eric Geddes, First Lord of the Admiralty, declared on 9 December: 'The Germans, if this Government is returned, are going to pay every penny; they are going to be squeezed as a lemon is squeezed – until the pips squeak. My only doubt is not whether we can squeeze hard enough, but whether there is enough juice.'*

The effect of the election campaign on the peace negotiations was not confined to the election promises given by Lloyd George and others. In sweeping away the old Liberal Party (even Asquith lost his seat) the electorate saddled Lloyd George with a Jingo majority in Parliament

---

* Bunselmeyer (p.137) suggests that one reason for the widespread electoral interest in the economic aspects of the peace settlement was that 17m people in Britain held government debt.

(383 Conservatives, many of them businessmen). Furthermore, at the height of the election, Lloyd George accepted a recommendation by the Imperial War Cabinet that Hughes and Cunliffe, the chief authors of what he later called the 'wild and fantastic report', should be the British representatives – together with a judge, Lord Sumner – on the Reparations Commission at the Paris Peace Conference. Keynes and the British Treasury were thus formally excluded from the reparations side of the peace talks. This decision had baleful consequences. When, in Paris, Lloyd George eventually turned to Keynes and others to provide him with more realistic figures, he found he was saddled with the 'Heavenly Twins', as Cunliffe and Sumner were known, who prevented a coherent British position from emerging.

Keynes and the Treasury view were not without supporters. Bonar Law, the Chancellor and head of the Conservative Party, was a notable force for moderation. Jan Christian Smuts, leading the South African delegation to Paris and also a member of the British War Cabinet (his double position was one of the war's constitutional anomalies), was full of admiration for Keynes's 'masterly memorandum on Indemnities'.[6] On the other side, Leo Amery, the Colonial Secretary, wrote to Smuts on 26 December:

> Hughes's figures seem to me exaggerated. On the other hand the Treasury memorandum goes much too far the other way and is full of crude economic fallacies such as one would naturally perhaps expect from a professor like Keynes. Neither of them take any account of what is really the most important question, which is to make sure that whatever the amount Germany does pay, we should get our fair share.[7]

Amery wanted, above everything, to avoid a rupture between Britain and the Dominions. He worked out a formula, based on 'total net loss', which would have given the British Empire a larger share of a still moderate indemnity.[8]

On the other hand, the U.S. and British Treasuries saw eye to eye. On 6 December, D. H. Miller, chief legal adviser to the American delegation, reported a conversation between himself, two American representatives and Keynes on the subject of reparations. Keynes took the view that the 'French demand for a huge indemnity was to be the basis for continued occupation and ultimate acquisition of the Rhine provinces'. Paul Cravath, one of the American lawyers present, urged a proper distribution of the indemnity and warned that the French would advance claims without regard to Wilson's Note of 5 November, to which the Germans had agreed.[9] In France it was accepted that no French government could survive which did not demand from Germany the whole cost of the war ('L'Allemagne paiera') since to raise taxes was considered political suicide. The political chiefs of Britain and France were united in their determination to wriggle out of their commitment to 'reparation only'. The point on which they differed was the division of the loot.

II

DR MELCHIOR

Keynes went to Paris on 10 January as the chief Treasury representative of the British delegation, assisted by Dudley Ward, Oswald Falk and Geoffrey Fry of 'A' Division. He had a room at the Hotel Majestic with the rest of the British delegation. His job was to handle the financial aspects of the transition to peace. Relief matters were in the hands of an Inter-Ally Supreme Council for Relief and Supply, of which the American Herbert Hoover was director-general, and on which Keynes served under Lord Reading. A decision to supply the Germans with 270,000 tons of food was taken by the Council on 12 January 1919, conditional on the Germans handing over their merchant marine. But at the Armistice Commission, over which Marshal Foch presided, the French Finance Minister, Louis-Lucien Klotz, objected that 'Germany should not pay for [the food] out of assets which were available for Reparation'.[10] Keynes, left to represent the British position, protested loudly: 'as a result deadlock and the matter referred to the Supreme War Council in the afternoon [of 13 January]'. Here President Wilson held forth eloquently on the dangers of Bolshevism if Germany were not fed; Hoover, desperate to unload his 'abundant stocks of low-grade pig products at high prices' on the Germans, added supporting arguments. Klotz reluctantly accepted a compromise whereby Germany should be allowed to earmark resources to pay for some of the food, subject to an investigation of the German financial position. Next day (14 January) Keynes, together with Norman Davis, Assistant Secretary to the American Treasury, and Comte de Lasteyrie and Professor Attolico, representing the French and Italian Treasuries, joined Marshal Foch's train en route for Trèves (or Trier), where the Marshal was due to meet President Erzberger of Germany. They had arranged to meet German financial experts to discuss means of payment. Keynes recalled that on the journey, and at Trèves itself, when not in conference, he made up an almost continuous Anglo-American bridge four.[11]

The financial discussions took place on the train. The German team was headed by Dr Kaufman, President of the Reichsbank. But it was another German who made the deepest impression on Keynes. This was Dr Carl Melchior, a partner in the banking firm of M. M. Warburg. 'Dr Melchior: A Defeated Enemy', posthumously published in

1949, is the most intimate and accomplished of all Keynes's writings, offering a highly emotional account of a personal drama. It was first read to Bloomsbury's Memoir Club in February 1920, where it greatly impressed Virginia Woolf with its 'method of character drawing'. She thought the 'set-pieces' were very brilliantly told. Here Keynes sets the scene:

> A sad lot they were in those early days, with drawn, dejected faces and tired staring eyes, like men who had been hammered on the Stock Exchange. But from amongst them stepped forward into the middle place a very small man, exquisitely clean, very well and neatly dressed, with a high stiff collar which seemed cleaner and whiter than an ordinary collar, his round head covered with grizzled hair shaved so close as to be like in substance to the pile of a close-made carpet, the line where his hair ended bounding his face and forehead in a very sharply defined and rather noble curve, his eyes gleaming straight at us, with extraordinary sorrow in them, yet like an honest animal at bay. This was he whom in the ensuing months I was to have one of the most curious intimacies in the world, and some very strange passages of experience – Dr Melchior ... This Jew, for such, though not by appearance, I afterwards learnt him to be, and he only, upheld the dignity of defeat.[12]

Fraternisation between victor and vanquished was forbidden, and the conference ended, as it had been conducted, with frigid formality, thawed only slightly by the natural gregariousness of the Americans. Little had been accomplished. The Germans agreed to hand over £4m in gold to pay for an immediate supply of fats and condensed milk. Mr Hoover's pigs remained uneaten; Klotz was still determined to get his hands on the bulk of Germany's gold reserve. German ships remained in German harbours, blockaded by the Allies. But Keynes and Melchior had made an unstated contact. The suffering in Melchior's face made a more vivid impact on Keynes than did the collective sufferings of France. The balance of his emotions was tilted even further in Germany's favour by his dislike of his French colleagues. De Lasteyrie, a 'genteel Catholic', represented to him the 'grasping sterility of France'; or of that part of France which, 'in spite of what Clive [Bell] and Roger [Fry] may say, *is* France'. Keynes recalled: 'I don't believe I have ever ... been so rude to anyone' – an awesome thought.[13]

Keynes was getting on no better with the French in other matters. On 19 February, back in Paris after a fortnight with the Bussys on the Riviera recovering from 'flu and a second fruitless conference at Trèves, he had another row with Klotz. He curtly told the French Finance Minister that Britain could no longer provide support for the French franc. The franc plummeted, followed soon afterwards by sterling, ending a hundred years of fixed exchange-rates. Klotz wrote a book in

1924, blaming Keynes's 'swollen vanity' for the 'financial catastrophe which has fallen on the world'. But Keynes was acting on the authority of Austen Chamberlain, the new Chancellor of the Exchequer, who had been told by Colonel House, Wilson's special adviser, that American official aid to Britain was being cut off.[14] Continuous contact with France's garrulous Finance Minister on the Supreme Economic Council (which had replaced the Council for Supply and Relief on 8 February) did nothing to increase Keynes's already limited sympathy for French demands. 'A short, plump, heavy-moustached Jew, well-groomed, well kept, but with an unsteady, roving eye, and his shoulders a little bent with instinctive deprecation',[15] Klotz represented, to Keynes, the other face of France's grasping sterility; a view not uninfluenced by the anti-Semitism which was normal to his class and generation.

On 4 March Keynes was once more negotiating with the Germans. This time the meeting took place in Belgium at Spa, Germany's war-time military headquarters, where he stayed with General Haking, Britain's chief military representative on the Armistice Commission, in Ludendorff's villa, surrounded by 'the theatrical melancholy of black pinewoods'. The head of the British delegation, Admiral Hope, opened the meeting by informing the German delegates that no foodstuffs would be allowed to enter Germany until 'substantial progress' had been made in handing over the German passenger and cargo vessels. The head of the German delegation, von Braun, replied that the delivery of the German merchant fleet was contingent on firm promises from the Allies to make available enough food to feed Germany till the next harvest (in August).[16] But there was no way such promises could be given, since the French had not yet agreed to allow the Germans to pay for any food beyond a small amount. Meanwhile, Haking told Keynes that the Germans were starving and the social order was on the point of collapse.

Keynes was convinced that some way had to be found of breaking the deadlock. If the Germans would agree to give way on the ships, he and the Americans would bring pressure on their political chiefs to overrule Klotz. As Keynes tells it:

> I looked across the table at Melchior. He seemed to feel as I did. Staring, heavy-lidded, helpless, looking, as I had seen him before, like an honourable animal in pain. Couldn't we break down the empty formalities of this Conference, the three-barred gate of triple interpretations, and talk about the truth and the reality like sane and sensible persons?

He tells how they escaped from Melchior's mutinous, bolshevised clerks to a small room where they were at last alone:

I was quivering with excitement, terrified out of my wits at what I was doing, for the barriers of permitted intercourse had not then begun to crumble, and somewhat emotional. Melchior wondered what I wanted ... I tried to convey to him what I was feeling, how we believed his prognostications of pessimism, how we were impressed, not less than he, with the urgency of starting food supplies ... that they [the Germans] must make up their minds to the handing over of the ships; and that, if only he could secure a little latitude from Weimar, we could between us concoct a formula which would allow the food supplies to move in practice and evade the obstructions of the French.

By now both Keynes and Melchior were in a highly emotional state. 'We both stood all through the interview. In a sort of way I was in love with him.' What Keynes and Melchior seem to have done is to agree a form of words, for Admiral Hope to present to the German delegation, to the effect that if the Germans agreed to hand over their merchant marine, the Allies would agree to supply the food the Germans required, subject to the approval of the Supreme War Council as to quantities, and to the approval of the Supreme Economic Council as to arrangements for payment.[17] 'We pressed hands, and I hurried quickly into the street ...'[18]

Weimar was contacted but refused to budge. Keynes left for Paris on 6 March determined to 'attract the attention of the Great Ones' who were frittering away their time debating how many votes Brazil should have on some sub-commission, and listening to endless speeches in unknown languages by Copts, Armenians, Slovaks, Arabs and Zionists.[19] This time he managed to engage Lloyd George's interest. A meeting of the Supreme War Council was called for 8 March.

The story of that dramatic meeting, in which Lloyd George turned with terrible fury on Klotz, stimulated Keynes to the most vivid piece of writing in his memoir; his account is substantially confirmed by Lord Riddell in his *Intimate Diary of the Peace Conference*. Lord Robert Cecil presented the British case. The Germans must promise to deliver the ships. The Allies must promise to start delivering the food as soon as Germany started releasing the ships. The Germans must be allowed to pay in gold. The blockade must be lifted to the extent of allowing them to start exporting some goods and buying food from neutrals. Lloyd George clothed Lord Robert's prosaic prose with tempestuous imagery: if the Allies refused to revictual the Germans they would be sowing the seeds of Bolshevism, of the next war. It was 'a superb farrago of sense and sentiment, of spontaneous rhetoric and calculated art'. Clemenceau gave way on the gold.

Lloyd George had another trick up his sleeve. Suddenly a secretary rushed in with a telegram. Tearing it open, the Prime Minister read out a message from General Plumer, commanding British occupation forces on the Rhine. It demanded food 'without delay'. Women and children were dying; the people were in despair and felt that an end by bullets was better than death by starvation. Despite the effect produced by this *coup de théâtre* Klotz, misjudging the atmosphere, still made difficulties.

> Never [Keynes wrote] have I seen the equal of the onslaught with which that poor man was overwhelmed ... Lloyd George had always hated and despised him; and now saw in a twinkling that he could kill him. Women and children were starving, he cried, and here was M. Klotz prating and prating of his 'goold'. He leant forward and with a gesture of his hands indicated to everyone the image of a hideous Jew clutching a money bag. His eyes flashed and the words came out with a contempt so violent that he seemed almost to be spitting at him ... Everyone looked at Klotz ... the poor man was bent over his seat, visibly cowering.

The Prime Minister had not finished. Unless Klotz ceased his obstructive tactics, he roared, three names would go down in history as the architects of Bolshevism: Lenin, Trotsky and ... 'All round the room you could see each one grinning and whispering to his neighbour "Klotzky".'[20] This was the moment when Maynard changed his mind about Lloyd George. He suddenly realized that 'he can be amazing when one agrees with him. Never have I more admired his extraordinary powers'. The seeds of Maynard's later 'betrayal' of Asquith, of his collaboration with Lloyd George in the Liberal Industrial Enquiry of the late 1920s, were planted in that inspired half-hour.

Four days later Keynes was on his way to Brussels with the First Sea Lord, Admiral Wemyss, who was authorised to accept the surrender of the German ships. The admiral was worried that the Germans might demur about handing over their ships unconditionally, which is what the Supreme War Council had insisted on. Would Keynes make sure that everything went smoothly? Once more he sought out Dr Melchior in his hotel room. He told him that the leader of the German delegation would be called upon to surrender the ships right at the start of the conference. But then, as Melchior's face fell, Keynes added that once the German statement to that effect had been made the Allies would immediately give their undertaking to revictual Germany. Could Melchior make sure that the German part of this script was followed to the letter? 'Yes,' he replied. 'There shall be no difficulty about that.' The next day everything went according to plan. Within days, 'the food trains started to Germany'.[21] There were to be further meetings, near Paris, with Melchior and other German bankers to discuss the handover of German gold and securities, but the battle had been won.

Throughout this period Keynes was living in an extreme state of nervous excitement. To his mother he wrote on 16 March:

I am Deputy for the Chancellor of the Exchequer on the Supreme Economic Council with full powers to take decisions; also one of the British Empire representatives on the Financial Committee of the Peace Conference; Chairman of the Inter-Allied Financial Delegates in Armistice Negotiations with the Germans; and principal Treasury Representative in Paris. All of which sounds rather greater than it is; but it's a full day's occupation.

He rushed about in 'draughty motor cars from one overheated room to another', eating excessively rich food and sometimes overwhelmed with work.[22] The Hotel Majestic swarmed with Scotland Yard officers. Members of the British delegation hurried from one committee to another. The red boxes circulated unendingly, full of unread memoranda; and the 'feverish, persistent and boring gossip of that hellish place had already developed in full measure the peculiar flavour of smallness, cynicism, self-importance and bored excitement that it was never to lose'.[23] To Vanessa Bell, Keynes wrote, 'I'm absolutely absorbed in this extraordinary but miserable game. I wish I could tell you every evening the twists and turns of the day, for you'd really be amused by the amazing complications of psychology and personality and intrigue which make such magnificent sport of the impending catastrophe of Europe.'[24]

III

THE REPARATIONS TANGLE

Keynes had, as yet, had little to do with drawing up the financial terms of the peace settlement. The detailed work of the conference was being done by the Expert Commissions, with contentious issues referred to the Supreme War Council, or Council of Ten as it was known, which became the Council of Four late in March. The Reparations Commission was divided into three sub-committees, on evaluation, capacity and guarantees. In the first sub-committee the Australian prime minister, Hughes, a blunt, impetuous man whose deafness was a considerable help in resisting counter-arguments, joined the French in claiming the whole cost of the war, his argument being that the tax burden imposed on the Allies by the German aggression should be regarded as damage to civilians. The claim came to about $125b, or £25b. The American John Foster Dulles took the line that there had been a contract with Germany, which limited her liability at most to $25b–$30b, or about £5b–£6b.

Faced with an American veto, the French abandoned their claim to war costs, being impressed by Dulles's argument that, having suffered the most damage, they would get the largest share of reparations. Once the percentage game started, the British discovered that their share would go up relative to the French by including in the Allied claim the costs of pensions paid to war widows, and separation allowances paid to the wives of combatants. The American Assistant Secretary to the Treasury Norman Davis 'finally agreed to include these items in the categories of damage because we thought it just, and because we thought it would not increase the amount which Germany would eventually pay, but would only change the basis of dividing what she did pay, which seemed to us more equitable '.[25] However, the French refused to set a figure on their claim, since they feared it would be too small to satisfy French public opinion.

All this was going on in February. In the second sub-committee, the chairman Lord Cunliffe thought that Germany could pay £25b, but finally agreed to recommend £8b if the Americans would agree. The French Minister of Reconstruction, Louis Loucheur, told Davis privately that he was satisfied that the Germans could not pay anything approaching this, but could not advocate a smaller sum than Lord Cunliffe was doing. On 1 March Keynes reported to Austen Chamberlain that the range of disagreement was between £6b and £9b.[26] Deadlock was reached when the banker Thomas W. Lamont, representing America, refused to go above £6b, of which half was to be paid in German currency. In Tillman's summary, 'Direct negotiations for a fixed sum through the determination of German capacity to pay had by early March failed as completely as the attempt to fix the sum through the evaluation of damages.'[27]

On 10 March, in an effort to break the deadlock, Lloyd George, Clemenceau and Colonel House (representing Wilson who was away in the United States) appointed a secret committee consisting of Edwin Montagu, Davis and Loucheur to determine what sum could be collected from Germany, and in what proportion it should be distributed. An agreement on percentages was reached, 55 per cent to the French and 25 per cent to the British. Montagu and Loucheur also agreed with Davis that the most Germany could be expected to pay over thirty years was £3b – the same figure as the British Treasury memorandum of 26 November 1918 – Loucheur telling Montagu that 'Germany could not ... pay more than £2b which would have to be supplemented by ... "monkey's money" '.[28] Lloyd George seemed to accept this on 15 March, saying to Davis that he would have 'to tell our people the facts'. But on 18 March, fortified by Lord Sumner's assurance that the Germans could be milked for £11b, Lloyd George decided to postpone the public enlightenment. These events marked Keynes's first involvement in the reparations question. Montagu naturally consulted him; there is a memorandum from Keynes, dated 11 March, stating that whereas Germany should be required to 'render payment for the injury she has caused up to the limit of her capacity', it was impossible at the present time to determine what her capacity was, so that the fixing of a definite liability should be postponed.[29] Since this is what the Treaty actually did, it would seem that Keynes's advice was contrary to his later view (expressed in *The Economic Consequences of the Peace*, pp. 85, 99) that the Allies should have fixed a definite sum in the Treaty. However, he was still assuming in March that the *total* of claims would not amount to more than £3b, the political leaders not yet having agreed to the inclusion of pensions and separation allowances.

Lloyd George's strategy at this point was still to bind Cunliffe and Sumner to a 'reasonable' sum. The experts worked out a flexible plan, allowing for a minimum of $25b (£5b) and a maximum of $35b (£7b). This was the nearest they got to harmonising the views of Davis and Lamont on the one hand, and Cunliffe and Sumner on the other. There is a letter Keynes's hand to Lloyd George, dated 22 March, enclosing a schedule of annual payments based on the smaller sum, which he had worked out with R. H. Brand of Lazards. Keynes's touch appears in the words: 'In our opinion, long before the amounts are collected, the Allied governments may, and probably will, find that such collection is doing them as much damage as to the enemy'.[30] But Lloyd George would not accept £5b unless Cunliffe and Sumner accepted it, fearing that their opposition would 'crucify' him in Parliament;[31] the Heavenly Twins refused to budge. Keynes was now taking a more charitable view of the Prime Minister. He wrote to his father on 30 March: 'For the last ten days I've had the experience of working intimately with the P.M. and have seen a fair amount of Wilson and Clemenceau. The fact is that Ll.G. has, at least for the time being, taken a turn towards a heaven place and away from a hell place, so that my services are not quite as inappropriate to him as usual.'

After a weekend at Fontainebleau, Lloyd George returned to Paris in a liberal mood, declaring once more (26 March) that he and Clemenceau should tell the people the truth. Wilson responded enthusiastically to this suggestion, especially as coming from such an unlikely quarter: 'I cannot fail to express my admiration for the spirit which manifests itself in Mr Lloyd George's words. There is nothing more honourable than to be driven from power because one was right.' This was the last thing Lloyd George had in mind. A couple of days later, he clutched at Klotz's proposal that they leave out of the Treaty any definite figures. A Reparations Commission was to be given until 1921 to work out what Germany owed, subject only to the proviso that it pay £1b on account. Twisting and turning, Lloyd George had eventually found a way out of his embarrassing commitments to the Jingoes and the Heavenly Twins.

As we have seen, the idea of including pensions and separation allowances in the claim for damages dated from February. But the American President had not yet agreed to this apparent breach of the Fourteen Points. At first he had strongly resisted it. But he was converted by a 'legal opinion' prepared by Smuts on 31 March 1919, at Lloyd George's request. Smuts argued that while direct war expenses could not be legitimately claimed from the Germans, 'disablement pensions to discharged soldiers, or pensions to widows and orphans or separation allowances paid to their wives and children during the period of their military service' could.[32] Smuts's aim was to get the British Empire a larger share of reparations. He recognized that it would increase the total claim against Germany; but assumed that this would anyway be scaled down to Germany's 'capacity to pay' which, like Keynes and the Americans, he estimated at between £2b and £3b.[33] Wilson, seeing a way of squaring British and French demands with his conscience, dismissed the legalistic objections of his advisers – 'Logic! Logic! I don't give a damn for logic. I am going to include pensions' – even though he recognized that 'it was not in the minds of those who drew up the Armistice . . . to include pensions'.[34] The fullest account of the dramatic meeting of 1 April has been left by John Foster Dulles. Before the President was a plan agreed by Montagu and Keynes providing for 'the determination by a commission of the amount of damage for which the enemy should make reparation and which further provided for a reference to arbitral decision of the question of the inclusion of any category of damage as to which any member of the commission entertained doubt and provided the capacity of the enemy to pay was not exhausted without the inclusion of such item'. Lloyd George had refused to accept this plan, insisting that pensions and separation allowances be included there and then. This compelled a decision by the President. Wilson said he had been very impressed by Smuts's memorandum. Vance McCormick pointed out that American legal advisers disagreed. Wilson replied that he didn't think this was a matter for 'legal principles'. He was 'continuously finding new meanings and the necessity for broad applications of principles previously enunciated'. Dulles pointed out that it was 'very difficult to draw any logical distinction between a family which had been damaged by having their bread-winner drafted and another which had been damaged to an equivalent extent by having to pay for the equipment of that soldier and that there was a danger that to accept pensions would involve admitting against the enemy all war costs . . .' Wilson replied that 'he did not feel bound by considerations of logic . . .' It was 'thereupon agreed that pensions, including those in the form of separation allowances, would be allowed'. Keynes's unflattering assessment of the President in *The Economic Consequences of the Peace* was largely based on this single episode, which he regarded as a prime example of Wilson's casuistry.[35]

The crucial defeat in the battle to limit Germany's bill came at a meeting of the Council of Four on 5 April 1919, when Lloyd George, citing Lord Sumner, agreed to extend the time-limit of annual payments beyond thirty years 'if it turns out that all cannot be paid in this period'. In Wilson's absence, it was Colonel House who sold the pass. This concession destroyed the assumption that the inclusion of pensions would make no difference to the total amount which Germany would be called on to pay.[36] As Florence Lamont wrote in her diary, 'L.G. does not want anything put in to limit the capacity of the Germans to pay.'[37]

The Americans complained that Keynes failed to stand up to Lloyd George.[38] But no one in the British delegation did. Smuts, who might have done, was away ill for most of March; he returned to write his fateful 'legal opinion' on pensions – a document which his biographer says 'did more to damage his reputation than any other document that he ever produced in his life'[39] – before being despatched on a mission to Hungary. The Foreign Secretary, Arthur Balfour, who had the authority to do so, was so cynically detached from the proceedings that when Margot Asquith visited Paris she found that 'no one seemed to know whether he was there or not'. Keynes encountered him one night 'in a rather elevated condition in the street. He seized me warmly by the arm and marching along linked embarked on a discussion on the merits of Tiepolo.'[40] Keynes himself was no more part of Lloyd George's circle than he had been in the war. Lloyd George used him, as he used Montagu, to wriggle out of his commitments to the Heavenly Twins. But he never thought of taking his advice. Keynes later told Margot Asquith that the British were the best-equipped delegation in Paris, but that for all the use the Prime Minister made of them 'we might have been idiots'. On the whole Lloyd George took a moderate line. He feared a German war of revenge if Germany felt badly treated; he was very alive to the dangers of Revolution. So he fought successfully against the French plan to dismember Germany. It was only where his own political fears and fortunes were involved that he became timid and slippery. On reparations he wanted devices not solutions. Keynes could not help him here. Eventually Keynes realised that he could do no more good at the Treasury; but not before he made one further attempt to influence events in the direction of sanity and moderation.

IV

'GRAND SCHEME FOR THE REHABILITATION OF EUROPE'

Keynes's closest political friend in Paris was the South African defence minister, Jan Christian Smuts. They 'found' each other by elective affinity, just as Keynes had found Melchior. A Cambridge graduate of 1894, Smuts was an intellectual general, a politician with philosophical interests and ambitions. (He later invented a philosophy called Holism.) He shared with Keynes a high-minded approach to peacemaking, as well as an antipathy to the French, and a marked distrust of Lloyd George. Their disillusion with events in Paris developed in parallel. After his return from Hungary, Smuts wrote to his friend Mrs Gillett on 9 April:

> This afternoon . . . Keynes came to see me and I described to him the pitiful plight of Central Europe. And he (who is conversant with the finance of the matter) confessed to me his doubt whether anything could really be done. Those pitiful people have little credit left, and instead of getting indemnities from them, we may have to advance them money to live.[41]

Smuts's account of the suffering in Central Europe concentrated Keynes's attention on a scheme which had been germinating in his mind. This was to link the reparations' question with the question of inter-Ally debts. The British and French wanted to milk Germany partly for the purpose of paying back America. If the Americans could be persuaded to scale down their claims this would ease the pressure on Germany. As early as November 1918 Keynes had pointed out the advantage to Britain of an all-round debt cancellation: Britain held a lot of bad debts from its European Allies, while America held a lot of good debts from Britain. If some means were not found of reducing Britain's obligations, Britain would be left open to 'future pressure by the United States of a most objectionable description' and its foreign investment potential would be crippled.[42] On 28 March 1919 he circulated a paper arguing that the attempt to collect all the debts arising from the last war (including reparations) would poison, and perhaps destroy, the capitalist system. 'I do not believe that any of these tributes will continue to be paid, at the best, for more than a very few years. They do not square with human nature or march with the spirit of the age.' The paper is notable for its sense of the fragility of capitalist civilisation, of the heightened conflict between nationalist hopes and international obligations. But Keynes recognised that total cancellation was not practicable. So he hinted at a scheme by which Allied governments would accept German reparation bonds 'in final discharge of the debts incurred between ourselves'.

On 12 April he returned to England. Five days later he wrote to his mother that he had been busy getting through the Cabinet a '*grand scheme for the rehabilitation of Europe*'. The plan had taken shape in discussions with Smuts, and Smuts gave it enthusiastic support, while acknowledging that the idea was Keynes's.[43] Austen Chamberlain recommended it to Lloyd George as being marked by 'all Mr. Keynes's characteristic ability and fertility of resource'.[44] Lloyd George was impressed too: scaling down demands on Germany in return for a remission of debt to the United States was something which he could sell to Parliament. He passed on the Keynes Plan to President Wilson with a warm covering letter. What Keynes's scheme provided for was the issue by the German government and its defeated Allies of £1345m worth of bonds, on account of reparations, and 'in payment of all indebtedness between any of the allied and associated governments'. No interest was to be paid on them for five years, and they were to be jointly guaranteed by the issuing governments and by the allied governments in certain specified proportions. Of the total, £1000m of bonds were to be paid to the European Allies, and the rest retained by the Central Powers. The bonds were 'to be acceptable as first-class collateral for loans'.[45]

Keynes was trying to kill a number of birds with one stone. All inter-Ally debts arising from the war were to be reduced and the balance discharged by means of a German debt which could be transferred without putting immediate strain on the German balance of payments. European credit would be rehabilitated; the United States would be assured of a demand for its exports; the Central Powers too would obtain funds to feed their people. Thus the plan served both the immediate purpose of providing the European countries with means of payment for imports pending the revival of their export industries, and also the long-term purpose of greatly reducing the overhang of debt arising from the war. It was compatible with decisions already taken on reparations – which provided for an initial German payment of £1b – while improving the prospect of getting an eventual sum within Germany's 'capacity to pay'. In an accompanying memorandum intended for Wilson and Clemenceau, Keynes wrote:

A proposal which unfolds future prospects and shows the peoples of Europe a road by which food and employment and orderly existence can once again come their way, will be a more powerful weapon than any other for the preservation from the dangers of Bolshevism of that order of human society which we believe to be the best starting point for future improvement and greater well-being.[46]

The American reaction was disappointingly cool. Thomas Lamont, writing with all the authority of a partner in J. P. Morgan, condemned

it as 'unsound in conception, and impracticable in execution'. He argued that its adoption would give the impression that the European
countries were insolvent, and would diminish the Europeans' incentive
to work. Furthermore, it would require Congressional approval which
would not be forthcoming. Lamont wanted American credits to be
extended through 'normal commercial and banking channels'. He
proposed setting up a private Finance Corporation in the United States
to channel American savings to Europe in co-operation with British
banking groups.[47]*

At dinner with Keynes and Smuts on 3 May, Davis and Lamont
revealed another objection to the Keynes Plan: 'They see that any
assistance they give to Germany will enable us to extract more reparation, and they are determined they will not assist.'[48] Any hope that
Wilson would forego part of the European debt to the United States
foundered on the rock of Lloyd George's reparations policy. On 3 May
the President wrote to the Prime Minister:

> You have suggested that we all address ourselves to the problem of
> helping to put Germany on her feet, but how can your experts or ours
> be expected to work out a *new* plan to furnish working capital to
> Germany when we deliberately start out by taking away all Ger-
> many's *present* capital?[49]

Keynes argued against this interpretation, but his heart was not in it.
As he told Philip Kerr, Lloyd George's private secretary, 'There is a
substantial truth in the President's standpoint'.[50]

Keynes's last hope that out of the horrors of Paris would at least come
a plan to put Europe back on its feet had gone. By early May a draft

---

* In a letter to R. H. Brand dated 10 June 1919, Lamont elaborated his scheme:

America has ample credit resources, Great Britain has wonderful credit machinery
all over the world. Why not make a combination of the two? You people have
splendid banks established in the Far East and all through South America. Now, we
in America are right on the verge of duplicating every bit of that banking machinery
... The result will be, you will make smaller profits, and so shall we, and we shall
be very keen rivals. Why don't we avoid all that by our buying a half interest, no
more, in a lot of your banks, and thus make a combination of your machinery and
our credit resources? I suppose the very idea sounds fantastic to you. It did to
Keynes when I sprang it on him the other night at dinner. His ready answer was,
that your banks wanted to run their business and didn't want any interference from
the outside. It was a very complete answer, because it showed the spirit of the whole
thing. When a man goes into partnership, of course, he is no longer free to manage
his affairs by himself. The same is the case when he takes a wife; but the state of the
married man is supposed to be more blessed than that of the single.

Now, I think that if the British and Americans were to start out towards a goal
of partnership, they would both make a lot more money than they ever will by
staying apart and competing against each other; and what is of infinitely greater
importance, they would establish such a rapprochement that the world could never
shake us out of peace and into war. (Lamont Papers, 165–10)

Treaty had at last been assembled out of the labours of fifty-eight specialist commissions and the deliberations of the Council of Four, giving Keynes for the first time an overall view of the proposed settlement. He was horrified. In a letter of 4 May 1919 he jotted down his immediate reactions in a note to Bradbury and Chamberlain. The reparations clauses were 'unworkable' and showed 'a high degree of unwisdom in almost every direction'. He did not object to the territorial or military clauses, though he thought they would arouse tremendous opposition from the Germans. The economic chapters contained 'a long series of pinpricks insisting upon innumerable small concessions without reciprocity' whose effect would be to 'diminish to an appreciable extent the sovereignty of Germany'. The transit and inland transport chapters contained a 'series of humiliating and interfering provisions'. No honourable country would sign a Treaty providing for the trial of its leaders. The chapter providing for the continued occupation of the Rhineland 'would appear to lend itself to the most terrible abuse'. He concluded, 'The settlement is a paper settlement which even if it is accepted cannot possibly be expected to last.' He doubted whether the Germans would sign it.[51]

To his English friends he revealed more of his true state of mind:

JMK to Duncan Grant, 14 May 1919:
My dearest Duncan,
It's weeks since I've written a letter to anyone, – but I've been utterly worn out, partly by incessant work and partly by depression at the evil round me. I've been as miserable for the last two or three weeks as a fellow could be. The Peace is outrageous and impossible and can bring nothing but misfortune . . . Certainly if I were in the Germans' place I'd die rather than sign such a Peace. Personally I don't think they will sign, though the general view here is to the contrary. But if they do sign, that will really be the worst thing that could happen, as they can't possibly keep some of the terms, and general disorder and unrest will result everywhere. Meanwhile there is no food or employment anywhere, and the French and Italians are pouring munitions into Central Europe to arm everyone against everyone else. I sit in my room hour after hour receiving deputations from the new nations, who all ask not for food or raw materials, but primarily for instruments of murder against their neighbours. And with such a Peace as the basis I see no hope anywhere. Anarchy and Revolution is the best thing that can happen, and the sooner the better.
Thank God I shall soon be out of it and I suppose it won't be many weeks before I've forgotten the nightmare. I'm writing to the Treasury to be relieved of my duties by 1 June if possible and not later than 15 June in any event.
One most bitter disappointment was the collapse of my Grand Scheme for putting everyone on their legs. After getting it success-

fully through the Chancellor of the Exchequer and the Prime Minister and seeing it formally handed to Wilson and Clemenceau, the American Treasury (of whom no more was asked than ours)* turned it down firmly as a most immoral proposal which might cost them something and which Senators from Illinois wouldn't look at. They had a chance of taking a large or at least a humane view of the world but unhesitatingly refused to sign it. Wilson, of whom I've seen a good deal more lately, is the greatest fraud on earth.

The weather is very fine. I spent last weekend at Fontainebleau Forest and tried to get to Chartres but was defeated by two punctures to my motor. Do write to remind me that there are still some decent people in the world. Here I could cry all day for rage and vexation. The world can't be quite as bad as it looks from the Majestic.

A week or two ago I went to a Matisse exhibition and enclose the catalogue. I like the latest least. Am I right that he is becoming almost academic? The singularity seemed vanishing ... I send also two reproductions of Bonnard to prove that he is not the least like you.

Your loving

JMK

To his mother he wrote the same day in similar terms regretting that he had been 'an accomplice in all this wickedness and folly'.

Now attempts were made to get him to stay on. Florence wrote on 19 May that 'perhaps things are not quite so desperate'. Austen Chamberlain begged him 'most earnestly . . . to continue for a time the public work in which you have been engaged'. General Smuts urged Keynes to fight for revisions: 'one only leaves the battlefield *dead*', he told him. But as Maynard replied to Chamberlain on 26 May: 'The Prime Minister is leading us into a morass of destruction. The settlement which he is proposing for Europe disrupts it economically and must depopulate it by millions of people'.[52] Lloyd George himself was beginning to have doubts. In the words of André Tardieu, later French Prime Minister,

> Those were atrocious days. Mr. Lloyd George thoroughly alarmed by the consequences either of a refusal to sign or of a crisis in Germany, suggested unthinkable concessions on almost every point. He excused himself for doing it so tardily. He spoke of consulting the Commons. The work of two months was threatened with ruin. M. Clemenceau stood firm.[53]

Lloyd George 'asked for a thoroughgoing revision of the Reparations Clauses, and inclined under the influence of Mr. Keynes to the lump

* The Keynes Plan provided a joint Allied guarantee of the German bonds in the event of a German default, with the U.S. and Britain each being responsible for 20 per cent. This makes it hard to maintain Stephen A. Schuker's view (*The End of French Predominance in Europe*) (1976, p.176) that Keynes planned to saddle the U.S. Treasury with worthless German reparation bonds in discharge of European obligations to the U.S.A.

sum proposed in March by the American experts'.[54] Keynes briefed him as well as he could. On 7 May Smuts wrote to his friend Mrs Gillett:

> Poor Keynes often sits with me at night after a good dinner and we rail against the world and the coming flood. And I tell him that this is the time for Grigua's prayer (the Lord to come himself and not to send his Son, as this is not a time for children). And then we laugh, and behind the laughter is Hoover's horrible picture of thirty million people who must die unless there is some great intervention. But then again we think things are never really as bad as that; and something will turn up, and the worst will never be. And somehow all these phases of feeling are true and right in some sense.

Mrs Gillett, referring to the Anti-Corn Law League, had reminded Smuts that economic reform had preceded franchise reform in the nineteenth century, and that 'now it seems as though in the same way the political and territorial questions won't be solved till the economic world is righted'. Smuts reported this remark to Keynes who said 'how true it was and he had never thought of it that way'.[55] Perhaps here we have the origin of the main theme of the *Economic Consequences of the Peace*.

Keynes was still trying to do good. At the end of May he attempted to get the successor states of the Austro-Hungarian empire relieved of their obligation to pay reparations. The minutes of the meetings held at the French Ministry of Finance, unusually for minutes, reveal the atmosphere as no summary can:

29 May 1919:
> Mr Keynes thereupon presented the general question as to whether the Reparation Clauses with Austria should follow the same lines as those with Germany. He explained that this was bad politically as the effect would be to give Austria the choice only between bolshevism with Hungary or to unite with Germany. The reports to the British Foreign Office from Vienna showed that the political effect of a treaty as proposed would be disastrous. The situation in Austria was critical and it was wholly impossible for Austria to make reparation along the lines proposed. Mr. Keynes suggested that we might abandon the present form for reparation and provide in general for a commission, not to be known as the Reparation Commission, which would have power to go to Austria and study the general economic and financial situation and with power to require reparation payments, if this should seem desirable, but also with power to recommend loans to Austria in case this should seem indispensable.
>
> After strong objections from Lord Sumner, Tardieu, Crespi and Baruch Mr. Keynes states that he wished he could adequately picture the frightful conditions in Austria. People were starving

on a large scale, and we were already loaning them substantial sums to buy food. A large part of the population were without clothing. The people were in desperate straits and already were frightfully punished for their participation in the war. We should hesitate to publish to the world a document such as the proposed draft of reparation clauses.

30 May 1919:
Discussion thereupon ensued with reference to Annex IV. Mr. Keynes particularly objected to the requirement of any immediate delivery of cattle, referring to the desperate starvation conditions prevailing.

Lord Cunliffe and Mr. Dulles pointed out that the figures given had been arrived at after consultation with experts, notably Dr. Alonzo Taylor, who had but recently been in Austria and who was deeply appreciative of the frightful food conditions. These experts had united, however, in agreeing that there were in outlying districts cattle which could be spared for Italy and Serbia, and which cattle, or the milk of which, could not on account of transportation conditions be carried to Vienna, where alone the situation was acute.

Mr. Crespi referred to the vital need of cattle and of milk in Serbia and in certain portions of Italy.

It was decided to retain Annex IV in its present form, recording the formal dissent of Mr. Keynes.

By this time Keynes had taken to his bed 'partly out of misery for all that's happening, and partly from prolonged overwork'. He had moved out of the Majestic to a flat on the edge of the Bois 'with an excellent French cook and a soldier servant to valet for me', rising only for meetings and interviews with the Chancellor, Smuts, the Prime Minister and suchlike. But it was all too late. Quite apart from Clemenceau's intransigence, Wilson had convinced himself that the draft Treaty was in conformity with his Fourteen Points. Besides, at the last moment he did not want any change in the Treaty 'simply because it was severe; . . . he wanted this to be a historic lesson, so that people might know that they could not do anything of the sort the Germans attempted without suffering the severest kind of punishment'.[57] It may also be that Lloyd George had received secret information that the Germans would sign, come what may, and that German protests were for form's sake only.[58]

The Treaty of Versailles was signed on 28 June 1919. By then Keynes had already left Paris and the Treasury. 'I can do no more good here', he wrote to Norman Davis on 5 June. 'You Americans are broken reeds'. To Lloyd George he wrote on the same day:

Dear Prime Minister,

I ought to let you know that on Saturday I am slipping away from the scene of nightmare. I can do no more good here. I've gone on hoping even through these last dreadful weeks that you'd find some way to make of the Treaty a just and expedient document. But now it's apparently too late. The battle is lost. I leave the twins to gloat over the devastation of Europe, and to assess to taste what remains for the British taxpayer.

Sincerely yours,

J. M. Keynes[59]

Mostly at Paris Keynes had been in touch with the circle with whom he had been dealing as a wartime Treasury official. But he made two new friends, who were to provide important links with American affairs in the years ahead: Felix Frankfurter, a young lawyer and professor at the Harvard Law School, who was a member of the Zionist Commission at the conference, and the journalist Walter Lippman. Frankfurter's views coincided with those of Keynes, for whom he developed an unbounded admiration: the Treaty was a breach of faith; Wilson, presuming to play a lone hand out of his self-sufficient principles, had been outwitted by unscrupulous European tricksters. Frankfurter got Keynes his American publisher for *The Economic Consequences of the Peace* and arranged serialisation of the book in the *New Republic*; in the 1930s he would be Keynes's main contact with Franklin Roosevelt and the New Deal. The disgust of both men at the standard of statesmanship achieved at Paris would spur their efforts to build a better world.

16   Civilisation under Threat

WRITING THE BOOK

On 25 June 1919 Keynes wrote to his mother from Charleston, 'On Monday I began to write a new book . . . on the economic condition of Europe as it now is, including a violent attack on the Peace Treaty and my proposals for the future . . . I was stirred into it by the deep and violent shame which one couldn't help feeling for the events of Monday, and my temper may not keep up high enough to carry it through.'[1] On Monday, 23 June, the Allies had finally cut off any hope of modifying the draft proposals presented to the Germans; but the idea of making a public protest was already in Keynes's mind. He had written to Smuts on his return to London (8 June): 'I hope immensely that you may come to the conclusion that some explanation of what is really happening and a protest against it is now the right course. If so, I am at your service by pen or any other way.'[2] At this stage, Keynes still saw himself as briefing Smuts; he did not yet see himself in a starring role.

The possibility of having to take the lead was forced on him by Smuts's own withdrawal. Although reproving Keynes for 'cutting the painter', Smuts had urged him on 10 June to start writing 'a clear, connected account of what the financial and economic clauses of the treaty actually mean, and what their probable results will be'. However, he had reserved his own position. 'Our actual course we need not decide just yet. Indeed, I have not yet made up my mind on the matter.' Smuts felt that the Treaty was bound to be a 'rotten thing'. On the other hand, 'it is necessary to have a formal Peace in order that the world may have a chance'.[3] These phrases reveal Smuts's ambiguity: for if he signed the Treaty, how could he lead a campaign against it? Keynes replied on 12 June from 46 Gordon Square:

> I was afraid you would be a little annoyed with me for clearing out. But after much reflection I felt, whether wisely or not, that I really had no alternative. So far as one can judge from the progress of events from the newspapers I should have done no good, at any rate so far,

by lingering on, whereas my rage and misery would certainly have become insupportable.

Short of a real and genuine miracle, I don't see how I can possibly contemplate coming back. If the Prime Minister turned a complete somersault and really wanted my assistance for business on really new lines that would be another matter. But this is not going to happen. In Paris I am sure the battle is lost.

As regards the future, I am taking a complete holiday in the country for the moment. But I shall be ready at any time you suggest and would be able to complete the work at short notice and with very little delay. The thing is quite clear in my head and only needs writing out.[4]

Smuts signed the Treaty of Versailles on 28 June, while publicly protesting its inadequacy. On 17 July, on the eve of his departure for South Africa, he wrote to Maynard once more, apparently reversing his previous advice:

After giving the matter my closest consideration I have seen no great profit in a regular attack on the Treaty. It is past and nothing can undo it except time and the Great Mercy which works away all our human follies. Better to be constructive. My protest on signing the Peace had a great effect both here and on the Continent ... You will find many opportunities to help the world, especially when the real trouble over the Reparations and financial clauses begins with Germany.[5]

Once the Germans decided to sign the Treaty, Smuts's own signature became inevitable. He had no British political base from which to oppose it. Besides South Africa needed the Treaty to secure its mandate over the former German colony of South-West Africa. Smuts also attached far more importance than did Keynes to setting up the League of Nations. Like many revisers he looked to the League to remedy the handiwork of the treaty-makers.

Keynes had no intention of leaving matters to the 'Great Mercy'. If Smuts disdained to be briefed there were others – like Lord Robert Cecil – who urged him, on 31 July, to write 'a brilliant article ... exposing from a strictly economic point of view the dangers of the treaty'.[6] Beyond Cecil there were the Asquithians, badly in need of political ammunition; beyond them the 'educated public', bemused by wartime propaganda, in need of enlightenment. For Keynes the role of civil servant/technical economist merged insensibly into that of educator/political economist. The unique qualities of the book he actually wrote can blind us to the fact that it fell into a pattern which had already started with *Indian Currency and Finance* – that of interpreting the official mind for the educated public, and bringing the force of enlightened opinion to bear on political action. The view he would expound, as in his earlier book, was that of the informed insider, but one who was just ahead of the possibilities of action.

This, of course, does not exhaust consideration of the frame of mind in which Keynes set to work. He had resigned from the Treasury in 'misery and rage' – a misery and rage which had been building up right through the war. It was compounded of the moral strain of working for a war he did not believe in, and of the guilt at having prospered, while his friends had suffered, for views which they had jointly held. These emotions give his writing its tension, its moral and stylistic force. He also wrote with the urgency of despair. Virginia Woolf who saw him at Charleston noted in her diary of 8 July:

> He is disillusioned, he says. No more does he believe, that is, in the stability of the things he likes. Eton is doomed; the governing classes, perhaps Cambridge too. These conclusions were forced on him by the dismal and degrading spectacle of the Peace Conference, where men played shamelessly, not for Europe, or even England, but for their own return to Parliament at the next election.[7]

To Lord Robert Cecil Keynes wrote on 26 July, 'I find I take a not less pessimistic view as to the prospects of Europe and of European order, unless early steps are taken to make and *admit* as a dead letter many of the *economic* clauses of the treaty. Do you agree?'[8]

Other influences played their part in shaping the book. Immediately following his return he was in touch with Margot Asquith. At a performance of *La Boutique Fantasque* on 12 June, Margot 'saw Keynes who told us the Paris peace conference had made him morally, spiritually & physically *ill*. He had resigned out of protest. The collapse of Wilson was agonizing.' Margot Asquith's comments on the Big Three in her diary of June 1919 foreshadow, in an astonishingly precise way, what Keynes was to write about them in his book. President Wilson's 'egoism, isolation, icy ignorance & mulishness has made him hated in his own country'. Of the French she wrote: 'They don't think of the future except with Fear, or the Past except with Hate & don't realize that Fear & Hate carry Death–not Life–in their development.' Clemenceau 'with eternal Youth, France on his breast, hate in his heart & a limited life (being 78) has scored all through. He knew exactly what he wanted.' As for the British, 'unfortunately neither a Statesman nor an Englishman had the last word but a Welshman ... Doped & bewildered the British Electorate went solid for money & revenge & the Bottomleys, Beaverbrooks, [Pemberton-] Billings & Bonars have been clamouring to keep Ll. G. up to his promises ever since.'[9] With these ideas in her mind, Margot Asquith wrote Keynes a rather incoherent letter on 13 June demanding that he give her a description of the men and meetings at Paris for her diary.[10] She may well have planted in his mind the thought of supplementing his economic exposition with an account of the characters of the Allied leaders, and the atmosphere in which they worked. A remoter influence was Lytton Strachey's *Eminent Victorians* which had appeared in 1918. David Garnett feels that it tempted Keynes to be 'more indiscreet than he was by nature: to have the courage to print what he would have said in conversation'.[11]

Before he could settle down to his writing, there was practical business to attend to. Resignation from the Treasury had naturally cost him his Treasury salary of £1200 a year. But he no longer hankered for the life of a full-time Cambridge don. Within a few weeks of his return he had turned down a new chair of Currency and Banking at the London School of Economics, and a professorship at Leeds. More tempting was the offer of the chairmanship of the British Bank of Northern Commerce, a subsidiary of a Scandinavian group controlled by two millionaire bankers, Gluckstadt and Wallenberg, whom he had met during the war, and which promised £2000 a year for one day's work a week. He finally turned it down after his City friends Brand, Kindersley and Falk as well as his father had advised against, on the grounds of the Bank's foreign control. 'I am sure they want me', he had written to his father on 25 June, 'because they think I shall be of use to them with the Treasury and the F.O.; whereas in fact I am not at all disposed to play the foreigners' game against our own Depts.' But he let it be known that he was open to other offers. Meanwhile, currency speculation offered a more amusing and lucrative way of making than selling economics by the hour. He returned briefly to Cambridge in mid-June to arrange the reduction of his college and university teaching commitments. From 20 June to 9 July he was at Charleston. From 10 to 24 July he was in Cambridge again. He wrote to Duncan Grant from King's on 17 July:

> Most of the day I think about my book, and write it for about two hours, so that I get on fairly well and am now nearly half-way through the third chapter of eight. But writing is *very* difficult, and I feel more and more admiration for those who can bring it off successfully. I've finished to-day a sketch of the appearance and character of Clemenceau, and am starting to-morrow on Wilson. I think it's worthwhile to try, but it's really beyond my powers.
>
> I have written a letter to the provost [Walter Durnford], jointly with another fellow, proposing that as a memorial to those killed in the war, King's should build a Picture Gallery, in which we should gradually form a collection of modern pictures (i.e., not later than the 19th century) and give temporary exhibitions. Isn't it a good idea? ... Isn't it shocking about Lopie? Has she been discovered yet? Clive

and I are giving a grand party on the 29th to which we hoped she would come.*

Keynes left Cambridge on Thursday, 24 July. He spent a weekend at The Wharf (26–27 July) where he found a 'rather amusing party ... the Grand Duke Michael and Countess Torby, Mrs. Keppel, the Countess of Crewe, etc, etc, old world celebrities as you see, off whom I won £22 at bridge'. In London on Tuesday, 29 July (he continued in a letter to his mother),

I gave a party at Gordon Square to round up the season which was judged a great success – I was too much preoccupied with the strenuous staff work of host to see much of it. We sat down twenty-three to supper shortly before midnight and did not rise from table until half-past one. It is astonishing what the resources of a household are, when pushed. The next evening [30 July] was amidst much excitement the last night of the ballet, all of my various worlds being there. I also kept various business appointments, gave evidence before the Indian Currency Committee, addressed the Fight the Famine Council, opened a discussion on the Peace Terms at a City Dining Club,† and lunched and dined out every day – after which I was quite ready for the country. It's amusing to pass from Cambridge where I'm a nonentity, to London where I'm a celebrity.[13]

From the beginning of August Keynes settled down to a regular routine at Charleston. He breakfasted at 8 a.m., and wrote till lunch time. After lunch he read *The Times* and then gardened till tea. After tea he did his correspondence. He had his own servants, Blanche and Jessie, and Gordon Square was shut up. By 17 August he was able to report to Falk that he was in the middle of the reparations chapter, and that the book was making fast progress. There were readings for his friends. 'I expect your psychological analysis of Wilson is absolutely correct. It explains everything,' wrote Leonard Woolf to him on 21 August. He added. 'I hope you're doing Lloyd George.'[14] Keynes did, in fact, write a sketch of the British Prime Minister, but was dissatisfied with it. On 3 September he informed his mother that he had 'managed to keep up my average of 1,000 words fit for the printer every day, seven days a week; but there are still some very difficult bits to do. I hope to finish by the first week of October and have it actually published

---

* In June 1919, in the Diaghilev season at the Alhambra, Lydia Lopokova had danced the Can-Can with Massine in *La Boutique Fantasque*. The 'shock' refers to her much publicised 'disappearance' on 10 July, when she left her husband, Randolfo Barocchi, and the Company.

† Keynes opened a discussion on the Treaty of Versailles at the Tuesday Club on 24 July.

before the last day of the month'. As soon as he had finished a chapter he would send it off to Miss Pate's at Cambridge to be typed. By 23 September he had sent the first five chapters to R. & R. Clark, Macmillan's Edinburgh printer, to be set up in galleys. This was nearly four-fifths of the whole. But he had not managed to start the two remaining ones, and so reckoned he was ten days behind schedule. 'They weigh rather heavily,' he told Florence, 'as I am getting stale and should like to take a month off . . . But I suppose I must persevere.'[15] By the beginning of October he had started on his last chapter and was postponing his departure from Charleston.

Meanwhile in the United States President Wilson had collapsed on a speaking tour which he had undertaken to rally support for the Treaty. Lytton Strachey wrote to Keynes from Pangbourne on 4 October:

> I seem to gather from the scant remarks in the newspapers, that your friend the President has gone mad. Is it possible that it should have gradually been borne in upon him what an appalling failure he was, and that when at last he fully realised it his mind collapsed? Very dramatic, if so. But won't it make some of your remarks almost too cruel?

Even when he was writing flat out, Keynes was not the person to be doing just one thing. He was not an author content to leave practical details to agents and publishers. On 28 July Daniel Macmillan had agreed to publish his book 'on our usual terms', by which he meant sharing expenses and profits with the author on a fifty-fifty basis. But during the summer Dan was away from the office, and Keynes got so irritated with his replacement, George Macmillan,[16] that he decided to pay for printing the book himself, leaving Macmillan with 10 per cent of the profits for distributing it. He signed a contract to this effect on 21 August. He was told that printing five thousand copies in full cloth binding would cost £653 18s – which determined him to raise the price from 7s 6d to 8s 6d per copy. Keynes hereafter paid for the printing of all the English editions of his books, supervised the details of their production, and reaped the profits. He never employed a literary agent. Felix Frankfurter, returning to the USA with a 'sample' at the end of August, managed to get an offer of an American edition from the new firm of Harcourt, Brace, and Howe, which Keynes accepted, despite discontent at the 'low' royalty of 15 per cent per copy sold.

Keynes's dealings with Macmillan in August were not confined to his own book. He arranged for the publication of a volume of Luce's poems, again at his own expense, writing to Daniel Macmillan, 'I regard the poems as quite the best very recent work in the grand tradition of English poetry. But I think it safer to go on the assumption that they will not pay.'[17] (They appeared in 1920 and did not pay.) From Rangoon, Luce wrote: 'You always send me the kindest and loveliest letters'.[18] At the same time, Maynard was helping two other friends, David Garnett and Frankie Birrell, to set up a bookshop in London.[19] Finally, to relieve the tedium of country life, he had begun speculating on the foreign exchanges which 'will shock father, but out of which I hope to do very well'.[20] 'Money is a funny thing,' he wrote to Florence on 23 September. 'It seems impossible to believe that the present system will be allowed to continue much longer. As the fruit of a little extra knowledge and experience of a special kind, it simply (and undeservedly in any absolute sense) comes rolling in.' Soon he was to discover that a little extra knowledge was no guarantee against financial catastrophe. At this stage, he was 'bulling' dollars, convinced that nothing short of a miracle would keep the pound above four dollars.[21] He also agreed to join the board of the National Mutual Assurance Society.

By 11 October Keynes had sent off chapter 6 and the greater part of chapter 7. As is common with authors, the story had grown in the telling – from an estimated 40,000 to 60,000 words. He now had to return to Cambridge to resume his lectures, though not before spending two days in Amsterdam from 13 to 15 October attending a bankers' conference called by Dr Vissering, Governor of the Netherlands Bank, to discuss a scheme for an international loan. It was in the context of this proposed loan – which would have to be furnished mainly by American banks – that Keynes received an important criticism of his book. He showed a copy of the proofs to Arthur Salter, secretary-general of the Reparations Commission. Salter thought that his portrait of the President being outmanoeuvred by the cunning Europeans would jeopardise the chances of securing American money.[22] Keynes agreed to tone down certain passages but was adamant on the main point.

> The moderate people [he replied to Salter] can do good and perhaps the extremist can do good; but it is no use for a member of the latter class to pretend he belongs to the former. Besides, it is such a hopeless business trying to calculate the psychological effects of one's anticipated actions; and I have come to feel that the best thing in all the circumstances is to speak the truth as bluntly as one can.[23]

To General Smuts, Keynes wrote on 27 November that 'attempts to humour or placate Americans or anyone else seem quite futile, and I personally despair of results from anything but violent and ruthless truth-telling – that will work *in the end*, even if slowly'.[24]

Florence was also urging her son to tone down the personal passages. The references to Don Quixote, Blind Man's Buff, and the spider and the fly 'give unnecessary offence to both Wilson & Ll.G.' she wrote. Keynes crossed out spider and fly, but kept the other two (p. 26 of the

Collected Writings edition). She objected to calling Wilson ignorant, Lloyd George the Artful Dodger, and 'I don't like *orgy*. It is not a nice word.' Keynes altered all these. She thought his references to Lord Sumner approached the libellous: they were cut out. She accused him of inconsistency in indicating the possibility of a Revolution in England on pp. 150–1, and denying any possibility of it on p. 160. This was allowed to stay. The gloom of chapter 6 was 'almost unbearable', Florence feeling that Maynard was committing himself 'to too much prophecy of the Jeremiah type'. She hoped he would eliminate

> all the nasty hits at Lloyd George ... You owe some loyalty to your Chief, even if you don't agree with him ... Also spare the President where you can ... Don't call him 'poor' ... I am doubtful about the taste of the Nonconf. minister comparison ... Broadly speaking – it is really important to be careful about international susceptibilities – so don't call the French demands preposterous – or call any 'great' man wicked or wanton. The work will gain–not lose–by restraint.

On Asquith's advice, Keynes decided to leave out his character-sketch of Lloyd George; otherwise he changed detail without altering the tone. Florence was able to get him the reference for Sir Eric Geddes's 'making Germany pay till the pips squeak' speech at Cambridge: it was her alertness which rescued the remark from oblivion. From Stanley Baldwin, Keynes got the equally famous phrase about the Parliament of 'hard-faced men who look as if they had done very well out of the war' (p. 91).

There were other interesting suggestions. Lowes Dickinson advised him to put the chapter on personalities at the end; Sheppard, the classical scholar, objected to the physical description of Wilson:

> The legs, I think, delightful, but of course they will be thought quite frivolous by everyone who doesn't know you – and all of us. Odysseus, like Wilson looked wiser when he was seated [see p. 25]. Could this be used to ... sound less rude? ... Again the fact that his hands were creased appeals, as evidence only to people like you and me who judge people in this sort of way. Most people will think it simply irrelevant rudeness. The fact that they lacked taste and finesse is all right.

Sheppard advised him not to call Lloyd George a representative of Neolithic Man and to leave out the bit about 'de-bamboozling' the President (p. 34). 'On the whole,' he wrote, 'I think this would get your effect and not put off your presbyterians and your Americans so much – and you can't do anything practical without their help.' Keynes cut out the legs and modified the hands; he crossed out the 'de-bamboozling' passage, but later reinserted it. Neolithic Man was omitted as well.[25]

The Economic Consequences of the Peace was published on 12 December 1919. By Christmas it had sold 2642 copies – satisfactory but not spectacular. On 29 December, Daniel Macmillan wrote, 'I have no doubt that you will be fully justified in printing the 5000 copies.'[26] Neither of them sensed that it was about to become an international best-seller and, over the coming months and years, one of the most influential books of the twentieth century.

II

THE ECONOMIC CONSEQUENCES OF THE PEACE

The Economic Consequences of the Peace has a claim to be regarded as Keynes's best book. In none of his others did he succeed so well in bringing *all* his gifts to bear on the subject in hand. Although the heart of the book was a lucid account of the reparation problem, the book was no mere technical treatise. The torrid *mise-en-scène* at Paris is vividly recreated; the failings of Clemenceau, Wilson and Lloyd George are displayed with cruel precision. The writing is angry, scornful and, rarely for Keynes, passionate: never again were his denunciations of bungling and lying, or his moral indignation, to ring so loud and clear. Giving shape to the whole is a brooding sense of menace; a sense of the travails of a civilisation *in extremis*; of the mindless mob waiting its turn to usurp the collapsing inheritance; of the futility and frivolity of states-manship. The result is a personal statement unique in twentieth-century literature. Keynes was staking the claim of the economist to be Prince. All other forms of rule were bankrupt. The economist's vision of welfare, conjoined to a new standard of technical excellence, were the last barriers to chaos, madness and retrogression.

Unless one keeps Keynes's perspective firmly in mind, the intensity of his denunciations may seem puzzling, even perverse. After all, the Treaty did accomplish some things of which a liberal could approve. It set up the League of Nations; it freed subject nations from autocracy; it prevented the dismemberment of Germany. Keynes does not weigh these achievements in the balance. His book was written very much from an Anglo-American point of view; and most British and American opinion was disposed to judge the Treaty on economic grounds – the Jingoes, by whether it had succeeded in making Germany 'pay' for its aggression; the liberals, by whether it had provided for the resumption of economic progress. With the war over, the security issues which dominated the French faded with extraordinary speed from the Anglo-American consciousness. Traditionalists could take comfort in the destruction of the German Navy, whose existence had been the chief pre-war threat to Britain. Liberals tended to pin their hopes on the

League. Hardly anyone was interested in the Treaties separately concluded with Austria and Hungary by which Eastern Europe was roughly divided up in accordance with Wilson's principle of 'self-determination'; and Keynes's book was not about them, except insofar as they impinged on his central theme. That theme was about how the war had damaged the delicate economic mechanism by which the European peoples had lived before 1914, and how the Treaty of Versailles, far from repairing this damage, had completed the destruction.

The argument is impressively set out in chapter 2. Here Keynes defined mankind's permanent economic problem as to establish a balance between population and the means to feed, clothe and house it. Despite the extraordinary rise of population in the nineteenth century, the 'Malthusian devil' had been chained by free trade and the capitalist ethic. In Europe, the 'interference of frontiers and tariffs was reduced to a minimum ... Over this great area there was an almost absolute security of property and person.'[27] Germany had been the pivot of that vast mechanism of transport, coal, distribution and foreign trade which made possible an industrial order of life in the dense urban centres of new population.

> Only by operating this machine, *continuously and at full blast*, could she find occupation at home for her increasing population and the means of purchasing their subsistence abroad ... Round Germany as a central support the rest of the European economic system grouped itself, and on the prosperity and enterprise of Germany the prosperity of the continent mainly depended [my italics].[28]

Free trade, coupled with the export of capital, had also established an equilibrium between the Old World and the New, based on the exchange of Europe's manufactures for the food and raw materials of the Americas, and the 'annual tribute' which the investment of Europe's surplus capital enabled it to draw from the New World. This global system, which sustained a growing population at an increasing standard of life, depended in turn on a shared morality, which emphasized above all the virtues of abstinence, prudence, calculation and foresight – the basis of the accumulation of capital. Throughout Europe 'all those instincts of puritanism' which in previous times had led people to withdraw from the world were redirected to the task of securing a prosperous future. A radically unequal distribution of income was sustained by a bluff or deception, by which the workers were subjected to an enforced abstinence on the tacit understanding that the capitalists 'saved' most of their profits. Thus the world's economic organization ultimately rested on the exercise of the Victorian virtues.[29]

Even before the war, Keynes argued, this 'economic Eldorado' was being threatened by the decrease of Europe's pull on the resources of the

New World, and by the instability of the 'psychological conditions' underlying the social order. What the war had done was to destroy Europe's economic organization, largely destroy Europe's stake in the New World, and shake the social order by disclosing 'the possibility of consumption to all and the vanity of abstinence to many'.[30] As a result it had set free the Malthusian devil. The first result of his rampage was seen in Russia. In one of the most interesting passages of the book Keynes explicitly links surplus population to Revolution:

> Thus the extraordinary occurrences of the past two years in Russia, that vast upheaval of society, which has overturned what seemed most stable – religion, the basis of property, the ownership of land, as well as forms of government and the hierarchy of classes – may owe more to the deep influences of expanding numbers than to Lenin or to Nicholas; and the disruptive powers of excessive national fecundity may have played a greater part in bursting the bonds of convention than either the power of ideas or the errors of autocracy.[31]

The mood of menace here conjured up also overhangs chapter 6, in which Keynes discusses the condition of Europe at the war's end. The problems out of which Bolshevism grew were now being reproduced all over the continent. As a result of the war Europe faced an 'absolute falling off' in its standard of living.[32] Moreover, all the belligerent governments had been forced by the war to embark on a ruinous course of inflation, which was potentially fatal for capitalist civilisation. Once more Keynes invoked Lenin who had said that 'there is no subtler, no surer means of overturning the existing basis of society than to debauch the currency'. The reason was that by inflation governments confiscate wealth arbitrarily and thus strike at 'confidence in the equity of the existing distribution of wealth. Those to whom the system brings windfalls ... become "profiteers", who are the objects of hatred of the bourgeoisie, whom the inflationism has impoverished, not less than of the proletariat.'[33] Inflation, in other words, undermines the *virtue* of the capitalist system on which its legitimacy, in Keynes's view, depends. Economic Bolshevism paves the way for political Bolshevism. The message would be sufficiently vivid in the minds of Keynes's readers, following the revolutionary outbreaks in Germany and Hungary, and the upsurge of working-class militancy in Britain.

The 'good peace', Keynes claimed, should have addressed itself directly to these problems, which affected European victors and vanquished alike. Instead the treaty-makers produced what he called a 'Carthaginian Peace' whose effect, if not intention, would be to impoverish Europe. He attributed this result to two things – the inadequacy of the statesmen's ideas, and the inadequacy of their characters.

The second of these explanations is the famous one, enshrined in chapter 3 of the book. But the condemnation of the Treaty as a whole rests much more on the first of them. Keynes's thesis, stated simply, is that the Big Three all gave politics precedence over economics. Thus having stated the economic problem facing Europe in chapter 2, Keynes writes, at the start of chapter 4:

> The thoughts which I have expressed in the second chapter were not present to the mind of Paris. The future life of Europe was not their concern; its means of livelihood was not their anxiety. Their preoccupations, good and bad alike, related to frontiers and nationalities, to the balance of power, to imperial aggrandisement, to the future enfeeblement of a strong and dangerous enemy, to revenge, and to the shifting by the victors of their unbearable financial burdens on to the shoulders of the defeated.[34]

Clemenceau's political conception is summarised in chapter 3:

> So far as possible . . . it was the policy of France to set the clock back and undo what, since 1870, the progress of Germany had accomplished. By loss of territory and other measures her population was to be curtailed; but chiefly the economic system, upon which she depended for new strength . . . must be destroyed. If France could seize, even in part, what Germany was compelled to drop, the inequality of strength between the two rivals for European hegemony might be remedied for many generations.[35]

But Keynes recognised that Clemenceau's political preoccupations, though not his aims, were shared by both Wilson and Lloyd George. Thus he writes on p. 92:

> To what a different future Europe might have looked forward if either Mr Lloyd George or Mr Wilson had apprehended that the most serious of the problems which claimed their attention were not political or territorial but financial and economic, and that the perils of the future lay not in frontiers or sovereignties but in food, coal, and transport.

And on p. 146:

> This [the feeding of the peoples of Central Europe] is the fundamental problem in front of us, before which questions of territorial adjustment and the balance of European power are insignificant. Some of the catastrophes of past history, which have thrown back human progress for centuries, have been due to the reactions following on the sudden termination . . . of temporarily favourable conditions which have permitted the growth of population beyond what could be provided for when the favourable conditions were at an end.

But the lack of vision on the part of the treaty-makers would not have mattered so much, Keynes suggests, had they stuck to the framework of the Fourteen Points, which ruled out a 'Carthaginian Peace' and specifically excluded punitive damages. It is to explain how the Versailles Treaty fell so far short of the Fourteen Points that Keynes penned his character-sketches of the Big Three.

Of the Allied chiefs Clemenceau comes off best. His is not only the most successful portrait – the account Keynes leaves of him 'throned, in his grey gloves, on the brocade chair, dry in soul and empty of hope, very old and tired, but surveying the scene with a cynical and almost impish air' is unforgettable – but his faults were faults of opinion not of character. He knew what he wanted – to crush Germany for a generation or more – and pursued his aim with single-minded determination, skilfully playing on the weaknesses of his colleagues. 'One could not despise Clemenceau or dislike him, but only take a different view as to the nature of civilised man, or indulge, at least, a different hope.'[36]

It is the President and Prime Minister who share the blame for the failure to make a wise peace, since together American money and British (or even Welsh) brains could have easily overcome French intransigence. One must remember that the American and British Treasuries were practically agreed about reparations. They should have prevailed; their failure to prevail was due to the temperaments of their political chiefs.

Wilson's first appearance prepares us for the role in which Keynes cast him, that of the 'blind and deaf' Don Quixote:

> His head and features were finely cut and exactly like his photographs, and the muscles of his neck and the carriage of his head were distinguished. But, like Odysseus, the President looked wiser when he was seated;* and his hands, though capable and fairly strong, were wanting in sensitiveness and finesse.[37]

Wilson, we are led to believe, was insensitive to his surroundings and atmosphere. His neck was stiff with rectitude. He descended on Paris trailing his Fourteen Commandments ('God had only ten', Clemenceau remarked wryly), to be defeated in a game whose rules he never mastered. Wilson's mind was packed with principles not policies. He was incompetent in council; and he had the theologian's capacity for self-deception. This last is the key point of Keynes's analysis. The President would do nothing that was contrary to his principles; but those principles

> became a document for gloss and interpretation and for all the intellectual apparatus of self-deception by which, I daresay, the

---

* The reference is to Book iii of Homer's *Iliad*. Since Odysseus was the cleverest of the Greek leaders the comparison is not especially apt.

President's forefathers had persuaded themselves that the course they thought it necessary to take was consistent with every syllable of the Pentateuch ... Then began the weaving of that web of sophistry and Jesuitical exegesis that was finally to clothe with insincerity the language and substance of the whole treaty.[38]

The spider who spun the fatal web which trapped the President was Lloyd George. Lloyd George was cast in the role of the enchantress, the Welsh witch, the *femme fatale*.

To see the British Prime Minister watching the company, with six or seven senses not available to ordinary men, judging character, motive, and subconscious impulse, perceiving what each was thinking and even what each was going to say next, and compounding with telepathic instinct the argument or appeal best suited to the vanity, weakness, or self-interest of his immediate auditor, was to realise that the poor President would be playing blind man's buff in that party.[39]

Although Keynes's character sketch of Lloyd George is unfair, it is a pity he left it out, and that it has not been reinserted at the end of chapter 3 in the new edition of his book; for without it the plot is incomplete. The key to Lloyd George, as Keynes saw it, was his lack of principle; he was

rooted in nothing; he is void and without content ... One catches in his company that flavour of final purposelessness, inner irresponsibility, existence outside or away from our Saxon good and evil, mixed with cunning, remorselessness, love of power, that lend fascination, enthralment, and terror to the fair-seeming magicians of North European folklore.[40]

Lloyd George's objectives were plucked from the circumambient atmosphere; and at Paris he was hostage to a parliamentary majority and public opinion created by his promise to demand of Germany the full cost of the war. Since this promise was in flat contradiction to the armistice agreement and the advice of his own experts his only hope of avoiding political defeat at home was to devise formulas designed to persuade the President that his (Lloyd George's) policy conformed completely to the Fourteen Points. Thus he set to work on the Presbyterian, with a success which eventually alarmed him. As Keynes tells it:

To his horror, Mr. Lloyd George, desiring at the last moment all the moderation he dared, discovered that he could not in five days persuade the President of error in what it had taken five months to prove to him to be just and right. After all, it was harder to de-bamboozle this old Presbyterian than it had been to bamboozle him.[41]

Keynes estimated that under the terms of the armistice agreement the Allies were legally entitled to claim between £1600m and £3000m which it would have been 'wise and just' to compound at £2000m.[42] This section of the book (pp. 73–85) largely recapitulates the arguments and estimates of the Treasury Memorandum of 26 November 1918. As in that memorandum he assumes that the cost of separation allowances and pensions was excluded. Keynes condemned the inclusion of these items in the claim against Germany in the Peace Treaty as a 'breach of contract'. He wrote:

> There are few episodes in history which posterity will have less reason to condone ... a war ostensibly waged in defence of the sanctity of international engagements ending in a definite breach of one of the most sacred possible of such engagements on the part of the victorious champions of these ideals.[43]

The section on Germany's capacity to pay (pp. 106–31) contains whole paragraphs lifted verbatim from the same Treasury document. Keynes emphasised the contradiction between reducing Germany's capacity by territorial and other confiscations and increasing its liability. Apart from immediate transfers of gold and movables, Germany could pay reparations only by means of an export surplus, which would give it the foreign exchange to pay its annual 'tribute'. However in the five years before the war Germany's adverse balance of trade averaged £74m a year. By increasing its exports and reducing its imports Germany might 'in time' be able to generate an annual export surplus of £50m, equivalent to £100m at post-war prices. Spread over thirty years this would come to a capital sum of £1700m, invested at 6 per cent a year. Adding to this £100m–£200m available from transfers of gold, property, etc., he concluded that '£2000m is a safe maximum figure of Germany's capacity to pay'.[44] Thus, by a bit of juggling with the figures, Germany's capacity could just about be squared with its 'legal' liability. Allowing £500m for ships and property already ceded, Germany should be required to pay £1500m in thirty annual instalments of £50m a year, free of interest payments.

French critics were to accuse Keynes of grossly underestimating Germany's productive potential. Here Keynes's theory of probability came to the rescue:

> The fact that all things are *possible* is no excuse for talking foolishly ... We cannot expect to legislate for a generation or more. The secular changes in man's economic condition and the liability of human forecast to error are as likely to lead to mistake in one direction as in another. We cannot as reasonable men do better than base our policy on the evidence we have and adapt it to the five or ten years over which we may suppose ourselves to have some measure of prevision; and we

are not at fault if we leave on one side the extreme chances of human existence and of revolutionary changes in the order of Nature or of man's relations to her. The fact that we have no adequate knowledge of Germany's capacity to pay over a long period of years is no justification ... for the statement that she can pay ten thousand million pounds.[45]

But the question of Germany's capacity was not just a technical one. Germany could not in practice be got to pay more than it itself accepted as reasonable and just, without a permanent army of occupation. More generally, the attempt to 'collect' debts arising from the war would sour international relations and damage social order. The theme is by now familiar:

> Even capitalism at home, which engages many local sympathies, which plays a real part in the daily process of production, and upon the security of which the present organisation of society largely depends, is not very safe. But however this may be, will the discontented peoples of Europe be willing for a generation to come so to order their lives that an appreciable part of their daily produce may be available to meet a foreign payment the reason for which, whether as between Europe and America, or as between Germany and the rest of Europe, does not spring compellingly from their sense of justice or duty? ... In short, I do not believe that any of these tributes will continue to be paid, at the best, for more than a very few years. They do not square with human nature or agree with the spirit of the age.[46]

In chapter 7 Keynes outlined his alternative economic peace treaty: German damages limited to £2000m; cancellation of inter-Ally debts; creation of a European free trade area to offset the economic disorganisation of 'innumerable new political frontiers'; an international loan to stabilise the exchanges; and encouragement of Germany's natural organising role in eastern Europe, including Russia. If these remedies were not adopted,

> vengeance, I dare predict, will not limp. Nothing can then delay for long that final civil war between the forces of reaction and the despairing convulsions of revolution, before which the horrors of the late German war will fade into nothing, and which will destroy, whoever is victor, the civilisation and the progress of our generation.[47]

He dedicated his book 'to the formation of the general opinion of the future'.

On 23 December 1919 Keynes wrote to Lytton Strachey:

> The book is being smothered ... in a deluge of approval; not a com-
> plaint, not a ... line of criticism; letters from Cabinet Ministers by
> every post saying that they agree with every word of it, etc, etc. I expect
> a chit from the PM at any moment telling me how profoundly the book
> represents his views and how beautifully it is put. Will it be my duty to
> refuse the legion of Honour at the hands of Clemenceau?

As always, Keynes exaggerated to amuse his friends. Bloomsbury was
enthusiastic: *The Economic Consequences of the Peace* was Keynes's reparation to them for his war service; and for once they were generous to their
old friend. Lytton Strachey wrote from Pangbourne on 10 December:

> Dearest Maynard, Your book arrived yesterday and I swallowed it at
> a gulp. I think it is most successful. In the first place, extremely im-
> pressive; there is an air of authority about it which I think nobody
> could ignore. I was rather afraid at Charleston that it might appear too
> extreme, but I don't think this is at all the case. The slight softenings in
> the Clemenceau & Wilson bits seem to me a distinct improvement,
> adding to the effect, rather than otherwise. Then the mass of informa-
> tion is delightful ... As to the argument it is certainly most crushing,
> most terrible. I don't see how anyone can stand up against it – but no
> doubt nobody will try to do that; what the wretches will try to do will be
> to turn their backs on it, and go on as if it didn't exist ... One thing I
> doubted – and that was, whether on your own showing, even your
> proposed terms were not far too harsh ... To my mind the ideal thing
> would be to abolish reparation altogether – but of course that is not
> practical politics – at any rate just yet ...
> I admire the style very much ... your affectionate Lytton.

Curiously, Strachey failed to recognise the quotation from Shelley's
Prometheus Unbound which ended the book, ascribing it to Thomas Hardy.
On 30 January 1920, Luce wrote from Rangoon:

> Your book ... I don't think anything so great on politics or so
> profoundly moving has appeared in English since [Burke's speech on
> Conciliation] ... Incidentally, your style too was a revelation to me.
> Where did you get it from? ...
> There are times when I long to see you back in politics, pilot of the
> state, and yet I would not sacrifice your happiness to the world's. What
> is so exhilarating is to find in your book the demonstrable proof of the
> rightness of my loving you as I do and have done.[48]

The earliest criticism came from Austen Chamberlain. While 'full of admiration for a brilliant piece of work', Chamberlain nevertheless wrote to him (22 December):

> Frankly I am sorry that one who occupied a position of so much trust and consequence . . . should feel impelled to write in such a strain of the part his country played in the peace negotiations . . . I cannot help fearing that our international course will not be made easier by such comments from a late public servant.

Chamberlain also tried to extenuate Lloyd George's conduct on the grounds that the experts disagreed. Keynes was quick to take him up on this:

> In the matter of Cunliffe and Sumner I was in a difficulty. But finding that I could not give a true and intelligible account of the part they played without some breach of confidence, I decided to leave them out altogether. This, as you justly point out, makes my story incomplete. But would it have served to excuse the Prime Minister, had I given it in full? Lord Cunliffe was not brought in as an expert: – for who that knows him could suppose that his opinion as to Germany's capacity to pay was of the slightest value? He was brought in for electioneering and parliamentary purposes; and for parliamentary and press purposes he and Lord Sumner were retained. The Prime Minister was never under the slightest illusion as to the value of their advice. They were, as he well knew, the price he had to pay for electioneering.[49]

On 27 December the banker R. H. Brand wrote that chapter 3 would 'do harm in America, and will impair your usefulness in helping in the near future'. Brand thought Keynes too pessimistic about the prospects for capitalism: 'I think myself that the capitalist system is stronger than you seem to indicate, since no other way exists of keeping alive the population we have allowed to come into existence.'[50] McKenna, who also wrote on 27 December, dismissed the suggestion that the book would do harm in America. 'Fudge! It will do nothing but good anywhere. Until we get back to the truth there is no hope for the world.'[51]

The earliest reviews were by no means unanimous. The Liberal and Labour press was laudatory; but the right-wing *Sunday Chronicle* of 21 December called Keynes a representative of 'a certain . . . dehumanised intellectual point of view' which failed to accept that Germany had to be punished. *Blackwood's Magazine* of 20 February 1920 accused him of being detached 'from all wholesome partisanship'. The charge that Keynes was pro-German became standard in such circles. One reader of the *Saturday Review* thought he should have been given an Iron Cross.

The book's sales soon started to leave Macmillan's gloomy projections far behind. Keynes had had to order an early reprint of 3000 copies following an unfortunate mishap in December, when 2000 unbound copies had been thrown into the North Sea to save the ship carrying them from Edinburgh to London from capsizing in a storm. (They were later washed ashore in Denmark, and sold as waste paper.) At the year's end he ordered a second reprint of 5000. By 21 January 1920 English sales had reached 7700, and Keynes ordered a third reprint of 5000. Handling the foreign rights himself, he arranged a French edition, which was published by *La Nouvelle Revue Française* in June. He also agreed to a cheap edition of 10,000 copies to be published by the Labour Research Department at 2*s* 6*d* per copy. By 9 February 12,300 copies had been sold out of 16,000, and Keynes ordered a fourth reprint of 5000; a fifth reprint of the same number followed a month later. The U.S. edition was doing even better. The first printing of 20,000 sold out immediately. By 22 April 1920, 18,500 had been sold in England, and nearly 70,000 in the United States. It was only in June that the sales started to fall off, Keynes ordering a sixth reprint of 3000 in August. By this time world sales were well over 100,000, and the book had been translated into German, Dutch, Flemish, Danish, Swedish, Italian, Spanish, Rumanian, Russian, Japanese and Chinese. Keynes had started to make a lot of money. His English profits, at three shillings a copy, came to £3000; there was £6000 from his American sales. Much of this went on his speculations; but his income rose from £1802 in the tax-year 1918–19 to £5156 in the year 1919–20.

As the book spread over the world, so the scrapbooks in which Florence had started to keep all printed references to her now famous son filled up with reviews by the hundred. Keynes's style was universally commended: 'as a piece of literature it is beyond praise', wrote J. L. Hammond in the *Manchester Guardian* of 24 December 1919. The same journal accepted Keynes's view that 'the economic losses inflicted on Germany made it absolutely impossible for her to carry out the terms of the Treaty'. There was little dissent from this proposition in Britain or the United States. Pigou, voicing the opinion of the economics establishment, congratulated Keynes on his 'absolutely splendid and quite unanswerable argument'.[52] Dennis Robertson, in an oversubtle review in the *Economic Journal* of March 1920, thought that within the covers of a single 'very powerful and important book' were two or even three – 'a mordant political pamphlet, a masterly technical discussion . . . and interwoven with both an impressive and largely original philosophical *critique* of the economic relations of nations and classes' which broke with the old nineteenth-century assumption of harmony.

The main British criticism was not that Keynes had got his figures wrong, but his priorities. 'The revision of political frontiers was an absolutely vital preliminary to the work of building a New Europe,' wrote the historian R. W. Seton-Watson.[53] Wickham Steed, editor of *The Times*, saw the book as a misplaced revolt of economics against politics.

If the war taught us one lesson above all others it was that the calcula-tions of economists, bankers, and financial statesmen who preached the impossibility of war because it would not pay were perilous non-sense . . . Germany went to war because she made it pay in 1870–1, and believed she could make it pay again.[54]

A notice in the *Iron and Coal Trades Review* of 9 January made the good point that it was 'the very nation which was extracting the chief profit from the machine' before 1914, which had set out to destroy it. Economic prosperity, evidently, was no guarantee of political good behaviour.

Liberals of the political, rather than the economic, kind were worried by Keynes's indifference to political aims in general and to the League of Nations in particular.[55] The 'ultimate' criticism of the book, according to a reviewer in the *Times Literary Supplement*, was that Keynes was interested 'in only one aspect of the work'.[56] Some critics also felt that Keynes had ignored the fact that politics is the art of the possible. The Treaty was the best that could have been done under the circumstances. A more robust defence of the treaty-makers, and especially Wilson, was provided by the idiosyncratic American economist Thorstein Veblen. Wilson, he argued, had shown a 'notable leniency' to Germany in the interest of combating Bolshevism. Veblen's praise for the 'insight, courage, facility and tenacity of purpose' with which Wilson had pur-sued this goal was taken up in the 1960s by the American historian Arno Mayer.[57] It is now accepted that Keynes's criticism of Wilson's charac-ter hinged on a mistaken assessment of the President's priorities. Wilson conceded on points which Keynes thought important, but which Wilson did not. It is also now recognized that the Treaty was much less a triumph for French diplomacy than Keynes made out.

Keynes attempted no general reply to his critics until the end of 1921 when Macmillan published his *A Revision of the Treaty*. By this time a number of leading American and French participants had had their say. The official Wilsonian response came in March 1920 with Bernard Baruch's *The Making of the Reparation and Economic Sections of the Treaty*, largely written by John Foster Dulles. The Wilsonians did not, on balance, dispute Keynes's economic logic or conclusions, though some felt that the Treaty contained adequate safeguards for revision. What they were mainly concerned with was to salvage Wilson's reputation, and their own hopes for US international leadership, from the damage done by what McCormick called Keynes's 'vicious' book. Their defence was that, given the state of public opinion, Wilson had made the best peace possible. Specifically, 'the repression and minimizing of the vengeful elements in the Treaty were due in large measure to Woodrow Wilson'.[58] If the Treaty had faults they were the faults of democracy.

Baruch's argument, together with the course of events in 1920–1, led Keynes to modify his view of Lloyd George. In *A Revision of the Treaty* he is transformed from a mere power-seeker into Faust. The defence of Lloyd George, Keynes wrote, was that he had made 'the best momentary settlement which the demands of the mob and the characters of the chief actors enjoined to permit', and 'that he had spent his skill and strength for two years in avoiding or moderating the dangers [of the settlement]'. Such a defence 'would be partly true and cannot be brushed away'. Keynes conceded that 'a preference for truth and sincerity *as a method* may be a prejudice based on some aesthetic or personal standard, inconsistent, in politics, with practical good'. But in any case 'private individuals are not under the same obligation to sacrifice veracity to the public weal'.[59] This amounted to a considerable retraction of Keynes's earlier stand. He is here conceding that intellectuals and politicians may have different obligations; that the intellectual's duty was to tell the truth in face of *necessary* political lying, with the bonus that if he did so politicians would not have to lie as much. Few intellectuals nowadays would make such a confident distinction between truth and falsehood in public affairs as was still possible for someone of Keynes's generation.

In *A Revision of the Treaty* Keynes has a chapter on the legality of the claim for reparation. In his *Economic Consequences* he had omitted all mention of Smuts's part in 'bamboozling' the President on this issue. But Baruch had published Smuts's crucial memorandum of 31 March 1919. This publication was embarrassing to both Keynes and Smuts. Keynes defended Smuts vigorously against the charge that he had *proposed* including the costs of pensions and separation allowances in the reparation bill (though he wrote to him 'I am not sure it won't serve you right for writing that memorandum');[60] nevertheless, when he dealt with the Smuts memorandum in his second book, he was highly dismissive of its contents.[61] Keynes's view that the armistice agreement with Germany was a contract and not an unconditional surrender on Germany's part stands up quite well in retrospect. The German armies in the West were undefeated; its conquests in the East were still unchallenged; it would have been very difficult for the Allies to prolong the war for another winter. Germany – and Keynes – were entitled to feel that the peace should have had elements of a negotiation.

As was to be expected, the reception of *The Economic Consequences of the Peace* was least enthusiastic in Paris. French critics like Raphael Georges-Lévy in his *La Juste Paix* argued that Germany could readily pay what the Allies claimed. Keynes had failed to appreciate the German power of production: *'cette omission vicie tout son travail'*. Henri Brenier accused Keynes of understating Germany's pre-war production, and minimizing the damage Germany had done to France's occupied regions. (Keynes replied tartly in his *Revision of the Treaty* that 'to add a couple of noughts to an estimate is not really an indication of nobility of mind'.)[62] On the question of Germany's capacity to pay the accepted French view was that the right course was to fix a large capital sum and adjust the annual payments from time to time in the light of Germany's enlarging export capacity.[63] This rather missed the point, for Germany would have no incentive to enlarge its exports, if the addition was to be confiscated. In the later 1920s some of Keynes's bitterest arguments over Germany's capacity were to be with the French economist Jacques Rueff.

Recent scholarship based on French governmental as well as American and European banking archives is kinder to France's financial motives and logic than Keynes was. French claims for reparations are now seen to be more modest and defensible than Britain's; while the important linkage is not between reparations and security but between reparations, inter-Ally debts, and an American loan. Schuker argues that in the absence of official American aid, reparations represented France's only hope for access to scarce capital and energy for reconstruction; Trachtenberg emphasises that the French object was to get access to German coal (through deliveries in kind) and American credit (by 'monetising' a fixed German debt). The inability of the peacemakers to agree a fixed sum was a defeat, not victory, for French aims. A perverse outcome of the reparations issue was inherent in the conflicting interests of the Great Powers. Lloyd George's election promises and Wilson's 'bamboozlement' form at best a sub-plot to the main story.

Keynes himself never had to deal with the most widespread charge against his book. This is that, by discrediting the Versailles Treaty, it encouraged the 'appeasement' of the dictators in the 1930s, and thus helped cause the Second World War. This attack was spearheaded by Etienne Mantoux's book *The Carthaginian Peace or the Economic Consequences of Mr. Keynes*, published in 1946, after Keynes's death. Mantoux, who was killed fighting the Germans in 1945, had a personal interest in the Versailles Treaty. His father, Paul Mantoux, the economic historian, had acted as interpreter at the private meetings of the Council of Four, and had challenged Keynes's description of the atmosphere of these meetings on the ground that Keynes had not been present at them.*

* *The Times* of 14 February 1920 carried the following statement by Captain Paul Mantoux:

Mr. Keynes had written a clever book about the Council of Four, but Mr. Keynes had never been present at one of its meetings. He, with other experts, was sometimes consulted on matters of detail by one member or other or their representatives in a room

Étienne Mantoux claimed that Keynes's book helped cause the United States to abandon the Treaty of Versailles legally, Britain to abandon it morally, and weakened even the French will to enforce it. America retreated into isolationism; Britain embarked on the 'appeasement' policy; France's morale was broken. As a result, Hitler was given a free hand to destroy the Treaty in the 1930s. Mantoux singled out two aspects of Keynes's pernicious influence : (1) the guilt-complex produced by his accusation that the Allies had broken faith, and (2) the indifference to Germany's territorial aggrandizement in the 1930s produced by his argument that 'frontiers and sovereignties' were unimportant.

The indictment is less formidable than it appears at first sight. Keynes did not destroy the Treaty of Versailles; it destroyed itself. Too harsh to conciliate, it was not harsh enough to secure compliance. Mantoux, in fact, concedes that an enforceable treaty would have required permanent Allied occupation of the Rhine bridgeheads.[64] But Keynes can hardly be blamed for this omission. Nor is Mantoux's claim that Keynes's book helped prevent the U.S. Senate ratifying the Treaty tenable, though it is often repeated. It is clear that the architect of the Treaty's defeat in Congress was President Wilson himself, who refused to accept the amendments which would have ensured its passage. There is more to the charge that Keynes's picture of the President's being 'bamboozled' by the wily Europeans strengthened isolationist sentiment. But American opinion was hardly ready for a U.S. assumption of world leadership; even the Anglophile eastern establishment was not prepared for America officially to underwrite the reconstruction of Europe.

Nor is there a much stronger case for saying that Keynes turned British opinion against the Treaty. The facts did so; Keynes merely pointed them out. Liberal opinion had already started to question the 'Carthaginian Peace' before Keynes's book appeared; no one in the British delegation, even Lloyd George, doubted that the economic clauses would have to be revised. It was the Lloyd George tactic of inserting unenforceable claims which destroyed the credibility of the Treaty. Constant revision of the schedules of German payments in the 1920s paved the way for Hitler's successful assaults on the territorial clauses in the 1930s. More generally the mood of appeasement in the 1930s was created more by the revulsion against the slaughter voiced by poets, novelists and playwrights than by rejection of punitive damages.

upstairs—for though the experts were regarded as bores, they had to be listened to—but certainly Mr. Keynes was never present at the meetings at Mr. Wilson's apartment downstairs, where the Council really met and decided the main points.

It transpired that the Big Four met sometimes with their advisers, sometimes without; Keynes was writing about the first set of meetings; Mantoux about the second. That Keynes's integrity should have been challenged testifies to the enormous resentment which his book caused in France. (See *Collected Writings*, XVII, ch.5.)

Mantoux attacks Keynes's 'economism'. He points out that it was the Second World War, not 'economics', that solved the German problem. Yet the Second World War came after the Great Depression which brought Hitler to power. The Great Depression in turn was brought about by the failure of economic leadership in the early 1920s. Had Keynes's 1919 programme been carried out it is unlikely that Hitler would have become German Chancellor. It is absurd to blame Keynes for events which took place because his advice was not followed.

None of this is to deny that *The Economic Consequences of the Peace* was a very influential book. Of the dozens of accounts of the Treaty which appeared in the 1920s it is the only one which has not sunk without a trace. It captured a mood. It said with great authority, flashing advocacy and moral indignation what 'educated' opinion wanted said. It also had an influence at a deeper level. Wickham Steed was right: it was a revolt of economics against politics. The war had been fought in the name of nation, state, emperor. These, Keynes argued, were false gods, from whom he sought to divert allegiance towards economic tasks. It was a message calculated to appeal to the nation of Cobden and Bright, once it had recovered from its intoxication with military victories. It helped form the outlook of a new generation. The nineteen-twenties saw a new breed of economist-politician, who talked about the gold standard and the balance of trade as fluently as pre-war politicians had talked about the Two-Power standard and the balance of power. There were even economist-poets like Ezra Pound and T. S. Eliot. The idea that the creation of opulence was the main task of rulers was born in 1919 though it came of age only after the Second World War. The Keynes of the *General Theory* whom Mantoux admired cannot be separated from the Keynes of the *Economic Consequences* whom he attacked.

In the main part of his book Mantoux took the standard French view that Germany could have paid much more than Keynes said it could pay, or than it did pay. But he did not support this contention by good arguments (though such arguments are available). He claimed that the Weimar Republic could have restricted German consumption to pay reparations as Hitler did to pay for rearmament.[65] This ignores not just the fact that in the first case German sacrifices would have been demanded for a much less appealing purpose, but also the additional problem posed by having to 'transfer' the sacrifice abroad. He argued that Germany had no trouble collecting 'indemnities' from conquered countries in the Second World War.[66] But Keynes was assuming peacetime conditions, not permanent armies of occupation on Germany's soil. Finally, he argued that the United States had lent Britain and France large amounts of capital in the First World War, and its exports had increased proportionately.[67] But this ignores the fact that the loans were specifically contracted to meet additional demand for munitions; in any case, no problem of lost jobs arose, because large numbers of British and French workers had been drafted into the army. It is hard to disagree with Harrod's conclusion that Mantoux's arguments are 'feeble in the extreme'.[68]

How well, then, does Keynes's polemic stand up in the light of all the attacks made on it? He can surely be acquitted of the absurd charge of having helped cause the Second World War. His case on reparations remains unshakeable, not because all his arguments were good, but because he understood that the political will to extract large payments from Germany for thirty years or more would not be available. His ground for calling the inclusion of pensions and separation allowances in the reparations bill 'a breach of contract' is strong, though not unchallengeable. As far as the motives and characters of the principal actors are concerned, he got Clemenceau about right, Wilson more wrong than right, and failed to get Lloyd George into balance. Above all, he was absolutely right to insist that no political structure for keeping the peace would stand up if its economic foundations were rotten. From the biographical standpoint *The Economic Consequences of the Peace* is a key document. It marked a radical shift in Keynes's thought from the nineteenth-century assumption of 'automatic' economic progress sustained by liberal institutions to a view of the future in which prosperity would have to be strenuously won in the teeth of the adverse circumstances which the war had created.

IV

A NEW BEGINNING

The Economic Consequences of the Peace made Keynes world-famous. By writing it he renounced the privacy which he had always valued so highly. Superimposed on private Keynes – the Cambridge don selling economics by the hour, the lover of clever, attractive, unworldly young men, the intimate of Bloomsbury – is the public Keynes of the 1920s – the leading authority on reparations, the monetary reformer, the adviser of governments, the City magnate, the feared journalist whose pronouncements caused bankers and currencies to tremble. Philosophic speculation gave way to financial speculation, conferences jostled with holidays, intimacy merged into patronage. In 1925 the world-famous economist would marry a world-famous ballerina in a blaze of publicity.

The contrast must not be overdrawn. Even before the war there had been tendencies towards public Keynes; after it private Keynes was never entirely crowded out. His life simply moved into a higher gear. There still seemed time and energy for everything.

In one important respect, there was a return to private life. Keynes resigned from the Treasury in June 1919; he would not return to it till 1940. A picture has been painted of him in the wilderness in these years, his advice spurned by official circles who regarded his book as a breach of faith, a proof of unsoundness. There is something in this, but it is greatly exaggerated. Keynes had never intended to stay in the Treasury; he deliberately rejected many chances of a political career; he was frequently consulted by governments and politicians, at home and abroad. Nor should the disapproval which his book aroused be overstated. Much of *Economic Consequences* expounded Treasury doctrine. Keynes's relationship with his old department between the wars was never one of hostility, as it is often depicted. The so-called Treasury View on how the economy should be run was always evolving towards his view. The official mind was not so much opposed to his as slower, less adventurous. It shared most of his fears and preoccupations, but saw its way forward less clairvoyantly to the remedies.

The war marked the start of Keynes's career as a radical economist. Fear for the future of the established order had been growing during the war; Paris confirmed it. The task of building the future would start, not end, with the Allied victory. For all its faults the bourgeois civilization of the late nineteenth century had seemed the stepping stone to a higher life. That promise had to be recreated out of the debris of the war.

The nightmare which stalked Keynes's book was the Malthusian nightmare of fecundity. Keynes feared a general impoverishment which would unleash chaos and Revolution. What frightened him was not so much the material as the organizational and moral destruction wrought by the war. The margin of resources which the old civilization had afforded philosophers to dream and politicians and generals to play their war games had disappeared. A new standard of political efficiency was needed to keep alive the hope of civilization. It is true that Keynes himself distinguished between the situation in England, where he did not perceive the 'slightest possibility of catastrophe', and that in Continental Europe; but much of his analysis of the fragility of capitalism could be applied to England, and Keynes himself started applying it to England almost immediately after his book was published. Keynes did not say, in the *Economic Consequences*, that the survival of the social order depended on inventing new methods to maintain permanent boom. But the vision of social decay which presupposed the need for such new methods was already in place.

From today's perspective it may seem that Keynes was being unduly and unnecessarily pessimistic. The elements of precariousness in the capitalist order were overemphasized; the resilience of the system was downgraded. Yet it must be remembered that a sense of precariousness was always implicit in the world view of Keynes's generation. Their parents had, after all, relied on God to maintain social cohesion. When belief in God waned they could not help feeling that the moral capital which sustained the accumulation of economic capital had been severely depleted. Keynes and his friends had not worried about this before the war. The death of God meant to them liberation from false beliefs and irksome duties. By 1919 it appeared in a different light. The vanished nineteenth-century certainties seemed curiously comforting in retrospect; the apprehensions of a Sidgwick more vivid than Bloomsbury's new dawn. In the last resort Keynes's post-war fear for the future of capitalism was profoundly influenced by the Victorian fear of a godless society. The prospect of civilisation briefly opened up by Moore's *Principia Ethica* had receded over the horizon. The rest of Keynes's life was spent in trying to bring it back into sight.

Bibliography and Sources

(1) MANUSCRIPT COLLECTIONS CONSULTED

Since it is impossible to divide up all the manuscript sources I have used in writing this volume into discrete collections I will indicate where the papers I have consulted are currently to be found. Unless otherwise stated they are originals.

CAMBRIDGE UNIVERSITY LIBRARY (CUL)

Add. 7827f. J. N. Keynes Diary, 1864–1917. Missing 1865–8, 1877–81.

Various items of correspondence relating to J. N. Keynes, Florence Keynes, Sir Geoffrey Keynes, Margaret Hill, Alfred Marshall. Where I have quoted from these, the catalogue number is given in the individual reference.

Kennet Papers

KING'S COLLEGE, CAMBRIDGE (KC)

The King's College Library houses the bulk of J. M. Keynes's 'personal' papers, as distinct from his 'economic' papers. The most important 'runs' for the purposes of this volume are JMK's correspondence with his parents, contained in Boxes 34–6, and JMK's correspondence with Lytton Strachey. Since the first edition of this volume appeared in 1983, a number of important letters from JMK to his parents, and one from JMK to Hawtrey, have been recovered from the Harrod estate. Other citations, from the Keynes Papers at King's, appear with the abbreviation KC, KP, followed by the Box number.

The Library also has photocopies of the Charleston Papers which contain correspondence between JMK and Clive and Vanessa Bell. Citations are introduced with the abbreviation CP. Other papers consulted include the Sheppard, Wedd, Miscellaneous, and College Papers.

BRITISH LIBRARY (BL)

Contains correspondence between, (1) Giles Lytton Strachey and Duncan Grant, 1902–31, Add. MSS 57932–3; (2) Giles Lytton Strachey and James Strachey 1905–31, Add. MSS 60706–12; (3) JMK and Duncan Grant, 1908–46, Add. MSS 57930–1; (4) JMK and Macmillan & Co., Add. MSS 55201–4. JMK's letters to O. T. Falk are listed under Add. MSS 57923.

MARSHALL LIBRARY, CAMBRIDGE (ML)

Contains JMK's economic papers, mainly correspondence, India Office and Treasury memoranda, notes for lectures, drafts of books and articles, financial accounts, engagement diaries, etc. Much of this material has now been published in the 'Activities' volumes of the *Collected Writings* (see below under Printed Sources). However, I have consulted some of this in the original, as well as other material which was not included in the *Collected Writings*. The most useful of the latter have been (1) JMK's undergraduate essays on Bernard of Cluny (first read to the Eton Literary Society), Peter Abelard and Edmund Burke, (2) his notes and essays written in preparation for the Civil Service Examination, 1905–6, including the economics papers he wrote for Marshall, and (3) the papers he read to the 'Apostles' and notes on moral philosophy, mainly in the years 1905–10. (His important philosophical paper 'Ethics in Relation to Conduct', which he read to the Society on 23 January 1904 is, however, in the JMK Papers at King's College.) In addition I have consulted the correspondence files for the years covered by this volume, and those dealing with *The Economic Consequences of the Peace*. Citations are introduced by ML, KP followed by catalogue number, where there is one.

In addition to the JMK Papers, there is a good deal of correspondence from Marshall, Foxwell, Edgeworth, Ward, Johnson, Jevons and Nicholson to J. N. Keynes, and some letters from JNK in J. N. Keynes Papers, Boxes I–IV; letters from JMK to Foxwell in Keynes (JMK) Box V; letters to Marshall, including two from JMK, in Marshall Papers, Box 1; letters from Alfred Marshall to various academic colleagues in Marshall Papers, Box 3; two boxes of Miscellaneous Correspondence; and a Red Box I which contains some material on the Parental Alcoholism controversy of 1910–11 in chapter 9.

TRINITY COLLEGE, CAMBRIDGE (TC)

Edwin Montagu Papers

CHURCHILL COLLEGE, CAMBRIDGE (CC)

Reginald McKenna Papers; Cecil Spring-Rice Papers

HOUSE OF LORDS LIBRARY (HLL)

David Lloyd George and Andrew Bonar Law Papers

BIRMINGHAM UNIVERSITY LIBRARY (BUL)

Austen Chamberlain Papers

BODLEIAN LIBRARY, OXFORD

Asquith and Gilbert Murray Papers

ETON COLLEGE

Records of the College Debating Society (College 'Pop')

INDIA OFFICE LIBRARY (BRITISH LIBRARY)

India Office Papers

NUFFIELD COLLEGE, OXFORD

Henry Clay Papers

Hubert Henderson Papers

PUBLIC RECORD OFFICE, KEW (PRO)

Treasury Papers

SCOTTISH RECORD OFFICE, EDINBURGH (SRO)

Lothian Papers

SUSSEX UNIVERSITY LIBRARY

Leonard Woolf Papers

BAKER LIBRARY, HARVARD UNIVERSITY (BLH)

Thomas Lamont Papers

BERG COLLECTION, NEW YORK PUBLIC LIBRARY (BERG)

Contains correspondence between JMK and Giles Lytton Strachey for 1906, between Giles Lytton Strachey and Leonard Woolf, and between JMK and Leonard Woolf.

LIBRARY OF CONGRESS

Oscar Crosby Papers

Felix Frankfurter Papers

PRINCETON UNIVERSITY LIBRARY

Bernard Baruch Papers

John Foster Dulles Papers

PRIVATE COLLECTIONS

Dr Simon Keynes: files relating to Keynes–Brown family history, including notes of JMK's own researches into the Keynes family tree, correspondence arising from it, and Simon Keynes's schoolboy essay 'The Dissemination of a Norman Family'. Cited SK.

Dr Polly Hill: correspondence between J. N. Keynes and his parents, Florence Keynes and her parents, Florence and J. N. Keynes. Cited PH.

Stephen Keynes: JMK's Eton Diaries 1900–2. The 1899 volume is at King's College.

Mrs Henrietta Couper: JMK letters to Duncan Grant 1906–44; James Strachey to Duncan Grant; Giles Lytton Strachey to Duncan Grant; Duncan Grant's Diary 1917–18; and material relating to Grant's application for exemption from war service on grounds of conscientious objection. Cited HC.
Mr Richard Shone: correspondence between JMK and Duncan Grant 1907–46. Cited RS.
Mr Richard Garnett: The Diary of David Garnett, 1915, 1917–18.
Mr Mark Bonham-Carter: The Diary of Margot Asquith (at present in the care of the Warden of Nuffield College, Oxford).
Tuesday Club: Records of Meetings and Recollections.
Dr Michael Finlay: letters from JMK to R. H. Dundas.

(2) PUBLISHED SOURCES

(a) WRITINGS BY J. M. KEYNES

These are cited wherever possible from *The Collected Writings of John Maynard Keynes* (29 vols., 1971 –83). The particular volumes that have been most relevant to the writing of this book are:
I. *Indian Currency and Finance* (1913) 1971
II. *The Economic Consequences of the Peace* (1919) 1971
III. *A Revision of the Treaty* (1921) 1971
VIII. *A Treatise on Probability* (1921) 1976
X. *Essays in Biography* (1933) 1972. This includes some other writings, notably 'My Early Beliefs' and 'Dr. Melchior, A Defeated Enemy', first published as *Two Memoirs*, ed. David Garnett (1949).
XI. *Economic Articles and Correspondence: Academic* 1983. This includes JMK's three attacks on Karl Pearson in the *Journal of the Royal Statistical Society*, July, December 1910, February 1911; but not Pearson's reply in the same journal of January 1911; and JMK's three articles on the 1914 financial crisis in the *Economic Journal*, September, December 1914, and *Quarterly Journal of Economics*, November 1914.
XII. *Economic Articles and Correspondence: Investment and Editorial* 1983
XV. *Activities 1906–14: India and Cambridge* 1971
XVI. *Activities 1914–19; The Treasury and Versailles* 1971
XVII. *Activities 1920–2: Treaty Revision and Reconstruction* 1971

(b) BOOKS BY OTHER WRITERS

Noel Annan: *Leslie Stephen: His Thought and Character in Relation to his Time* (1956)
Bernard Baruch: *The Making of the Reparation and Economic Sections of the Treaty* (1920)
Basileon, A Magazine of King's College, Cambridge (1900–14)
Lord Beaverbrook: *Politicians and the War, 1914–1916* (1928)
——: *Men and Power, 1917–18* (1956)
Sybille Bedford: *Aldous Huxley* (1973–4)
Clive Bell: *Peace at Once* (1915)
——: *Civilisation: An Essay* (1928)
——: *Old Friends: Personal Recollections* (1956)
Quentin Bell: *Virginia Woolf, A Biography*: vol. ii: *Virginia Stephen, 1882–1912* (1972); vol. ii: *Mrs Woolf, 1912–1941* (1972)
——: *Bloomsbury* (1974)
Hugh Hale Bellot: *University College, London, 1826–1926* (1929)
Robert Blake: *The Unknown Prime Minister: The Life and Times of Andrew Bonar Law, 1858–1923* (1955)
Frances M. Brookfield: *The Cambridge 'Apostles'* (1906)
Oscar Browning: *Memories of Sixty Years at Eton, Cambridge and Elsewhere* (1910)
Richard Buckle: *Diaghilev* (1979)
Robert E. Bunselmeyer: *The Cost of the War 1914–1919: British Economic War Aims and the Origins of Reparations* (1975)
Philip M. Burnett: *Reparations at the Paris Peace Conference from the Standpoint of the American Delegation* (1940)
Ronald W. Clark: *The Life of Bertrand Russell* (1975)
Peter Clarke: *Liberals and Social Democrats* (1978)
Bernard Crick: *George Orwell, A Life* (1980)
Hugh Dalton: *Call Back Yesterday* (1953)
Marcello de Cecco: *Money and Empire* (1974)
Leon Edel: *Bloomsbury: A House of Lions* (1981)
Howard Elcock: *Portrait of a Decision, The Council of Four and the Treaty of Versailles* (1972)
Eprime Eshag: *From Marshall to Keynes: An Essay on the Monetary Theory of the Cambridge School* (1963)
Inga Flote: *Colonel House in Paris: A Study of American Policy at the Paris Peace Conference, 1919* (1973)
Penelope Fitzgerald: *The Knox Brothers* (1977)
E. M. Forster: *Goldsworthy Lowes Dickinson* (1934)
David Gadd: *The Loving Friends, A Portrait of Bloomsbury* (1974)
David Garnett: *The Golden Echo* (1954)
——: *The Flowers of the Forest* (1955)
——: *Great Friends* (1979)
David Lloyd George: *The Truth about Reparations and War Debts* (1932)
——: *War Memoirs* (1933–6)
Phyllis Grosskurth: *John Addington Symonds, A Biography* (1964)
W. K. Hancock: *Smuts: The Sanguine Years, 1870–1919* (1962)
W. K. Hancock and Jean van der Poel: *Selections from the Smuts Papers*, vol. iv (1966)
Lord Hankey: *The Supreme Control at the Paris Peace Conference, 1919* (1963)
Gerd Hardagh: *The First World War* (1977)
G. H. Hardy: *A Mathematician's Apology* (1940)
Roy Harrod: *John Maynard Keynes* (1951)
Cameron Hazlehurst: *Politicians at War*, July 1914 to May 1915 (1971)
Burton J. Hendrick: *The Life and Letters of Walter Hines Page* (1928)
Gertrude Himmelfarb: *Victorian Minds: A Study of Intellectuals in Crisis and of Ideologies in Transition* (1970)
Christopher Hollis: *Eton* (1960)
Michael Holroyd: *Lytton Strachey: A Critical Biography* (1967–8)
T. W. Hutchison: *A Review of Economic Doctrines, 1870–1929* (1953)
Gilbert E. Jackson and Philip Vos (eds.): *The Cambridge Union Society Debates, April 1910–March 1911* (1911)
Allan Janek and Stephen Toulmin: *Wittgenstein's Vienna* (1973)
Roy Jenkins: *Asquith* (1974)
L. E. Jones: *A Victorian Boyhood* (1955)

Denis Judd: *Lord Reading* (1982)
F. A. Keynes: *By-Ways of Cambridge History* (1947)
——: *Gathering up the Threads* (1950)
Sir Geoffrey Keynes: *The Gates of Memory* (1981)
J. N. Keynes: *Studies and Exercises in Formal Logic* (1884)
——: *The Scope and Method of Political Economy* (1891)
Milo Keynes (ed): *Essays on John Maynard Keynes* (1975)
——: *Lydia Lopokova* (1983)
Robert Lekachman (ed.): *Keynes's General Theory: Reports of Three Decades* (1964)
Paul Levy: *G. E. Moore and the Cambridge Apostles* (1979)
Arthur S. Link: *Wilson's Campaigns for Progressivism and Peace, 1916–1917* (1965)
Percy Lubbock: *Shades of Eton* (1929)
R. B. McCallum: *Public Opinion and the Last Peace* (1944)
Desmond MacCarthy: *Portraits* (1931)
Sir Andrew McFadyean: *Recollected in Tranquillity* (1969)
Alasdair MacIntyre: *A Short History of Ethics* (1967)
——: *After Virtue: A Study in Moral Theory* (1981)
Stephen McKenna: *Reginald McKenna, 1863–1943: A Memoir* (1948)
Rita McWilliams-Tullberg: *Women at Cambridge* (1975)
Étienne Mantoux: *The Carthaginian Peace, or the Economic Consequences of Mr Keynes* (1946)
Alfred Marshall: *Principles of Economics* (1890; 8th ed. 1920)
——: *Memorials*, ed. A. C. Pigon (1925)
——: *Official Papers*, ed. J. M. Keynes (1926)
——: *Early Economic Writings, 1867–1890*, ed. J. K. Whittaker (1975)
Arno Mayer: *Politics and Diplomacy of Peace-Making, Containment and Counter-Revolution at Versailles, 1918–1919* (1968)
J. S. Mill: *Autobiography* (1873)
G. E. Moore: *Principia Ethica* (1903; paperback 1959)
E. V. Morgan: *Studies in British Financial Policy, 1914–1925* (1925)
Lady Ottoline Morrell: *Ottoline: The Early Memoirs*, ed. Robert Gathorne-Hardy (1963)
——: *Ottoline at Garsington: Memoirs 1915–1918*, ed. Robert Gathorne-Hardy (1974)
D. P. O'Brien: *The Classical Economists* (1975)
Jean van der Poel: *Selections from the Smuts Papers*, vol. v (1973); vol. vii (1973)
John R. Presley: *Robertsonian Economics* (1978)
Gwen Raverat: *Period Piece: A Cambridge Childhood* (1952)
Lord Riddell: *My Intimate Diary of the Paris Peace Conference and After, 1918–1923* (1933)
S. P. Rosenbaum (ed.): *The Bloomsbury Group* (1975)
Sheldon Rothblatt: *The Revolution of the Dons: Cambridge and Society in Victorian England* (1968)
Royal Commission on the Depression of Trade and Industry: *Third Report*, Appendix C (1888)
Bertrand Russell: *Autobiography*, vols. i and ii (1967–8)
J. B. Schneewind: *Sidgwick's Ethics and Victorian Moral Philosophy* (1977)
Stephen A. Schuker: *The End of French Predominance in Europe* (1976)
Jordan A. Schwartz: *The Speculator, Bernard Baruch in Washington, 1917–1965* (1981)
Richard Shone: *Bloomsbury Portraits* (1976)
A. and E. M. Sidgwick: *Henry Sidgwick: A Memoir* (1906)
Henry Sidgwick: *Methods of Ethics* (1874)
Osbert Sitwell: *Great Morning* (1948)
——: *Laughter in the Next Room* (1949)
Frances Spalding: *Roger Fry* (1980)
George Spater and Ian Parsons: *A Marriage of True Minds: An Intimate Portrait of Leonard and Virginia Woolf* (1977)
Adrian Stephen: *The 'Dreadnought' Hoax* (1936)
Barbara Strachey: *Remarkable Relations* (1980)
Lytton Strachey: *Eminent Victorians* (1918)
——: *The Really Interesting Question and Other Papers*, ed. Paul Levy (1972)
André Tardieu: *The Truth about the Treaty* (1921)
A. J. P. Taylor: *Politics in Wartime* (1964)
Seth P. Tillman: *Anglo-American Relations at the Paris Peace Conference of 1919* (1961)

Marc Trachtenberg: *Reparation in World Politics* (1980)
S. Waley: *Edwin Montagu: A Memoir and an Account of his Visit to India* (1964)
Beatrice Webb: *The Diary*, ed. Norman and Jeanne Mackenzie, vol. i, 1873–92 (1982)
Sidney and Beatrice Webb, *The Letters*, ed. Norman Mackenzie, vols. i and ii (1978)
Martin J. Weiner: *English Culture and the Decline of the Industrial Spirit, 1850–1980* (1982)
Patrick Wilkinson: *A Century of King's, 1873–1972* (1982)
——: *Kingsmen of a Century, 1873–1972* (1980)
Francesca Wilson: *Rebel Daughter of a Country House* (1967)
Esmé Wingfield-Stratford: *Before the Lamps Went Out* (1945)
D. A. Winstanley: *Late Victorian Cambridge* (1947)
Sir Llewellyn Woodward: *Great Britain and the War of 1914–1918* (1969)
Leonard Woolf: *Autobiography*: vol. i: *Sowing* (1960); vol. iii: *Beginning Again* (1964)
Virginia Woolf: *Letters*, ed. Nigel Nicolson, vols. i and ii (1975–76)
——: *Diary*, ed. Anne Olivier Bell, vols. i and ii (1977–8)
——: *Moments of Being*, ed. Jeanne Schulkind (1978)
H. E. Wortham: *Victorian Eton and Cambridge, being the Life and Times of Oscar Browning* (1956 edition)

(c) ARTICLES

N. G. Annan: 'The Intellectual Aristocracy' in J. H. Plumb (ed.), *Studies in Social History – a Tribute to G. M. Trevelyan* (1955)
Bernard Bergonzi: 'Who are You?' (critique of Bloomsbury Group), *New Review*, November 1974, 50–4
K. Burk: 'J. M. Keynes and the Exchange Rate Crisis of July 1917', *Economic History Review*, 2nd series, xxxii, 3 (1979) 405–16
——: 'The Diplomacy of Finance: British Financial Missions to the United States, 1914–1918', *Historical Journal*, xxii, 2 (1979) 351–72
S. G. Checkland: 'Economic Opinion in England as Jevons Found it', *Manchester School*, xix (May 1951), 143–69
A. W. Coats: 'The Role of Authority in the Development of British Economics', *Journal of Law and Economics*, vii-viii (1964) 85–106
——: 'Sociological Aspects of British Economic Thought (1880–1930)', *Chicago Journal of Political Economy*, lxxv (October 1967), 706–29
——: 'The Historicist Reaction in English Political Economy, 1870–1890', *Economica*, xxi (May 1954), 143–53.
John Milton Cooper, Jr: 'The British Response to the House-Grey Memorandum', *Journal of American History*, lix (1973) 958–71
——: 'The Command of Gold Reversed: American Loans to Britain, 1915–1917', *Pacific Historical Review*, xlv (May 1976) no. 2, 212–30
Charles P. Dunbar: 'The Reaction in Political Economy', *Quarterly Journal of Economics*, i (October 1886), 1–27
H. S. Foxwell: 'The Economic Movement in England', *Quarterly Journal of Economics*, ii (1888) 84–103.
Sir Roy Harrod: 'Clive Bell on Keynes', *Economic Journal*, December 1957, 692–9
T. W. Hutchison: 'The Collected Writings of John Maynard Keynes, vols. i-vi and xv-xvi', *Economic History Review*, 2nd series, xxvi (February 1973) 141–52
Syed Anwar Husain: 'The Administrative Departments of the India Office, 1858–1919', *Indian Journal of Public Administration*, xxvii, no. 2 (April-June 1981), 430–43
Elizabeth Johnson: 'Keynes' Attitude to Compulsory Military Service', with 'A Comment by Sir Roy Harrod', *Economic Journal* (March 1960), 160–7
Arnold P. Kaminsky: 'The India Office in the Late Nineteenth Century' in Robert I. Crane and N. Gerald Barner (eds.): *British Imperial Policy in India and Sri Lanka 1858–1912 – A Reassessment* (1981)
J. N. Keynes: 'Obituary of Sidgwick', *Economic Journal* (1902) 586–91
Q. D. Leavis: 'Henry Sidgwick's Cambridge', *Scrutiny* (December 1947) 3–11
J. S. Nicholson: 'The Vagaries of Recent Political Economy', *Quarterly Review*, ccxix, no. 437 (1913), 406–25
Talcott Parsons: 'Wants and Activities in Marshall', *Quarterly Journal of Economics*, xlvi (November 1931), 101–40

——: 'Economics and Sociology: Marshall in Relation to the Thought of His Time', *Quarterly Journal of Economics*, xlvii (February 1932) 316–47

Karl Pearson: 'Influence of Parental Alcoholism', *Journal of the Royal Statistical Society* (January 1911) 221–9

J. P. Roach: 'Victorian Universities and the National Intelligentsia', *Victorian Studies* (December 1959) 131–50

D. H. Robertson, Review of *The Economic Consequences of the Peace*, in *Economic Journal* (March 1920) 77–84

E. A. G. Robinson: 'John Maynard Keynes 1883–1946', *Economic Journal* (March 1947)

S. P. Rosenbaum: 'Keynes, Lawrence and Cambridge Revisited', *Cambridge Quarterly*, xi (1982) 252–64

——: 'The Intellectual Origins of the Bloomsbury Group', *Times Higher Educational Supplement*, 29 October 1982

Arthur Smithies: 'Keynes Revisited', *Quarterly Journal of Economics* (August 1972)

Sir Richard Stone: 'Keynes, Political Arithmetic and Economics', British Academy 7th Keynes Lecture in Economics (1978)

Stephen Toulmin: 'Moore: G. E. Moore and the Cambridge Apostles by Paul Levy', *New Republic* (30 August 1980)

Thorstein Veblen: Review of *The Economic Consequences of the Peace*, in *Political Science Quarterly*, xxxv (October 1920) 467–72

N. Wedd: 'Goldie Dickinson: The Latest Cambridge Platonist', *Criterion*, xii, no. xlvii (January 1933) 175–83

Bernard Williams: 'The Point of View of the Universe: Sidgwick and the Ambitions of Ethics', *Cambridge Review*, 7 May 1982

Raymond Williams: 'The Significance of "Bloomsbury" as a Social and Cultural Group' in Derek Crabtree and A. P. Thirlwall (eds.), *Keynes and the Bloomsbury Group* (1980)

(3) UNPUBLISHED THESES

J. A. Hemery: 'The Emergence of Treasury Influence in the Management of British Foreign Policy', M. Phil., Cambridge, 1982

R. M. O'Donnell: 'Keynes: Philosophy and Economics: An Approach to Rationality and Uncertainty', D. Phil., Cambridge, 1982

References

These reference notes are intended to be used in conjunction with the Bibliography. Books or articles listed in the Bibliography have been cited by author alone – or if the author has several works listed, by author and short title.

The following abbreviations have been used:

BL: British Library
BLH: Baker Library, Harvard University
BUL: Birmingham University Library
CAB: Cabinet Papers
CC: Churchill College, Cambridge
CP: Charleston Papers
CUL: Cambridge University Library
CW: *The Collected Writings of John Maynard Keynes*
DG: Duncan Grant
DNB: The Dictionary of National Biography
ECP: The Economic Consequences of the Peace

EcHR: *Economic History Review*
EJ: *Economic Journal*
FAK: Florence Ada Keynes
GLK: Sir Geoffrey Langdon Keynes
GLS: Giles Lytton Strachey
HLL: House of Lords Library
JBS: James Strachey
JMK: John Maynard Keynes
JNK: John Neville Keynes
JNKP: J. N. Keynes Papers
JRSS: Journal of the Royal Statistical Society
KC: King's College, Cambridge

KP: Keynes Papers
ML: Marshall Library, Cambridge
MLK: Margaret Keynes (later Hill)
MP: Marshall Papers
PH: Dr Polly Hill
PRO: Public Record Office
PSQ: Political Science Quarterly
q.: quoted in

QJE: Quarterly Journal of Economics
QR: Quarterly Review
RS: Richard Shone
SK: Dr Simon Keynes
SRO: Scottish Record Office
TC: Trinity College, Cambridge
TLS: The Times Literary Supplement

Chapter 1: Dynastic Origins

1. P. H. Reaney: *A Dictionary of British Sur-names* (3rd Imp., 1966)
2. Albert Dauzat and Charles Rostaing, *Dictionnaires des Noms de Lieux de France*, 129
3. This is JMK's version. Dr Simon Keynes in 'The Dissemination of a Norman Family' (unpublished schoolboy essay) omits the intermediate Ralph.
4. SK, JMK to Mrs Keynes, Kenynton, S. Australia, 20 May 1907.
5. *Ibid.*
6. FAK, *Gathering*, 3.
7. *D.N.B.*
8. See *Gardener's Magazine, Gardener's Chronicle*, 23 February 1878.
9. The *Garden*, 4 May 1878.
10. FAK, *Gathering*, 46.
11. *Ibid.*, 45.
12. PH, JNK to John Keynes ?1865.
13. Bellot, 298.
14. JNK Diary, 1 June 1870.
15. PH, Anna Keynes to JNK, 13 February 1871.
16. JNK Diary, 21 January 1873.
17. PH, JNK to John Keynes, 19 October 1872; to Anna Keynes, 20 October 1872.
18. JNK Diary, 20 February 1873.
19. *Ibid.*, 16 August 1873.
20. *Ibid.*, 13 March 1875.
21. *Ibid.*, 13 June 1874.
22. *Ibid.*, 26 January 1875.
23. CUL. Add. 7562, Item 7.
24. JNK Diary, 16 March, 31 August 1875.
25. James Ward to JNK, transcribed JNK Diary, 13 December 1875.
26. JNK Diary, 10, 11 August 1876.
27. *Ibid.*, 20 June 1877.
28. ML, JNKP: Box 1, H. S. Foxwell to JNK, 11 August 1877.
29. JNK Diary, 3 May 1877.
30. *Ibid.*, 13 May 1877.
31. Woman's Hour, Transcript of FAK's interview with Ruth Drew, 1951; published in *The Listener*, 12 July 1951.
32. PH, Florence Brown to Ada Brown, ?October 1878.
33. FAK, *Gathering*, 29–32.
34. *Ibid.*, 11–12.
35. GLK, *Gates*, 12.
36. PH, FAK typescript 'On Growing Old'.
37. FAK, *Gathering*, 33.
38. McWilliams-Tullberg, 58.
39. CW, x, 237.
40. The information is pieced together from John Keynes's will and JNK's Diary.
41. JNK Diary, eg., 22 September 1881, 28 July 1882.
42. *Ibid.*, 25 June, 18 July 1882.
43. *Ibid.*, 5 October 1881.
44. *Ibid.*, 21 February 1882.
45. *Ibid.*, 7 February 1881.
46. *Ibid.*, 31 August, 15, 16 September 1881.
47. *Ibid.*, 31 December 1881.
48. *Ibid.*, 24 January 1882.
49. *Ibid.*, 23 July 1882, reference to 1881.
50. *Ibid.*, 25 January 1882.
51. *Ibid.*, 21 October 1881.
52. *Ibid.*, 10 April 1881.
53. *Ibid.*, 13 June 1881.
54. *Ibid.*, 28 February, 13 March 1881.
55. *Ibid.*, 25–27 February 1882.
56. *Ibid.*, 30 April 1882.
57. *Ibid.*, 30 April 1882.
58. PH, John Brown to FAK, 18 June 1882.
59. JNK Diary, 30 July 1882.
60. PH, Ada Brown to FAK, 17 October 1882.
61. JNK Diary, 25 July 1882.
62. *Ibid.*, 13 October 1882.
63. *Ibid.*, 30 July 1882.
64. *Ibid.*, 8 August 1882.
65. *Ibid.*, 10 August 1882.
66. *Ibid.*, 13 August 1882.
67. *Bedford Mercury*, 16 August 1882.
68. JNK Diary, 30 September 1882.
69. *Ibid.*, 11 October 1882.
70. KC, KP, Box 34, John Brown to FAK, 6 June 1883.

Chapter 2: Cambridge Civilisation: Sidgwick and Marshall

1. Mill, *Autobiography*, 225–6.
2. Quotations from Paley, Sedgwick and Whewell all from Schneewind, 105, 124, 150. This book has influenced my discussion of the Victorian search for 'doctrine'.
3. Himmelfarb, 219.
4. Rothblatt's conclusion was foreshadowed in J. P. Roach, 'Victorian Universities and the National Intelligentsia', *Victorian Studies* (1959), 131–50.
5. See for example Weiner.
6. Schneewind, 163–6.
7. Sidgwick, 463–4.
8. Bernard Williams, 'The Point of View of the Universe: Sidgwick and the Ambition of Ethics', *Cambridge Review* 7 May 1982. quotation, Sidgwick, 489–90.
9. A. and E. M. Sidgwick, 347.
10. *Ibid.*, 466–7.
11. Rothblatt, 135, writes that Sidgwick was 'probably' impotent.
12. A. and E. M. Sidgwick, 357.
13. Harrod, *Keynes*, 2, 214–5.
14. A. and E. M. Sidgwick, 399, 442.
15. CW, x, 162–3.
16. *Ibid.*, 166.
17. *Ibid.*, 167.
18. Foxwell, 'Economic Movement in England'.
19. CW, x, 177.
20. B. Webb, *Diaries*, i, 285.
21. CW, x, 205–10.
22. ML, JNKP, 3:81, JSN to JNK, 27 July 1890.
23. JNK Diary, 11 May 1886.
24. ML, JNKP, 1:108.
25. CUL, Add. 7562:117, Ward to JNK, 21 September 1900.
26. ML, JNKP, 1:125, Marshall to JNK, 30 January 1902.
27. ML, MP, 3:44, Marshall to Foxwell, 14 February 1902.
28. ML, MP, 3:41, Marshall to Foxwell, 8 May 1901.
29. Parsons, 'Wants and Activities in Marshall'.
30. Marshall, *Memorials*, 101.
31. *Ibid.*, 227–56.
32. *Ibid.*, 304.
33. CUL, Add. 8069/M.256, Marshall to Kidd, 27 May 1902.
34. Marshall, *Memorials*, 443–4.
35. *Ibid.*, 298–30.
36. ML, MP, 1;121, Jowett to Marshall, 24 July 1890.
37. ML, MP, 1:124, Marshall to JNK, 22 May 1901.
38. Marshall, *Memorials*, 342–6.

Chapter 3: Growing up in Cambridge

1. GLK in M. Keynes, *Essays*, 26.
2. JNK Diary, 8 July 1883.
3. *Ibid.*, 10 January 1889.
4. FAK, *By-Ways*, xix.
5. JNK Diary, 12 June 1895.
6. *Ibid.*, 26, 30 September, 3 October 1896.
7. GLK, *Gates*, 24.
8. JNK Diary, 4 June 1886.
9. *Ibid.*, 27 July 1898.
10. *Ibid.*, 22 February, 17 March 1890.
11. *Ibid.*, 9 December 1883.
12. *Ibid.*, 30 June, 10 November 1895.
13. FAK, *Gathering*, 65.
14. JNK Diary, 25 March 1891.
15. *Ibid.*, 29 April 1887.
16. Marshall, *Principles* (8th ed.), 59.
17. JNK Diary, 30 March 1891.
18. *Ibid.*, 18 June 1883.
19. *Ibid.*, 3 January 1900.
20. *Ibid.*, 5 February 1885.
21. *Ibid.*, 9 April 1886.
22. KC, KP, Box 34, JNK to JMK, 13 July 1891.
23. JNK Diary, 10 February 1884.
24. *Ibid.*, 11 November 1885.
25. KC, KP, Box 34, JNK to JMK, 29 January 1901.
26. For Neville's attitude to Florence's C.O.S. work see JNK Diary, 6 February 1897.
27. *Ibid.*, 25 October 1883.
28. q. *Ibid.*, 16 February 1884.
29. q. *Ibid.*, 14 February 1884.
30. q. *Ibid.*, 27 June 1884.
31. JNK obituary, *The Times*, 16 November 1949. JNK's chief innovation was said to be a kind of immediate inference to which he gave the name 'inversion' and in which from a given proposition another is inferred having for its subject the contradictory of the original subject.
32. ML, JNKP, 3:62.
33. PH: FAK to JNK 17 December 1884.
34. ML, JNKP, 1:71.
35. JNK Diary, 1 February 1885.
36. *Ibid.*, 6 June 1885.
37. q. *Ibid.*, 2 June 1885.
38. ML, JNKP, 1:67.
39. Marshall, *Early Writings*, i, 18.
40. ML, JNKP, 3: 66, 69, 70, 74.

41. ML, MP, Marshall, 3:43, Marshall to Foxwell, 29 January 1902.
42. JNK Diary, 13, 14 January 1888.
43. Tr. *Ibid.*, 28 January 1888.
44. ML, JNKP, 1:27, Foxwell to JNK, 15 January 1888.
45. ML, JNKP, 1:80, Marshall to JNK, 17 March 1888.
46. JNK Diary, 21 April 1888.
47. ML, JNKP, 3:130, JNK to F. Edgeworth, 14 December 1890.
48. F. Y. Edgeworth, 'The Method of Political Economy', *Nature*, 26 February 1891, 387.
49. JNK Diary, 14 June 1891.
50. *Ibid.*, 17 January 1891.
51. ML, JNKP, 1:101, Marshall to JNK, 18 March 1891.
52. JNK Diary, 26 March 1892.
53. CUL, Add. 7562: 72.
54. JNK Diary, 26 March 1892.
55. CUL, Add. 7562: 178, 9.
56. JNK Diary, 6, 10 June 1883.
57. PH: FAK to JNK, 31 July 1883.
58. JNK Diary, 4 November 1885.
59. Interview with GLK, 6 September 1979.
60. JNK diary, 21 October 1894.
61. GLK, Gates, 19.
62. See JNK Diary, 31 August 1889, 18 April, 26 July, 15 August 1890; 14 June, 7 November 1891.
63. M. Keynes, *Essays*, 28–9.
64. GLK, *Gates*, 24.
65. JNK Diary, 11 August 1889.
66. M. Keynes, *Essays*, 30.
67. JNK Diary, 11 March 1885.
68. *Ibid.*, 11 February 1888.
69. *Ibid.*, 19 August 1888.
70. *Ibid.*, 2 December 1888.
71. *Ibid.*, 13, 17 April 1889.
72. CW, x, 213.
73. M. Keynes, *Essays*, 29.
74. JNK Diary, 14 March, 28 September 1892.
75. *Ibid.*, 30 April 1893.
76. *Ibid.*, 6 October 1893.
77. q. *Ibid.*, 4 April 1896.
78. *Ibid.*, 5 November 1895.
79. M. Keynes, *Essays*, 29.
80. JNK Diary, 26 June, 28 June 1897.
81. *Ibid.*, 4–8 July 1897.
82. KC, KP, Box 36, JNK Holiday Diary, 23 August 1897.

Chapter 4: Eton

1. Jones, 152, 176f.
2. C. Bell, *Civilisation*, 85–6.
3. Jones, 165.
4. Crick, 48.
5. Browning, 68.
6. M. Keynes, *Essays*, 31.
7. This was what Hope-Jones, one of Maynard's election, told Sir Roy Harrod; see Harrod, *Keynes*, 16–17.
8. q. Harrod, *Keynes*, 50.
9. Fitzgerald, 38.
10. *Ibid.*, 28.
11. KC, KP, Box 20. The letter is addressed to 'Adolphe', which was Keynes's name for Knox.
12. Fitzgerald, 67.
13. JNK to JMK, 24 October 1899.
14. JMK to JNK, 11 February 1900.
15. JMK to JNK, 18 March 1900.
16. JMK to JNK, 20 May 1900.
17. Dr G. E. Hale to FAK, 9 November 1900.
18. FAK to JMK, 25 July 1900.
19. JMK to JNK, 21 October 1900.
20. JNK Diary, 18 November, 21 December 1900.
21. JNK to JMK, 28 October 1901; S. G. Lubbock to Nathaniel Wedd, 9 May 1901. (Wedd Papers, III).
22. JMK to JNK, 17 December 1901, quoting from Leigh's letter.
23. Harrod, 45.
24. JMK to JNK, 23 March 1902.
25. JNK Diary, 31 March 1902.
26. *Ibid.*, 16 July 1902.
27. *Ibid.*, 30 March 1902.
28. These extracts are taken from the Records of the College Debating Society, Eton. Each member wrote out a summary of his own speech.
29. JMK to JNK, 23 March 1902.
30. GLS to L. Woolf, 20 June 1905, q. Holroyd, i, 222.
31. KC unclassified, B. W. Swithinbank, 'Note on Eton in JMK's Time' dated 9 March 1948.
32. JMK to FAK, 10 July 1902.

Chapter 5: The Cambridge Undergraduate

1. Browning, 15.
2. Wingfield-Stratford, 145.
3. KC, KP, Box 2.
4. MacCarthy, 37–8.
5. Wilkinson, *Century*, 13.
6. Wingfield-Stratford, 179.

7. *Basileon*, June 1912, 280.
8. Wingfield-Stratford, 151.
9. JNK Diary, 15 October 1902.
10. KC, KP, JMK to Swithinbank, 10 December 1902.
11. *Ibid.*, 17 December 1902.
12. JNK Diary, 12, 18 February 1903.
13. Wingfield-Stratford, 158.
14. KC, KP, Box 18(M), J. E. McTaggart to JMK, 25 February 1903.
15. Levy, 66.
16. Russell, i, 66.
17. Stephen Toulmin, reviewing Levy's *Moore* in *The New Republic*, 30 August 1980.
18. JMK to GLS, 18 October 1905.
19. KC, KP, JMK to Swithinbank, 30 May 1903.
20. *Granta*, 28 November 1903; JNK Diary, 29 November 1903.
21. JNK Diary, 12 September 1903.

22. *Granta*, 28 January 1905.
23. JNK Diary, 15, 16 June 1904.
24. C. R. Fay in M. Keynes, *Essays*, 37.
25. Russell, i, 71.
26. JMK to GLS, 20 July 1904.
27. Russell, i, 72.
28. L. Woolf, *Sowing*, 201
29. KC, KP, Box 32, G. M. Trevelyan to JMK ?1904.
30. q. Holroyd, 211–12.
31. *Ibid.*, 213; Holroyd calls Hobhouse 'Sir Edgar Duckworth'.
32. Russell, i. 74.
33. KC, KP, Box 32.
34. KC, KP, Box 31A, JMK to Hobhouse, 27 March 1905.
35. *Cambridge Review*, 16 March 1905.
36. JBS to GLS, 16 July 1906; JMK to GLS, 5 May 1906 (Berg).
37. JNK Diary, 20 June 1905.

Chapter 6: My Early Beliefs

1. MacIntyre, *After Virtue*, 63.
2. q. Levy, 223–5.
3. L. Woolf, *Sowing*, 131.
4. Russell, i, 64.
5. Russell to Alys Pearsall Smith, 18, 21, February 1894, q. Levy, 125–6.
6. Levy, 105.
7. *Ibid.*, 179–81.
8. *Ibid.*, 127.
9. Russell, i, 114.
10. CW, x, 444, 'My Early Beliefs'.
11. *Ibid.*, 438.
12. KC, KP, Box 18, Norton to JMK c. 1906.
13. q. Levy, 198–9.
14. *Ibid.*, 145.
15. Moore, (paperback ed) 76.
16. In Strachey, *The Really Interesting Question*, 104.
17. Moore, 81–96.
18. *Ibid.*, 188.
19. *Ibid.*, 189.
20. *Ibid.*, 99.
21. *Ibid.*, 105, 107.
22. *Ibid.*, 27.
23. CW, x, 436.
24. *Ibid.*, 436–7.
25. *Ibid.*, 445.

26. *Ibid.*, 441.
27. *Ibid.*, 442.
28. *Ibid.*, 445.
29. *Ibid.*, 446.
30. *Ibid.*, 445–6.
31. *Ibid.*, 447–9.
32. Russell, i, 70–1.
33. L. Woolf, *Sowing*, 148–9.
34. Levy, 7, 9.
35. Harrod, *Keynes*, 76–81.
36. In M. Keynes, *Essays*, 242–6.
37. Leavis, 'Keynes, Lawrence and Cambridge', reprinted from *The Common Pursuit* (1953) in Rosenbaum, 391.
38. KC, Keynes Library.
39. ML, KP, UA/10$_2$.
40. ML, KP, UA/10$_1$, paper to Apostles 'read again' on 22 January 1921.
41. KC, KP, Box 1, 28.
42. ML, KP, unclassified.
43. Moore, 203.
44. ML, KP, UA/10$_1$, paper read to Apostles on 8 February 1908, 19 November 1910.
45. *Ibid.* 'Posterior Analytics', paper read to Apostles c. 1905–6.
46. *Ibid.*, 'Science or Art', paper read to Apostles, 20 February 1909.

Chapter 7: Cambridge and London

1. JMK to GLS, 24 June 1905.
2. *Ibid.*, 8 July 1905.
3. KC, KP, JMK to Swithinbank, 21 September 1905.
4. *Ibid.*
5. JMK to GLS, 15 October 1905.

6. JMK to GLS, 20 January 1906.
7. JMK to GLS, 24 October 1905.
8. JMK to GLS, 26 October 1905.
9. GLS to JMK, 4 November 1905.
10. JMK to GLS, 6 November 1905.
11. JMK to GLS, 7 December 1905.

12. JMK to GLS, 6 April 1906.
13. ML, KP, unclassified.
14. q. Harrod, 117.
15. CW, xv, 2.
16. JMK to GLS, 3 February 1906.
17. KC, KP, Box 20(A).
18. GLS to DG, 24 March 1906.
19. B. Strachey, 234.
20. JNK Diary, 20 December 1905.
21. JMK to JNK, 29 June 1905.
22. JMK to JNK, 21 September 1905.
23. Kaminsky, 30.
24. CW, xv, 3-4.
25. JMK to GLS, 1 March 1907.
26. JMK to JNK, 1 March 1907.
27. JMK to GLS, 31 January 1907.
28. CW, xv, 11-12.
29. JMK to JNK, 22 March 1907.
30. JMK to GLS, 14 March 1907.

31. JMK to FAK, 17 March 1907.
32. KC, KP, Box 21(S), 16 March 1907.
33. JMK to GLS, 12 October 1906.
34. JMK to JNK, 17 December 1906.
35. KC, KP, Box 21(T), R. C. Trevelyan to JMK, 16 March 1907.
36. JMK to GLS, 13 July 1907.
37. JMK to JNK, 4 September 1907.
38. KC, JMK, *The Principles of Probability*. The quotation is from the 1908 version of his thesis.
39. CW, xv, 15-17; KC, KP, Box 20D, 1 July 1908.
40. BL, India Office Library, Public Works Dept. Orders and Memoranda, L/PWD/5/28, no. 133.
41. CW, xv, 17.
42. *Ibid.*

Chapter 8: Lytton, Duncan, Maynard

1. GLS to JMK, 30 October 1905.
2. DG to GLS, 7 April 1907.
3. JMK to DG, 5 April 1907.
4. DG to JMK, 9 April 1907.
5. Holroyd, i., 262.
6. Garnett, *Flowers*, 29-30.
7. DG to JMK, 25 June 1908.
8. GLS to JBS, 14 July 1908.
9. Holroyd, i, 338.
10. JMK to DG, 24 July 1908.
11. JMK to DG, 5 February 1909.
12. JMK to GLS, 13 September 1908.
13. JMK to JNK, 13 September 1908.
14. RS, 'Maynard Keynes as a Picture Buyer', Notes for BBC talk by Grant.

15. JMK to DG, 24 October 1908.
16. GLS to JBS, 27 October 1908.
17. JBS to GLS, 2 November 1908.
18. GLS to JBS, 23 November 1908.
19. JMK to FAK, 13 November 1908.
20. JMK to DG, 20 November 1908.
21. JMK to DG, 24 November 1908.
22. JMK to DG, 16 December 1908.
23. JNK Diary, 4 December 1908.
24. JMK to DG, 22 December 1908.
25. JMK to DG, 31 January 1909.
26. JMK to MLK, 7 January 1909.
27. JMK to DG, 26 December 1908.
28. JMK to DG, 22 January 1909.
29. JMK to DG, 8 February 1909.

Chapter 9: Economic Orthodoxies

1. JMK to JNK, 10 April 1908.
2. CW, xv, 46-7.
3. Hutchison, *EcHR*, February 1973.
4. CW, xxii, 294.
5. KC, KP, Box 2.
6. JMK to Dundas, 30 September 1905.
7. CW, ii, 6.
8. Dalton, 157-8.
9. q. Nicholson, 1913.
10. Hutchison, *Review*, 284n.
11. CUL, Add. 7562. Item 229.
12. JMK to DG, 19 January 1909.
13. CW, xv, 65-6.
14. JNK Diary, 27 January 1910.
15. JMK to DG, 20 January 1909.
16. JMK to DG, 24 October 1909.
17. JMK to DG, 16 February 1909.
18. KC, KP, Box 2.
19. ML, KP, 'Can We Consume our Surplus

or the Influence of Furniture on Love', Paper read to Apostles *c*. 1909.
20. ML, KP, Correspondence L/12. Angell to JMK, 19 February 1912.
21. JMK to DG, 24 November 1908.
22. See Presley, 37-8.
23. KC, KP, Box 2.
24. On 20 May 1909, *CW*, xv, 31-3.
25. KC, KP, Box 21R.
26. See O'Brien, 162-4.
27. Royal Commission, Appendix C, 415-17.
28. Eshag, 34.
29. KC, KP, Box 19, Williams to JMK, 1 August 1911.
30. CW, xii, 693.
31. *Ibid.*, xi, 388-94.
32. *Ibid.*, xii, 755.
33. *Ibid.*, 708.
34. *Ibid.*, 778.

35. *Ibid.*, 783.
36. *Ibid.*, 713–16.
37. *Ibid.*, 717–18.
38. *Ibid.*, 765.
39. *Ibid.*, 767.
40. JMK to DG, 18 December 1908.
41. JMK to DG, 10 May 1909.
42. CW, xii, 711.
43. CW, xi, 104f.

44. Stone, 7th Keynes Lecture, 3 May 1978.
45. CW, viii, 349. See R. M. O'Donnell, ch. 10 for an illuminating discussion.
46. CW, viii, 368.
47. Harrod, 57.
48. *JRSS*, July 1910, 773; repr. in CW, xi, 195.
49. *Ibid.*, February 1911, 344–5; repr. in CW, xi, 216.

Chapter 10: Private Lives

1. Dennis Robertson in *Basileon*, June 1911.
2. JMK to DG, 11 February 1909.
3. JMK to DG, 25 January 1909.
4. JMK to DG, 2 February 1909.
5. JMK to DG, 28 February 1909.
6. Wilkinson, *A Century of King's*, 51.
7. BL, Strachey, Add. MSS 60668, DG to JBS, 22 April 1909.
8. GLS to JBS, 25 June 1909.
9. GLK's memoir of Henry James's visit, 'Henry James at Cambridge' (1967), is reproduced in *Gates*, 64–80.
10. JMK to DG, 23 July 1909.
11. JBS to GLS, 26 August 1909.
12. JBS to GLS, 1 October 1909.
13. GLS to JMK, 13 August 1909.
14. CUL, Hilton Young, 'In and Out', 25: Kennet Papers, 82/1.
15. Virginia Stephen to Vanessa Bell, 19 April 1911, V. Woolf, *Letters*, i, 462.
16. KC, KP, Box 18.
17. KC, KP, Box 32.
18. Clarke, 132.
19. Jackson and Vos, 79–87.
20. Virginia Stephen to Vanessa Bell, 25 December 1909, V. Woolf, *Letters*, 415.

21. Q. Bell, *Bloomsbury*, 28–9.
22. The quotations from Virginia Woolf are from her *Moments of Being*, 164, 169, 172.
23. Q. Bell, *Virginia Woolf*, i, 135.
24. KC, CP, Box 3: 30.
25. V. Woolf, *Moments of Being*, 126.
26. CUL, Hilton Young, 'In and Out', 22: Kennet Papers 82/1.
27. KC, CP, Box 18, Item 7.
28. L. Woolf, *Beginning Again*, 35–7.
29. DG to JMK, 28 February 1910.
30. KC, CP, Box 12, Item 1.
31. Garnett, *Golden Echo*, 207.
32. CW, viii, 241.
33. JMK to DG, 13 August 1910.
34. JMK to DG, 21 August 1910.
35. JBS to GLS, 29 August 1911.
36. JMK to JNK, 14 July 1911.
37. JMK to JNK, 29 June 1911.
38. JMK to GLS, 17 July 1911.
39. JMK to GLS, 8 September 1911.
40. JMK to DG, 7 September 1911.
41. JMK to DG, 12 March 1911.
42. KC, KP, Box 32, JMK correspondence with Sarkar.
43. JMK to FAK, 24 September 1911.

Chapter 11: An Indian Summer

1. KC, KP, (unclassified), G. H. Luce to JMK, 7 October 1913.
2. JMK to DG, 12 February 1913, 19 September 1912; JMK to FAK, 17 September 1912.
3. ML, KP: Waterlow to JMK, 6 October 1931; JMK to GLS, 13 October 1912.
4. JMK to DG, 15 November 1912.
5. KC, KP, Box 32, Wittgenstein to JMK, 16 July 1913.
6. KC, KP, Box 32, Rose to JMK.
7. Holroyd, ii, 28.
8. KC, KP, Box 37, JMK to MLK, 12 February 1911.
9. JMK to DG, 12 February 1913.
10. GLS to JMK, 30 October 1912.
11. Q. Bell, *Virginia Woolf*, i, 175.
12. KC, CP, Box 12, Item 9, V. Bell to C. Bell, 11 October 1911.

13. Virginia Stephen to Ottoline Morrell, 9 November 1911; to L. Woolf, 2 December 1911; V. Woolf *Letters*, i, 480, 484.
14. GLK, *Gates*, 115.
15. V. Woolf to K. Cox, 4 September 1912, V. Woolf, *Letters*, ii, 6.
16. JMK to DG, 3 February 1911.
17. ML, KP, Correspondence L/12, Leaf to JMK, 8 February 1912.
18. JMK to DG, 23 November 1911.
19 CW, xv, 66, Abrahams to JMK, 29 April 1911.
20. *Ibid.*, 62.
21. *Ibid.*, 67–85.
22. JMK to M. Macmillan, 12 August 1910, BL, Add. MSS 55201.
23. CW, xv, 90.
24. ML, KP, 5:5.
25. JMK to JNK, 20 March 1913.

26. JMK to JNK, 4 April 1913.
27. JMK to DG, 17 April 1913.
28. CW, xv, 98.
29. JMK to JNK, 4 April 1913.
30. See JMK to Lydia Keynes, 16 November 1924: 'In 1913 when he [Montagu] was at the India Office, it was he who got me put on the Royal Commission on Indian Currency ...'.
31. JMK, *Indian Currency and Finance*, CW, i, 51.
32. *Ibid.*, 124–6.
33. *Ibid.*, 102.
34. *Ibid.*, 69–71.
35. *Ibid.*, 165–6.
36. *Ibid.*, 255.
37. Smithies, 'Keynes Revisited', *QJE*, 465.
38. Austen Chamberlain to JMK, 12 August 1913, CW, xv, 100.
39. ML, KP, 5:10, JMK to Foxwell, 3 November 1913.
40. CW, xv, 107.
41. Editor's summary of Abrahams memo, CW, xv, 131.
42. JMK to JNK, 13 August 1913.
43. q. B. Strachey, 289; see also Holroyd, ii, 90.
44. CW, xv, 143.
45. For the whole memo, see 'An Indian State Bank', CW, xv, 151–203.
46. q. CW, xv, 221.
47. KC, KP, Box 17.
48. JMK to JNK, 11 January 1914.
49. FAK, *Gathering*, 81.
50. CW, xv, 258–63.
51. CW, xv, 237.
52. A. Marshall to JMK, 9 March 1914, CW, xv, 268.
53. q. Shone, 135.
54. *Ibid.*, 101.
55. In her obituary of Diaghilev, repr. in M. Keynes, *Lopokova*.
56. Sitwell, 209.
57. JMK to JNK, 28 July 1914.

Chapter 12: Adapting to War

1. ML, KP, L/14. B. Blackett to JMK, 1 August 1914.
2. *EJ*, September, December 1914: *QJE*, November 1914, repr. CW, xi, 238–328.
3. CW, xvi, 7–15.
4. CW, xvi, 16–19.
5. BUL, Austen Chamberlain Papers, AC 13/4/4, Bradbury to Chamberlain, 13 August 1914.
6. Morgan, 15–18; for the deeper issues, see De Cecco, ch. 7.
7. JMK, *EJ*, September 1914, 472; cited Morgan, 30.
8. ML, MP 1:67. cf. Sir Felix Schuster's letter to JMK 30 November 1914 in ML, KP, L/14, in which he assured Keynes that it had been the pressure of himself and Holden which had prevented the suspension of specie payments which was being urged by the Governor of the Bank of England.
9. CW, xi, 318–19; reprinted from *EJ*, November 1914.
10. See Blackett's diary (q. Harrod, *Keynes*, 197) 4 August 1914: 'Keynes' memorandum given by Hamilton to Lloyd George, who asked who Keynes was, and on being told that he was friend of mine, expert in currency, said it was monstrous that Treasury officials should call in outsiders on their own responsibility.'
11. ML, KP, L/14, Blackett to JMK, 13 August 1914.
12. JMK to JNK, 28 August 1914.
13. TC, Montagu papers, 2072(1), JMK to Montagu, 4 September 1914.
14. CW, xvi, 36.
15. CUL, Hilton Young, *In and Out*, Kennet Papers 81/2.
16. KC, KP, Box 17. JMK to DG, 10 October 1914: JMK to Hardman, 25 October 1914.
17. KC, CP, Box 12, Folder IV, Item 114, V. Bell to C. Bell, 2 October 1914.
18. Hutchison, *EcHR* 2nd Series, xxvi, February 1973, 145.
19. Garnett, *Golden Echo*, 270–1.
20. *Ibid.*, 271.
21. JMK to FAK, 9 August 1914.
22. KC, KP, Box 30, Békássy to Noel Olivier, ?May 1915.
23. Holroyd, ii, 117.
24. GLS to JMK, 24 September 1914.
25. Levy, 279.
26. Harrod, *Keynes*, 201.
27. JMK to Lydia Keynes, 16 November 1924.
28. q. JNK Diary, 22 January 1915.
29. E. Johnson in CW, xvi, 57.
30. TC, Montagu Papers 86(1), Holderness to JMK, 3 February 1915.
31. q. JNK Diary, 30 January 1915.
32. TC, Montagu Papers, AS/4/3, Lloyd George to Montagu, 24 January 1915.
33. Garnett Diary, 1, 2 February 1915.
34. CW, xvi, 67–74.
35. HLL, Bonar Law Papers, 107/2/67, JMK to Bonar Law, 10 October 1922.
36. CW, xvi, 67.

37. Quotations from a lecture, 'The Civil Service and Financial Control', JMK gave to the Society of Civil Servants in 1921, CW, xvi, 296–307.
38. Cited Harrod, *Keynes*, 201.
39. CW, xvi, 299.
40. Garnett, *Flowers* 21–3.
41. Holroyd, ii, 160.
42. CUL, Kennet Papers, 28/8, DG to Hilton Young, ?April 1915.
43. KC, CP, Box 12, Item 118, V. Bell to C. Bell, Monday ? 1915.

44. Garnett, *Flowers*, 42.
45. Clark, *Russell*, 260–1; Morrell, *Ottoline at Garsington*, 60.
46. V. Woolf, diary, i, 17, 13 January 1915.
47. Hazlehurst, 232.
48. *Ibid.*, 297.
49. JNK Diary, 22 June 1915.
50. JMK to DG, 24 July 1915: JMK to FAK, 17 July 1915.
51. Morrell, *Ottoline at Garsington*, 50.

Chapter 13: Keynes and the First World War

1. See Lloyd George's speech in the Commons, 4 May 1915, q. Hazlehurst, 224.
2. *DNB*, 'McKenna'.
3. Beaverbrook, *Politicians*, 155.
4. Margot Asquith Diary, 6 August, 14, 20 September 1915.
5. CW, x, 58–60.
6. CW, xvi, 104. See also PRO: CAB 37/129/29.
7. *Ibid.*, 125–8. See also PRO: T 170/73.
8. Morgan, 355–6.
9. TC, Montagu Papers, AS/1/12, 252 (1).
10. Margot Asquith Diary, 20 August 1915.
11. CW, xvi, 110–15.
12. Jenkins, 289n.
13. *Ibid.*, 371.
14. CW, xvi, 117–25; final version in PRO: T.170/85. See also JMK's note for the PM on the Financial Position, 30/10/15 in MS Asquith (31–4).
15. Cooper, 'Command of Gold', 212.
16. Lloyd George, *War Memoirs*, ii, 684.
17. CW, xvi, 117–25.
18. *Ibid.*, 154.

19. Jenkins, 388.
20. *Ibid.*, 387.
21. C. Bell, *Old Friends*.
22. KC, CP, Box 3:30.
23. Holroyd, ii, 172.
24. KC, KP, Box 17. A first draft of this letter was kindly given me by Richard Garnett.
25. Garnett, *Flowers*, 97.
26. TC, Montagu Papers, AS/1/1, 45.
27. *Ibid.*, AS/VI/10: 2104(1).
28. Jenkins, 389.
29. q. Holroyd, ii, 172.
30. In M. Keynes, *Essays*, 68.
31. Holroyd, ii, 172.
32. Levy in M. Keynes, *Essays*, 68.
33. GLS to JBS, 22 February 1916.
34. Woodward, 220; see also Cooper, 'British Response'.
35. KC, CP, Box 4:18.
36. In the possession of Mrs Henrietta Couper.
37. Garnett, *Flowers*, 121.
38. *Ibid.*, 122.

Chapter 14: Touch and Go

1. KC, CP, Box 14: 6, Bell to V. Bell, ?May 1916.
2. Morrell, *Ottoline at Garsington*, 107.
3. q. Bedford, i, 69.
4. JMK to JNK, 5 June 1916.
5. CW, xvi, 213.
6. *Ibid.*, 189–96. See also PRO: CAB 37/151:9.
7. JMK to FAK, 10 September 1916.
8. KC, CP, Box 18, JMK to V. Bell, 25 August 1916.
9. V. Woolf, *Letters*, ii, 95, V. Woolf to V. Bell, 14 May 1916.
10. JMK to FAK, 29 October 1916.
11. Garnett, *Flowers*, 144–5; see also his *Great Friends*, 136.
12. CW, xvi, 85, 187.

13. *Ibid.*, 197–209, JMK memoranda are dated 10, 24 October 1916.
14. See Cooper, 'Command of Gold', 219–21.
15. Lloyd George, *War Memoirs*, ii, 854–5.
16. CW, xvi, 198.
17. *Ibid.*, 211–12, 24 September 1939.
18. V. Woolf, *Letters*, ii, 812, 29 December 1916.
19. Hendrick, ii, 269–70.
20. CW, xvi, 215–21.
21. q. Cooper, 'Command of Gold', 227.
22. MacFadyean, 64.
23. JMK to FAK, 30 March 1917.
24. Hemery, 90.
25. JMK to JNK, 29 May 1917.
26. CW, x, 34, JMK, 'Andrew Bonar Law'.

27. For an account see Burk, *EcHR*, 1979, 405–16.
28. CW, xvi, 249–50.
29. *Ibid.*, 253–4. See also T 172/443: 61–2
30. Burk, *EcHR*, 415.
31. CW, xvi, 255–63.
32. Blake, 351–4.
33. JMK to FAK, 10 July 1917.
34. FAK to JMK, 1 August 1917.
35. JMK to FAK, 19 August 1917.
36. JMK to FAK, 28 September 1917.
37. 'He has been my mainstay out here in finance and has given me most valuable assistance.' Reading to Bonar Law, q. CW, xvi, 264.
38. CC, Spring Rice Papers, 2/13, n.d.
39. HLL, Lloyd George Papers, F. 23/1/25; F. 23/4/43, 8.
40. Blackett to Hamilton, 1 January 1918, q. CW, xvi, 264.
41. JMK to FAK, 14 November 1917.
42. JMK to FAK, 6 December 1917.
43. JMK to FAK, 15 December 1917.
44. JMK to DG, 15 December 1917.
45. JMK to Blackett, 30 January 1918, q. CW, xvi, 264
46. Garnett Diary, 30 January 1918.

47. For the whole memo see CW, xvi, 274–85.
48. JMK to Chalmers, 30 April 1918. CW, xvi, 290–3.
49. CW, xvi, 289–90.
50. *Ibid.*, 287.
51. JMK to FAK, 14 November 1917.
52. JMK to FAK, 24 December 1917.
53. FAK to JMK, 26 December 1917.
54. JMK to FAK, 10 February 1918.
55. V. Woolf, *Diary*, i, 86, 7 December 1917.
56. For Maurice Debate, see Beaverbrook, *Men and Power*, 248–64.
57. JMK to FAK, 14 April 1918.
58. KC, KP, Box 32. JMK to B. Webb, 11 March 1918.
59. V. Woolf, *Letters*, ii, 208, V. Woolf to Margaret Llewellyn Davies, 2 January 1918.
60. Garnett Diary, 23 January 1918.
61. See JMK to DG, 26 June 1918. Duncan's commission fell through.
62. KC, CP, Box 18, JMK to V. Bell, 23 March 1918.
63. JMK to FAK, 22 March 1918.
64. KC, CP, Box 14: 44.
65. *Ibid.*, Box 17.
66. JMK to FAK, 3 November 1918.

Chapter 15: *Zigzagging*

1. CW, xvi, 313–34.
2. *Ibid.*, 341.
3. *Ibid.*: 'Memorandum by the Treasury on the Indemnity Payable by the Enemy Powers for Reparation and Other Claims', 348, 357, 375, 378.
4. Bunselmeyer, 16.
5. *Ibid.*, 97.
6. Hancock and Poel, iv, Doc. 876.
7. *Ibid.*, iv, Doc. 871.
8. Bunselmeyer, 176.
9. Elcock, 49–50.
10. CW, x, 398, 'Dr Melchior'.
11. *Ibid.*, 399.
12. *Ibid.*, 395, 403.
13. *Ibid.*, 402–3.
14. For the 1924 dispute see BUL, Austen Chamberlain Papers, AC 35/7/4–11; also CW, xvi, 406–15.
15. CW, xvi, 422.
16. BLH, Lamont papers, 170–15, Reports of Admiral Hope and T. W. Lamont on meetings held at Spa, 4 and 5 March 1919.
17. *Ibid.*
18. CW, x, 413–15, 'Dr Melchior'.
19. *Ibid.*, 409.
20. *Ibid.*, 422–3.
21. *Ibid.*, 425–6.

22. JMK to FAK, 12 February 1919.
23. CW, x, 390, 'Dr Melchior'.
24. KC, CP, Box 18, JMK to V. Bell, 16 March 1919.
25. BLH, Lamont Papers 164–15; Norman Davis, 'Peace Conference Notes', 5 July 1919.
26. HLL, Lloyd George Papers, F/30/3/27.
27. Tillman, 239.
28. TC, Montagu Papers, 249(1), memorandum by Montagu, 4 April 1919.
29. Lothian Papers, G040/17/64.
30. HLL, Lloyd George Papers, F/213/5/9.
31. q. Tillman, 241.
32. For the text of the Smuts memorandum see Hancock and Poel, iv, pp. 926–8.
33. See Hancock and Poel, vii, Doc. 841, Smuts to R. F. Harrod, 24 March 1949. Harrod's letter of enquiry to Smuts is in the Smuts Papers vol. 89, No. 5, 26 February 1949. I am indebted to Dr Iaian Smith for giving me a copy of the Harrod letter.
34. BLH, Lamont Papers, 168–4, T. W. Lamont, 'Note of a Conversation with Woodrow Wilson', 3 April 1919.
35. John Foster Dulles Papers, Box 2, 79.
36. BLH, Lamont Papers, 166–11, 'Memor-

andum of Conference held 5 April at the President's House'. Present were Clemenceau, Klotz, Loncheur and de la Chaume (France); Lloyd George, Lord Sumner and Col. Hankey (G.B.); Col. House, Baruch, Davis, Lamont and McCormick (U.S.A.); and Orlando and Crespi (Italy).

37. *Ibid.*, 164–20. Typed copy of Florence C. Lamont's Diary.
38. *Ibid.*, 164–20. Florence C. Lamont's Diary, 4 May 1919; Diary of Vance McCormick, 22 May 1919.
39. Hancock, *Smuts*, i, 515.
40. KC, CP, Box 18: 11. JMK to V. Bell, 20 January 1919.
41. Hancock and Poel, iv, Doc. 936.
42. CW, xvi, 418.
43. Hancock and Poel, iv, Doc. 943.
44. HLL, Lloyd George Papers, F/7/2/27; Austen Chamberlain to Lloyd George, 17 April 1919.
45. CW, xvi, 429–31.
46. *Ibid.*, 436.
47. BLH, Lamont Papers, 165–12; T. W. Lamont, 'Comments upon the so-called Keynes Memorandum as to European Credits'.

48. CW, xvi, 439; JMK to Bradbury, 4 May 1919.
49. q. CW, xvi, 441.
50. *Ibid.*, 442.
51. *Ibid.*, 450–6.
52. *Ibid.*, 460.
53. Tardieu, 120.
54. *Ibid.*, 298.
55. Hancock and Poel, iv, DOC. 962.
56. BLH, Lamont Papers, 169–11, 12: 'Memorandum of Conference held at the Ministry of Finance to deal with Reparation Clauses in the Treaty with Austria'. Present on 29 May were Lamont (presiding) Baruch, Davis, McCormick, Dulles, Smith and Whitney (U.S.A.); Lord Sumner, Lord Cunliffe, Keynes and Ward (G.B.); Tardieu, Klotz, Sergent and Jouasset (France); and Crespi and D'Amelio (Italy).
57. Bernard Baruch Papers, Section IV, Diary, 2 June 1919.
58. CW, x, 429, 'Dr. Melchior'.
59. HLL, Lloyd George Papers, F/7/2/32.

Chapter 16: Civilisation Under Threat

1. Letter discoverd in Harrod's papers, now at KCC.
2. Hancock and Poel, iv, Doc. 1012.
3. *Ibid.*, 1013.
4. *Ibid.*, 1016.
5. *Ibid.*, 1054.
6. q. CW, xvii, 4.
7. V. Woolf, *Diary*, i, 288.
8. q. CW, xvii, 4.
9. Margot Asquith Diary 1918/19, 173.
10. KC, KP, Box 30.
11. Garnett, *Great Friends*, 140.
12. BL, Falk Papers, Add. MSS 57923, JMK to Falk, 25 June 1919; also JMK to JNK, 25, 27 June 1919. JMK wrote to Madsen-Mygdal refusing the offer on 2 July 1919: 'I have not enough experience of the City to justify me in plunging at once into so responsible a position; and I do not feel that I know enough about the whole situation to take the step suggested'. A directorship in the National Discount Bank also fell through at this time. See R. H. Brand to JMK, 3 July 1919, ML, KP, L/19/1919.
13. JMK to FAK, 6 August 1919.
14. In KC, KP, Box 32.
15. JMK to FAK, 23 September 1919.
16. See ML, KP, EC/1/4. On 12 August 1919

George Macmillan wrote to him to say that a printing of 5000 would be excessive; he also refused him a separate American edition.
17. BL, Macmillan Papers, Add. MSS 55201, JMK to D. Macmillan.
18. KC, KP, 27 September 1919.
19. *Ibid.*, Box 17.
20. JMK to FAK, 3 September 1919.
21. BL, Falk Papers, Add MSS 57923, JMK to Falk, 1 September 1919.
22. CW, xvii, 5–6, Salter to JMK, 14 October 1919.
23. *Ibid.*, 6–7, JMK to Salter, 18 October 1919.
24. *Ibid.*, 7.
25. The comments of FAK, Lowes Dickinson and Sheppard on the proofs of *ECP* are in KC, KP, Box 35a.
26. ML, KP, EC/1/4.
27. CW, ii, 9.
28. *Ibid.*, 7, 9–10.
29. *Ibid.*, 11–12.
30. *Ibid.*, 13.
31. *Ibid.*, 8–9.
32. *Ibid.*, 146.
33. *Ibid.*, 148–9.
34. *Ibid.*, 35.
35. *Ibid.*, 22.
36. *Ibid.*, 18.

37. *Ibid.*, 25.
38. *Ibid.*, 32.
39. *Ibid.*, 26.
40. CW, x, 23–4, *Essays in Biography*.
41. CW, ii, 34.
42. *Ibid.*, 85.
43. *Ibid.*, 91.
44. *Ibid.*, 126.
45. *Ibid.*, 128–9.
46. *Ibid.*, 179.
47. *Ibid.*, 170.
48. KC, KP.
49. BUL, Chamberlain Papers, AC 35/1/8.
50. ML, KP, ECP 1/19 Corr.
51. *Ibid.*
52. *Ibid.*
53. FAK Scrapbook, *New Europe*, 1 January 1920, xiii, 168.
54. *The Times*, 5 January 1920.
55. FAK Scrapbook. An editorial in the *Liverpool Courier*, 15 January 1920, referring to a speech by JMK to the Liverpool Branch of the League of Nations Union, said he had failed to mention the League once, and that his appearance on a League platform was likely to destroy confidence in the League. In *ECP* (CW, ii, 163–5) JMK doubted whether the League could become an effective instrument for revising the Treaty.
56. FAK Scrapbook, *TLS*, 15 January 1920.
57. Thorstein Veblen, *Political Science Quarterly*, October 1920, 467–72; Arno Mayer, *Politics and Diplomacy of Peacemaking, Containment and Counter-Revolution at Versailles 1918–1919* (1968).
58. Baruch, 6, 8. For Keynes's review in the *Manchester Guardian* of 2 December 1920, see CW, xvii, 91–8. For the genesis of Baruch's book, see Schwartz, 153–60.
59. Vance McCormick's remark is in a letter to Dulles dated 16 March 1920, in Dulles Papers, Box 3. For a symposium of Wilsonian views, see the *Bulletin* of the League of Nations Association, April 1920.
60. Poel, v, Doc. 32, JMK to Smuts, 22 October 1920.
61. CW, iii, 103–4.
62. CW, iii, 70; for the Brenier controversy see CW, xvii, 154–62, 302–3.
63. See Tardieu, 307–9.
64. Mantoux, 21–2.
65. *Ibid.*, 122–3.
66. *Ibid.*, 126.
67. *Ibid.*, 121.
68. Harrod, *Keynes*, 276.

Dramatis Personae

AMOS, SIR MAURICE (1872–1940), lawyer, served in Egyptian judiciary. Ed. Trinity College, Cambridge. 1st in Moral Sciences, 1893. On his visit to Egypt in 1913, JMK stayed with him in Cairo.

ASQUITH, EMMA MARGARET ('Margot') (1864–1945), Asquith's second wife. JMK won substantial amounts of money playing bridge with Margot and her step-daughter Elizabeth (later Princess Bibesco). As he told Duncan Grant, 'Margot always ends by going into the next room and thrusting a wad of notes into [my] hands saying "I don't know how much there is but I should think it is right" – it always being too much.'

ASQUITH, HERBERT HENRY (1852–1928), lawyer and Liberal statesman. Ed. City of London School and Balliol College, Oxford, 1870. 1st in Classics. Home Secretary, 1892–5; Chancellor of the Exchequer, 1906–8; Prime Minister, 1908–16. Married (1) Helen Melland, who died in 1891, leaving him with five children, and (2) Margot Tennant, in 1891, who bore him a further five, only two of whom survived infancy. JMK got to know Asquith during the First World War, spending bridge evenings at No. 10, and many weekends at the Wharf. He was a convinced Asquithian.

ATTOLICO, BERNARDO (1880–1942), lawyer. Italian representative on the Wheat, War Purchase, and Maritime Transport Committees in London during the war. Legal counsel to the Italian delegation to the Paris Peace Conference, and member of the Supreme Economic Council, 1919. Italian Ambassador to Berlin 1935–40 – not a good time.

BAGENAL, BARBARA (née Hiles) (b. 1891). One of the wartime Bloomsbury 'bunnies' or 'cropheads'. Studied at the Slade School 1913–14; employed at the Hogarth Press 1918–19. She had a brief affair with David Garnett, a flirtation with JMK, and a lifelong friendship with Saxon Sydney-Turner; she married Nicholas Bagenal in 1918.

BALFOUR, ARTHUR JAMES (1848–1930), philosopher and Conservative statesman. Ed. Eton and Trinity College, Cambridge, 1866. Studied moral philosophy under Sidgwick, who later married his sister Eleanor, subsequently Principal of Newnham College; another sister married John Strutt (later Lord Rayleigh), the Cambridge physicist. Prime Minister, 1902–05; First Lord of the Admiralty, 1915–16; Foreign Secretary 1916–19. JMK briefed him in the anti-conscriptionist cause, to which he inclined. But Balfour's inclinations were never very strong in any direction, and he later served happily enough under Lloyd George. To JMK he appeared 'perfectly poised between the past and the future'. The most striking summary is by Hugh Kingsmill: 'Men of affairs admired him as a philosopher. Philosophers admired him as a man of affairs. Thinkers of plebeian origin were flattered that an aristocrat should condescend to enquire into the mystery of things; and aristocrats were heartened by the rumour that one at least of their order was capable of sustained thought.'

BARUCH, BERNARD MANNES (1870–1965), financial wizard. Member of the American Commission to Negotiate Peace, and Supreme Economic Council, 1919. Disliked JMK.

BÉKÁSSY, FERENC (1893–1915), poet. Son of a Hungarian landowner. Ed. Bedales and King's College, Cambridge, 1911, where he read history. Apostle, 1912. Served as a Lieutenant in the 5th Honvéd Hussars; killed in Bukovina, 25 June 1915. King's put up a (separate) memorial to him in its chapel. His book of poems, *Adriatica*, was published posthumously by the Hogarth Press. JMK visited him in Hungary in 1912. Békássy wrote to Noel Olivier in May 1915: 'I wanted to write much more about Maynard... Do you know I think there's a difference between poets (who write poetry) and other people, that poets take hold of the feelings they have and won't let them go and other people let feelings have their natural effects and don't write poetry.'

BELL, CLIVE (1881–1964), art critic. Ed. Marlborough and Trinity College, Cambridge, 1899. A sportsman, with a passion for modern French painting and good living, he married Vanessa Stephen in 1907 and invented the aesthetic theory of 'significant form'. Virginia Woolf wrote of his book *Civilisation* (1928): 'He has great fun in the opening chapters, but in the end it turns out that civilisation is a lunch party at 50 Gordon Square.' JMK and Clive constantly saw each other in the Bloomsbury Group, but in his memoir, *Old Friends* (1957), Bell implied that old friends might not always be the best of friends..

BELL, VANESSA: *see* STEPHEN

BERENSON, MARY and BERNARD: *see* PEARSALL SMITH family

BIRRELL, FRANCIS FREDERICK LOCKER ('Frankie') (1889–1935), translator. Son of the Liberal politician, Augustine Birrell. Ed. Eton and King's College, Cambridge, 1908, where he read history. 'A tousled, gnome-like creature in spectacles' (David Garnett), he charmed JMK and appalled D. H. Lawrence, making him dream of beetles. In 1920 he and David Garnett started a bookshop, Birrell and Garnett, Ltd, in London with JMK's assistance. Birrell wrote to JMK in 1918: 'It is sickening to see you so little, as I can never forget that if I am a presentable person at all, it is to a great extent, to a very great extent, due to you.'

BLACKETT, SIR BASIL (1882–1935), financial administrator. Ed. Marlborough and University College, Oxford. Entered the Treasury in 1904. Secretary of the Royal Commission on Indian Finance and Currency, 1913–14, when JMK got to know him. Treasury representative in U.S.A. 1917–18. Went to India in 1922 as Finance Member of the Viceroy's Council.

BOND, HENRY (1853–1958), friend of J. N. Keynes; Master of Trinity Hall, Cambridge, 1919–29.

BRADBURY, JOHN SWANWICK, BARON BRADBURY (1872–1950), civil servant, Ed. Manchester Grammar School, Brasenose College, Oxford. Joint Permanent Secretary, Treasury, 1911–19. The Treasury pound notes issued in 1914 were known as 'Bradburys'.

BROOKE, JUSTIN (1885–1963), fruit farmer. Ed. Bedales, Abbotsholme and Emmanuel College, Cambridge, 1904, where he read law. Founder of the Marlowe Dramatic Society, 1907: friend of Rupert Brooke.

BROOKE, RUPERT CHAWNOR (1887–1915), poet. Ed. Rugby and King's College, Cambridge, 1906. Apostle, 1908. Fellow, 1913. Died of blood poisoning at Skyros, 23 April 1915, on active service. He and JMK were good, but not intimate friends, Brooke being closer to JMK's brother Geoffrey, a fellow Rugbeian. Brooke's younger brother, Alfred, who came to King's as an exhibitioner in 1909, was also killed in the war.

BROWN family. DR JOHN BROWN (1830–1922), father of Florence Ada Keynes and grandfather of JMK. Minister, Park Chapel, Cheetham Hill Road, Manchester, 1855–64; Minister, Bunyan Meeting, Bedford, 1864–1903; chairman of the Congregational Union, 1891; author of numerous works on Puritanism, including *John Bunyan, his Life, Times, and Work* (1885). Married ADA HAYDON FORD, 1859, by whom he had three sons and three daughters. Apart from JMK's mother, there were ALICE (1864–1958), a doctor; JESSIE (*d.* 1949), who married Albert Lloyd; WALTER LANGDON-BROWN (1870–1946), an eminent physician; HAROLD (1873–1957), and KENNETH (1879–1958), a solicitor.

BROWNING, OSCAR (1837–1923), schoolmaster and famous Cambridge character. Ed. Eton and King's College, Cambridge, 1856. Apostle, 1858. Assistant-master at Eton, 1860–75, dismissed 'on unsubstantiated charges of misconduct' (*DNB*), returned to King's, where he became college lecturer in history, 1880. Died in Rome.

BUTLER, HAROLD BERESFORD (1883–1951), international civil servant. Ed. Eton and Balliol College, Oxford, 1902. Fellow of All Souls, 1905–12. School friend of JMK.

CARRINGTON, DORA HOUGHTON (1893–1932), painter. At the Slade School, Mark Gertler fell violently in love with her; but she developed an implausible passion for Lytton Strachey in 1915, which consumed the rest of her life, and drove her to take her own life after his death. A fine painter, she reminded Ottoline Morrell of 'a wild moorland pony'.

CHALMERS, ROBERT, BARON CHALMERS (1858–1938), civil servant. Ed. City of London School and Oriel College, Oxford. Permanent Secretary to the Treasury, 1911–13. Governor of Ceylon, 1913–16. Joint Permanent Secretary, Treasury, 1916–19. Master of Peterhouse, 1924–31. 'His pomposity and cynicism concealed sensitivity and many benefactions.' (*DNB*).

CHAMBERLAIN, SIR (JOSEPH) AUSTEN (1863–1937), Liberal Unionist statesman. Eldest son of Joseph Chamberlain. Ed. Rugby and Trinity College, Cambridge, 1882 – Oscar Browning's only success in producing statesmen. Chairman of the Royal Commission on Indian Finance and Currency, 1913–14, when JMK first got to know him, and concluded that his intellect might be adequate for the premiership. Chancellor of the Exchequer, 1919–21, Foreign Secretary, 1924–9.

CLEMENCEAU, GEORGES (the 'Tiger') (1841–1929), statesman. Prime Minister of France 1917–19, and President of the Paris Peace Conference. JMK encountered him in extreme old age, not as the translator of John Stuart Mill and fiery Radical Deputy of the early days of the Third Republic.

COLE, ARTHUR FREDERICK ANDRÉ (1882–1968), barrister and bibliophile. Ed. Clifton College and King's College, Cambridge, 1901. Lifelong correspondent with JMK on book-collecting.

COSTELLOE, RACHEL and KARIN: see PEARSALL SMITH

COX, KATHERINE LAIRD ('Ka') (1887–1938), civil servant. Ed. Newnham College, Cambridge, 1910, 'neo-pagan' and friend of Rupert Brooke. In 1919 she married William Arnold-Forster.

CRAVATH, PAUL DRENNAN (1861–1940), lawyer. Advisory Counsel, American Mission to the Inter-Ally Council for War Purchases and Finance, London and Paris, 1918.

CROSBY, OSCAR TERRY (1861–1947), director of a street-car company who became Assistant Secretary of U.S. Treasury, and President of the Inter-Ally Council for War Purchases and Finance, 1917–19. Author of *Electrical Railway in Theory and Practice* (1926).

DALTON, EDWARD HUGH JOHN NEALE (1887–1962), Labour politician. Ed. Eton and King's College, Cambridge, 1906, where he studied economics under Pigou and JMK. Always known as 'Daddy' in JMK's circle. Already possessed of a booming voice and habit of addressing people as if they were a public meeting.

DARWIN family. CHARLES DARWIN (1809–1882) had three sons who became prominent in science, all of them graduates of Trinity College, Cambridge – SIR GEORGE HOWARD DARWIN (1845–1912), professor of astronomy at Cambridge, SIR FRANCIS DARWIN (1848–1925), a botanist, and SIR HORACE DARWIN (1851–1928), an engineer and designer of scientific instruments. Sir George Darwin's daughter, GWEN (1885–1957), married JACQUES RAVERAT (1885–1925); her sister MARGARET (d. 1974) married JMK's brother Geoffrey in 1917. Sir Francis Darwin's daughter FRANCES (1886–1960) married the classical scholar FRANCIS CORNFORD (1874–1943). It was of Sir George Darwin that JMK wrote to his father in 1899: 'His hands certainly looked as if he might be descended from an ape.'

DAVIES family. The Rev. John Llewelyn Davies (1826–1916), a graduate of Trinity College, Cambridge, follower of F. D. Maurice, and noted preacher and theologian, had two sons Crompton (1868–1935) and Theodore (1870–1905), who were both Apostles of the Moore–Russell generation. Their sister Margaret (1861–1944), a supporter of women's rights, was Virginia Woolf's friend. Their aunt Sarah Emily (1830–1921) was the founder of Girton College, Cambridge.

DAVIS, NORMAN HEZEKIAH (1878–1944), banker. Assistant Secretary of State, U.S. Treasury, 1917; member of the American Commission to Negotiate Peace and Supreme Economic Council, 1918–19. Active in U.S. financial and disarmament diplomacy between the wars.

DICKINSON, GOLDSWORTHY LOWES (1862–1932), humanist and philosopher. Ed. Charterhouse and King's College, Cambridge, 1881. Apostle, 1885. Fellow of King's, 1887. Best known for his books, *A Greek View of Life* (1896), *Letters from John Chinaman* (1901) and *International Anarchy* (1926), the last an investigation into the origins of the First World War. Sheppard thought that this book would be recognised as 'the greatest contribution Cambridge ever made to historical research'.

DRAKE, FRANCIS COURTNEY (1868–1915), civil servant. Ed. Winchester and New College, Oxford. Assistant Secretary, Revenue and Statistical Department, India Office, 1907–12.

DULLES, JOHN FOSTER (1888–1959), lawyer and statesman. Advisory Counsel to American Commission to Negotiate Peace, and member of the Supreme Economic Council, 1918–19. U.S. Secretary of State 1952–9.

DUNDAS, ROBERT HAMILTON (1884–1957), classics don. Ed. Eton and New College, Oxford, 1903. Lecturer in Greek History and Censor, Christ Church, Oxford. Eton friend of JMK.

FALK, OSWALD TOYNBEE ('Foxy') (1879–1972), financier. Ed. Rugby, Balliol College, Oxford. In 'A' Division of the Treasury, 1917–19. Founder of the Tuesday Club, 1917. Partner in the stockbroking firm of Buckmaster and Moore, his clients 'either made a killing in the market or [were] wiped out completely' (Nicholas Davenport). Collector of Post-Impressionist paintings and a ballet-lover, he wrote (1950) about the pre-war era that 'those who were young on the night of Mafeking lived for an Edwardian decade the life of a delicious novel by Henry James. There were threatening clouds, but we hardly noticed them, and when the storm broke in 1914 we believed it was merely an interlude to be followed by another and even more secure nineteenth century.'

FAWCETT, HENRY (1833–1884), economist and politician, Ed. King's College School, London, and Peterhouse, Cambridge, 1852. Professor of Political Economy at Cambridge, 1863–84. An orthodox expositor of the doctrines of Ricardo and John Stuart Mill.

FAY, CHARLES RYE (1884–1961), economic historian. Ed. Merchant Taylors' School, King's College, Cambridge, 1902. 1st in History. Fellow and Lecturer of Christ's College, Cambridge, 1908–22. Professor of Economic History, Toronto University, 1921–30. First met JMK when they were freshmen in 1902. Thought him 'the most brilliant man I have ever met or can hope to meet'. JMK thought Fay's essays on money were mainly off the point.

FORSTER, EDWARD MORGAN (1879–1970), writer. Ed. Tonbridge and King's College, Cambridge, 1897. Apostle, 1901. His great Cambridge friends were Dickinson and H. O. Meredith. Brought up in a 'haze of elderly ladies', he grew up into a sharp and demure old maid. Lytton Strachey called him a *taupe*, or mole.

FOXWELL, HERBERT SOMERTON (1849–1936), economist and bibliographer. Ed. Wesleyan College Institute, Taunton, University College, London, and St John's College, Cambridge, 1868. Senior Moralist, 1870. Fellow of St John's, 1874. Professor of Political Economy, London University, 1881–1928. President, Royal Economic Society, 1927–30. Foxwell collected nearly 60,000 books, pamphlets, and rare MSS on economics, which were sold to Goldsmith's Library in London, and also to Harvard University. On his engagement to Olive Dorrington in 1897 he wrote to J. N. Keynes: 'I grieve to add that Miss Dorrington is not a bit advanced or cultured, knows no political economy ... and couldn't possibly pass in any Tripos except perhaps modern languages. On the other hand, she doesn't sing, which is a great comfort ...'

FRY, SIR GEOFFREY STORRS (1888–1960). Ed. Harrow and King's College, Cambridge, 1905. Served under JMK in 'A' Division of the Treasury 1917–19. Later private secretary to Bonar Law and Baldwin.

FRY, ROGER ELIOT (1866–1934), art critic and painter. Ed. Clifton College and King's College, Cambridge, 1885. 1st in Parts I and II Natural Sciences. Apostle, 1887. Slade Professor of Art at Cambridge, 1933. 'The greatest influence on taste since Ruskin' (*DNB*). His particular friend in Bloomsbury was Vanessa Bell, but he and JMK had financial and artistic dealings.

FURNESS, SIR ROBERT ALLASON (1883–1954). Ed. Rugby and King's College, Cambridge, 1902. 1st in Classics. JMK's closest undergraduate friend at King's. Egyptian Civil Service, 1906–23; thereafter a variety of posts in Egypt. JMK stayed with him in Egypt in 1913.

GARNETT, DAVID (known as 'Bunny') (1892–1981), writer. Ed. Royal College of Science, South Kensington. Friend of JMK and his main defender in Bloomsbury Group. JMK described him as 'earthy'. His best-known novel was *Lady into Fox* (1922).

GODLEY, JOHN ARTHUR, first Baron Kilbracken (1847–1932), civil servant. Ed. Rugby and Balliol College, Oxford, 1866, Permanent Under-Secretary of State for India, 1883–1909.

GRANT, DUNCAN JAMES CORROWR (1885–1978), painter. Ed. St. Paul's School, London, Westminster School of Art, Slade; studied under Jacques-Émile Blanche in Paris. Portrayed as the painter Duncan Forbes in D. H. Lawrence's *Lady Chatterley's Lover* – 'that dark-skinned taciturn Hamlet of a fellow with straight black hair and a weird Celtic conceit of himself'. Cousin of Lytton Strachey, and JMK's best and lifelong friend. Emotional lynch-pin of the Bloomsbury Group.

GREENWOOD, LEONARD HUGH (1880–1965), classical scholar from New Zealand. Ed. King's College, 1899. 1st in Classics. Apostle, 1902. Fellow and Director of Studies in Classics at

Emmanuel College. Whether or not through his influence, Emmanuel became, in the late 1900s, a considerable source of Apostles and 'embryos'.

HAMILTON, GRANVILLE, *see* PROBY.

HARDMAN, FREDERICK MCMAHON (1891–1914). Ed. Eton and King's College, Cambridge, 1905. JMK taught him economics. Lytton Strachey said that he belonged 'to the small, chiselled, fair and futile type – with an infinitely aristocratic voice'. Killed in action, October 1914.

HARDY, GODFREY HAROLD (1877–1947), mathematician. Ed. Cranleigh, Winchester and Trinity College, Cambridge, 1895. 4th Wrangler, 1898. Fellow, 1898. Sadleirian Professor of Pure Mathematics, Cambridge, 1931–42. In his autobiographical essay, *A Mathematician's Apology* (1940), he defended the mathematical vocation on the ground that it is, at least, harmless.

HAWTREY, SIR RALPH GEORGE (1879–1975), civil servant and economist. Ed. Eton and Trinity College, Cambridge, 1898. 19th Wrangler. Apostle, 1900. Entered the Treasury, 1904.

HILL, ARCHIBALD VIVIAN (1886–1977), scientist. Ed. Blundell's School, Trinity College, Cambridge. 3rd Wrangler, 1907. 1st in Natural Science, Pt 2 (Physiology), 1909. Fellow of Trinity College, 1910–16. Nobel Prize in Physiology and Medicine, 1922. He married JMK's sister Margaret (1885–1970) in 1913.

HOBHOUSE, SIR ARTHUR LAWRENCE (1886–1965), solicitor and farmer. Ed. Eton, St Andrews University, Trinity College, Cambridge, 1904. Apostle, 1905. Friend of JMK. 'Really Arthur is a triumph ... of hereditary muddles' (JMK to Lytton Strachey, 10 December 1905).

HOLDERNESS, SIR THOMAS WILLIAM (1849–1924), civil servant. Secretary to the Revenue, Statistics and Commerce Department of the India Office, 1901–12. Permanent Under-Secretary of State, 1912.

HOOVER, HERBERT (1874–1964), statesman. In charge of U.S. relief to Europe during the War and Armistice; member of Supreme Economic Council, 1919. President of the United States, 1929–33.

HOUSE, EDWARD MANDELL ('Colonel') (1858–1938), President Wilson's special adviser and *éminence grise*. Represented the President on the Supreme War Council and Armistice Negotiations. As a member of the American Commission to Negotiate Peace, 1918–19, he often sat in for Wilson, and took crucial decisions in his name.

HUGHES, WILLIAM MORRIS (1862–1952), Australian politician. Born in London of Welsh parents, educated in Llandudno, he emigrated to Australia and was Federal Prime Minister, 1915–23. A strong supporter of a total Australian war effort, he expected Australia to be fully compensated by Germany for its sacrifices. According to Bernard Baruch he 'insisted that every Australian who had placed a mortgage on his house to buy a war bond was as definitely entitled to reparation as was every Frenchman whose house had been burned by the Germans'.

HURST, GILBERT HARRISON JOHN (1872–1930), schoolmaster, later lawyer. Ed. Eton and King's College, Cambridge, 1890. 2nd Wrangler. Taught JMK mathematics at Eton.

JEVONS, WILLIAM STANLEY (1835–1882), economist and logician. Ed. University College, London, 1851. Professor of Political Economy, University College, London, 1876. Famous for his theory of marginal utility, and the sunspot theory of trade depressions. JMK found his style of writing electrifying.

JOHNSON, WILLIAM ERNEST (1858–1931), logician. Ed. Perse School, Liverpool Royal Institution, and King's College, Cambridge, 1879; 11th Wrangler 1882; 1st in Moral Sciences, 1883. University Lecturer in Moral Sciences, 1896–1901; Fellow of King's and Sidgwick Lecturer in Moral Sciences, 1902–31. His *Logic* appeared in three volumes between 1921 and 1924. The most ingenious problems in J. N. Keynes's *Studies and Exercises in Formal Logic* were devised by W. E. Johnson whose 'fertility in producing problems on the syllogism seemed inexhaustible'. As a boy JMK would fidget as his father and Johnson discussed logical problems at interminable lunches.

KEELING, FREDERIC HILLERSDON ('Ben') (1886–1916). Ed. Winchester and Trinity College, Cambridge. Refounded University Fabian Society, 1906. Later assistant editor of the *New Statesman*. Killed on the Somme.

KEYNES, FLORENCE ADA (1861–1958), JMK's mother. Eldest daughter of the Rev. John and Ada Haydon Brown. Ed. privately and at Newnham College, 1878–80. Married J. N. Keynes, 1882. Secretary, Cambridge branch of Charity Organisation Society, 1894–1928. Chairman, Cambridge Board of Guardians, 1907. Founder and Chairman of National Union of Women Workers, 1912. First woman member, Cambridge Borough Council, 1914; Alderman, 1931; Mayor, 1932–3. Founded Papworth Village Settlement, 1917. President, National Council of Women, 1930. Started Cambridge Juvenile Employment Exchange. Hon Fellow, Newnham College, 1954. 'The busiest woman in Cambridge'.

KEYNES, SIR GEOFFREY LANGDON (1887–1982), surgeon, bibliographer, author, JMK's younger brother. Ed. Rugby and Pembroke College, Cambridge, 1906. 1st in Natural Sciences. He had a distinguished surgical career at St Bartholomew's Hospital. In the world of letters he is best known for his bibliographies of William Blake and editions of his works.

KEYNES, JOHN NEVILLE (1852–1949), logician and university administrator, JMK's father. Only son of JOHN KEYNES of Salisbury (1806–1878) and ANNA MAYNARD KEYNES (1821–1907), though he had a half-sister FANNY MARIA PURCHASE, née Keynes (1836–1933). Ed. Amersham Hall, University College, London, and Pembroke College, Cambridge, 1872. Senior Moralist, 1875. Fellow of Pembroke College, 1876–82; Hon. Fellow, 1911. University Lecturer in Moral Sciences, 1884–1911; Assistant Secretary of the Local Examinations and Lectures Syndicate, 1882–92; Secretary, 1892–1910; Registrary of Cambridge University, 1910–25. Author of *Studies and Exercises in Formal Logic* (1884) and *Scope and Method of Political Economy* (1891).

KLOTZ, LOUIS-LUCIEN (1868–1930), lawyer and politician. Several times French Minister of Finance – 1910, 1911, 1917–20; played a leading part in drawing up the financial clauses of the Versailles Treaty. His career was ended by a financial scandal, and his name does not appear in *Grand Larousse Encyclopédique*. Clemenceau called him 'the one Jew I know with no capacity whatever for finance'.

KNOX, ALFRED DILWYN (1885–1943), classics don and cryptographer. Ed. Eton and King's College, Cambridge, 1903. At Station X, Bletchley Park, Knox (together with Oliver Strachey) played a key part in breaking the German 'Enigma' cipher in the Second World War.

LAMONT, THOMAS WILLIAM (1870–1948), banker. As a partner in J. P. Morgan & Co., 1911–40, he was chiefly responsible, with Henry P. Davison, for organising financial assistance to Britain and France before the United States came into the war. Representative of the U.S. Treasury on American Commission to Negotiate Peace, 1918–19. Much engaged in international financial negotiations between the wars.

LASTEYRIE, CHARLES, COMTE DE (1879–1936), archivist and civil servant. An Inspecteur des Finances, he represented the French Treasury at the conferences at Trèves, Spa, and Paris. Minister of Finance, 1922–4.

LAVINGTON, FREDERICK (1881–1927), economist. Ed. Emmanuel College, Cambridge. 1st in Economics, 1910–11. After working in the Labour Exchange Department at the Board of Trade, he returned to Cambridge in 1918, becoming Girdler's Lecturer in Economics (1920) and a Fellow of Emmanuel College (1922).

LAW, ANDREW BONAR (1858–1923), Conservative statesman; JMK's chief as Chancellor of the Exchequer, 1917–18. Prime Minister, 1922–3. JMK got on very well with him, partly because he was 'almost devoid of Conservative principles'. JMK's summary of Law's character: 'too pessimistic to snatch present profits and too short-sighted to avoid future catastrophe'.

LLOYD GEORGE, DAVID (1863–1945), Liberal statesman. Chancellor of the Exchequer, 1908–15; Minister of Munitions, 1915–16; Secretary of State for War, July–December 1916; Prime Minister 1916–22. In the war years JMK detested Lloyd George for his commitment to total victory and his deviousness. In *Old Friends* (1957) Clive Bell writes (p. 47): 'I remember his cutting from a French paper . . . a photograph of "the goat" . . . in full evening dress and smothered in ribbons, speaking at a banquet in Paris; and I remember his writing under it "Lying in State". He pinned it up in the dining-room at forty-six [Gordon Square]'. In the 1920s Keynes's view of Lloyd George changed.

LOUCHEUR, LOUIS (1872–1931), industrialist and politician. Minister of Munitions and Minister of Reconstruction.

LUBBOCK, SAMUEL GURNEY (1873–1958), schoolmaster. Ed. Eton and King's College, Cambridge, 1892. 1st in Classics, 1895. JMK's Tutor at Eton.

LUCE, GORDON HANNINGTON (1889–1979), poet and teacher. Ed. Dean Close, Cheltenham, and Emmanuel College, Cambridge, 1906. 1st in Classics, 1911; 2nd in Medieval and Modern Languages, 1912. Professor of English, University of Rangoon. Lifelong friend of JMK, to whom he dedicated his *Poems* (1920), published by Macmillan at JMK's expense.

LUXMOORE, HENRY ELFORD (1839–1926), schoolmaster. Ed. Eton and Pembroke College, Oxford. Assistant-Master (Classics) at Eton, 1864–1904.

MCADOO, WILLIAM GIBBS (1863–1941), lawyer and businessman. Married Eleanor Wilson, daughter of President Wilson, 1914; Secretary of the Treasury, 1913–December 1918. Successfully floated four Liberty Loans, collecting over $18b. Later a U.S. Senator and a leader of the Democratic Party.

MACCARTHY, SIR (CHARLES OTTO) DESMOND (1877–1952), literary and dramatic critic. Ed. Eton and Trinity College, Cambridge, 1894. Apostle, 1896. Literary Editor, *New Statesman*, 1920–7; senior literary critic, *Sunday Times*, 1928–52. Leonard Woolf thought him 'perhaps the most charming man I have ever met'. A marvellous raconteur, he never wrote the great book which his friends expected.

MCFADYEAN, SIR ANDREW (1887–1974). Ed. University College School, London and University College, Oxford, where he got a 1st in Lit. Hum, 1909. Appointed to 'A' Division of the Treasury, 1917 but spent most of the next two years as Treasury representative in U.S.A.

MCKENNA, REGINALD (1863–1943), Liberal politician and banker. Ed. abroad, King's College School, London, and at Trinity Hall, Cambridge, 1882, where he read mathematics. President of the Board of Trade, 1907–8. First Lord of the Admiralty, 1908–11. Home Secretary, 1911–15. Chancellor of the Exchequer, 1915–16. Appointed chairman of the Midland Bank, 1919. He and JMK mounted a formidable, though unsuccessful, Treasury opposition to Lloyd George's 'great gun' programme, when McKenna tried to convince Lloyd George that 'the same man could not at the same time be in the navy and the army, in a factory and an arsenal, on the land and down a mine' (Stephen McKenna, *Reginald McKenna*, 229).

MACMILLAN, DANIEL DE MENDI (1886–1965), publisher. Ed. Eton and Balliol College, Oxford, 1904; director, Macmillan & Co, 1911. Eton friend and later publisher of JMK.

MCTAGGART, JOHN ELLIS (1866–1925), Idealist philosopher. Ed. Clifton College and Trinity College, Cambridge, 1885. Apostle, 1886. Fellow, 1891–7. Fellow and Lecturer, 1897–1923. His breakfasts were notorious for their lack of food and conversation. C. D. Broad wrote that 'McTaggart, though an atheist, could never have been anything but an Anglican'.

MALLORY, GEORGE LEIGH (1886–1924), mountaineer and schoolmaster. Ed. Winchester and Magdalene College, Cambridge. Died on Everest. Friend of JMK, who lent him £50 in 1910, but more so of Geoffrey Keynes.

MARSHALL, ALFRED (1842–1924), economist. Ed. Merchant Taylors' School and St John's College, Cambridge, 1862. 2nd Wrangler. Fellow of St John's, 1868–77, Principal of University College, Bristol, 1877–81. After two years at Balliol College, Oxford, succeeded Henry Fawcett as Professor of Political Economy at Cambridge, retiring in 1907. One of the great Victorian synthesisers, he published his *Principles of Economics* in 1890, which reconciled the classical tradition to Jevons, abstract theory to history, and science to morals. JMK thought him 'a very great man, but I suppose rather a silly one . . .'

MARTEN, SIR CLARENCE HENRY KENNETT (1872–1948), schoolmaster. Ed. Eton and Balliol College, Oxford, where he took a 1st in Modern History. Taught JMK history at Eton and Queen Elizabeth II history when she was a girl.

MEREDITH, HUGH OWEN (1878–1964). Ed. Shrewsbury and King's College, Cambridge, 1897. 1st in Classics Part I and in History Part II, 1903–8. Apostle, 1900. Girdler's Lecturer in Economics, 1908–11, Professor of Economics, Queen's University, Belfast, 1911–45. Friend of Lowes Dickinson, E. M. Forster and G. E. Moore. Oscar Browning told him: 'You are very brilliant, but you will never do anything.' James Strachey called him the 'Rupert Brooke of his time'. Meredith preserved in Belfast 'a one-man atmosphere of the Cambridge of Lowes Dickinson, E. M. Forster – and, indeed, of H. O. M.' (S. Gorley Putt). H. O. M. (as he was known to his friends) suggested to G. E. Moore 'the whole plan of the last chapter of *Principia Ethica*'.

MONTAGU, EDWIN SAMUEL (1879–1924), Liberal politician. Ed. Clifton College, City of London School, Trinity College, Cambridge, 1898. As President of the Cambridge Union (1902) he gave JMK the first of many helping hands in his career. Private Secretary to Asquith, 1906–10. Parliamentary Under-Secretary of State for India, 1910–14. Financial Secretary to Treasury, 1914–16. Chancellor of the Duchy of Lancaster, 1915. Minister of Munitions, June–December 1916. Secretary of State for India, June 1917–March 1922. L. E. Jones (in *Edwardian Youth*) remembers that, as an undergraduate, 'his long, ugly bony face was pockmarked like a photograph of the moon, but his eyes held me: sombre, patient, unhappy eyes of extraordinary intelligence'. Waley in his life of Montagu (p. 3) calls him 'the most melancholy and the gayest of friends'. JMK called him a 'natural tool and victim'.

MOORE, GEORGE EDWARD (1873–1958), philosopher. Ed. Dulwich College and Trinity College, Cambridge, 1892. Apostle, 1894. Fellow of Trinity, 1894–1904. University Lecturer in Moral Science, 1911–25. Professor of Philosophy, Cambridge University, 1925–39. In professional philosophy famous as the leader, with Russell, of the revolt against Idealism. But to JMK and his friends, he was the author of the 'religion' of *Principia Ethica* (1903).

MORRELL, LADY OTTOLINE (1873–1938), hostess. Half-sister of the 6th Duke of Portland, married Philip Morrell (1870–1943), a Liberal MP. Lover of Bertrand Russell, patron, protector and butt of Bloomsbury. JMK was often at Garsington during the war.

NICHOLSON, JOSEPH SHIELD (1850–1927), economist. Won the Cobden Prize, 1877. Professor of Political Economy, Edinburgh University, 1880–1927. Pioneer of economic history in Scotland. 'On questions of imperial policy and currency and banking he attained a position of exceptional authority' (*DNB*).

NORTON, HENRY TERTIUS JAMES (1887–1936), mathematician. Ed. Eton and Trinity College, Cambridge, 1905, of which he became a Fellow in 1910. Apostle, 1906. Brilliant and excitable friend of JMK, he eventually gave up mathematics after a nervous breakdown.

OLIVIER family. SYDNEY HALDANE, BARON OLIVIER (1859–1943), Fabian, civil servant and politician, had four daughters, MARGERY, BRYNHILD (1887–1935), DAPHNE (1889–1950) and NOEL (1892–1969). JMK rode with Brynhild, 'the outstanding beauty of the four' (David Garnett), who married A. E. Popham, and whose daughter Anne Olivier (*b*. 1916) married Quentin Bell, the younger son of Vanessa and Clive Bell. David Garnett wrote of the four sisters, who were his childhood friends: 'They were all aristocratic creatures; pride was the moving force of their lives; they felt contempt easily; pity did not come naturally, except for animals. Their minds were free; but though loving discussion of all things and eager to hear all sides, they were violently prejudiced and swayed by their emotions and the views in which they had been brought up.'

PAISH, SIR GEORGE (1867–1957), statistician and writer. Adviser to the Chancellor of the Exchequer, 1914–16. JMK wrote 'As usual, however, Mr. Lloyd George soon got bored with him and stopped reading his lengthy memoranda.'

PEARSALL SMITH family. ROBERT (1827–99) and HANNAH (1832–1911) PEARSALL SMITH, Quakers from Philadelphia, who settled in England in 1880s, had three children, MARY, LOGAN and ALYS. Mary (1864–1945) married BENJAMIN FRANCIS COSTELLOE (1855–1899), by whom she had two daughters, RACHEL CONN (1887–1940) and KARIN ELIZABETH CONN (1889–1938), both of whom went to Newnham College, Cambridge. Rachel married Lytton Strachey's elder brother OLIVER (1874–1960) in 1911 and took up women's causes. Karin, who Russell thought had 'more philosophical capacity than I have ever before seen in a woman', married ADRIAN STEPHEN in 1914. Their mother Mary became the mistress and then the wife of the art dealer and historian BERNARD BERENSON (1865–1959), and they lived at I Tatti, outside Florence. Logan (1865–1946) was a writer. Alys (1867–1951) Pearsall Smith was BERTRAND RUSSELL's first wife. JMK first met the sisters Ray and Karin on his motor-tour of Italy with their mother in 1906. The Pearsall

Smiths were 'one of the interesting intersecting points between the Fabians and what became the Bloomsbury Group' (Norman Mackenzie).

PEARSON, KARL (1857–1936), statistician and eugenicist, a pioneer of applying statistical methods to human behaviour. Ed. University College School, London and King's College, Cambridge, 1875. Professor of Applied Mathematics (1884), Geometry (1891), and Eugenics (1911) at University College, London. JMK's main intellectual opponent before the First World War. David Garnett describes him as 'a tall stiff man who wore one of those hard hats with straight sides and a flat top, and had a very blank and wooden face with thin, compressed lips'.

PIGOU, ARTHUR CECIL (1877–1959), economist. Ed. Harrow and King's College, Cambridge (1896), 1st in History, 1899 and in Part II, Moral Sciences, 1900. Fellow of King's, 1902; succeeded Marshall as Professor of Political Economy, Cambridge University, 1908–48. Like Marshall, he saw economics as a branch of applied ethics; founder of the British School of Welfare Economics. Donald Corrie, an undergraduate friend of Pigou, recalled that they would indulge in 'Cumberland wrestling . . . in the seclusion of the grass area on the north of the Chapel at dead of night'. Pigou wrote his male friends sentimental letters laced with Italian couplets.

PROBY, GRANVILLE (1883–1947), lawyer. Ed. Eton and Balliol College, Oxford, 1902. Clerk in the House of Lords, 1907–44. JMK knew him at Eton as Granville Hamilton, his father changing his name to Proby by deed poll.

PURVES, PATRICK JOHN CHESTER (1890–1960), international civil servant. Ed. Fettes, and King's College, Cambridge, 1909. Worked with League of Nations, and, later, WHO and UNESCO

RAMSAY, SIR MALCOLM GRAHAM (1871–1946), civil servant. Ed. Winchester and New College, Oxford. Assistant Secretary to the Treasury, 1914–19.

ROBERTSON, SIR DENNIS HOLME (1890–1963), economist. Ed. Eton and Trinity College, Cambridge, 1908. 1st in Part I Classics, 1910 and Part II Economics, 1912. Fellow of Trinity College, 1914. His *A Study of Industrial Fluctuations* was published in 1915. A prominent collaborator of JMK's in the 1920s. JMK wrote to Duncan Grant on 24 November 1908: 'Mr Robertson of Eton and Trinity came to lunch and for a walk with me yesterday. There's a good deal in his favour, but a little pudding-headed perhaps . . .'

ROSE, CHARLES ARCHIBALD WALKER (1880–1961), diplomat and businessman. Ed. Bedford School and King's College, London. Entered King's College, Cambridge in 1911 as Advanced Student, after thirteen years in consular service in China. Later joined the British-American Tobacco Company, and became a director of the Chartered Bank. JMK taught him economics and he taught JMK riding. His 'supreme gift was for friendship' (*KCC Annual Report*, 1961, 55–7).

RUSSELL, BERTRAND ARTHUR WILLIAM, EARL (1872–1970), mathematician and philosopher. Ed. by tutors, at crammer, and Trinity College, Cambridge, 1890. Apostle, 1892. 7th Wrangler, 1893, 1st in Moral Sciences, 1894. Fellow of Trinity, 1895–1901, and Lecturer in Mathematics, 1910–1916. In latter year deprived of his lectureship after being convicted for writing and distributing seditious anti-conscriptionist pamphlet. In his autobiography he wrote 'What I most desired was to find some reason for supposing mathematics true'. Wrote *Principles of Mathematics* (1903) and (with A. N. Whitehead) *Principia Mathematica* (1910). In his autobiography (i, 71) he wrote: 'Keynes's escape [into the great world] . . . was not complete. He went about the world carrying with him everywhere a feeling of a bishop *in partibus*. True salvation was elsewhere, among the faithful at Cambridge. When he concerned himself with politics and economics he left his soul at home . . . There was one great exception, *The Economic Consequences of the Peace* . . .'

RUSSELL-COOKE, SIDNEY (1895–1930), stockbroker. Ed. Cheltenham, and King's College, Cambridge, 1913. Friend of JMK. 'A good looking young man with dark brown hair and brown eyes, an aristocratic nose and the somewhat arrogant manner of the upper-class' (Nicholas Davenport), he committed suicide in 1930.

SANGER, CHARLES PERCY (1871–1930), statistician and barrister. Ed. Trinity College, Cambridge, 1890. 2nd Wrangler, 1893. Fellow, 1895–1901. An Apostle (1902), who bridged the gap between the Russell and Keynes generations. Virginia Woolf wrote of him in 1916: 'He is very red-eyed and wizened and overworked but he pumps up the most amazing quips and cracks, and his eyes glow and he looks like one of the dwarfs in the Ring'.

SCOTT, GEOFFREY (1883–1929), writer. Ed. New College, Oxford. Friend of JMK and Mary Berenson. He married Lady Sybil Cutting in 1918, and had an affair with Vita Sackville-West in 1923.

SHEPPARD, SIR JOHN TRESSIDER (1881–1968), classics don. Ed. Dulwich College and King's College, Cambridge, 1900. Apostle, 1902. Fellow of King's, 1906, and lecturer in Classics, 1908–33. Vice-Provost of King's, 1929–33. Provost, 1933–54. A great College character, he was at his best in his Sunday evening 'At Homes', where the 'hypnotic power of those slightly protruding eyes' and his mixture of dignity and clowning, snobbery and subversiveness 'made us feel a community with him in original sin' (Patrick Wilkinson). His great friend was Cecil Taylor, later a housemaster at Clifton. Best known in the University for his productions of the triennial Greek Plays, starting with *Oedipus Tyrannus* in 1912.

SHOVE, GERALD FRANK (1887–1947), economist. Ed. Uppingham and King's College, Cambridge, 1907. Switched from classics to economics, in which he got a 1st in 1911, on the strength of a few answers. Apostle, 1909. Generally silent and taciturn, but with flashes of ebullience (as when he proposed the toast of 'The King, God damn him' at the Carbonari dinner of 1909), and moral passion. In 1915 he married FREDEGOND CECILY MAITLAND, daughter of Sir Frederic Maitland, the legal historian and cousin of Virginia Woolf. Became a Fellow of King's in 1926. Between the wars, Cambridge's hardest working economics don; published almost nothing.

SIDGWICK, HENRY (1838–1900), philosopher and university reformer. Ed. Rugby and Trinity College, Cambridge, 1855. Apostle, 1856. Resigned his Fellowship at Trinity in 1869 to avoid 'dogmatic obligations' of a lost faith. Knightbridge Professor of Moral Philosophy, 1882–1900. A leading late Victorian 'pious agnostic'. JMK wrote 'He never did anything but wonder whether Christianity was true and prove that it wasn't and hope that it was'; but in the intervals of doubts, he founded Newnham College.

SMUTS, JAN CHRISTIAN (1870–1950), South African lawyer, statesman, and philosopher. Ed. at Christ's College, Cambridge, 1894, where he obtained a 1st in both parts of the Law Tripos. Fought for the Boers 1899–1902, negotiated peace in 1902. Minister of Defence, 1910–19; member of the British War Cabinet, 1917–19, and of the British Empire Delegation to the Paris Peace Conference, where he and JMK fought for a magnanimous peace. Subsequently Prime Minister of South Africa, 1919–24 and 1939–48. His *Holism and Evolution* was published in 1926.

SPOKES, ARTHUR HEWETT (1854–1922), lawyer. Friend of J. N. Keynes. Recorder of Reading, 1894.

STEPHEN family. One of the leading Evangelical, intellectual and administrative families of Victorian England. SIR LESLIE STEPHEN (1832–1904), philosopher and man of letters, was educated at Eton, University College, London, and Trinity Hall, Cambridge, of which he became Fellow and tutor, resigning his tutorship in 1862, following religious doubts. According to Quentin Bell, his 'agnosticism made him not less, but more anxious to preserve the proprieties'. He was the younger brother of the lawyer SIR JAMES FITZJAMES STEPHEN (1829–1894), author of a famous attack on John Stuart Mill. Sir James Fitzjames, as well as his second son JAMES KENNETH STEPHEN (1859–1892), hero of the Eton Wall Game and Fellow of King's, were both Apostles; unlike Sir Leslie and his two sons THOBY ('the Goth') (1880–1906) and ADRIAN (1883–1948), both of whom went to Trinity College, Cambridge. In addition to his two sons, Sir Leslie had two daughters by his second wife JULIA PATTLE–VANESSA (1879–1961), who married CLIVE BELL, and VIRGINIA (1882–1941), who married Leonard Woolf. The Stephens exemplify the passage from pious agnosticism to impious atheism.

STRACHEY family. Another central transitional family, with roots in the British imperial service. EDWARD STRACHEY (1774–1832), a judge in India, had six sons of whom three – SIR EDWARD STRACHEY (1812–1901), SIR RICHARD STRACHEY (1817–1908) and SIR JOHN STRACHEY (1823–1907) made their mark, the second and third in Indian administration. Sir Edward's son, JOHN ST LOE (1860–1927) became editor of the *Spectator*; his son, EVELYN JOHN ST LOE (1901–1963) was the Labour politician and Marxist intellectual of the 1930s. Sir Richard Strachey, soldier and scientist, had by his second wife JANE MARIA GRANT (1840–1928), ten surviving children (she forgot one of them in her entry in *Who's Who*), of whom GILES LYTTON STRACHEY (1880–1932) was the eighth and JAMES BEAUMONT STRACHEY (1887–1967) was the youngest. The others, in descending order, were ELINOR (1860–1945), married to JAMES MEADOWS RENDEL, another Indian administrator; RICHARD (1861–1935), who served as a soldier in Borneo; DOROTHEA (1866–1960), translator and married to the French painter SIMON BUSSY; RALPH (1868–1923); PHILIPPA ('Pippa') (1872–1968), an 'inconspicuous but indefatigable force at the centre of the constitutional women's movement' (Anne Olivier Bell); OLIVER (1874–1960), a historian and civil servant, who married RACHEL COSTELLOE; JOAN PERNEL (1876–1951), Principal of Newnham College, Cambridge, 1923–41; MARJORIE (1882–1969), a writer and teacher.

SWITHINBANK, BERNARD WINTHROP (1884–1958), administrator. Ed. Eton and Balliol College, Oxford, 1903. Career civil servant in Burma, before retiring in 1946. JMK's best friend at Eton.

SYDNEY-TURNER, SAXON (1880–1962), civil servant. Ed. Westminster and Trinity College, Cambridge, 1899. Apostle, 1902. Disappeared into the Treasury, where he remained till he retired. The silent man of Bloomsbury, short, with straw-coloured hair. Leonard Woolf called him an 'atrophied Shelley', but he had a passion for Wagnerian opera.

TAYLOR, CECIL FRANCIS (1886–1955), schoolmaster. Ed. Emmanuel College, Cambridge, 1905. Apostle, 1910. From 1912 till his retirement, a schoolmaster at Clifton College. J. T. Sheppard's lifelong friend, he was known in JMK's circle as 'Madame'; at Clifton his nickname was 'Babe'.

TREVELYAN family. The three sons of SIR GEORGE OTTO TREVELYAN (1838–1928), historian and Liberal politician, and HANNAH MORE, Macaulay's sister, were SIR CHARLES PHILIPS TREVELYAN (1870–1958), Liberal and Labour politician, ROBERT CALVERLEY TREVELYAN (Bob Trevy) (1872–1958), and GEORGE MACAULAY TREVELYAN (1876–1962). All three brothers were educated at Harrow and Trinity College, Cambridge; the last two were Apostles, in 1893 and 1895 respectively, as their father had been (1862). Bob Trevy and GMT were both friends of JMK; the former, a 'very scholarly but not very inspired poet' (Russell), but a great mimic; the latter an austere historian, Regius Professor of Modern History, 1927–40, Master of Trinity, 1941–50, and pillar of the Liberal establishment. It was he who advised JMK to go into politics in 1904. All the Trevelyans were prodigious walkers.

VENN, JOHN (1834–1923), logician and historian of Cambridge University, Fellow of Caius College, Cambridge, 1857, President 1912–23. One of the founders of the Cambridge Moral Science Tripos. His book, *Logic of Chance* (1866), was criticised by JMK in his *Treatise on Probability*, 101–9.

WARD, DUDLEY (1885–1957), civil servant and banker. Ed. Derby School and St John's College, Cambridge. JMK taught him economics; he served under JMK in 'A' Division of the Treasury, 1917–19, accompanying him to the Paris Peace Conference. Friend of Rupert Brooke.

WARRE, EDMOND (1837–1920), schoolmaster. Ed. Eton and Balliol College, Oxford. Headmaster of Eton, 1884–1915. Much admired for improving its moral tone.

WEBB, BEATRICE (*née* Potter) (1858–1943), wife of SIDNEY JAMES WEBB (1859–1947); both leaders of the Fabian Society. Although JMK found lunch with Beatrice in 1913 'a deep spiritual experience' he did not repeat it till 1926.

WILSON, WOODROW (1856–1924), 28th President of the United States, 1912–20. Professor of Jurisprudence and Politics at Princeton, 1897–1910. JMK thought better of him as a professor than as President.

WITTGENSTEIN, LUDWIG JOSEF JOHANN (1889–1951), philospher. Born in Vienna, studied philosophy under Russell at Trinity College, Cambridge, 1912–13, when JMK first met him. Apostle, 1912. A genius, he had a difficult relationship with both Cambridge philosophy and Cambridge people, of whom JMK was one he got to know best.

WOOLF, LEONARD SIDNEY (1880–1969), author and publisher. Ed. St Paul's School and Trinity College, Cambridge (1899). 1st class in Part I Classics, and Apostle, 1902. Colonial civil servant in Ceylon, 1904–11; married Virginia Stephen in 1912. Wrote on 'international government' during First World War; with Virginia Woolf founded the Hogarth Press in 1917; literary editor of the *Nation*, 1923–30. Called JMK a 'lovable character' in his autobiography (*Sowing*, 144), but it is hard to detect much affection on his part.

YOUNG family. Had strong connections with Eton, Cambridge and administration. Of the three sons of Sir George Young (1837–1930), a progressive civil servant and intrepid mountain climber, Sir George Young (1872–1952) was a diplomat, Geoffrey Winthrop Young (1876–1958) was assistant-master at Eton, 1900–05 and a famous mountaineer, and Edward Hilton Young (1879–1960), later 1st Baron Kennet of the Dene, was a Liberal politician, who proposed to Virginia Woolf, and whom Desmond MacCarthy called 'the sphinx without a secret'. JMK's Eton friend Gerard Mackworth Young (1884–1963) was the son of Sir William Mackworth Young (1840–1924), an Indian civil servant and brother of the first Sir George Young.

Yule, George Udny (1871–1951), statistician. JMK was instrumental in getting him appointed University Lecturer in Statistics at Cambridge, 1912, on the strength of his *Introduction to the Theory of Statistics* (1911). His next book was in 1944.

Index